D1130965

THE ORDER OF MERIT

THE ORDER OF MERIT

One Hundred Years of
Matchless Honour

Stanley Martin

I.B. TAURIS

LONDON · NEW YORK

Published in 2007 by I.B.Tauris & Co. Ltd
6 Salem Road, London W2 4BU
175 Fifth Avenue, New York NY 10010
www.ibtauris.com

In the United States and Canada distributed by Palgrave Macmillan
a division of St Martin's Press
175 Fifth Avenue, New York NY 10010

ISBN: 978 1 86064 848 9

A full CIP record for this book is available from the British Library

A full CIP record for this book is available from the Library of Congress

Library of Congress catalog card: available

Typeset in Sabon by Newgen Imaging Systems (P) Ltd, Chennai
Printed and bound in Great Britain by
TJ International, Padstow, Cornwall

To Hanni, Nick and Birgit, who have lived with the notion of this book for as long as they have known me – and who must often have wondered whether they would ever see it.

And to Oliver, who ensured that they did.

CONTENTS

ILLUSTRATIONS

PREFACE

The family story is that I swallowed *Whitaker's Almanack* at the age of nine – it was the 1943 edition – and continued thereafter to display an unusual, possibly even unhealthy, interest in orders and decorations.

As a schoolboy, I was hugely encouraged in this interest by two men: Ivan De La Bère, the Secretary of the Central Chancery of the Orders of Knighthood, who fed my ceaseless desire for more information on a rather esoteric subject; and Philip Banfield, who gave me a love of history and was the sort of teacher we all have one of in our lives – if we are lucky.

Although I learned a good deal about orders and decorations generally, and have written spasmodically about some of them, my real interest soon centred on the royally-nominated Order of Merit and, to a lesser extent, the politically-nominated Order of the Companions of Honour. The result was the accumulation of a frightening amount of material – books, pamphlets, press cuttings and manuscripts – the sifting of which has proved an enormous challenge in writing this book.

What appealed to me about the OM was its simplicity and the sheer standard of its membership. Here, by careful selection, was the nearest to an official roll-call of Britain's great of the twentieth century, an honour really worth having – and studying.

Over the years, I have been fortunate in meeting some 30 OMs and in corresponding with a number more. They were invariably charming, helpful – and modest.

The need for a study of the Order has been recognised occasionally but not at the length I have devoted to it. G. M. Trevelyan, an OM's OM in more ways than one, once told Stanley Baldwin that some young woman might write a PhD thesis on it. Also, one of the Queen's Private Secretaries told the Secretary of the Order that he doubted whether there would be sufficient material for a book. I await his judgement.

Facing me, as I wrote, were bookshelves containing over 500 biographies or autobiographies of OMs, as well as some of their writings. All of this was a tiny proportion of what has been written about or by these renowned people. The OM features briefly in many of these books. I have tried to bring together as much as I can of what has been written about it in one place for the first time and present a coherent history of its first century. Both the publishers and I wanted to avoid an unwieldy and unreadable tome of reference: a 'doorstop' book. It is designed to be liftable and readable. There is a serious thread going through the book but larded, I hope, with sufficient anecdotage to make it interesting.

The most daunting thought is that what I have written may well be read by over 20 of the brightest brains of Britain.

ACKNOWLEDGEMENTS

It is usual for any author who has been given access to material in the Royal Archives and Library to acknowledge that first. It is particularly appropriate where the subject of the book is the Order of Merit, which is in the personal gift of the Sovereign. I am therefore most grateful to Her Majesty the Queen for gracious permission to publish extracts from documents in the Royal Archives relating to the Order from 1902–1952 and to reproduce portraits from the Royal Collection.

I am also very grateful to His Royal Highness The Prince Philip, Duke of Edinburgh, for writing the Foreword. He is the senior Member of the Order and has held it for longer than anyone else.

Successive Private Secretaries to the Queen have given me help and encouragement over the years: the late Lord Charteris of Amisfield, Lord Moore of Wolvercote, Sir William Heseltine, Lord Fellowes (now Secretary and Registrar of the Order) and the present incumbent, Sir Robin Janvrin. Within the bounds of confidentiality, they have explained to me the working of this particularly royal Order and their pivotal role in appointments to it. Mr Simon Hitchens, former Assistant Private Secretary to The Queen, lit the fuse, without which this book might not have got off the launch pad.

My greatest debt over the years of gestation of the book has been to the late Sir Edward Ford, Secretary and Registrar of the Order of Merit from 1975 to 2003. His interest and friendship were unflagging and I am very sad that he missed the publication of this book by only a few weeks. In the book itself, I have paid tribute to the great work he did for the Order in the last quarter of its first 100 years.

To the Royal Archives and Library, I am endebted for speedy, cheerful and meticulous help whenever I needed it. Ever since the idea of the book began to take concrete shape, Mr Oliver Everett (for many years Librarian of the Royal Library and Assistant Keeper of the Royal Archives) has been the most keen supporter of my efforts. He obtained crucial financial support, suggested necessary reductions in the text and cajoled when necessary. He thoroughly deserves his inclusion in the dedication of the book. Without his infectious enthusiasm, which has extended generously into his retirement, my own might well have flagged. Among his colleagues, I should like particularly to thank Miss Jane Langton, Lady de Bellaigue, the Hon Lady Roberts and Miss Pam Clark.

At the Central Chancery of the Orders of Knighthood, I have received ready assistance from Lt Col Anthony Mather and Lt Col Robert Cartwright, the former Secretaries, the late Mr George Harris, the former Assistant Secretary, and Mr Jeremy Bagwell Purefoy, the present Insignia Clerk.

My links with the College of Arms extend over several years and I am endebted for the help received from the late Sir Colin Cole and his successor as Garter King of Arms, Sir Conrad Swan, and from the late Mr John Brooke-Little, when Norroy and Ulster King of Arms. From their colleague and my friend, Mr Phillip O'Shea, New Zealand Herald of Arms Extraordinary, I have received valuable information about the OMs who had links with New Zealand.

At various times, I have received assistance from diplomatic missions in London: the German Embassy (Herr Volker Dreike), the Austrian Embassy (the late Ambassador Reginald Thomas) and the Japanese Embassy. I am also indebted to the officials of the German Order Pour le mérite, particularly the former Chancellor of the Order, Professor Dr Helmut Coing. My gratitude goes to two former British Ambassadors to Japan, Sir John Whitehead and Sir Sydney Giffard, for advice on the political background to the appointment of three Japanese Honorary OMs in 1906.

I have been greatly assisted by those at the two premier intellectual bodies, to which so many OMs were elected. First, the Royal Society – initially by Sir Andrew Huxley, OM, when he was President, but whose help has continued at intervals since; and more recently by Mr Stephen Cox, the Executive Secretary, and his staff. Secondly, the British Academy – again, initially by the Revd Professor Owen Chadwick, OM, KBE, when he was President, and later by Mr Peter Brown, the Secretary.

Other institutions have also helped me: the British Association for the Advancement of Science the Classical Association; the Royal Society of Literature; the Imperial War Museum; the National Army Museum; and the Royal Air Force Museum.

I received help from Mr Robin Harcourt Williams (Hatfield House), Mrs Molly Clark (Broadlands) and Mr Stuart Holmes (Westminster Abbey).

Mr Kenneth Rose, who knows so much about the Order of Merit and the personalities of the twentieth century, has been generous with his time, particularly in pointing me in various useful directions.

Professor Peter Hennessy, the eminent contemporary historian, has been similarly helpful. Mr Hugo Vickers, another authority on the last century, kindly helped me to use the important private note by Sir Alexander Hardinge in Chapter 5.

To numerous friends I owe thanks for constant encouragement. They include Mr John Morrison, who has kept me regularly supplied with material from the American press about OMs; Major Albert Abela, who has written authoritatively on honours matters; the late Mr James Risk, one of the leading authorities on British honours; and some of my co-authors of *Royal Service: The History of the Royal Victorian Order, Medal and Chain* – the late Judge Henry Pownall, QC, Mr John Tamplin and Mr David Stanley. My friends at the Royal Over-Seas League, the Director-General, Mr Robert Newell, and his assistant, Mrs Fatima Vaniček, have been consistently helpful.

My greatest personal debt in finally producing the book is to my family – all of it. This is no ritual tribute. I thank my wife, Hanni, not only for her forbearance when my ever-growing material on the Order of Merit crept into corners of the house where it had no place but also for the mammoth task she undertook in transcribing my manuscript into printed form. To achieve this, she embarked, without any experience, on the new, challenging and disturbing world of the computer. She was wonderfully assisted, in frequent moments of difficulty, by our son, Nick, and daughter-in-law, Sarah, and by our daughter, Birgit, son-in-law, Michael, and their au pair, Helena. At times, Birgit took a hand in the typing and printing; at other times, Nick, with his considerable knowledge of Germany and its language, helped me with the many references to the Order Pour le mérite, the model for the Order of Merit. No author can ever have been blessed with a more supportive family.

To my publishers, I.B. Tauris, and their Chairman, Mr Iradj Bagherzade, I owe a particular debt of gratitude. They took on an unknown author with an esoteric subject and were forbearing when problems arose along the way. My commissioning editor, Dr Lester Crook, was helpful in getting the project underway. More recently, Ms Kate Sherratt ensured that the revised text was brought to contract stage. Most recently, however, Ms Liz Friend-Smith has brought her skill and determination to bear to ensure a finished product within a tight timescale. Finally, Dr Richard Willis has helped me to the finishing line.

In time-honoured fashion, I apologise to anyone deserving of my thanks whom I have inadvertently omitted. I am also very sorry if through oversight my publishers and I have failed to obtain permission to reproduce copyright material.

Although the Order of Merit is likely to be mentioned in biographies of its members, this is the first time that it has had a book to itself. Mr. Stanley Martin has obviously taken a keen interest in the Order for many years and now offers this first history of it.

King Edward VII, the founder of the Order, intended that it should recognise 'exceptionally meritorious service in Our Navy and Our Army, or who may have rendered exceptionally meritorious service towards the advancement of Art, Literature and Science'. His successors have tried to remain faithful to his vision while broadening it to include the Royal Air Force, Engineering and other exceptional services. As with anything that requires human judgement, opinions can vary and it is up to the reader to decide whether they succeeded.

The author combines the fruit of considerable research with a light touch and, with the benefit of hindsight, he is not afraid to discuss whether the right people were always appointed and who he thinks might have been better candidates. His anecdotes help to bring to life many of its members, particularly those, whose names and talents may be better known than their personalities.

This is certainly a very special Order and I am sure that it has always been highly prized by its members. It may not be as well known as some other Honours, but that does not mean that it has not acquired an enviable prestige. I believe that it fully deserves this illuminating history.

Philip

You see, my good wenches,
how men of merit are
sought after...

Falstaff
(Henry IV, Part 2;
Act II, Scene IV)

1

INTRODUCTION

On 26 June 1902, the British public awoke to find that they had acquired a new Order – not of knighthood, but of merit for those who 'may have rendered exceptionally meritorious service in our Navy and our Army, or who may have rendered exceptionally meritorious service towards the advancement of Art, Literature and Science'. The public had hoped to awake also to a coronation but two days earlier they had been told that King Edward VII must undergo an immediate operation for acute appendicitis. By the king's command, however, the generous Honours List that traditionally accompanies a coronation was published as originally planned.

Thus, the quality newspapers announced, under a headline 'New Order of Merit', that 12 of the nation's most distinguished men – three soldiers, two sailors, four scientists, two men of letters and a painter – had been appointed to it. Only the painter was without a title or prefix of some kind; for the rest, the simple letters 'OM' and a simple neck badge were to be added to far more resplendent letters and insignia. All 12, however, knew that they were receiving a very special distinction from their Sovereign and so it has been with the 150 or so British subjects who have followed them as Members of the Order of Merit.

Some of them were, and have remained, household names; others were renowned in their day but today have faded or limited reputations; a few were never known beyond a restricted circle. With rare exceptions, however, all were – in the lights of their own day – being given the highest state honour they could receive. In real terms, the Order of Merit is the peak of the most complex honours system in the world. That makes its story well worth telling.

A glance at the chapter headings will show that I have told the story thematically, rather than chronologically, since that would have resulted in a rather disjoined work, jumping from one appointment to another in completely unconnected fields. After a review of the British honours system up to 1902, I describe how the need for an Order of Merit came to be recognised, how it was established in 1902 and how it has developed, in principle, over the twentieth century. I then move on to the various categories of members: the military, the scientists, the scholars, and so on. Even they are too large to avoid further subdivision. For instance, the 44 scientists appointed after the initial four have been broken into homogenous groups: the Physical (physicists, mathematicians, astronomers); the Chemical (chemists, biochemists/molecular biologists); the Medical (physiologists, immunologists, pathologists, surgeons); the Natural (botanists, zoologists, geologists); and the Engineering (engineers in various fields).

The book is intended, however, to be a history of the Order and its development and not the story of its individual members. Many of them are so well known, with so many biographies of them, that it is not necessary to include more than short thumbnail sketches. The reader does not need to be told very much about figures as great and diverse as Churchill, Mountbatten, Eliot, Hardy or Elgar, but, nevertheless, their appointments to the Order need to be put in context, for instance on timing. I have deliberately written more about some of the lesser-known figures, partly because the average reader will not be familiar with their lives and partly to explain why they received the OM. Some groups like the Honorary Members or those who refused the Order make more interesting reading than some of what, even with such a great honour, might be called the 'routine' appointments.

These portrait sketches are deliberately not uniform; they are very selective and must certainly not be relied on as authoritative mini-biographies. They draw heavily on secondary sources and emphasise relationships or contacts with other OMs. The most they can claim to be are possibly amusing or enlightening vignettes which bear on the development of Britain's 'premier society of honour'.

Having described the Members individually, I attempt to draw various conclusions regarding their backgrounds, lives, links and memorials.

It would not be reasonable to expect the confidential papers of the present reign to be opened for some years. This has resulted in an imbalance between the amount I can say about the appointment of recipients in the first 50 years of the Order, as compared with those of the second 50 years. The book is also unbalanced because the OM archives are erratic. That said, it seemed best to let the words of the Sovereign's private secretaries, those they consulted and the recipients to speak for themselves. It is the first time that many of these views have appeared in print. Of course, there is an uneven result because some appointments generated a good deal of correspondence, while there is little on others. Either it has not survived or the consultation was verbal and not recorded, except sometimes to say simply that X or Y supported the proposal or that the Sovereign decided on a particular appointment.

To anyone with the remotest interest in honours, the knighthood is the quantitative leap. The differences between CB and MVO or CMG and LVO or even between CBE, OBE and MBE are lost on many people. So why should the OM or CH be so special? Are they not just two more sets of initials after a name, maybe a sort of glorified 'OBE'? It is the 'Sir' (or 'Dame') before the name that attracts attention. It is precisely that lack of a title, denying them the opportunity to genuflect mentally, which makes the OM rather boring to most of the press and the public. Perhaps that is why, according to Jacob Epstein's biographer: 'The knighthood gave him immense pleasure: to be seen to be somebody, to have recognition obvious to all, was much better than the initials of some rarer honour after your name.'[1]

If, however, it is rarity rather than recognition that appeals, the OM has no equal. There are approximately 3,500 knights and dames but never more than 24 OMs; the ratio is 150:1. That rarity – almost a Victorian austerity – is what appealed to the likes of G. M. Trevelyan, whose biographer, in discussing whether he refused a peerage, wrote: '... in any case, Cambridge men of Trevelyan's background and generation – like Vaughan Williams and E M Forster – only accepted honours which came after their name, but not before it.'[2]

In order to reduce the repetition of long names and titles, I have usually referred to dead OMs by their surnames only (after first describing their appointment), unless it is necessary to distinguish those with the same name, such as Trevelyan, Moore, Fisher, James, Hodgkin or Sutherland. As a matter of courtesy, however, I have referred to living OMs by their first and surnames, again omitting titles or other prefixes, except where they are relevant in context. This is consistent with my view that titles intrude on the simplicity and dignity of the Order of Merit, which is what this book is all about. Whatever other adornments OMs might enjoy, in the writing of this book it is their appointment to the Order that has been overriding. Between them, they represent much of the history of Britain in the twentieth century. To describe them is dangerously like writing, in staccato form, the story of our country over the last 100 years.

2

THE NINETEENTH CENTURY WITHOUT AN ORDER OF MERIT

The developing honours system

The United Kingdom of Great Britain and Ireland came into being on 1 January 1801, with an elaborate honours system that was wide in theory but limited in practice. At its peak was the peerage, a complicated structure, consisting of four separate parts: the peerages of England (conferred in that country before the Union with Scotland in 1707), of Scotland (conferred in that country before 1707), of Great Britain (conferred between that Union and the one with Ireland in 1801) and of Ireland (conferred not always in close connection with that country and amounting sometimes to a second-class peerage).

What replaced the peerage of Great Britain in 1801 was the peerage of the United Kingdom, in which, with some rare Irish exceptions, all peerages since that date have been created. As before, titles could be granted at any of five levels: duke, marquess, earl, viscount and baron, the last commonly referred to as lord. Below the peerage, but before knights, came the baronetage. Baronetcies were hereditary but gave no seat in the House of Lords.

In addition to the hereditary peerage and baronetage there were four orders of chivalry:

- the Most Noble Order of the Garter, founded in 1348
- the Most Ancient and Most Noble Order of the Thistle, founded or technically revived in 1687
- the Most Illustrious Order of St Patrick, founded in 1783
- the Most Honourable Order of the Bath, founded in 1725

These were limited to 25, 16, 22 and 35 knights, respectively, and the first three were virtually confined to the aristocracies of England, Scotland and

Ireland. The Bath served two purposes: to reward political figures who were not suited (at least yet) for the Garter, which might well have no vacancy anyway; and to reward senior naval, military or diplomatic officers.

Coming below the four orders was the much older rank of knight bachelor, which stemmed from the immediacy of dubbing on the battlefield but had moved to the more sedate field of country gentlemen and others whom the monarch wished to keep on his side or win to it. Unlike the knights of the four orders, knights bachelor had no robes or elaborate insignia; they simply enjoyed the title 'Sir' by virtue of the monarch having conferred, usually in person, the accolade upon them with a light touch of a sword on each shoulder.

In 1801, there were approximately 300 knights, some 100 in the orders and the remainder knights bachelor. This was out of a male population in Great Britain of, say 5.5 million, half of the total registered in the first census of that year. Of course, there were no honours for women, who did not participate in the activities that brought rewards to a few men; they were not landed magnates or country squires or politicians or admirals or generals or explorers. Indeed, as can be seen, even for men the chance of an honour was very slight. There was no provision for rewarding those below the very top level of society, particularly if they were not involved in the civil or military governance of the country.

By the end of the nineteenth century, the enormous growth in the economic, military and colonial power of the United Kingdom had affected the honours system – but not much. It had spread laterally but still had precious little depth.

The first change came in 1815, at the end of the Napoleonic Wars. That lengthy and wide-ranging conflict had demonstrated the inadequacy of a single class order (Knight of the Bath – KB) for rewarding all levels of naval and military service. The Bath was therefore expanded on the military side, to three classes: all KBs became Members of the First Class or Knights Grand Cross (GCB) and below them were instituted a Second Class or Knights Commander (KCB) and a Third Class or Companions (CB) – the grades which still exist today. This expansion enabled 'lesser' admirals or generals and middle-ranking officers (captains or colonels) to drink at the fountain of honour, from which they had previously been largely excluded.

Additionally, the Bath was given a specific civil division, but only at the level of GCB. Not until 1847 was the civil side equated to the military with the addition of the KCB and CB. That move was the first to have any significance in relation to the sort of men for whom the Order of Merit would eventually be founded: the scientists, artists, writers and musicians.

In 1818, the Prince Regent instituted the Most Distinguished Order of Saint Michael and Saint George. As a result of the Napoleonic Wars, Britain had acquired a Mediterranean empire: the island of Malta, and Corfu, Cephalonia and the other Ionian Islands. This new order had the extraordinarily limited objective of keeping the leading citizens of these small possessions contented with British rule. Unlike the Bath, however, it was primarily a civilian award. In 1868, it was expanded to reward services anywhere in the colonies and in 1879, the Foreign Office got in on the act by securing its conferment also for diplomatic services anywhere in the world.

In 1861, the Most Exalted Order of the Star of India was instituted with one class of knight (KSI); but the lessons of the Bath and Saint Michael and Saint George were quickly learned and, in 1866, the Order was restructured into three classes: Knights Grand Commanders (GCSI) – 'Cross' was not used in order to avoid offending Muslim (and Hindu) susceptibilities – Knights Commanders (KCSI) and Companions (CSI).

When Queen Victoria happily accepted Disraeli's suggestion of assuming the title of Empress of India in 1877, another order quickly followed; in 1878, the Most Eminent Order of the Indian Empire was instituted, again with only one class. This class however, was the lowest one of Companion and the new order was clearly intended as a poor relation of the Star of India for rewarding those middle-ranking officials in the expanding Indian Civil Services who could not reasonably aspire to the grander order. Within ten years, however, the Order of the Indian Empire was brought into line with the others by the introduction of two higher classes: Knights Grand Commanders (GCIE) and Knights Commanders (KCIE).

The increasingly elaborate honours jigsaw was not yet complete. In 1896, Queen Victoria established the Royal Victorian Order, which was to be in her personal gift and not, as with other honours, on the recommendation of ministers. It was to recognise personal services to her or the monarchy in general and followed the pattern set by other European royal houses. It was the most complicated piece of the jigsaw. It had five, rather than three, classes: Knights Grand Cross (GCVO), Knights Commanders (KCVO), Commanders (CVO) – originally ranking immediately after Knights Bachelor and before the differently-styled Companions of the existing four orders – Members of the Fourth Class (MVO (IV)) – styled Lieutenants since 1984 – and Members of the Fifth Class (MVO (V)). There was also a Medal of the Order, in Gold, Silver and Bronze (RVM).

Thus, by the end of the nineteenth century, the British honours system has been considerably enlarged but still basically within the governing classes. Not until the establishment in 1917, to meet the pressures of wartime, of the Most Excellent Order of the British Empire, was there a large, multi-purpose award to recognise, in theory, the efforts of men *and women* in all classes and walks of life. Like the Victorian Order, it had five classes but only one medal: Knights and Dames Grand Cross (GBE), Knights and Dames Commanders (KBE or DBE), Commanders (CBE), Officers (OBE), Members (MBE) and Medallists (BEM). This weighty structure made it the Heineken of the honours system, able to reach those parts of society that the other orders could not – and were not designed to.

The Order of the Companions of Honour (CH) is the stablemate of the Order of the British Empire and ranks between Knights and Dames Grand Cross and Knights and Dames Commanders but it confers no title. The two were created on the same day – 4 June 1917 – to meet, at different levels, the same needs brought about by the First World War. The CH, however, is the slim racehorse, with originally only 50 members, male and female (increased in the Second World War to 65), whereas the Order of the British Empire, with its thousands and thousands of members is the brewer's dray horse.

The CH is often referred to, somewhat glibly, as a Second Class Order of Merit. I shall need to refer to it many times later in the book and I introduce it now simply to fit it in the overall constellation of honours.

The use made of the honours system

Against that background of the honours system as it developed in the nineteenth century, I want to look at how far it met the need, eventually filled by the Order of Merit, to give exceptional recognition to exceptional men, particularly in the fields of science and the arts. The short answer is not very much, because the official honours system was geared overwhelmingly to rewarding official service to the State. For those in, or closely associated with, Crown service, there was the possibility of appointment to one of the growing number of orders.

Thus, Rowland Hill, the inventor of the modern postage stamp in 1840, was made a KCB 20 years later for being Secretary of the Post Office. Anthony Panizzi, the Italian-born bibliographer who, as Principal Librarian of the British Museum, designed the famous reading room, was made a KCB in 1869. Henry Cole, writer and art critic, was similarly honoured in 1875, after 15 years as Director of the South Kensington Museum; Edwin Chadwick, the social reformer, was made a KCB at the age of 88, having been Secretary of the Poor Law Board many years before.

Someone who held no official position surprisingly received the higher GCB in 1900: Henry Morton Stanley, the explorer and journalist, who had discovered Livingstone at Ujiji 28 years earlier.

The lists of Knights Bachelor in the nineteenth century are full of officials and state and municipal worthies in Britain and the colonies, particularly those peopled with British stock which had become self-governing in Canada, Australia, New Zealand and South Africa. For writers and artists, usually freelance without official connections, there was much less chance of preferment.

Among writers, honours were slim indeed. Walter Scott's baronetcy in 1820 and Alfred Tennyson's barony in 1884 stand out for precisely that reason. Scott, however, was close to the Crown (and stage-managed King George IV's historic visit to Scotland in 1822 – 'The King's Jaunt – one and twenty daft days') and Tennyson had been Poet Laureate for 34 years.

The list of unhonoured writers in a great century for English literature is endless: Sheridan, Hazlitt, Lamb, Coleridge, Wordsworth (Tennyson's predecessor as Poet Laureate, but for only seven years), Thackeray, Dickens, Mill, George Eliot, Trollope (despite being also a senior Post Office official and the inventor of the postbox) the Rossettis, Arnold, Browning, Ruskin. Others, as brilliant, died too young to have been honoured even today: Byron, Shelley, Keats, Jane Austen, Stevenson and the Bronte Sisters. Southey, Poet Laureate from 1813–43, declined a baronetcy but accepted a pension and, to do nineteenth-century governments justice, pensions were often their more practical way of 'honouring' those in the arts.

Historians fared only slightly better. There were baronies for Thomas Macaulay in 1857 (recognising his four-volume *History of England* but also his role as an MP and Minister) and for John Acton in 1869 (at the age of 35, having succeeded to a baronetcy at the age of three). In 1874, Thomas Carlyle persisted in declining a GCB offered by Disraeli, in an exchange foreshadowing the Order of Merit and referred to in more detail in the next chapter; a few months earlier he had accepted the Prussian Order Pour le mérite, founded by his idol Frederick the Great, whose biography he wrote in six volumes.

Artists, with a Royal Academy under the monarch's patronage, reaped more honours than writers. Every President of the Academy from Sir Joshua Reynolds has been knighted, with the exception of two in the early nineteenth century: Benjamin West, the American painter, and James Wyatt, the architect, whose presidency lasted only one year. In the nineteenth century, those honoured included Thomas Lawrence, Frederic Leighton and John Everett Millais. The last two did better than a mere knighthood: Leighton progressing from that to a baronetcy and, the day before he died in 1896, to a barony while Millais went straight to a baronetcy. Henry Raeburn was knighted, as were others who were Presidents of the Royal Scottish or Hibernian Academies or portrait painters to the royal family. Edwin Landseer, whose lions guard Nelson's Column, and Francis Chantrey, whose estate became the bequest named after him, were also knighted, as were architects such as Richard Westmacott, John Soane, Joseph Paxton, George Gilbert Scott and Charles Barry.

Missing from this list are the really great artistic names: George Stubbs, William Blake, John Nash, John Constable and J. M. W. Turner. Of course, even if the OM had existed, it might not have been offered to Turner; according to King George V, Queen Victoria always said he was mad.[1]

In contrast to literature and painting, British music did not excel in the nineteenth century: 'das Land ohne Musik', as the Germans called us. There were few honours for musicians. The most famous names were knighted in pairs: in 1883, Arthur Sullivan (leaving W. S. Gilbert to wait another 24 years for his knighthood) and George Grove; and in 1888, Charles Hallé and John Stainer.

Science fared better, with knighthoods for Benjamin Thomson (Count Rumford) the physicist and social reformer; Joseph Banks, the botanist on Cook's expeditions and later President of the Royal Society; Humphrey Davy, the discoverer of sodium and potassium and also President of the Royal Society – knighted at the age of 34, a baronet at 40 and PRS at 42; Marc Isambard Brunel, the civil engineer and father of the unhonoured civil engineer and inventor, Isambard Kingdom Brunel; Joseph Bazalgette, designer of London's sewage system; and Henry Bessemer, whose 'process' was the first cheap large-scale method of converting pig-iron into steel. Of the famed Armstrong–Whitworth team, both William Armstrong, inventor and arms pioneer, and Joseph Whitworth, mechanical engineer, were knighted and Armstrong went on to a barony.

Unhonoured were many other great names of what was a vital century in Britain's scientific and industrial development. There was nothing for Joseph Priestley, Henry Cavendish, James Watt, William Herschel, Edward Jenner, Thomas Telford, John McAdam, George Stephenson, Charles Babbage, James Clerk Maxwell (only 48 when he died, he would still have been only 71 when the OM was founded in 1902); and the most famous of all, Charles Darwin.

T. H. Huxley, the biologist who was President of the Royal Society and did much to promote scientific advance and popular understanding of it, cared little for honours ('CBships and KCBships') but accepted the non-titular one of a privy counsellorship. The most notable refusal of an honour by a scientist in the nineteenth century was that by Michael Faraday, probably the greatest experimental scientist of his time. The son of a poor blacksmith, he declined both a knighthood and the presidency of the Royal Society in the following terms: 'I must remain plain Michael Faraday to the last; and let me tell you, that if I accepted the honour which the Royal Society desires to confer upon me, I would not answer for the integrity of my intellect for a single year.[2] There is a picture in the Royal Society of his resisting the blandishments of three Fellows.

Many men in public life in the nineteenth century received no public recognition, since presumably a knighthood or a peerage held no appeal. Among political figures, an Order of Merit would have sat easily upon Pitt the Younger, Warren Hastings, John Bright, Richard Cobden (who declined a privy counsellorship and a GCB in 1860), Robert Peel (who had inherited a baronetcy) and Robert Owen. The same distinction would have fitted the influential thinkers Jeremy Bentham, Thomas Malthus and John Stuart Mill.

While Disraeli happily accepted an earldom (and thereafter, in the House of Lords, was 'dead, dead, but in the Elysian fields'), Gladstone steadfastly refused one. The OM would surely have claimed both, as it might also have done William Morris, the socialist designer and writer, whom Max Beerbohm described thus: 'a wonderful all-round man, but the act of walking round him has always tired me.'[3]

On the social and philanthropic side, Elizabeth Fry, the Quaker prison reformer (who is now on the UK £5 bank note), William Wilberforce, the successful campaigner against the slave trade, and the (Seventh) Earl of Shaftesbury, the eminent factory reformer and philanthropist, would have qualified for consideration under the rules that developed for the Order during the twentieth century. (Shaftesbury, by reason of his aristocratic position, received the Garter, after having first declined it.) It is interesting that, a century later, the Sovereign's Private Secretary wrote: 'Shaftesbury and Wilberforce were both "politicians" but wouldn't they have deserved the OM for what is nowadays called "social service"?'[4]

The military men would have fared badly after the end of the Napoleonic Wars. Peace for the rest of the century, except for a short and localised Crimean War and various colonial-type conflicts of short duration, offered little scope for 'exceptional' service by the leaders of the Navy and Army. Nevertheless, admirals and generals do not need much sympathy. At the heart of the Establishment, close to the monarch and government, they never go unrewarded. All of those who might have received the OM in the nineteenth century were already amply provided for.

3

MOVES TOWARDS THE ORDER
OF MERIT

Dissatisfaction in the first half of the nineteenth century

The aim of the previous chapter was to show the serious deficiencies in an honours system that failed to recognise the achievements of many of the most significant people in the country. In this chapter, I shall look at the growing awareness during the century of the shortcomings of the system and the resultant searching after some sort of 'Order of Merit'.

Just after Trafalgar, when awards for the victorious Fleet were under discussion, there is a reference in correspondence between Lord Barham (First Lord of the Admiralty) and William Pitt (First Lord of the Treasury) to a new 'Order of Merit'. On 9 November 1805, Barham writes: 'As far as I can judge of the nature of the new Order, I think it will lead to a very considerable degree of disappointment if any material retrospect was to take place...As soon as the first order is determined on, the second will be easy but the old proverb of *Bis dat qui cito dat* is as true in honours as in positions...' Pitt replied on 7 December 1805: 'Lord Hawkesbury [Home Secretary, and later, as Earl of Liverpool, First Lord of the Treasury, 1812–27] will bring you in a day or two the plan for the Order of Merit, I hope nearly in a complete state...'[1] No more is heard of this particular Order of Merit, although from remarks by Lord Castlereagh in the House of Commons in 1815 about its being 'an object to which Mr Pitt's mind had been earnestly directed...towards the close of his life', it seems clear that it was the extension of the military side of the Bath which was contemplated.[2]

The perennial problem with recurring references to an 'Order of Merit' is that it is a generic term that applies to all orders based on so-called meritocratic, rather than old-fashioned aristocratic, principles. At various times during the nineteenth century, however, the idea was mooted of an order like the one we have today, to remedy the deficiencies of the honours system outlined in the last chapter. During the same debate in which Castlereagh spoke in 1815, soon after the expansion of the Order of the Bath on the military side, Sir Charles Monck Bt MP 'condemned in strong terms the almost utter exclusion of the civil classes of society, under the new modification, from participating in the honours of this Order.'[3]

The Bath was again an opportunity to query the vacuum in the honours system when the question of abolishing the fees its members had to pay on appointment (including £6 to the king's barber) came up in the Commons on 18 April 1834. Joseph Hume, an ex-army surgeon who had bought a seat in Parliament and sat as a Philosophic Radical, widened the debate thus:

> Although England was a civil country, distinguished from the military despotisms of the Continent, yet all the honorary distinctions, with very few exceptions, went to naval and military officers. There was no Order of Knighthood in this country for men of great genius, or those who distinguished themselves by their intellectual requirements... the King of Prussia rewarded men of literary or scientific attainments... There was, however, nothing of the kind in England and yet England was quite as proud of her arts as her arms.[4]

Hume found no support in the Commons. That heavyweight, Sir Robert Peel, Bt, deplored any new order:

> The prerogative was already vested in the Crown to confer honours upon persons distinguished for their high literary and scientific attainments... The establishment of a new Order would depreciate [those] honours... not in the least calculated to raise the character of this country for literary and scientific acquirements [sic].[5]

A lesser Member, Henry Warburton, also attacked Hume's idea. He thought: 'that the dignity of literary and scientific pursuits could not be heightened by such honours.' In other words, writers and scientists are really rather above the sordid world of honours.[6]

It was not only radical politicians who voiced dissatisfaction with the inadequacies of the honours system. In his four-volume work, *History of the Orders of Knighthood of the British Empire*, published in 1842, Sir Nicholas Harris Nicolas, Chancellor of the Order of St Michael and St George, wrote in his Introduction, referring to a technical anomaly, 'This is, however, only one of the numerous circumstances which seem to render the creation of an Order for Civil Merit, and the reconstruction of the Order of the Bath, highly proper and expedient.' He subsequently observed that,

> In the Century that has elapsed since the revival of the Order [of the Bath], the discoveries made in Science have been transcendent . . . In Literature and the Arts, British Genius has shone with equal brightness; but the list of Knights of the Bath will be explored in vain for even one solitary Name among the host of illustrious men who adorned the past, and give lustre to the present generation, by their profound attainments in these pursuits which at once dignify and benefit mankind . . . The singular neglect of claims of this nature was, however, most strongly shewn on the Extension of the Order to Three Classes in 1815, when Civil merit was not deemed worthy of admission into even the lowest of the new Degrees . . . Not a single Cross was appropriate to Science or Letters.[7]

The expansion of the Order of Bath owed a lot to the interest taken by Prince Albert, consort of Queen Victoria since 1840 and Great Master of the Order since 1843. Sir Robert Peel, although no longer Prime Minister, was consulted at the last moment in 1847 and suggested to Prince Albert that the term 'or by great eminence in Art, Science or Literature have deserved our Royal Favour' should be added to the appropriate section;[8] the suggestion was not taken up.

Peel, while Prime Minister, had been involved in an earlier consultation of honours for 'merit'. In 1844, Prince Albert's manuscript diary (transcribed by his daughter, Princess Helena) records for the 16 January: 'Prince has a conference with Sir R. Peel . . . Prince suggests idea of institution of a civil Order of Merit.' Queen Victoria's Journal for the 19 January gives a fuller account:

> Albert saw Sir Robert Peel and I joined them a little later . . . Albert and I then suggested the desirability of some day considering, and perhaps establishing an Order (as we have nothing of the kind), which might be given only for Merit or as a mark of particular favour, in fact, for Distinguished Talents, & Personal Service to the Sovereign. Sir Robert thought this might be a very good thing, particularly if the Order were carefully bestowed.

So here is the germ of royal consideration of an Order of Merit but rather confused with the Royal Victorian Order and Royal Victorian Chain; all three distinctions were over 50 years away. Attention was really concentrated on extending the civil side of the Bath and it was that rather than a new order which Queen Victoria and Prince Albert discussed with Peel's successor as Prime Minister, Lord John Russell at Osborne on 27 August 1846.[9]

Around this time, of course, Prince Albert in particular would have been very conscious of the reshaping in 1842 of the Prussian Order Pour le mérite to include those men of science, literature and the arts whom the British honours system was, by and large, failing. The influence of this order on the development of our own Order of Merit is discussed in later chapters and a fuller account of it will appear in the *Journal of the Orders of Medals Research Society*.

1873: The House of Lords debate

The most important airing of the perceived need for an Order of Merit as we know it came in 1873, in a debate in the House of Lords.[10] In February of that year, Lord Houghton deplored the restrictions (of long standing and still in force today) on British subjects accepting foreign honours. He was supported by (the Fifth) Earl Stanhope, a former Under Secretary for Foreign Affairs (1834–35), who went on, however, to regret 'that an Order of Merit, or some such Order, was not instituted in this country. He hoped that some day it would be.'

Stanhope's foray in February encouraged him to raise the matter more fully later in the year. He was very well qualified to do so. He was a Fellow of the Royal Society, the Founder and Chairman of the Trustees of the National Portrait Gallery, a Trustee of the British Museum, President of the Royal Literary Fund, a member of the Historical Manuscripts Commission, President of the Society of Antiquaries and a historian of some repute.

On 27 June 1873, Stanhope tabled a motion in the House of Lords for an Address to be presented to the Queen, 'praying Her Majesty to take into her gracious consideration the institution of an Order of Merit, by which her Majesty would be enabled to bestow a sign of her royal approbation on men who have deserved well of their country in science, literature, and art.'[11]

In his speech, Stanhope set out cogently the arguments for such an order and compared Britain unfavourably with the other leading countries of Europe in its lack of recognition of men outside the military or civil service of the State. Most states had been tardy in recognising merit in literature, art or science but this had been rectified on the Continent, with Britain still 'discreditably lagging in the rear'. He maintained, with examples, that all the other four Great Powers, France, Austria, Russia and Prussia, found room in their honours systems for such non-official luminaries. He singled out Prussia for particular praise, extolling the Pour le mérite for its recognition of 'men who had obtained eminence in any branch of knowledge or of art' (für Wissenschaften und Künste). In Britain (or England, as he, like so many others then and now, persist in calling it), the 'recognition of literature, science and art far from advancing, had actually retrograded'.

Stanhope suggested three rules: first, 'the new Order of Merit should be open to all parties and to all or nearly all professions and ranks' (the qualification probably referred to the exclusion of theologians from Pour le mérite); second, 'the number should be limited'; and, third, 'the Order should not carry with it any change of title, as distinct from the name of the recipient'. He referred to the refusals of titular honours by the historians Henry Hallam and George Grote.

In conclusion, Stanhope expressed confidence in Ministers who would carefully consider his proposal, compared with the 'contempt and disdain often felt for literature and science by underlings in office'. His final plea was 'to seek to do honour to those men who had done honour to their country'.

Granville, the Foreign Secretary, responded courteously but vigorously. Of course, he respected 'the deservings of distinguished men of science, literature, and art, of whom the country had good reason to be proud' but 'the difficulties of dispensing a new Order of Merit...were by far greater than [Stanhope] seemed to think'. He mocked the Légion d'Honneur 'because almost every third or fourth person one met in the streets displayed that riband'. (This was long before the Paris Metro faced bankruptcy because too many of its passengers, with the red riband, were exempt from paying fares.)

While conceding that, 'it was illogical to confine rewards to servants of the Crown; but it should be remembered that it was the object of the State to tempt the best men into the public service', he concluded by doubting whether the distinguished potential members 'would derive the slightest increased consideration from an Order of that character' and by disagreeing with Stanhope's proposal because 'the Government saw no means of giving practical effect' to it.

Three other peers spoke to the motion. Lord Houghton recognised that, 'it was doubtless easier to reward public servants than to select men distinguished in art, science and literature', but 'believed the advantages that would accrue [from Stanhope's proposal] would considerably outweigh the defects'. He referred to three men who 'had guided and influenced the mind of England' but who 'would hardly come under the cognizance of those who distributed decorations': Samuel Taylor Coleridge, Thomas Carlyle and John Stuart Mill. Houghton's final question was: 'Why should there not be a distinct recognition of mental eminence?'

The other two speakers were against Stanhope's motion. The (Second) Earl of Harrowby, another Garter Knight, thought 'the recognition of literary and scientific men as a separate class was undesirable'. It was wisest to leave matters as they were and to allow literary and scientific men 'to enjoy...that unbought honour which sprang from the admiration and gratitude of their countrymen'.

Finally, yet another Garter Knight, (the Third) Earl Grey, opposed a new order and cited earlier opposition even to extending the Order of the Bath to civilians eminent in literature and art. In the government of Lord John (now Earl) Russell in 1846, in which he had been Colonial Secretary, such an extension 'was very carefully considered, and it was determined that it would not be expedient to take that course . . . Some of the most distinguished literary men concurred in that view.'

The motion was negatived and so ended the only full public debate on the pros and cons for the sort of Order of Merit we have today. Many of its arguments are relevant to any discussion of the Order today: the preponderance of officials, military and civil, in the honours lists; the lack of recognition of men in the fields of art, literature and science but the accompanying problem of selection where there are less clear hierarchies; the doubt that public honours add anything to the reputations of such people; and the attraction of an honour which brings no title with it.

Stanhope died, aged 70, in 1875. He deserves an honoured place in the pre-history of the Order of Merit.

The year after the Lords debate provided evidence of the continuing problem of titular honours for many eminent men. Disraeli wanted to honour Carlyle.[12] He sought, and received, the Queen's agreement to offer Carlyle a GCB (because no KCB was vacant!) and a pension. He devoted much effort to composing the offer to a man who had always treated him as 'a superlative Hebrew conjurer'. Carlyle was embarrassed at receiving this from a man 'I almost never spoke of except with contempt . . . yet see, here he comes with a pan of hot coals for my guilty head'. Disraeli's letter (of 27 December 1874) was bold:

> A Government should recognise intellect. It elevates and sustains the tone of a nation . . . When I consider the literary world, I see only two living names which . . . will be remembered . . . I have advised the Queen to offer to confer a baronetcy on Mr Tennyson and the same distinction should be at your command, if you liked it . . . You are childless and may not care for hereditary honors . . . recommend Her Majesty to confer on you the highest distinction for merit at her command and which, I believe, has never yet been conferred by her except for direct services to the State. And that is the Grand Cross of the Bath.

Carlyle declined the honour – as did Tennyson, although he took the barony offered ten years later. Disraeli recorded the refusal in a letter as follows:

> Alas! The Philosopher of Chelsea, tho' evidently delighted with the proposal, and grateful in wondrous sentences, will accept of nothing – 'Titles of honor, of all degrees, are out of keeping with the tenor of my poor life' . . . Nevertheless the proposal is 'magnanimous and noble, without example in the history of governing persons with men of letters' and a great deal more in the same highly-sublimated Teutonic vein.

Significantly, a footnote by Disraeli's biographer, G. E. Buckle, against a statement that Disraeli's imagination had supplied 'the unique distinction which might not unfitly be offered to the doyen of English letters' reads: 'The Order of Merit was not founded until the Coronation of King Edward VII'.

Prime Ministers continued to have intermittent feelings of guilt about top-level recognition for the arts. After Tennyson's peerage in 1884, Gladstone turned his mind to artists and in June 1885 wrote to the Queen that he had 'for many years felt it to be a matter of regret as well as of anomaly that the grade of Baronet so frequently conferred in the Medical profession (for example) has not been tendered to any Artist'. After consulting Sir Frederic Leighton, the President of the Royal Academy (to whom he virtually promised a baronetcy at a later date), he submitted the names of G. F. Watts and John Everett Millais for the honour; Watts declined (but accepted the OM in 1902), Millais accepted.[13]

The approaching Golden Jubilee of Queen Victoria in 1887 aroused, as is common on such royal occasions, interest in – and, possibly, expectation of – honours. A doctor who had suggested an 'Order for Medical Merit' was satirised in *Punch* by 'Sawbones', who said something more than a decorative order was needed. Why not distinguishing titles, such as the Marquis of Magnesia or Baron Bluepill? A distinguished physician or surgeon might be useful in the House of Lords but 'fancy Harvey or John Hunter . . . going about with a medal or strip of silk or satin attached to the portion of attire anterior to his pectoral region'.[14]

Just before the Jubilee, a weightier article in *Nature* deplored the fact 'that during the Queen's reign, since the death of the lamented Prince Consort, there has been an impossible gulf between the highest culture of the nation and Royalty itself. The brain of the nation has been divorced from its head. Literature and science, and we might almost add art, have no access to the throne.' It criticised two future OMs for preferring politics to literature: Sir George Trevelyan for saying that literature was 'a good thing to be left' and John Morley for looking back 'with a half-contemptuous regret to the days when he occupied a 'more humble sphere' as a leader of literature. Again, there was an unfavourable comparison with the leading continental countries, where 'men of science and literature are recognized as subjects who can do the State some service'.[15]

1887: Proposed Order of Merit in Science and Art

Queen Victoria's Golden Jubilee Year saw the most serious attempt to create a new order for science and the arts. It was the brainchild of Sir James Linton, the recently-knighted first President of the Royal Institute of Painters in Water Colours, which he had reorganised in order to elevate the status of that particular art form. He had been encouraged by the 'condescending kindness' of the artistically-inclined Princess Beatrice, Queen

Victoria's youngest daughter, who was also her constant companion and close confidante. He therefore put to the princess on 20 January 1887 a proposal for 'an order comprising the degrees of Knight and companion to those [including ladies] who have distinguished themselves in', 'the Arts and Letters, and more especially the Arts'.[16]

After stating that 'this is the only country where men who have devoted themselves to the cause of culture and the advancement of Art have no special decoration', he expressed the hope that the order would be 'absolutely personal to The Queen (non-political, non-official and non-academical) in order that all who form in the highest sense the Aristocracy of their day and generation may be gradually led to look to The Queen (without the intervention of any official of a public character) for the supreme appreciation of their merits.'

This back-door approach was quickly re-routed to the front. It was referred by the Queen's Private Secretary, Sir Henry Ponsonby, to the Prime Minister's (Henry Manners), who responded that Lord Salisbury 'can hardly consider that the suggestions of Sir J. Linton are altogether practical or practicable...The creation of a new order of the kind suggested would require much consideration, as altogether the number of Orders in existence in England is considerable.'[17] In an accompanying private letter, he said that Lord Salisbury 'would not be obdurate altogether on the matter, if Her Majesty saw the way to make a small and easily managed distinction of the sort'.[18]

In replying to Linton, on the princess's behalf, Ponsonby said the Queen 'had no directions to issue on the subject' and added that he did not understand the proposals: 'You contemplate a merely private or personal ornament. I cannot think the Artist would like this.'[19]

The project now gained pace, with correspondence between Linton, Ponsonby, Salisbury, the Queen and a 'back-room boy', Sir Owen Burne (the Secretary in the Political and Secret Department of the India Office since 1874). Linton, worried that he had 'overstepped the kindness and condescension of Her Majesty and of Her Royal Highness', assured Ponsonby that he did not intend 'personal' to mean 'private' but simply to be as purely a civil order as possible, distinct from the existing orders awarded for naval, military and political service.[20]

Burne wondered whether any new order should have only a level of companion, although he recognised that a knighthood was perhaps what the artists wanted; he also agreed with Linton's idea of kicking 'out the Royal Academy as having any voice in the matter' and of including ladies 'if there be no objection to make them "She Knights"'. He passed on the views of the Prime Minister that 'the whole subject requires a good deal of deliberation before coming to a conclusion one way or the other'. Finally, Burne thought literature and science should be included as well as art.[21]

Salisbury now went ahead and consulted the Cabinet, reporting to the Queen that such an order would be 'desirable if agreeable to the leading men of those vocations [for which it was intended]'. Some Ministers were apprehensive, however, 'that any obtrusive activity of the Ministry in pushing a project of that kind at a moment of such gravity as the present [of Ministerial resignations], might be open to unfavourable comment.'[22]

The Queen nevertheless urged Salisbury to go ahead with consulting Sir Frederic Leighton 'and other leading men in the artistic and literary worlds'. There followed one of those slightly steely sentences which feature in Queen Victoria's correspondence with Ministers: 'The Queen hopes you do not mean that the Cabinet are opposed to the idea but rather that there are other more important questions that must postpone the consideration of this one.'[23] In reply, Salisbury reassured Ponsonby that while there is no opposition to the idea, 'it is felt that there are other more important questions under consideration, and there is a fear lest our activity in the present case might be disadvantageously compared with what is supposed to be, but unjustly supposed to be, our inactivity in other more important matters.'[24]

By mid-June, Salisbury was telling the Queen that 'whenever Your Majesty has leisure, he also desires to speak concerning the proposed Order of Merit for Science and Art'.[25] On 25 July, the Queen sent Salisbury the rules of the Order Pour le mérite sent to her by her eldest daughter, the Crown Princess of Prussia.[26]

On 5 January 1888, Salisbury submitted 'the rough draft of the proposed Statutes for an Order of Merit in Science and Art, in order to ascertain, before consulting any other person, whether it meets Your Majesty's general approval.'[27] There was to be 'an Order of Knighthood to be bestowed on those who have attained great and recognized distinction in science, or in the arts of painting, sculpture, or music'. There would be one grade, divided into two branches: 20 Knights of the Order of Scientific Merit and 20 Knights of the Order of Artistic Merit, five of which would be reserved for eminence in music. The knights were to be named in the original statutes and, within six months, each branch should submit a list of 40 other persons from whom future selection should 'generally' be made and the number should be kept up to 40 by further selections.

There would be a Chancellor and Vice-Chancellor, also to be named in the original statutes, who would have the duty of convening the selection meetings. If the Sovereign nominated someone who was not on the reserve list, 'special reasons for such exceptional nomination' would be given. Although the insignia was not spelled out at this stage, the initials to be used by knights were: KMS (Knight of Merit in Science) and KMA (Knight of Merit in Art).

A couple of days later, the Queen received Salisbury at Osborne and 'again talked of many things, – and of the new order of Merit...'.[28] No details are given.

A month later, Salisbury was pouring cold water on the scheme. He reported to the Queen that he had spoken to Leighton about the list that was submitted to her (of which there is no trace in the Royal Archives) and found him 'very discouraging'. Leighton 'laid great stress upon the heart-burnings the proposed proceedings were likely to cause, and could not be induced to speak plainly what he wished for'. Presumably, the President of the Royal Academy knew his artists and was terrified at the prospect, akin perhaps to elections to the Academy itself, of the furore that would be caused by the selection processes envisaged for the new order. This helped to get Salisbury off the hook.

Although Sir James Linton's scheme had run into the ground, he must have derived some satisfaction from the institution of the Order of Merit in 1902. Of course, he did not receive it, as perhaps he had hoped to be included among the much larger number of KMAs. He died, at the age of 86, in 1916, without achieving even the distinction of an entry in the *Dictionary of National Biography*.

The 1890s

In the decade or so between the unsuccessful Order of Merit in Science and the Arts and the successful plain Order of Merit, the honours system, under both Salisbury and Gladstone (and, briefly, Rosebery), moved towards greater recognition of science and the arts.

The three Prime Ministers differed in their personal approach to honours. Salisbury was a marquess (who had declined a dukedom), with titles going back three centuries, and a Garter that more or less went with what we would now call 'the territory' (Hatfield and Cranborne in his case). Gladstone was the Grand Old Man, a determined commoner, who would never take the earldom that was his due. Rosebery, the short-lived Premier in 1894–95, was not averse to the Garter and the Thistle (an unusual combination for a non-royal), the Royal Victorian Chain and a United Kingdom earldom to top up his older Scottish one.

In his dealings with Queen Victoria, Salisbury was showing a desire to broaden, however marginally, the basis of the Upper House. In December 1891, he submitted his draft New Year Honours List, proposing names over which she had previously had reservations:

> Sir Frederick Leighton and Sir William Thomson are, whatever their merits, respectively at the head of the Art and Science of England [and Scotland also, Thomson must have thought]. Is very desirable to give the feeling that the House of Lords contains something besides rich men and politicians ... The more the House of Lords can be provided, as occasion serves, with elements of eminence of a different kind, the greater will be its moral authority, and its chance of doing useful service ... to the institutions of this country.[29]

Thomson received his peerage as Lord Kelvin in 1892 and, indeed, other future civil OMs were to be honoured in the decade: Sir Archibald Geikie in 1891, Sir William Crookes in 1897, Sir Lawrence Alma-Tadema in 1899 and Sir Richard Jebb in 1900.

As we have seen, 1892 also saw a privy counsellorship for T. H. Huxley. In 1893, there was a knighthood for John Tenniel (the cartoonist for *Punch* and illustrator of *Alice in Wonderland*), in 1894 a baronetcy for Edward Burne-Jones, the painter, and in 1895 a knighthood for Henry Irving, the first for an actor but quickly followed by one in 1897 for Squire Bancroft.

1896 brought Leighton his peerage (the day before he died) and a privy counsellorship for Friedrich Max-Müller, the Oxford philologist. He had refused a knighthood ten years earlier as being inadequate recognition when foreign countries (including Germany) had given him their highest honours reserved for literary work; he died in 1900, otherwise he would have been a prime candidate for early appointment to the OM.

At the end of 1896, after discussing the New Year Honours, which included a peerage for Lister (who would be an inaugural OM), Queen Victoria recorded: 'Lord Salisbury explained that he wished to bring into the House of Lords men of science and art. I quite agreed with his view.'[30]

She did not, however, agree with artists being admitted to the Privy Council. It was alright for scientists (Huxley) or scholars (Max-Müller) but not for artists, like G. F. Watts, the future OM, whose appointment she vetoed in 1897. Salisbury had urged it on her because

> he is accused of never submitting to your Majesty any honour in favour of *Art*; and that many people are alienated by this consideration.[31]

This reads rather oddly in view of his recent successful attempts on behalf of Leighton, Burne-Jones and Millais.

It can be seen that, throughout the nineteenth century, there is recurring discontent with the failings of the honours system, particularly in regard to science, the arts and literature. It finds expression in Parliament and in the writings of commentators on the system. There are moves towards remedying the matter but they come to nothing. Nobody bites the bullet until the appearance of an unlikely figure in the rotund shape of the new king, who accedes in the fourth week of the new century: Edward VII.

4

THE ESTABLISHMENT OF
THE ORDER OF MERIT

The founder

King Edward VII was an unlikely figure as the founder of the Order of Merit. George III and Queen Victoria (with Prince Albert at her side) appear much more likely founders; it is a pity that the opportunities of 1844 and 1888 were missed.

Much has been written about Edward VII, as about all British monarchs. In his case, very little relates to any serious interest in the sciences, the arts or learning. He had undergone the ritual training of an heir to the throne, including educational visits to the continent and studies at Oxford and Cambridge; indeed, in his youth, he had attended lectures at the Royal Institution given by that great refuser of honours, Michael Faraday, whose attitude was one of the pointers towards having a non-titular Order of Merit.

A glance at any index of any biography of Edward VII is illuminating. The list of his sporting pastimes is far longer than that of his cultural interests. Queen Victoria had scant regard for her eldest son's serious side, particularly his capacity for paperwork. She warned Gladstone: 'The P. of W. has *never* been fond of reading, and from his earlier years it was *impossible* to get him to do so. Newspapers and, *very rarely*, a novel, are all he ever reads.'[1] His father was equally scathing: 'his intellect is of no more use than a pistol packed in the bottom of a trunk if one were attacked in the robber-infested Apennines.'[2]

The biographer Christopher Hibbert opined that Edward 'seems rarely to have even so much as opened a book, and almost never to have finished one, a notable exception being Mrs Henry Wood's romantic novel, "East Lynne".' Shown a picture by Holman Hunt (an early OM) of a London street scene on the night of his marriage, Edward enquired, 'Where am I?'[3] Another future OM, Henry James, deplored the accession of 'Edward the Caresser', whom he considered an 'arch vulgarian'. 'Corpulent voluptuary' was the term employed by another writer, Rudyard Kipling, who was twice to decline the OM.

His woeful ignorance of literature is often highlighted by the story of his comment at a dinner of the Royal Society of Literature organised by Sir Sidney Lee to celebrate the publication of the *Dictionary of National Biography*. Asking why a particular cleric was there and being told that he was a very great authority on Lamb, Edward retorted, in bewilderment: 'On *lamb!*'[4]

On music, Edward VII's reputation fares better. He patronised the opera, enjoying gargantuan meals in the hour-long intervals, and he was a sponsor of the school that became the Royal College of Music; he lobbied for knighthoods for musicians, including Arthur Sullivan. As regards the stage, 'he fancied lighter plays only and was hardly interested in the cause of serious dramatists'.[5]

Such interest as he had in science was focused on medicine. Perhaps because he had sat on Royal Commissions on the Housing of the Working Classes (on which he made his only speech in the House of Lords) and on Investigation into Relief for the Aged Poor, improved medicine caught his attention. He met Louis Pasteur (along with Charles Darwin) at the International Congress of Medicine in London in 1881, he visited the Pasteur Institute in Paris in 1888 and later the same year he called a meeting at Marlborough House to found a National Association for the Prevention of Consumption. He encouraged Joseph Lister (due to be one of his first OMs) to found in 1891 the British Institute of Preventive Medicine, later renamed the Lister Institute. He started what became King Edward's Hospital Fund, to raise badly-needed money for the hospitals of the capital, he supported his friend Agnes Keyser in founding the hospital that is now the King Edward VII's Hospital, Sister Agnes, much patronised by his descendants, and towards the end of his life he told the surgeon, Sir Frederick Treves, that his 'greatest ambition was not to quit this world until a real cure for cancer' had been found. He would almost certainly have played a greater role in public life had his mother allowed it.

Edward's official biographer was muted when it came to the intellectual side of life. Sir Sidney Lee wrote in the *Dictionary of National Biography*:

> While he derived ample amusement from music and the drama, chiefly from the theatre's more frivolous phases, he showed small capacity for dramatic criticism. A man of the world, he lacked the intellectual equipment of a thinker, and showed on occasion an unwillingness to exert his mental powers. He was no reader of books. He could not concentrate his mind on them.[6]

In his vast two-volume biography, Lee's concluding paragraph ran thus:

> Literature and science he could not appreciate. His outlook was essentially practical. Not for him the 'dreams and desires and sombre songs and sweet'; not for him the tumultuous mighty harmonies of the poetic imagination; but for him essentially the blazing pageantry of court ceremonial, the activities and interests of an intensely patriotic sovereign. He had the temperament of a king, and as a king he was eminently successful. *Son métier était Roi.*[7]

The founding

The Order of Merit did not emerge in a neat, orderly, typewritten way, as would a governmental creation. Neither King Edward VII nor Lord Salisbury kept diaries that have survived.[8] According to Arthur Balfour, consulted years later by King George V's Private Secretary: 'The whole idea originated with King Edward: I have no reason to believe that it was a subject in which Lord Salisbury took a deep interest; and I was not consulted.'[9] (He had become Prime Minister three weeks after the institution of the Order.) The only living ex-Prime Minster, the Liberal Lord Rosebery, was consulted, however, as he told George V's Private Secretary many years later.[10]

The first letter of any substance on the matter is in manuscript, dated 28 March 1902, from the Royal Yacht Victoria and Albert and it presupposes previous discussion. In it, the King's Assistant Private Secretary, wrote to the Comptroller of the Lord Chamberlain's Department thus:

> Re Order of Merit
> The King says you have got all the salient points of the Order. Two classes (1) & (2)
> I Naval & Military
> It is to be instituted as a reward for *exceptionally meritorious service* for Military & Naval Officers. [The word 'Senior' before 'officers' was crossed out.]
> II Civil
> For *exceptionally meritorious service* towards the advancement of Art, Literature, Science & c & c (all the different branches of the liberal professions to be quoted generally (i.e. in general terms)).
> There is to be only one class. The Order is to carry no Knighthood & confers no rank or precedence.
> The King approves of your asking Pom McDonnell (on behalf of the P.M.) to submit a draft outline of the Statutes & would like you to submit it, with your own remarks, additions, to here, as soon as possible, together with the translation of the Prussian Statutes & H.M. will then

go through them & will make such additions or alterations as he may think necessary.[11]

Ellis must have acted as requested because by 12 April he was telling McDonnell (Salisbury's Private Secretary) that the King was grateful for his carefully drawn up Statutes but enclosing a letter including some suggestions by His Majesty. He mentioned also the question of precedence and of consulting Garter King of Arms, to which reference is made later in the chapter.

By mid-April, the consultation between King and Prime Minister and others was in full swing. On 17 April, Salisbury wrote (in manuscript) to the King, putting forward the views of St John Brodrick, the Secretary of State for War (later Ninth Viscount and First Earl of Midleton), strongly supported by Lord Roberts, the Commander-in-Chief of the Army, that:

> an extension of the 'Ordre pour le Mérite' to the military service would be productive of confusion, and would add to the difficulty of duly distributing other honours among military officers according to their merits. The number of honours which are now open to them is very large, far beyond all precedent. The peculiar class of merit which the new Order is intended to recognise will not, ordinarily, have any close relation to military service, and some confusion will probably result from an attempt to mix up with such claims the kind of distinction which the Ordre pour le Mérite will confer.

After adding the view of Lord Selborne, the First Lord of the Admiralty that the new Order should also not apply to naval officers, Salisbury concluded with firm views about limiting the number of the Order:

> I hope that in fixing the Statutes of the Order, Your Majesty will see fit to select some number beyond which the creation of members shall not go. *What* that limit shall be is not a matter of primary importance: what is essential is that it shall be known that there *is* a limit fixed by the Statutes of the Order. Otherwise it will not keep its hold in public estimation.[12]

To this démarche from three of his most senior ministers, the King responded speedily, firmly and in detail. Writing from Sandringham on 20 April, he expressed

> some surprise, and I fail to see any arguments brought forward [by Brodrick and Selborne] why the 'Order for Merit' should not be conferred on officers of the Army & Navy who have greatly distinguished themselves on active service.

The Order which will be instituted will have only one class, & no rank given for it. It will consist of a Red cross worn round the neck, the only difference being that the order conferred on officers of the Army & Navy will have two swords crossed, as was the case in the Hanoverian Order of the Guelph.

For many years it has been my great wish that this 'Order of Merit' should be instituted so as to reward in a special manner officers of the Navy & Army, & Civilians distinguished in Arts, Sciences and Literature. I have always been so much impressed by the Prussian Order 'Pour le mérite', which was I believe instituted originally by Frederick the Great conferring such distinctions, that I have always wished that a similar one might be created for England.

Your view that there should be a limited number is well worthy of consideration & possibly 12 for the Army & Navy & 12 for Civilians would be the right number.

I shall be glad to see Mr. Brodrick on the subject on my return to London.

I should wish it to be a decoration entirely vested in the Sovereign's hands, who would naturally consult the Prime Minister, & the Ministers at the head of certain Departments.[13]

In his reply the next day, Lord Salisbury said he had told both Selborne and Brodrick that the King did not agree with their views but would be ready to give Brodrick an audience if he wished. By the end of April, Brodrick was ruefully writing to the Viceroy of India:

The King is giving us much trouble with Orders ... There is to be a new 'Order of Merit' – limited to 24. I got it reduced from 60. It is for savants and soldiers. Its chief objects are that it is worn round the neck, and puts Edward VII on a par with Frederick the Great, who invented a similar one![14]

Since the King was already suggesting a limit of 24 in his letter of 20 April, it is not clear when Brodrick 'got it reduced from 60', although that would have been a natural number for an order based on the Prussian order with its 30 German and 30 foreign members.

May and June were taken up with the routine of arranging, between the Palace, Downing Street and Garter King of Arms, the drafting of both the empowering Letters Patent and the Statutes that would follow them. The Prime Minister's Private Secretary, Schomberg McDonnell, seems to have taken the lead in the drafting. By the time he sent 'revised' Statutes to Sir Arthur Ellis in the Lord Chamberlain's Office on 28 April, they are virtually the same as those finally promulgated.

Only small points were later changed: the colour of the seal was to be white rather than blue; 'distinguished and meritorious' was inserted before the bald description of military 'services'; and the deletion of the words 'Military and Civil Division of' before 'Order' in the Statute on Honorary Members seems to show some original idea of having a formal separation between Military and Civil Members.

All was now set for the passing of the Letters Patent under the Great Seal of the Realm by the Clerk of the Crown in Chancery, Muir Mackenzie, on 23 June and the gazetting on 26 June (Coronation Day) of those Letters Patent alone, it having been decided (following a 'protest' from Garter King of Arms) not to publish the actual Statutes, which were to be dated 23 June. (Copies of the Letters Patent and the Statutes are given in Appendices A and B, respectively.)

On 26 June also, the names of the first OMs would be announced, within the main Coronation Honours List, together with an explanation of the institution of the new Order.

On 24 June, however, a dramatic *London Gazette Extraordinary* was published, saying simply that the 'Coronation had been cancelled indefinitely from 26th instant'. Edward VII had been diagnosed as having acute appendicitis, which required an immediate operation. He insisted, however, that the honours list should proceed, as planned, for 26 June. On 2 August, the first OMs were formally gazetted.

The Coronation Honours were announced in the press on 26 June with the first headline being 'New Order of Merit'. There followed the list of appointments which the King had approved: the Knights of the Garter, the Thistle and St Patrick, the peers, privy counsellors, baronets, knights bachelor and those in the civil division of the Order of the Bath. After the name of Dr Benjamin Whitelegge, Chief Inspector of Factories, came the announcement:

ORDER OF MERIT
The King has been pleased to institute an Order of Merit, to which his Majesty, as Sovereign of the Order, has made the following appointments:
Field Marshal Earl Roberts of Kandahar, KG, KP, VC
Field Marshal Viscount Wolseley, KP, GCB
General Viscount Kitchener of Khartoum, GCB, GCMG
Lord Rayleigh, FRS
Lord Kelvin, GCVO, FRS
Lord Lister, FRS
Admiral of the Fleet the Hon Sir Henry Keppel, GCB
The Right Hon John Morley, MP
The Right Hon WEH Lecky, MP
Admiral Sir Edward Hobart Seymour, GCB
Sir William Huggins, KCB, PRS
George Frederick Watts, Esq, RA

In the Honours List were a number of other appointments relevant to the new Order. Two of its original Members, Lord Lister and Lord Kelvin, were made privy counsellors, along with R. B. Haldane, the lawyer MP who was to receive the OM in 1915. Among the appointments to the military division of the Order of the Bath were two future OMs: Admiral Sir John Fisher (as a GCB) and Vice Admiral Arthur Knyvet Wilson (as a KCB), who became OMs in 1905 and 1912.

Two of the men behind the foundation and development of the Order were also honoured as KCBs: Viscount Esher, the eminence grise who was officially Secretary to the Office of Works, and the Hon Schomberg McDonnell, who, following the resignation of Lord Salisbury, was just succeeding Esher at the Office of Works.

Other notable names in the List were the composers, Hubert Parry (baronet) and Charles Stanford (knight bachelor) and the writer, Arthur Conan Doyle (knight bachelor). Leslie Stephen, the editor of the *Dictionary of National Biography* and father of Virginia Woolf and Vanessa Bell, was rather curiously made a KCB and Winston Churchill's mother, Mrs George Cornwallis-West, received the Royal Red Cross decoration for serving on the hospital ship, *Maine*. As the wife of the late Lord Randolph Churchill, some time Secretary of State for India, she had received the much higher distinction of the Imperial Order of the Crown of India but CI did not follow her name in the *Gazette*.

As regards the selection of the first Members, the Prime Minister's Private Secretary refers to the King having 'written the names on Lord Salisbury's list: I will get them and send them to you in due course'.[15] In later years, Balfour wrote:

> The names no doubt had been settled some time before this so as to be ready for announcing on the original date fixed for the coronation [26 June].[16]

The new Order was greeted with dignified acclaim in *The Times*. A leading article on 27 June referred to:

> The keen and general interest aroused by the creation of the new 'Order of Merit', a measure, it may be said, that has met with general approval.
>
> The impression produced by the publication of the names of those selected by the King as the original members of the Order of Merit is that all are worthy of the high honour for which they have been chosen. Some would plead for additional names, but would not desire to strike out any. [There followed fulsome tributes to the original members.] What is wanting, perhaps, is a representation of the imaginative elements, of poetry and fiction, as well as of pure philosophy. The names of Mr Herbert Spencer and of Mr George Meredith have been suggested,

and it will be generally agreed that these as well as others might be appropriately associated with the illustrious twelve. But it must be borne in mind that there will certainly be a few additional members, though it was not thought wise or expedient to fill up the whole number at once. It might, perhaps, be advisable that later additions should be made subject, in a modified form, to the principle of co-optation adopted in the Friedensklasse of the Prussian Order. However made, they will be governed by the characteristics which are visible in the rules of that Order and which we believe have at once commended the idea to the British people. The simplicity of the Order of Merit, the absence of title or precedence or any form of parade, the perfect equality between its members whether they represent eminent services in the Army or the Navy or solid work done in science, in literature, and in art, the comprehension of nearly every form of achievement and intelligence, are all in accord with the temper now prevailing in the nation. The Coronation honours – and the Order of Merit in especial – are, in great measure, a tribute to the ideal of efficiency which we have been taught, in a hard school, to hold up before us.

The part played in the preparations for the new Order by the College of Arms is hazy. Garter King of Arms, the 86-year-old Sir Albert Woods, had been a herald for 64 years and Garter for 32; his father had held the office before him. Because he was old and infirm, however, a Deputy Garter had been appointed: Sir William Weldon, Clarenceux King of Arms, who had once managed a circus and was to perform in Garter's place at the impending coronation. It was probably he with whom McDonnell and Ellis were in touch but, busy as he would have been with the coronation, he could probably not summon up much interest in this new-fangled and very simple Order. It did not have much to offer in heraldic terms.

In 1902, by order of the King, Garter King of Arms, the aged Sir Albert Woods, was consulted about the drafting of the Statutes of the new Order as 'an expert in these matters [who] will be able to say better than I can whether anything has been omitted'.[17] The 'advice' of 'Garter' is referred to and, at one point, the Prime Minister's Private Secretary consulted him in person. Later, a revised copy of the draft Letters Patent and Statutes were shown to him. But, alas, a later Garter explained to me, 'He did not keep a record of anything which he said in response to the approaches made to him in 1902.'[18]

Edward VII told Lord Salisbury in the beginning that he wanted to base his new order on the German Order Pour le mérite. His links with that order went back to his baptism on 25 January 1842, at which the chief sponsor, in person, was King Frederick William IV of Prussia, who was to reconstitute the Pour le mérite with a civil class only four months later. In the King's suite at the baptism was the great naturalist, Alexander von Humboldt, who was the first Chancellor of the new civil class.

Edward VII sent for and received from the British Embassy in Berlin in March 1902 the statutes of the German order and coloured drawings of its insignia (much as his mother had done in 1887 when the earlier British Order of Merit had been under consideration). In November 1902, the German Ambassador was asking for copies of the Statutes of the new British Order of Merit. Having looked at the Founder and the details of his founding of the Order of Merit, it is reasonable to ask: why did he do it? He gave a superficial explanation to Salisbury: he had always wanted a British Order Pour le mérite and his desire would only have been accentuated by the death in 1888, after a 99-day reign, of his brother-in-law, the Liberal-minded Frederick III of Germany, whom he described as being 'too good for this world'. More to the point probably was his extraordinary interest, common to monarchs before and after him, in orders and decorations and in etiquette generally.

I think it was therefore, partly because he was a king (Lee's *'Son métier était Roi'*) that he wanted an order, appointments to which were entirely in his hands. The Prime Minister and others might help him in the choice but, ultimately, it would be his. In choosing the field of art and learning, he was, perhaps unknowingly, following the example of many early modern monarchs, who considered that patronising scholars and artists was the right thing to do, even thinking (in the case of autocratic rulers) that it gave them a legitimacy in the twilight period between reigning by divine right and reigning by popular will.

Edward VII's enthusiasm for new decorations did not end with the Order of Merit. He founded two other decorations on the occasion of his coronation in 1902, at different ends of the social spectrum. The first was the Royal Victorian Chain, also in the Sovereign's personal gift, for foreign Heads of State and very distinguished subjects who have rendered high-level service to the Sovereign. (I have written in detail on this elsewhere.[19]) The second was the Imperial Service Order, for middle-ranking civil servants.

A key feature of the Order of Merit and the one that gives it such a high standing is its freedom from political influence. That has always been so but nowhere in its birth was this publicly stated. The Statutes are silent on the point, which is indicative in itself but not conclusive since the monarch is presumed to act on political advice in all public actions. There has been no statement as in the case of the Orders of the Garter and the Thistle, when appointment to them was transferred to the monarch personally in 1946/47. So, over the years, the point has had to be constantly reiterated informally.

The Statutes: including insignia and other details

The Statutes of the Order of Merit, in their present form, are set out in Appendix B. In fact, they have changed textually little over the years but the effect has been to widen the scope of the Order and this I shall describe in the next chapter – on its development.

Here, I want to recount them as they were promulgated on 23 June 1902. The Preamble, with all its royal flourishes, recites the authority of the Letters Patent passed under the Statutes. (The Letters Patent are set out in Appendix A.)

The Order of Merit is to have a Sovereign and one class of Members. That class is to consist of Ordinary and Honorary Members. The Ordinary Members are to be subjects of the Crown who:

> may have rendered exceptionally meritorious service in Our Navy and our Army, or who may have rendered exceptionally meritorious service towards the advancement of Art, Literature and Science.

There shall not be more than 24 of them. (There is no provision, as in other orders, including the Companions of Honour, for Additional Members to be appointed above the limits laid down in the statutes.) The Honorary Members are such foreigners:

> upon whom We may think fit to confer the honour of being received into the Order.

There is no limit to their number.

Members are to be appointed by a Warrant under the Sovereign's signature, sealed with the Seal of the Order. The Members are to be invested by the Sovereign personally, although the usual provisions are made for occasions when that is not possible. (These are described in more detail in Chapter 23.)

There is to be only one Officer of the Order, a Secretary and Registrar. His duties and Badge and the role that successive incumbents have played in the development of the Order are described in Appendix D. Last, but by no means least, the Sovereign (as usual) reserves:

> full power of annulling, altering, abrogating, augmenting, interpreting, or dispensing with these Statutes and Regulations, or any part thereof

by a Warrant under the Sovereign's signature.

The Badge, which has remained unchanged to this day, was described in Statute IX as being:

> a Cross of red and blue enamel of eight points, having, within a laurel wreath upon a centre of blue enamel, the motto of the Order, that is to say: 'For Merit,' in letters of gold; on the reverse, within a laurel wreath, upon a centre of blue enamel, our Royal and Imperial cypher in gold (with the addition of two silver swords with gold hilts, placed saltirewise

between the angles of the Cross, to be worn by such Members as may be appointed for distinguished and meritorious services in Our Navy and Our Army), the whole being surmounted by Our Imperial Crown enamelled in proper colours, and suspended by a parti-coloured riband of garter blue and crimson of the breadth of two inches.

(The description of military services was later broadened to include the Air Force.) The badges and riband are shown in Illustration 1.

I have not been able to discover who designed the Badge. Collingwood, the manufacturers then and now, have illustrations of various designs, all based on a cross, surmounted by a crown, usually with laurel wreath and with swords, where appropriate, leading to the eventual design. The initials on them appear to be HAW. The firm consulted a former employee: a woman who was assistant to the insignia manager, who had joined the firm in 1913 but whose memory, at the age of 93 in 1986, was beginning to fail. Nevertheless, she was clear that the designer was a man and probably from outside the firm because the initial expenses for the order include £3.2s.6d for 'drawings'.[20]

The Royal Mint kindly searched their records but

failed to produce any reference to the Order. It therefore looks as if the Mint may not have been consulted officially, though I suppose some form of semi-official consultation remains a possibility.[21]

1 Insignia of the Order of Merit. On the left, Badge of a Civil Member (reverse) and on the right, Badge of a Military Member (obverse).

The crossed swords, to denote a military recipient, were new to a British order, although a common device in other European orders. They had not been used in the Order of the Bath but had been in the Royal Hanoverian Guelphic Order, which played a fleeting role in the British honours system. Edward VII had referred specifically to them in his letter to Salisbury of 20 April. Although the German Pour le mérite inspired much about the Order of Merit, it did not inspire the Badge.

The simplicity of its two-word English motto – 'For Merit' – stood out against the longer mottos of existing British orders. (Only 'Victoria', for the Royal Victorian Order, was shorter.) In its short and direct wording, it bore comparison with the 'For Valour' of the existing Victoria Cross and the 'For Gallantry' of the future George Cross.

It was provided in Statute XII that, as in other orders, Members might suspend a representation of the Riband and Badge from their coats of arms. In addition to the Badge, there was the matter of the Seal of the Order, provided for in the Letters Patent as follows:

> upon a white field, a representation of the Badge to be worn by Members of this Order, impaled with Our Royal Arms, with this circumscription, 'The Seal of the Order of Merit'.

Although the Royal Mint has no trace of being involved in the design of the Badge, it was in that of the Seal. Letters (in manuscript – because of the secrecy?) from a Mint official (Horace Ferguson) to the Lord Chamberlain's Department in May and June 1902 show that they produced drawings, which originally used the badge of the Secretary and Registrar, pointing out that the Badge of a Member differed, according to whether he was military or civil. The decision was made, in those heady days of a great military empire, to use the military version of the Badge. Laurel wreaths were added as an embellishment.

This has looked increasingly odd as the civilian element has grown steadily larger. Today, it is positively misleading. With only 30 out of the 182 Members having worn the military version and with none wearing it today, or in the foreseeable future, this small change in the Seal would be, if nothing more, a courtesy to the present membership.

The question of the precedence of the Order of Merit as an order or of its Members personally was deliberately not covered in the Statutes. In the preparations for establishing the Order, Edward VII had made his position quite clear:

> His Majesty wished you clearly to explain to Lord Salisbury that it will be impossible to grant precedence to the recipients of this Order which may be bestowed on a Captain or on a Field Marshal, and that precedence would complicate the whole matter. That in Germany the 'pour

le Merite' carries with it no precedence, social or military, for the same reason, and bestowing no knighthood or rank, the wives of recipients will remain as before.[22]

The lack of any official guidance, however, immediately aroused problems in a precedence-ridden society. The two men most closely involved, with the King, in its foundation were soon corresponding. In a manuscript letter, the Comptroller of the Lord Chamberlain's Office asked the King's Private Secretary:

> Questions are asked! Are members of the Order of Merit to be permitted (like VC) to have the letters 'OM' after their names?

'Yes', scribbles the Private Secretary on the letter.[23] Later, the Private Secretary needed guidance from the Comptroller:

> Can you tell me where the Order of Merit comes in the order of precedency [sic]?

Instantly comes the reply:

> *immediately after* Grand Crosses of the Bath, GCBs, by the King's order – and tomorrow [at an investiture] Mr Lecky OM will be introduced and follow Admiral Fisher GCB and precede Aga Khan GCIE.[24]

Years later, the anomaly in the non-Statutory precedence of the OM was noted by an heraldic expert on the subject. He noted that, by its Statutes, the later Order of the Companions of Honour *did* have a precedence – after the first class of the Order of the British Empire (GBE) – but that individual CHs had no personal precedence.[25] In practice, it is now customary to accord both OMs and CHs the courtesy precedence accorded to their respective orders, i.e. an OM follows a GCB and a CH follows a GBE, assuming that they enjoy no higher precedence by virtue of another honour or social status.

It was not always so, to judge from Elgar's experience in 1914, recounted in a letter:

> After all I did not dine at the RA – I went in, found they had *omitted* my OM & put me with a crowd of nobodies in the lowest place of all – the bottom table – I see no reason why I should *endure* insults...I left at once and came here [the Athenaeum] & had a herring.[26]

With the Order instituted and the first appointments announced, the men had to be invested. One, as explained later, had got ahead of the others: Kitchener, who received it from the King on his triumphal return from South Africa. The others (except Lecky, who was recuperating in Germany) were summoned to an investiture at the Palace on the afternoon of 8 August, along with many other notables who needed to receive their new awards before attending the postponed Coronation the next day.

It is worth noting, in passing, that the Order of Merit was founded around the same time as three other institutions of intellectual standing, with which its fortunes have been intermittently linked ever since. In December 1901, the Nobel Prizes were first awarded and, as will be seen, many OMs have been Nobel Laureates, in all five of the original categories.

In January 1902, the *Times Literary Supplement* was launched separately from its parent newspaper; again, over the years, many OMs have written for, or had their work reviewed in, what is now known as the TLS. On 8 August, the British Academy was founded as a counterpart, in the humanities and social sciences, of the much older Royal Society; a glance at the list of OMs (Appendix C) will show that a quarter of the Civil Members were or are Fellows of the Academy.

It is fitting to end this chapter on the establishment of the Order of Merit by recording a tribute to this new official 'intellectual élite' from the unofficial home of that élite: the Athenaeum Club. On 25 July 1902, the Club gave a dinner in honour of the Members of the new Order, all seven of whose civilian recipients, as well as Roberts and Wolseley, were long-standing members of the Club. The occasion was recorded at length in *The Times*, in accordance with the custom of the day. Ten of the 12 came to the reception before the dinner; the two absentees were Wolseley, who was cruising off Scotland and Lecky, who was recuperating abroad. Eight stayed for the dinner itself but Morley had a long-standing political engagement and Watts was too frail at 85. Kitchener was the only one who had received the Badge and was therefore able to wear it, the first time it was seen in public.

It was a distinguished gathering, with barely an untitled man in sight. In the chair was the banker and naturalist, Lord Avebury, who received the German Order Pour le mérite in 1902 – but never the OM. In addition to the Lord Chancellor and the Speaker, there were several peers, a couple of bishops, many knights (including Henry Irving, Arthur Conan Doyle and Hubert Parry) and eight men who were to receive the Order themselves in the next 20 years: the scientists, Hooker, Geikie and Crookes, the painters, Alma-Tadema and Holman Hunt, the classical scholar, Jebb, the writer, Barrie, and 'Mr Balfour, MP', who just happened to have been Prime Minster for the previous two weeks. Kipling, who was to turn the Order down twice, was also there, as was St John Brodrick, who had been so sceptical about its creation.

In response to the toast of 'The Guests', each of the eight responded, although Seymour responded for his fellow-sailor, Keppel, who (at 93) 'never flagged throughout the long dinner but . . . did not trust himself to speak'.[27] A message was sent to the King congratulating him on recovering from his operation and he responded:

> I thank sincerely you and the committee and members of the Atheneaum assembled at dinner in celebration of the establishment of the Order of Merit for your telegram and kind good wishes.

The dinner of 11 courses, with five wines, had cost 35s (£1.75) a head.

As it was the first, so it was to be the last time the Members of the Order of Merit met as a group – until the Queen instituted, on the Order's seventy-fifth anniversary in 1977, the practice of quinquennial lunches, on which I shall elaborate in Chapter 25 on the present standing of the Order.

Over the century of its existence, well over half of the Members of the Order of Merit have been members of the Athenaeum, at one time or another. It was therefore fitting that the club gave a dinner for OMs during the Order's centenary year, 2002.

5

DEVELOPMENT OF THE ORDER
OVER THE YEARS

Political independence

In the previous chapter, I referred to the crucial importance, as regards its standing, of the Order of Merit being considered free from political influence. It is so highly valued because it is thought of as outside the ordinary honours system, in which ministers advise the Sovereign on, and take responsibility for, the awards from GCB to MBE, including the CH.

Because, however, there was no simple, official public statement of the 'independence' of the Order in 1902, it has been necessary continually to seek clarification on the point. As early as 1905, the Prime Minister was reassuring the King's Private Secretary:

> Though I do not think that any formal arrangement was ever come to by the late Lord Salisbury when the establishment of this Order was discussed between the King and him, I imagine that it was thought that this decoration was intended to be given, like the Victorian Order, on the initiative of the Sovereign rather than on that of His advisers for the time being, and that what you want is, as it were, any *unofficial* assistance which I can give in the matter.[1]

This accords with what Salisbury's Private Secretary had told Knollys when the Coronation Honours List was being prepared in 1902. After saying that Salisbury was writing to all intended recipients, he concluded:

> he has not written to any of those who are to be appointed Members of the Order of Merit as this intimation should of course come direct from HM.[2]

Much later, Lloyd George attempted, successfully, to block a proposed appointment to the Order by George V: that of Gilbert Murray in 1921. What it caused the King's Private Secretary to do, however, was to seek reassurance about the monarch's powers with regard to conferring the Order. Stamfordham consulted his predecessor and two former Prime Ministers. He recorded:

> Lord Knollys was very positive that, in creating the Order, King Edward's intention was that it should be in the gift of the Sovereign, independent of Ministerial advice – though any appointments would be, naturally, communicated to the Prime Minister.
>
> This principle was rigorously adhered to during King Edward's reign and no question was ever raised by the Prime Minister in opposition to the King's suggestions. At the same time, His Majesty considered, though did not always approve, any suggestions made by the Prime Minister for appointment to the Order.[3]

Balfour, Salisbury's successor, was still equally clear on the matter, telling Stamfordham:

> I have, however, no doubt at all that the intention of the King, accepted by the then Prime Minister, was that the new Order should resemble the Victorian Order rather than that of the older Orders, which are commonly given on the advice of the Prime Minister of the day. It was on this theory that I systematically acted during my tenure of Office ... did not preclude private and unofficial suggestions being made to the Sovereign by his First Minister. [He recalled Edward VII not accepting his suggestion of Florence Nightingale, which is discussed in Chapter 16.]
>
> In any case, it is, I think conclusive as to the views taken by the King and his Ministers in the early days of the Order; and I am not aware that they have ever been altered.[4]

All this reassurance would have encouraged Stamfordham in stating clearly to the Royal Commission on Honours in late 1922 that:

> ... the Sovereign maintains the right of personally selecting Members for the Order of Merit.[5]

When the first Labour Government came to office in 1924, George V had a memorandum prepared to guide the inexperienced Prime Minister, Ramsay

MacDonald, on relations with the Sovereign. It included the following sentence:

> All recommendations for Honours are submitted in conjunction with the Prime Minister with the exception of the Order of Merit and the Royal Victorian Order (which are made on the King's initiative).[6]

During the second Labour Government a few years later, MacDonald's Private Secretary gave him a brief on the Order of Merit to use in discussion with the King's Private Secretary (to whom he unwittingly gave it). It set out the division of the members at the time into four each for Science and Learning, two for Literature and one each for Painting, Music and Politics; against the last four, MacDonald had written: 'This group should be strengthened if at all possible.' The note began, however:

> As you know, you do not initiate appointments to the Order of Merit, but the general public always gives you the credit (or reverse) for any appointments made.[7]

By 1936, the status of the Order of Merit was enshrined in the constitutional textbooks. A leading authority wrote:

> The King is the fountain of honour and of precedence by common law ... The general rules of ministerial responsibility apply to every class of honour. The Prime Minister bears the general responsibility, and on him depend the rewards given for eminence in art, science and literature, and for political services ... two exceptions to the rule of ministerial responsibility. [The Royal Victorian Order.] The Order of Merit created in 1902 Edward VII regarded as a personal business, though the Prime Minister might put forward suggestions, and the Order therefore has proved acceptable to great writers like Thomas Hardy, who would not have welcomed ordinary honours. The Companionship of Honour seems to be more of an ordinary distinction, and has been given to miscellaneous recipients of varying degrees of distinction.[8]

The relationship between the Sovereign and the Prime Minister

Overall, this relationship is complex and subtle, covering the whole range of state and dynastic matters and obviously varying according to individuals and periods. I am naturally concerned only with that tiny aspect relating to their dealings over appointments to the Order of Merit.

Initially, as can be seen from the preceding section, the Order seems to have been beset by its own difference from other orders: no title, no precedence for Members, no political advice on appointments. All this was so different from the rest of the honours system that it confused people, not least those at the top who were administering it.

Judging from the degree of interest, amounting almost to interference, shown by Prime Ministers in the early years of the Order, they seemed scarcely able to believe that a predecessor – admittedly in his old age and about to retire (and die) – could have given away such a potent part of his patronage. (The analogy with the Royal Victorian Order was rather false, since that was intended to reward personal services to the monarchy and not exceptional services to the nation.)

Alarm bells had rung at the Palace when Asquith successfully nominated Alfred Russel Wallace, the naturalist, for the Order in 1908. Knollys wrote to Edward VII:

> I am sure Mr Asquith does it from ignorance but will it not be dangerous to allow the Prime Minister to take the initiative *officially* and recommend some one for the Order of Merit. Of course, this need not prevent him from mentioning *privately* the name of a person whom the Prime Minister thinks deserving.
>
> Also, ought not the enquiry respecting Dr Wallace . . . to come from your representative and not from the Prime Minister. It is otherwise taking the matter rather out of Your Majesty's hands.
>
> If Your Majesty should so desire, I could point this out *personally* on my return to London to Mr Asquith.[9]

The King was more relaxed than his Private Secretary but Knollys nevertheless made his point at official level by informing the Prime Minister's Private Secretary:

> On every occasion when the Order of Merit has been given, I have written from the King by his desire to the recipient to offer it, and he thinks therefore I had better do so in regard to Dr Wallace.[10]

George V demonstrated his interest in the Order by asking for a list of Members and a copy of the Statutes within a month or so of his accession. Kenneth Rose, in his biography of that monarch, commented that he

> was neither indifferent to the repute of authors nor ignorant of their works. He took much care in selecting candidates for the Order of Merit (including both Hardy and Bridges) and would have bestowed it on Kipling, Shaw and Housman had not all three of them refused.[11]

His private secretaries were still confused. When Stamfordham asked his former assistant, Ponsonby (who was to become Keeper of the Privy Purse), whether he had arranged the gazetting of Geikie's OM in the 1914 New Year Honours, Ponsonby telegraphed Number 10. Stamfordham promptly put him straight:

> The Prime Minister has nothing to do with gazetting of the Order of Merit. I have written to the Lord Chamberlain to say the King wishes the gazette to appear tomorrow morning.[12]

The interplay between the Sovereign and Prime Minister will be demonstrated frequently in the descriptions of individual conferment of the Order in succeeding chapters. In the memorandum Stamfordham prepared in 1921 for George V's meeting with Lloyd George described below, he had recounted various occasions on which the Order had been conferred on the suggestion of the Prime Minister: Nightingale and Hooker (1907); Wallace (1908), when the King had specifically asked his Private Secretary to 'explain to Mr Asquith that the Order is in the Sovereign's hands and not in that of the Government'; and Hardy and Crookes (1910). The memorandum also recalled the King's rejection of two of the Prime Minister's suggestions: Birrell and Sargent in 1911.[13]

The only Prime Minister to receive the Order of Merit while in that office and clearly for services as such was David Lloyd George. It was as a war leader who would accept no other honour that it came to him in August 1919. Two years after his appointment to the Order, Lloyd George achieved another first in its development: he intervened more decisively and effectively in its affairs than any Prime Minister before or since.

In the argumentation that then arose, there is a need to distinguish it from the on-going discussion about whether there should be politicians in the Order, even under a literary guise. Here I am concerned only with that aspect of the discussion that impinged on what can be dramatised, within the narrow confines of the Order, as the 'Murray Affair'.

In October 1921, A. J. Balfour suggested that, if the King wished to appoint a scholar to succeed Henry Jackson (who had just died), he might well consider Gilbert Murray, a leading Greek scholar. Murray, however, led a political life outside classical Greece and Stamfordham sensed a possible problem with Lloyd George. He therefore began to assemble, from those who ought to know, information on the original intentions regarding the role of the Prime Minister in relation to appointments to the Order. To his trusted correspondent, A. J. Balfour, Stamfordham wrote:

> As you know, the Order is in the gift of the Sovereign, but it is customary to inform the Prime Minister, which I propose to do. Politically, I suppose the PM does not smile upon Gilbert Murray![14]

He would have been encouraged by Balfour's reply:

> I have no reason to believe that he is in opposition to the present
> Government, though he may be. I was not aware that politics were
> taken into account in the bestowal of the OM.[15]

On 17 October, Stamfordham informed Lloyd George in plain terms that,
after consulting 'those who are in a position to judge', the King proposed
to confer the OM on Murray, an appointment which 'would be generally
welcomed'.[16] Number 10 were soon reacting. Wigram, the King's Assistant
Private Secretary, reported to Stamfordham:

> I told the King of our conversation on the telephone about the Order of
> Merit for Gilbert Murray. His Majesty says that the Prime Minister is
> wrong in thinking that the Order is in any way connected with politics.
> The King is giving it to Gilbert Murray on account of his distinction as
> a literary genius.[17]

Number 10 did not let up, as Stamfordham recorded:

> Sylvester [one of Lloyd George's private secretaries] rang me up now
> about the OM for Gilbert Murray – and I endeavoured to tell him quite
> plainly the King's views and begged him to try and make the PM realise
> that politics has nothing to do with the OM. My feeling is that on this
> occasion the PM thinks that it is not the King but *I* who is at work –
> and for this reason if the King cannot see LG it would be something if
> he wrote to LG.[18]

Stamfordham's confidence was shaken, however, when Ponsonby (Keeper
of the Privy Purse and former Assistant Private Secretary) told him that he
regarded

> the Order of Merit in the same light as the Garter, Thistle and St Patrick
> and only to be conferred on the recommendation of the Prime Minis-
> ter: and that the King could not give it to anyone in opposition to the
> Government. This is to me an astonishing theory.[19]

The crunch came on 3 November when the Prime Minister saw the King,
who told him of his wish to confer the OM on Murray for his scholarly
attainments:

> Mr Lloyd George strongly urged His Majesty to reconsider this pro-
> posal on account of Dr Murray's pronounced political views: that
> during the War he had shown himself as a Passivist [sic] and almost

a Pro-German: and such an Honour bestowed upon him at the present moment would cause much annoyance to the Unionist Party, who were already in a mood which required to be placated rather than irritated.

The Prime Minister said he had spoken to Mr Austen Chamberlain and Colonel Leslie Wilson, the Leader of the House of Commons and the Head Whip, respectively, and they confirmed this opinion.

The King represented to the Prime Minister that politics had never come into the question of ineligibility for the Order, and that, moreover, its disposal was entirely in the hands of His Majesty, and he merely intimated to the Prime Minister his intentions.

Mr Lloyd George answered that he was sure the King would not wish him to withhold advice in order to prevent His Majesty committing an unpopular act.

The King finally consented to do nothing further in the matter of Dr Murray.[20]

To Murray's biographer:

Lloyd George's objections seem very strange when he had himself offered Murray first a CH and then a Knighthood in 1917 (both of which Murray refused). Presumably it was Murray's defence of the Lansdowne letter at the end of 1917, and of Conscientious Objectors in 1918, his criticism of the Treaty of Versailles, and of Lloyd George himself in his book of early 1921, *Problems of Foreign Policy*, which had offended the Prime Minister. There is no indication that the Murrays had any inkling of the proposal of 1921.[21]

Stamfordham recorded that the Murrray case, 'is the first instance of the Prime Minister declining to concur with a proposal made by the Sovereign for the conferring of the Order'.[22] The Murray episode seems to have dented Stamfordham's belief in the King's primacy in respect of the Order of Merit. A year after it, he wrote in manuscript to Sir Francis Bryant (the secretary of his office):

I think it is correct that although the King nominates, no one can be gazetted to the OM until the King has signed a submission made by the PM – which is of course *not* the same in the VO.

Bryant underlined the middle phrase in red and wrote in the margin:

No – the procedure is for the King to nominate and intimate the appointment to the Prime Minister – The Private Secretary instructs the Lord Chamberlain to gazette the appointment.[23]

After a brief moment of concord, when Lloyd George readily agreed to the OM being offered to Kipling and secured the King's agreement to offer it also to Barrie, there was again dissent:

> The King showed the Prime Minister Lord Stamfordham's Memorandum of November 2nd on the Order of Merit. Mr Lloyd George, apparently, only read the first page, and when His Majesty asked whether he agreed to what the Memorandum laid down, replied that he would not like to commit his successors to the principle set forth in the Memorandum.[24]

After Lloyd George, however, no Prime Minister employed the same blunt instrument to get his way. They showed varying degrees of interest in the Order of Merit and continued to 'suggest' names for it. Baldwin, although appearing to appreciate the proper position in the case of Kipling in 1924 (the details of which are in Chapter 21), nevertheless still thought the Prime Minister had a formal role to play. Thus, while cautioning Kipling (his cousin) that 'of course, it is in the King's gift alone', he proposed to the Palace (in the mistaken belief that the writer would accept) that he should make the offer to him. The King did not approve of that channel and directed his Private Secretary to write.[25]

By 1927, the situation between Palace and Number 10 seemed to have become clear. When Parsons, the maritime engineer, was to be appointed, Stamfordham wrote to Baldwin:

> The King, after careful consideration and consultation with what he regards as sound judges, has *decided* to confer . . . His Majesty will like to feel that this appointment will have your *concurrence* [my emphasis].[26]

Baldwin's Private Secretary replied:

> The Prime Minister very fully endorses The King's *decision* [my emphasis] . . . and received your note to this effect with great satisfaction.[27]

The following year when consulting Sir Walter Lawrence about the appointment of Grierson, the expert on Indian languages, Stamfordham felt able to write:

> The King guards jealously, and rightly so, the Order, which is entirely at the Sovereign's disposal.[28]

In 1931, Morshead expressed concern to the new Private Secretary, Wigram, about possible 'political contamination' of the Order:

> Baldwin told me that...he never attempted to wrest the OM from the sovereign's personal control because it was one of the few things left to his unfettered action, because he felt it had been well administered...
>
> The Labour Government...want the OM because of its unstained character [which] it owes to the sovereign's detachment...They must be content with being Companions of Honour.[29]

Morshead thought that the 'utmost limit of concession should be the institution of a third branch of the Order, a maximum number being appointed for each branch – perhaps as follows: Military 6; Civil 12; Political 6.'[30] Hardinge (Assistant and future Private Secretary) commented:

> excellent...if ever politicians, as such, are admitted, the Order will surely be debased.[31]

In 1931, the Labour Prime Minister, Ramsay MacDonald, '...assured the King that he could always rely upon his rigidly adhering to the rule that there was no interference with His Majesty's personal right of appointment to the Order'.[32] Such threat as there might have been to the integrity of the Order had been dispelled. This did not mean that Prime Ministers lost interest in the Order but they resisted the temptation to assert themselves. At the height of the Abdication crisis in 1936, as I shall show in Chapter 9, Baldwin still found time to seek Rutherford's views on the astronomer, Jeans. He could be seen at house parties making notes of names suggested for the Order in discussions between the guests.

The attitude of Churchill (who must have confidently expected to receive the Order, as he did) was benign and, with a couple of exceptions, uninterfering. George VI showed caution, however, when informing him in 1940 of his desire to confer the OM on Gilbert Murray, which is dealt with in detail in Chapter 13. The Private Secretary told Churchill:

> The King, in the same way as his Father, has been reluctant to honour someone who is in open opposition to his Government of the day, as it might lead to misunderstanding and possible misuse for political purposes...would like to be assured that such an award would not be embarrassing to you, in the event of His Majesty deciding to make it.

Churchill gave Murray an immediate 'all-clear'.[33]

When, in 1943, Churchill proposed both Pound, the First Sea Lord, and Viscount Cecil, the veteran peace worker, for the Order, George VI eventually accepted Pound but demurred on Cecil. The details are in Chapter 8. Here it is sufficient to note that Churchill was told:

> The King wishes me to assure you that such suggestions from you for the Order of Merit are always welcome.[34]

The two examples of 'interference' by Churchill were in 1941, in respect of Hailey, the eminent administrator in India, and in 1944, regarding Portal, the Chief of the Air Staff. Churchill's objections were that Hailey would lower the standard of the Order and that Portal had enough honours to be going on with. The Palace tacitly accepted the objections and did not renew the proposals until Churchill was no longer Prime Minister.

Macmillan was another Prime Minister who was interested in the Order, to the extent of its being the only one he wanted or, eventually, accepted. His hand is evident in the OM conferred on John Anderson (Viscount Waverley) on his deathbed in 1957.

In the later years of the century, I have the impression that Prime Ministers strictly kept their place in relation to the Order. Those who liked sticking to the rules held firmly to the view that this honour was nothing to do with them and refrained from any form of lobbying. What has continued is the scrupulous informing of Number 10 by the Palace of impending appointments, thus preserving the opportunity for the Prime Minister to comment. This practice also helps to avoid, more often than not, the appointment as a CH of someone who was nudging the OM tape.

I hope I have shown that the Order of Merit has now developed into what it was always intended to be: a highly exclusive award in the personal gift of the Sovereign, with the Prime Minister having no formal role. This has been achieved, as the papers demonstrate, somewhat by trial and error, particularly as there was no clear written 'memorandum of understanding' in the first place.

It would be wrong to pretend, however, in a simplistic way, that the Order is nothing *whatever* to do with the Prime Minister because, as I explain later (when describing the important role of the Sovereign's Private Secretary) the monarch is acting personally but publicly – and not privately – when appointing to the Order.

In the highly unlikely event of an 'outrageous' appointment, especially if it had political overtones, the Prime Minister could not realistically absolve himself from all involvement. He has the ultimate constitutional responsibility for all the Sovereign's public acts and would be held accountable for not having pressed his advice against an 'outrageous' appointment. Equally, he would have to answer if it could be shown that he had persuaded the Sovereign, against her better judgement, into making such an appointment.

All of this is what Lloyd George realised when he cleverly pressed home the point that he was 'sure the King would not wish him to withhold advice in order to prevent His Majesty committing an unpopular act' by appointing Gilbert Murray. He was probably exaggerating the unpopularity in political circles of an appointment that would have been popular in the intellectual and academic circles for which the Order was primarily intended. Nevertheless, he was daring the King to over-rule his advice – and have it known that he had done so. No monarch could afford to do that, then or now.

A careful – and apparently successful – balance has therefore been struck between the Sovereign's special rights in relation to the Order and the Prime Minister's ultimate constitutional responsibility. The procedure of informing the Prime Minister in advance not only minimises the risk of overlap between OM and CH appointments but also enables the Sovereign to take advantage of the experience that any Prime Minister builds up in the honours field. The Prime Minister's restraint in making 'suggestions' is also an important part of the equation.

The balance is now sufficiently well understood to ensure that no Prime Minister would attempt to use the Order for political purposes, as he can quite properly do with the CH on occasion. The Crown therefore has little need to feel possessive about the OM because, nowadays, no Prime Minister is likely to show signs of wanting to possess it himself.

To end this section, it is interesting to remember that, whatever envious eyes it may be thought that Prime Ministers have cast on this precious personal royal honour, only five (out of the 20 since the foundation of the Order) have received it for services as Prime Minister: Lloyd George, Churchill, Attlee, Macmillan and Margaret Thatcher. The political impartiality of the Order is demonstrated by the fact that three of them – Churchill, Attlee and Macmillan – received it when Her Majesty's Ministers were of a different political persuasion.

The role of the Sovereign's Private Secretary

This role is so crucial in the history of the Order of Merit that it would be as well to list the holders of the office, by the title they held for all or most of their tenure. The reader will encounter the names of the first five frequently in the Royal Archives papers of 1902–52, from which I quote frequently in succeeding chapters.

1. 1901–13   Lord (later Viscount) Knollys (jointly with Lord Stamfordham from 1910–13)
2. 1910–31   Lord Stamfordham
3. 1931–36   Sir Clive (later Lord) Wigram
4. 1936–43   Sir Alexander Hardinge (later Second Lord Hardinge of Penshurst)

5. 1943–53   Sir Alan Lascelles
6. 1954–72   Sir Michael Adeane (later Lord Adeane)
7. 1972–77   Sir Martin Charteris (later Lord Charteris of Amisfield)
8. 1977–85   Sir Philip Moore (now Lord Moore of Wolvercote)
9. 1985–90   Sir William Heseltine
10. 1990–99   Sir Robert Fellowes (now Lord Fellowes)
11. 1999–   Sir Robin Janvrin

The importance of the Private Secretary must be obvious to anyone who stops to think for a minute. No monarch could be expected to have such a wide-ranging personal knowledge of all the potential OMs across the whole spectrum as to be able to decide, in a truly personal way, on those to be appointed. The decision has to be based on evidence and opinions from various sources and the Private Secretary is the logical and, indeed, the only co-ordinator of them. Since, as we have seen, the Sovereign is not receiving advice, at least in the usual formal way, from the Prime Minister, this particular task must fall to the Private Secretary.

When the Sovereign confers the Order of Merit, she is acting – as is rightly and constantly emphasised – in a personal way. Nevertheless, she is also acting in a public, and not private way. Her decision is made public and is the object of legitimate public scrutiny. It is not, to use the current jargon, an invasion of the monarch's privacy, for the press or public to comment on OM appointments. This only reinforces the care with which the Private Secretary must marshal the material on which the Sovereign has to make the final decisions.

I had the advantage of discussing this in some detail with three of the Queen's former Private Secretaries. Much of what they told me is incorporated, without specific attribution, in what follows. The responsibility rests with the Private Secretary, although he will often discuss proposals with the two Assistant Private Secretaries. He conducts any necessary correspondence, however, as is very clear from the files I saw.

There is no selection committee, even in an informal sense. The Private Secretary will write or talk to a few trusted contacts, including existing Members of the Order, who are obviously disinterested parties. In the case of scientists, there is evidence in the files of successive Secretaries of the Royal Society (who are unlikely to be serious candidates themselves) being consulted. Once a President of the Royal Society is admitted to the Order, as every one has been so far, he is a natural contact and will continue to be so after his term finishes.

Over the years, certain existing Members have lent themselves more to consultation than others, either because they had wider contacts or because they took more interest in the development and quality of the Order. To take one example, and there have been others before and since: G. M. Trevelyan. Once he was a Member, at the early age of 54, his advice was regularly sought and given, as will be evident from correspondence quoted in later chapters. The OM was very close to his heart, as he was to its.

The consultation of and among existing Members of the Order will have increased over the years, particularly since 1977, when the Queen began the practice of a lunch for them every five years. On these occasions, with which I shall deal in more detail in Chapter 25, the Members meet not only each other but also the Sovereign's Private Secretary and the Secretary and Registrar of the Order. All of this has led to a greater collegiality, to something approaching its German model, the Order Pour le mérite: a self-perpetuating academy.

The Private Secretary will keep careful note of every serious suggestion made to him (one called these his 'little black book') and a file will be made where necessary, particularly if a candidate is clearly heading towards the Order. He must always have regard to the overall balance of the Order but not at the expense of individual quality; it is better for the reputation of the Order to have three outstanding painters than a less than outstanding composer, historian and poet.

There is little lobbying from the street, as in the case of lesser honours. It is not often that somebody thinks his friend or neighbour is a possible OM but, if he does, he is likely to be discreet in his lobbying, as the 'great and the good' invariably are. A verbal, and often indirect, approach is likely to precede a written one.

There are times when the Private Secretary can stimulate a particular idea but, while it could well be imaginative, it could never be just a maverick. What has to be resisted, however, is any temptation to make a choice that would be simply 'popular', since that can be safely left to the main honours list. On the other hand, it is no bad thing if some OMs are known to the general public.

The close involvement of the Private Secretary only rarely makes itself evident. In 1942, Sir Alexander Hardinge wanted his papers on the Order of Merit reorganised and his office sent a plea to the Central Chancery:

> Sir Alexander is so often wanting the OM papers that they really should be kept in the Private Secretary's office, as was the case up to 1940.[35]

Private Secretaries do not write their memoirs but Hardinge did record privately his role in the relationship to the Order:

> One of the duties that interested me most was finding suitable candidates for the Order of Merit – the only Order (other than the Victorian Order) which the King then gave without any recommendation from the Prime Minister. I noticed that covetous eyes were occasionally cast on this Order from 10 Downing Street, but we fortunately had strong written evidence, as well as precedent, to support our case. It was my ambition

only to make suggestions to the King that would maintain the very high standard of this Order, and I naturally took a lot of outside advice before suggesting anybody. During my time I put forward the names of Augustus John, Lutyens, Gilbert Murray and Adrian, among others, and I do not think that any of these could be said to have let the standard down. Since my day it has been given to several octogenarians, which I think is a pity, and was certainly contrary to the practice in Lord Stamfordham's time, when it was held – and I think rightly – that if a man had ever been worthy of the OM he would have got it when in his prime, ie long before he was eighty.[36]

In 1963, Sir Alan Lascelles (in retirement at Kensington Palace) was moved to write to *The Guardian*, after it had criticised the length of time that the 90-year-old historian G. P. Gooch had had to wait for his OM:

In one of your leading articles, you deplore the fact that the mills of the Order of Merit, like those of the Almighty, grind slowly. May I remind you that the Order is limited by its charter to a membership of 24 persons, and consequently the Sovereign is precluded from appointing new members, however eligible they may be, until death provides a vacancy?[37]

I referred earlier to the Private Secretary's regular 'contacts'. I am tempted to call them 'éminences grises' but that tends to imply a murky or underhand or self-serving role when it was actually none of those things. They were (and are) men whose wide knowledge and judgement made them eminent and usually disinterested advisers of the Sovereign's principal adviser.

The reader will find the same names frequently recurring in the correspondence from the first 50 years of the Order, quoted in succeeding chapters. A. J. Balfour, both before and after his own appointment to the Order, and Stanley Baldwin were two Prime Ministers who took a particular interest in the Order, as I have noted in the preceding section.

In the papers I studied, certain names constantly recurred and their opinions undoubtedly influenced the Private Secretaries who sought them. The Sovereign was able to be assured that the names being presented for his consideration and choice had the support of a number of his eminent and trusted subjects. The decision was his but it would be based on carefully gathered information. Among the recurring names, that of Reginald, Second Viscount Esher, looms large: 'the enigmatic Edwardian' as his own biographer described him. One of Edward VII's biographers was more forthright:

As a supposedly self-seeking éminence grise, Esher was disliked and distrusted by those who suspected his motives for so sedulously acquiring authority and influence to be less disinterested than they were.

He cited the unflattering comments of a number of Esher's contemporaries.[38] As Secretary of the Office of Works, he had been an adept showman when helping to organise Queen Victoria's Diamond Jubilee. From the time he played his part in advising Edward VII on the foundation of the Order until his death in 1930, he had an important role in the development of its membership.

Another name is that of Sir Frederic Kenyon, the Greek scholar who was Director of the British Museum from 1909–30. Only briefly a candidate for the Order himself, he was well placed to advise on the scholarly appointments to it. From Paris, in the mid-1920s, advice came from the Marquess of Crewe, who was then British Ambassador but had previously been in every Liberal Cabinet from 1905 to 1916. His 'definite views' pleased Lord Stamfordham, who found some other opinions too hedged about with caveats. On one occasion, Crewe worried about the lack of first-rate candidates and wondered whether this was because it was a second-rate age or simply that he was getting old.

Also prominent among those whom Stamfordham sometimes called his 'referees' was the Twenty-seventh Earl of Crawford (and Balcarres), a former Cabinet Minister who wrote about Italian sculpture. Across the Thames from Windsor, the Provost of Eton, M. R. James, was another source of advice and eventually received the Order himself. There are others, as the reader will see from the correspondence cited in succeeding chapters.

I cannot say who the contacts are now but anyone looking at the list of present OMs is likely to be able to make a pretty intelligent guess, in the light of the criteria I quoted earlier, as to those who have followed in the footsteps of G. M. Trevelyan.

Two officials have been well placed to offer advice to the Private Secretary, if asked to do so. The Librarian of the Royal Library at Windsor was, until very recently, also the Assistant Keeper of the Royal Archives, which are housed at Windsor. In that second capacity, with immediate access to the archives of the Order of Merit, he has been able to advise particularly on the considerations affecting earlier appointments. Owen Morshead, who held that office from 1926 to 1958, was in constant correspondence with successive Private Secretaries – about future as well as past appointments. His influence, or what he once called his 'small part', can be judged from the correspondence in the succeeding chapters. I imagine that his successors have been able to play a similar role, if later Private Secretaries have wished it.

The other official is the Secretary and Registrar of the Order. As I point out in Appendix D, the earlier holders of the office seemed to play very little part in the selection process, often being informed of appointments only shortly before they were announced. The former Secretary, Sir Edward Ford, was invited to play a more active advisory role, aided by his long experience as an Assistant Private Secretary.

Precedence – of the Order and its Members

The question of precedence would not go away. Pretending to ignore it in Edwardian Britain simply would not work. The new Secretary and Registrar of the Order was soon writing to his predecessor:

> I notice none of the Peerages seem to give any precedence to the Order of Merit. (*Whitaker's* say they have no precedence.) Is this right? I have an idea you told me there was a precedence.

The speedy response came:

> The OM *as an Order*, inter se, ranks after the GCB and before the GCMG [and presumably GCSI also]. It does not however entitle the holder to any precedence.[39]

After the accession of George V in 1910, the Lord Chamberlain's Office thought it right to address this question formally in a memorandum sent to his Private Secretary:

> The Order of Merit confers no precedence upon the Members of the Order. When the Order was instituted in 1902 the question arose as to whether the Members were to be permitted to place the letters 'O.M.' after their names. King Edward VII ruled that they should do so, when a further question arose to the order in which the letters 'O.M.' were to be placed with regard to letters designating that Members of the Order possessed other Orders. His late Majesty ruled that the letters 'O.M.' should be placed immediately after 'G.C.B.'. The question now arises as to the position of the Order of Merit with regard to other Orders when announcing appointments to the various Orders in the *London Gazette*.
> [There followed a statement of relative precedence of other orders.]
> From the above it will be seen that there is no general rule which governs the precedence of the various Order of Knighthood. This being the case, and bearing in mind His late Majesty's ruling as to the placing of the letters 'O.M.', it is humbly recommended for The King's consideration that the Order of Merit might be given place after the Order of the Bath and before the Order of the Star of India.[40]

A few days later, the Lord Chamberlain's Office noted:

> His Majesty rules that the Cypher of the OM shall remain with King Edward's Cypher'. That the Order shall come directly after the GCB and as an Order has precedence immediately after the Bath.[41]

Institution of the CH in 1917

When the Order of the Companions of Honour was instituted in 1917, it superficially resembled the Order of Merit. It had a simple neck badge, it had a fixed limit of membership – of 50, later increased to 65 – and, while conferring no title, it ranked above many titles; a CH came above all Knights Commanders but below Knights Grand Cross, while an OM ranked above all Knights Grand Cross, except those of the Bath.

There were, however, two vital differences: the OM was in the personal gift of the Sovereign, whereas the CH was on the recommendation of the Prime Minister; the OM was for 'exceptionally meritorious service', while the CH was for the clearly less demanding 'Conspicuous service of National importance'.

The OM was not intended to reward political services and, for many years, it did not, whereas the CH was, from its inception, intended as an important part of the Prime Minister's political patronage. It was after the developing use of the CH to reward distinguished services to the arts and science that comparison with the OM was invited and the phrase 'second class OM' began to be used.

Nevertheless, it was 30 years before any CH became an OM and it was three statesmen who were the first: Churchill (1946), Smuts (1947) and Attlee (1951). After that, political figures have been either OM *or* CH – or, in the case of Prime (or near-Prime) Ministers, KG or KT.

After those first three, 18 more CHs later became OMs: all in the artistic or scientific fields.

Amendments to the Statutes of the OM

In the first 85 years of the Order of Merit, there were only three amendments to its Statutes: in 1907, 1935 and 1969. The first merely detached the office of Secretary and Registrar from the office of Comptroller of the Lord Chamberlain's Department and gave it a separate existence, which is explained more fully in Appendix D.

By 1935, the Royal Air Force was clearly established as the third arm of the British defence forces. The King's Private Secretary noticed, however, that only the Navy and the Army were eligible to receive the Order of Merit. He brought this to the attention of George V, who ordered that the Air Force should be added to the list.[42]

The Private Secretary thought this provided an opportunity to improve the Statutes generally and asked the Permanent Secretary of the Treasury (who was also Head of the Home Civil Service) for suggestions. Not surprisingly, the Permanent Secretary thought that the eligibility of the Navy and Army should be widened to include *all* Crown Services, civil at home and overseas as well as military. He also wrote that:

> The limitation in the general sphere to 'Art, Literature and Science' has been proved by experience to be too narrow; and I would suggest the substitution of 'the Arts, Learning, Literature, Science and Philanthropy'. 'Philanthropy' would provide for another Baden-Powell or an English President Wilson. You will recall that there is a Nobel Peace Prize.[43]

At the same time, the Permanent Secretary's Private Secretary (who was at the helm of the honours system in Whitehall from 1928 until his death at the age of 76 in 1965) gave expert advice on the word 'philanthropy', citing from *Webster's Dictionary*.[44] The King's response was in the negative:

> His Majesty did not like the word 'philanthropy' which smacks of a cash order, and neither do I.[45]

As in 1902, there was consultation with the Garter King of Arms, who happened to be the healthy Sir Gerald Woods Wollaston, the maternal grandson of the frail Sir Albert Woods. The Secretary of the Central Chancery also realised that the Statutes needed to make proper provision for the wearing of the Badge by a female – on a bow rather than round the neck.

The upshot of all this was that, on 16 December 1935, barely a month before he died, George V approved an Additional Statute to include the Air Force, to change 'Art' to 'Arts' and include 'Learning' and to provide for a proper wearing by a woman of the Badge.

In 1969, the Statutes were amended to take account of the constitutional changes that had taken place within the Commonwealth in the preceding 20 years. In 1949, it was agreed that India could remain within the Commonwealth when it became a republic. Although no longer owing allegiance to the King, it accepted him as 'Head of the Commonwealth'. Over the years, many other Commonwealth countries followed suit, either as republics or as monarchies with their own monarchs.

The statutes of orders provided for *honorary* awards to foreigners because they were not subjects of the British Crown. Such statutes had to be amended so that honorary awards could be made to those Commonwealth citizens who were no longer subjects of the Crown but who were not legally 'foreigners'. When this anomaly was pointed out to the Private Secretary[46], he commented:

> The Queen did, in fact, give an Honorary OM to President Radhakrishnan [of India, in 1963] but I suppose no one realised, any more than I did, that this was technically beyond the scope of the Statute.[47]

On 7 November 1969, an Additional Statute provided that, in Statute V the old description of Ordinary Members as 'subjects of Our Crown' should be altered to 'citizens of countries of which We are Queen'. In Statute VI, the description of Honorary Members was altered, rather clumsily, to 'persons other than those referred to in Clause V', which presumably meant Statute V.

In 1986, the Secretary and Registrar of the Order decided it was no longer proper to send new Members their copy of the Statutes with extra bits of paper inserted showing the changes made since 1902. It was time, as happens with most orders as they age, to 'consolidate' the Statutes. Some of the changes were merely for historical or grammatical reasons. For instance, in Statute IX, the wording on the wearing of the Badge, now by both men and women, was simplified and the description of the Cypher was reduced to 'Royal' since the Queen has never been an Empress and therefore never ER*I*. It was decided, however, not to change the Imperial (high-arched) Crown to a Royal (dipped-arch) Crown: the St Edward's Crown, which has been used for most purposes in this reign.

The original description of the Order as having 'one class of' Members was altered by the deletion of those words (in Statute IV).

An odd anomaly was removed in Statute XI. It is no longer necessary, in this non-political order, for a Warrant delegating the power of investiture to be countersigned by a Secretary of State. It was always illogical for a Minister to be involved formally in the operation of an order in which no Minister had any formal role in respect of appointments.

The provision (in Statute VIII) for the Sovereign's Badge to be different from the Member's Badge was removed.

By far the most important change was to Statute V, describing the services for which the Order could be awarded. I have already outlined the problems on the early appointments of political figures, thinly disguised as being for their services to Literature. Later appointments were also difficult to fit within the strict wording: Baden-Powell, Churchill, Attlee, Stockton, Cheshire – none was being honoured for 'service in Our Crown Services, or towards the advancement of the Arts, Learning, Literature and Science.'

The solution was to bring Ordinary Members into line with Honorary Members, for whom there has never been any specific qualification. So, to Statute V, was added after 'Science' the words 'or such other exceptional service as We see fit to recognise'. The Order can now be conferred for any form of exceptional contribution to national life. Margaret Thatcher was the first political figure to benefit from the change; her appointment was four-square within the Statutes.

Two other possibilities for bringing the Order into line with reality were not achieved. Its precedence (not specified in the Statutes) *after* the GCB remained unaltered, despite the OM always having been conferred after a GCB as a distinctly higher honour. Also, the Seal of the Order continues to bear the military version of the Badge, despite there having been only 30 military awards out of the total of 182 and there having been no Military Member living since 1979.

After this, the question again rose of the returnability of insignia. The outcome in 1991 is that the Badge now has to be returned after the death of a Member.

6

THE ORIGINAL MEMBERS

The original members of the Order of Merit were:

1. Field Marshal Earl ROBERTS (Military)
2. Field Marshal Viscount WOLSELEY (Military)
3. Field Marshal Earl KITCHENER (Military)
4. Lord RAYLEIGH (Civil)
5. Lord KELVIN (Civil)
6. Lord LISTER (Civil)
7. Admiral of the Fleet Sir Henry KEPPEL (Military)
8. Viscount MORLEY (Civil)
9. William LECKY (Civil)
10. Admiral of the Fleet Sir Edward SEYMOUR (Military)
11. Sir William HUGGINS (Civil)
12. George WATTS (Civil)

No British Order has come on to the honours stage with such an outstanding cast as the OM. It has run twice as long as *The Mousetrap*, where the limited cast also changes from time to time.

I have described the appointment and gazetting of the original 12 members. They were at the top of their callings at the time, as I hope to demonstrate by outlining what they had done by the time they appeared in this very special list.

All the five military OMs had the Grand Cross of the Bath already, the three older men from as long before as 1871 (Keppel) and 1880 (Wolseley and Roberts), the younger two from only 1898 (Kitchener) and 1900 (Seymour). This progression, for senior officers from the GCB to the much rarer OM, became the norm for the Order. All military OMs (except the

Japanese honorary Members, who were never GCBs) were already GCBs while, of course, the vast majority of GCBs never became OMs. Speaking of precedence, I have already referred to the fact that while the new Order was supposed to be based purely on 'Merit', without any consideration of the recipient's place in society, the first list of Members adhered rigidly to the Order of Precedence. First, the earl (Roberts), followed by two viscounts (Wolseley and Kitchener, in their own order of precedence), the three barons (again in their own order, the Third Lord Rayleigh's title naturally being older than the first creations of Kelvin and Lister), the younger son of an earl (Keppel), the two privy counsellors (Morley and Lecky) the GCB (Seymour), the KCB (Huggins) and the mere Mr or Esquire (Watts).

The military five

Field Marshal Earl Roberts of Kandahar, Pretoria and Waterford – 'Bobs' – was probably the most famous man in the country in 1902. In full uniform, he was the most splendid: with the stars of the Orders of the Garter, St Patrick, the Bath, the Star of India and Indian Empire on his left breast, below a row of medals, headed by the Victoria Cross. At his neck, he would now wear the new Order of Merit. He is still the only man ever to hold the Victoria Cross, the Order of the Garter and the Order of Merit.

He symbolised, second only to the monarch, Victoria or Edward VII, the British Empire. He was a child of the Empire and grew with it. Born, the son of a general, in India in 1832, and blind in one eye from infancy, he yet went back as a young officer and served for *Forty-One Years in India, from Subaltern to Commander-in-Chief* – the title of his autobiography. On his way to Commander-in-Chief, he had won the VC in the Mutiny, been mentioned in despatches 24 times and had led the march of a force in 1880 to relieve the garrison at Kandahar, from which Afghan town he took his peerage title.

In December 1899, by then a Field Marshal and C-in-C Ireland, he was summoned to take command of the British forces in South Africa after the military disasters of 'Black Week'. Within six months, the Boer general Cronje had surrendered, Ladysmith, Kimberley and Mafeking had been relieved, and the two Boer capitals, Bloemfontein and Pretoria, had been captured. A large two-volume illustrated history, *With the Flag to Pretoria*, embodied the victorious spirit of Britain. Its frontispiece is a drawing of Roberts kneeling before Queen Victoria at Osborne on his triumphal return to this country. She conferred on him the Order of the Garter, the first victorious general to receive it since Wellington, and he was made an earl. He became the last C-in-C of the British Army until the abolition of the post in 1904.

In 1905, Roberts resigned from the Imperial Defence Council and began an unsuccessful campaign for the introduction of compulsory national service.

When war broke out in 1914 he was nearly 82 but, as Colonel-in-Chief of the Overseas Forces in England, he went to visit the Indian troops in France. He caught a chill and died of pneumonia at the British GHQ at St Omer on 14 November. Kipling wrote, in the tenor of the time:

> He passed to the very sound of guns;
> But, before his eye grew dim,
> He had seen the faces of the sons
> Whose sires had served with him.[1]

Roberts' body was brought back to Britain and, on the gun-carriage his son had died trying to save in South Africa, borne to St Paul's Cathedral where, in the presence of the King, he was buried in the crypt close to Wellington and Nelson, under a stone inscribed simply 'Roberts 1832–1914'. Yet, as a biographer recorded already half a century ago: 'his name nowadays is curiously little remembered.'[2]

Field Marshal Viscount Wolseley (formerly Sir Garnet) was nine months younger than Roberts but senior to him militarily. He had been firmly overtaken by him, however, in popular esteem and official honours. The public loved 'Bobs' but the catchword 'All Sir Garnet' came to mean unqualified success or everything being shipshape, for which there was respect but little love.

The two men were contemporaries but, although Roberts took over a post from Wolseley in India in 1858, the men did not actually meet until 40 years later. Wolseley's career had scarcely been in India but almost everywhere else in the Empire: in Canada, against the Red River rebels in 1870; in West Africa, against the Ashantis in 1874; in Cyprus, taken over from the Turks in 1878; in Egypt, against the Egyptian army rebels in 1882, thus saving the Suez Canal for Britain.

He refused the GCB in 1874 at the age of 41, for fear of creating jealousies among powerful senior officers. He also declined a baronetcy, supposedly telling friends that he did not want to share the honour with the Duke of Devonshire's gardener (Sir Joseph Paxton had been knighted after the Great Exhibition many years before.) Despite his arrogance, Wolseley did receive a GCMG, a KCB and £25,000 from Parliament.[3]

It was this abrasive and rather cold attitude that made him an easy target for the caricaturists: he was the inspiration for 'the very model of a modern Major-General' in Gilbert and Sullivan's *Pirates of Penzance* in 1880. In Cyprus, he wanted to kick almost all the inefficient people he had to deal with or, as he put it, to 'introduce my bootmaker to the fellow's tailor'. Later, however, he could see the funny side of a Commander-in-Chief (who had served in India) having to step aside into the snow at Balmoral to make room for the carriage taking the Munshi, Queen Victoria's Indian servant, out for his daily drive.

His row of colonial successes was dented by his failure in 1885, at the head of the relief expedition despatched tardily by Gladstone, to rescue Gordon in Khartoum. Had he succeeded, we might now talk of Wolseley of Khartoum, rather than Kitchener.

After being Adjutant-General, Wolseley was Commander-in-Chief in Ireland (he had been born in Co. Dublin) and finally, in 1895, after much jockeying, Commander-in-Chief of the Army, in succession to the Queen's cousin, who had held the post for 40 years. He handed it over to Roberts at the end of 1900.

His barony had come in 1882 after his victory in Egypt. The previous year, Queen Victoria had refused to give him a peerage so that, as a serving offer, he could advocate Gladstone's proposed army changes in the Upper House.[4] He was proud of being a writer, on various military subjects, including Marlborough, von Moltke, Napoleon and, disappointingly, himself. Henry James was a friend and Thomas Hardy invited him to be one of the 30 authors who signed a congratulatory seventieth birthday letter to George Meredith.[5]

In his last years, he and his wife lived at Hampton Court Palace but wintered at their villa on the Riviera, where he died in 1913. Like Roberts, he was brought back in style to be buried in the crypt of St Paul's.

Today, **Field Marshal Earl Kitchener of Khartoum** is the most remembered of the three soldiers. Sadly, the irrepressible Margot Asquith's indiscreet quip that 'if he was not a great man, he was, at least, a great poster' has come to be almost true. (Kitchener retorted that 'all his colleagues repeated military secrets to their wives, except Asquith, who repeated them to other people's wives'.[6])

His accusing finger and his moustache (comparable, as twentieth-century political moustaches go, only with the Kaiser, Stalin and Hitler) have been converted from the plain and very successful recruiting call of August 1914 – 'Your Country Needs You' – into whatever the advertiser or cartoonist chooses to make of them.

Born in Ireland, Kitchener's military career had not got off to a good start. He was reprimanded by the Commander-in-Chief for serving briefly with the French army in the Franco–Prussian War of 1870, while waiting for his commission in the Royal Engineers. He surveyed Cyprus after its acquisition by Britain in 1878 and most of his service was in the East, particularly Egypt and the Sudan.

He served under both his fellow OMs, being considerably younger than they were. He was on both of Wolseley's expeditions, to Egypt in 1882 and to the Sudan in 1885; he sent the first authoritative report of Gordon's death. And it was he who was to avenge that death and the shame it had brought to the British Empire.

As Sirdar of the Egyptian Army, he became convinced that the only solution to the problem of the Nile was to advance into the Sudan and defeat the

2 Earl Kitchener of Khartoum.

dervishes. This he finally achieved, with considerable ferocity, at and after the Battle of Omdurman in 1898. He was a national hero, with a peerage and £30,000 from Parliament.

In 1899, he was called to be Chief of Staff – and, in effect, second-in-command – to Roberts in South Africa. On Roberts' triumphal return to Britain at the end of 1900, Kitchener took over as C-in-C to wind up the campaign. Boer guerrilla tactics, however, prolonged it for another 18 months.

Kitchener's second triumphal return coincided with the establishment of the Order of Merit. Although much junior to Roberts and Wolseley, he was the hero of the hour and an inevitable recruit for the new Order. It was but one of a clutch of honours: promotion to general, to GCMG and to a viscounty. A bachelor, this peerage, like Roberts' and Wolseley's, came with a special remainder, in his case to his brothers.

In fact, Kitchener was the first to be invested. Just as Roberts had gone straight to see Victoria, so Kitchener (after lunch with the Prince of Wales and other royalties) went to see the sick Edward VII at Buckingham Palace. Recovering from the operation that had delayed his Coronation, the King gave Kitchener the OM from his bed – and Queen Alexandra cried.

Unlike the two older soldiers, Kitchener's military career was far from over. He had a turbulent spell as Commander-in-Chief India from 1902–09, emerging victorious not from a military campaign but from the historic row with the Viceroy, Lord Curzon, over ultimate control of the Indian Army.

Morley, another original OM, and by 1910 Secretary of State for India, declined (despite pressure from Edward VII) to nominate Kitchener as Viceroy of India and, instead, he became the ruler of Egypt, still with the modest title enjoyed by Cromer for so many years (British Agent and Consul-General). Like Cromer, he was rewarded with an earldom.

Kitchener was actually on board ship at Dover, about to return to Egypt, when the First World War broke out. The most popular man in the British Empire was summoned to join the government as Secretary of State for War. 'His country needed him' to give the public confidence in the conduct of the war. Even when he lost the confidence of his political colleagues and various of his responsibilities were transferred elsewhere, he had to be retained to reassure the public.

Kitchener was to avoid political downfall or humiliation by sudden death, with Wagnerian overtone. On 5 June 1916, five days after the Battle of Jutland, the cruiser in which he was sailing on a special mission to Russia hit a German mine off the Orkneys and sank within 15 minutes. He was not among the few survivors or the bodies washed ashore. Jellicoe (soon to be an OM for Jutland) blamed himself for choosing the wrong route; in any case, he felt responsible as Kitchener had been in the care of the Navy. The King and Queen, unusually, attended a memorial service for Kitchener in St Paul's.

Kitchener of Khartoum has not been short of biographers since his death and his name is probably the only one of the original military OMs that still rings a bell with most people. Of course, the ever-increasing enquiry into the sexuality of historical figures has done nothing to diminish interest in Kitchener.

The first three military OMs look out on Horse Guards Parade: equestrian statues of Roberts and Wolseley flank the arch to Whitehall, while Kitchener stands in the back wall of 10 Downing Street. They have now been joined by a statue, sited on Foreign Office Green, of Mountbatten, the last military OM.

The two naval OMs pale in comparison with the three soldiers, not only in their place in the military history of the country but also in the public knowledge of them at the time. This is not surprising. Since the Napoleonic

Wars, the Navy had had little opportunity to shine; it had supported the Army in building up and defending the Empire, by transporting troops and guarding the sea routes.

The two admirals represented the old Navy and the new. **Sir Henry Keppel** was 93, the oldest person appointed to the Order of Merit until the spate of nonagerlan appointments in the 1990s: de Valois, Gielgud and Denning. He had retired in 1876 and had been an Admiral of the Fleet since August 1877, 25 years earlier. Seymour was a mere 62, still a serving officer.

Keppel was the twelfth child of the fourth Earl of Albemarle. The family were Dutch in origin and had come over with the Little Conqueror, William of Orange, in 1688 and the first four earls were all Knights of the Garter.

3 Sir Henry Keppel.

Harry was so weak at birth that only a sharp-eyed nurse ensured that he was christened rather than buried. He never grew to be more than five feet tall.

His career was pretty varied: he was a great friend of the first 'White Rajah' Brooke of Sarawak, whom he helped to suppress piracy; he smuggled an 11-year-old nephew aboard his ship in the Baltic; he refused a CB because 'I feel more distinguished as I am' (referring to the superiority of an earl's son); his term as Commander-in-Chief, Cape Station, ended prematurely when he made the mistake of providing a shoulder for the Governor's wife to cry on; in 1886, he even accepted an offer to command the (river) navy in Paraguay.

To his aid, however, came his friend, the Prince of Wales. The following description of their relationship in the official biography of Edward VII goes a long way to explaining the eventual choice of Keppel as the first naval OM:

> Characteristic, too, were the Prince's relations with a naval officer considerably his senior, Sir Henry Keppel, to whom he gave proofs of attachment through a period of five-and-forty years. 'The Little Admiral', as Keppel was called in the Prince's family circle, was an amusing companion, and no mean sportsman. The Prince did all he could to help his professional advancement. As early as 1866, the Prince successfully busied himself to obtain . . . the command for Keppel of the China and Japan station.[7]

His last active appointment was as C-in-C Devonport from 1870–76. A special Order-in-Council retained him on the active list as an Admiral of the Fleet and, at his death in 1904, he had served for 82 years.

In 'retirement', Keppel's links with the royal family flourished. Prince George of Wales (later George V) wrote to him:

> Sir, That is the proper way for a lieutenant to address an Admiral of the Fleet, but I hope I may be allowed to begin: My dear Little Admiral, which is what I always call you.[8]

His sister Princess Maud had a reputation for bravery and was therefore nicknamed 'Harry' after the courageous old admiral. There are photographs of Edward VII and Queen Alexandra with protective arms around their small friend. He was, incidentally, the great-uncle of the complaisant husband of Alice Keppel, Edward VII's last mistress.

Sir Edward Seymour was also from a family of admirals. As a midshipman, he served in China alongside Arthur Wilson, who was also to become an OM. When serving in West Africa, he solved the perennial problem of young sailors ashore by having the British Consul direct them to a particular establishment where the madam ensured that the girls remained healthy and

4 Sir Edward Seymour.

clean. The Navy sent its thanks, which prompted the establishment to erect a sign 'By appointment to HM The Queen'.

Like other naval officers of the time, he had long periods on half-pay, when there was no work for them ashore or afloat. In 1882, he was fortunate enough to have command of a battleship, in succession to Jacky Fisher, who was to be the next naval officer to receive the OM after him.

Seymour's career reached its peak, and he achieved what was not much more than 15 minutes of fame, in 1900 as Commander-in-Chief China Station. The Boxer rebels were threatening the foreign legations in Peking and, as the commander of a hastily assembled international brigade, he set out to relieve the diplomats. In the face, however, of considerable rebel forces and with the railway cut, he had to retire to Tientsin to await the arrival of land forces. He was promoted to Admiral in March 1901 and it was therefore as relatively junior in that rank that he became one of two original naval OMs. Nevertheless, he had recently been in the public eye in a fighting role.

Seymour's career ended, like Keppel's, as Commander-in-Chief Devonport, from 1903–05, after which he was promoted to Admiral of the Fleet. He was a member of the Mission, led by Prince Arthur of Connaught, to present the Order of the Garter to the Emperor Mutsuhito of Japan in 1906. For that, he was made a GCVO and in 1909 he became a privy counsellor, when he had the unusual distinction of flying his flag as an Admiral of the Fleet commanding a squadron sent to Boston for special celebrations.

The civil seven

The four representatives of 'Science' – Rayleigh, Kelvin, Lister and Huggins – were the undoubted great men of British science at the time but three were past their peak of activity. Only Rayleigh, at 59, had a future, the average age of the other three being 77. The Order of Merit had a lot of catching up to do.

Lord Kelvin, born William Thomson, was precocious, to say the least. His father, a professor of mathematics, educated him at home, before sending him at the age of ten to the University of Glasgow. After going on to Cambridge, he returned to Glasgow at the age of 22 as Professor of Natural Philosophy, a post he held for the next 53 years. An FRS at 27 and knighted at 42, he received a peerage at 68, halfway through his Presidency of the Royal Society. He was a very early GCVO, only weeks after the foundation of the Royal Victorian Order in 1896. 1902 brought him his last two honours: a privy counsellorship and the new Order of Merit – on his seventy-eighth birthday. He narrowly missed winning the first Nobel Prize for Physics in 1901.

He first proposed the use of the absolute scale of temperature and the degree used in it is called the Kelvin. He created the first physics laboratory in a British university. His knighthood came because the transatlantic telegraph table was successful only when, at the third attempt, his ideas on using low voltages were adopted.

Though he was one of the greatest researchers of the nineteenth century, Kelvin's lectures were less outstanding. When he went to Windsor

5 Lord Kelvin by Elliott and Fry.

to receive his knighthood and his assistant, Dr Day, lectured in his place, students (irreverent even in 1866) chalked on the blackboard: 'Work while it is yet Day for the Knight cometh when no man can work.'[9] He was always concerned with the utilisation of science for practical ends and was very conscious of his place in the line of great practical scientists. He was proud of his acquaintance, in youth, with the aged giant, Michael Faraday. In his own old age, he 'like Sir Isaac Newton, was impressed with the small-ness of that which had been actually achieved in comparison with what had been attempted. For instance, in his speech at his jubilee [in 1896] he said that... he knew little more of electricity and magnetism than he did at the beginning of his career'.[10]

Joseph Lister is still renowned as the founder of antiseptic surgery and a pioneer of preventive medicine. He was directed towards science by his Quaker father, an FRS – and wine merchant. As a student, he attended the first operations under ether in Britain in 1846.

6 Lord Lister by Elliott and Fry.

He did much of his pioneering work while holding chairs of surgery at both Glasgow and Edinburgh, before taking up a similar position at King's College, London in 1877, where he remained for 15 years. At that time nearly half the patients undergoing major surgery died from post-operative septic infection. Influenced by the work of Pasteur, Lister set about remedying the situation and did. By the use of carbolic acid, he eliminated septic diseases.

He took an active part in founding the Institute of Preventive Medicine in 1891, which was renamed after him in 1903. It remains a research organisation embracing a wide variety of biological disciplines that makes many notable contributions to medical science.

Honours came richly to Lister: a baronetcy in 1883 and a barony in 1897 – the first peerage conferred for services to the science of medicine, although it also took account of his current presidency of the Royal Society (of which he had become a Fellow at the age of 33). In 1902, came a privy counsellorship and one of the first OMs.

Lister was the one OM to whom the King felt most personally indebted. He had been consulted over the operation that had caused the postponement of the Coronation and the King told him: 'I know well that if it had not been for you, I should not have been here today'.[11] There was a small hitch in the actual investiture; the ribbon was too small and would not go over his head and the badge therefore came to rest on his nose; he told the King he had better take it away in his hand.[12]

Lister's death, in 1912, brought fulsome praise:

> If true worth be measured by work accomplished for the benefit of mankind, very few worthier have lived and died...saved more human lives than all the wars of the nineteenth century had sacrificed...It is a most wonderful achievement for one man and not easy to grasp...true type of scientific genius. He had the idea and the capacity to work it out with infinite pains. He saw surgery revolutionised.[13]

William Huggins was President of the Royal Society when he was made one of the first OMs and this established a precedent that has been followed to this day: every PRS has received the Order, either before or during his term of office. No other office, from Prime Minister downwards, has achieved this distinction.

Huggins had not come to his high scientific office by the usual academic route. As a youth, he had busied himself with microscope and telescope but, instead of going to Cambridge as originally intended, he took charge of the family drapery business in the City of London for a dozen years. Only after selling that and moving to Tulse Hill in South London, where he built his own observatory, did he devote himself to astronomy and astrophysics, with his wife as his sole assistant.

With his own telescope (to which he attached a spectroscope) and, later, with telescopes lent to him by the Royal Society, he revolutionised astronomy. By using spectroscopy, he determined that stars contained elements such as hydrogen, calcium, sodium and iron; he used photography in stellar spectroscopy. He investigated the visible spectra of the sun, stars, planets, comets and meteors and discovered the true nature of the 'unresolved' nebulae. He was a pioneer, who left astronomy in his debt.

When his telescopes were returned to the Royal Society, they were given to Cambridge University Observatory with a plaque reading:

> These telescopes were used by Sir William Huggins and Lady Huggins at their observatory at Tulse Hill in researches which formed the foundation of the Science of Astrophysics.

Huggins' pioneering work brought him many honours: FRS at 41 (after a slow start), the Presidencies of the British Association for the Advancement of

Science and of the Royal Astronomical Society, as well as the Royal Society itself. His small private means were augmented by a civil list pension of £150 and, despite not holding any official position, he was made a KCB in the Diamond Jubilee Honours List of 1897.

John Strutt, **Lord Rayleigh** was a premature baby, a frail child (with intermittent schooling at both Eton and Harrow) but an exceptional adult, graduating as Senior Wrangler at Cambridge: 'Strutt's answers were better than the books', said one examiner.

An FRS at 32, he succeeded to the family title and estates in Essex. Leaving the management of the estates to a younger brother, he behaved in what was considered a rather eccentric manner for a rich landowner by concentrating on physical research. This was to bring him eventually the Nobel Prize for Physics in 1904 for the discovery of the element argon, with Sir William Ramsay, who received the Prize for Chemistry. This discovery initiated the uncovering of a whole new family of elements, the inert, or noble, gases. One of his other important contributions to physics was what is now known (because of a later correction by another OM, James Jeans) as the Rayleigh-Jeans equation, describing the distribution of wavelengths in black-body radiation.

After five years as Cavendish Professor of Experimental Physics at Cambridge, he did most of his further research in the private laboratory on his estate. He was also active in public life, as Lord Lieutenant of Essex for ten years, as Chancellor of Cambridge University from 1908 until his death in 1919, as chairman of government committees on the formation of the National Physical Laboratory and on aeronautics. For him, with his inherited peerage, the OM was the first public recognition of his standing; a privy counsellorship followed in 1905.

After Kelvin's death in 1907, Lord Rayleigh was generally recognised as the leader of British science on the physical side. The *Dictionary of National Biography* (*DNB*) summarised his achievement in a way that explains why his name no longer ranks alongside those of Kelvin or Lister:

> Of striking discoveries or inventions practically none stand to his credit with the single exception of the discovery of argon. His special aptitude was for arranging and levelling up existing knowledge rather than for taking giant strides into unexplored country. The outstanding qualities of his writings were thoroughness and clearness: he made everything seem obvious.[14]

'Literature' was represented among the original 12 members of the Order of Merit by two historians, both with political connections.

John Morley's connections were very strong. After leaving Oxford with only a pass degree, he became a journalist and edited, for 15 years, the *Fortnightly Review*, an influential organ of liberal opinion, for a few months the moribund *Morning Star*, a reforming paper; and, for a couple of years, the *Pall Mall Gazette*. He was much influenced by early friendships with the aged John Stuart Mill, the 'saint of rationalism', and the middle-aged George Meredith (who was later to join him as an OM). He had a long career as a biographer – of Burke, Voltaire, Rousseau, Cobden, Cromwell and, finally, Gladstone (in three large volumes, published in 1903).

With his writing, Morley combined a full political career, entering the Commons in 1883 and remaining there (except for a few months) until he went to the Lords in 1908. He described the life of an MP as 'work without industry and idleness without leisure'.[15] He speedily entered the Cabinet, as Chief Secretary for Ireland, in Gladstone's short-lived 1886 government. He held the same office throughout the next Liberal administrations from 1892–95. He was opposed to the war against the Boer republics and, as it dragged on, he argued for negotiation rather than a demand for unconditional surrender. The OM came to him a month after the end of the war, along with the victorious generals, Roberts and Kitchener.

His biography of Gladstone was enormously successful, selling 30,000 copies in the first year and another 100,000 in the next ten. It was his last great literary work but his greatest time in politics lay ahead. From 1905–10, Morley was Secretary of State for India. Although initially indignant at being 'exiled to the Brahmaputra',[16] he collaborated with the Viceroy in what became known as the Morley-Minto reforms, designed to associate the people of India gradually with the civil administration of their country. He published much of his correspondence with Minto in *Recollections* in 1917. Lytton Strachey commented that

> though Lord Minto might perhaps be described as an average Viceroy, Lord Morley was certainly not at all an average Secretary of State.

As Lord President of the Council from 1910–14, Morley read to the Upper House in 1911 the famous paper stating that, in the event of rejection by the Lords of the Parliament Bill, the King would create enough peers to avoid a second rejection and, in 1914, resigned over the declaration of war. When later rebuked for drinking German wine, he replied: 'I am interning it.'[17]

On the award of the OM to Morley, there were later some doubtful views. Esher thought it was Morley's 'pagan philosophy [which] obtained for him the OM'.[18] When commenting adversely on a later proposal that Augustine Birrell should get the OM, Balfour said had Birrell not distinguished himself as a politician, nobody would have thought of giving it to him for literary work.

> Morley has just escaped this charge; but only just: and his work is of course on a far more extensive scale than any which Birrell has attempted.[19]

William (or W. E. H.) Lecky was an Irish Protestant landowner, whose private income allowed him to write from an early age, although he was always attracted by politics. By the age of 30, he had written two very successful books on *Rationalism in Europe* and on *European Morals*. He became famous very quickly and began to move in high literary and political circles.

His early success prompted him to move on to his magnum opus, the eight-volume *History of England in the Eighteenth Century*, which took him 19 years to write and was published between 1878 and 1890. Despite its title, much of it was devoted to the history of Ireland and was later published separately under that title. He had earlier written a successful book on *Leaders of Public Opinion in Ireland*. His scholarship led Salisbury to offer him the Regius Chair of Modern History at Oxford in 1892 but he refused.

In politics, Lecky was a theoretical nationalist, with great regard for the intellectual stirrings in Ireland, but he was against Home Rule and, when elected to the Commons in 1895 for his alma mater, Trinity College, Dublin, it was as a Liberal Unionist. His privy counsellorship came in the Diamond Jubilee Honours List and recognised his writing as much as his political activity. In 1902, he was one of the founding members of the British Academy.

For many years after his death in 1903, Lecky was completely neglected and relegated by historians like Namier to the graveyard of Victorian Whig writing. He has not, however, been completely forgotten; a full-length biography was published as recently as 1994.[20]

'Art' had only one representative among the original OMs. Lord Leighton, Sir Everett Millais, Bt and Sir Edward Burne-Jones, Bt had all died in the previous six years and Mr **George Frederic Watts**, who had twice declined Gladstone's offer of a baronetcy, was the outstanding living painter and sculptor. He was 87 and was to enjoy the honour for only two years.

The second time Watts refused a baronetcy, in 1894, he said 'I must own that if thought worthy, I should like to be the first of a new Order.' Salisbury was anxious for him to accept a privy counsellorship in 1897 and he said he would accept it 'not because it would be anything to me personally, but I should like to inaugurate this honour as suitable for literary and artistic labours.' Queen Victoria rejected the recommendation, however, believing the Privy Council was not a suitable vehicle for the rewarding of artists.[21]

As a young man, the son of a piano maker and tuner, Watts had had an early success in gaining a commission for a painting for the rebuilt Houses of Parliament. He enjoyed the patronage of Lord and Lady Holland, both in Italy and England and it was his long stay in Italy that perhaps led to his being called 'Signor' by his near friends. He was not elected an RA until he was 51, a much later age than Millais and Leighton, but he had been candid in criticising the Academy's shortcomings and errors.

His allegorical paintings, some immense, bore titles such as 'Time and Oblivion', 'Death Crowning Innocence', 'Time, Death and Judgement' and 'Love Steering the Boat of Humanity'. The Great Hall of Lincoln's Inn is dominated by his 'Justice, a Hemicycle of Lawgivers' ranging from Alfred the Great and Edward I to Moses and Justinian. His total output is reckoned to have been over 800 and he once had a room to himself at the Tate.

Watts' portraits – many in the National Portrait Gallery, to which he donated them – included Edward VII (as Prince of Wales), Carlyle, Gladstone, Cardinal Manning, John Stuart Mill, Cecil Rhodes and three other OMs (Roberts, Lecky and Meredith), as well as a self-portrait, which Carlyle described as looking 'like a mad labourer'. He also painted Julia Margaret Cameron, who obliged by photographing him.

His sculptures include the powerful statue of a rider on a rearing horse, 'Physical Energy', in Kensington Gardens and the statue of Tennyson outside Lincoln Cathedral.

Twice, Watts married women 30 years his junior. At 47, he married the 17-year-old actress, Ellen Terry, who modelled for many of his pictures before soon running off with the stage designer, Edward Godwin. At 69, he married the 36-year-old Mary Fraser-Tytler. She became his devoted companion and nurse and not only wrote a biography of him but also established in their home at Compton in Surrey the memorial gallery which is still there. For many years, Wilfrid Blunt was its curator and he chose for the title of his biography the name that Leighton had given to Watts: *England's Michelangelo*.

For most of the twentieth century, Watts was written off as 'largely forgotten' or a 'nineteenth-century phenomenon'. In a TV programme about him in 1981, Hugh Casson, then President of the Royal Academy, described him as 'hopelessly unfashionable...much of his work lies unseen under dustsheets and in the storage rooms of museums...the fame he enjoyed in his lifetime died with him'.

His stock has risen. Reviewing a Tate Gallery exhibition in 1997 of 'The Age of Rossetti, Burne-Jones and Watts', Richard Cork wrote:

> Watts is a revelation. Neglected and even mocked for much of the present century, he is ripe for reassessment...more rewarding than either Rossetti or Burne-Jones...a retrospective survey of Watts's achievement is long overdue.[22]

The financial reassessment had started a decade earlier when Watts' most famous painting 'Hope' (sitting on a globe with bandaged eyes, plucking the one remaining string of her lyre) sold at auction for £869,000, a record for a Victorian painting.

Of the original 12 OMs, the first to die was Lecky, 18 months later, in October 1903; the last was Seymour, nearly 27 years later, in March 1929.

A hundred years later, how have their reputations fared? I suspect that, among the general intelligent public, only four names would be recognised, even if their precise roles might not be easily identified: Kitchener, Lister, Watts and Kelvin. The other eight would probably be recognised by present practitioners in their fields, although I doubt even that in the case of the two admirals. I have found a number of senior naval officers completely unaware of them.

7

DIVISIONS OF DISTINCTION

The original Statutes of the Order of Merit in 1902 envisaged that its strictly limited number of 24 Members should be divided between certain stated categories. What has never been stated, however, is the number to be allotted to any particular category. In this respect it differs from its model, the German Order Pour le mérite and the aborted British Order of Merit in Science and Art. Its Statutes are guidelines not rules and the Sovereign therefore has a wonderfully free hand – in theory.

At the beginning, the OM was talked of as an order to be divided more or less equally between Military and Civil 'divisions'. There are no such 'divisions', even though the Palace has frequently fallen into wrongly describing appointments (sometimes in the *London Gazette* or the *Court Circular*) as belonging to one or other division. There are simply two types of Badge, with crossed swords distinguishing those Members appointed for military services.

The first list in 1902 achieved rough parity between military and civil: five to seven. Since then, the military side has never remotely compared in numbers with the civil side. The original five has risen occasionally to six (particularly after the two world wars) but only between March and June 1912 has it gone as high as seven: under a third of the total of 24. By 1970, the number had dwindled to two and, since the death of Lord Mountbatten in 1979, there have been no military Members.

The Statutes naturally provided that the military Members would come from the two services in existence in 1902: the Navy and the Army. Despite its smaller size, the 'Senior Service' has managed to maintain more than parity over the years: 11 sailors and nine soldiers, with the addition of three airmen after the newest service, the RAF, became eligible in 1935.

Civil Members were, likewise, to come from different stated categories. Originally, they were to be from Art, Literature and Science; later this was broadened to include Learning, to make Art into Arts and to include civilian Crown Service; finally to include any 'exceptional service'.

In the years, however, before the broadening of scope, there was sometimes concern about maintaining a balance between the different fields, informally in the way that Pour le mérite did formally. There was often talk of a particular artist or writer taking the 'place left vacant' by a recently deceased artist or writer. This has never been so, because the country might possess four brilliant artists and only two brilliant writers at a particular moment. It does no credit to the Order to appoint a second-rate composer when there are two first-rate playwrights in the wings. The Order of Merit should reflect the state of British excellence as it is, not as it ideally should be.

So, there is always an attempt to keep a balance between acknowledging exceptional individual merit, in whatever field, and recognising excellence across the board of national activity. Nevertheless, because individual excellence has to be the overriding criterion, there have been oddities, not least because increasing longevity has caused 'bunching-up' in some fields. Over the years, there have always been some strange overall distributions at particular times, as the figures from 1935, 1955 and 1975 show.

In 1935, there were three sailors but no soldiers; five scientists, of whom three were physicists; eight from the world of letters, including philosophy, poetry, history and classical scholarship; one composer; one painter; and one ex-Prime Minister – 19 in all. The Order is not always full, although in recent years there seems to have been more effort to fill the vacancies reasonably soon.

In 1955, the Order was full: only ten years after the Second World War, there were ten from all three Armed Services and public affairs, including two ex-Prime Ministers and one 'near-miss'; seven from the world of letters, including three poets, two philosophers, one classical scholar and one historian but no novelist or playwright; three from the arts: painter, composer and architect; four scientists, including three from the field of medicine, one chemist but no physicist or engineer.

In 1975, there were again only 19 Members: one sailor; nine scientists, including three physicists, three from the field of medicine, one chemist, one zoologist and one engineer; six from the arts: two painters, two composers, one sculptor and one architect; two from the world of letters: one historian and one philosopher; two men of affairs. The next year, four were added: two historians, one engineer and one ex-Prime Minister.

In 2002, there were 21 Ordinary Members of the Order, divided thus:

- Science – 11 (three molecular biologists, two physiologists, two engineers, two mathematicians, one biochemist and one chemist)
- Arts – four (one singer, one painter, one sculptor and one architect)

- Learning – two (one historian and one in public affairs)
- Literature – one (playwright)
- Public Affairs – two (one Consort of the Sovereign and one ex-Prime Minister)
- Humanitarian – one

There is no novelist or poet, no composer, no philosopher. The reader can probably think of someone to fill each of those 'vacancies'.

In any case, many of the labels are misleading. In succeeding chapters I have tried to discuss the Members over the century in terms of their categories: the military (who are self-evident), the scientists, the writers, the artists, the musicians, the men of affairs and so on. There is, however, much overlapping and, as I shall show, the categories of some of the early Members were blurred. For instance, men in the world of politics happened also to be active in the world of letters and thus could be fitted, however narrowly, into the ambit of the Order: Morley, Bryce, Balfour, G. O. Trevelyan, Haldane and H. A. L. Fisher. Such men are not common nowadays and, in any case, the ambit has been extended to its limit.

Within science itself, developments have caused descriptions to change. The physicist, chemist, biologist or zoologist, to be found among the earlier OMs, have given way in many cases to the biochemist or the molecular biologist.

In the humanities and the arts, the novelist or playwright may well also be a poet and the painter also a sculptor. What also of the spanning between science and the arts? The philosopher is often also a mathematician and could therefore figure under either heading.

What I am saying is that the categories I have used must not be taken as rigid. They are for convenience only, to enable the study of the Order of Merit to be made within reasonably coherent frameworks rather than in the more common chronological sequence, which I find rather random and meaningless.

Many readers will disagree with my categorisations but I ask only that they look at the overall picture – of individuals who have been appointed to the Order of Merit for excelling in a field important in the life of the nation, whatever name is given to their achievements.

Honorary Members have never been subject to any categorisation or limitation of number, being simply 'such persons, who are not subjects of Our Crown, upon whom We may think fit to confer the honour of being received into the Order'. This allowed the admissions of Schweitzer in 1955 and Mother Teresa in 1983 for humanitarian services, neither of whom would, strictly speaking, have been admissible as British Civil Members at those times.

8

THE MILITARY MEN

1. 1902 Field Marshal Earl ROBERTS
2. 1902 Field Marshal Viscount WOLSELEY
3. 1902 Field Marshal Earl KITCHENER
4. 1902 Admiral of the Fleet Sir Henry KEPPEL
5. 1902 Admiral of the Fleet Sir Edward SEYMOUR
6. 1905 Field Marshal Sir George WHITE
7. 1905 Admiral of the Fleet Lord FISHER
8. 1906 Field Marshal Prince YAMAGATA (Honorary)
9. 1906 Field Marshal Prince OYAMA (Honorary)
10. 1906 Admiral of the Fleet Marquis TOGO (Honorary)
11. 1912 Admiral of the Fleet Sir Arthur WILSON
12. 1914 Field Marshal the Earl of YPRES
13. 1916 Admiral of the Fleet Earl JELLICOE
14. 1918 Marshal of France Ferdinand FOCH (Honorary)
15. 1919 Admiral of the Fleet Earl BEATTY
16. 1919 Field Marshal Earl HAIG
17. 1919 Marshal of France Joseph JOFFRE (Honorary)
18. 1931 Admiral of the Fleet Sir Charles MADDEN
19. 1936 Field Marshal Lord CHETWODE
20. 1937 Lieutenant General Lord BADEN-POWELL (really 'Civil')
21. 1939 Admiral of the Fleet Lord CHATFIELD
22. 1940 Marshal of the RAF Lord NEWALL
23. 1943 Admiral of the Fleet Sir Dudley POUND
24. 1945 General of the Army Dwight EISENHOWER (Honorary)
25. 1946 Marshal of the RAF Viscount PORTAL
26. 1946 Field Marshal Viscount ALANBROOKE
27. 1946 Admiral of the Fleet Viscount CUNNINGHAM

28. 1951   Marshal of the RAF Viscount TRENCHARD
29. 1959   Field Marshal Earl ALEXANDER
30. 1965   Admiral of the Fleet Earl MOUNTBATTEN

Of the 30 recipients of the Military Badge of the Order of Merit, I have already described in some detail in Chapter 6 the five who were among the first 12 Members appointed in 1902. I shall also deal separately in Chapter 17 with the six honorary recipients: the three Japanese in 1906; the two French in 1918/19; and the one American in 1945. I shall also cover in Chapter 15, among those who received the Order for humanitarian services, the award to Baden-Powell, which although technically military was really for civil work.

That leaves 18 British servicemen to be covered in this chapter. They divide into five time categories: before the First World War; the First World War; between the wars; the Second World War; and after the Second World War.

A noticeable feature is how many of the military recipients were born in Ireland or whose families came from there. It was George Meredith, an early OM, who wrote in his only really popular novel, *Diana of the Crossways*: 'Tis Ireland gives England her soldiers, her generals too.' He might have added 'and admirals also'. The list includes Roberts, Wolseley, Kitchener, White, French, Alanbrooke among the generals, as well as Beatty, Madden and Cunningham among the admirals

Before the First World War

After the original list of 12 OMs in 1902, there was no effort to fill the remaining 12 places until 30 June 1905, by which time three of the first 12 had died. To the remaining nine, six were added, of whom two were military – a field marshal and an admiral.

The soldier was **Sir George White**, who had won the VC in 1879 in Afghanistan under Roberts, whom he later succeeded as Commander-in-Chief in India. When the South African War broke out, he was 64 and limping from a riding accident. Wolseley told him this might keep him from the front. He responded: 'I beg your pardon, sir, my leg is well enough for anything except running away.'

So he went out to command the forces in Natal in 1899 but was besieged in Ladysmith with 10,000 troops for four months. On one occasion, a Boer shell buried itself under his horse but did not explode; he continued talking without flinching or even altering his voice. It was as the 'Defender of Lady-smith' that he became a famous hero, rather like another OM, Baden-Powell, at Mafeking.

His rewards were two more Grand Crosses and the Governorship of Gibraltar, which was then a military fortress of Empire rather than a source of diplomatic friction with Spain. While there he was made a field marshal and, on his return in 1904, be became the Governor of Chelsea Hospital, where he died in 1912.

Edward VII was fond of this brave soldier and hence his incorporation into the Order of Merit. Balfour, the Prime Minister, was distinctly less enthusiastic:

> I have little to say about this most excellent officer, except that nobody has ever supposed that he is a man of great abilities, military or otherwise. So far as courage and character are concerned, he has, and can have, no superior; but though the OM would add to his reputation, I do not think he would add to the reputation of the OM.[1]

White's reputation has not survived. Indeed, one of the most recent OMs thought little of the equestrian statue in London:

> General or Field Marshal Sir somebody or other White. I don't know who on earth he was. Yet he takes up a lot of public space in Portland Place.[2]

The admiral in the 1905 list was the flamboyant **Sir John Arbuthnot ('Jacky') Fisher**. He was another intimate of Edward VII and, after a career that began in 1854 (on the nomination of the last of Nelson's captains) and included the Crimean War, China during the opium wars, the Mediterranean and the West Indies, he had reached the top as First Sea Lord in 1904. He was determined to drag the Navy out of its almost sail-like mentality and fit it for twentieth-century warfare. He introduced the Dreadnoughts.

He was a man of fierce temper, who brooked no opposition, declaring dramatically:

> If any man oppose me, I will make his wife a widow, his children fatherless and his home a dunghill.[3]

He was loved or loathed. The great American naval historian, Arthur Marder, described him as:

> regarded by the Royal Navy in his own lifetime either as a saint or a devil, as a genius who raised the efficiency of the Fleet to a peak never reached before, or as an evil old man who raised havoc with naval discipline and efficiency... there was no half-way house.[4]

Fisher's closeness to Edward VII, commented on in the *DNB* entry on that monarch, led to an extensive correspondence, although Fisher burnt nearly all the King's letters.[5] He once suggested to the King that, before it grew too large, the German fleet should be 'Copenhagened', recalling Gambier's pre-emptive strike against the Danes in 1807. 'My God Fisher, you must be mad!' said the King.[6] In March 1905 he threatened to resign and go into the armaments industry. The King was opposed to this and in June Fisher got the OM; and in December promotion to Admiral of the Fleet.

Fisher retired in 1910 but, on the enforced resignation of Prince Louis of Battenburg after the outbreak of war in 1914, he resumed the office of First Sea Lord, at the age of 73. He resigned suddenly, however, in May 1915 to the consternation of the country's leaders. George V thought, 'that he should have been hanged at the yardarm for desertion of his post in the face of the enemy'.[7] Fisher is best remembered, however, as the man who modernised the Royal Navy.

Fisher was succeeded as First Sea Lord in 1910 by the man who also followed him as the next military OM: Admiral of the Fleet **Sir Arthur Knyvet Wilson,** who received the honour on his resignation in 1912. He had won the VC on land, at the battle of El-Teb in 1884, while serving as a captain with the Naval Brigade in Egypt. As an admiral, he commanded both the Channel and Home Fleets. He disliked the new submarine service, which he described as underhand, underwater and un-English.

His short period as First Sea Lord, from 1910–12, was because he fell out with Churchill (First Lord of the Admiralty), who wanted to create a Naval War Staff. Churchill respected him as a man:

> He was, without any exception, the most selfless man I have ever met or even read of. He wanted nothing, and he feared nothing – absolutely nothing... Everything was duty... There was nothing else... It made him seem very unsympathetic on many occasions... He never opened up, never unbent.[8]

Having declined a peerage offered by Churchill, Wilson accepted the King's OM, offered by way of compensation. It was announced on 8 March 1912, shortly after his retirement. He succeeded to a baronetcy on his brother's death in 1919, only a couple of years before his own death. During the War, he had worked at the Admiralty, without any official post or salary, and often urged his pet scheme to invade and hold Heligoland.

The First World War

It is not surprising that the first of the four British military OMs in the war went to a soldier. It was predominantly a land war and it is rather surprising that the Army received only two of the four awards.

The first of the military OMs had spent four years in the Navy before transferring to the Army. The aptly named **Sir John French** had commanded the British Expeditionary Force in France (the Kaiser's 'contemptible little army') since the outbreak of war. By way of obvious encouragement,

George V conferred the Order of Merit on him on 3 December 1914, during the King's first visit to the front. It was Asquith's idea:

> The Prime Minister asked me to suggest to you that it might be suitable to give the OM to Sir J. French now. Lord Roberts' death leaves Lord Kitchener as the only English military member of the order. The grant would of course be without prejudice to anything that may be done for him hereafter . . . PS There are three naval members . . . [9]

French irritated the King by wearing too many stars of orders on his khaki uniform: 'always covered himself with foreign baubles.' Henry Wilson (another Field Marshal) said about him:

> He is a nice little man in his bath, but when he puts his clothes on you can't trust him, and you never know what he will wear.[10]

All French's decorations, including presumably the OM, were pawned by his grandson, the Third and Last Earl of Ypres, in 1970 and had to be redeemed by his second son, who spent much of his life trying to redeem also the military reputation of his father.

A year and a day after receiving the OM, French was recalled by Asquith, acting under pressure from Haig and other generals and at the insistence of the King. This followed the disasters of Neuve Chapelle, Festubert and Loos. He was appointed Commander-in-Chief Home Forces and created a viscount. Haig remembered this when offered only a viscounty after the victory in 1918 and complained: 'When FM French was *recalled* from the command of the Armies in France for *incompetence*, he was made a Viscount![11] As one of French's biographers concluded:

> History has dealt too harshly with French . . . He was not a great general. He was a brave man and a good cavalry leader, and cared deeply about his profession. But in many respects he never transcended the nineteenth century . . . [But Churchill said that he] in the sacred fire of leadership, was unsurpassed . . . [12]

French, however, survived his dismissal to fight another fight – against the Irish, as the penultimate Viceroy of Ireland from 1918–21, for which he was promoted to an earldom (of Ypres).

In 1975, the Imperial War Museum acquired two different portions of French's writings: love letters to his mistress, with indiscreet references to troop and VIP movements; and his war diaries from 1914–15.

The next military OM of the First World War was 'won' at sea, the only operational award of the Order in the sense that the recipient was in the face of the enemy at the time and could have lost his own life. He was

7 Earl Jellicoe by R. G. Evans.

Sir John Jellicoe, the Commander-in-Chief of the Grand Fleet, pithily described by Churchill as the only commander on either side, whose orders 'in the space of two or three hours might nakedly decide who won the war.[13] His OM headed the Honours List announced on 15 September 1916 for the Battle of Jutland nearly four months earlier, a list which also included a posthumous VC for the 16-year-old John Cornwell for remaining at his gun turret.

Jutland, the first great sea battle since Trafalgar, began when *HMS Galatea* signalled 'enemy in sight' on the afternoon of 31 May and ended when Jellicoe signalled 'enemy fleet returned to harbour' early on 1 June. In between, the British Grand Fleet had lost 14 ships (totalling 115,000 tons), including the battlecruisers *Queen Mary*, *Invincible* and *Indefatigable*, with nearly 7,000 men killed and wounded. The German High Seas Fleet had lost 11 ships, (totalling 61,000 tons), including the battlecruiser *Lutzow* and the cruisers *Wiesbaden* and *Pommern*, with around 3,000 men killed and wounded.

This Battle of the Mists was indecisive and both sides claimed victory. 'The spell of Trafalgar has been broken', claimed the former Admiral of the

Fleet and Knight of the Garter, Kaiser Wilhelm II, but his fleet ventured out only once more before it mutinied in 1918. George V was more circumspect in his message to Jellicoe:

> Though the retirement of the enemy immediately after the opening of the general engagement robbed us of the opportunity of gaining a decisive victory, the events of last Wednesday amply justify my confidence in the valour and efficiency of the fleets under your command.

The battle has provided naval historians with material for dispute ever since; the Jellicoe–Beatty controversy has raged endlessly about the responsibility for the tactical indecisiveness of the action. With his overwhelming superiority, had Jellicoe preserved his Grand Fleet but at the expense of letting the High Seas Fleet off? Had Beatty deployed his Battle Cruiser Squadron effectively?

In the press at the time there was questioning as to whether the Grand Fleet should not be given over to younger men, like David Beatty and Charles Madden (future OMs). In December, that happened. Jellicoe became First Sea Lord and Beatty succeeded him in command of the Grand Fleet.

When Beatty succeeded him again, as First Sea Lord in 1919, Jellicoe (by this time a viscount) went out to New Zealand as Governor-General, where he stayed until 1924, when he was promoted to an earldom. It was a considerably more comfortable 'billet' than that given to French in Ireland. When Jellicoe died in 1935, he was buried in St Paul's Cathedral, alongside Nelson and Collingwood.

At this point, between discussing the OMs for Jellicoe and Beatty, it may be appropriate to observe that, with one exception, all the British naval OMs who were not dead or too old served at the Battle of Jutland:

- Jellicoe, in overall command
- Beatty, in command of the Battle Cruiser Squadron
- Madden, as Chief of Staff to Jellicoe
- Chatfield, as Flag Captain to Beatty on *Lion*
- Pound, as Captain of *Colossus*
- Mountbatten, as a midshipman 'doggie' or general dogsbody to Chatfield

The exception was Cunningham, who was where he spent much of his career: in the Mediterranean.

Also at Jutland was 20-year-old Prince Albert, second son of George V, who was mentioned in despatches for his service in 'A' turret of the battleship *Collingwood*. Chatfield and Pound would not reasonably have thought that this young sub-lieutenant, as George VI, would one day confer the Order of Merit on them.

The two British commanders – of fleet and field – had to wait until the Birthday Honours of 3 June 1919 when came the announcement that Admiral of the Fleet **Sir David Beatty** and Field Marshal **Sir Douglas Haig** had been appointed to the Order of Merit. They were invested by the King on 12 June.

Beatty, at 48, was the youngest OM ever appointed, until the Duke of Edinburgh received the Order on his forty-seventh birthday in 1968; Beatty's first ship, as a cadet and midshipman, was the flagship in the Mediterranean of the previous Duke of Edinburgh, Queen Victoria's second son.

From an Irish family, Beatty had won a DSO in Kitchener's Sudan campaign in 1896 and served under Seymour in China in 1900. With his cap at the jaunty angle that took his name and having a rich American chain store heiress for a wife, he was the dashing figure he always remained. He was popular with his sailors – and other men's wives.

As the youngest flag officer for a century, Beatty caught the eye of an even younger First Lord of the Admiralty, Winston Churchill, when he was Naval Secretary; his advice to his successor was: 'You have a bloody awful row with Winston once a month and you are all right.' He was given, over the heads of many others, the much-coveted command of the Battle Cruiser Squadron in 1912 and held it until 1916.

In the first two years of the war, his squadron engaged the Germans in the Heligoland Bight and on the Dogger Bank. Jutland was the great test and I have already discussed that battle above. Beatty's remark to his flag captain has entered the history books: 'There seems to be something wrong with our bloody ships today, Chatfield' and 'and with our bloody system', which is less often quoted. Beatty was conscious of the faults in the construction of the British ships and their guns and signalling and, as well, of the rigid and highly centralised command structure.

In charge of the Grand Fleet from 1916–19, he fought no more battles but maintained the morale of his men claiming that his fleet 'preserved a cheerfulness which is extraordinary'. The year 1919 was his *annus mirabilis*. At the end of 1918, he was a Vice-Admiral with a GCB; by October 1919 he was an Admiral of the Fleet, an earl, First Sea Lord and £100,000 richer (by courtesy of Parliament, which voted Jellicoe half that sum). For four days, in April 1919, he enjoyed the unusual distinction of flying the Union Flag of an admiral of the fleet while commanding the Grand Fleet immediately before its dispersal.

Their respective protagonists portrayed tension between him and Jellicoe, but he was very careful to assure George V on his visit to the Grand Fleet in June 1917 ('What with Monarchs and Submarines, we are having a hectic time') that 'my relations with Jellicoe are very friendly'.[14]

As First Sea Lord, from 1919–27, Beatty presided over a period in which the days of British naval supremacy went for ever. With the airman,

Trenchard, a much later OM, he was a member of the first Chiefs of Staff Committee in 1926.

His own winter death was precipitated by two others, when he had walked behind gun carriages through the streets. He rose from his sick bed to attend Jellicoe's funeral in November 1935 and only two months later, against doctors' advice, he went to George V's: 'He was not only my King, he was my friend.'[15] He died in March 1936, aged only 65. Like Jellicoe, he was buried in St Paul's, beside Nelson and Collingwood. Fifty years later, a leading military historian wrote that Beatty 'was generally accounted to be Britain's greatest sailor since Nelson'.[16]

Beatty's companion in the June 1919 Honours List, **Douglas Haig**, has become by far the most controversial of the military OMs. In terms of human life, Jutland is insignificant compared to the carnage on the Western Front. Words like Somme and Passchendaele have entered the English language as symbolising the waste of human life.

As the twentieth century progressed and human life became more valued, the controversy increased. Can one imagine the outcry today if hundreds of thousands of body bags came home, instead of resting quietly in some corner of a foreign field? No government, let alone a single general, could survive it.

Was Haig a cold-hearted butcher, indifferent to the deaths of so many of his troops or was he the master of attrition – the 'master of the field', as the Germans called him? Hardly a year passes now without some reassessment following re-assessment.

I am certainly not qualified, nor indeed would I have the space, to attempt yet another 'judgement'. What I can say firmly is that, in his lifetime, Haig was respected and almost revered. It would have been impossible *not* to give him the OM. 'Donkeys leading lions' came later, much later. It was Beaverbrook who said that, with the publication of his *Private Papers* (in 1952), Haig had committed suicide 25 years after his death.

At the end of the war, Haig was the victorious general and, moreover, one who did not take the sizeable honours and rewards that came his way – an earldom, the OM and £100,000 from Parliament – until he had satisfied himself about proper pensions provision for his troops. He founded the British Legion and its Poppy Day Appeal, which has grown from £106,000 in 1921 to over £20m in 2001.

Haig was a cavalryman who had served in Egypt and South Africa and held the prestigious Aldershot Command, before taking a corps across to France in 1914 with the BEF, under French, whom he managed to displace at the end of 1915. He had married a royal lady-in-waiting and he was close to George V, who encouraged him to maintain a private correspondence throughout the war.

When the great German offensive of March 1918 tried to divide the British and French and capture the Channel ports, Haig issued his famous 'Special Order of the Day' to his troops:

> Every position must be held to the last man: there must be no retirement. With our backs to the wall, and believing in the justice of our cause, each one of us must fight on to the end.

> [These] grave and moving words must be taken to heart by every man and woman in these islands.[17]

On Haig's death in 1928, aged 67, it was written that:

> he bore a burden more terrible and prolonged than ever was borne by any other British general...He was never perturbed by danger however imminent, by mishaps or disappointments however unexpected, by responsibilities however grave.[18]

It is precisely that imperturbability that has been turned against Haig over the years. I shall leave this contentious issue with some remarks by one of our leading contemporary military historians:

> Haig, whom his contemporaries found difficult to know, has become today an enigma...in whose public manner and private diaries no concern for human suffering was or is discernible [and who] compensated for his aloofness with nothing whatsoever of the common touch...[19]

Between the wars

The 1920s were a fallow time for the military side of the Order of Merit. The war to end wars was over and the top military commanders in it had received the Order. The idea of 'exceptional' military service in peacetime was rather hard to justify.

The three military appointments to the Order between the wars went to men who had been middle-rank commanders in the First and had reached the top of their profession before the Second: two sailors, Madden and Chatfield, and a soldier, Chetwode. The awards recognised what was spelled out in Madden's case as 'distinguished services rendered to his Country in Peace and War'.

Admiral of the Fleet **Sir Charles Madden** received the OM in the New Year Honours of 1931, shortly after relinquishing the post of First Sea Lord, in which he had succeeded Beatty in 1927. His selection, from out of retirement, by Beatty has been attributed by one naval historian to the latter's 'desire to heal the schism which had developed in the Navy between his own and Admiral Jellicoe's supporters over the unsatisfactory outcome of the battle of Jutland'.[20]

As already noted, Madden was Jellicoe's Chief of Staff at that time, as well as being his brother-in-law, their wives being daughters of the shipping magnate, Sir Charles Cayzer. In his despatch on the battle, Jellicoe had commended his 'brilliant work' over 21 months of war:

> His good judgement, his long experience in fleets, special gift for organisation, and his capacity for unlimited work, have all been of the greatest assistance to me...he was always at hand...his judgement never at fault. I owe him more than I can say.[21]

Madden's reward at the end of war was promotion to full admiral, a baronetcy and £10,000 from Parliament. After commanding the Atlantic Fleet, he retired in 1924, only to be recalled three years later. He did not have an easy time as First Sea Lord, settling (almost to the point of resignation) for 50 cruisers rather than the 70 the Navy thought it needed. Perhaps the OM was the 'Sailor King's' way of compensating this admiral for the rough time the government had given him. He lived only another four years.

Madden's early career had been that of a high flyer. That early OM, Jacky Fisher, thought he was one of the five best brains in the Navy below flag rank and picked him out to be his naval assistant and a member of the Dreadnought design team. His next sea appointment was to command *Dreadnought* itself.

The last OM appointment made by George V was of Field Marshal **Sir Philip Chetwode** in the New Year Honours of 1936. He was invested at Sandringham on 1 January by the King, who was already unwell and died there three weeks later. In a manuscript letter to his aged soldier uncle, the Duke of Connaught, the King included the remark: 'Hope you will approve of my giving the Order of Merit to Philip Chetwode, he is now one of our greatest soldiers.'[22] This is hardly a statement that would resonate through today's Army but, in 1936, Chetwode was a man who had narrowly missed being Chief of the Imperial General Staff; as Commander-in-Chief India from 1931–36, he had gone a long way to modernising, and in the process Indianising, the officer corps. He created an Indian Sandhurst, an Indian Air Force and converted the Indian Marine into a Navy.

The eldest son of a baronet, Chetwode's early military career had included serving under White in the defence of Ladysmith and winning a DSO. He later served under French. In the First World War, he commanded cavalry brigades and divisions on the Western Front before moving to the Near East to command the Desert Column, under Allenby, which was instrumental in levering the Turks out of their defences ahead of Jerusalem. Years later, Ataturk told him: 'You beat us because you had more money' – to hire camels to carry water for the horses.

During the Second World War, Chetwode was Chairman of the Executive Committee of the joint organization set up by the Red Cross and St John, for which he received a barony. There had been a short-lived plan to send him as Ambassador to Spain when relations were established with Franco in 1939 but it came to nothing.[23]

Chetwode achieved somewhat dubious posthumous fame as the father-in-law of John Betjeman, particularly because of the story that, when the poet asked him what he should call him instead of the pre-nuptial 'Sir', he received the considered reply 'Field Marshal'.

In the New Year Honours of 1939 came the third inter-war appointment: Admiral of the Fleet **Lord Chatfield**. He had been First Sea Lord from 1933–38 and, by the time of his OM, had become Minister for the Co-ordination of Defence. This was highly unusual – a Service Chief of Staff becoming a Minister of the Crown. He did not last very long as a Minister, finding he did not possess the powers necessary to prepare the nation for war; 'co-ordination' was an important caveat and he left office in March 1940.

He had been the most influential of the Chiefs of Staff in the 1930s, critical of a government that based its defence policy not on solid reasoning but on the question: 'What is the cheapest way in which we can face the world?'[24]

Chatfield was a Beatty man, as Madden had been a Jellicoe man. Beatty had nurtured him and, after being the great man's flag captain, Chatfield was his Assistant Chief of Naval Staff, before becoming Third Sea Lord and commanding both the Atlantic and Mediterranean Fleets. His overall experience for the top naval job was unrivalled.

He lived to be 94 and when he died in 1967, the Queen's representative at his funeral was the last naval (the last military) OM: Lord Mountbatten, who had been his midshipman dogsbody at Jutland.

The Second World War

The five military OMs of the Second World War were all Chiefs of Staff. They had played a far more pivotal role in the strategy of the world-wide conflict than their predecessors in the first, more limited 'world' war. So, in contrast to that war, no fleet, field or air commander received the honour; although it does now seem strange that some of the great military names of the Second World War are not on the OM roll of honour.

On 1 January 1946, there were only 14 living OMs and only three (Chetwode, Chatfield and Newall) were military men. So, with ten vacancies, there was room for more than the three Chiefs of Staff who were appointed that year. Perhaps it was the old problem of invidious choices.

It had been agreed before the war that the Chiefs of Staff and the principal operational commanders would hand over their responsibilities after the opening phases of the conflict. The first to go was General Sir Edmund

Ironside in May 1940, after having held the post only since the first day of war; he was promoted to Field Marshal and, later, made a baron.

The next to go, in October 1940, was the airman, Marshal of the Royal Air Force **Sir Cyril Newall**, who had held the post of Chief of the Air Staff since 1937. One of his successors said:

> He was among the least well known of our military leaders in that war, and never really received the credit that was his due... It was not his fault that the RAF was called upon to make so many bricks without straw in the opening stages of the war.[25]

The significance of his appointment to the Order of Merit was that he was the first RAF officer to receive the honour, by virtue of the change to the Statutes in 1935 altering 'Our Navy and Our Army' to 'the Crown Services of Our Empire'. There are, however, no papers in the Royal Archives relating to his appointment.

Newall was one of the pioneers of the Royal Flying Corps, to which he was attached from the Gurkhas. In 1915, he was awarded the Albert Medal of the First Class (Gold) – a forerunner of the George Cross – for entering a burning bomb store and, with others, extinguishing a fire that had broken out. He transferred to the new RAF and was promoted steadily between the wars.

After leaving the top RAF post, Newall was appointed Governor-General of New Zealand, like Jellicoe before him. He stayed there until 1946. Once, when addressing men of all three services, he began: 'Men of the Army, Men of the Navy, Gentlemen of the Air Force.' He was not the first Briton to fail to realise that our sense of humour does not always travel well. He died in 1963.

The second wartime Chief of Staff to be made an OM enjoyed the honour for six weeks and the Badge itself for only two. He was Admiral of the Fleet **Sir Dudley Pound**. As we have seen, he commanded a ship at Jutland and by the 1930s he had become Second Sea Lord and then Commander-in-Chief Mediterranean. He became First Sea Lord by the unexpected resignation and death of the incumbent in the summer of 1939.

Controversy has raged about some of Pound's decisions: over the Norwegian campaign, the despatch of the capital ships *Prince of Wales* and *Repulse* to Malaya without sufficient air cover and his order to Convoy PQ17 to disperse, with resulting heavy loss of ships. He was recently described in a radio programme as one of the most controversial figures in the Royal Navy in the twentieth century: a 'cunning old badger', who had used guile to frustrate Churchill's dramatic idea of sending a battle fleet into the Baltic early in the War.[26]

Early in 1943, Pound declined a peerage on the grounds that he was not 'well-to-do'. Churchill was anxious, however, that he should receive some special recognition and telegraphed the Palace from Washington in May 1943:

> The record month in the sinking of U-boats and possibly the turning point of the U-boat war would seem a good occasion to offer some recognition to the services of this pre-eminent officer. There is no comparison between the responsibilities he has borne and those of any other naval officer during the war.[27]

The reply was that:

> As you know, His Majesty was hoping to keep the OM for service afloat rather than in Whitehall, as his Father did in the last war – but he is very conscious of Pound's remarkable record, and will be prepared to give further consideration to the matter either at the New Year or on some earlier occasion.[28]

George VI's inclination towards keeping the OM for active service reflected the views not only of his father but also of his grandfather, when founding the Order.

In July, Lady Pound died and that added to the strain of four years of war on Pound himself. The OM was offered to him on 30 July

> in recognition of your long and most eminent service in the Royal Navy, particularly during the four arduous years of war throughout which you have held the post of First Sea Lord.

It was the King's idea that it should be announced on 3 September, the fourth anniversary of the outbreak of war. Pound's health had seriously deteriorated, however, and in August in Quebec he told Churchill that he must resign; he had had a stroke and was no longer fit for duty. Churchill immediately relieved him of responsibility and he returned to Britain a very sick man. Pound went into hospital on 21 September and suffered a second stroke, which paralysed him completely. He resigned formally on 5 October.

The next day, the King's Private Secretary (Sir Alan Lascelles) called at the Royal Masonic Hospital and gave the dying admiral the insignia of the Order of Merit. Pound died on 21 October and, after a funeral in Westminster Abbey, his and his wife's ashes were scattered at sea.

Cunningham, in his memoirs, summed up Pound's contribution thus:

> It cannot be doubted that Dudley Pound was the right man in the right place. For four most difficult years of trial and disappointment, he bore the brunt and responsibility of the war at sea. Fearless and outspoken, he stood like a rock against the waves of adversity. They beat against him

in vain, leaving him unshaken and unmoved, even in the face of criticism in Parliament and the press, some of it cruelly unjust and bitter, when the tide of the war at sea was running against us.[29]

After Pound's resignation and Cunningham's arrival, the Chiefs of Staff Committee remained unchanged until the end of the war two years later. The first then to leave and therefore the first to receive the OM was Marshal of the Royal Air Force **Lord Portal of Hungerford**. He would have received it earlier but for Churchill. In April 1944, the King wanted to bestow the OM on him but Churchill was against it:

> He was only made Marshal of the Royal Air Force a short time ago and I think it would be better to keep the OM till we get a little nearer winning the war, or even have won it.[30]

The testy exchange continued a year later, when the proposal was renewed. Churchill minuted:

> My opinion has not changed. If you start giving the OM to high Commanders or Chiefs of Staff, it opens a very wide door.[31]

In Churchill's resignation honours list in August 1945, Portal and his fellow Chiefs of Staff were given mere baronies. Attlee promoted them all to viscounts in the 1946 New Year Honours. Ironically, Portal's appointment to the OM was also announced in that list, along with that of Churchill. Attlee had 'warmly support[ed] the proposal' when the King renewed it.[32]

Charles (known as 'Peter') Portal's service career started, like many others, with a move from undergraduate to private soldier in 1914, initially as a despatch rider. It was 'on his bike' that he quickly came to the attention of both French and Haig; he was commended in the former's first despatch of September 1914 and he crashed into the staff car of the latter. By the end of that war, he was a lieutenant colonel with two DSOs and an MC and, as one of Trenchard's protégés, he ascended the ranks of the RAF. On the outbreak of the Second World War, Portal was Air Member for Personnel but quickly moved to head Bomber Command before succeeding Newall as Chief of the Air Staff – and being succeeded in turn by 'Bomber' Harris.

It is, of course, the bombing offensive of the RAF – 'area' bombing – that has produced most of the controversy over air warfare in the Second World War. Portal has had stern critics:

> By his indecision and weakness in handling Harris and the bombing offensive, Sir Charles Portal disqualified himself from consideration as a great, or even an effective, commander of air forces, whatever his merits as a joint-service committee man.[33]

Equally, he had praise in abundance:

> The Americans considered Portal to be the ablest of the British Chiefs
> of Staff, and they were probably right. He never lost his temper or his
> sense of proportion... insisted on bowing out so quietly [and] refused
> to take part in any post-war controversies.[34]

Despite Portal's reputation for calmness and equanimity under pressure,
he was once goaded by Churchill into speaking more strongly than usual.
Afterwards, he apologised:

> I'm sorry if I seemed a bit over-assertive or hot under the collar, Prime
> Minister.

To which he got a typical retort:

> In war, my boy [Churchill was 70, Portal was 50], you don't have to be
> sorry – you only have to be Right![35]

The remaining two wartime Chiefs of Staff went in June 1946 and they
received the OM together in the Birthday Honours that month. For **Field
Marshal Alanbrooke,** the Chief of the Imperial General Staff, despite his
viscounty and the Garter that was to follow at the end of the year, it was
quite simply the greatest honour of his career:

> Of all the orders and decorations that I received none of them have ever
> seemed in the same category. I felt intense gratitude that my services
> should have been recognised in such a manner.[36]

Montgomery was always a great admirer of 'Brookie': 'the greatest soldier – soldier, sailor or airman – produced by any country taking part in the
war.' With surprising candour, he also praised his chief's way of handling
him:

> there have been moments when I have gone 'off the rails': due to impetu-
> osity, irritation, or some such reason. You have always pulled me back
> on the rails, and I started off down the course again.[37]

Sir James Grigg, the Permanent Under Secretary and Secretary of State for
War, who had observed Brooke at close quarters throughout the war years
thought that 'those on the inside of affairs would assess his contribution to
victory as second only to Churchill'.[38]

Not everyone was so enthusiastic and much controversy was aroused by
the publication of his diaries. Brooke was forthright in his comments on

8 Viscount Alanbrooke.

Churchill and was the first prominent critic to challenge the idea of a strategic genius. One of his biographers also wrote, in the *DNB* notice, this summary of the relationship:

> Neither Churchill nor Brooke could have done so much without the other – yet each found the other abrasive as well as stimulating and indispensable ... Brooke wrote of the prime minister as someone whom 'he would not have missed working with for anything on earth' ... It was a high-spirited, high-tempered, exhausting, and astonishingly successful partnership.[39]

Born of an Ulster family with a soldiering tradition (26 of his family fought in the First and 27 in the Second World War), Brooke had lived abroad as a child and spoke French and German before he did English. He had emerged from the First World War as a lieutenant colonel in the Royal Artillery and, after being one of the first students at the new Imperial Defence College, he rose rapidly to be a lieutenant general commanding a corps in France in 1939–40. After Dunkirk, he commanded the Home Forces until becoming CIGS in December 1941; he quickly took the chair of the Chiefs of Staff Committee. He had hoped to command the Allied forces invading the continent but recognised that an American would have to.

Brooke had one high day of glory at the Coronation in 1953, when he was Lord High Constable (and Field Marshal Commanding the Troops) and rode immediately behind the Queen's state coach; the office of Constable was once so powerful that monarchs now appoint to it only for the single day of their coronation, which gives even an ambitious soldier too little time to mount a coup. (The only example of a monarch suspecting such an attempt in modern times is the reported remark of George VI, in response to Churchill saying that he thought Montgomery was after his job: 'Thank goodness, I thought he was after mine.')

Andrew Browne Cunningham (known as ABC) received his OM with Alanbrooke. At the beginning of the Second World War, ABC was commanding the Mediterranean Fleet, in which he had served for much of a career that had brought him three DSOs in the First World War. In 1940–41, his fleet had routed the Italians by air attack at Taranto and by sea at Cape Matapan. The arrival of the Germans in the area, however, left the British sadly short of air cover. On being made a GCB in 1941, Cunningham remarked: 'I would sooner have had three squadrons of Hurricanes.' The next year (unusually for an active commander in the Second World War), he was made a baronet.

After a spell as Head of the Admiralty delegation in Washington in 1942, Cunningham returned to the Mediterranean, first in command of the naval forces in the invasion of French North Africa and later in command again of the Mediterranean Fleet. From that, he was summoned to succeed the dying Pound as First Sea Lord; he was the only one of the three Chiefs of Staff at the end of the war to have spent more of it in active operational command than at the centre.

A pleasant surprise came Cunningham's way in the New Year Honours of 1945. After a meeting ending at 1.30am, Churchill, with whom his relations were not easy, called him aside. Having confirmed that he was a Scot (although born in Ireland), Churchill said he was recommending that the King should create him a Knight of the Thistle. Cunningham, who may not have been aware of the comparable award (in 1917) to Haig, before the end of hostilities, wrote:

> realising that the honour was even more a compliment to the Navy than it was to me, I thanked him warmly. I could remember no naval officer outside the Royal Family who had ever received this great distinction.[40]

By the end of the war, like Beatty before him, Cunningham was being hailed as 'the Nelson of our times'.

In retirement, in both 1950 and 1952, Cunningham was Lord High Commissioner to the General Assembly of the Church of Scotland, ranking second only to the Sovereign in Scotland during the sitting of the Assembly. He died in a taxi in London in 1963, five days before Alanbrooke, who was the same age – 80. Portal, younger than them by ten years, lived until 1971.

After the Second World War

Of the last three military OMs, appointed after the Second World War, the first, in the New Year Honours of 1951, was a very belated award, a real 'catching-up' with the past. **Hugh Trenchard** – 'Boom' as the ' Father of the RAF' was called – had won the DSO as long ago as 1906, had been a baronet since 1919, a GCB since 1924, the first Marshal of the Royal Air Force since 1927, a baron since 1930 and a viscount since 1936.

His service career had started badly. Having failed to get into the Navy, Trenchard just scraped into the Army. He served in unfashionable, and unhealthy, West Africa, from where he was invalided home in 1912, just in time to become interested in the developing Royal Flying Corps. After commanding it on the Western Front, he became the first Chief of Air Staff on the formation of the Royal Air Force on 1 April 1918, a post he retained (except for a few months) until 1929.

It was Trenchard's work in those ten years that led *The Times* to describe him as 'A Great Captain':

> Now that the conception of an airforce equal to its elder sister services is an accepted commonplace it would be easy to forget how much the nation owes to Trenchard and to others who had the courage and the imagination to leave the broad highways of professional advancement while flying was still being regarded as an exercise in dangerous acrobatics.[41]

When the Americans were forming an independent Air Force after the Second World War, they came for advice 'to the patron saint of air-power'.

After leaving the post of CAS in 1929, Trenchard was Commissioner of the Metropolitan Police. During the Second World War, as 'Father of the RAF', he visited many establishments in Britain and overseas. While the Battle of Britain raged, he received a letter from George VI:

> I must tell you how much the wonderful spirit and efficiency of the air force which we see daily at this moment is due to your leadership and foresight in laying well and truly the foundations in the early days.[42]

Trenchard's name had first come up as a possible OM at the time of the 1937 Coronation, two years after the RAF became eligible for the honour. Geoffrey Dawson, editor of *The Times*, thought he had 'created something that will endure'.[43] Even by then, however, he 'was considered to have been out of the Service for too long'.[44] His case was urged again in 1944 and the final push came in October 1950 from the RAF itself. The Chief of the Air Staff wrote a 'strictly private and confidential' letter 'on a subject which I know is nothing to do with me' to the King's Private Secretary. He argued that Trenchard:

> was really responsible for our victory in the Battle of Britain and for the great achievements of the RAF in the war ... but for his single-minded devotion to the principle of a single autonomous air Service, the RAF in 1939 would have found itself in the same position as the Tank Corps – and that I believe would have meant our defeat in the Battle of Britain, with repercussions on the outcome of the war which no one can assess.[45]

The award of the OM came three months later and the 78-year-old Trenchard confessed to feeling 'rather overwhelmed by this very pleasant surprise'.[46] Newall and Portal must have felt that justice had been done when Trenchard joined them in the Order. He died in 1956 and his ashes are buried in the RAF Chapel in Westminster Abbey.

Trenchard was already dead by the time the next military OM was appointed. In the New Year Honours of 1959 (the last time such a routine method was used), **Harold Alexander** added the OM to his earldom, Garter and GCB. He was already Lord Lieutenant of London and was soon to become Grand Master of the Order of St Michael and St George, an unusual distinction for a non-royal person. He had been the last British Governor-General of Canada after the war and, rather less successfully, Minister of Defence in Churchill's peacetime government.

Scion of an Anglo-Irish aristocratic family (the Earls of Caledon), Alexander led what was described as a charmed life in the trenches of the First World War, ending it as a lieutenant colonel, with a DSO and MC. After two unusual appointments – in Latvia and Turkey – he progressed until, in 1939–40, he was leading a division and then a corps in the BEF in France. He was the last off the beaches at Dunkirk in the same way as, two years later, he was the last out of Burma when it fell to the Japanese.

It was, however, in the Middle East that Alexander found fame and success as Commander-in-Chief, often in an uncomfortable position between Churchill at home and Montgomery in the field. His triumphal moment was the routing of the Axis forces in North Africa and it was from that that he eventually took his peerage title: Alexander of Tunis. He went to command the Allied Armies in Italy until the end of the war.

9 Earl Alexander of Tunis.

The Americans had a high regard for Alexander. Omar Bradley called him 'the outstanding general's general of the European war'. Mark Clark (who had disobeyed his orders in capturing Rome) described him as an 'outstanding leader and a selfless soldier' and Eisenhower thought he was 'the ace card in the British Empire's hand'.[47]

Mountbatten thought, however, that 'he had the average brain of an average English gentleman...who was beloved by everybody because he had never harmed anybody.'[48] Harold Macmillan paid a striking tribute. After praising Alexander's character, charm and simplicity, he wrote: 'If Montgomery was the Wellington, Alexander was certainly the Marlborough of this war.'[49]

Alexander was appointed to the Order of Merit shortly after suffering two heart attacks, but he lived on for another ten years, with his modesty unscathed. Supposedly at a reunion of wartime leaders, Macmillan said: 'Wouldn't it be wonderful, Alex, if we could have our life over again?' The reply was: 'Oh no, Harold, we might not do as well.'[50]

Like Alexander before him, when **Louis Mountbatten** received the OM he was already an earl, a Knight of the Garter, a GCB and much else besides. But when he did receive it from the Queen in 1965, he was thrilled. He recorded:

> She then handed me the Military badge of the Order of Merit. This really was an absolutely wonderful gesture on her part. The Order of Merit . . . as far as I know, had only been given once before to a sailor for work in peacetime and that was the great Admiral Jackie Fisher in the 1900s. In the First World War Beatty and Jellicoe got it, and in the Second World War ABC[unningham], Chatfield and Pound. So far as I know I am only the seventh sailor to get it.[51]

10 Earl Mountbatten of Burma.

He was not the first or last person to forget Keppel, Seymour, Wilson and Madden! His arithmetic was corrected in subsequent editions.

If the military side of the Order of Merit was to go out with a bang and not a whimper, the choice of Louis Mountbatten to be the last such holder was inspired. He lived and died in the glare of publicity. There was a fascination for the public in this minor member of the royal family, who achieved such distinction on his own merit. His egocentric character was not to everyone's taste and it was said that if he was a good man to get you out of a tight spot, it was because he was the most likely man to have got you into it in the first place.

Mountbatten was born at Frogmore House, in the grounds of Windsor Castle, in 1900 and his great-grandmother would be on the throne for another six months. His mother was a daughter of Queen Victoria's second daughter, Alice, Grand Duchess of Hesse; his father was Prince Louis of Battenberg (as indeed was he) until anti-German feeling had compelled the relinquishment by the royal family in 1917 of the German titles. His naval career was as a midshipman at Jutland, a signals specialist, a wartime destroyer captain (losing his ship, *HMS Kelly*, but being put on screen by Noel Coward in the film *In Which We Serve*), a phenomenal promotion to be Chief of Combined Operations, an even grander promotion to be Supreme Commander in South East Asia, a bump down afterwards to mere rear admiral commanding a cruiser squadron before becoming Fourth Sea Lord, Commander-in-Chief Mediterranean and, finally, the coveted post of First Sea Lord from which his father had had to resign in 1914 because of his German name. Of course, on the way, he took time out, at Attlee's request, to be the last Viceroy of India, and stayed on for a year as the first Governor-General of independent India.

After being First Sea Lord, Mountbatten became the first effective Chief of the Defence Staff in 1959 and set about the highly unpopular task, in which he thought he had only half-succeeded, of achieving greater integration of the Armed Forces. It was on his retirement from that post in 1965 that he received the OM.

It was Mountbatten's status generally in British society that made him a target for the IRA, who struck successfully when they blew up his fishing boat in 1979. His funeral, which he had planned in detail himself, was a grand semi-state occasion. With Mountbatten's death the line of military OMs, seen originally as so important an aspect of the Order, was extinguished and it has never been restored.

General observations

What of notable Second World War commanders who did not receive the OM?

Two soldiers were considered for the Order. When Alanbrooke tried to secure a peerage for his ousted predecessor as CIGS, Field Marshal Sir John Dill, Churchill 'jumped at it. He only asked whether he might perhaps prefer an OM. I must now see that he sticks to it.' Later, after Dill's death in 1944: 'this was never turned down by the PM but nothing ever came of it.'[52]

Much later, Mountbatten tried to secure the Order for Field Marshal Sir Claude Auchinleck, the last Commander-in-Chief India: 'If there is any sign that it is feasible I will certainly follow it up but if there is any difficulty about it, I know that "The Auk" himself would hate me to do anything further about it.'[53] He did pursue it further with the Queen's Private Secretary but nothing came of it.[54]

At this distance, the absence of two other soldiers from the Order of Merit looks strange: Field Marshal Viscount Montgomery, whose military career continued until his retirement from NATO in 1958, and Field Marshal Viscount Slim, whose military reputation steadily grew and who concluded his public service as a long-serving and very popular Governor-General of Australia.

'Monty' and Churchill (who described him as 'in defeat, unbeatable; in victory, unbearable') are Second World War faces recognised by the present generation. Montgomery lobbied Mountbatten (unsuccessfully) for an earldom, an honour (along with the OM) enjoyed by both Mountbatten and Alexander.[55] 'Bill' Slim received the Garter and four Grand Crosses but never the OM.

After the appointment of Mountbatten to the Order in 1965, there were no other officers whose wartime roles would have been an important factor in their joining him. Such appointments would have had to come from those who stood out from their contemporaries by holding the post of a Chief of Staff or, after 1965, of Chief of the Defence Staff. But no such appointments came. Instead, they have received a peerage and possibly the Garter also. Probably the most significant pointer to the intentional disuse of the OM came with the Falklands War of 1982. Unlike Suez, this was a successful, and primarily naval, operation to recover invaded British territory. The CDS, Admiral of the Fleet Sir Terence Lewin, received a peerage and the Garter. Even in clear warlike conditions, the OM was not the ultimate reward.

I shall return to this issue when considering the future of the Order.

9

THE SCIENTISTS

The physical

Physicists

1. 1902 John (Lord) RAYLEIGH*+
2. 1902 William (Lord) KELVIN*
3. 1912 Sir Joseph John THOMSON*+
4. 1925 Ernest (Lord) RUTHERFORD*+
5. 1931 Sir William BRAGG*+
6. 1957 Sir John COCKCROFT+
7. 1967 Patrick (Lord) BLACKETT*+
8. 1969 William (Lord) PENNEY

Mathematicians

9. 1969 Sir Geoffrey TAYLOR
10. 1973 Paul DIRAC+
11. 1992 Sir Michael ATIYAH*
12. 2000 Sir Roger PENROSE

Astronomers

13. 1902 Sir William HUGGINS*
14. 1938 Sir Arthur EDDINGTON
15. 1939 Sir James JEANS

The chemical

Chemists

16. 1910   Sir William CROOKES*
17. 1949   Sir Robert ROBINSON*+
18. 1960   Sir Cyril HINSHELWOOD*+
19. 1965   Dorothy HODGKIN+
20. 1977   Alexander (Lord) TODD*+
21. 1989   George (Lord) PORTER*+

Biochemists/Molecular Biologists

22. 1935   Sir Frederick Gowland HOPKINS*+
23. 1986   Frederick SANGER++
24. 1988   Max PERUTZ+
25. 1991   Francis CRICK+
26. 1995   Sir Aaron KLUG*+

The medical

Physiologists

27. 1924   Sir Charles SHERRINGTON*+
28. 1942   Edgar (Lord) ADRIAN*+
29. 1973   Sir Alan HODGKIN*+
30. 1983   Sir Andrew HUXLEY*+

Pharmacologists

31. 1944   Sir Henry DALE*+
32. 2000   Sir James BLACK+

Immunologists

33. 1958   Sir Macfarlane BURNET+
34. 1981   Sir Peter MEDAWAR+

Pathologist

35. 1965   Howard (Lord) FLOREY*+

Surgeons

36. 1902   Joseph (Lord) LISTER*
37. 1953   Wilder PENFIELD

The natural

Botanist

38. 1907   Sir Joseph HOOKER*

Naturalist

39. 1908   Alfred Russel WALLACE

Geologist

40. 1914   Sir Archibald GEIKIE*

Zoologists

41. 1968   Solly (Lord) ZUCKERMAN
42. 2002   Robert (Lord) MAY

The engineering

Engineers

43. 1927   Sir Charles PARSONS
44. 1962   Sir Geoffrey de HAVILLAND
45. 1971   Sir George EDWARDS
46. 1976   Christopher (Lord) HINTON
47. 1986   Sir Frank WHITTLE
48. 1997   Sir Denis ROOKE

Preliminary

While the non-scientific side of the Order is spelled out in the Statutes into 'The Arts, Literature and Learning', 'Science' is simply that. It includes many disciplines, which sometimes overlap and have blurred boundaries, especially to a non-scientific author. Purely for convenience of study and in order to break down the largest single group of recipients, I have divided them into the five groups shown above. I am comforted to have the endorsement of Sir Andrew Huxley, OM, a former President of the Royal Society and Master of Trinity College, Cambridge (and Nobel Laureate) in my choice of divisions and allocation of individuals to them.

Naturally, there has always been a scientist in the Order but not always one from a particular discipline. Five of the longest-holding scientist OMs span the century of the Order between them: Rayleigh (1902–19), Thomson (1912–40), Sherrington (1924–52), Adrian (1942–77) and Edwards (1971–2003).

The Royal Society has occupied a key position in British science since it was founded when Charles II was restored to the throne in 1660. It is the ambition of most scientists to be elected to its fellowship, since it is the recognition of one's professional peers. The last President, Lord May of Oxford, has described it as 'democratically elitist'. It is natural therefore that virtually all the scientist OMs have been Fellows of the Royal Society (FRSs); only Geoffrey de Havilland, the aircraft designer, was not.

In addition, 18 other OMs have been elected FRSs, either because of their scientifically-inclined scholarship (the philosophers, Whitehead and Russell) or because they had 'rendered conspicuous service to the cause of science or are such that their election would be of signal benefit to the Society'. Those 16 are Morley, Cromer, Bryce, Haldane, Balfour, Frazer, G. M. Trevelyan, H. A. L. Fisher, Churchill, Smuts, Attlee, Waverley, Mountbatten, Prince Philip, Stockton and Margaret Thatcher.

The Presidency of the Society is highly prized and is very much a roll call of the country's scientific 'greats'. It is hardly surprising therefore that every president since 1902 has received the Order of Merit. This unbroken succession (enjoyed by no other office-holder in the country) has sometimes been questioned on grounds of apparent automaticity. I prefer to believe that the Fellows of the Royal Society do not elect a president simply because he is a good administrator or chairman of committees, though he may well have to be those things too, but primarily because he is extremely distinguished in his own field and that distinction brings him easily into the range of the OM.

Of the presidents who have been OMs, three had already held the office when the Order was created. Of the 21 who have completed a term of office since 1902, six received the Order before becoming President and 15 during or immediately following their tenure.

The British Association for the Advancement of Science was founded in 1831 in order to strengthen the relationship between science and public interests. It meets annually and now emphasises the social and technological aspects of science rather than new discoveries. Originally 'an association of our nobility, clergy, gentry and philosophers', in the mid-nineteenth century its presidents included three dukes, three marquesses and three earls, as well as a number of clergymen. Before the end of the century, professional scientists had come to the fore and 28 OMs have held the presidency, from Hooker in 1868 to Denis Rooke in 1991 and including three who were not scientists: Balfour (in 1904, while Prime Minister), Smuts and Prince Philip.

Of the 48 scientists, 26 have won the Nobel Prize. Since the three scientific prizes do not cover the natural sciences or engineering, it is only the 37 OMs in the physical, chemical and medical spheres who could really have been awarded the Prize: 26 out of 37. The OM and the Prize are not Siamese twins, however, and many more Nobel Laureates have not received the OM than have.

The physical

Physicists

By the time that **J. J. Thomson** was appointed to the Order in 1912, Kelvin was dead but not Rayleigh, Thomson's mentor, whom he had succeeded as Cavendish Professor of Experimental Physics at Cambridge in 1894.

He became a physicist by accident, since his family originally intended him to be an engineer. While waiting for an apprenticeship, he entered Owens College, Manchester (the forerunner of the university) at the age of 14, before winning a scholarship to Trinity College, Cambridge in 1876. He was 18 and he stayed there, as undergraduate, fellow and Master until his death 64 years later.

Thomson's early research on vortex rings led him to begin investigations into cathode rays and these led to his most famous discovery – of the electron in 1897. The *DNB* described this as

> not merely a discovery, it was a revolution. The chemical atom had stood for nearly a century as an indivisible unit in the structure of matter. It now appeared that there was a more fundamental unit, an atom of pure electricity, a common constituent of all the chemical atoms. They were originally called corpuscles by Thomson, but later this was dropped in favour of electron.
>
> For the rest of his life most of his personal experimental work was directed towards improving the technique which had succeeded so well with the electron, and applying it to ascertain the masses, energies, and electricity charges of the other particles occurring in electric currents through gases . . . [1]

Honours came rapidly to Thomson: a knighthood in 1904; the Nobel Prize for Physics in 1906 'in recognition of his theoretical and experimental investigations on the conducts of electricity by gases'; and the OM in 1912. Like other OMs of that time, Thomson was suggested by Asquith, the Prime Minister. Haldane was also involved and sent the King's Private Secretary an account of their views:

> Thomson is a man of the very highest distinction in the application of mathematics to the great physical problems, e.g. the electrical constitution of matter. He is showing signs of holding as great a position in

the scientific world as did Kelvin... has the real quality of genius, and is looked on abroad and at home as our greatest Man of Science.[2]

Quite apart from his own research, Thomson developed the Cavendish Laboratory into what would now be called a world 'centre of excellence', training a whole generation of leading physicists. Seven of his research assistants (including his only son, George) later won Nobel Prizes.

He was also active in public life and, among other activities, he chaired the Royal Commission on Secondary Education in 1916. His appointment by the Crown to be Master of Trinity in 1918, during his tenure as President of the Royal Society, surprised many since it had for long been the preserve of literary men. In making such a success of the post, he was helped not only by his own unassuming personality and equable temperament but also by the devotion of his wife; she was the daughter of a Cambridge professor and one of the first women to work in the Cavendish Laboratory, where she met her husband.

Thomson's appearance belied his fame and genius:

tramp-like in dress and appearance even after he became Master of Trinity, clumsy with his hands but able, after a few moments' scribbling on the back of an envelope, to tell a baffled researcher exactly how to put right his equipment.[3]

As Thomson had followed Rayleigh into the Cavendish chair and into the Order of Merit, so it was Thomson's successor in that chair – **Ernest Rutherford** – who followed him as the next physicist OM but not for another 13 years. When endorsing the appointment of the physiologist Sherrington in 1924, Balfour was already singing the praises of Rutherford:

probably the greatest living man of science, except Einstein, among men of his standing; but his work is a development of JJ Thomson's, who has already got the Order. He must wait; but I cannot doubt that he will some day obtain what he already deserves.[4]

'Some day' was only six months later, in the New Year Honours of 1925.

About Rutherford's suitability there was 'no question', as Stamfordham told the Archbishop of Canterbury in December 1924, when passing on the views of both Esher ('the King would be justified in the eyes of all men') and Crewe ('first-rate and does credit to any order – Cambridge again, which shows what a brilliant university we are').[5] On 19 December, Stamfordham conveyed the King's offer 'in recognition of the conspicuous services which

11 Lord Rutherford by Sir James Gunn.

you have rendered both in research and teaching to the world of Physical Science'.[6] Rutherford's reply was speedy and generous in its wording:

> sensible of the great honour conferred on me by including my name in the list of this most distinguished Order. I appreciate that this award is not so much in recognition of my own personal services to Science, for an individual can hope to accomplish but little, but rather a recognition by His Majesty of the importance of science and scientific study to the welfare of the Empire.[7]

There spoke, very genuinely, a son of Empire when that concept had meaning.

Another Fellow of Trinity, A. E. Housman (who was to decline the OM four years later) wrote:

> This is a sad day for poor old England, and will put new and unnecessary pep into the All Blacks; but I am afraid there was no avoiding it . . . if a Trinity prime minister [Baldwin] had failed to do his duty he would have been unpopular in Trinity.[8]

Rutherford had come from the far end of the Empire, from Nelson on the South Island of New Zealand. He was a poor boy but his mother and grandmother were teachers. He benefited from a postgraduate scholarship to Cambridge, financed from the proceeds of the 1851 Exhibition, but only because the man originally awarded it chose to get married. He always blessed his good fortune and years later, when it was proposed to reduce these scholarships, Rutherford

> was too upset to speak: at last he blurted out: 'If it had not been for them, I shouldn't have been.'[9]

Having failed to secure a fellowship at Cambridge, Rutherford did not stay long. At the age of 27, he became Professor at McGill University, Montreal, where the motto over the entrance to the physics laboratory read 'Prove All Things' and it was there that he did the work that gained him the Nobel Prize for *Chemistry* in 1908: 'for his investigations into the disintegration of the elements, and the chemistry of radioactive substances.'

Rutherford moved to Manchester in 1907 and, later, made two other fundamental discoveries. Cockcroft described one:

> by remarkable insight, [he] concluded that the atom must be like a miniature solar system – a central electrically charged sun, the nucleus, with the electrons circulating around it like planets. This picture was confirmed by a series of beautiful experiments.[10]

The other was to produce the first artificial transformation, changing one element into another – he was almost an alchemist.

While at Manchester, Rutherford was knighted, in 1914 aged 43. He enjoyed his worldly success and status. He once said in a speech:

> As I was standing in the drawing-room at Trinity, a clergyman came in. And I said to him: 'I'm Lord Rutherford.' And he said to me: 'I'm the Archbishop of York.' And I don't suppose either of us believed the other.[11]

Rutherford naturally resented any hint of being patronised, as a New Zealander with a west country cum cockney accent. When Archbishop Lang (of Canterbury) suggested that a famous scientist could have no time for reading, he turned the tables by listing the books he had read recently and asking what the other man had:

> 'I am afraid,' said the Archbishop, somewhat out of his depth, 'that a man in my position really doesn't have the leisure.' 'Ah, yes, your Grace,'

said Rutherford in triumph, 'it must be a dog's life! It must be a dog's life!'[12]

He was not immodest about his scientific prowess. He once assured a large audience: 'There is no room for this particle in the atom as designed by *me*.'[13] When the 'inevitable' peerage came in 1931, at the end of his term as President of the Royal Society, he showed his pride in being the first New Zealander to achieve that honour. His title was Rutherford of Nelson and his coat of arms featured a Kiwi crest and a Maori supporter; his Latin motto translated as 'To seek the origin of matter'. To his aged mother, he sent a telegram: 'Now Lord Rutherford, more your honour than mine – Ernest.'[14] His father had died only three years earlier and so both his parents lived to know of his OM.

Rutherford played to the full the role of Great Scientist. He presided over the *annus mirabilis* in Cambridge in 1932, which will be described in the achievements of his successor physicist OMs: Cockcroft and Blackett. Indeed, years later Cockcroft described him as coming 'to dominate the scientific world as no other scientist has ever done'.[15] He was the father of nuclear physics, who was acknowledged in due course as the founder of modern atomic theory. After 1933, he took a leading role in welcoming the Jewish refugees from Nazism, many of whom contributed so much to British science over the following decades.

Rutherford's death came speedily, as the result of a strangulated hernia, in 1937.

When **William Bragg** was admitted to the Order of Merit in 1931, he joined two other living physicists: Thomson and Rutherford. Like both of them, he was a Trinity man and, like Rutherford, he was a professor in a dominion in his twenties. At 24, as a mathematician, he was appointed to a chair in Adelaide that combined his own subject with physics, the field in which he was to make his name. He stayed in Australia for 23 years and did not achieve significant success until after his return to chairs in Britain, first in Leeds and then in London. He was 45 when elected an FRS.

Within ten years, however, Bragg had won the 1915 Nobel Prize for Physics, with his 25-year-old son (Lawrence), 'for their services in the analysis of crystal structure by means of X-rays':

> Between them they founded the modern science of crystallography. They established for the first time how the atoms are arranged in crystals such as rocksalt and diamond, and it is hardly too much to say that the whole science has been nothing but an elaboration of their work.[16]

In the First World War, Bragg worked on underwater acoustics for the Admiralty and in 1917 was appointed one of the first Commanders of the new Order of the British Empire, being promoted to KBE only three years later. It was his lecturing skills, combined with his geniality, which made him such a successful Fullerian Professor and Director of the Davy-Faraday Laboratory at the Royal Institution.

Not surprisingly, Bragg's name was being mentioned for the Order of Merit. In 1928, Esher wrote of him as an 'obvious' candidate, although the Private Secretary thought that science was already well represented – 'but no doubt Sir William Bragg might be considered later on'.[17] Bragg's name was in the Birthday Honours of 1931.

Bragg's scientific work became more directional than personal, as he took on the role of one of the most prominent scientific figures in the country. At the rather advanced age of 73, he was elected President of the Royal Society in 1935 and this brought him, on the outbreak of war in 1939, the chairmanship of the Cabinet committee on scientific policy. He did not long survive the end of his five-year presidency, dying in 1942, aged 82.

John Cockcroft was the son of a Lancashire cotton manufacturer; he studied electrical engineering and mathematics at Manchester University and did a two-year apprenticeship with Metropolitan-Vickers before continuing his mathematical studies at Cambridge. Like Bragg, he had no formal training in physics. He began work at the Cavendish Laboratory, as a student of Rutherford, in what he later described irreverently as 'the Old Stone Age of nuclear physics'.

In 1932, he (and his Irish colleague, Ernest Walton) demonstrated that accelerated protons were able to split atomic nuclei. A story that has entered Cambridge and scientific mythology (but the truth about which he would never admit) is that he skipped along King's Parade shouting at anyone who would listen: 'We've just split the atom and the Americans have been spending *millions*!' They had made a dramatic discovery in what was a dramatic age for physics.

Of this period, he used to tell a story of paying $ 10 for a gallon of 2 per cent heavy water in the United States, bringing it with difficulty through British customs ('they did not understand why I should be importing a liquid which looked very much like water') and being told by Rutherford that he had paid too much and should have sought authority for the purchase.

Cockcroft was elected FRS in 1936 but not until 1951, well on into the 'nuclear age' he had helped to create, did he and Walton receive the Nobel Prize for Physics 'for their pioneer work on the transmutation of atomic nuclei by artificially accelerated atomic particles'.

Meanwhile, during the war, Cockcroft had headed the Air Defence Research and Development Establishment and was closely involved in the development of radar before becoming head of the Canadian Atomic Energy Commission. He returned to Britain to become the first Director of the Atomic Energy Research Establishment, at Harwell. It was from there that from 1946–58 he exercised his greatest influence on the development of the British nuclear programme, in close collaboration with two other future

OMs: Hinton, on the engineering side and Penney, on the weapons side. Cockcroft's own OM – the first of the three – came in the 1957 New Year Honours.

Twenty-five years after the splitting of the atom, Cockcroft was able to announce that a ZETA machine at Harwell had produced temperatures of 5 million degrees centigrade (one-third of the temperature of the interior of the sun), 'held' them for a few thousandths of a second and repeated the process 'many thousands of times'. This was a major step forward in fusion research.

In 1959, Cockcroft accepted the formidable task of starting Churchill College, Cambridge, as its first Master. He died in the Master's Lodge in 1967, having been Chancellor of the Australian National University in Canberra, won the Atoms for Peace Award and being about to be President of the Pugwash Conference on science and world affairs and President of the Liberal Party.

The Times obituary revealed something of his character:

> he did not pretend not to like the honours that gathered round him . . . All his medals and ribbons were on display in his house and this was a rather lovable characteristic of him.

> He was a fine scientist, one of the most reliable and upright human beings of his time, and a man of absolute good will. As a friend, he was a rock.[18]

The next physicist OM, **Patrick Blackett**, appointed two months after Cockcroft's death, had been, like his predecessor, in the hothouse that was the Cavendish Laboratory under Rutherford in the 1920s. His route there had been unorthodox. As a young naval officer, who had seen action at the Battles of the Falkland Islands and Jutland *and* designed a revolutionary new gunsight, he had been sent on a six-month course to Cambridge; within six weeks, he had resigned from the Navy, confident that he could make a successful career in academic science. Fifty years later, with a Nobel Prize, the Presidency of the Royal Society, the OM, CH and a life peerage under his belt, he must have reckoned that he took the right decision.

Blackett was the son of a stockbroker but an undergraduate friendship with Kingsley Martin, later editor of the *New Statesman*, helped to lead him into a firm commitment to the left and he was always more active politically than many of his fellow scientists. His scientific career took him from Cambridge to London (Birkbeck), to Manchester and back to London (Imperial College). It was at Cambridge that he made the first photograph of an atomic transmutation and, some years later, he used a cloud chamber to discover the positive electron; at Birkbeck, he went on to investigate cosmic rays. His Nobel Prize, in 1948, was for the discoveries he had made with the cloud chamber method 'in the fields of nuclear physics and cosmic radiation'.

12 Lord Blackett.

In the Second World War Blackett initiated the main principles of operational research and was Director of that new management tool in the Admiralty from 1942–45. He was critical of the RAF strategic bomber offensive. He also wrote the only memorandum that disputed the strategic and diplomatic justification for a British atomic bomb, telling Attlee that it would diminish rather than increase the country's security.

During the 13 years of Conservative Government from 1951–64, Blackett acted as a leading scientific adviser to the Labour opposition. He was behind the establishment of a Ministry of Technology in 1964 ('the white heat') and became personal scientific adviser to the Minister; two weeks before the 1964 election he had told Harold Wilson that he would have, at the most, a month to save the British indigenous computer industry.[19] He believed that an important part of the problem facing Britain at the time was to redress the imbalance between the prestige attaching to pure science and to applied science, respectively.

As a left-wing radical, Blackett had refused a knighthood but the return of Labour in 1964 brought him a plethora of honours: governmental, scientific and royal, tumbling upon each other. In 1965, he was made a CH and elected President of the Royal Society, an honour he thought would elude him because of his strong political views; a peerage followed in 1969.

In between, in 1967, came the Order of Merit, for which Blackett's name had first been mentioned over 20 years earlier. He received the OM in an unusual way. The day after it was announced, the Queen opened the new premises of the Royal Society in Carlton House Terrace and

> handed the Insignia of the Order of Merit to Professor Blackett at the conclusion of her speech.[20]

The investiture went unrecorded in the *Court Circular* detailing Her Majesty's visit.

Blackett had enjoyed his CH for only two years and was rather loathe to lose sight of it. After receiving the OM, he wore the CH to a Royal Academy dinner and was rebuked by Mountbatten (a new OM himself) for not wearing the senior order. Blackett responded: 'I was just giving the CH an airing.'[21] He was not able to air either decoration for all that long. He died in 1974.

The last physicist to be appointed to the Order of Merit, **William Penney**, received the honour while Blackett was still living – in 1969. Their origins were very different. Penney was the son of an army sergeant major and progressed from Sheerness Technical School to Imperial College (London) and to that seemingly inevitable destination – Trinity College, Cambridge. On appointment to the Order, he was Chairman of the UK Atomic Energy Authority: the 'Father of the British atom bomb'. Unlike all the other OM physicists, he was neither President of the Royal Society nor a Nobel Laureate.

When Penney completed his four-year course at Imperial College in two, with a first-class degree, his response to a suggestion that this was rather brilliant was: 'I was a bit good at mathematics and that helped, of course.'

In the Second World War, Penney was in the British team working on the atomic bomb at Los Alamos, in New Mexico. He forged close links with the Americans in his field and he was one of the two British observers on the aircraft that dropped the bomb on Nagasaki in August 1945; the other was a young group captain with the VC: Leonard Cheshire.

When attempts at United Nations control of atomic energy failed, Penney, who would like to have returned to academic life, was prevailed on to remain in government service. Lord Cherwell described him as:

> our chief – indeed our only – real expert in the construction of the bomb and I do not know what we should do without him ... The Americans admit frankly that they would give a good deal to get him back ...[22]

Penney himself said:

> There was near unanimity on the decision to develop the bomb, but with heavy hearts.[23]

Penney was in charge of the British nuclear tests in Australia, first off the coast at Monte Bello in 1952 (for which he was knighted) and thereafter at Maralinga in the South Australian desert.

Harold Macmillan, whom he accompanied to the Bermuda meeting with the Americans in 1962, liked to tease Penney about his residual Cockney accent. When he asked how many Russian 100-megaton bombs it would take to destroy Britain, Penney replied:

> Five or six will knock us out, to be on the safe side, seven or eight. I'll 'ave another gin and tonic, if you'd be so kind.[24]

On being created a life peer in 1967, Penney included in his arms 'three representations of the symbol Paramagnetic Electron' and took the motto 'Science and the Useful Arts'. In the same year, he went back to Imperial College as its Rector, retiring in 1973. The William Penney Laboratory commemorates his time there. He died in 1991, having destroyed his papers. He asked that there should be no memorial service and said he would be quite content if a few of his friends remembered him momentarily.

Mathematicians

The first mathematician to receive the Order of Merit, **Geoffrey Taylor**, received it at the same time (1969) as the last physicist – William Penney. They had both been at Los Alamos. The far-ranging effect of Taylor's work was summed up on his death:

> ...one of the most notable scientists of this century. Over a period of more than 50 years he produced a steady stream of contributions of the highest originality and importance to the mechanics of fluids and solids and to their application in meteorology, aeronautics, and many branches of engineering. He occupied a leading place in applied mathematics, in classical physics, and in engineering science and was equally at home with the methods and attitudes of these three disciplines... Many of his scientific contributions opened up whole new fields; he had the knack of being first. He was the personification of the peculiarly British tradition of applied mathematics, and carried forward the type of thought represented by Newton, Maxwell, Stokes and Rayleigh.[25]

A Trinity man (what else?), Taylor began his research work under J. J. Thomson and soon had a temporary readership founded to encourage the study of meteorology; he was meteorologist on a ship sent to initiate an ice patrol in the North Atlantic after the sinking of the *Titanic*. He continued his meteorological work in the First World War and was the first scientist to qualify as an air pilot (in 1915).

With a number of other bright young scientists, including Adrian (another future OM), George Thomson (son of J. J.) and F. A. Lindemann (later Lord Cherwell), Taylor worked at the Royal Aircraft Factory at Farnborough. In a biography of Cherwell, there is an account of how he and Taylor ('with his bubbling vivacity') engaged in many heated arguments:

> they delighted the mess by differing on the question of the closest packing of spheres as instanced by a dish of oranges...cheered on by the rest...Taylor saying: 'but don't you see, stoopid'...

The argument was settled by the onlookers throwing the oranges at the arguers.[26]

After the war, Taylor was drawn into Rutherford's web at the Cavendish until a Royal Society Research Professorship began an especially productive phase of his life, when he made his most substantial and significant contributions to continuum mechanics. In the Second World War, his work ranged from underwater explosions to dispersal of fog, from parachute design to the atom bomb. Even after his official retirement in 1952, he continued

> to be equally interested in the trivial and the profound but anything he touched turned to scientific gold and no longer looked trivial.[27]

Taylor's OM came when he was 83, 20 years after he was first considered. He enjoyed it for only six years. He wrote no books but, after his death in 1975, over 200 of his articles were published in book form and the G. I. Taylor Chair of Fluid Mechanics was endowed at Cambridge.

The second 'mathematician' to be appointed to the Order might equally figure among the 'physicists'. **Paul Dirac** is often described as a 'theoretical physicist', indeed the greatest since Maxwell, or a 'mathematical physicist'. Whatever the most accurate description, an account of his amazing early achievements will show he was worthy of the OM, when he eventually received it – in 1973, at the age of 70, 40 years after he had won the Nobel Prize.

Dirac was born (of a Swiss father and English mother) in 1902. After a spell as an engineering apprentice, he turned to the study of mathematics at Bristol and Cambridge, with startling results. He published a paper establishing the fundamental principles of quantum mechanics, of which he is generally regarded as a founder alongside Heisenberg and Schrödinger: the second great scientific theory of the twentieth century, along with Einstein's theory of relativity. Dirac's greatest discovery was the formulation of the relativistic equation of the electron, closely followed by the theory of the positron, the first example of anti-matter. His book, *The Principles of Quantum Mechanics*, is a classic of scientific literature.

Dirac was elected FRS at 28 and Lucasian Professor of Mathematics at Cambridge (Newton's old chair) at 30. The Nobel Prize for Physics came to him at the age of 31, in 1933, jointly with Schrödinger, 'for the discovery of new productive forms of atomic theory'. (Heisenberg received the 1932 Prize.) He held the chair at Cambridge for 37 years and after that taught in the United States. He never achieved again, however, the successes of his early work. Nevertheless, in 1952, the German Physics Institute awarded him the Max Planck Medal, his only predecessors being Planck himself and Einstein.

In his early life, Dirac was regarded as a reserved and diffident bachelor, whose only recreation was his sports car. He eventually married at the age of 35. For God, he had unusual praise:

> A theory with mathematical beauty is more likely to be correct than an ugly one that fits some experimental data. God is a mathematician of a very high order, and He used very advanced mathematics in constructing the universe.[28]

Long before he received the OM, Dirac's name was mentioned to the Palace as a 'mathematical physicist of international reputation but quite young'.[29] He was then 41 and had another 30 years to wait. He died in the United States, at the age of 82.

Among its living Members, the Order of Merit now has two mathematicians: Michael Atiyah and Roger Penrose, appointed in 1992 and 2000, respectively.

Michael Atiyah was born in London and schooled in Egypt and Britain before going to Trinity College, Cambridge. Elected FRS at 32, he lectured in Cambridge and Oxford, where he became Savilian Professor of Geometry at 34, winning the Fields Medal (the mathematical equivalent of the Nobel Prize) three years later. Apart from a spell at Princeton, he remained in Oxford until his appointment as Master of Trinity College, Cambridge and as the first Director of the Isaac Newton Institute for Mathematical Sciences – and election as President of the Royal Society, all in 1990. He was knighted in 1983.

His work has been on algebraic geometry and on the mathematics of the quantum field theory; one of his concerns has been bridging the gap between physicists and mathematicians. As PRS, he urged more effort to raise the morale of younger scientists, for example by longer-term fellowships awarded on an individual basis. The Public Orator at Oxford, in presenting him for an honorary degree in 1998, described him as 'most ingenious among the ingenious' and as possessing 'an extraordinarily wide grasp of the wide subject, which he insists is one and indivisible'.

Roger Penrose, son of an FRS (Lionel, the geneticist), took his first degree at University College, London, his doctorate at Cambridge and was himself elected FRS at the age of 41. In 1960, he collaborated with Stephen Hawking in studying black holes in space, showing that they were inevitable, once the collapse of a massive star at the end of its life had started. After holding a chair at Birkbeck College, London, he was Rouse Ball Professor of Mathematics at Oxford from 1973 until his retirement in 1998. He was knighted in 1994.

His researches have been published in books with intriguing titles like *Spinors and Space-time*, *The Emperor's New Mind* and *The Large, the Small and the Human Mind*. He has won the Dirac Medal and Prize, the Eddington Medal (of the Royal Astronomical Society) with Stephen Hawking – and the Einstein Medal. It is not surprising, in this overlapping of disciplines, that he has been described as a 'mathematical astronomer'.

Shortly before his retirement, he made unusual headlines when he sued the makers of Kleenex for unauthorised use of the 'Penrose Pattern' of diamond shapes. (Geometrical figures were something he had first worked on with his father.)

Astronomers

The 'mathematical astronomer' leads naturally on to those I have described as primarily 'astronomers'. William Huggins, an original Member, has already been discussed in Chapter 6. The only other two astronomer OMs, **Arthur Eddington** and **James Jeans**, ran neck and neck for the honour during the 1930s; Eddington won by a short head. They were not so far apart in age – Jeans was five years older – and, with one major exception, their careers ran in parallel.

Jeans was elected FRS in 1906 (aged 28) and President of the Royal Astronomical Society in 1925 and knighted in 1928; as his first wife was a well-to-do American and he made money from his books, he retired early from academic life and never held a chair. Eddington, a staunch Quaker, was elected FRS in 1914 (aged 32) and President of the RAS in 1921 and knighted in 1930 but, for many years, he was Plumian Professor of Astronomy and Director of the University Observatory at Cambridge.

Jeans' achievements included his theory of continuous creation of matter and his publicising of astronomy. He wrote the *The Universe Around Us* and *The Mysterious Universe*, in which (like Dirac) he concluded that God was a pure mathematician. Eddington's achievements included showing that the luminosity of a star depends almost exclusively on its mass. He wrote

Stellar Movements and the Structure of the Universe, in which he created the new subject of stellar dynamics.

In this history of the Order of Merit, it may be best to let the story of the so-called 'rivalry' or 'controversy' between these two men be told mainly through an account of the consideration of them for the Order.

The great Rutherford responded to an enquiry from the Prime Minister, Stanley Baldwin, who was by then embroiled in the Abdication crisis:

> Jeans is a man of great natural ability both in science and in affairs generally ... gifts as a writer ... [but] the OM on the 'science' side should be awarded only to those who have made original contributions to knowledge of exceptional importance, the value of which is everywhere recognised in the scientific world. Jeans does not seem to me to quite satisfy this criterion ... Possibly ... unlucky in not making any outstanding original contribution ... falls somewhat below the level of performance I set in my own mind for the award of the OM.[30]

In 1938, the two astronomical physicists were compared, by the Secretary of the Royal Society:

> best known to the public is Sir James Jeans, who has the happy gift of describing complicated scientific facts in simple language ... *Mysterious Universe* was a best seller. But ... Sir Arthur Eddington has rendered greater service to science inasmuch as he has made more real contributions to knowledge ... not of the same standard as Thomson and Sherrington but he may well be compared with Bragg. [Rutherford was dead.] In the world of Physics, I know of no one more worthy of recognition ...[31]

To this recommendation, there was added verbal support from the Prime Minister, the former Prime Minister (Lord Baldwin) and Sir Robert Vansittart (Permanent Under Secretary of the Foreign Office). Eddington's appointment to the Order was announced in the Birthday Honours of 1938.

The turn of Jeans, the older man, came the following year. Towards the end of 1938, an existing OM, Thomson, gave his views:

> besides the great work he has done in arousing public interest in science, he has himself made very important discoveries in pure science ... took up the subject of dynamical astronomy and found solutions which had baffled his predecessors, such as the origin of the solar system, the formation of binary stars and of spiral nebulae. His success in exciting popular interest in science has tended to draw attention away from his scientific work.[32]

Eddington died, unmarried, in 1944. Jeans' second marriage was to a young Austrian organist; he died in 1946 but she survived until 1993. He played the organ himself and one of his books, dedicated to her, was *Science and Music*.

The chemical

Chemists

The first 'chemist' OM, **William Crookes,** was also a physicist and the *DNB* described him as:

> a man of science in the broadest sense, an influential personality, and a doyen of his profession ... The breadth of his interests, ranging over pure and applied science, economic and practical problems, and psychical research, made him a well-known personality ... [his] work extended over the regions of both chemistry and physics.[33]

Crookes was the eldest of the 16 children of a tailor/businessman, from whom he inherited enough money to make him independent for life. He founded, and edited for nearly 50 years, the weekly *Chemical News* and, in his own laboratory, he discovered the element thallium; he was 29 and was elected FRS two years later. In physics, he invented the Crookes radioscope or radiometer. Again, in the *DNB*:

> Crookes's experimental work in this field was the foundation of discoveries which have changed the whole conception of chemistry and physics.[34]

It was men like Thomson (the electron) and Rontgen (the X-ray), who pursued some of Crookes' observations.

His excursions into spiritualism struck many of his scientific colleagues as akin to heresy and

> certainly led him into some very curious situations but they show that he thought all phenomena worthy of investigation, and refused to be bound by tradition and convention.[35]

It was barely a month after George V's accession that the Prime Minister's Private Secretary wrote to the Palace that Asquith:

> would be much gratified if the King would allow him to suggest two names for His Majesty's consideration for the Order of Merit [Hardy] ...

Sir Wm Crookes FRS, whose claims as a distinguished man of science rank very high.[36]

There was not much detail but Crookes was appointed, with Hardy, on 8 July 1910, one of the few Presidents of the Royal Society to receive the honour *before* being elected to that office. When summoned to an investiture, his response was mildly quaint, even for those days:

> I will do myself the honour of being at Marlborough House on Tuesday the 19th inst to receive the Insignia of the Order of Merit from the hands of His Most Gracious Majesty the King.[37]

Crookes appreciated the Order of Merit the more because 'he had been disappointed in 1897 at being made only a knight bachelor 'like any little local mayor'.[38] He must, at that time, have expected a KCB or a baronetcy.

Crookes died in 1919 and it was another 30 years before another chemist was appointed to the Order of Merit: **Robert Robinson**. Son of one of the inventors of cottonwool, Robinson studied at Manchester before becoming a professor at Sydney at the age of 26. He went on to work in Manchester, Sydney, Liverpool and Manchester (again) before coming to Oxford in 1930 to the Waynflete Chair in Chemistry, which he held for 25 years. His research there was wide-ranging: the colouring of flowers, the production of synthetic penicillin, the constitution of strychnine and basic work on tuberculosis. Some of his research on steroids paved the way for the contraceptive pill and infertility treatment for women.

Knighted in 1939, Robinson became President of the Royal Society in 1945 and was awarded the Nobel Prize for Chemistry in 1947, 'for his investigations on plant products of biological importance, especially the alkaloids'. When, in the same year, he received the Albert Medal of the Royal Society of Arts, he was described as 'the greatest organic chemist of our time'. When Robinson was considered in 1949, the opinion of Sir Charles Darwin (Director of the National Physical Laboratory and son of one of the five knighted sons of *the* Charles Darwin) was that he

> is undoubtedly one of the leading chemists of the world, and *the* leading one of this country, and no one would question his receiving the honour.[39]

Lascelles was told by the Secretary of the Royal Society:

> Organic chemistry is the chemistry of carbon and its compounds and there are about a million known. Robinson is at home amongst them all! He has an amazing type of memory and an instinct to convert one compound into another and know how to build up new

molecules . . . his extraordinary knowledge of chemistry made it possible for him to synthesise some of the natural hormones (sex hormones). He discovered too an artificial hormone – stilboestrol (the first synthetic oestrogen) . . . Robinson's contribution to discovery of the constitution of penicillin and its synthesis was more than anyone's . . . He is undoubtedly the greatest living organic chemist.[40]

He was appointed to the Order in the Birthday Honours of 1949.

In 1955, Robinson took the opportunity of his presidential address to the British Association to criticise the premature building of nuclear power stations, advocating coal and oil instead. He also disputed the alleged safety of the H-bomb, warning against the danger of a nuclear explosion that would create a catastrophic and uncontrollable uranium fire.

Robinson's first wife was also a chemist and worked with him in the laboratory. After her death, he claimed that he married his second (American) wife because she allowed him to teach her one of his many passions – chess.

In 1944, **Cyril Hinshelwood**, at the age of 46, was simply an 'also ran' in the list sent to the Private Secretary. Eleven years later he was President of the Royal Society and, near the end of his term of office, he was made an OM. With Graham Sutherland, he was appointed – along with two Garter Knights – on St George's Day, 1960; they broke the custom of OMs normally being included in the six-monthly honours lists and none has appeared in such a list since.

One comment immediately highlighted the unusual nature of Hinshelwood:

> he must be [the Order's] most redoubtable polymath. Who else has ever been president both of the Royal Society and of the Classical Association – and can, on top of that, discourse with Russian and Chinese scholars in their own tongues?[41]

He had started work as a chemist in an explosives factory in the First World War and it was only after that that the 'boy wonder' studied at Oxford, where he was to remain for the rest of his working life. From 1937–64, Hinshelwood was Dr Lee's Professor of Chemistry.

Knighted in 1948, Hinshelwood was President of the Chemical Society in its centenary year (1947) and of the Royal Society in its tercentenary year (1960). His presidency of the Classical Association reflected his strong interest in the classics and in the arts generally: music, painting, Chinese porcelain and languages (of which he spoke half a dozen). He believed strongly in the essential unity of the intellectual disciplines.

Hinshelwood was strongly critical of scientists who thought they had discovered the ultimate. In *The Structure of Physical Chemistry*, published in 1951, he quoted *Alice in Wonderland*: 'Somehow it seems to fill my head with ideas, but I don't know exactly what they are.' In his presidential address to the Royal Society, he spoke of the three stages through which most scientific theories usually passed: the first, of gross over-simplification in order to achieve elegance of form; the second, in which symmetry is distorted by recalcitrant facts; and the third, in which a new order emerges 'of nature's and not of man's conception'.[42]

Hinshelwood shared the 1956 Nobel Prize for Chemistry with a Russian, Nikolai Semenov, 'for their researches into the mechanism of chemical reactions'. In close personal touch for 25 years, despite the political difficulties, they had pursued independent but parallel research in chemical kinetics – the study of the rates at which chain reactions proceed. Their work had important practical applications in the plastics industry and in the production of more efficient automobile engines.

Hinshelwood was unmarried and died in 1967, in the same small Chelsea flat he had shared with his widowed mother since 1904; she died the year before his OM. He had only a brief retirement, in which he continued his research work, dying at the age of 70. A year later, there was an exhibition at Goldsmiths Hall in London of over 100 of his oil paintings.

When **Dorothy Hodgkin** was admitted to the Order of Merit in 1965, the press concentrated on her being the first woman appointed since Florence Nightingale in 1907. The year before, when she became the first (and, so far, only) British woman to win a Nobel Prize, there was similar emphasis on her gender. 'Grandmother wins Nobel Prize', '£18,750 award to mother of three' and 'an affable-looking housewife' were some of the comments. Of course, perhaps not intentionally, they were compliments to her tenacity in a particularly male-dominated world. That tenacity had also been needed to cope for 30 years with the rheumatoid arthritis that is evident in the painting by Maggi Hambling in the National Portrait Gallery, and in the sketches of her hands by her fellow OM, Henry Moore, in the Royal Society.

The first woman academic at Oxford to receive paid maternity leave, Hodgkin was eventually able to respond to the view that things must have been quite difficult for female scientists: 'Not after I won the Nobel Prize.'[43] That had come 'for her determinations by X-ray techniques of the structures of important biochemical substances'.

The daughter of a colonial civil servant, Hodgkin was born in Cairo in 1910, shortly before Nightingale's death. Her mother, denied a medical career herself, encouraged her, not least by giving her Bragg's Royal Institution lectures; it was Hodgkin who was to follow him in the field of X-ray crystallography. After taking her degree in chemistry at Oxford (where her professors were Robinson and Hinshelwood), she went to Cambridge to study under the left-wing J. D. Bernal, with whom she had a professional, political and personal relationship. Returning to Somerville College, Oxford, as a lecturer, she was allowed to address the University's chemistry society but not to join it.

She married Thomas Hodgkin, who had left the colonial service on political grounds. He became a Communist and an academic historian, especially of Africa; the marriage reinforced her own political views:

> She shared her husband's faith in the socialist paradise, no matter whether this was in the Soviet Union, China or Vietnam, and tended to close her eyes to the evils of the Communist dictatorships.[44]

An occasion on which I met her was at a Vietnamese party to celebrate their victory in 1975. I rescued her from a miners' union official who was laboriously telling one of the most intelligent people in the country about a Chinese miner with pneumoconiosis, named 'Wun Lung Foo'. She talked interestingly about her own career – 'I can't envisage doing nothing' – and the time it was taking to dispel the notion of Florence Nightingale as 'the only woman OM'.

Hodgkin was active in the Pugwash movement and received the Lenin Peace Prize in 1987. Her last overseas visit, against her doctor's advice, was to a crystallography conference – in Beijing. She died the following year (1994), after a fall at her home.

At Oxford, Hodgkin received no chair in the University until her appointment as the Royal Society Wolfson Research Professor from 1960–77. By then, she had discovered the molecular structure of penicillin and vitamin B12, as later (after the Nobel Prize) she was to do of insulin. All these discoveries had important implications for the treatment of diseases, including pernicious anaemia and diabetes.

Hodgkin's work brought her election as one of the early women FRSs, at the age of 37 in 1947, the year in which her most famous pupil graduated: Margaret Thatcher, who eventually joined her in the Order of Merit. Her left-wing views did not incline her to accept a title

> 'and when I saw [a letter] from Buckingham Palace, I left it sealed, fearing that they wanted to make me Dame Dorothy.' It would have made her feel like a 'femme formidable', which she so happily was not. She was relieved to find that the Queen offered her the Order of Merit, a much greater honour.

So wrote her fellow-untitled-OM, Max Perutz.[45] It is said that when summoned to the Palace to receive the honour, she arrived on foot, approached one of the guards and simply said: 'I want to see the Queen.'[46]

In her life, Dorothy Hodgkin had provided an exemplary role model for aspiring women scientists and, in her old age, she took some comfort from the slowly increasing number of women appointed to chairs in the sciences – and the humanities. Only a couple of years after her death, a portrait of the young Dorothy Hodgkin appeared on one of the British stamps commemorating Women of Achievement, alongside her molecular model of vitamin B12 which features also in the Hambling portrait.

The organic chemist, **Alexander Todd**, who became an OM in 1977, was a Glaswegian with a doctorate from Germany. After working at Oxford under Robinson and at the Lister Institute in London, he held a chair at Manchester before becoming Professor of Organic Chemistry at Cambridge from 1944–71. From 1963, he was also Master of Christ's College, as well as being the first Chancellor of the University of Strathclyde in his native Glasgow. He was knighted in 1954.

Todd's researches were into natural substances and many proved to be of fundamental importance, especially his work on anthocyanins, vitamins, nucleotides and coenzymes, organic compounds which make up DNA and RNA, the molecules of heredity. His Nobel Prize in 1957 was 'for his work on nucleotides and nucleotide coenzymes', but he declared it was 'much more of a tribute to a lot of the boys who have worked with me'.

Todd was big in body and mind. His physical size (6 feet 4 inches) led to his being called 'Todd Almighty', with the young scientists around him known as 'Toddlers'. A limerick ran:

> Doesn't it strike you as odd
> That a commonplace fellow like Todd
> Should spell, if you please,
> His name with two Ds,
> When one is sufficient for God?'

Todd was active in the politics of science, taking the chair of various bodies, including (after his peerage in 1962) the House of Lords committee on science and technology. His authoritative and sometimes remote attitude did not endear him to all. When he was chairman of the Advisory Council on Scientific Policy, disgruntled physicists renamed it the 'Association of Chemists for the Suppression of Physicists'. Tony Benn, when Minister for Technology, thought he was 'an impossibly arrogant and vain man'.[47]

Todd married the daughter of Henry Dale, the pharmacologist, and he once told me – with justifiable pride – that he shared four distinctions with his father-in-law: the Order of Merit, a Nobel Prize, the German Order Pour le mérite and the Presidency of the Royal Society (which he held from 1975–80). In that last capacity, he was forthright about scientific research:

> In these days of rampant egalitarianism, our concern for an elite in science may be regarded by some as outmoded. But it is not. In science the best is infinitely more important than the second best.[48]

Todd's death in 1997, at the age of 89, brought forth impressive tributes to a man who had acquired great stature in science, academia, industry and national science policy:

> Olympian in scale, international in outlook and achievement . . . perception was extraordinary in its power and precision; he was among the greatest and most creative organic chemists of the century. Among Scottish scientists, only Kelvin matches his stature.[49]

The last chemist in the Order of Merit was **George Porter**, who received it in 1989, towards the end of his time as President of the Royal Society. He received a life peerage six months later and he used his maiden speech in the Lords to criticise the level of public support for science, which he thought seemed to come not only sparingly but grudgingly, with all sorts of strings attached.

Porter graduated from Leeds in the Second World War, in which he later served as a Navy radar officer. Afterwards, he did research at Cambridge before becoming Professor of Physical Chemistry at Sheffield in 1955, at the age of 34. Five years later, he was elected FRS. His Nobel Prize in 1967 was for 'studies of extremely fast chemical reactions, effected by disturbing the equilibrium by means of very short pulses of energy'. The technique, on which he had begun work in 1947, is flash photolysis and this, combined with his expertise on the dance floor, led the irreverent to call him 'Flash Porter'.

Porter moved from Sheffield to London in 1966 to become Fullerian Professor and Director of the Royal Institution, where, like Bragg 40 years earlier, he established a reputation as an exciting lecturer and broadcaster. In his case, he was also able to pioneer televised science programmes for young people. He was knighted in 1972. Porter's election as President of the Royal Society in 1985 was reported as being because he was perceived as the man to speak for science at a time of low morale. He encouraged scientists not to regard popularisation of science as necessarily vulgarisation or lowering of standards: 'This attitude is not only quite mistaken but, in the modern world, positively dangerous.'[50] Later, Porter criticised the funding of research and development: 'a deliberate policy of the downgrading of the pursuit of knowledge for the pursuit of affluence.'[51] In the Dimbleby Lecture in 1988, he said:

> For over three centuries, Britain played a leading role in the scientific revolution that changed our lives. The revolution will continue, but we shall not be part of it if, by pursuing only short-term goals, we forfeit the science base that makes it all possible.[52]

Biochemists and molecular biologists

Before describing the five OMs in this section, I ought perhaps to define these two disciplines of which, like many other non-scientists, I was only hazily aware. Biochemistry is the science concerned with the chemistry of living organisms, while molecular biology is the study of the molecular basis of life.

The first biochemist to be admitted to the Order of Merit, in 1935, was **Frederick Gowland Hopkins**, a great pioneer in the field. He was articled to a consulting analyst and did a course in chemistry before qualifying as a doctor at Guy's Hospital in 1894. He was already publishing research that was noticed and in 1898 he was invited to teach at Cambridge. His researches there, pursued despite ill health, led him to the clear conclusion that vitamins, the substances present in natural, fresh foods, were essential to a healthy diet. He was Professor of Biochemistry for 30 years and around him grew a 'school', thus establishing a separate discipline concerned with this active chemistry of the life process. One of his young collaborators

> once made the provocative statement that he could not regard him as a great experimentalist ... because he had no need to make experiments ... only went to the bench to confirm his own insight. Intuition, insight, are certainly the words to emphasise.[53]

Eventually, in 1929, Gowland Hopkins shared (with a Dutchman) the Nobel Prize for Physiology or Medicine 'for his discovery of the growth-stimulating vitamins'. This was reflected in the citation for his OM, which he received in George V's Silver Jubilee Honours List in 1935 (in company with Masefield and Vaughan Williams): 'eminent services to Biochemistry especially in connection with the discovery of Vitamins.'

Elected FRS in 1905, at the age of 44, he was a member of the first Medical Research Committee in 1913 and President of the Royal Society from 1930–35. The OM came at the end of his term.

In 1986, after 50 years, there followed Gowland Hopkins into the Order of Merit a man, **Frederick Sanger**, who had appropriately won in 1971 the memorial medal named after the discoverer of vitamins. That award came just over halfway between winning two Nobel Prizes and thus becoming the only British person, and one of only four people overall, to achieve that distinction. He won both while simply 'on the staff of the Medical Research Council from 1951–1983', working for most of the time at the Molecular Biology Laboratory in Cambridge. Unlike many scientists, he did retire at 65.

The first Nobel Prize, in 1958, was 'for his work on the structure of proteins, especially that of insulin'. He was the first man to determine the complete chemical structure of any protein and it involved working out the exact order in which the 49 sub-units (amino-acids) are joined together.

The second Prize, shared with others, in 1980 was 'for contributions concerning the determination of base sequences in nucleic acids'. He had synthesised segments of the DNA strand by adapting an earlier discovery about how the molecules in living cells reproduce themselves, so inventing the first workable technique for reading DNA.

Fred Sanger keeps the two Prize gold medals in the bank and the certificates in the loft. That sort of modesty, which includes declining a knighthood, does not make you a household name. He has, however, more substantial testaments to his fame, ranging from Sanger Road in the research park of Surrey University to the Sanger Centre, funded by the Wellcome Trust (the largest charity in Britain) at Cambridge, which is the British home of the international Human Genome Project. When this is completed, the entire human genome will have been sequenced, revealing the order in which the billions of chemical building bricks in the human body are assembled, with immense implication for the study of diseases. In an interview given in 2000, Fred Sanger confessed amazement at the pace of progress in his field:

> What they do now is nothing like I used to do. I was messing about with chemicals and test tubes, and nowadays it's sitting in front of your PC.[54]

In that same interview, some views on honours were given by this social-ist Quaker, who had been a conscientious objector in the Second World War and therefore embarked on research immediately after graduating from Cambridge in 1939. It was recorded that he

> even turned down a knighthood. He didn't care to be called Sir: 'A knighthood makes you different doesn't it and I don't want to be different. But I did accept an Order of Merit, which is higher, so I suppose there's a bit of snobbery there.'

Only two years after Frederick Sanger's appointment to the Order of Merit, he was joined (in 1988) by his fellow Cambridge pioneer in the field of molecular biology, **Max Perutz**. He had come to Cambridge from Vienna in 1936 and, as a lapsed Catholic of Jewish extraction, he decided to stay. He had hoped, but failed, to work under Gowland Hopkins and instead, after a spell with J. D. Bernal, he became a research assistant at the Cavendish to Lawrence Bragg (son of William).

In an article in the *New Yorker* in 1985, entitled 'Enemy Alien', Perutz recounted his sudden internment in 1940 and transportation to Canada, where his companions included Klaus Fuchs, the atomic spy, and Hermann Bondi, later Chief Scientific Adviser to the Ministry of Defence. On release, instead of taking a proffered chair in New York, he returned to Britain to work on a project (once supported enthusiastically by Churchill and

Mountbatten and code-named 'Habakkuk') for creating floating ice landing strips in the Atlantic.

Soon after the war, Perutz began his remarkable career at Cambridge, as Director of the two-man Medical Research Council Unit for Molecular Biology. With the 'other man' (John Kendrew), he went on to win the 1962 Nobel Prize for Chemistry, 'for their studies of the structures of globular proteins'; his contribution was to solve the structure of the haemoglobin molecule, the red protein in blood that carries oxygen from the lungs to the body's tissues. It was not until 1959 that the breakthrough had come:

> It was an overwhelming experience to see a vital part of ourselves that is a thousand times smaller than anything visible under a light microscope revealed in detail [on a University computer] for the first time, like the first glimpse of a new continent after a long and hazardous voyage.[55]

The Unit, which became a Laboratory in new quarters in 1962, attracted researchers who became not only FRSs but also Nobel Laureates and OMs, including Fred Sanger (after his first Nobel), Francis Crick and Aaron Klug. The celebrations after each success led Perutz to remark that, 'All these parties will give the lab a bad name!'

Perutz's way of running the laboratory, which had grown to 90 by 1962 and is 400 today, was exemplified by his choosing to become chairman, rather than director:

> I tried to attract talented people by giving them independence. Had I tried to direct them, the mediocrities would have stayed and the talented ones would have left.[56]

When, in 1977, Francis Crick (to whom I shall come later) emigrated to the United States and *The Times* suggested that Perutz was thinking of doing likewise, he quashed it with a one-liner: 'I have no intention of emigrating.'[57] Perutz was a frequent speaker and writer, on political subjects such as asylum (naturally), Ulster, the Falklands, Eastern Europe and government funding, as well as on purely scientific ones.

On reaching the MRC retirement age of 65, in 1979, he evaded their rule that no director should continue to work in the same laboratory by pointing out he had not been 'director'. He continued to pursue research in the laboratory and wrote a number of books, including a scientific autobiography, *Science is No Quiet Life*, and a series of essays on science and scientists, *I Wish I'd Made You Angry Earlier*, the title of which was inspired by an incident when criticism had caused him to erupt. In addition to the books, Perutz produced over 100 papers; the last was sent for publication an hour before he entered hospital. He died on 6 February 2002.

The tributes on Perutz's death were unanimous in praising not only his scientific prowess but also his humanity:

> Max Perutz spoke with the same respect to young students, and to college and laboratory staff, as he did to Prime Ministers and royalty. He often used to quote Albert Schweitzer: 'Example is not the main thing in influencing others; it is the only thing.' Perutz was a wonderful human being: the great can also be good.[58]

It was in Max Perutz's laboratory in 1951 that he brought together two scientists, who collaborated in trying to unravel the mysteries of the genetic code. One was a British physicist turned molecular biologist, **Francis Crick** (who was made an OM in 1991), the other an American biologist, James

13 Francis Crick by Tom Coates.

D. Watson (who was made an honorary KBE in 2001). Perutz was not very impressed with their manner of working:

> When Crick and Watson lounged around, arguing about problems for which there existed no firm experimental data, instead of getting down to the bench and doing experiments, I thought they were wasting time. However, like Leonardo, they sometimes achieved most when they seemed to be working least, and their apparent idleness led them to solve the greatest of all biological problems, the structure of DNA. There is more than one good way of doing science.[59]

Later, Perutz knew that he was responsible 'for the best known double act in 20th century science'.[60]

What the two men had discovered, on 7 March 1953, was described by Peter Medawar, the OM immunologist, as 'the greatest achievement of science in the 20th century'. It was the molecular structure of DNA (*d*eoxyribo-*n*ucleic *a*cid), which makes possible the transmission of characteristics from parents to child. They showed that it was made up of two strands that paired up with each other to form a double helix (or spiral or coil). On seeing this for the first time, Perutz described it 'as beautiful as the Matterhorn'.[61]

The influence of the discovery has been enormous. It marked a new era in the study of biological inheritance and the methods employed in medicine, agriculture and industry were radically changed by the work done over following decades. We are now all familiar with DNA fingerprinting and the use of DNA in establishing paternity and other relationships.

Crick and Watson had used work done at King's College, London, by Maurice Wilkins and Rosalind Franklin, to assist in their discovery and, in 1962, the Nobel Prize for Medicine or Physiology was shared between the first three. Rosalind Franklin was dead. The Prize was 'for their discoveries concerning the molecular structure of nucleic acids and its significance for information transfer in living material'. The accompanying citation explained that the work was of major importance to the study of heredity and could lead to an explanation of why one species differed from another and why each individual was unique in some respect.

After school and university in London (University College), Francis Crick worked, as a physicist, on radar and magnetic mines. Later, inspired by Schrödinger's book *What is Life?*, he wanted to investigate the genes at a molecular level and this led him to biology and the Cambridge laboratory, where he stayed until 1977, when he went to the United States. In his case, it was to the Salk Institute in California, where he remained. This caused *The Times* to comment on the 'ridiculous level of British taxation' that compelled such a distinguished scientist to leave because he was unable to provide a satisfactory income for the remainder of his life. Before he left Britain and his

Cambridge house, 'The Golden Helix', he had been awarded both a Royal and the Copley Medals (the highest) by the Royal Society, to which he was elected in 1959.

Crick's research at the Salk Institute concentrated on consciousness and the brain, on which he wrote, especially in *The Astonishing Hypothesis: the Scientific Search for the Soul* (1994). Perhaps, after the Nobel Prize, he gradually felt that further research on DNA would be detail, or, as Rutherford called it, 'stamp-collecting'. In his autobiographical book, *What Mad Pursuit* (1988) – the title taken from Keats's 'Ode on a Grecian Urn' – he was quite laconic about the DNA work:

> Finally, after many ups and downs, Jim and I guessed the correct structure, using some of the experimental data of the London group together with Chargaff's rules about the relative amounts of the four bases in different sorts of DNA.[62]

This was in marked contrast to Watson's much earlier book, The *Double Helix* (1968), which many sedate scientists thought had made light of a serious subject. He opened the book with the comment:

> I have never seen Francis Crick in a modest mood . . . Already, he is much talked about, usually with reverence, and some day maybe considered in the category of Rutherford or Bohr.[63]

In the perspective of the Order of Merit, it seems that 'some day' was a long way off: the DNA discovery in 1953, the Nobel Prize in 1962 and the OM in 1991. He died in California in 2004.

Aaron Klug, the molecular biologist, was appointed OM in 1995 just before entering on his five-year term as President of the Royal Society. He went to school and university in South Africa, where his family had emigrated from Lithuania when he was two. With the aid of one of the 1851 Exhibition awards that had brought Rutherford to Britain over 50 years earlier, Aaron Klug came to the Cavendish Laboratory in Cambridge in 1949 and took a doctorate. He moved on to Birkbeck College, London, and worked on the study of the tobacco mosaic virus with Rosalind Franklin. In 1962, he returned to Cambridge on the staff of the Medical Research Council Laboratory of Molecular Biology, becoming its director from 1986–96. Elected FRS in 1969, he was knighted in 1988.

In his researches, he used electron microscopy, X-ray diffraction and structural modelling to study the structures of different viruses (including polio) that are too small to be visible with a light microscope or to be trapped by filters. The Nobel Prize for Chemistry came in 1982 'for his development of crystallographic electron microscopy and his structural elucidation of biologically important nucleic acid-protein complexes'.

When presenting Aaron Klug for an honorary degree at Oxford in 2001, the Public Orator drew particular attention to the wide range of his interests in an age of increasing specialisation, ranging also to connoisseurship of ancient Greek coins. Roy Jenkins, Chancellor of the University and fellow OM, welcomed him as a:

> Penetrating researcher into the unknown and most acute observer of nature, you uncover and reveal to us the secrets of life itself.

The medical

Physiologists

Like many of the scientific appointments, that of **Charles Sherrington** in 1924 was accepted without qualms by those from the humanities who considered the nominations. Stamfordham simply told Balfour that he knew it would have his 'whole-hearted approval'. Balfour confirmed that it would.

Sherrington had been President of the Royal Society since 1920 and was knighted in 1922. His professional life was devoted mainly to the study of the nervous system and his research work rendered possible many of the great advances in the surgery of the brain. He made important findings about the nerve supply to muscles, reflex actions and the regions of the brain that govern movement and sensation in particular parts of the body.

After a completely classical education at school, Sherrington studied natural sciences and medicine at Cambridge and qualified as a doctor at St Thomas's Hospital in London. He did graduate work in France and Germany, where he was taken to hear Bismarck in the Reichstag. He was already specialising in physiology and his researches earned him election as FRS at the age of 36, shortly before he took up the chair in the subject at Liverpool in 1895. Many of the results of the researches described above were embodied in *The Integrative Action of the Nervous System*, which was published in 1904 and reprinted without alteration in 1947 by the Physiological Society, 'so that it might be read by all students of physiology and reread by their teachers'.

Shortly before the First World War, Sherrington visited St Petersburg where he met the famous physiologist, Pavlov, and Tsar Nicholas II. When the latter asked for news of his cousin, George V, Sherrington had to reply that he had not seen much of the King of England lately.[64]

Sherrington moved to Oxford as Waynflete Professor of Physiology in 1913 and stayed there until retiring in 1935. He was engaged on many government committees and, in the First World War, in order to study industrial fatigue, he worked at a lathe in a shell factory. After retirement, the philosopher in him came to the fore and he published *Man on His Nature*. The Nobel Prize for Physiology or Medicine came late to him, in 1932 – shared with the much younger E. D. Adrian – 'for their discoveries regarding the functions of neurons' (or nerve cells).

There was another side to Sherrington. He published a volume of poetry in 1925, at the end of his presidency of the Royal Society. His poetic imagination led him to describe the brain as ' "an enchanted loom" with nerve impulses like lighted shuttles passing to and fro, weaving complex patterns'.[65] He had a large collection of nineteent-century paintings of the East Anglian school and, with a strong interest in bibliography, presented many volumes to the collection of the British Museum, of which he was a trustee. He was painted by his fellow-OM, Augustus John. He lived to be 94, dying in 1952.

Sherrington was to be joined in the Order of Merit by his young co-winner of the Nobel Prize, **Edgar Adrian**. The path to the Order of the youngest-ever scientist Member was swift and clear. In 1938, around Adrian's forty-ninth birthday, the support for him was mounting, even though it was from

14 Lord Adrian.

those who disclaimed any intimate knowledge of his work. Bragg considered him 'a great biologist . . . a charming man . . . an excellent teacher'. Thomson believed his work to be 'of quite exceptional importance . . . confirmed by Nobel Prize in 1932. I think that the quality of his work is quite up to the standard required for the OM.' To these were added the powerful view of Gowland Hopkins:

> his accomplishment as a whole reaches a standard quite exceptionally high, equal, I venture to think, to that of any one of the existing scientific members of the Order . . . his reputation among expert neurologists in this country and in America stands very high.[66]

By June 1941, the Private Secretary thought he was a 'strong candidate' and, in the Birthday Honours a year later, he was appointed to the Order.

Adrian had been Professor of Physiology at Cambridge since 1937 but had begun his researches there before the First World War, after graduating in natural sciences. He completed his medical degree in the war and worked on nerve injuries and shell shock. On his return to Cambridge, he was much in demand as a lecturer on subjects such as sleep, dreams, hysteria and multiple sclerosis. Elected FRS in 1923, at the age of 34, his researches led to the Nobel Prize only nine years later, which he shared with Sherrington, as noted above. His work, with the aid of modern electrical recording and display, was complementary to that of the older man; he concentrated on electrophysiology, especially nerve impulses. He was one of the first to study the electrical activity of the brain. From working on the physiology of sensation, he moved to the spinal cord and the brain itself.

On the retirement in 1951 of his fellow-OM, the historian G. M. Trevelyan, from the Mastership of Trinity College, Cambridge, Adrian was appointed by the Crown to succeed him. He had just been elected President of the Royal Society and in 1954–55, he was President also of the British Association. Encouraged by Trevelyan, he took a peerage at the end of his term as PRS. Later, he served as Vice-Chancellor of the University, was extended in the Mastership and, after retiring, was elected Chancellor, the first to be resident in Cambridge for 400 years. He was also the first to resign, at the age of 86, a year before he died. He was succeeded by Prince Philip, who also succeeded him in 2003 as the longest-serving Member of the Order of Merit.

The longevity of Adrian helped to ensure that he overlapped with the next physiologist to be honoured with the Order of Merit, **Alan Hodgkin**, who was appointed in 1973, four years before Adrian's death. Like his pupil, collaborator and co-Nobel Laureate, Andrew Huxley (to whom I shall refer in more detail later), Hodgkin came from a long intellectual line. One forebear founded meteorology, while Hodgkin's Disease is named after another; his grandfather was a banker-cum-historian. His cousins included

Howard, the painter, and (by marriage) Dorothy, the OM chemist. His father-in-law won a Nobel Prize for Medicine – three years after his own.

At Cambridge, Hodgkin presided over the exclusive debating group of 12, the Apostles, and was rebuked by Keynes for letting the membership dwindle to two. He was also quickly elected to the Natural Science Club, which was remarkably successful in picking out future FRSs – he became one at 34. A fellowship at Trinity came a year after his graduation. He soon began the research on the chemistry of nerve function that was to occupy him, except for the years of the Second World War, for the next 30 years.

Hodgkin's Quaker upbringing posed a problem in 1939 but his first-hand experiences of Nazi Germany earlier in the decade enabled him to overcome his pacifism and contribute to the war effort in the development of airborne radar, which became a decisive weapon against German submarines in the Atlantic. He was a very good physicist and mathematician, despite his lack of formal training.

On returning to Cambridge, he continued the research he had begun with Andrew Huxley in 1939 on measuring the electrical and chemical behaviour of individual nerve fibres to see how nerve impulses are produced and transmitted. The nerves of giant squids, which are 50 times larger than those in humans, proved a vital part of the research. It led to their sharing the 1963 Nobel Prize for Physiology or Medicine 'for their discoveries concerning ionic mechanisms involved in excitation and inhibition in the peripheral and central portions of the nerve cell membrane'. As Andrew Huxley has described it to me: 'the mechanism by which a nerve fibre conveys its messages'. Hodgkin's own description was:

> for finding out how nerves work, how they conduct messages, how pain and sensations reach your brain and how they travel back … As a result of our work, whole areas of medicine have shifted in emphasis.[67]

The outcome of their research is now known as the Hodgkin-Huxley model.

Hodgkin was a Royal Society research professor at Cambridge before holding the chair of biophysics there. He was President of the Society from 1970–75, during which he was knighted and made OM. In his retiring address, he called for the appointment of a chief scientific adviser to the Cabinet, a suggestion that was later followed. On the retirement of R. A. Butler as Master of Trinity in 1978, Hodgkin was appointed to succeed him and he held the post until 1984, when he was 70. He died in 1998.

I have already acknowledged the help and guidance I have received many times from **Andrew Huxley**. Much of his scientific work was described when writing of Hodgkin. It was a close collaboration (originating in that of teacher and pupil), which made them joint winners of the 1963 Nobel Prize for Physiology or Medicine. Like Hodgkin, Andrew Huxley comes from the intellectual, and particularly scientific, purple. His grandfather was T. H. Huxley, the great Victorian scientist to whom I referred in Chapter 2.

His half-brothers were Aldous, the writer, and Julian, zoologist and first Director-General of UNESCO. He also has family connections, of varying degrees, with three OMs: G. M. Trevelyan, Ralph Vaughan Williams and Veronica Wedgwood.

Andrew Huxley graduated from Trinity College, Cambridge, just before the Second World War and when that interrupted his research with Hodgkin, he was involved in operational research for both the Army and the Navy. After the war, he and Hodgkin resumed the research that led to the 1963 Nobel Prize. Meanwhile, he had been elected FRS in 1955 before, unlike so many of the Cambridge stalwarts, moving to London – to chairs of physiology. While working in London, he was knighted in 1974 and, in 1980, elected President of the Royal Society, an office his grandfather had held a century before.

His election to the presidency came at a time when there was criticism that the Society was too cautious about expressing opinions on political and social issues relating to science. Andrew Huxley's response was clear:

> It isn't always good to upset applecarts. A great deal of damage can be done which has then only to be undone... If it's a case of ideology interfering with the development of actual scientific ideas, then I think the Royal Society has a clear duty to speak out. But if it's a case of scientists acting as *political* dissidents, I think we have to be very careful about getting the society bogged down in politics.[68]

In his first presidential address, Andrew Huxley found himself drawn into a renewed argument about evolution, the topic his grandfather had so famously debated with Bishop Wilberforce in Oxford in 1860. The press announced that 'Another Huxley takes up arms in the defence of Darwin'.

In November 1983, Andrew Huxley joined his old friend and collaborator in the Order of Merit. In 1984, he returned to Cambridge to succeed Hodgkin as Master of Trinity College, thus breaking a long tradition of the post alternating between science and the humanities. Michael Atiyah, the other 'front-runner', had to wait six years before succeeding Andrew Huxley – as the third scientist in a row.

Pharmacologists

The pharmacologist, **Henry Dale**, was appointed in 1944, in the year before he relinquished the Presidency of the Royal Society. Dale was measured in his estimation of the honour:

> When asked at an interview on his 90th birthday which honour, if any, he would single out as being particularly gratifying he replied: 'Well, I think the OM – anybody would be gratified by that. Also by the Nobel Prize.'[69]

Dale was one of the seven children of the manager of a manufacturing firm and he needed (and won) scholarships to take him through school and Trinity College, Cambridge. At a late stage, he lost out to Rutherford for a studentship. When the New Zealander left for a chair in Canada the next year, however, the studentship was shared between Dale and R. J. Strutt, son and heir of Rayleigh, the physicist OM.

Dale subsequently went to London where, after qualifying as a doctor, he embarked on the first key post of his career. At the age of 29, he was appointed to the staff of the Wellcome Research Laboratories and, within two years, he was the director. In 1914, the year he was elected FRS, Dale was recommended by Sir Frederick Hopkins for a second key post. He became Director of the Department of Biochemistry and Pharmacology of what was to become, in 1920, the National Institute for Medical Research and of which, in 1928, he became the first director. It soon became a Mecca for researchers in his field.

In his pharmacological research, Dale was instrumental in discovering the nature of histamine in 1910 and in isolating acetylcholine from biological material in 1914. These and subsequent investigations showed both substances to be natural constituents of animal tissue and they provided the first definite proof that chemical substances are involved in the transmission of nerve impulses. It was for his work that he and a German pharmacologist, Otto Loewi, were jointly awarded the 1936 Nobel Prize for Physiology or Medicine. Adrian later said of Dale's research:

> Often enough his evidence has led to elaborate theorising by others... whereas Dale was more concerned to apply the brake than to be the first in the gold rush [but] the gold he has found will keep its value.[70]

In addition to his own original research, Dale was active, on behalf of the Medical Research Council, in ensuring that new discoveries, such as insulin, would be standardised by sound methods. An international committee, which he chaired, brought order where there could have been chaos in the field of the biological standardisation of hormones, vitamins, antibiotics and immunological products in general. He thus made an immense contribution to therapeutics throughout the world.

Following the death of Sir Henry Wellcome in 1936, Dale became a trustee and soon chairman of the eponymous foundation. His role, as what is sometimes called its 'patron saint', was summarised:

> It was the skill and devotion of Wellcome's trustees, notably Sir Henry Dale, that rescued both the company and the Trust, now the greatest single private contributor in Britain to medical research and study of the history of medicine.[71]

He continued as the Foundation's chairman until 1960 (when a Royal Society research professorship was endowed in his honour) and as its scientific adviser until 1968.

Dale, who had been knighted in 1932, was invited to become President of the Royal Society in 1940. To his responsibilities, however, he quickly added the chairmanship of the Scientific Advisory Committee of the War Cabinet and (in succession to William Bragg) the Directorship of the Royal Institution, both of which he held until shortly after the war. As chairman of the advisory committee, he was naturally involved with the development of the atomic bomb. Many years later he gave his views:

> Of course I wanted to do my best, so far as I had anything to do with it at all, to help the enterprise along, and there was the fear at the back of everybody's mind that the Germans might get the bomb first, but subject to that I had always the hope that the bomb would be demonstrated to be possible, but that it would not be used.[72]

During Dale's presidency of the Royal Society, a meeting was held outside Britain (in India) for the first time, the number of fellows elected annually was increased from 20 to 25 and women were admitted for the first time. During his term he was made a GBE, the year before his OM. In addition to presiding over many other scientific associations and bodies he found time, later, to be Chairman of the British Council.

Dale died in 1968, aged 93. The conclusion, on his death, was that he had been:

> an outstanding leader of medical research in Great Britain [with] an extraordinary instinct for choosing problems of importance, for planning experiments ... for describing the results ...

and that:

> British scientific medicine had lost its greatest genius ... one of the most prodigious minds in the whole of medical history.[73]

The second of the physiologists, who are more properly described as pharmacologists, is **James Black,** who received the Order of Merit in 2000, having been knighted in 1981. When the Academy of Medical Science nominated its first six Honorary Fellows in 1999, he had been among them, with three existing OMs (Andrew Huxley, Max Perutz and Frederick Sanger) and a CH (Sydney Brenner). Son of a mining engineer, his career, which he has

15 Sir James Black by Michael Clark.

described as entirely unplanned and heavily reliant on daydreaming, began at St Andrews University during and after the Second World War.

Much of his subsequent career was spent in major drug companies. At ICI in 1962, he discovered the first beta-blocking drugs for treating angina, blood pressure and cardiac disease by reducing the heart's demand for oxygen and thus its workload. At Smith, Kline and French in 1972, he developed cimetidine, the active ingredient of the drug Tagamet to prevent peptic ulcers. After a spell as Professor of Pharmacology at University College, London, he returned to business as Director of Therapeutic Research at the Wellcome Laboratories.

It was after another brief spell as an academic, holding the chair of Analytical Pharmacology at King's College Hospital Medical School, that he received the 1988 Nobel Prize for Physiology or Medicine, 'for work on the principles governing the design of new drug treatment'. Like so many Nobel Laureates, he was quick to say the award had resulted from teamwork by many people.

A successor at University College, Professor Desmond Laurence, commented:

> Black in the laboratory has relieved more human suffering than thousands of doctors in a lifetime at the bedside. He has a totally original mind. I think he is a genius. He is tough, genial and a marvellous leader.[74]

His successor at Wellcome, Dr Salvador Moncada, thought that:

> Jim Black changed the whole scenery [of the drugs industry]. It is not random any more, it's drug-designing. Largely due to him, we are into tailor-made molecules.[75]

Since leaving his post at King's, James Black has worked in new laboratories in Dulwich, with a relatively small staff. Since 1992, he has been Chancellor of Dundee University, which was part of St Andrews University when he was a student.

Immunologists

The appointment as an OM of **Macfarlane Burnet**, the immunologist, in the Birthday Honours of 1958, marked an important stage in the development of the Order but it came rather late and was not pursued as vigorously as perhaps it might have been. *The Times* immediately seized on the point with its leading article 'Australian OM':

> ...sets a happy precedent...although...Gilbert Murray never forgot his Australian origin...[Burnet] is the first recruit to the Order whose home and life's work have been in Australia.
>
> He is outstanding among the explorers of those domains of infinitesimal life, or sub-life, on the comprehension and manipulation of which human health in innumerable ways depends...[He] has elucidated the obscure mutations of viruses...through the results of his research science is able to throw its reserves into the battle on the side of the microscopic forces friendly to man, and so to check the progress of a great variety of virus-carried diseases...Medical practitioners all over the world and their patients stand in [his] debt.[76]

Burnet's journey to the Palace for his audience with the Queen was rather fraught and he was 'so het-up by the experience' that he needed a glass of water, which was supplied by 'one of the footmen, who was dressed in a kilt' – presumably the pipe-major on duty.[77] His wife was furious at not being invited to accompany him but was mollified by his 'detailed description of [the Queen's] clothes . . . the way her hair was done, down to the shoes she was wearing, as well as her jewellery!'[78] That evening, at a Royal Society conversazione, Burnet 'was able to sight at least half a dozen members of the Order of Merit in one room.'[79]

After qualifying in medicine in Melbourne, Burnet had two spells in Britain, at the Lister Institute and the National Institute for Medical Research, but unlike other Antipodean OMs such as Rutherford and Florey, he returned home to pursue his career. He worked at the Walter and Eliza Hall Institute in Melbourne for 38 years, for the last 21 of them as its Director; elected FRS in 1942, he was also, from 1944 until his retirement in 1965, Professor of Experimental Medicine at Melbourne University. He was knighted in 1951.

Unusually, the OM had come to Burnet *before* the Nobel Prize. In 1960, he received the one for Physiology or Medicine, jointly with Peter Medawar (whom I shall be discussing shortly) 'for discovery of acquired immunological tolerance' (the principle that a body can be made to tolerate foreign tissues). This was a development of major importance in the field of skin and tissue grafting.

Burnet took full advantage of his standing as the Grand Old Man of Australian science to speak out on various subjects: calling for a ban on uranium mining in Australia in order to set a moral lead in controlling nuclear weapons; predicting that in 100 years a selective breeding process would have to be used to ensure that superior genetic qualities were passed on; and saying that the human brain would be the greatest field for biological research in the future, in an effort to explain the nature of aging.

The pattern of Burnet's honours was unusual. After the knighthood, Order of Merit and Nobel Prize, he was appointed a KBE, a much lower award than the OM. It was in the Australian New Year Honours List of 1969 and, although he was listed as 'President of the Australian Academy of Science', it was shown as being 'for services to medical research', which is why he had received the OM. He had been, however, the first Chairman of the Commonwealth Foundation, created in 1965 to increase interchanges between Commonwealth organisations in the professional fields.

Burnet's last honour, in 1977, was as a Knight of the newly instituted Order of Australia (AK), one of the handful appointed in the few years that that grade of the order existed; it ranked immediately after the OM. It was natural, however, that, regardless of his other honours, his own country should wish him to have the highest honour in its indigenous system.

He died, in 1985, of cancer. He was given a state funeral and, in Canberra, the Prime Minister moved a motion of condolence in Parliament, which was highly unusual for someone who had not sat in it. In his foreword to a biography of Burnet, Prince Philip wrote that he

> was Australia's most distinguished scientist. It will be a very great man
> who ever supplants him. Genius is a word that can easily be used

lightheartedly but in the case of the subject of this book it can be used in all seriousness.[80]

The name of **Peter Medawar,** who received the Order of Merit in 1981, is linked with Macfarlane Burnet by virtue of their sharing the Nobel Prize for Physiology or Medicine in 1960, as described above. Their work, conducted 12,000 miles apart, was complementary rather than joint. What the research of Medawar and his colleagues confirmed was Burnet's hypothesis that the ability of an animal to produce a specific antibody develops during the animal's lifeline and is not inherited. This was crucial in the development of human organ transplants.

Medawar, like Burnet, had been born outside Britain – in Rio de Janeiro, of a British mother and a Lebanese father. He graduated in zoology from Oxford, where he was much influenced by Florey. From an Oxford fellowship he went, aged 32, to a chair in zoology at Birmingham and later to one at University College, London, where his department is now the 'Medawar

16 Sir Peter Medawar.

Building'. Elected FRS at 34, he followed his Nobel Prize-winning research by moving in 1962 to be Director of the National Institute for Medical Research, 20 years after Dale had relinquished the post.

Medawar's mischievous sense of humour (a hilarious game of snooker usually followed dinner at the Athenaeum) was apparent in the titles of some of the books in which he exercised his skills as a communicator of science: *Pluto's Republic*, tilting at misconceptions in scientific thought; *From Aristotle to Zoos: A Philosophic Dictionary of Biology* (written with his wife); and his last, his autobiography, *Memoirs of a Thinking Radish*. In that book, he recounted meetings with various OMs over the years. Gombrich – 'the wisest and most learned man I have ever known' – told him (contrary to C. S. Lewis' view) that 'some of Nietzsche's poetry is really rather good'. Florey told him to rewrite a paper because 'it sounds more like philosophy than science to me'. Zuckerman believed 'it was a little vulgar to accept every honorary degree that was offered, but then he was not playing, as I am, the diverting indoor pastime of trying to secure an alphabetic full house of doctorates'. (Medawar counted Exeter as an 'X' but lamented 'that Yale and Zimbabwe are unaccountably dragging their feet'.) At Harvard, Mother Teresa, seeing him in a wheelchair,

> walked over to me and without further ado blessed me, not at all perfunctorily but in the deeply earnest way that I believe to be characteristic of her.

An earlier book, *The Art of the Soluble*, took its title from a statement in it that, 'if politics is the art of the possible, research is surely that of the soluble'.

The last 18 years of Medawar's life were cruelly disrupted by a series of strokes. The first, in 1969, when he was 54, occurred as he was reading the lesson at the service for the annual meeting of the British Association for the Advancement of Science, over which he was presiding. As it was, he gave up the Directorship of the NSMR a couple of years later and moved to the Clinical Research Centre, where he was able to continue his research, as well as write, lecture and travel. All this, despite having lost half his eyesight, the use of his left arm and having to walk with a stick and a heavy splint on his left leg. His many honours came at regular intervals: CBE in 1958, a knighthood in 1965, CH in 1972 and OM in 1981. The CBE was in time to be worn at the Nobel ceremonies in Stockholm in 1960.

In his wife's book about their life together, *A Very Decided Preference*, she amusingly recalled the love/hate reaction to titles in England. Their housekeeper said: 'I'll never be able to say Sir Peter or Lady Medawar, never.' But she did, as did the telephone operators at the NIMR, who were quick with their 'Yes, Sir Peter' and 'No, Sir Peter'. An Italian waiter ensured the other diners heard him say 'May I pour your wine, m'lady?', until he slipped back into his usual 'a spot of vino?'

Unusually, Jean Medawar accompanied her crippled husband to both CH and OM investitures. Of the first, she recorded:

> I helped him to sit down, after he had received the Order and the Queen firmly held the back of the chair for him, as Peter said afterwards, 'To prevent me rolling backwards out of the Presence' on the well-oiled castors of the gilt chair.

After two serious strokes in 1980 and 1985, Medawar died in 1987.

Pathologist

Howard Florey received the OM in 1965 at the end of his Presidency of the Royal Society, just after a life peerage. The background to this was that in March 1944, when Attlee was the Lord President of the Council, it fell to him to make proposals to the then Prime Minister for honours for men of science. He wrote:

> I am . . . proposing two other medical men for the honour of knighthood, Professor A. Fleming and Professor H. W. Florey. I have to stress that Professor Fleming and Professor Florey should be considered together and that it would be most unfortunate if one were honoured and not the other. Professor Fleming discovered Penicillin, but Professor Florey discovered its real value.[81]

The Ministry of Health also stated at that time that if an order of merit was required, they would place Florey before Fleming. Those two men were joint recipients of the Nobel Award, together with Dr Chain. This advice obviously set the Palace back on its heels in relation to Fleming and Florey. Consequently, Fleming never received the OM and died in 1955; and Florey had to wait till 1965.

There was a lot of ill feeling over the true credit for penicillin. As one biographer of Florey, Trevor Williams, records:

> relations between Florey and Chain were strained, to say the least, and one of the few bonds between them was resentment at what they regarded as Fleming's immodest claims . . . Florey was never disposed to forgive Fleming, aided and abetted by St Mary's Hospital [Paddington] for . . . totally unwarranted claims . . .[82]

Another biographer and Oxford colleague of Florey, Professor Gwyn Macfarlane (who also wrote his *DNB* entry), sub-titled his book 'The making of a Great Scientist', while his biography of Fleming a few years later was sub-titled, 'The Man and the Myth'. In reviewing the latter, the medical historian, Professor Roy Porter, wrote:

> The world hailed [Fleming] as the pioneer of the greatest life-saver in the whole history of medicine... the wonder drug, rescuing from the jaws of death those struck down by killer diseases, like pneumonia and meningitis... saving the lives of thousands of badly wounded soldiers... What a debt humanity owed to Fleming... What an achievement! What a myth!... The tale of Fleming as traditionally told is but a half-truth... All of that [testing, purifying and manufacturing sufficient for medical use] – the truly difficult and heroic bit – was the work of Howard Florey in Oxford, at the head of a team... names which never became household, unlike Fleming's.
>
> Why did Fleming get all the glory? Florey sent the news-men packing with a flea in their ear (he wanted to get on with his work, and thought it unethical for medics to give stories to the press); but Fleming, by contrast, basked in the publicity. Not that he was self-seeking or vain... finding the 'Fleming myth' the media wove around him so amusing, he couldn't be bothered to set the record straight.[83]

Howard Florey, having qualified as a doctor in Adelaide, came to Oxford as a Rhodes Scholar in 1922. There he worked under Sherrington, who became his lifelong guide, supporter and friend. In a BBC programme on penicillin, he was described as being, in his early career 'rough, tough, Australian – tense and prickly – taciturn'.[84] Nevertheless, when he moved on briefly to Cambridge, he attracted the attention of giants, outside his own discipline, like J. J. Thomson and Rutherford; his biographer suggests that, despite his bluntness, 'people in many walks of life found Florey what for lack of a better generalization might be called "good value", a phrase he often used himself.'

Florey's rise was rapid. With Sherrington's backing, he obtained a chair at Sheffield at the age of 34 and three years later, by a narrow vote, the chair of Pathology at Oxford, which he was to occupy for 27 years, until elected Provost of Queen's College, Oxford. The work on penicillin began in 1939 with a Medical Research Council grant of £25.

Unlike Burnet, Florey never returned to live permanently in Australia but, in his later years, he renewed his associations with his native country. He was concerned with the foundation of the Australian National University in Canberra (of which he was later Chancellor). After the Australian Academy of Science was established, he became one of only ten corresponding members elected in its first 25 years; the others included Adrian, Robinson and Todd. Near the close of his life, he declined the Governorship of his home state, South Australia.

Florey continued to make his home in Oxford, where his next-door neighbour was Hinshelwood. His chair was based at Lincoln College, where he encouraged the building of the first Middle Common Room (for graduates) but declined the offer of the Rectorship. He was later also to reject an approach from Brasenose College to be its Principal but, with the end of his professorial term in sight, he accepted the Provostship of Queen's College. He helped in the foundation of Iffley, later Wolfson, College.

Outside Oxford, Florey was elected the fiftieth President of the Royal Society in 1960; rather surprisingly, he had not been elected a Fellow until 1941, when he was 43. When, as the immediate Past President, Florey thanked the Queen in 1967 for opening the new Royal Society premises (when she conferred the OM on Blackett), he fell into the same historical trap as Queen Victoria in referring to Charles I and II as 'royal *ancestors*'. On the earlier occasion, Lord Macaulay had rebuked his Sovereign: 'I think Ma'am, you mean your royal *predecessor*'. (The House of Hanover/Windsor is descended from Charles I's sister, Elizabeth of Bohemia.) There is no record of Queen Elizabeth II similarly rebuking Florey.

Unknown to most people, Florey had suffered from angina and he died of a heart attack in Oxford in 1968, aged 69. He was commemorated in many ways: buildings in Oxford (Queen's College and the Science Park) and in Melbourne; an Australian $ 50 bank note; and, in Westminster Abbey, a memorial stone inscribed 'His vision, leadership and research made penicillin available to mankind'.

Surgeons

Only two practising surgeons have been appointed to the Order of Merit: Lister among the original Members in 1902 (as already described in Chapter 6) and **Wilder Penfield** half a century later, in the first New Year Honours List of the Queen's reign, on 1 January 1953.

Although the appointment was the first OM of the Queen's reign, it caused little stir in the British press, which noted it as that of 'a Canadian, Dr Penfield', 'the distinguished Canadian neuro-surgeon' or 'a Canadian neurologist'. The *Manchester Guardian* noted that he was 'known only in medical quarters in this country' but the *Daily Telegraph* did observe that he was 'the first Commonwealth academic figure to receive the Order of Merit', since the New Zealander, Rutherford, had done much of his work in Britain. To do them justice, however, both the *The Guardian* and the *Telegraph* included summaries of Penfield's career and achievements in their diary columns, to explain to British readers how this man from across the Atlantic had come to justify inclusion in this select Order.

Penfield's biographer observed that the Order was 'the highest civilian honour in the empire', which only one other Canadian (Mackenzie King) had received previously and which was the only award Churchill would accept after the war.[85]

Penfield and his wife spent two months of the summer of 1953 in Britain, their first engagement being the Coronation on 2 June, in company with the Dales. On 7 July, Penfield went to receive the OM at Buckingham Palace but his way to the Queen's room was obstructed by the four-year-old Prince Charles, who plied the escorting equerry with questions about his medals. In his diary, Penfield recorded his investiture by the Queen in a detail that is rarely reproduced in a published work:

> [He] found himself in a large room with a desk in one corner and the door closing behind him. 'I was startled when I realized that there was a woman standing quietly in the centre of the room. She was dressed in a yellow silk gown. She smiled slightly but did not move. I recognized the queen with a curious feeling – no royal coach, no trumpeters and the thought occurred to me – could it be someone else. I approached her. She was holding a brown leather case in her hand. She opened it and gave it to me. I looked down at it – a dark red cross in the centre in gold – 'For Merit.' 'It gives me great pleasure to give you this. You deserve it.' I thanked her and said 'But I don't deserve it. You have been badly advised.'[86]

What route had this West Coast American followed to bring him, as a Canadian, to receive an honour primarily regarded as British? At Princeton he was a prize quarter-back and his closest friend was Gil Winant; little can these two young Americans have imagined that one day they would both be awarded the same high honour by the monarch of faraway Britain. (Winant's tragically short membership of the Order is described in Chapter 17.) Penfield came over to Merton College, Oxford, as a Rhodes Scholar in 1914; he was the first such scholar to receive the OM, appropriately in the centenary year of Rhodes' birth.

At Merton, Penfield encountered another American, T. S. Eliot, who was also to become a subject of the Crown and an OM. Whereas, however, the poet fled to London in search of intellectual stimulus, Penfield found all he wanted in Oxford, under the tutelage of his two great heroes: his fellow-Canadian, Sir William Osler, the Regius Professor of Medicine, and Sir Charles Sherrington, Wayneflete Professor of Physiology. It was Sherrington's 'place' in the Order of Merit that Penfield had taken. In 1954, not wanting to leave Canada, he turned down the offer of Osler's old chair.

When the United States came into the First World War in 1917, Penfield served with an American Red Cross hospital in France before returning to Oxford to continue his studies, which also took him to London, Edinburgh,

Germany, Spain, Harvard and Johns Hopkins University in Baltimore. He moved to Canada in 1928 and in 1934, the year he became a naturalised Canadian citizen, he was elected Professor of Neurology and Neurosurgery at McGill University in Toronto. His fast-growing reputation was instrumental in persuading the Rockefeller Foundation to endow in 1935 the Montreal Neurological Institute, of which he was the director until his retirement in 1954. It was there that he pioneered treatments that now allow millions of epileptics to lead near-normal lives; he performed more operations for epilepsy than anyone of his era and wrote extensively on it; and he pioneered electrical stimulation of the living brain.

In the Second World War, Penfield was a colonel in the Canadian Medical Corps and travelled between Ottawa, London and Washington organising the teams that treated servicemen with brain injuries. At the ripe old age of 52, he was elected FRS and made a CMG. (The Canadians had resumed the acceptance of non-titular honours during the war.) When Penfield wrote to the Secretary of the Order in 1966, asking for an up-dated list of Members, he was still so little known that the recipient passed it to the Central Chancery of the Orders of Knighthood for action with the comment:

> When I opened this I thought it was from some odd Yank who mixed the OM with the Buffaloes. But I see it is a most distinguished Canadian.[87]

In 1967, when the Order of Canada was instituted, Penfield was among those in the first class of Companion (CC), very much as Burnet was to be honoured in Australia. Also in the mid-1960s, he had a disconcerting encounter with Madame Vanier, the wife of the Governor-General, who asked him:

> Dr Penfield can you tell me where the soul is?'... He looked at her, blinked his eyes and then fixed her with that disarmingly bright stare and said: 'We can't answer that quite yet.'[88]

A month after the publication of his last book, *The Mystery of the Mind*, Penfield died of stomach cancer aged 85. He was described in the British press as 'one of the pioneers of human brain surgery' and 'one of the greatest neurosurgeons of all time'. Sir George Pickering, who accepted the Oxford chair that Penfield refused, wrote:

> Wilder was not only a great surgeon and a great scientist, he was an even greater human being... He held that most people had it in their power to adopt a second career upon retirement from their first. He himself exemplified this by writing a number of enchanting novels and biographies.[89]

The natural

In this section, I consider five OMs whose work was in various spheres of the natural world but who did not fit neatly into the other categories. There is one botanist, one naturalist, and one geologist, and there are two zoologists.

Botanist

Joseph Hooker's appointment to the Order came from a straightforward recommendation from the Prime Minister (Henry Campbell-Bannerman). He asked Knollys:

> Will you ascertain what the King's feeling would be about the Order of Merit – two names for which suggest themselves...
>
> [The first was Florence Nightingale, over which Edward VII demurred, as recounted in Chapter 16 on 'Women'.] The second is Sir Joseph Hooker and I shall save time by referring you to the enclosed letter to Haldane [Secretary of State for War and future OM] from Sir W. Thistelton-Dyer. It seems a strong case.[90]

It was a strong case, put by Hooker's son-in-law and successor as Director of Kew Gardens, William Thistelton-Dyer. Hooker's predecessor at Kew had been his father, Sir William Hooker – a remarkable succession of botanical expertise in one family. The honour was timed to coincide with Joseph Hooker's ninetieth birthday on 30 June 1907. Because he was too frail to attend an investiture, the Badge was presented to him by Sir Douglas Dawson (Secretary and Registrar of the Order) at his house in Sunningdale. He died in 1911.

At Glasgow University, a fellow student was the future Lord Kelvin, who remained a lifelong friend. After qualifying as a doctor, Hooker went as a surgeon and naturalist on an expedition from 1839–43 to the southern hemisphere, led by the famous explorer, James Clark Ross. On his return, he began the publication of a six-volume work on the flora he had seen. It established his reputation as a botanist of the highest calibre and he was elected FRS in 1847, at the age of 30.

Hooker then sailed to India to study (from 1847–51) Himalayan plant life, vividly describing in his journal and letters home various hardships and dangers he encountered in this expedition to the borders of Sikkim and Tibet. He collected hundreds of unknown species of flowers, including 27 of rhododendron, which now flourish not only at Kew but in parks and gardens all over Britain.

Hooker became assistant director at Kew in 1855, succeeding his father as director ten years later. In his 30 years at Kew, Hooker continued his father's policy of making it a combination of scientific research institution and public pleasure garden. He also began the seven-volume *Flora of British India*, written jointly with other botanists and published over 25 years (1872–97).

Hooker's connection with Darwin was close. He produced the botanical volume on the specimens from the voyage of the *Beagle* and he received many letters from Darwin, particularly about whether the geographic distribution of plants could be explained by migration. Darwin believed they could. Hooker was one of the small circle to whom Darwin confided his ideas on evolution.[91] Indeed, in 1862, Darwin wrote to Hooker:

> For years I have looked to you as the man whose opinion I have valued more on any scientific subject than anyone else in the world.[92]

Hooker's eminence led to his election as President of the Royal Society in 1872. At the end of his five-year term he was made KCSI and in 1897 he was promoted to GCSI. These honours recognised his close connection with India but were rare awards for someone not directly involved in the administration of that Empire.

Naturalist

Alfred Russel Wallace, the naturalist whose name is linked with Charles Darwin as co-founder of the theory of evolution by natural selection, was put forward for the Order of Merit by the Prime Minister (Herbert Asquith) in 1908, 50 years after the publication of the theory. In a handwritten submission to Edward VII, Asquith asked

> whether it might not be a graceful and generally appreciated mark of Your Majesty's interest in the progress of Natural Science to confer the distinction of the Order of Merit on Dr Alfred Russel Wallace, FRS. The scientific world has this year been celebrating the fiftieth anniversary of the announcement of the biological doctrine of Evolution, which commonly goes by the name of the Darwinian hypothesis. As Your Majesty is aware, the same conclusion had been independently and simultaneously reached by Dr Wallace, who still survives at the great age of 85. It would seem, therefore, not unfitting that he should this year be admitted to the Order of Merit.[93]

The King told Asquith he would give the recommendation his fullest consideration and meanwhile accepted the Prime Minister's offer to consult the

President of the Royal Society, Lord Rayleigh, one of the original OMs.[94] Asquith soon reassured the King that:

> Lord Rayleigh was of opinion that Dr Wallace would be a very fit recipient ... would be regarded as an appropriate honour by the scientific world ... [95]

The appointment was the last to be made by Edward VII His successor was, however, to show anger at the appointment. In 1912, George V's Private Secretary wrote to the Prime Minister's:

> The King is rather scandalised that the possessor of the Order of Merit should avow himself to be a Socialist. I allude to Dr Alfred Russel Wallace who in a letter which appears in today's *Times* ... glories in being a Socialist.
>
> The King says he does not care whether a man is a Liberal, Radical or a Tory, but he thinks the Order of Merit should not be given to Socialists. Could you ask the Prime Minister whether he can remember any of the circumstances connected with the bestowal on Russel Wallace?[96]

I have traced no reply to show whether Asquith owned up to his prime role in the appointment.

The eighth of nine children, Wallace left school at 14 and was apprenticed to a watchmaker before helping his brother with surveying. After a spell as a schoolmaster, the turning point in his life came when he met the naturalist, Henry Bates, to whom he later suggested a collecting trip to the Amazon in 1848. Wallace returned after four years but the ship caught fire and sank. After ten days in open boats, the ship's company were rescued but Wallace lost all his specimens, except those he had sent home earlier. Wallace thought, however, that it was a blessing in disguise because it turned his attention to *The Malay Archipelago*, the title of the book (published in 1869) in which he described his work in the Malay peninsula and the East Indies from 1854–62. While there, he noticed marked differences between the animals of Australia and Asia divided by a hypothetical line (now named after him) running between the islands of Borneo and Celebes and between those of Bali and Lombok.

In 1855, Wallace wrote *On the Law Which Has Regulated the Introduction of New Species*, propounding the idea that 'every species has come into existence coincident, both in time and space, with a pre-existing closely-allied species'. This led him to the same conclusion as Darwin had reached independently but had not published – that species evolve by natural selection. He sent a summary of his ideas to Darwin and the findings of both men were combined in a joint paper given at the Linnean Society on 1 July 1858. Next year, Darwin published his famous work, *On the Origin of Species*.

The relationship between the older and established Darwin and the younger and inexperienced Wallace was a delicate one. The joint paper has been described as

> a monument to the natural generosity of both the great biologists . . . Darwin had been working privately on the identical theme for years, but insisted on this joint publication; while Wallace, who might have raised a technical claim to priority as having been the first to write out his views for publication, never dreamt of such a procedure.[97]

The *DNB* summarised Wallace's career:

> There was a certain element of the crank in him; but, when he was handling the facts of nature and the sample speculations of evolutionary theory, this could not show itself . . . his name will be permanently remembered as long as the theory of evolution is discussed.[98]

In the twentieth century, however, Wallace's name was more or less eclipsed by that of Darwin. A sign of Wallace's slippage in public estimation was given in a recent radio programme when the Science Correspondent of the BBC was moved to ask why the Natural History Museum was paying £150,000 for the papers (including the famous letter to Darwin) of this 'obscure Victorian naturalist' – later amended to 'great forgotten naturalist'. Perhaps that sums Wallace up: great but largely forgotten.[99]

Geologist

The only geologist appointed to the Order of Merit was **Archibald Geikie**, in 1914. No consultation about, or sounding of, him is apparent in the OM archives. He was just finishing a five-year term as President of the Royal Society and, since he had been made a KCB in 1907, it must have been assumed (correctly) that he would welcome the OM. He received a letter on New Year's Eve:

> I am commanded by the King to inform you that it gives His Majesty great pleasure to confer upon you the Order of Merit, in recognition of the eminent services which you have rendered to your Country and to the world at large in the Science of Geology.[100]

The announcement in the *London Gazette* made no mention of Geikie's services to geology. It described him simply as 'President of the Royal Society'. His career, however, had been spent entirely with the Geological Survey of Great Britain, which he entered at the age of 20. Elected FRS at the age of 30, he was the 'father' of the Society at his death in 1924, at the age of 88. In the Geological Survey, he rose to be Director in Scotland (combining it with a new chair of Geology at Edinburgh University) before becoming Director-General for Great Britain from 1882 until his retirement in 1901. He was knighted in 1891.

Geikie wrote many books, based on his work in Britain and study expeditions overseas. His great work was *Ancient Volcanoes of Great Britain*, but a smaller one, *Old Red Sandstones of Western Europe*,

> was without question, his greatest original contribution to stratigraphical geology . . . Although he had a great volume of original scientific work to his credit his *Text-Book of Geology* and other publications destined for the student did much to enhance his reputation by their lucid, orderly, and attractive presentation of geological facts and principles.[101]

Just before his death, Geikie published his autobiography, *A Long Life's Work*, an outstanding feature of which had been his devotion to the learned societies with which he was associated: the Royal Society, the Royal Society of Edinburgh and the Geological Society, of which he was twice President.

Zoologists

Long before Aaron Klug, the molecular biologist, came from South Africa to find scientific eminence in Britain after the Second World War, another South African preceded him on the same trail, which culminated in the Order of Merit, though not in the Presidency of the Royal Society. He was **Solly Zuckerman**, who summed up his life in two volumes of autobiography: *From Apes to Warlords* and *Monkeys, Men and Missiles*. A zoologist who became a powerful scientific adviser to the government ('Boffin-Extraordinary' was one description), he was appointed OM in 1968.

Born into a Cape Town family of merchants that had emigrated from Eastern Europe, Zuckerman studied zoology before coming, at the age of 22, to London in 1926 to study medicine; he never lived again in South Africa, the 'backwood', as he called it. Equally, he was a cool Zionist. Asked what he had ever done for Israel, he replied: 'At least I have not changed my name.'[102] In Britain, he acquired doctorates and made his mark early with *The Social Life of Monkeys and Apes*, in 1931. His pre-war research, as a lecturer in human anatomy at Oxford, was primarily concerned with the physiology of primate reproduction and his war work began with advising on the effect of bomb blast on the body.

Zuckerman's close association with Louis Mountbatten began in 1942 when he became the new Chief of Combined Operations' scientific adviser. It was to be renewed on the official level in 1960 when, after serving on many official committees and while still holding a chair of anatomy at Birmingham University, he became Chief Scientific Adviser to the Minister of Defence, by which time Mountbatten was Chief of the Defence Staff. He was reluctant to take the job and told Mountbatten and his wife (Edwina) that he would need both arms twisted; they duly obliged to the point where it hurt and he accepted the position.

Mountbatten and Denis Healey, however, advised him to decline Wilson's request to become Minister of Disarmament in 1964. Instead, he became Chief Scientific Adviser to the Government from 1964–71. On his retirement, he was made a life peer, having had a steady accumulation of honours: CB in 1946 for his war work; a knighthood in 1956 for his official committee work; and a KCB in 1964, for his services at the MOD.

Zuckerman recalled that he presented his credentials for the wartime job with Mountbatten as 'I know about apes'. Many years later, Mountbatten said:

> I heard he had written a book about the sex life of primates and I thought at first it was about what happened after the Archbishop of Canterbury switched off the light.[103]

Later, referring to his own autobiography, Zuckerman said: 'I liked the monkeys but I understood the war-lords better.'

Elected FRS in 1943, Zuckerman's war work continued as planning adviser in the Mediterranean, under Tedder and Eisenhower, and he enjoyed their support in his successful argument with 'Bomber' Harris and 'Prof' Lindemann over whether the Allied bomber force was better used on German cities and factories or, as he advocated, on the rail network of North-West Europe. His OM came on St George's Day 1968.

Zuckerman devoted much of his energy to the London Zoo, despite his many other activities, from the time he became its research anatomist in 1928, through 20 eventful years as its secretary until the time he retired as its president in 1984.

Zuckerman always had a wide circle of friends from areas beyond science. Ben Nicholson (who became an OM on the same day) and Barbara Hepworth were early friends as, later, were Henry Moore, Alfred Hitchcock and Charles Laughton, as well as political figures like Nye Bevan and Roy Jenkins, who wrote in his foreword to a biography of Zuckerman:

> No one but Solly ever invited me to a country dinner *a cinq* with the Queen and Prince Philip.[104]

When Zuckerman died in 1993, at the age of 88, Roy Jenkins, writing only a few months before his own appointment as an OM, said:

> Over the next 40 years, up to, say, his 1968 OM, he proceeded to storm every bastion of British establishment life ... became almost universally

accepted as the best man to explain any corner of science...But although he conquered the Establishment he never allowed it to conquer him ... [he] maintained a critical iconoclasm, a 'radical chic' I suppose his detractors might call it...firmly on the liberal side on every issue of interest and controversy.[105]

No special scientific achievement was credited to Zuckerman and possibly my brief account of his life would place him as much in Chapter 14 on 'The Men of Affairs' as in this one on 'Scientists'. His OM must certainly have been intended to recognise an outstanding contribution to the national life beyond that of zoology and anatomy.

The second zoologist to receive the Order also came from overseas and was also Chief Scientific Adviser to the British Government. Unlike Solly Zuckerman, however, **Robert, Lord May of Oxford**, settled in Britain relatively late in his career.

His life has been divided between Australia (for nearly 40 years), the United States (for 15) and Britain (for nearly 20). He grew up in Sydney, where he took a PhD in theoretical physics in 1959. After a couple of years teaching at Harvard, he returned to Sydney and progressed to a personal chair before leaving again for the United States in 1973. He held chairs in biology and in zoology at Princeton and was chairman of the university research board.

In 1988, he moved to Britain, where he had already held visiting appointments at Oxford, Cambridge and Imperial College, London. An FRS since 1979, he became a Royal Society Research Professor in Zoology at Oxford and Imperial in 1988.

In Britain, he has served on many public and academic boards and councils, notably as President of the British Ecological Society and Chairman of the Natural History Museum. Most important was the position that brought him to the notice of the public at large: from 1995–2000, he was Chief Scientific Adviser to the Government and Head of the Office of Science and Technology.

Bob May (as he likes to be called) was a very public President of the Royal Society – from 2000–05. He has particularly urged that scientists should carefully consider which advances in scientific knowledge they should pursue and which they should leave alone. He has talked of their embracing the 'role of citizen scientist'. He noted the increasing concern of people about risks such as GM crops or the MMR vaccination and argued that, by taking account of those concerns, we should move to a position where decisions on scientific issues were taken more deliberately rather than by just letting them happen. In the ongoing debate about the empty fourth plinth in Trafalgar Square, he advocated a sculpture of the aesthetically beautiful double helix structure of the DNA molecule to commemorate one of the most important scientific achievements of the twentieth century.

In Britain, public honours have come to Bob May in quick succession. In the British 1996 New Year Honours, he was knighted 'for services to science.' Two years later, his native Australia honoured him with the AC (ranking above most knighthoods) and a more precise citation: 'for service to science and scientific research, particularly in the area of biological conservation involving the interaction between population, resources and the environment, to scholarship and to the formulation of scientific policy.' In 2001, he was in the first list of 'people's peers' that resembled most previous lists drawn from the ranks of 'the great and the good.'

In October 2002, his appointment to the Order of Merit maintained the tradition that the President of the Royal Society receives this personal mark of royal favour. He is now chairman of the independent specialist committee that advises the government on honours in the fields of science and technology.

The engineers

Engineers

It may sometimes seem that engineers are rather the cinderellas of British science and yet engineering is something at which the British have always excelled, as the great achievements of the Industrial Revolution bear witness, with names like Watt, Stephenson and Brunel. Of the six OM engineers, however, only one was appointed in the first 60 years of the Order. The pace has now somewhat quickened. There also appeared in 1976 the Fellowship of Engineering, which became the Royal Academy of Engineering, with a status alongside the older Royal Society and British Academy. Its Fellows are denoted as FR Eng.

The first appointment of an engineer to the Order of Merit was decided in a week and announced only two weeks later, in the Birthday Honours of 1927. It was for **Charles Parsons**, the inventor of the steam turbine engine. Lord Rayleigh, son of an original OM and, later, a candidate for the Order himself, organised a powerful lobby. He said:

> [Parsons] has not received from the government quite the recognition which is due to him. It cannot be doubted that in engineering he is *facile princeps* in the whole world and that too in a predominantly mechanical age. He is no longer young [he was 72].[106]

Rayleigh listed three OMs as supporting his proposal (of which Parsons knew nothing): Balfour, Thomson and Rutherford.

Stamfordham immediately checked with Balfour and Thomson, emphasising how greatly the King relied on opinions such as theirs. Both responded enthusiastically. Thomson described Parsons as:

> the greatest Engineer this or any other Country has produced for
> many generations. His invention and development of the turbine has
> revolutionised the production of power from fuel. His work is charac-
> terised by remarkable originality and courage; at first his ideas met with
> but little favour or encouragement but he kept on working away and
> proved most triumphantly that he was right and his critics wrong.[107]

The Prime Minister's 'concurrence' in the King's 'decision' (based on these
'sound judges') to confer the OM on Parsons was sought; Baldwin's endorsement was swiftly given.[108] Before the Prime Minister's views were confirmed,
the OM was offered to Parsons

> in recognition of your pre-eminence in the World of Practical Engi-
> neering and of the fact that through your inventive genius, patient,
> undaunted study and research the great problem of the turbine was
> solved, thereby revolutionising the power of the ship alike in peace
> and war.[109]

Parsons had been born into the Anglo-Irish landed (and intellectual)
aristocracy. He was a brilliant student of mathematics at Cambridge
before serving an engineering apprenticeship with the renowned firm of
W. G. Armstrong on Tyneside. After a few years as a partner with another
firm there, he founded his own company, C. A. Parsons, which still survives.
Parsons soon turned his attention to developing the marine turbine and built
the experimental vessel *Turbinia*. She was 100 ft long, with a displacement
of 44 tons, and her three turbines could attain a speed of 34.5 knots; this
she did when, with Parsons as chief engineer, she sped saucily along the lines
of ships assembled at Spithead for the Diamond Jubilee Naval Review in
1897, causing a mixture of consternation, amazement and interest among
watching naval officers. The Commander-in-Chief sent out a picket boat to
catch the intruder but it was not fast enough to catch her and, indeed, was
nearly rammed when trying to cut across the path of the daring new vessel.

The interest of the British Navy was soon made manifest. Two destroyers
were equipped with the new means of propulsion but foundered, through no
fault of the engines. Nevertheless, after a turbine-propelled cruiser easily out-
paced three others with conventional engines, the Admiralty decided that all
future warships would adopt the new invention. In 1906, the *Dreadnought*
was the first turbine-driven capital ship to be commissioned. Commercial
shipping kept pace: in 1901, a Clyde steamer; in 1903, a private steam
yacht (the first turbine-driven vessel to cross the Atlantic); and, in 1906,
the two Cunard liners, the *Lusitania* (sunk by a German U-boat in 1915)
and the *Mauretania*. The *Turbinia* has now been restored and is on show in
Newcastle-upon-Tyne.

Parsons had other inventions besides the marine turbine and, indeed, the steam turbine itself had important uses elsewhere, especially in power stations. His inherited interest in optics led to work on searchlights and optical instruments and he revitalised the British optical glass industry. He invented an auxetophone for increasing the volume and richness of musical stringed instruments but, although supported by Henry Wood, it was not liked by musicians.

Honours came fast to Parsons after his marine turbine success. Elected FRS in 1898, he was made CB in 1904 and promoted to KCB in 1911. Nevertheless, he had to wait another 16 years – and the age of 72 – for the OM. Parsons relaxed by cruising on liners and it was as the *Duchess of Richmond* sailed into Kingston harbour in Jamaica in 1931 that he died on board.

Over 30 years were to elapse before another engineer received the Order of Merit – and he was of the air rather than the sea: **Geoffrey de Havilland**, in 1962. He was born at just the right time to be inspired by the new science of aviation. He was 22 when the Wright brothers made their historic flight and de Havilland was already embarked on an engineering career.

Son of a clergyman, de Havilland took an engineering course and did an apprenticeship before being employed as a draughtsman. He built a revolutionary motorcycle and, in 1909, designed his own aeroplane and engine, which he taught himself to fly. He was quickly employed by the new government aeronautical establishment. De Havilland was heavily involved in the great expansion in aviation in the First World War, five of his eight DH designs going into active service. He ended the war with an OBE and the Air Force Cross.

In 1920, founded his own de Havilland Aircraft Company, supplying the new civil airlines and in 1927 his first aero-engine appeared. The Moth light aircraft, in its many guises, was everywhere between the two wars. De Havilland continued to fly himself until he was 70.

In the Second World War, while his Tiger Moth trainer was used by RAF throughout, de Havilland's most famous contribution was the wooden Mosquito, perhaps the most versatile warplane ever built and the fastest for much of the conflict. They accounted for over half of de Havilland's total wartime production of 14,000 aircraft. De Havilland was knighted in 1944.

After the war, de Havilland remained in military aviation with fighters like the Vampire, Venom and Sea Vixen and, after 1951, guided weapons. In the civil sphere, the Comet was the first jet age airliner, but crashes caused by metal fatigue delayed its development and enabled the Americans to seize the lead in the market.

De Havilland, who was never elected FRS, retired in 1955. The OM was recognition of a designer who

saw clearly the right direction to go and unerringly judged the right step forward; he was often unorthodox, yet acted within the boundaries of existing knowledge ... was first in the field with many revolutionary ideas.[110]

He died in 1965. In 1997, Prince Philip was able, following a public appeal, to unveil a statue of de Havilland (holding a Tiger Moth) at his old airfield at Hatfield.

The second aircraft designer to be awarded the Order of Merit was **George Edwards**. The honour came to him in 1971, when he was Chairman of the British Aircraft Corporation, a position he held from 1963–75. After graduating in engineering from London University, he spent seven years in what he described as 'general engineering'. He joined Vickers Aviation in 1935, and became experimental manager in 1940. He was involved in designing the Wellington bomber. He was made an MBE at the end of the war, when he became Chief Designer. He led the team that designed the Vickers Viscount, the world's first turboprop airliner. It first flew commercially from London–Cyprus in 1953, after George Edwards had been promoted to CBE. It was manufactured for nearly 20 years, sold to nearly 60 airlines and some continue to fly in Britain and overseas. Many consider it to be the greatest British commercial airliner.

Edwards was a director of Vickers from 1955–67 and was knighted in 1957, at the age of 49. During his chairmanship of BAC, he was elected FRS, in 1968. Honours, in the form of medals and honorary fellowships, came to him from aeronautical bodies – and more widely: the Albert Medal of the Royal Society of Arts and the Royal Medal of the Royal Society.

After the engineers of the sea and the air, the next such appointment, of **Christopher Hinton** in 1976, was from the post-Second World War growth industry of atomic energy. I have shown how Penney was reluctantly drawn into the post-war military development of the new source of energy. Hinton came from an engineering background to mastermind the civil development. He had started work as an apprentice with 'God's Wonderful Railway' in Swindon, before going to Cambridge. With a degree in mechanical sciences, he was with ICI until the war took him into munitions.

After the war, Hinton joined two other OMs, Cockcroft and Penney, to work under the overall direction of a fourth, Portal, in the Ministry of Supply. The three stayed as technical members of the UK Atomic Energy Authority when it was created in 1954, the year in which Hinton was elected FRS. He had been knighted in 1951 and to him fell the responsibility for the design and production of the first nuclear power stations, especially after his appointment as Chairman of the new Central Electricity Generating Board (CEGB) in 1957. Hinton's standing at that time, as one of the tokens of a better age, was illustrated by the tribute paid to him on receiving an honorary degree at Cambridge (1960):

> the genius who had enabled the discoveries of the great atomic scientists to be put to the service of men. Cyclopean power-stations were

needed: he was the Vulcan who superintended the raising of these great piles and their equipment with most intricate machinery. Calder Hall was his memorial.[111]

On leaving he CEGB in 1965, Hinton received a peerage and took the title Hinton of Bankside (of Dulwich). This title has proved a link with two other OMs: Gilbert Scott, who designed the original Bankside power station and Norman Foster (now Lord Foster of Thames Bank), who has transformed it into the Tate Modern art gallery.

Hinton became the first President of the Fellowship of Engineering in 1976, the year in which he was admitted to the Order of Merit, along with Harold Macmillan, who had been Prime Minister for most of Hinton's time at CEGB. He died in 1983, aged 82.

Of all the 47 scientist OMs, **Frank Whittle** is probably the name best known to the public at large, particularly in the second half of the twentieth century. This is hardly surprising since it is his invention of the jet engine which has transformed many of their lives, enabling them to travel, for business or pleasure, long distances in short times. His invention was in the

17 Sir Frank Whittle by Michael Noakes.

1930s, it was fully operational in the 1950s and he received the OM in 1986, by which time he had gone to live in the United States.

Slow recognition, however, was nothing new to Whittle. He had had a hard struggle to get his invention off the ground. First of all, it had been a struggle to get himself off the ground. Son of a mechanic with a small and not very successful machine tools business, there was not enough money to send him to the RAF College at Cranwell. Instead, he went to the apprentice school at Halton, after considerable difficulty in reaching the physical requirements. He did well and the RAF always recognised his personal worth, for which he later gave them full credit. He won a prized cadetship to Cranwell and, in the mid-1930s, was sent to Cambridge, where he got a First in Mechanical Sciences.

The RAF was much slower, however, in recognising the worth of Whittle's invention. In a thesis in 1928, aptly entitled 'Future Developments in Aircraft Design', he had put forward the idea of a gas turbine to produce a propelling jet. He took out a patent on his design (amazingly not safeguarded by any security classification) and continued to publicise his idea but received no official encouragement, rather the reverse.

Whittle was criticised, as a cadet and young officer, for 'over-confidence' and he was seen by many of his superiors as a bit of an upstart. In any case, as war approached, the Air Ministry became increasingly concerned with improving the design, performance and quantity of conventionally-propelled aircraft. Only with the help of friends, initially to the tune of £5 to renew the patent but later more substantially, was he able to keep his idea alive. The vehicle for doing so was a company called Power Jets, to which he was seconded from the RAF in an unusual arrangement. Progress was slow; not until 1937 was the first jet engine successfully run and two years later it was decided to test fly it. On 15 May 1941, the Gloster-Whittle E 28/39 flew successfully – appropriately at Cranwell – at a higher speed than any existing conventional aircraft. One onlooker exclaimed: 'My God, Frank, it flies,' to which Whittle responded, 'Of course it does; it was bloody well meant to.'[112]

Whittle's main pre-war rival was the German, Han von Ohain, whose ample financial backing enabled him to produce the jet Heinkel 178, which made the world's first jet-powered flight on 27 August 1939. An Italian jet aircraft flew in 1940. Neither was pursued as they might have been. After the War, von Ohain worked in the United States and he and Whittle met there; they were awarded the same prize by the American National Academy of Engineering.

The delays of the 1930s led Whittle to declare in 1987:

> My only bitterness is at the officialdom which did its best to frustrate me in the early years. We could and should have had jets to fight the Battle of Britain.[113]

As it was, the first British operational jet aircraft, the Meteor, never saw air-to-air combat during the war but did shoot down V1 flying bombs. Shortly after the war, Whittle himself flew a Meteor at 450 mph, a rare occasion of an engine designer piloting an aircraft powered by one of his own engines.

Towards the end of the war, Power Jets was turned over to state ownership and, having relinquished his shares in it to the government, Whittle left it and took up an RAF post in the Ministry of Supply.

The immediate post-war years saw both honours and a premature retirement. He was made CBE in 1944 and CB in 1947 but nearly missed a knighthood, which was not normally given to air commodores, let alone those with only the acting rank. Nevertheless, June 1948 was a good month for Whittle: a KBE in the Birthday Honours and £100,000 tax-free from the Royal Commission on Awards to Inventors, although he had made no claim himself. He had been elected FRS in 1947.

His health had suffered from his years of struggle and he retired from the RAF in 1948 on medical grounds at the age of 41. In 1950, Whittle and George Edwards flew on the world's first commercial turbine-powered air service from London to Paris in the Viscount prototype. In 1952, he was the first recipient of the Churchill Medal of the Society of Engineers for his 'incalculable service to British engineering'. To some extent, over the next couple of decades, Whittle was lost to sight. He worked as a consultant while the world of the jet developed around him.

In 1976, on his second marriage, Whittle moved to the United States, where he became a professor at the Naval Academy at Annapolis. He returned occasionally to Britain. Lord King's Norton, himself a distinguished aeronautical engineer, described Whittle as 'a genius, one of the great engineers of all time'; he had earlier said that Whittle's

> name in the annals of engineering comes after those of Watt, Stephenson and Parsons, only for reasons of chronology or alphabetical order ... [He had] an idea ... The technical and executive ability to give it flesh ... [and] the tenacity of purpose to drive through to success.[114]

The award of the Order of Merit in 1986 brought Whittle great pleasure. I happened to be at Buckingham Palace at a ceremony on the day he came to be invested. Such was his loyalty to the RAF that he had rather hoped to receive the military rather than the civil badge but seemed to accept that his services had been as much in the civil as in the military sphere – and he had been retired for nearly 40 years. Nevertheless, had he been able to find an air commodore's uniform in London that fitted, he said he would have worn it. That afternoon, at the opening of the Queen Elizabeth II Conference Centre (where one of the rooms is named after him), he could not remember – unlike Wilder Penfield years before – what the Queen had worn in the morning;

I was able to tell his wife that it was a salmon pink dress. When I reminded him of his sense of humour in putting on the envelope of a letter he had sent me a stamp showing an aircraft with *piston* engines, he laughed and said it simply commemorated the fiftieth anniversary of the first trans-Pacific airmail flight in 1935.

Whittle died in the United States in 1996, aged 89. At the memorial service in Westminster Abbey, the then Chief of the Air Staff said:

> It is given to few people, and even fewer in their own lifetime, to open up new horizons for their fellow human beings. This is what Frank Whittle did by paving the way for popular air travel on a scale that few people thought possible at the time. This practical realisation of a soaring vision is surely the essence of genius.[115]

The last engineer to be appointed to the Order, 1997, was **Denis Rooke**, an outstanding figure of his generation of engineers and from a hitherto unrecognised sector of the profession – the gas industry, in which he spent his working life and with the transformation of which he was closely involved. He is now 82.

His schooling and university education in London (University College) were interrupted by service in the Royal Electrical and Mechanical Engineers. He started with the South Eastern Gas Board as an assistant engineer in 1949 and ended as Chairman of British Gas in 1989, having held the post for 13 years. In between, he worked in Britain and the United States on liquefied natural gas and was in the technical team on board the first ship that brought it to this country; later, he was Member for Production and Supplies of the old Gas Council.

He has been very active outside the confines of his own industry. Elected FRS in 1978 and later winning its Rumford Medal, he was instrumental in founding the Fellowship of Engineering, to which I referred earlier, and the culminations of his presidency from 1986–91 was its transformation into the Royal Academy of Engineering; he received its Prince Philip Medal in 1992.

More widely, Denis Rooke has been Chairman of the Royal Commission for the Royal Exhibition of 1851 (from the funds of which Rutherford and many others got their kick-starts), of the Council for National Academic Awards (CNAA) and the Trustees of the Science Museum, as well as being Chancellor of Loughborough University (formerly a University of Technology).

10

THE ARTISTS

Painters

1. 1902 G. F. WATTS
2. 1905 Sir Lawrence ALMA-TADEMA
3. 1905 William HOLMAN HUNT
4. 1931 Philip Wilson STEER
5. 1942 Augustus JOHN
6. 1960 Graham SUTHERLAND
7. 1968 Ben NICHOLSON
8. 1983 Sir Sidney NOLAN
9. 1993 Lucian FREUD

Sculptors

10. 1963 Henry MOORE
11. 2000 Sir Anthony CARO

Architects

12. 1942 Sir Edwin LUTYENS
13. 1944 Sir Giles Gilbert SCOTT
14. 1962 Sir Basil SPENCE
15. 1997 Norman (Lord) FOSTER

Preliminary

There is an interesting but not very surprising difference between the scientists and the artists in their attitude to the Establishment, whether of their own profession or the state at large. Whereas all but one of the 47 scientist OMs were Fellows of the Royal Society, only nine of the 15 artists were Royal Academicians: five of the nine painters, all four architects but neither of the sculptors. Indeed, as I shall show, the relationship of some of the artists with the Academy was distinctly troubled. Only one President of the Royal Academy since 1902 has been an OM (Lutyens, the architect), while, as we have seen, every President of the Royal Society has received the Order. The aim of most scientists is to be elected FRS; for many artists, election as an RA is to be avoided at all costs.

Another difference between the two groups is in their attitude to titles. Of the 48 scientists, only seven were untitled, while of the 15 artists, eight remained 'Mr' and this was particularly true of the painters – seven out of nine.

The painters

G. F. Watts, whose appointment as one of the original Members of the Order of Merit was described in Chapter 6, died in 1904. His loss was compensated for by the simultaneous appointment, in 1905, of two painters: Lawrence Alma-Tadema and William Holman Hunt, both highly acclaimed at the time. One was a man renowned for his portrayal of (suitably classical) female nudes; the other was a man whose most famous painting was of Christ at a door – *The Light of the World.*

Lourens Alma Tadema can be compared to Rubens and Van Dyck in three respects: all were Dutch painters, who came to England and were knighted. The comparison probably ends there. Alma-Tadema was fascinated from an early age by archaeology and, at the Antwerp Academy, he was influenced by the historical painter, Baron Hendryk Leys, whose assistant he became. Many of his early paintings were of ancient Egypt. He was a meticulous man who numbered his paintings with Roman numerals, reaching CCCCVIII shortly before his death.

He had quickly established himself in England after his arrival in 1870. He was naturalised in 1873; painted prolifically (84 of the 408 paintings mentioned earlier were painted between 1871–76); and gained election to the Royal Academy, as an Associate in 1876 and as a full Academician in 1879. By this time, he was 'Lawrence' and the hyphenating of his last two names put him conveniently at the front of exhibition catalogues.

By then also, his painting was almost entirely of imperial Rome–languorous Mediterranean idylls frequently set in bath-houses and thus providing great scope for nudity. Alma-Tadema was the foremost provider of this form of art to the Victorian age and sometimes it shocked as well as titillated. For instance, *Tepidarium* shows a reclining naked girl using one hand to neatly obscure her genitalia with feathers and the other to

18 Sir Lawrence Alma-Tadema by William Strang.

hold a phallic scraping tool for examination. His depiction of marble was described as 'marbellous' by *Punch*, which also suggested he should be made a KCMB (Knight of the Cool Marble Bath); perhaps it led to his serving on the committee to oversee the redecoration of the Athenaeum Club.

Many fellow-painters, while enjoying his company and his technical brilliance, thought little of his work. John Singer Sargent went so far as to say:

> I suppose it's clever. Of course, it *is* clever ... but, of course, it's not art in any sense whatever.[1]

Perhaps Sargent did not approve of Alma-Tadema relying heavily on photographs.

Official recognition came relatively late to Alma-Tadema. He was not knighted until he was 63, in Queen Victoria's eightieth Birthday Honours List in 1899, only six years before his appointment to the Order of Merit. When, in 1901, he designed the elaborate sets for Sir Henry Irving's last new Shakespearian production, *Coriolanus*, with incidental music by Sir Alexander MacKenzie, the stage manager remarked: 'Three blooming knights – and that's about as long as it will run!'[2]

Alma-Tadema's growing prosperity – by the mid-1880s, he was one of the richest painters ever in Britain – led him to buy and extend a house in Grove End Road, St John's Wood, formerly owned by the French painter, James Tissot. When completed, the *Pall Mall Gazette* called the house 'The Palace of the Beautiful'. In this grand house, Alma-Tadema (known to his friends as Tad) and his wife entertained vigorously over many years. Their guests included the Prince of Wales, T. H. Huxley, Henry James and Winston Churchill, who was in a group with whom Alma-Tadema visited Egypt. A. J. Balfour sat for the artist a decade before he became Prime Minister. A strong interest in music led to the guests also including Tchaikovsky, Paderewski, Caruso and Melba.

Alma-Tadema's great success in his lifetime was reflected in the prices fetched by his paintings: between £2–6,000 each. Interest in him and his work fell dramatically after his death in 1912 and there was no exhibition of his paintings in this country between the memorial one in 1913 and 1976. By the 1970s, however, the market in his genre was picking up and prices were back in the thousands of pounds. In 1995, *The Finding of Moses* was sold at auction for £ 1.5 m; it had been dumped in the 1950s in an alley in St James's, without its (more valuable) frame.

One rumour persists about Alma-Tadema:

> It is even said that he executed a series of mildly pornographic sketches for the Prince of Wales [Edward VII] but that these – if they ever really existed – were purged from the Royal Collection by Queen Mary.[3]

Not surprisingly, the Royal Collection refuse to be drawn on this.

As his prices fell and rose, so did Alma-Tadema's reputation, although art critics over the years never seem to have thought as highly of him as buyers.

Alma-Tadema died in 1912 in the German spa town of Wiesbaden, where he had gone reluctantly, on the advice of his doctors, after a couple of years of deteriorating health. He was too famous to 'go to Paradise by way of Kensal Green' (where his wife was buried) and so he was placed in the crypt of St Paul's Cathedral, alongside Turner, Leighton, Millais – and Holman Hunt, his fellow-OM.

Like Alma-Tadema, **William Holman Hunt** also had a strong interest in the Mediterranean but in the Holy Land rather than in Egypt or Rome. The son of a warehouseman, his second name was really Hobman (from a

Danish ancestor) but it became changed by mistake. He escaped from a City clerkship to the Royal Academy Schools, where he met Millais and Dante Gabriel Rosetti, with whom he founded the Pre-Raphaelite Brotherhood (PRB) in 1848. All were under 21. They agreed with Ruskin that artists should go to Nature and draw what was really there. Their admiration of the early Italian masters before Raphael (with whom great art was then believed to start but whom they thought over-praised) earned them the name of Pre-Raphaelite.

The story of Hunt's most famous picture *The Light of the World* spread over 50 years. It shows Christ, lamp in hand, knocking at a closed door: the human heart that can be opened to Him only by each individual. The original was painted over three years and exhibited at the Academy in 1854, when Ruskin pronounced it 'one of the very noblest works of sacred art ever produced'. The model who posed for Christ, Domenico Mancini, was an ice-cream vendor with a stall outside the Lyric Theatre in Hammersmith.[4] It was bought for 400 guineas by Thomas Combe, Printer to Oxford University, whose widow presented it to Keble College, Oxford, where it is today.

Because Hunt was not happy with the way the College treated the picture, he decided to paint it again, twice the size, from 1901–04. By then partially blind, he needed help. The philanthropist, Charles Booth, bought it and sent it on a tour of Canada, Australia, New Zealand and South Africa, where it was seen by seven million people before it came home to rest in St Paul's, where it remains the only painting in the cathedral. Hundreds of thousands of prints of the painting were sold around the world and it became the most significant religious painting of its era. It also earned Holman Hunt a fortune.

A devout Christian, Holman 'Holy' Hunt visited the Holy Land in 1854 so that he could better portray the life of Christ and make His divine teaching more tangible. He wanted veracity in the landscape, flora, buildings and people he painted. Above all, he wanted 'to find out with his own eyes what Christ was like'.[5] *The Scapegoat*, painted while encamped by the Dead Sea, was the main product of the visit: a tethered goat ready for sacrifice, just as Christ was 'despised and rejected of men'. Hunt visited Palestine again in 1869–71, 1875–78 and 1892.

There were secular counterparts of the religious paintings but they usually conveyed some moral message. *The Awakening Conscience* (1854), which is now in Tate Britain, is full of detailed symbols emphasising the sudden repentance of a mistress.

Hunt's relationship with Millais was close; until his death he wore a ring given to him by the man who became a baronet and President of the Royal Academy. Hunt's own relations with the Academy were distinctly less cordial. After securing only one vote for election as ARA in 1857, he sent no more pictures to the Academy until 1860 and he stopped sending them altogether in 1874. He criticised the Academy before a royal commission in 1863 and resisted later suggestions from Millais that he would be welcomed into it. He was, however, elected to the Athenaeum in 1868.

Holman Hunt's paintings sold well in his lifetime and they kept their value rather better than Alma-Tadema's. In 1973, *Rienzi Vowing to Obtain Justice* (for which Millais modelled) fetched £48,000 and, 20 years later, *Master Hilary – The Tracer* (a portrait of his young son) sold for just under £1m, while *The Shadow of Death* was estimated to be worth £1.5m.

A month before receiving the OM, Hunt, at the age of 77, produced what *The Times* called 'a new and independent masterpiece, *The Lady of Shalott*, which proved that "he is still a great painter" and that "his eye is not dim nor his natural force abated" '.[6] Based on Tennyson's poem, the painting took nearly 20 years to complete. It was the last great Pre-Raphaelite painting, almost art nouveau.

Holman Hunt's death in 1910 was regarded as the end of an epoch:

> England is sensibly the poorer . . . a name that will long be identified with the history of art in the latter half of the nineteenth century . . . Unlike his early friend Millais, he remained throughout constant to his artistic ideals and principles; and there can be no question that his fame will gain thereby . . . the ideals of the PRB were his to the end . . . [On suggestion of burial in St Paul's, it] would be in every way appropriate. The painter of The *Light of the World* . . . should rest among the long series of illustrious artists who lie in the crypt beneath it; for none of them ever worked more strenuously or more successfully than he to inspire his fellow men with lofty ideals, and to wed beauty to religion.[7]

Five days later, Hunt's ashes were buried in St Paul's.

After the deaths of Holman Hunt in 1910 and Alma-Tadema in 1912, nearly 20 years passed before another painter was appointed to the Order of Merit. **Philip Wilson Steer** is probably the least well known of the nine OM painters. Even in his own day, his reputation was a little variable and it is significant that his appointment to the Order in the New Year Honours of 1931 was 'in recognition of his eminent position in the World of Art both as Painter and Teacher'.

In his later years, Steer's reputation stood high as a teacher – at the Slade School of Fine Art, where he taught from 1895 until his retirement in 1930. Although he was not a good teacher in the conventional sense, being rather inarticulate, his judgement on a student's work and worth was deferred to by the others.

In 1930, Owen Morshead recommended Steer to Stamfordham. It shows the forceful, but not always balanced, views that, early in his 30 years as Assistant Keeper of the Royal Archives (and Royal Librarian), he was beginning to exert. Because art was unrepresented in the Order of Merit, he consulted the Keeper of Pictures at the National Gallery:

> without a moment's hesitation [he replied] Wilson Steer...a century hence anyone surveying the field of English landscape artists would recognise the main 'peaks' viz. Crome, Constable, Turner & Steer...[8]

But when Steer was sounded about receiving the OM, he was 'very difficult' about it. 'He didn't care a damn about that sort of stuff.' According to his old friend and colleague, D. S. MacColl, Steer declined the offer of a knighthood from Ramsay MacDonald. He listened to the argument that in honouring him art would be honoured and, finally, he agreed. When Steer received the letter from the King's Private Secretary, he put it in his pocket and, when he met Henry Tonks a week later, he showed it to him saying, 'I expect you've got one of these too'. He was now inclined to refuse the honour but Tonks 'persuaded him that here was a distinction that even he must accept'.[9]

Steer's father was a portrait painter, who taught his son drawing and painting. After failing to enter the Royal Academy Schools, he went to Paris where his studies were hindered by his inability to speak French. He settled in Chelsea and exhibited at the Academy but, like Holman Hunt, he was never elected to it. Soon, in the late 1880s, he began to stay at Walberswick on the Suffolk coast, where the sea, beaches, pier and playing children came together in some of his most famous paintings. He painted also in France, notably *The Bridge, Etaples*. He became a leading exponent of English impressionism.

Another critic drew the distinction between Steer's early and later work:

> Before 1900 he is a man in love with light and colour and the sheer joy of putting paint on canvas. After 1900 he is careful, self-conscious, tasteful, technically highly proficient, and just inescapably inclined to be dull...impossible to diminish the wonder and delight of his early years...for 10 or even 15 years, Steer was a great painter.[10]

The novelist, Maggie Hemingway, decided she knew the answer to this change in Steer's style: 'cherchez la femme'. In her book, *The Bridge* (later filmed), she described a love affair with a married woman in Suffolk and was amazed when Steer's great-grandchildren introduced themselves to her; their grandfather was the offspring of the liaison.[11]

Steer died in 1942, aged 81. One of Steer's paintings of Chepstow Castle was bought by the Duchess of York (later The Queen Mother) in 1928 and she visited his memorial exhibition at the National Gallery in 1943 with the then Princess Elizabeth. In recent years, Steer's paintings have fetched reasonably high prices: £24,000 for a portrait in 1989, only a year after his record of £60,000 was broken within a week by £187,000 for *A Girl Reclining on a Sofa*.

Michael Holroyd, biographer of Augustus John and Bernard Shaw, described Wilson Steer's essential Englishness thus

> built upon a pattern very dear to his fellow-countrymen. He was a large, genial, small-headed, slow-moving man, very easygoing, incurious and inarticulate. People loved him for his modesty – you'd never guess he painted, especially since he locked up his painting equipment in a cricket bag, explaining: 'I get better service that way'.
>
> His virtues were total shyness and a monumental calm. Despite his eye for painting pretty girls, he was triumphantly unromantic; and as England's most avant-garde painter he remained, very properly, a deeply conservative man.[12]

The next painter OM (in June 1942), **Augustus John**, was everyone's idea of the Bohemian artist, in both dress and lifestyle. He dressed like a flamboyant gypsy, with a temperament that was unpredictable and often fierce and an unrestrained lust for women. His children were numerous, although slightly uncertain in number. His life had started respectably enough as the son of a Welsh solicitor, who was widowed when Augustus was six. He left an unhappy childhood behind him at 16 to go to the Slade School of Fine Art in London. A holiday accident to his head seemed to transform him from a methodical and unremarkable student into a brilliant 'enfant terrible', who drew compulsively, instinctively and powerfully. The John legend had begun.

Early success in selling his art enabled John to indulge his passion for travel – on foot or in a caravan – around Britain, France and Italy. His sympathy with gypsies and their way of life led to his becoming a persistent champion on their behalf. He was constantly on the move, believing that a studio 'shut the door on nature'. Once, he was arrested in Normandy as a vagrant, after sleeping under a hedge and having his money stolen. His ever-growing family were often with him on his travels.

In 1901, John married Ida Nettleship, who had been at the Slade with him, but, after bearing him five sons, she died in 1907. By then, he had introduced Dorothy McNeill (known as Dorelia and later Dodo) into a ménage a trois and she bore him the first of their three children before Ida's death. He had at least three other illegitimate children. At the age of 72, he fell in love with a young art student and, to separate them, his daughter dragged him away to France.[13] In a moment of introspection, John confessed to a woman friend: 'What inconsiderate buggers we males are!'[14] John's relations with his many children were often unusually difficult. The only one of the John children who broke free and made a life for himself elsewhere was Caspar, who found a 'new and orderly society' in the Navy; when he read the lesson at his father's memorial service, he was the First Sea Lord.

John was unfit for service in the First World War (he was in his late thirties anyway) and Lord Beaverbrook eventually arranged for him to be commissioned as a war artist with the Canadian Forces. He 'held court' at the Paris Peace Conference in 1919, painting many of the leading Empire delegates.

Other notable figures attracted his brush and pencil over the years, including at least nine OMs: Balfour, Hardy, Sherrington, de la Mare, Murray, Schweitzer, Lloyd George, Churchill and 'Jacky' Fisher, of whom John wrote:

> The night before his sittings, he might have been dancing indefatigably, or sitting up to all hours drinking champagne with Winston Churchill; as far as I could see, he was never the worse for it.[15]

When T. E. Lawrence backed once more into the limelight with his *Seven Pillars of Wisdom*, John contributed drawings of him and his hero, Emir Feisal.

Augustus John's relationship with the Royal Academy was suitably volatile but at least, unlike Hunt and Steer, it did exist and, indeed, nearly ended with his becoming President. Although he recognised the Academy as a good showcase for his works, he was no keener to belong to it than many of its members were to have him. He was elected an Associate in 1921 and a full Academician in 1928. Ten years later, he resigned when the Academy rejected a portrait by Wyndham Lewis of T. S. Eliot. He was re-elected in 1940.

Just as the Academy had to begun to feel uncomfortable at not having John among their number, so the Palace gradually became concerned about his absence from the Order of Merit. His name was first mentioned for the Order as early as 1922 but, at the age of 44, he was considered too young. By 1936, it was his lifestyle rather than his painting that impeded his appointment. A new Private Secretary was noting: 'In spite of his morals, I think he ought to have it.'[16] By June 1941, John was 'much in the running'[17] and, by April 1942, the Private Secretary was:

> feeling unhappy that the Order should not include Augustus John . . . far the greatest English painter. His respectability is certainly a doubtful factor but, within limits, I do feel that this ought not really to be allowed to count.[18]

Two months later, in the Birthday Honours of 1942, John was appointed to the Order.

According to John's biographer, 'rumours of a knighthood had been blowing about the previous year' but Dorelia did not want to be 'Lady'. His disappointment was easily removed by the OM – 'a far more distinguished award' and one in which he expressed both pride and humility in 'succeeding' Steer.

John made prolonged attempts to be a painter of royalty. He had been rejected in 1925; George V's Private Secretary dismissed the notion: 'No! HM wouldn't look at AJ!! And so AJ wouldn't be able to look at HM!!' (In 1928, the King, when required to sign John's diploma as an Academician, exclaimed: 'What, that fellow! I've a damned good mind not to sign it.')[19]

Early in George VI's reign, however, John was 'invited to meet the new Queen – provided he arrived dead sober'. There were sittings in the winter of 1939–40, but there were problems. Sensing the root of these, the Palace provided sherry and brandy. The Blitz interrupted proceedings and John shut the uncompleted portrait away. Not until 1961 was it rediscovered in a cellar below John's studio and a shipping company presented it to the sitter, by then Queen Mother, who thanked the artist shortly before his death: 'I want to tell you what a tremendous pleasure it gives me to see it once again . . . It looks so lovely in my drawing-room and has cheered it up no end!'[20]

John's experience with other distinguished sitters was sometimes fraught. When Queen Mary's brother (the Earl of Athlone) and his wife burst out of John's studio, looking furious and drove heatedly off, he 'tore the painting to pieces. I suddenly couldn't stand it.'[21] Much more publicised was the mauling of John's portrait of 'His Margarine Majesty', Lord Leverhulme, by the sitter himself, who cut off the offending head and face and put it in his safe. His housekeeper mistakenly returned the rest of the portrait to John, who demanded an explanation for 'the grossest insult I have ever received in the course of my career'.

Even before his death, John's reputation had begun to fade. The Royal Academy mounted a major retrospective exhibition for him in 1954 but 'pundits wrote off his entire production, early as well as late: John just "couldn't draw".'[22] However, in the entry on John in the *Dictionary of National Biography*, John Rothenstein wrote:

> It is scarcely an exaggeration to say that – outside academic circles – he was worshipped: . . . a draughtsman of rare mastery, and a notable painter . . . although, on account of changing fashion and indiscriminate praise, his reputation declined, he is likely to be remembered as one of the masters of his age.[23]

John's death was followed by a decade of almost total neglect; his works were 'removed from the walls of our public collections and his talent has been neatly analysed away to nothing in the text-books'. A two-volume biography by Michael Holroyd (updated in a single volume in 1996), the occasional exhibition and a play *Portraits*, by William Douglas-Home in 1987 all helped to keep John in the public eye. His critical and commercial reputation, however, has never returned to that he enjoyed between the wars, when it was enhanced by his notorious lifestyle.

Ironically, in death, Augustus John is increasingly compared to his sister, Gwen, who painted in Paris for many years and died there in 1939. He himself had said that 50 years after his death he would be remembered as Gwen John's brother. Perhaps, he will be proved right. By 1991, her auction record stood at £165,000 while his was £34,000.

While it has been said that John had 'succeeded' Steer in the Order of Merit three months after the latter's death, the same could not be said of **Graham Sutherland**, who was appointed to the Order on 23 April 1960, 18 months *before* the death of John. His appointment served to show me how the Prime Minister was given advance warning of awards of the OM. One evening, as a young private secretary in the civil service, I had to go to the Prime Minister's office. Business over, his private secretary asked me what I thought of Sutherland's work. When I said I liked it, he replied: 'Good, because he's going to get a rather nice medal soon.'

The appointment, with that of Cyril Hinshelwood, the chemist, was made along with two new Knights of the Garter. Now that OM appointments were no longer to be made in the routine honours lists, this seemed to be an experiment in linking two of the great orders in the personal gift of the Sovereign. It was repeated only once, in 1968, after which appointments to the two orders have always been announced separately. Nevertheless, the linkage provoked comment from *The Guardian*:

> The Order of Merit and the Order of the Garter are in their very different ways the two most distinguished bodies of their kind. It is a red-letter day that sees two new members added to each.

The Guardian described Sutherland as:

> an unexpected but a very welcome recruit to the Order. He is a great painter though a difficult and exacting and even yet hardly a popular one ... [He] has wrought nobly with – until the portraits of the last few years – too little public recognition. It is a finely conceived as well as a deserved appointment.[24]

In the authorised biography of Sutherland, Roger Berthoud described it as an award which 'is generally considered the most distinguished available'. Congratulations naturally flowed in. In reply to those from his old friends, Jane and Kenneth Clark (the latter a CH and future OM), Sutherland responded:

> To Jane: That K's advice is responsible for this rather extraordinary thing that has overtaken me I can have no doubt ... I am moved beyond words.

To Kenneth: Had we lived at the time of the Renaissance, I like to think
that we would have been a typical example of the relation between artist
and patron...[25]

Henry Moore (also a CH and future OM) wrote: 'It's the very top of
all.' While Vita Sackville-West (another CH, who had been considered for
the OM) wrote: 'How much more satisfying than being given the Garter.'
Herbert Read (the radical art critic who dismayed his anarchist friends by
accepting a knighthood because he did not feel grand enough to refuse) saw
Sutherland's OM as the final canonisation of modern art.[26]
Sutherland himself, in one of his replies 'showed the conflicting emotions
it had aroused in his breast':

I've never been a great chap for wanting honours. I am certain it is
intended as a mark of awareness of the work and direction which many
of us have been obsessed with over a number of years. That does not
mean to say that I am not glad to represent all this. One would be hardly
human not to be pleased. I can only pray that I will not be thought
respectable.[27]

Son of a barrister in the civil service, Sutherland started work as a railway
engineering apprentice but poor mathematics turned him to art, which he
studied at Goldsmith's College from 1921 to 1926, the year in which he
became a Catholic. It was as an engraver and print-maker that he hoped to
make a living but that market, based on the United States, collapsed in 1929.
While teaching at the Chelsea School of Art, he joined with other artists, such
as John Piper, Paul Nash and Rex Whistler, in designing advertisements for
Shell Mex and BP, as well as London Transport.
Sutherland also turned to painting and became captivated by Wales,
especially Pembrokeshire, of which he painted semi-abstract landscapes, of
gnarled or blasted trees and hedges, with thistly and spiked plants. (Later, he
endowed the art gallery of the National Museum of Wales, which is named
after him.) His patron, Kenneth Clark, helped him both financially and with
arranging his first one-man show in 1938. He also invited Sutherland to join
his team of official war artists, which resulted in studies of air-raid devasta-
tion in South Wales and the East End of London, as well as of flying-bomb
sites in Normandy.
Another patron, Canon Walter Hussey, drew him into the realm of religious painting by commissioning a *Crucifixion* for St Matthew's Church,
Northampton and, later, *Noli Me Tangere*, the altarpiece for Chichester
Cathedral. In 1962, he completed *Christ in Glory*, the tapestry that
dominated the rebuilt Coventry Cathedral.

Sutherland did not begin to paint portraits until 1949, when a full-length 'warts and all' painting of Somerset Maugham startled a public accustomed to more conventional portraiture. It provoked Sir Gerald Kelly, the rather wistful President of the Royal Academy, into saying:

> To think that I have known Willie since 1902 and have only just recognised that, disguised as an old madame, he kept a brothel in Shanghai.[28]

At a degree ceremony in Oxford years later, Sutherland was described as 'a portraitist of shocking insight'.

Sutherland's most famous, and controversial, portrait was that of his fellow-OM, Winston Churchill. It was commissioned as the gift of Parliament on the eightieth birthday in 1954 of the man who was still Prime Minister. The sitter, while subtly describing it as 'a great example of modern art', took an instant dislike to it: 'it makes me look half-witted, which I ain't.' It was secretly destroyed within a couple of years.

Rumours of its disappearance flourished but it was not until after the death of Lady Churchill in 1977 that Sutherland later had confirmation of this from the couple's surviving daughter, Mary Soames, who wrote to tell him that her mother

> had been greatly distressed to see how much it preyed on Churchill's mind and she had promised him that it would never see the light of day.[29]

Sutherland replied in a dignified but sorrowful strain:

> the whole undignified affair is for me past history. Nonetheless, some others may well feel differently... for whatever reason the portrait was caused to be destroyed, it was an act of vandalism perhaps not without precedent, but rare in history, except in war time.[30]

There was an outcry when the destruction was made public. *The Times* lamented the loss:

> A portrait of the greatest Englishman of his time by an artist who is arguably the best living English portraitist is an object of outstanding historical importance... Its destruction is a great misfortune.[31]

Sutherland's other portraits include one of Kenneth Clark but those of the Queen Mother and his fellow-OM, Dorothy Hodgkin, never progressed beyond the sketch stage.

In the early 1970s, Sutherland returned to drawing Welsh scenes. One sketch of a pink erect column of rock excited Greta Garbo when she visited him at his French home, to which he had repaired for tax reasons:

> 'O, la, la,' she said when she came to the penile monolith. Graham peered over. 'Oh, madame, c'est un peu phallique,' he conceded apologetically, and explained that he was not guilty – the rock really looked like that and was that colour too. 'Mais, je l'aime!' said Garbo. 'C'est fantastique.'[32]

Like Steer and unlike John, Sutherland was always a neat and elegant dresser; also like Steer and unlike John, he was never a Royal Academician. Sutherland died in 1980, at the age of 76. The summary of his work in the *DNB* was:

> In the last twenty years of his career he was a celebrity but, understandably in the heyday of abstract painting, his reputation suffered an eclipse and he had few advocates among English critics. His work continued to be admired abroad and it is symptomatic that the memorial exhibition held in 1982 was warmly received in Darmstadt but less so at the Tate.[33]

While there was only that brief overlap of a year or so between John and Sutherland, there was a much longer one between the appointment to the Order of the next painter, **Ben Nicholson**, in 1968 and Sutherland's death in 1980. Nicholson lived in Switzerland from 1958–71. When he returned to live in England, it was partly because of the confusion of language – 'when I picked up a phone I never knew what language I might hear' – and, in any case, 'my roots are in England and I wanted to return to them'.[34]

Nicholson's appointment to the Order was greeted as entirely appropriate:

> Ben Nicholson is – sometimes to a maddening extent – a perfectionist in everything connected with his painting, and it is safe to say that the Order of Merit will strike him as a very happy choice of honour … That he remains a towering figure in the recent history of British painting goes, for most people, without saying.[35]

Nicholson was, as one critic said, 'born to the purple of English art'. His father, Sir William, mother, Mabel Pryde, and uncle, James Pryde, were all painters of distinction. After his first fiancée married his widowed father, he threw the engagement ring into the Thames and went on to marry three artists: the painter, Winifred Roberts (or Dacre); the sculptor, Barbara Hepworth; and the photographer, Felicitas Vogler. Two of his daughters became artists and one married a future Director of the Tate Gallery, Alan Bowness.

Nicholson attended, briefly and rather perfunctorily, the Slade School of Art and claimed he learned more at a nearby hotel playing billiards with Paul Nash. Because of chronic asthma, from which he always suffered, he did not serve in the First World War and spent many of his early years in warmer climates.

With his first wife, in the 1920s, Nicholson painted still lifes and landscapes, with only an occasional abstract. In Paris, he encountered the Cubism that was to be so influential in his work. In Cornwall, he (and fellow-painter, Christopher Wood) discovered Alfred Wallis, a retired fisherman cum rag-and-bone merchant turned 'primitive' painter.

In 1932, Nicholson began his professional and personal relationship with Barbara Hepworth. With Henry Moore and Paul Nash, they founded the group, Unit One. Nicholson's work, influenced by contacts with Miro, Braque and Mondrian, became increasingly abstract and his first all-white reliefs were completed in 1934. According to the *DNB* entry (written by his son-in-law):

> The white reliefs are today generally agreed to be Nicholson's major contribution to English and European Modernism. They gave Nicholson a leading position in the avant-garde in art of the time.[36]

In the Second World War, Nicholson and Hepworth moved from Hampstead to St Ives and were followed by Naum Gabo, the Russion constructivist sculptor, with whom Nicholson had edited the notable *Circle, an International Survey of Constructive Art*. In Cornwall, Nicholson

> was pursuing what might be described as post-Cubist still-life painting, in which the shapes and colours of jugs and bottles on a table top were abstracted into grand pictorial compositions. It was these in particular that gave Nicholson an international reputation in the late 1940s. He won numerous awards...[37]

Indeed, championed by Herbert Read, he became, alongside Henry Moore, the British Council's 'official artist' and featured in 40 of their exhibitions between 1947–60. A retrospective exhibition in 1954 toured continental Europe before coming to rest at the Tate, which staged another retrospective in 1969 to mark Nicholson's seventy-fifth birthday. After his death, a 1956 work *La Boutique Fantasque* sold at auction for £1.1m. Like Sutherland, he was never a Royal Academician.

Nicholson was always a keen ball-player (which he linked with proficiency in art) and he often timed his London exhibitions to coincide with Wimbledon; at the age of 86, he regretted that he could no longer play tennis with quite his old enthusiasm. He went on painting (and making puns) to the end.

He died in 1982. On the occasion of the 1993 Tate retrospective, a critic wrote:

> The cross that Ben Nicholson has to bear is that he is Britain's best-known abstract painter. This is a cross, because Britain has a national antipathy to abstraction...[He] emerges from this exhibition as the creator of a true, and truly British, modern art.[38]

Nicholson's death had left the Order of Merit without a painter but the 'seat' was taken within two years by the Australian, **Sidney Nolan**, who was appointed OM in 1983. He was a sixth-generation Irish immigrant; his father was a tram driver in Melbourne and his grandfather (a self-taught artist) was one of the policemen who pursued the gang of another Irish immigrant in the 1880s: the bushranger, Ned Kelly. It was on that famous episode in Australian folklore that Nolan was to base the paintings that made him famous.

Nolan left school at 14 and did odd jobs. While painting posters for a hat factory, he enrolled for night classes at the National Gallery in Melbourne, as well as absorbing in libraries as much as he could of Western art and literature. He stowed away unsuccessfully on a ship for Britain. Then, along with other young painters, he was taken up by a rich solicitor and art patron, John Reed, in the artistically-renowned district of Heidelberg. They were the 'Angry Penguins', who flourished from 1940–45 around an avant-garde magazine of that name, reflecting the anger of young Australian artists trying to fire their indigenous art with a new and radical spirit. In 1988, on the Australian bicentennial, an exhibition in London entitled *Angry Penguin* included all 23 of Nolan's first series of Kelly paintings.

During the Second World War, Nolan was sent to an army camp in the north of Victoria and this later inspired a series of landscapes of the vast space and light of Australia: *Outback* and *Interior*. To avoid front-line service in New Guinea, he deserted and lived under a false name but was able to take advantage of a post-war amnesty.

Immediately after the war, Nolan began work on his first series of Kelly paintings: the outlaw depicted wearing a black pot with a wide slit for his eyes or on a horse like a centaur. Nolan himself said:

> Kelly isn't only Kelly for me. He's a symbol – the thing in the bush, if you like.[39]

Later, Nolan also made series of paintings on other Australian historical episodes: Mrs Eliza Fraser, who was shipwrecked in 1836, captured by aborigines and rescued by a convict whom she later betrayed; Burke and Wills, the explorers who starved to death after completing the first south–north crossing of the continent by white men; and Gallipoli, where Australia was blooded as a nation.

In 1949, Kenneth Clark, the art critic and historian (and future OM) encouraged the young painter to come to England but warned him that he might never go back to Australia. That proved to be largely true and, much later, Nolan talked of being 'suspended' between the two countries. Clark promoted him in Britain as:

> the first artist to give us the real flavour of that strange continent. He has extracted its essences: the red desert, the dead animals, the stranded, ridiculous towns.[40]

Nolan was always involved with the theatre, from 1939, when he designed the sets for Serge Lifar's *Icare* in Australia, through *The Rite of Spring* at Covent Garden in 1962 to *Samson et Dalila* there in the 1980s. In 1970, he toured Central Australia with Benjamin Britten. Nolan often painted to music – the same Beethoven quartets 30–40 times a day.

Nolan's ascent of the honours ladder was initially slow but accelerated rapidly in the last few years of his life. The awards illustrated the division of his life between Australia and Britain. His first honour (CBE) was in the British Prime Minister's List in 1963, while his next, a knighthood in 1981, was in the Australian List, although he no longer lived there permanently. When – four years after the OM – he received the highest Australian honour (AC) in 1988, while his London address was shown, the citation was 'for service to the visual arts and to the advancement of art appreciation in Australia and overseas'.

Recognition from the Royal Academy came late, after most of his official honours; he was elected an Associate in 1987 and a full Academician in 1991, the year before his death at the age of 75.

To outsiders, there was something distasteful about Nolan's long public quarrel with Patrick White, the Nobel Prize-winning author of *Voss*, the dust jacket of which Nolan had illustrated in the days of their friendship. After Nolan's second wife committed suicide in 1974, White blamed him for it and, in an autobiography, accused him of 'throwing himself on another woman's breast before the ashes were barely cold'. Nolan retaliated by portraying White and his lover in an unfavourable light in his work and by secretly buying the film rights of *Voss*. Outliving White by two years, Nolan was able to have the last word: 'I'm fit, heterosexual; I produced the goods and he couldn't.'[41] A few weeks later, he himself was dead.

Nolan's critical success in the 1940s and 1950s, when his pictures entered the Tate and the Royal Collection, was not maintained. His *Notes for Oedipus* series in 1976 sold only one painting – to his own dealer. He was pained when the Melbourne Cultural Centre commissioned but rejected a series of paintings. His old champion, Kenneth Clark, still defended him, in 1977:

> When time has weeded out his colossal output and the didactic snobbery of abstract art has declined, he will be of even greater importance.[42]

Nolan died at his Jacobean home in Herefordshire on 27 November 1992. The obituaries were quite fulsome:

> a born painter with magical gifts, who arrived on the scene at just the right time to make a major contribution to Australia's collective imagination and sense of national identity... able to embody the essence and atmosphere of the island continent and to give it its own mythology.[43]

> Australia's most famous painter... In time to come it is his critics, not Nolan, who will be found wanting. He was one of the great artists of the 20th century.[44]

Only a year elapsed after Sidney Nolan's death before the appointment of the next painter to the Order of Merit: **Lucian Freud**, in 1993, two days before his seventy-first birthday. Ten years before he had accepted a CH. Like a number of earlier painter OMs, however, he is not a Royal Academician.

His lifestyle is closer to Augustus John than to any other painter OM but it does not attract the same attention, since it is now much more readily accepted than in John's day. He has been married and divorced twice; his first wife was the daughter of Jacob Epstein, the sculptor, and his second was the daughter of the Fourth Marquess of Dufferin and Ava. In addition to two children from his first marriage, he has had seven others by two women; in his mid-80s his partner is now a woman 50 years his junior.

Lucian Freud's father was an architect in Berlin and his grandfather was Sigmund, the founder of psychoanalysis. With many (but sadly, not all) of the family, Lucian came to Britain in the Jewish exodus of the 1930s, was naturalised and served as an ordinary seaman on a merchant ship during the Second World War. Having been to the East Anglian School of Painting and Drawing, he settled in London and began exhibiting at an early age, as well as teaching at the Slade School of Art, with only a brief spell painting in France and Greece.

He was briefly interested in surrealism and his first major picture from that time, an image of a sofa and a zebra's head, sold 50 years later for £0.5 million. Now, he is variously described as 'one of the great British painters of the twentieth century' or (sometimes with the cautionary 'arguably') 'Britain's greatest living figurative painter'. There are frequent references, however, to the sharp brutality and the cold detachment of his work. One critic of the eightieth year retrospective at Tate Britain in 2002 had no doubts:

> all sorts of rubbish about him…salacious stuff…tabloid pap… absolute seriousness and purposefulness of his art…This retrospective proves that Freud is more interested in beauty than he is in cruelty…we find it so easy to mistake truth for ugliness. Freud doesn't. Is he the greatest living painter? Without a shadow of doubt.[45]

Lucian Freud is meticulous and honest in his approach to portraiture, requiring his subjects to come to him for many sittings. A dozen or so women have posed for him repeatedly, frequently naked on a low bed in a bare studio. He met his mother every morning for breakfast in a patisserie and she sat for him over 1,000 times in six years. He has painted his wives, daughters and others in his family and his largest portrait, with (unusually for him) five people in it – *Large Interior, W11 (After Watteau)* – sold in 1998 for £3.5 million; it was the highest price ever paid for a work by a contemporary British artist. He is a tough critic of his own work, sometimes taking years to complete a painting or never doing so. He demands, of a painting by himself or anyone else, that it 'astonish, disturb, seduce and convince'.[46]

Lucian Freud is a ruthless self-portraitist – starting at 17 – and he is (probably) the only OM artist to have painted a full-length full frontal nude of himself, at the age of 70 and wearing only shoes. Jeffrey Bernard once drew a portrait in the words of Lucian Freud:

> He has cracked the nut of how to conduct a double life. This is very important to him. I have spent endless afternoons with him in betting shops; but then Lucian goes home, puts on the flannel suit, shaves and bathes, then appears pristine and lovely, standing toe to toe with Andrew Devonshire.[47]

In fact, he has done more than stand toe to toe with the late Duke of Devonshire, who owns 12 of his works. He has painted the Duke, his wife and other members of the family and the portraits hang in Chatsworth House, alongside those by Joshua Reynolds and John Singer Sargent. The Duke described his first glimpse of his wife's portrait at the artist's studio in the 1950s:

> Not unusually, Lucian was having financial trouble and the bailiff was in. I heard the bailiff asking Lucian who the portrait was of and then saying, 'Thank God that woman's not my wife.'[48]

In 1994, the Dulwich Picture Gallery was the scene for an interesting contrast between four recent rough Freud nudes and the older smoother ones of Rubens and Lely. Two of the Freud paintings were a contrast in themselves: the towering and masterful male *Leigh under the Skylight*, standing on a table, and the enormous female with roll of fat falling upon roll as she slumps on a sofa that looks dangerously unsafe under her weight: the arresting title is *Benefits Supervisor Resting*.

Lucian Freud's eventual agreement to paint the Queen was ascribed to his friendship with Robert Fellowes, who was for many years Her Majesty's Private Secretary. The eventual portrait startled some people. So did the artist's unflinching approach to painting the face of the 75-year-old monarch. The reaction of *The Times* was:

> The outcome is a painting about advancing age, defined with great insight by a painter who now seems closer in spirit to Rembrandt than to any of his contemporaries ... [This is a] painful, brave, honest, stoical and above all clear-sighted image.[49]

The measured Palace comment on what is clearly no work of sycophancy was: 'an intensely powerful image'. In years to come, perhaps it will be taken to mark the later years of the Queen's long reign, rather as Annigoni's 1955 portrait symbolised the early years.

The sculptors

In addition to the nine painters honoured with the Order of Merit, there have been two sculptors: Henry Moore in 1963 and Anthony Caro in 2000. (G. F. Watts, one of the original 12 OMs, was honoured more for his painting than his sculpting.)

Henry Moore received the offer in August 1963 when, despite his instructions that no mail should be forwarded, an envelope from Buckingham Palace disturbed a holiday with family and friends in Dubrovnik, on the Croatian coast. The letter inside asked him to respond with a telegram saying 'Yes Moore' or 'No Moore'. A friend recalled:

> 'When Henry handed in a telegram saying "Yes Moore" addressed to Buckingham Palace, the porter thought we were drunk.' They went out to celebrate and, when they returned to the Excelsior [Hotel] they *were* a bit high.[50]

The honour was greeted as deserved but late. *The Times* wrote that he

> is often quite simply referred to as the greatest of living sculptors. His art is a distinct creation – so distinct that to speak of 'a Henry Moore'

19 Henry Moore.

at once calls up a mental image ... the word 'grandeur' must be used to describe the effect he has produced on a generation.[51]

As early as 1944, when he was 47, Henry Moore was being seriously promoted for the Order of Merit. The King's Private Secretary noted that:

E. Maclagan [Director of the Victoria and Albert Museum] and others have strongly recommended Henry Moore, sculptor, as a possible OM. I know nothing of his work, but they said he was in the Rodin category – anyhow a clear alpha. His age (46) is in his favour.[52]

Lascelles, like Hardinge before him, was keen on keeping down the age of appointment to the Order.

Kenneth Clark also supported Moore as the:

> greatest artist of his generation, not only in England but anywhere else
> [but] those who can't swallow modern art can't swallow Moore...Has
> however recently done a number of drawings of tube shelters and
> of war ruins which even the most academically minded have had to
> admit are masterly...not simply a good or clear artist...largeness and
> nobility...eminently suitable recipient of the OM.[53]

It was to be another 20 years before Moore was sufficiently acceptable to
be admitted to the Order of Merit – in 1963, at the age of 65. In the meantime,
he had declined a knighthood, because he thought it would distance him from
his assistants; 'Good morning, Sir Henry' was a greeting he did not relish.
He passed through the halfway house of the CH – and even that not until
1955. Moore explained his reluctance to accept a knighthood:

> I didn't want to be rude, but titles change one's name and one's opinion
> of oneself. The initials aren't so bad. No one comprehends them.[54]

His biographer explained the puzzlement of Americans at Moore's decision:

> [They] could never understand that the CH and to an even greater extent
> the Order of Merit were vastly greater honours than a knighthood. To
> them it seemed anomalous that Epstein could call himself Sir Jacob while
> Moore remained plain Mr. All explanations about the proliferation of
> knighthoods among backbench MPs and businessmen were wasted: no
> initials, however distinguished, had the courtly associations of a title.[55]

Well before his honours, Moore was certainly a 'successful artist', who
had come a long way from his roots as a miner's son in Yorkshire. A father,
who saw schoolteaching as a way out of the coalfields for his children, and
an art teacher, who recognised the young Henry's talents, set him on the
road to being an art teacher himself. Gassed in the First World War, Lance
Corporal Moore's ex-serviceman's grant enabled him to go to proper art
school in Leeds. He wanted to be a sculptor and won a scholarship to study
at the Royal College of Art, where he later taught.

In the 1930s, Moore was already demonstrating the originality of carving
in stone and wood on which his fame was to rest but he had yet to make
money. When Robert Sainsbury bought one of his works in 1933 for £160,
it represented half-a-year's income.

When his Hampstead studio was bombed in 1940, Moore moved to Perry
Green in Hertfordshire, where he was to live and work until his death nearly
50 years later. He was diverted by Kenneth Clark to be an official war artist

and his drawings of those sheltering in the London underground and of miners at the coalface added to his reputation.

Moore's return to sculpture was marked by a number of his works being bought for public spaces, outside major buildings from New York to Bonn, from Washington to Rome. Our parliamentarians are constantly interviewed in front of his *Knife Edge Two Piece* opposite the Houses of Parliament. One suggestion, from Prince Philip to design a fountain for Windsor, he declined, adding 'Why don't you design it and I'll sign it!'[56] His contribution to Coronation year was a *King and Queen* above a remote Scottish loch. In his old age, the Queen opened the extended galleries of the Moore Sculpture Gallery in Leeds and he presented her with a copy of his facsimile *Sheep Sketch Book*.

Moore's female figures of the 1950s gave way to more abstract works in the 1960s. Their rounded forms (which reminded him of his mother's back which he had rubbed with liniment) – often punctuated by holes – became unmistakable. As they were usually made in editions, they numbered around 6,000 in all, making Moore a rich man. At his peak, nine-tenths of Moore's income came from abroad and his international fame was recognised by many countries, including Italy, Austria, Germany and, eventually, France.

While he enjoyed from his early days the staunch support of men like Kenneth Clark and Herbert Read, Moore was publicly reviled by the conservative elements of the Royal Academy, of which he was never a member. He was active, however, in other aspects of public artistic life: a trustee of the National and Tate Galleries and a member of the Arts Council, the Royal Fine Art Commission and the National Theatre Board; in 1967, he was elected to a distinction more usually accorded to literary figures: the fellowship of the British Academy.

A strong social conscience led Moore to establish in 1977 a foundation (with assets of £20–30m), which not only arranged his own exhibitions but funded many activities devoted to sculpture. His work was summarised by Alan Bowness in the *DNB* entry:

> his best work [has] a universal relevance which speaks to people of whatever race or religion in a way that no artist before Moore had been able to achieve. He was regarded, and is likely to remain, a towering figure in twentieth-century art.[57]

Moore's obituaries were epic – and kind – and went beyond his art:

> Since the death of Sir Winston Churchill, Henry Moore had been the most internationally-acclaimed of Englishmen...attained a stature almost unknown in the history of British artists...those of us who are not geniuses can still draw encouragement from so impressive an example.[58]

Ironically, the greatest sculptor of our century came from England, a country that has never played a significant role in the field of sculpture. However, his insistence on the close relationship between art and nature appears typically English.[59]

At his memorial service, the Queen was represented by Moore's friend from Hampstead days – and fellow-OM – Solly Zuckerman. Margaret Thatcher attended.

A few years later, on his centenary in 1998, there was questioning of Moore's reputation. While paying tribute to him as a 'heavyweight' and to his foundation as 'the most influential force behind the resurgence of British sculpture', a *Times* leader commented on the sheer volume of his work, which

> became over familiar. It lost its power to surprise. Only time will judge if his reputation is merited. But as far as the contemporary world is concerned, less would have been more.[60]

Henry Moore had been dead for nearly 14 years when his one-time assistant, **Anthony Caro**, was appointed to the Order of Merit in 2000. The older man had lived to see his pupil receive a CBE in 1969 but just missed Caro's knighthood in 1987. Nor did he see him gain the Henry Moore Grand Prize in 1991. Moore also missed the publicity surrounding the younger man's rejection in 1990 of an offer to join the Royal Academy, the institution of which he also had never been a member. Anthony Caro declined the offer because he did not share the beliefs and aims of the Academy and doubted whether his work would be shown to its best advantage in the summer exhibitions.

Anthony Caro admits to being sheepish about his knighthood:

> I realise Bacon and Moore didn't accept theirs but I think I felt a bit less secure than they did . . . and my Mum was pleased. It really made a difference to me. Not to my work, though. It was just nice.[61]

The son of a stockbroker, Anthony Caro served in the Fleet Air Arm at the end of the Second World War and studied engineering at Cambridge and art at the Regent Street Polytechnic and the Royal Academy Schools. He was Henry Moore's assistant from 1951–53.

According to Moore's biographer, the older man

> appreciated [Caro's] quick and sensitive mind (honed at Cambridge), for the two established an affectionate master–pupil relationship that was unique [at the Moore studio].[62]

Not surprisingly, Caro's early work bore the imprint of Moore. He was 'a quite traditional figure sculptor, with relatively lush bronze nudes'.[63] Then came what one critic called

> his sudden apostasy from figuration to abstraction around 1959, a move inspired by meeting pioneer American sculptor David Smith [which led to a] progressively elegant repertoire of welded metal forms.[64]

Later he turned also to what were described as 'table-top' sculptures. He did away with pedestals so that his work could be seen on the ground itself. He also moved to working in bronze, wood and clay on various scales. He also found time to be an influential teacher at St Martin's College of Art for many years.

In the Swinging Sixties, Henry Moore, as the Grand Old Man of British sculpture, was ripe for dethroning and, in 1967, 41 younger artists (including Anthony Caro and other former assistants or pupils of Moore) wrote to *The Times* about the proposed housing in an extension to the Tate Gallery of a gift of his works from Moore. They repudiated 'any attempt to predetermine greatness for an individual in a publicly financed form of permanent enshrinement'. Moore took unkindly to this but Caro assured him that they had not meant the letter in any personal way. Anthony Caro said that his wife (an artist) had advised him not to sign the letter, to which Moore replied that he should have followed her advice.[65]

Anthony Caro indulges in what he calls dialogues with great artists of the past, such as his *Descent From the Cross (after Rembrandt)*, *Le Dejeuner sur l'herbe* – after Manet – and *Chair* – after Van Gogh. Nevertheless, he confesses to being daunted at the comparisons:

> Take someone big from history, stand beside them and you feel a bit intimidated ... [but] painting can feed sculpture ... old art can feed new art. Art feeds on art ... I don't think there's a divide between abstract and figurative art. That's a mistake a lot of people make. Good or bad is the divide.[66]

His exhibition at the Tate in 1991 was entitled *Sculpture towards architecture* and he has produced large pieces called 'sculpitecture', which he liked people to enter, climb up and walk around inside. One such was *Octagon Tower*, which weighed 25 tons and spiralled 22 feet into the air. He collaborated with his fellow-OM, the architect Norman Foster, in the design of the Millenium footbridge across the Thames.

Like Moore, his first 'father in sculpture' (Smith was the second), Anthony Caro has been accorded a great exhibition in Italy. His was in Rome in

1992, 20 years after Moore's in Florence. When he had an exhibition at the National Gallery in 1998, one critic concluded:

> blast of sculptural vitality...fertility of his inventiveness. If Caro continues to perform with as much acrobatic zest as he displays here, his late period will be prodigious and full of surprises.[67]

In acknowledging his mission to push the boundaries of the possible and the acceptable, Anthony Caro recalled that his son (when six) talked about 'the onward of art'. 'That's rather nice. I do think about the onward of sculpture.'[68]

The architects

The four architects who have been honoured with the Order of Merit were all knighted Royal Academicians by the time they received the Order. They were all Fellows of the Royal Institute of British Architects and three of them – Spence was the exception – were awarded the Royal Gold Medal of the Institute. None of them overlapped in the Order. The first architect to become an OM was **Edwin Landseer Lutyens**, in 1942. It took him a long time to reach the Order and he enjoyed it for only two years.

In 1928, that inveterate adviser, Lord Esher, in a review of possible OMs, was saying: 'In due course, I feel sure that Winston and Lutyens will be recognised as possessing *genius*.'[69] Esher had been influential in having Lutyens' design for the British pavilion at the Rome Exhibition of 1911 transformed into the headquarters of the British School there.

In 1937, Morshead was asked to consult Kenneth Clark as to whether he rated Lutyens or Scott highest for the OM, who he reported as saying:

> Lutyens, without a moment's hesitation...his reputation stands today probably as low as it will ever stand...fashion has moved on, past him. But even now, at the nadir of his fortunes, while his style is out-of-date without yet being historical, he overtowers all rivals, including the honest plodder Gilbert Scott [who could not] have conceived and carried through the truly Imperial glories of Delhi...Lutyens would add lustre to the Order, and would be approved in their heart of hearts by the members of the profession too.[70]

At the same time, strong support came from Vincent Harris, RA, architect of government buildings in Whitehall, who told Morshead:

> Lutyens is head and shoulders above the rest...greatest architect since Wren...posterity will realise his influence upon his whole generation;

20 Sir Edwin Lutyens.

his loftiness of perception has raised the whole level of architectural achievement.[71]

In 1941, Churchill, now Prime Minister, also supported Lutyens' case and so, in 1942, Lutyens was appointed OM. He described the insignia as a 'wee locket' to his grandson, Nicholas Ridley, and signed the letter 'Your Grand O-Man Grandfather'.[72]

Lutyens was knighted in 1918. His puckish sense of humour, for which he was renowned, came to the fore at the Palace investiture:

a very nervous man next to him asked what the procedure was. 'Quite simple,' Father told him. 'The Lord Chamberlain will call out your name and lead you up to the throne; then all you have to do is to go down on one knee on a cushion and sing 'God Save the King'. 'But I don't even know the words!' 'Don't worry, the King will help you out with them.'[73]

In 1930, on the conclusion of his great work in New Delhi, he was made Knight Commander of the Order of the Indian Empire.

'Ned' Lutyens was the son of an army officer, who painted horses and helped Edwin Landseer to sculpt the lions at the foot of Nelson's column in Trafalgar Square. Landseer wished to adopt the baby Lutyens (who was the eleventh of 14 children); although his mother declined the offer, she did name the child after the sculptor. Lutyens is a German name and the family had come over and acquired British nationality in the 1740s.

At 16, Lutyens was a pupil in an architect's office and, by 20, he had his own practice in London. He made his name by designing a brilliant series of country houses, mostly in the Home Counties and especially in Surrey. The 'Elgar of architecture' was one description of him. The early influence in these houses came from the Arts and Crafts school of William Morris but it developed into a Queen Anne style, with dominant roofs, chimneys and windows and, even later, into what his biographer, who also wrote the *DNB* entry, described as 'a high-Renaissance palazzo in the Roman Doric key' at Heathcote, Ilkley. It is as the designer of so many sought-after country houses that Lutyens is now most frequently recalled. His Home Counties houses are now reproduced in 'Lutyensesque' executive homes.

One of the last of Lutyens' 'country houses' was, in fact, a castle, the last to be built in this country: Drogo, on Dartmoor. It was designed for Julius Drewe, who had made a fortune from the grocery chain of Home and Colonial Stores. Lutyens also designed the renovation of his wife's family home: Knebworth House in Hertfordshire and the conversion work on Lindisfarne Castle, off the Northumbrian coast. When he visited grand houses, the humour would still come out. Staying with Sir George Sitwell and his wife, he loved to ask the butler in the morning; 'Is Lady Ida down?'[74]

Lutyens married well. He designed an extravagant jewel case with which to win the hand of Lady Emily Lytton, daughter of the First Earl of Lytton, a former Viceroy of India; it worked, although her family were less enthusiastic.

In 1911, at the Imperial Durbar in Delhi, King-Emperor George V announced that the capital of India would be moved there from Calcutta. Lutyens, a Viceroy's son-in-law, was chosen to design the new centre of British India, in collaboration (at his suggestion) with an old friend, Herbert Baker, who had designed the South African Capital Buildings in Pretoria. The original plan to complete New Delhi in four years was frustrated by the First World War and it took until 1930; a mere 17 years later, the British Raj had ended. Indian legend, anyway, said that a new city in Delhi foretold the end of the current dynasty.

Lutyens' crowning glory was the Viceroy's House, now Rashtrapati Bhavan, the residence of the President of India – according to some, he built the last palace in the world. It embodied the British imperial ideal but its great dome was based on an Indian ruin he had seen.

Lutyens designed other government buildings, the most notable of which was the British Embassy in Washington, an impressive echo of the imperial grandeur he had built in New Delhi. He designed some commercial buildings in London: Grosvenor House in Park Lane, the Midland Bank in Poultry, the headquarters of what is now BP in Finsbury Circus and a small gem, 120 Pall Mall, next to what is now the Institute of Directors. Late in life, he designed the George V memorial at Windsor and, appropriately for Landseer's godson, the fountains in Trafalgar Square, as memorials to the sailor-OMs, Jellicoe and Beatty.

After the First World War, Lutyens designed memorials which have come to symbolise the enormous human sacrifice in that conflict. The Cenotaph itself, of which he produced a sketch for Lloyd George on the day he was asked, was made permanent in stone and is now central to the national remembrance of the two wars. On the battlefields themselves, he designed, for the Imperial War Graves Commission, a number of the cemeteries and memorials, including the largest, at Thiepval, to the 73,000 'Missing of the Somme'; he also designed the simple Stone of Remembrance, which is in many of the cemeteries. It is easy to sideline such work but it is difficult to deny its place in the national psyche.

Lutyens' work also included the church and the surrounding houses in the central square of Hampstead Garden Suburb and Campion Hall in Oxford. And he designed the first stage sets for the whimsical play *Peter Pan*, written by another OM, J. M. Barrie, and the miniature dolls' house for Queen Mary at Windsor Castle.

After his death, Lutyens' reputation, in the austere post-war period, slumped. But by 1981, Lutyens was the first twentieth-century architect to have a major Arts Council exhibition in London, and one critic spoke of his 'restoration to critical respectability after two generations of disdain'.[75] Another referred to a

> ... flood of new books whose authors are divided only between those who believe that Lutyens was a better architect than Christopher Wren and those who content themselves merely with the thought that he was just as good ... When modernism was in the ascendant, Lutyens' standing was at its lowest. Now that modernism is in decline, he is being promoted ...[76]

Giles Gilbert Scott had, unknowingly, been stalking Lutyens for a place in the Order of Merit for some years. Some of the papers dealing with him were in the style of 'Lutyens v Gilbert Scott', since there was thought not to be room in the Order for two architects – and Scott was 11 years younger. With Lutyens dead, however, Scott was quickly back in consideration in early 1944.

Morshead considered that while he was not 'so great a man as Lutyens', he was 'definitely up to OM standard in a rather meagre generation. The one question is – when?' As Scott was unlikely to be elected PRA in succession to another architect, Lutyens, Morshead suggested he might receive it 'now'.[77] Lascelles pretended to be horrified:

> you, whose very initials [OM] should safeguard you against such back-sliding, urge that Giles Scott might be given an OM 'to compensate his loss of the PRA'.
>
> O tempora; O Morshead! Surely the only point we ought to allow ourselves to consider is whether he is, or is not, an alpha plus architect?
>
> You might as well recommend an officer for the VC because the Colonel had seduced his wife.[78]

The King approved Scott's appointment and informed the Prime Minister, who had no comment. The Private Secretary had told the King that with nine vacancies in the Order, three new Members (Passfield, Dale and Scott) was not excessive.[79] The new OM was welcomed by *The Times Weekly Edition* in those familiar terms:

> as a great architect who has attained a position perhaps unparalleled since Wren.[80]

And Lutyens was scarcely cold in St Paul's.

Scott was born into the purple of his profession. His grandfather, Sir (George) Gilbert Scott was a notable Victorian architect and is buried in Westminster Abbey. He designed the Martyrs' Memorial in Oxford and, in London, the Albert Memorial, St Pancras Station and the complex of government buildings that is today the Foreign and Commonwealth Office.

The young Gilbert Scott was even more precocious than Lutyens. By the age of 22, he had designed an Anglican cathedral (in Liverpool), somewhat to the embarrassment of the selection committee when they discovered both his age and his religion – he was a Roman Catholic. The older architect who was assigned to be his 'collaborator' died within three years, after which Scott worked on his own. The foundation stone was laid by Edward VII in 1904, but it was his great granddaughter, Elizabeth II, who attended the service of dedication on its completion in 1978; the notoriously slow building of cathedrals had not been helped by two world wars. The part-completed building had been consecrated in 1924 and the topmost stone of the large central tower had been laid by Scott himself in 1941. The completed building was described as

> one of the largest cathedrals in the world ... a gigantic, soaring barn yet full of hidden corners and surprises ... Wonderful also is the quality of the stonework and masonry, and its carving and detail.[81]

Other churches that Scott was naturally commissioned to design relied, like Liverpool, on mass for effect, with a look of strength but careful regard for detail. They include the chapels of Charterhouse and Ampleforth, the Roman Catholic cathedral in Oban and the Carmelite Church in Kensington, close to St Mary Abbot's, which his grandfather had designed. The young Scott also designed a large religious building, the tower of which dominates the South London skyline: the Salvation Army training college at Denmark Hill.

Scott was far from being an exclusively ecclesiastical architect. In the 1930s, he had provided both Cambridge and Oxford with new library buildings and Guinness with its Park Royal brewery. When Rennie's Regency Waterloo Bridge was demolished in 1936, it was Scott who designed the simple five-arch bridge that replaced it in 1945. He was familiar with building on the Thames; both Battersea and Bankside power stations were his. The latter (controversially sited across from St Paul's) was opened only in the year of his death, 1960, and fulfilled its purpose for only a couple of decades. After skilful interior conversion, it now thrives as the home of Tate Modern, with Scott's original turbine hall left empty to the building's original height.

The heavy bombing of the Second World War provided many architectural opportunities and Scott was entrusted with two of the major restorations in London. He had to rebuild the House of Commons chamber in its original confrontational form, although without the Gothic ornamentation still to be found in the House of Lords. He also rebuilt the Guildhall with a finely proportioned interior.

Scott's smallest 'building' is also probably the best-known: the red telephone box. He won the Royal Fine Art Commission competition in 1924 (the year he was knighted), with a prototype that came to stand in the courtyard of the Royal Academy. Its distinctive roof was supposedly based on the urns on the exterior of Dulwich Picture Gallery and, eventually, nearly 80,000 were erected throughout the country.

When Scott died in 1960, he was buried alongside his wife in the tomb he had designed for them against the walls of Liverpool Cathedral, while a commemorative plaque was placed in the centre of the floor of the nave.

In the way that Lutyens was linked with New Delhi and Scott with Liverpool, so their successor in the Order of Merit, **Basil Spence**, was best known as the architect of the rebuilt Coventry Cathedral. Indeed, one obituary recorded:

> The climax of official recognition came to him in 1962 when, in the wake of all the attention Coventry Cathedral had aroused, he was awarded the OM.[82]

Spence had been knighted and elected an RA only in 1960 and, at 55, was a relatively young recruit to the Order. Lutyens and Scott were both knighted and elected RAs over 20 years before their admission to the Order. The son of an analytical chemist in the Indian Civil Service, Spence was born in that country not long before Lutyens began his long association with it and, after an outstanding career at architecture schools, Spence worked briefly in Lutyens' London office. Like his master, he began by designing country houses. After war service in the Royal Artillery, he made a name as the designer of exhibitions, including the Sea and Ships pavilion at the Festival of Britain on the South Bank.

Spence's career took a deliberate – and dramatic – turn in 1951, when he won the competition to design the new cathedral at Coventry. In his *Phoenix at Coventry*, he described his first visit to the ruins:

> one of the most deeply stirring and moving days I have ever spent...I saw the old Cathedral as standing clearly for the Sacrifice, one side of the Christian Faith, and I knew my task was to design a new one which would stand for the Triumph of the Resurrection...in my mind's eye, I got one of those pictures that architects sometimes get...a great nave and an altar that was an invitation to Communion, and a huge picture behind it...In those few moments the idea of the design was planted. In essence it never changed.[83]

When Spence was told on the telephone that he had won the competition, he fainted. He became an immediate celebrity and discovered a flair for public relations, especially in relation to fund-raising.

In 1956, the Queen laid the foundation stone, attending the consecration six years later. In addition to Sutherland's tapestry, the cathedral included sculpture by Joseph Epstein and stained glass by John Piper. Henry Moore was approached but his dislike of constraint put paid to his involvement. Spence's obituarist concluded that:

> His Coventry design showed one masterly stroke of imagination: the notion of preserving the ruins of the burnt-out, medieval cathedral as an approach to the new one. The building itself was orthodox in conception and structure, and so cannot be said to have made a permanent contribution to the art of architecture.[84]

Before the completion of Coventry Cathedral brought him many new commissions, Spence had designed houses, schools, churches and university buildings all over the country. After 1962, with the aid of partners in London and Edinburgh, he worked on the layout and initial design of Sussex University, sensitively exploiting its downland setting, and on a new library for Edinburgh University. Some of Spence's public buildings aroused considerable controversy. The plans for Knightsbridge Barracks and the Home Office in Queen's Gate were attacked for intruding on the leafy skylines of Hyde Park and St James's Park. He defended them passionately and they were built. The new Kensington Town Hall was completed after his death.

Abroad, Spence drew up the original plans in 1965 for the 'Beehive' in Wellington, the distinctive circular building with a honeycomb appearance that provides executive offices for the New Zealand Government. Another overseas project in 1971 was the chancery for the British Embassy in Rome (described in the *DNB* as 'not one of his happiest designs'), which had to stand comparison with a nearby masterpiece by Michelangelo.

Spence was an active President of the Royal Institute of British Architects (from 1958–60) and a conscientious member of the Royal Academy. He died in 1976. One obituary commented on his

> somewhat isolated position [as someone who] never became involved, early in his career, with the movements and groups seeking new ideals in architecture which occupied the energies of so many other young architects of his generation.
>
> He worked hard and was always confident of the validity of his own ideas, with which he became emotionally involved, causing him to feel persecuted when subjected to criticism of a kind that other architects might have accepted as all in the day's work.[85]

Over 20 years were to elapse after Spence's death in 1976 before another architect was to be admitted to the Order of Merit. The early 1990s saw a triumvirate of knighted British architects in the headlines. James Stirling died suddenly in 1992, only 12 days after his knighthood, leaving Norman Foster and Richard Rogers in possession of the high ground. By 1999, both were peers, with fluvial titles: Foster of Thames Bank and Rogers of Riverside. Foster had become an OM on 25 November 1997.

Norman Foster started with no particular advantage. One interviewer wrote:

> as a multimillionaire, he is as lean and hungry as he was when, as a cash-strapped, working-class student in Manchester, he sold ice cream and worked as a bouncer at nightclubs to pay his way through

architecture school. This was very unusual: then, as now, architecture was predominantly a middle-class profession.[86]

After leaving school at 16, Foster went through the Manchester and Yale Schools of Architecture before founding his own firm. His most famous early building, for an insurance company in Ipswich, was listed after only 25 years.

Two of Norman Foster's latest London commissions have aroused considerable public interest. The Millenium Footbridge across the Thames, on which Anthony Caro collaborated, closed two days after its opening in 2000 because of a dangerous wobble but the fitting of shock absorbers enabled it to re-open in 2002. The headquarters of the Greater London Authority, close to Tower Bridge, was also opened by the Queen, in 2002. Comment on its completion gave full credit to its unusual design:

> the craziest-looking building that has risen in the capital. Inside, columns lean, windows slant and slope, every office is on the curve . . . provocative and sensational . . . showpiece is the astonishing stair ramp circling through eight storeys . . . energy costs [have been kept] to a quarter of the average modern office building . . . cooled by borehole water from below the site . . . The guiding principle . . . is that it should be as open and accessible as an assembly or council debating chamber can be . . .
>
> [Outside is] the most beautifully paved space that London has seen in a century.[87]

Earlier, in London, the Foster partnership (which has 170 architects) had designed the cleverly contrived Sackler Gallery in a narrow courtyard of the Royal Academy, the Canary Wharf Tube Station, with its bank of escalators under one giant tunnel arch, and the renovation of the Great Court at the British Museum, surrounding the famous Reading Room where Marx and Gandhi had studied. This last development was described as

> a breathtaking refurbishment [which] at last does justice to one of the world's greatest collections.[88]

Outside London, Foster has designed for the universities of Oxford (the Economics Building) and Cambridge (the Law Faculty). In 1998, he won the Stirling Prize for the American Air Museum at Duxford near Cambridge. This award seemed to confirm the 'Fosterisation of Britain' by one who had 'a commanding position in British architecture' and whose 'reputation rides higher, the world around, than that of any other living architect'.[89]

Overseas, Foster's most publicised design has been for the rebuilding of the Reichstag in Berlin. It is a building unusually charged with history, the seat of the parliament of a recently united Germany from 1894 until the fire in 1933, which provided the excuse for the imposition of Nazi dictatorship. The

Russian captors in 1945 scrawled graffiti on the walls, which are preserved in the renovated building. The German Communist government used it as offices. In April 1999, Norman Foster symbolically handed a gigantic blue steel key to the President of the German Bundestag. If Goethe could see the new Reichstag, perhaps he would think it justified his description of architecture as frozen music.

Earlier overseas, Norman Foster's 42-storey headquarters building for the Hong Kong and Shanghai Bank in the former colony was the most expensive building of the 1980s. His design of the Stansted Airport terminal led on to that for Hong Kong international airport, the largest construction project in the world. There followed the towering Commerzbank headquarters in Frankfurt, the tallest building in Europe, with conservatory gardens rising through its 58 floors. In the hills behind Barcelona is the telecommunications tower, the express lift of which has glass doors facing outwards. In Riyadh, is the Al Faisaliah Tower, the first skyscraper in Saudi Arabia.

The Norman Foster partnership is frequently mentioned when large-scale schemes for the future are being discussed. These include the pedestriani-sation of much of Trafalgar and Parliament Squares; a similar project for the Elephant and Castle in South London; an enormous apartment block on the Thames at Battersea; a 98-storey Millennium Tower on the Baltic Exchange site (withdrawn after widespread opposition); London headquar-ters for Swiss Re, the re-insurers (called an 'erotic gherkin' by some); and a new Wembley Stadium. The drawingboard must be groaning under the weight of so many diverse commissions. Norman Foster himself, however, sees his greatest career achievement not as a building but as a quest:

A passion to change preconceptions, to question the status quo and stereotypes.[90]

11

THE MUSICIANS AND PERFORMERS

Composers

1. 1911   Sir Edward ELGAR
2. 1935   Ralph VAUGHAN WILLIAMS
3. 1965   Benjamin (Lord) BRITTEN
4. 1967   Sir William WALTON
5. 1983   Sir Michael TIPPETT

Choreographers

6. 1977   Sir Frederick ASHTON
7. 1992   Dame Ninette DE VALOIS

Performers

8. 1987   Yehudi (Lord) MENUHIN
9. 1991   Dame Joan SUTHERLAND

Actors

10. 1981   Laurence (Lord) OLIVIER
11. 1996   Sir John GIELGUD

The composers

It was not until 1911, in the Coronation Honours of George V, that the first musical figure was appointed – **Edward Elgar** – and even then doubts were expressed. Morley told the King's Private Secretary that he had 'always

21 Sir Edward Elgar by William Strang.

understood that he is the best English musician since Purcell', and Balfour wrote:

> Probably Elgar – in the opinion of the best judges – is the greatest living English composer; he is certainly thought to be so by the general body of concert-goers, and his name is better known abroad than that of any other English musician.[1]

Elgar was fulsome in expressing 'greatest gratitude ... my deep appreciation of the distinction'.[2] His wife described it as 'the one thing which really delights him'. A biographer records his concern

> that the Worcestershire people did not attach enough significance to the honour, for it had only been in existence for nine years and had not

yet acquired the almost mystical significance it holds today. He wrote
to Troyte in July 1911: 'I wish you wd write to the Worcester paper
and say a little what the Order of M really is! Some...think it is a
sort of degradation & quite unworthy of me...At the Investiture Sir
G. Trevelyan & I were marshalled next GCB & *before* GCMG (which
is Ld Beauchamp's highest distinction!) & of course before GCSI etc. It
was very nice.'[3]

The OM was not Elgar's last honour. After becoming Master of the King's
Musick in 1924, he was made a KCVO in 1928, a baronet in 1931 and a
GCVO in 1933, the year before he (and Delius and Holst) died. A peerage
eluded him. Although accused of lusting for honours, his reaction to the
KCVO was far from lustful:

HM has offered me the wretched *KCVO* (!!!) which awful thing I must
accept! Alas![4]

In the musical world, Elgar did not receive the highest honour (the Gold
Medal of the Royal Philharmonic Society) until 1925, after Delius and when
he was already 68.

Elgar had a self-reliant childhood and a fortunate marriage to a woman
who believed in his genius but he was afflicted with dramatic changes
of mood. After being a provincial bandmaster, who conducted both the
Worcester Glee Club and the county lunatic asylum band, he made his mark
in 1899 with the *Enigma Variations*, which have delighted and intrigued
audiences ever since. *The Dream of Gerontius* (based on the poem by
Cardinal Newman, who first offered it to Dvorak) followed in 1900 and
Elgar wrote on the score, 'This is the best of me'. The first performance was
disappointing: 'As far as I'm concerned music in England is dead,' wrote
Elgar. Initially, it fared better in Germany, where Richard Strauss famously
toasted 'the first English progressivist, Meister Edward Elgar'.

Over the following 20 years (until the death of his wife in 1920), Elgar
is credited with his greatest creativity, breaking the musical 'ice age' after
Purcell and becoming the 'first English composer since Purcell to achieve
more than provincial status',[5] who 'single-handedly propelled Britain back
into the mainstream of music'.[6] There were the concertos for violin, performed first by Fritz Kreisler in 1910 and later by the youthful future OM,
Yehudi Menuhin, and for cello, regularly the best-selling classical recording
in the country 70 years later.

Elgar produced two Coronation pieces: the *Ode* in 1902 and the *March* in
1911, in which year his *Second Symphony* was dedicated to the memory of
Edward VII. He had already produced the *Pomp and Circumstance Marches*,
including that 'alternative' national anthem, *Land of Hope and Glory*, which
has grown progressively more popular as the empire it lauded has dwindled.

In his declining years, Elgar wrote another royal piece: the *Nursery Suite*, dedicated to the Duchess of York and her two young daughters, Princesses Elizabeth and Margaret Rose. Appropriately, in the next royal generation, the Prince of Wales is Patron of the Elgar Foundation.

On his death in 1934, Elgar was hailed as

> The Laureate of English Music ... who was distinguished from many of his contemporaries in the fact that music for him was always first and foremost beautiful sound.[7]

In the *DNB*, one of Elgar's biographers wrote that he

> will be remembered as the man who so far lifted the status of English music that the once fashionable description of England as 'the land without music' became an absurdity ... The splendid attainments of succeeding English composers, especially in symphonic writing, have been so much the more notably excellent for the vantage-ground gained by Elgar ...[8]

As so often happens after the death of an artist of any kind, interest in Elgar's work declined dramatically. A centenary verdict, in 1957, was that he 'wandered on into a hostile age that judged him harshly. Coming generations may reverse that verdict'.[9] They did.

Just over a year after Elgar's death in 1934, **Ralph Vaughan Williams** was made an OM, almost as if to take the musical 'seat' in the Order. He had refused a knighthood and, in fact, is the only OM in the musical and performing field to have died untitled. He was 'Dr' Vaughan Williams but, unlike Elgar, came from a prosperous, upper middle-class background (his mother was a Wedgwood). Yet his succession to Elgar was by no means certain. In 1952, it would be written:

> Thirty years ago there was little to suggest that it would be Vaughan Williams who would assume Elgar's position as the outstanding contemporary composer, but, like Verdi, Vaughan Williams has produced his finest works in old age.[10]

In youth, Vaughan Williams's abilities had been severely doubted. Between spells at the Royal College of Music, he took a degree at Cambridge (Trinity, of course). When Vaughan Williams was 80, his music was described as 'the authentic voice of Britain', which had been misjudged originally as 'parish-pump' or 'folky' but which by 1935 (the year of his OM and a 'violent' fourth symphony) had become 'the embodiment of a challenging and distinctively English voice in European music'.[11] He had found his personal idiom and nationalist creed in the folk-song and had challenged British composers to

> take and purify and raise to the level of great art the forms of musical expression that surrounded them in the music-hall, the Salvation Army, Welsh hymn-singing, and other equally humble manifestations of native popular music.[12]

Vaughan Williams's composition was disturbed by service in the First World War as a medical orderly and artillery officer and, to a much lesser extent, by the energy he devoted in the Second World War to growing his own food and serving in the Home Guard. For the Coronation Service of George VI, he made a festival setting of the Te Deum.

On Vaughan Williams's death, *The Times* leading article concluded:

> his achievement was to cut the bonds that ... had bound England hand and foot to the Continent. He found in the Elizabethans and folk-song the elements of a native English language that need no longer be spoken with a German accent ... The emancipation he achieved thereby was so complete that the composers of succeeding generations like Walton and Britten had no longer need of the conscious nationalism which was Vaughan Williams's own artistic creed. There is now an English music which can make its distinctive contribution to the comity of nations.[13]

In recent years, Vaughan Williams's music has been championed by, among others, Simon Heffer, one of his biographers. In an article in 1991, he recalled many of Vaughan William's notable works: *On Wenlock Edge, Fantasia on a Theme by Thomas Tallis* and, above all, his nine symphonies, the last six composed when he was aged between 62 and 85, in the years after he received the OM. He quoted Malcolm Sargent's withering comment that any city whose concert goers could not understand the sixth symphony (written in 1944–47) 'deserved to be bombed'.[14]

The obituary of Vaughan Williams in 1958 had pointed the finger at Walton and Britten as his successors at the head of English music. Already then, the younger of the two was clearly in view as his 'successor' in the Order of Merit. **Benjamin Britten** had been made a CH in the Coronation Honours of 1953, at the age of 39; he waited another 12 years, however, before being appointed to the higher Order at the still relatively young age of 51.

On receiving the OM, Britten wrote to Menuhin (still over 20 years away from the honour himself):

> Honours, as you know only too well, don't really touch me; but there are moments in one's depressions, when one feels one's work to be hopelessly inadequate (all too often!) that they *do* encourage ...[15]

22 Benjamin Britten, on the right (and Peter Pears) by Kenneth Green.

Britten was a man of East Anglia, appropriately born on St Cecilia's Day, who first began composing at the age of six and owed much of his early technical skill to Frank Bridge and John Ireland. He worked with W. H. Auden on that memorable documentary film *Night Mail* in 1936. Three years later, with the singer Peter Pears (who was to be his lifelong companion), he followed Auden to the United States. In 1942, however, they returned to Britain and registered as conscientious objectors, obliged to give concerts for the forerunner of the British Council.

The opera *Peter Grimes* was Britten's first great work, immediately after the end of the war. Soon he settled, with Pears, in Aldeburgh, on the Suffolk coast, founded the eponymous festival and produced a series of operas (11 in all), including *The Rape of Lucretia, Albert Herring, Billy Budd, The Turn of the Screw* and *Death in Venice.*

In 1953, encouraged by the Queen's cousin, Lord Harewood, he wrote *Gloriana* about Elizabeth I and Essex. It had a Royal Gala premiere at Covent Garden a week after the Coronation but before that he and the librettist, William Plomer, had briefed the Queen and Prince Philip:

> They couldn't have been more amiable, and although neither is musical, both paid close attention. Prince Philip is quite as Germanically thorough as the Prince Consort, but has a more practical and varied experience of life, is versatile, and has a much lighter touch and a sense of fun.[16]

Later, Plomer commented: 'I think he [Prince Philip] now knows the libretto better than I do.'[17] Unfortunately, the premiere pleased neither audience nor critics. Britten's reaction was that of many artists over many years: 'if I had listened to the critics I would have given up writing music long ago.'[18]

Britten's *War Requiem* accompanied the dedication of the rebuilt Coventry Cathedral in 1962. Using Wilfred Owen's war poems, including the piercing line, 'I am the enemy you killed, my friend', Britten created music which one writer called 'a savage indictment of human folly'.[19]

Britten's name equipped him admirably to be the representation of British music such as none of his predecessors had enjoyed. Courteous and gentle as a man, he could be ruthless as a musician. Britten was already dying when, in the Birthday Honours of 1976, he was made a life peer. His peerage – the honour that Elgar never achieved – was the first bestowed on a British composer. His nurse and friend, Rita Thomson, threatened: 'if you don't take this, I'll never speak to you again.'[20] Others were puzzled by his acceptance: Lord Harewood – 'curiously unnecessary' and his *DNB* biographer, Donald Mitchell – 'it didn't seem sensible to me'[21]; although it did make him feel 'he was back on the musical map'.[22] His assistant, Rosamund Strode, thought: 'He just felt it was marvellous for music.'[23] He himself joked that signing simply 'Britten' 'saved energy'.

Britten's life lasted another six months and he was buried not in the proffered Westminster Abbey but in Aldeburgh graveyard. The obituaries were glowing. Tippett, his natural successor, wrote:

> Benjamin Britten was the most absolutely gifted man of music I have ever known. Music spurted, as it were, from his body...He knew that if there is a heritage within a nationality, it is that of those creators who pass over the frontiers. His music did just that...I loved him...Dear, dear Ben, to the end I keep a place warm in my heart.[24]

The Queen sent a message of sympathy to Pears 'as a representative of all who had worked with Lord Britten', which Pears regarded as 'a recognition of the way we lived'.[25]

Three years after Britten's appointment to the Order of Merit, he was joined in 1968 by **William Walton**, almost 12 years his senior and already knighted. For the first time, there were two living composer OMs. Walton was much affected by the honour. According to his wife's account, he broke down and cried. 'To think,' he said, 'the Queen actually knows I am alive.'

Walton's musical career began early. At the age of ten, he had become a chorister in Christ Church Cathedral, Oxford, and at 16, he entered the college as an undergraduate. The first of his patrons were Thomas Strong, the Dean of Christ Church, and Hugh Allen, the Professor of Music. He left Oxford without a degree and soon acquired the patronage of the Sitwells 'and sacheverell other people', as Dylan Thomas punned it. Walton himself said: 'I was a scrounger and scrounge I certainly did.'[26] From this patronage emerged *Façade* in 1923. When *Belshazzar's Feast* followed in 1931, it was 'widely recognised as the biggest event in English choral singing since *The Dream of Gerontius*.'[27] In 1937, aged 35, Walton wrote his first royal piece: the Coronation march, *Crown Imperial*. In 1953, came his second, another march *Orb and Sceptre*, and a Coronation *Te Deum*.

During the Second World War, in between driving ambulances 'very badly', Walton wrote two ballet scores for Ashton: *The Wise Virgin* and *The Quest*. He also collaborated with Olivier, composing the musical scores for *Henry V*, *Hamlet* and later, *Richard III* – some of his most widely heard music. After the war, despite a knighthood in 1951, he found himself overtaken by Britten in the regard of a new intelligentsia.

At the age of 46, Walton married a young Argentine woman, whom he had met at a conference in Buenos Aires. After moving with his wife to the island of Ischia, in the Bay of Naples, he composed the opera *Troilus and Cressida*. Later, came a cello concerto, a second symphony and *Variations on a Theme by Hindemith*.

When Walton died in 1983, the obituaries were a little lack-lustre:

> a composer whose work had...experienced the vicissitudes of being considered in turn, notorious, fashionable and finally popular...In spite of composing relatively few works, he did nonetheless build up a substantial corpus of large-scale works in every form and enriched the world's repertory.[28]

In 2002, the centenary of his own birth and of the Order in which he took such delight, Walton's music was featured, as representing the 1950s, in a concert in the grounds of Buckingham Palace to celebrate the Queen's Golden Jubilee.

Only six months after Walton's death in 1983, **Michael Tippett** was made an OM; he had been knighted in 1966 and made a CH only four years earlier, in 1979. Like Britten (who was nine years younger), Tippett matured musically in the Second World War, particularly with the oratorio, *A Child of Our Time*, which drew on the pre-war murder of a German diplomat that precipitated the notorious 'Kristallnacht'.

A socialist (briefly a communist) and pacifist, Tippett served three months in prison in 1943 for failing to do the farm work into which he had been directed as a conscientious objector. Vaughan Williams pleaded for him, describing his compositions as 'very remarkable...a distinct national asset...Music is forming a great part in national life now...everyone able to help with that work is doing work of national importance.'[29] Prison was not a pleasant experience, in a cell between a rapist and a black marketeer, sewing the traditional mail bags and regarded by the warders as 'the lowest

23 Sir Michael Tippett by Adam Birtwhistle.

of the low'. His mother, who had been imprisoned as a suffragette, was immensely proud of him.

During his appointment from 1940–51 as Director of Music at Morley College, where Holst had served before him, Tippett's concerts became legendary and, after leaving the college, he devoted himself to composition. A foray into 'royal' music came in 1948 with the *Suite for the Birthday of Prince Charles*.

Tippett's first opera, *The Midsummer Marriage*, in 1955, owed something to his absorption in Frazer's *The Golden Bough*. In the midst of some hostile comment, Tippett took comfort that

> Walton himself, whose *Troilus and Cressida* was being held up as the true alternative to my confused effort, saw it and told me, I believe in all sincerity, that this was the real opera.[30]

Other operas followed: *King Priam* (the premiere of which was in Coventry to celebrate the opening of the new cathedral), *The Knot Garden* and *The Ice-Break*. There were symphonies and concertos, one dedicated to Britten on his fiftieth birthday 'with affection and admiration'. In the year following the OM, he produced *The Mask of Time*, an oratorio in which he hoped 'to offer fragments or scenes for a possible 'epiphany' for today'.[31]

An obituarist wrote of Tippett:

> Although a challenger of received order, Tippett was also a traditionalist. Rejecting the romanticism of Elgar no less than the folk-song revivalism of Vaughan Williams, he followed Holst's example in turning to earlier English sources for his music. Purcell was an inspiration ... His attraction to popular music, especially to the blues, gave him familiarity with jazz ...[32]

Since Tippett's death in 1998, there has been no composer in the Order of Merit.

The choreographers

To the five composers were added two great figures from that world of music and drama – dance. The two had brought to fruition after the Second World War the phenomenon of British ballet: Frederick Ashton and Ninette de Valois.

Frederick Ashton, the choreographer, acknowledged the influence of three women in his professional life. He saw Anna Pavlova dance in Lima (where his father was a businessman and honorary consul) when he was 13 and was 'injected with her poison' because she was 'the greatest theatrical personality I have ever seen'. After seeing her, all he wanted to be was Nijinsky.

Marie Rambert was his first teacher and, although she thought he was 'passionately lazy', she also confided that the most passionate English ballet was Ashton's *Façade*. He agreed with her about his laziness: 'People think I'm working out wonderful things. I say not at all. I'm just in a state.'[33]

The third woman, de Valois, congratulated Rambert on having discovered 'a real choreographer' and, indeed, he is now regarded as the first British choreographer of note. His cooperation with her began in 1931 and, with the exception of his war service in the RAF, continued until his retirement in 1970 from what had by then become the Royal Ballet.

Ashton's corpus of work was enormous: over 150 ballets, as well as directing operas like Britten's *Albert Herring*. Critics have written:

> Most of his ballets have this instantly recognizable English quality, such as *La Fille mal gardée*, *The Two Pigeons* or *A Wedding Banquet* ... the diffident artless grace of an English lyric poet ...[34]

and

Ashton's ballets have been the biggest single influence on the way the Royal Ballet dance.[35]

As a dancer, Ashton delighted audiences in his early years, partnering Karsavina, Lopokova and Markova. Younger people will remember best the gentle humour of his Ugly Sister in *Cinderella*.

Ashton enjoyed the friendship of Queen Elizabeth The Queen Mother and, on her eightieth birthday, it was his *Rhapsody* that had its world premiere at Covent Garden. On the sixtieth birthday of the Queen, his choreography accompanied the performance, also at Covent Garden, of Elgar's *Nursery Suite*.

Ashton often professed amazement at the public recognition he received – OM, CH and a knighthood:

> nobody is more surprised than I was. I can honestly say that I've never scrabbled for them... I often think to myself, well imagine little Freddie Ashton from Lima, Peru, ending up with all this.[36]

Even privately, he expressed surprise and was glad of reassurance. After one of the Queen's lunches for OMs, a neighbour recorded that Ashton:

> seemed pleased that I thought ballet ranked as an art form. 'Most people,' he said, 'think an Order of Merit for service to the ballet – how inappropriate!'[37]

Ashton had received the OM at the age of 73 as a great choreographer. His mentor, **Ninette de Valois**, had to wait until after his death to receive it, when she was 94. Her honour was not for creating ballets but for creating British ballet itself. The influence on the young Edris Stannus (her real name) of an army background may have contributed to her strong sense of discipline, which gave her the name of 'Madam' to her face and 'The Games Mistress' behind it.

After dancing, in a child troupe, 'on every pier in England', de Valois gravitated to Covent Garden Opera and the Diaghilev Ballet. She moved, however, to teaching and arranging ballets. In 1931, with the support of Lilian Baylis (who 'liked her face'), she formed the Vic-Wells Ballet. Through the following decade, she choreographed several ballets but, during and after the war, she concentrated on developing the Vic-Wells into the Sadlers Wells and, finally, the Royal Ballet, with a royal charter in 1956. She brought, among others, Robert Helpmann and Margot Fonteyn into the Royal Ballet and, just before her retirement (and succession by Ashton) as Director in 1963, the Russian refugee, Rudolf Nureyev. In 'retirement', de

Valois devoted her undiminished energy to the Royal Ballet School and it was fitting that she should visit it on her hundredth birthday.

Despite her apparently autocratic style, de Valois admitted to being shy:

> I have never felt comfortable taking a curtain call – Fred Ashton had to tell me not to hold the flowers upside down like an umbrella. I still try to remember that advice.[38]

Honours followed de Valois' work in jerky progression: CBE in 1947 and DBE in 1951. Nothing more, however, until 1981 when, with Ashton still alive and an OM, she was made a CH. The incredibly late arrival of the OM, long after she had ceased to be active, must be attributed to her longevity causing even greater awareness of the great institution she had created.

There had always been royal interest in de Valois' work. The King and Queen, with the two princesses, had attended the re-opening of the Royal Opera House in 1946. The present Queen attended de Valois' ninetieth birthday concert there when she was told, 'Madam, you have hit 90. But there is not much evidence that 90 has hit you!' Again in 1996, the Queen went to 'The Garden' and watched *The Sleeping Beauty*, as she had at that re-opening 50 years earlier; de Valois, by then an OM, was there.

On de Valois' death at 102 (the longest-lived OM), the tributes concentrated on her legacy to British theatre and dance:

> [She] leaves, for future British dancers, the prospect of a career that did not exist when she was young; for audiences, two great companies that would not have existed without her; and for her country, a national asset beyond price.[39]

The performers

Since honorary OMs are so rare and since creativity and not 'mere' performance has always been rated so highly in the conferment of the Order, it was a long time before the child prodigy violinist, **Yehudi Menuhin**, could have been seriously considered for the honour.

Acclaimed in France and the United States at the age of ten, this American of Russian Jewish parentage made his debut in London only two years later. *The Times* declared that, 'judged by the absolute standard, Menuhin's performance [of Brahms's *Violin Concerto*] was very good.' He was soon repeating such performances, famously with the aged Elgar conducting his own *Cello Concerto*; later, Menuhin was to call Elgar 'My Musical Grandfather'.

Menuhin's playing took him all over the world, where he also played an increasing role in trying to heal, with the aid of his music, some of the divisions afflicting that world, particularly in Europe and the Middle East. He was Mr Music in many countries. He was concerned about young musicians

24 Yehudi Menuhin by Mfanwy Pavelic.

and founded the famed school of music in Surrey. He directed the Bath
Festival for ten years. Walton composed a sonata for him. He developed a
rapport with musicians as diverse as Stephane Grapelli and Ravi Shankar.
One of the experiences that moved him most was his visit, with Britten, to
Belsen concentration camp only a few weeks after its liberation in 1945.

Menuhin lived more and more in Britain, although retaining his American
citizenship. His first British honour was an honorary KBE in 1965 but, on
naturalisation 20 years later, he received the accolade from the Queen and
was able to use the title 'Sir'. Only two years after that, came the OM and,
in 1993, a life peerage, only the second for a musician, after Britten. This
accumulation of British honours did not seem strange to a man who said:

> I like to be rather old-fashioned and call myself a British subject. I've
> lived much of my adult life here, my wife is British, my school is here
> and my recording contract with EMI goes back to 1929, the year I made
> my British debut. Britain has always seemed very like home.[40]

Whatever the critics' view of his later playing, Menuhin continued to enjoy
the full admiration of the Establishment for a life that had gone well beyond
the violin. The Prince of Wales hosted an eightieth birthday party for him.
On that occasion, *The Times* hailed him as 'music's ambassador to the world'

and rejoiced that his adopted country had been able to honour him 'with a knighthood and then a peerage' – no mention of the Cinderella OM.

Menuhin died, in Berlin, after cancelling a concert, at the age of 82. It was in that city, 70 years earlier, that Albert Einstein, after hearing him play, had exclaimed: 'Now I know there is a God in Heaven!' The many obituary tributes tried to match a musical talent that had diminished, with a man whose influence had ranged so widely. Thus:

> not the finest violinist of his age...Outshone in youth by Fritz Kreisler and in maturity by Jascha Heifetz...In old age, he become a conductor...Yet quite simply the most famous musician on Earth, a synonym for music itself and, no less impressively, a force for good.[41]

George Steiner had described Menuhin as 'probably the best-loved personality in the history of the performing arts'.[42]

Joan Sutherland was an unusual addition to the Order of Merit: out of her 158 predecessors, she was only the seventh woman, fourth Australian

25 Dame Joan Sutherland by Michael Stennett.

and second performer. She had left her native country at the age of 25, like so many young Australian musicians and artists before her, in search of a bigger stage than could then be found at home. Their destination was usually London and it was to Covent Garden that the young singer soon gravitated in 1952. From being Edward Downes' 'clumsy, awkward lump with little promise', she developed into one of the greatest and best-loved sopranos of the twentieth century, excelling in the 'bel canto' roles of neglected romantic operas of the eighteenth and nineteenth centuries. Her famed breakthrough was in 1959, as Donizetti's *Lucia di Lammermoor* at Covent Garden.

She was soon dubbed 'La Stupenda' (The Marvel) and her dazzling international career took off, around the opera houses of London, New York, Paris, Milan – and Sydney – in company with Richard Bonynge, her coach, conductor and husband. The marvel is that she seems an ordinary women with an extraordinary voice, demonstrating such un-diva like qualities as modesty, courtesy and generosity; these endeared her to the musical world, even those who were unenthusiastic about the dramatic aspect of her performances. She was inevitably compared throughout her career with her great but older contemporary, who was an early inspiration: Maria Callas.

Joan Sutherland's career brought her early honours: CBE in 1961, AC (one of the first) in 1975 and DBE in 1979. Her husband was made CBE and AO. In 1990, she announced her retirement so that she would 'be remembered by her past performances'. Her farewells in Sydney and London were moving occasions. In 1959, *The Times* had written:

> She poured out warm rounded tone in the Italianate manner, sustained the line and controlled the ornaments superbly.[43]

Of her 1990 performance, the same newspaper remarked:

> The Sutherland voice may have lost a little of its youthful power, yet here was a fitting reminder of the reason she has dominated the bel canto repertoire for three decades: nobody ever produced coloratura singing of more purity or accuracy.[44]

The Order of Merit and other honours in the personal gift of the Queen remain open to Australians, unlike the mainstream British honours, which they had used for so many years before adopting sole use of the Order of Australia in the 1980s. Joan Sutherland's appointment as an OM came only a few months after her retirement, and she was invested by the Queen on the lawns of Admiralty House in Sydney in February 1992. She declared her belief in an Australian monarchy: 'Republicans! I've no sympathy with the republicans at all.'[45]

In her retirement, Joan Sutherland has contributed her vast experience to encouraging young singers.

The actors

Actors would certainly not have been in the minds of the founders of the Order of Merit. It was only in 1895 that Henry Irving (surely an OM a century later) had become the first knighted actor. As the twentieth century went on, knighthoods for the acting profession proliferated and on some of the recipients, the honour sat with gentlemanly ease. Soon the female actors (then known as actresses) were able to join them as 'Dames', of the non-pantomime variety. Where would the press be now without its 'knights (and dames) of the theatre'?

Later in the century, the knighthoods were topped up, in a few cases, with the CH. Only two, however, have so far made their way into the Order of Merit – Laurence Olivier and John Gielgud.

Laurence Olivier was the son of a clergyman. A gentleman actor, Sir Johnston Forbes-Robertson, told the young Laurence's father of a school performance at the age nine: 'Your boy does not play Brutus, he *is* Brutus.' Ellen Terry saw the performance and noted in her diary: 'The small boy who

26 Lord Olivier as Richard III by Salvador Dali.

played Brutus is already a great actor.' Drama school led to Barry Jackson's Birmingham Repertory Company and his astonishing career was launched.

A 'dream team' production of *Romeo and Juliet*, in 1935, with Gielgud producing and alternating with Olivier the roles of Romeo and Mercutio, is generally seen as a high-water mark in the history of the British stage. Unlike his great contemporaries, Gielgud and Richardson, Olivier achieved a film career to compare with that on stage. The man whom one obituary described as 'probably the greatest actor of his generation and certainly the most handsome'[46] narrowly missed being simply a matinee-idol after his performances in *Wuthering Heights*, *Rebecca* and *Lady Hamilton*.

When war came, Olivier joined the Fleet Air Arm (with Richardson). He was called from the Navy to probably more worthwhile war work: the patriotic film, *Henry V*, in which Charles Laughton said he was 'quite simply England'. He was knighted in 1947 at the relatively early age of 40, six months after Richardson (who was five years older) and six years before Gielgud (who was three years older).

Olivier's award-winning films of *Hamlet* and *Richard III* came before two rather different roles: the *Prince* to Marilyn Monroe's *Showgirl* and Archie Rice in John Osborne's *The Entertainer*. After a short 'rehearsal' as Director of the new Chichester Festival, he became (in 1963) the first Director of the National Theatre. While at the National Theatre, he became the first actor to receive a peerage. Of course, it recognised his pre-eminence as an actor and director. It was another 11 years before Olivier received the Order of Merit, the first actor or performer of any kind to be so honoured. While waiting to receive it from the Queen, the 73 year old joked with Lady Medawar, with whom he had once danced: 'Couldn't do it now.'[47] A British ambassador-designate who was received by the Queen immediately after Olivier commented that the actor had made such an impression that it was some time before the conversation turned to the country to which the ambassador was going.[48]

Of Olivier's versatility, there was never any doubt. Kenneth Tynan, the critic, remarked that, although turbulent, he was 'pound for pound, the greatest actor alive'[49] but 'that the end of his reign was like the days of Stalin; no one knew who the successor would be because Larry would not name one.'[50] He played *Lear* on television at the age of 76 and when queried on the role:

> Like all the rest of us really. A stupid old fart, completely selfish and utterly inconsiderate.[51]

Olivier's three marriages were all to actresses. The second, to the temperamental Vivien Leigh, attracted vast media attention. The third, to Joan Plowright, gave him stability and happiness, and more children, in his last three decades. Gradually, his career wound down, especially as he was increasingly plagued with ill health. He gave up the stage in 1974 and the cinema in 1987, after a series of cameo parts.

In Olivier's lifetime, he saw his name given to the main theatre in the National and to the annual awards of the Society of the West End Theatre (previously the SWETs!). After his death, he appeared (with Vivien Leigh) on one of the stamps issued in 1996 to celebrate '100 years of Going to the Pictures'.

The obituaries of Olivier were uniformly fulsome: 'Player of spellbinding power and versatility' (*The Times*); 'First lord of the stage...the greatest actor of the twentieth century, maybe even the greatest in recorded history' (*The Guardian*); 'king of the British stage, indeed, if the title has meaning, the greatest actor in the world' (*The Independent*); 'whose name came to symbolise the art of acting in this century, as those of Burbage, Kean and Irving did in theirs' (*Daily Telegraph*).

On 20 October 1989, Olivier's memorial service took place in Westminster Abbey and the ashes were later laid beside those of Irving and Garrick, beneath the bust of Shakespeare and close to the graves of Henry V and Richard III's wife. In his address, Alec Guinness said, 'there can never and will never be a second Olivier' and referring to his many honours, including the OM, quoted Othello: 'I have done the state some service, and they know't' – a remark that could be made by or about many other OMs, even if they never played Othello. One of the readings was by **John Gielgud**, then a knighted CH but destined to follow Olivier as the only other actor OM of the century.

Olivier and Gielgud had been linked, and compared, throughout their careers. Donald Sinden summed up the continuing debate:

> They cannot be compared. [Olivier] a more physical, [Gielgud] a more cerebral performer. They are both giants. We are privileged to have seen them both.[52]

Others concurred in this assessment by describing Gielgud as 'the greatest actor in the world from the neck up'.

In 1996, at the age of 92, Gielgud joined Olivier in the ranks of the Order of Merit, thus ensuring that history would be able to draw no distinction, in the award of the supreme artistic honour, between the two giants of the twentieth-century British stage. The award may not have pleased Kenneth Rose, an authority on the Order who frequently wrote about it in his Albany column in the *Sunday Telegraph*. To him, the *Daily Telegraph* (of 10 December 1996) attributed the remark that he would only exclude three categories of recipients: 'Actors, photographers and hairdressers.'

Gielgud's first two state honours had come on occasions of royal celebration: his knighthood in the Coronation Honours of 1953 and his CH in the Silver Jubilee Honours of 1977. The first he got by a hairsbreadth. Only four

27 Sir John Gielgud by John Ward.

months later, he was fined £10 for homosexual importuning, an event that, 50 years ago, endangered his career and would have put paid to any chance of a knighthood for many years. The Garrick Club debated his removal; 44 years later, it gave him a celebratory dinner for his OM.

Neither Gielgud nor any one else was ever allowed to forget that he was Ellen Terry's great-nephew. That connection, and talent, helped in his career. He claimed that, like all the Terrys, he had 'weak lachrymal glands' and could therefore cry at the drop of an adjective.

RADA led to the Old Vic where he first played *Hamlet*. (Gielgud was often described as the finest of contemporary Hamlets.) His Richard in *Richard of Bordeaux* in 1934 placed him firmly in the front rank of actors. His voice became legendary, famously described by Alec Guinness as 'a silver trumpet muffled in silk'.

One of Gielgud's earliest film performances was in Priestley's *The Good Companions*, in 1933. Much later, his film roles included (appropriately for a future OM) the Master of Trinity College, Cambridge in *Chariots of Fire* and the butler to the alcoholic Dudley Moore in *Arthur*. The Oscar he received for that he described as 'extraordinary after wonderful things like a knighthood'. (Years later, his obituary in the *Daily Sport* was headed: 'Butler in Dudley Moore film dies.')

Gielgud went on to many other film and TV roles, increasingly cameo-like, after he gave his last stage performance in 1988. He was concerned, even in very old age, if offers of work fell away; when complaining to a friend how terrible it was to be out of work and being asked how long this had been going on, he replied: 'Oh, since Friday.'[53] He resisted writing for a long time but *An Actor and his Time* came out in 1979. One of his recollections was of the famous critic James Agate, coming to see him in the interval of *Macbeth* to say:

> I thought I'd tell you how good you are now; I might have changed my mind by the end of the play.[54]

Gielgud became renowned for his indiscretions, like telling Emlyn Williams (after a Dickens recital) that 'one should keep those one-man shows for one's old age' or like confiding in Elizabeth Taylor that Richard Burton had sacrificed theatrical greatness by marrying 'some Hollywood star or other'.[55]

Gielgud hankered for a theatre to be named after him. After the opening of Shakespeare's Globe on Thameside, the old Globe in Shaftesbury Avenue was re-named the Gielgud.

On Gielgud's death, in May 2000, the obituary headlines echoed those of Olivier: 'Fastidious performer with a matchless voice, who stood centre stage through the whole history of modern British theatre' (*The Times*); 'Actor whose reputation as the greatest of the 20th century was challenged only by Olivier' (*Daily Telegraph*); 'He could steal a scene just by wearing a hat' (*The Independent*).

12

THE WRITERS

Novelists and playwrights

1. 1905 George MEREDITH
2. 1910 Thomas HARDY
3. 1916 Henry JAMES
4. 1922 Sir James BARRIE
5. 1929 John GALSWORTHY
6. 1969 E. M. FORSTER
7. 1977 J. B. PRIESTLEY
8. 1986 Graham GREENE
9. 2000 Sir Tom STOPPARD

Poets

10. 1929 Robert BRIDGES
11. 1935 John MASEFIELD
12. 1948 T. S. ELIOT
13. 1953 Walter DE LA MARE
14. 1998 Ted HUGHES

Preliminary

The writers in this chapter are those of fiction. Other men of letters – philosophers, classical scholars and historians – are studied in the next chapter. In this chapter, I have drawn a simplistic line between novelists and dramatists on the one hand and poets on the other. Of course, some, like Meredith and Hardy, spanned the line.

More has probably been written about the men of fiction, by literary critics and other men of letters, than about any other group in this book, except for the most famous of the men of affairs. Their novels, plays and poems are endlessly dissected, interpreted and appraised. Even more therefore than with the other groups, I have had to restrict the number of (often conflicting) views of their work that I can reasonably record. In their heyday, each was readable and read. Now, some of them are seldom read.

One notable feature of this group is their almost unanimous dislike of titles. Only two of the 14 accepted one: J. M. Barrie and Tom Stoppard. Of the other 12, at least five are known to have actually refused before their appointment as OMs and others may well have done so. In this respect, they differ greatly from the musicians and performers, of whom ten out of 11 accepted titles.

Novelists and playwrights

'Literature' had been represented in the original 12 Members of the Order of Merit by two historians, Morley and Lecky. The name of **George Meredith**, however, was specifically noted by *The Times* as missing, although he could have been 'appropriately associated with the illustrious'.[1] It was therefore no surprise when he was included in the second list of OMs, published on 30 June 1905.

There is nothing in the Royal Archives on the background to the award but, to judge from his own letters, the offer was made to him initially in March by the Prime Minister, Arthur Balfour, and he had little doubt that the instigator was Morley, a friend of 40 years standing. On 21 June, Meredith received formal confirmation from the King's Private Secretary that the award was to be 'in recognition of the great services you have rendered to Literature for so many years'.[2]

There is one dubious, but none the less tellable, story about Meredith's OM. Fred Karno, the Edwardian comedian, had a particular catch-phrase and one account of its origin is that a friend of Meredith, who also figured in the 1905 Birthday Honours List, burst into his study shouting, 'Meredith, we're in'. In December, he told Morley:

> At last I am entitled to be hailed by you as Brother Merit. Sir Arthur Ellis came here by our King's command to invest me with the Insignia.[3]

If, as Kenneth Rose was told by Max Beerbohm (who had drawn Meredith for *Vanity Fair*), Morley had objected to the OM for Meredith,[4] he must have been somewhat embarrassed by all this effusive gratitude.

Meredith had come a long way to become the Grand Old Man of English letters. His background, about which he was sensitive, was a tailoring family in Portsmouth. His father went bankrupt. His grandfather, known as 'Great

Mel', figured in a novel *Evan Harrington*, about a tailor's son torn between continuing the business or bettering himself in society. Meredith was educated at a Moravians school in Germany and started to write poetry after a spell in a solicitor's office.

The title of Meredith's first prose work, *The Shaving of Shagpat*, suited the elaborate Eastern fantasy but it already showed his 'extraordinary power of concealing his thought in verbal flourishes'. Nevertheless, George Eliot called it 'a work of genius, and of a poetical genius'. His novel, *The Ordeal of Richard Feverel*, describing seduction and adultery, was a scandal in 1859 but it did include the very straightforward thought 'Kissing don't last: cookery do!' Among his other works were *The Adventures of Henry Richmond*, *Beauchamp's Career* (which included the only recorded use of the word 'obtumescent' – remaining wilfully mute), *The Egoist* and the most popular, *Diana of the Crossways*.

Meredith supplemented his income from writing with other activities. He was the model in 1856 for the painting *The Death of Chatterton* by Henry Wallis, who repaid him by seducing his first wife, a daughter of Thomas Love Peacock. That bitter experience produced *Modern Love*, 50 sonnets that were described as 'the first marriage-torture, marriage-strife poem'. From 1860–94, he was a publisher's reader and among the books he spotted was Olive Schreiner's *The Story of an African Farm*, which is arguably the first sustained imaginative work to come out of white Africa. He encouraged Thomas Hardy. In 1867, he was even, briefly and inactively, a war correspondent in Italy.

In his old age, Meredith received numerous tributes, apart from the OM. On his seventieth birthday, an address of congratulation was signed by 29 fellow-writers, including nine future OMs. While acknowledging it gracefully, his private opinion was more forthright:

> I know what they mean, kindly enough. Poor old devil, he *will* go on writing; let us cheer him up. The old fire isn't quite out; a stir of the poker may bring out a shoot of gas.[5]

On Meredith's death in May 1909, at the age of 81, the leading obituary reflected his very high standing at the time:

> for more than half a century his intellectual force had been active in the midst of us . . . difficult to believe that that great brain is at rest, that there is no George Meredith in the flesh to spur men to endeavour, or to laugh at them for their good . . . in the end he achieved the position of the greatest man of letters of his age . . . [6]

Among the 'younger writers' influenced by Meredith were Thomas Hardy, who often visited him and wrote a poem on his death, Henry James and the historian, G. M. Trevelyan, another frequent visitor. In his Clark Lectures in 1953, Trevelyan (by then long an OM himself) gave a view of Meredith's work and reputation:

> Recognition as a poet followed slowly after his recognition as a novel-ist, partly because the new poems that he published in the 'eighties and 'nineties were many of them difficult and obscure, too heavily weighted with thought and imagery imperfectly digested, to be readable by ordi-nary mortals... It is as a poet, not as a poetical philosopher, that he has claim to immortality... [After the First World War] his work in verse and prose no longer appealed to the new generation. He had sunk once more below the capricious horizon of literary fashion.[7]

Oscar Wilde described Meredith's style as 'chaos, illumined by flashes of lightning' and said that he had mastered everything but language: as a novelist he could do anything but tell a story.

Despite periodic attempts to restore his reputation, not least in a biog-raphy by David Williams in 1977, Meredith has failed to keep his place among the immortals. By 1981, Meredith was written of as 'England's Great Unreadable'.[8] So, unless there is a startling revival in his fortunes, the first literary OM seems destined to be revered but not read.

Less than a year after Meredith's death, **Thomas Hardy** was appointed to the Order of Merit, one novelist/poet thus succeeding another. It was Asquith who put forward Hardy's name, in May 1909:

> The death of G. Meredith creates a vacancy in the Order of Merit... poet and a great writer of fiction... his place should be taken by some one who possesses – even if not in the same degree – the same qualifications. There is only one man in England of whom this can be said, and he is Mr Thomas Hardy...[9]

The unbookish Edward VII wrote on the letter:

> It does not create a vacancy but I should like to hear more about Mr Hardy.

If he did hear more, he took no action for Hardy had not received the honour before the King died in May 1910.

A month after the accession of George V in 1910, Asquith again recom-mended Hardy for the OM. Hardy had declined a knighthood in 1908, when one might have expected Edward VII to have 'heard more' about him. Hardy was appointed OM on 8 July 1910 and is now among the best-remembered

28 Thomas Hardy by William Strang.

of its Members. According to the biography written by his second wife,

> though he accepted the award with characteristic quietude, it was
> evident that this sign of official approval of his work brought him
> pleasure.[10]

Hardy was received by the King on 19 July. He was also immensely pleased
with the freedom of Dorchester, which he received later in the year at a
ceremony at which he wore his new Order. Despite the Palace's contacts
with him at this time, he does not seem to have been the foremost Hardy in
their minds. According to one biographer of George V:

> He had scarcely reigned one month when Asquith's private secretary
> telephoned the palace on Thomas Hardy's seventieth birthday to suggest

that a telegram to 'old Hardy' might be appreciated. 'It shall be done,' came the reply, and Mr Hardy, of Alnwick, who made the King's fishing rods, was astonished to receive royal congratulations on attaining an age he had not attained, on a day which was the anniversary of nothing.[11]

In a letter written in 1905, Hardy had set out his views:

> on honours for men of letters, I have always thought that any writer who has expressed unpalatable or possibly subversive views on society, religious dogma, current morals, and any other features of the existing order of things, and who wishes to be free and to express more if they occur to him, must feel hampered by accepting honours from any government – which are different from academic honours offered for past attainments merely.[12]

It looks as though Hardy later drew a clear distinction between a personal honour from the monarch and routine honours from the government. He was certainly aware of the special nature of the honour he had accepted.

The newly-honoured Hardy was suitably generous when it came to the dispersal of his manuscripts in 1911. He endorsed the suggestion that the Royal Library should receive the original autograph manuscript of *The Trumpet Major*, with its account (that had interested Queen Victoria in 1880) of George III's stay at Weymouth.

Thomas Hardy was born in 1840 in Dorset, the county which, with its surrounding area, he was to recreate fictionally with the historic name of Wessex. Its county town, Dorchester, became Casterbridge and other places such as Weymouth, Shaftesbury and Bridport emerged as Budmouth, Shaston and Port Bredy. Even faraway Oxford was barely disguised as Christminster.

Many would now associate the earldom of the Queen's youngest son, Prince Edward, more with 'Hardy country' than with the ancient kingdom of Anglo-Saxon England. Indeed, *The First Countess of Wessex* is a story in a set of tales published by Hardy in 1891: *A Group of Noble Dames*.

On both sides, Hardy came from old Dorset families and among earlier Hardys was Nelson's flag-captain, another Thomas. The future writer, however, was thought to be stillborn until an alert midwife noticed a spark of life and slapped some more into him. He inherited the aptitude of his father and grandfather (both Thomases) for music, church and secular.

Son of a stonemason builder, Hardy was eight before he went to the village school. After a year he moved to a private school in Dorchester, where he learned Latin and French. (In his own time, he was later to study Greek and German.) From rural society, such as the dances at which he played the fiddle, he imbibed much of the atmosphere that was to permeate his writing. Later, he was to use stories from old newspapers to reinforce his own experience.

At 16, Hardy became pupil to an ecclesiastical architect and embarked on the profession he was to follow for the next 15 years. By 20, he was working on the restoration of old churches. He had also begun to write both prose and verse. He had to earn a living and, at this stage, it had to be by architecture. At 22, Hardy went to London and was immediately employed by Arthur Blomfield, the noted ecclesiastical architect. He stayed in the capital for five years, worked hard at architecture, widened his education (with reading, evening classes, galleries and concerts) and wrote, mostly poetry.

Ill health compelled Hardy to return to Dorchester: to architecture for a few years, to marriage within a few years and to writing – prose fiction in order to make money. His first novel (with a rather socialist view of society) was not published and the manuscript was destroyed. It earned him praise, however, from John Morley for its rustic part but George Meredith (as a publisher's reader) urged on Hardy the importance of 'plot'.

The success of *Under the Greenwood Tree* (1872) enabled Hardy to become a professional writer and, for the next 23 years, a number of books, many produced in serial form, established him as a major novelist. Leslie Stephen, editor of the *Cornhill* magazine, offered to serialise *Far from the Madding Crowd*, which appeared in book form in 1874, shortly after Hardy's marriage. His bride was Emma Gifford.

> The marriage soon produced intolerable strains, but it also produced, after Emma's death in 1912, some of Hardy's most moving poems.[13]

He admitted publishing them as the only way he could make amends for the way he had treated her in later life. In happier times, even before their marriage, he had fictionalised their courtship in *A Pair of Blue Eyes* (1873).

The Return of the Native (1878) was followed by *The Trumpet Major* (1880). Close together came 'The Mayor of Casterbridge' (1886) and *The Woodlanders* (1887). Finally, were two novels that shocked many at the time, despite their having been 'deliberately modified to suit the delicacy of editors': *Tess of the D'Urbervilles* (1891) and *Jude the Obscure* (1895). The outcry nettled Hardy and appeared to contribute to the end of his career as a novelist. To the long-standing criticism of his 'pessimism' were added attacks on his 'immorality'.

In his new specifically poetic career, Hardy turned first to collecting in volume form the poems he had written at various times over the previous 30 years. They appeared as *Wessex Poems* (1898) and *Poems of Past and Present* (1901).

> But a grand project had long been gradually taking shape in his mind and was now ripe for execution...the vast theme of the Napoleonic

wars as a whole had presented itself to his poetic ambition... The three parts of *The Dynasts* were published in 1903, 1906 and 1908... [and] in one volume in 1910... by far his greatest single achievement, and the fullest and most complete expression of his genius.[14]

A recent biographer claimed that it was this vast drama in prose and blank verse, 'which, above all else, got him his Order of Merit'.[15] The papers in the Royal Archives do not clearly prove such a claim and, today, it is Hardy's novels which would justify the award in the eyes of most of his admirers.

In 1885, Hardy had moved to Max Gate, a house he had designed for himself near Dorchester. He lived there until his death 43 years later. After years of virtual estrangement, his first wife, Emma, died in 1912 and, two years later, he married a much younger woman, Florence Dugdale, who had been his companion and secretary for many years.

Like other writers, Hardy was soon caught up in the war propaganda effort in 1914. A particular target was the German philosopher, Friedrich Nietzsche. The writers, including the future OMs, Barrie and G. M. Trevelyan, continued their work through the war. Arnold Bennett recorded a meeting in Barrie's house in 1917:

> Hardy was very lively; talked like anything. He has all his facilities, unimpaired. Quite modest and without the slightest pose... Soon after Shaw and Wells came, Hardy seemed to curl up. The spectacle of Wells and GBS talking firmly about the war, in their comparative youth, in front of this aged, fatigued and silent man – incomparably their superior as a creative artist – was very striking.[16]

Hardy made his last visit to London in 1920, staying with Barrie (soon to be an OM) for the wedding of Harold Macmillan (eventually to be an OM). In that year, Oxford (his 'Christminster') gave him an honorary degree and he saw *The Dynasts* performed by the University Dramatic Society. In 1923, he spent his last night away from home – also in Oxford. In the same year, his last substantial verse work, *The Famous Tragedy of the Queen of Cornwall*, was published and performed. Hardy's last collection of poems, *Winter Words*, was published posthumously. It was also in 1923 that Hardy received a much-publicised visit from the Prince of Wales. Such a visit was scant compensation for the continuing lack of the Nobel Prize for Literature, which in the remaining five years of Hardy's life was to go to two British (Irish) writers: W. B. Yeats and Bernard Shaw.

On 11 December 1927, Hardy 'found himself, for the first time in his life, quite unable to work'.[17] Exactly a month later, he died peacefully at Max Gate. His ashes were interred in Westminster Abbey. At that ceremony, the pall-bearers included not only the Prime Minister and the Leader of the Opposition and OMs such as Barrie and Galsworthy but also the three literary figures who declined the Order: Kipling, Housman and Shaw. The newspapers had greeted Hardy's death on 12 January 1928 in a manner befitting the 'Grand Old Man of English Letters', such as *The Times*:

> a life that has a touch of the heroic in its long span, its unquenchable creative force, and its unflinching artistic sincerity ... he fought his way to the place he gained in the loving esteem of his countrymen only by prolonged patience and courage.

Although 39 years younger, his second wife survived him by only nine years. Soon after his death, she published two volumes of biography. They are commonly thought to have been dictated by Hardy himself.

A critic, writing a decade or so after Hardy's death, attempted to explain his work:

> Life to him was essentially tragic; a grim battle, in which man was almost certainly defeated by Fate. Yet he faces it with a brave tender resignation, an unfailing compassion for helpless mortality, which somehow draws the sting from despair.[18]

W. H. Auden, wrote of him in 1940, on the centenary of his birth:

> Hardy was my poetical father ... his humility before nature, his sympathy for the suffering and the blind, and his sense of proportion are as necessary now as they ever were.[19]

Hardy's continuing fame has been helped by films of his major novels, which even if not always doing full justice to his work have nevertheless brought him many more readers.

During Thomas Hardy's reign over English letters, another writer slipped into – and out of – the Order of Merit for exactly two months, only a few months shorter than the period of his British nationality: **Henry James.**

By 1915, James had been living in England for nearly 40 years. The memorial tablet to him in Chelsea Old Church records that he

> renounced a cherished citizenship to give his allegiance to England in the 1st year of the Great War.

He surrendered his American passport and found four persons to testify to his literacy and good character. They were his literary agent, the editor of a literary review, a noted critic (Edmund Gosse) and the Prime Minister

(Herbert Asquith). He took the oath of allegiance on 28 July

> and happily announced 'Civis Britannicus sum', and then rather thoughtfully said that he felt no whit 'different'.[20]

On being asked what qualities in the British had made him decide to acquire their nationality, James replied: 'I would say it is their decency ... and their dauntlessness.'[21] He had already helped the war effort by trying to persuade his fellow-Americans to come in on the Allied side.

A fervent admirer of most British institutions, James had an ambivalent attitude to the monarchy, as Kenneth Rose recounted in his life of King George V:

> On the death of Queen Victoria in 1901, James had written 'The Prince of Wales is an arch-vulgarian ... the wretched little Yorks [the future George V and Queen Mary] are less than nothing ... I am very pessimistic.'[22]

A few months after becoming a British subject, James suffered a serious stroke – on 5 December 1915. The former Prime Minister and future OM, Arthur Balfour, wrote to the King's Private Secretary:

> A friend, who wishes to be anonymous [in fact, Edward Marsh, the civil servant and literary critic and patron], has written me a letter of which the following is a copy: 'Henry James ["the novelist" added in manuscript] is lying at death's door. If he ever recovers sufficiently to *care* or realise things at all, would it be possible to persuade the Prime Minister to bestow on him the Order of Merit? It is the *only* thing that would at all appeal to him in the way of Honours and glory, and he is now such a passionate Englishman that he would appreciate it, and America would be proud ... '[23]

John Morley, however, the historian and only literary figure left from the original 12 Members of the Order, was firmly opposed to the award. But the Prime Minister, prompted by Marsh, supported it. Marsh sent a lengthy and vigorous memorandum to Asquith on 18 December:

> I think there should be little doubt of his right to stand beside George Meredith and Thomas Hardy – the only novelists yet admitted to the Order. If they have qualities which he has not, the converse is also true ... No writer of his time gives the same impression of knowledge and mastery in the architectural structure of his works, and in the gradual building up of atmosphere, character and situation.[24]

Asquith subsequently told Stamfordham:

> I have reconsidered the case of Henry James, & got the views of other
> literary authorities with the result that (despite Morley's criticisms) I
> have come to the conclusion that HM would be well advised to give him
> the OM. I believe it would have a really beneficial effect in America.[25]

The way was clear for Stamfordham to inform James of the King's intention to confer the Order 'in recognition of your eminent achievements in
the world of Literature'.[26] *The Times* greeted the announcement in the New
Year Honours with enthusiasm:

> The high honour now conferred on him will give the keenest satisfaction
> to lovers of literature all over the world, and not least in France, with
> whose national spirit and national culture he is deeply imbued ... a cit-
> izen of the world. The variety and subtlety as well as the fertility of his
> genius have placed him with Mr Thomas Hardy unquestionably at the
> head of living masters of English. Now he joins Mr Hardy in the Order,
> membership of which is the highest distinction attainable by a writer,
> and in which they are the only two representatives of pure literature.[27]

The question remained of how best to present the insignia to James, who
was clearly unable to attend an investiture. Lord Bryce, who had been
Ambassador in Washington and was an OM himself, duly went to Chelsea
and reported to the Palace:

> I took the Order of Merit to our poor friend Henry James, and placed
> it in his hands as he lay on his couch. He was conscious, and recognised
> me, and quite understood what the thing was, but he could not frame a
> complete sentence. He murmured 'Very touched' several times.[28]

Henry James lingered on, in a confused state of mind, until 28 February.
In its obituary the next day, *The Times* concluded:

> The one and most fitting distinction that could be offered him as an
> Englishman was the Order of Merit ... that he was able to appreciate
> the gift and to take pleasure in the thought of all that it meant, we know
> and should gratefully remember.[29]

Sixty years later, a stone commemorating 'Henry James, OM, Novelist' was
unveiled in Poets' Corner in Westminster Abbey.

Appropriately for the author of *Washington Square*, Henry James was
born in Washington Place in New York in 1843. His family, from Ireland
and Scotland, had been in America for a couple of generations. His Irish

grandfather had made a fortune in business. His father, also Henry, wrote on theology and his elder brother, William, became a notable philosopher. The family travelled a lot and James' rather desultory education was spread between New York, London, Paris and Geneva. He lived with his parents in Cambridge, Massachusetts and went there to Harvard Law School. Further visits to Europe in 1869 and 1872 intensified

> what he afterwards called the 'European virus', the nostalgia for the old world which made it impossible for him to live permanently elsewhere . . . when he came again, in 1875, it was with the decided intention of remaining for good.[30]

After a year in Paris, James settled in London. He was 33 and England was to be his home until his death 40 years later.

> He came because he was convinced that here only could an American really strike root in European soil.[31]

James bade farewell to his homeland with the remark that you couldn't have literature in the United States because it had no society.

James had not been shackled by any of the common parental pressures to pursue a profession. He had begun his writing ten years before settling in Europe – short stories, book reviews and two novels: *Watch and Ward* and *Roderick Hudson*, the latter having one of the first 'marginalized males' in his fiction.

On the question of James' much-debated sexual orientation – his 'consciousness of alternative masculinity' – the *DNB* (written within ten years of his death) was naturally silent, except for the traditional hint: 'He was never married.' Fifty years later, his main biographer, Leon Edel

> was timid or rash by turns. At first, he postulated a long celibacy for James, then decided, without proof, that the aged James released his longing in relations with younger men.[32]

Within a year or two of settling in London, James began dining with 'the great and the good' – in London and the country – at a fierce rate: 107 times during one winter. He met Gladstone, Browning, Trollope, Tennyson, George Eliot and Schliemann of Troy; over the years, he made friends with Burne-Jones, George du Maurier and Robert Louis Stevenson. He became an established figure on the social scene. The next 40 years were spent mostly in London, although from 1898 he lived at Lamb House in Rye during the summer and wrote his later novels there. He retained a room in the Reform Club. For the last three years of his life, James had a flat in Cheyne Walk, Chelsea.

James was renowned for his talk, which

> was memorably opulent and picturesque. To listen to him was like watching an artist at work; the ample phrases slowly uncoiled, with pausing and hesitating for the choice word, and out of them was gradually constructed the impression of the scene or the idea in his mind; when it was finished the listener was in possession of a characteristic product of Henry James's art.[33]

According to the *DNB*, James' work is commonly divided into three 'periods' or 'manners'. In the first period, the early years of his residence in England, he wrote about the impact of inexperienced Americans (especially young women) and American life on the 'older, richer, denser civilization of Europe'. This clash and the 'situations' it created were explored in novels published between 1876 and 1886, such as *The American*, *The Europeans*, *Washington Square*, *The Portrait of a Lady* and *The Bostonians*.

In the mid-1880s, James moved on to English life, with which he was obviously now more familiar:

> although it remained true that the England of his knowledge was confined to a comparatively small circle of London life.[34]

James was 'the master of the drawing room', far removed from Hardy's rural scenes. Typical of this period, extending to the end of the century, were *The Princess Casamassima* (in which, however, he did descend to the streets of London), *The Tragic Muse*, *The Spoils of Poynton*, *The Awkward Age* and *What Maisie Knew*. From the end of the century came also two of his most famous tales, both of which have been dramatised: *The Aspern Papers* and the ghost story, *The Turn of the Screw*.

In the early years of the new century, between 1902 and 1904, James returned to his original theme of the contrast between American and European character but brought to his writing much greater maturity and imagination. The result was demonstrated in his last three novels: *The Wings of the Dove*, *The Ambassadors* and *The Golden Bowl*.

James' ventures into drama, in the early 1890s, were not successful. Equally unsuccessful, as far as bringing him income, was the elaborate *New York*, revised and collected 24-volume edition of his novels and stories in 1907–1909. Between 1904–14, he wrote a few short stories and two long novels. *The Ivory Tower* and *The Sense of the Past* were unfinished at his death. They were published posthumously, with notes he had composed to guide him in completing them. Beside his novels and short stories, James' work included travel sketches and literary criticisms, as well as two completed volumes of reminiscences of his early years.

In 1909, in a fit of deep depression, James burnt many of his personal papers. In 1920, not long after his death, a collection of his letters was published. These were re-edited by Leon Edel, who for many years monopolised the study of James, culminating with a vast five-volume biography (1953–72).

Following his death, James' main biographer noted:

> The obituaries – in newspapers filled with the war – were of great length. The homage was profound... [but] very few of the Master's novels were in print... James would indeed sink from sight; swallowed up by the war, his would be among the forgotten reputations of the 1920s... It would take time for the world to rediscover him... his work itself gained an audience, slowly at first, until in the mid-twentieth century, his books were in print in great numbers.[35]

Much later came the TV serials and the films: *Portrait of a Lady*, *Wings of the Dove*, *Washington Square* and *The American*. They have completed the resurrection of 'The Master'.

J. M. Barrie's appointment to the Order of Merit arose from a bargain between George V and Lloyd George:

> At an Audience which the King gave the Prime Minister on 3rd November, 1921, His Majesty told Mr Lloyd George that he proposed conferring the Order of Merit upon Mr Rudyard Kipling. Mr Lloyd George thought the appointment would be a good one, but asked whether His Majesty would at the same time give the Order to Sir James Barrie. The King promised to do so.
>
> As Mr Kipling declined the Honour, the King decided to proceed no further with regard to Sir James Barrie, but on 20th December, Mr Lloyd George's Private Secretary, at the Prime Minister's direction, wrote to remind His Majesty of the promise, and subsequently the Order of Merit was offered to Sir James, who accepted it.[36]

According to Stamfordham (reporting a conversation with Lloyd George):

> the King's only wish was to do nothing to lower the standard of the Order of Merit... his one wish was to find, if possible, the proper person for such high recognition... [The PM] asked whether light literature was to be debarred from recognition by the OM? He regarded Barrie as the Sheridan or Oliver Goldsmith of today: his literature, though light, was well written, pure, clever, amusing: and he believed that both his works would be read and his dramas played in a hundred years' time... [37]

29 Sir James Barrie by W. T. Monnington.

The offer must have been a pleasant New Year gift for Barrie:

> in recognition of all that you have achieved as an author of fiction and as a dramatist, in both of which fields of literature your powers as an imaginative writer are unsurpassed.

The award was gazetted in the New Year Honours of 1922 as being, 'In recognition of his services to literature and the drama'. There were instant doubts about Barrie's appointment. John Murray, the publisher, observed:

> There are three or four names . . . [with] as great a claim as J. M. Barrie or even greater [including Kipling and Bridges].[38]

Many years later, these doubts were expressed more forcibly by another Private Secretary when the appointment of the poet, Walter de la Mare, was being considered:

> he is admittedly a greater literary figure than Barrie, who, in my opinion, was a bad appointment to the Order.[39]

The public announcement of the OM was not greeted with universal acclaim. *The Nation & Athenaeum* commented that:

> no touch is lighter than his; no gift blends more skilfully with the sentiment of his time. But the OM has been a jealously guarded preserve. It is our substitute for an Academy of Letters: the one high, unsoiled reward which bears the mark of a true aristocracy of mind.[40]

It thought his work was charming but lightweight and well behind other writers of 'more marked and more solid achievement', ranging from Shaw to Galsworthy and Conrad.

Barrie's undoubted popularity had already been officially recognised, although not originally to his liking. In the Birthday Honours of 1909, Herbert Tree, the actor, and Arthur Wing Pinero, the playwright, were knighted. In one of his depressive moods, Barrie had declined (gracefully) the same honour, saying 'only that he preferred to go on being Mister Barrie'.[41] The preference did not last long because although childless (and by then divorced) he did not resist the offer of the hereditary honour of a baronetcy in 1913.

James Matthew Barrie had come a long way as the ninth child of a handloom weaver in Kirriemuir, Forfarshire. Education was important, however, and it was furthered by an older brother being a teacher and, later, inspector of schools. Barrie went to Glasgow and Dumfries Academies before graduating from Edinburgh University. He was determined to write and began as a journalist but also wrote stories in which Kirriemuir became *Thrums*. These were 'kailyard' or cabbage-patch tales. Against professional advice, he moved to London in 1885, at the age of 25, and never struggled financially again. His pen names disappeared and, in his early thirties, his first novel, *The Little Minister* was published and his first plays were produced. When the novel was adapted for the stage in Britain and America, it earned Barrie £80,000 before he was 40.

It was the stage that really attracted Barrie and his last two novels of Scottish life, *Sentimental Tommy* and *Tommy and Grizel*, were published by the time he was 40. Even they had hints of *Peter Pan*, which was to be his enduring success. There were other plays, however, which were very successful in their day and continue to be revived occasionally today.

Quality Street (1901), a sentimental comedy set in a small English town during the Napoleonic era, established Barrie as a successful dramatist on both sides of the Atlantic and even ran in Berlin during the First World War. *The Admirable Crichton* (1902), with a star cast, was a great success; the critic, Ivor Brown, described it later as telling the Best People that the servants' hall contained their betters. *What Every Woman Knows* (1908), a politically-based comedy, and *Dear Brutus* (1917), about whether people would make the same mistakes if given a second chance, both proved successful.

Peter Pan (1904) is certainly Barrie's most enduring legacy, watched by successive generations of children. Originally only Barrie had any confidence in an unconsciously Freudian story. He had befriended the Llewelyn Davies family of five boys, whom he adopted after the early death of their parents. He transformed them into the Darling family of the play, with its Red Indians, pirates, Captain Hook and a crocodile inside which is a ticking clock. Much has been written of Barrie's relationship with the Davies boys. Peter, later a publisher (who committed suicide in 1960), described that with his brothers, George and Michael, as comprising 'a dash of the paternal, a lot of the maternal and much, too, of the lover.[42]

Peter Pan never dies and nor, almost, do the royalties from the productions. The rights to the character were left by Barrie to the Great Ormond Street Hospital for Children, of which he was a trustee.

With two OM-writers, so commonly assumed to be his superiors, Barrie enjoyed close relations. Meredith was 'royalty at its most august to [Barrie]'[43] and Hardy had 'a simplicity that merits the word "divine"'.[44] Another famous figure to whom he was once close was the explorer, Captain Robert Scott, one of whose death-tent letters was to Barrie:

> We are pegging out...I want you to help my widow and my boy/your Godson...Goodbye – I am not at all afraid of the end...I may not have proved a great explorer, but we have done the greatest march ever made and come very near to great success.[45]

Barrie did what he could to help Kathleen and Peter Scott.

In 1922, as Rector of St Andrews University, Barrie made one of his most famous speeches, later published as *Courage*. Haig, the Chancellor of the University, was to confer honorary degrees on Barrie's nominees, including Hardy, Galsworthy and a man who was the epitome of 'courage': Bernard Freyberg, the New Zealand VC and triple DSO. Barrie, however, was still badly affected by Michael Davies' death by drowning and he wrote that

> it was not St Andrews students I was seeing on the occasion, but an Oxford one.[46]

Towards the end of his life, Barrie (who greatly enjoyed his encounters with the royal family) played an elaborate charade with the very young

Princess Margaret, the first royal baby so close to the succession to be born in Scotland since Charles I in 1600. At her third birthday party, the princess placed one of her prized presents between Barrie and herself with the words 'It is yours and mine' and soon afterwards, overhearing Barrie being discussed, said: 'I know that man. He is my greatest friend, and I am his greatest friend.' Barrie incorporated both phrases in his last play, *The Boy David*. He agreed that she should have a penny for every night the play ran. It was a flop but nevertheless George VI playfully threatened Barrie with legal proceedings if he did not pay his debt. Barrie drew up a mock-indenture that, with his and Princess Margaret's signatures, is still in the Royal Library. Three days before he was due to go to the Palace with a bag of new pennies, Barrie was taken ill and died on 19 June 1937.

On the writer's centenary in 1960, the critic Ivor Brown wrote:

> A writer who has greatly pleased and who had lived a full life of years and triumphs is a certain target for disparagement... weakest of his work is apt to be brought up in evidence against him while the strongest is forgotten... Barrie... had enjoyed everything in the honours course... had gratified the Best People; he had so pleased the next-best that some of his plays could be called Middle Classics... the pet of the Establishment.[47]

Much later, it was written of Barrie that, 'his unfashionable whimsicality has come to obscure the best of his work: *Peter Pan*, however, remains popular.'[48]

John Galsworthy, before he was considered for the Order of Merit, had had the unusual distinction of receiving and declining a knighthood – in public. A letter offering the honour was sent on Christmas Eve 1917. The letter did not arrive. His reply to a chaser telegram was: 'Most profoundly grateful but feel I must not accept.'[49] His telegram did not reach Number 10 before the honours list was sent to the press and his knighthood was gazetted in the 1918 New Year Honours. He telegraphed again to Lloyd George, 'that I must persist in my refusal to accept and asked for his contradiction in the Press'.[50] This was duly forthcoming.

Thomas Hardy was quite philosophical in his letter:

> I don't think that mistake about the knighthood a disaster for you exactly, and probably you don't by this time. A friend of mine who happened to be here said, 'He has scored both ways. He has had the honour of being knighted, and the honour of having refused a knighthood. Many men would envy him.'[51]

Galsworthy's reply to press enquiries about his refusal was that 'Literature is its own reward' and his reasoning to Lloyd George states:

> I have long held and expressed the conviction that men who strive to be artists in Letters, especially those who attempt criticism of life and philosophy, should not accept titles.[52]

When Galsworthy was being considered as an OM in 1928, Kipling (by then an adviser on the Order, rather than a recipient of it) commented:

> by virtue of good work, general acceptance by critics and large popularity – would be a good name and ought to have a good Press.[53]

The Prime Minister, Stanley Baldwin, also suggested Galsworthy, who was now 'a bigger name in Europe than Shaw'.[54] It was also Baldwin's point about Galsworthy's reputation on the continent which informed the Private Secretary's submission to the King:

> His great prose work, *The Forsyte Saga*, is a complete chronicle of the typical English family of upper middle class at the beginning of the present century, and is regarded as a standard English work by foreigners, especially Germans. His influence in Europe is widespread and all for the good in favourably representing England to other Nations...[55]

The letter offering the OM referred to

> the admiration in which your writings are held not only by your fellow Englishmen, but also by a wide circle of readers among other Nations.[56]

Ramsay MacDonald (two days before becoming Prime Minister for the second time) wrote:

> My only regret is that I am now deprived of the opportunity of carrying out my own intentions.[57]

His intentions – in respect of the Order of Merit? Galsworthy was in little doubt as to whom to thank. He wrote to Stanley Baldwin, the outgoing Prime Minister:

> I write to you in briefest measure of my gratitude, for I know that you can have no time just now for reading of the pleasure you have given...[58]

Galsworthy received the OM from the Prince of Wales, the only time the Order has been conferred by the Heir to the Throne. George V was recovering from a serious illness.

Although Galsworthy was proud of his OM, he did take his publishers to task for overplaying it:

> By the way, I think JOHN GALSWORTHY, O.M. is a mistake in your advertisements. D.D. (dog's dinner) would have been better but no letters at all would have been best. May they be suppressed, please?[59]

John Galsworthy lived from 1867 to 1933. His background was thoroughly upper middle-class Forsytian: son of a solicitor/businessman, he went to Harrow and New College, Oxford before being called to the Bar. As a budding marine lawyer, he travelled in merchant ships in the Far East to gain experience and on one of them the mate was 'a capital fellow called Conrad'. Later, the established novelist was to help Galsworthy by reading his work, introducing him to other writers and finding publishers. Galslworthy's wife, Ada, was also instrumental in his becoming a writer.

Galsworthy's early writings were under a pseudonym but in 1906 he published under his own name the first novel in the Forsyte Saga, *Man of Property*, and his first play, *The Silver Box*. He continued the Saga with a number of novels in the 1920s and it is by them that he is now most remembered. Indeed, he called *The Forsyte Saga* his 'passport to permanence' and the original readership has been vastly increased by adaptations on TV in 1967–68 and 2002 and on radio in 1990. He acknowledged his own family as their base: 'Old Jolyon' as his father and the country house as Kingston Hill, where he was born and brought up. Gilbert Murray described the Saga as

> a highly critical, but not altogether unsympathetic, description of Victorian upper-class commercial society, narrow in sympathies but strong in will and in the prudential virtues.[60]

Most of Galsworthy's plays had a moral or social theme: *The Silver Box*, on the different treatment of rich and poor offenders; Strife, on conflict in industry; *Justice*, in which the law grinds down a minor felon (and which was part of his long campaign against solitary confinement); *The Skin Game*, about the rivalry between old and new money; *Loyalties*, on the clash between old England and intrusive Jewry.

At the end of his life, in November 1932, Galsworthy became the third Briton to receive the Nobel Prize for Literature; his two predecessors, Kipling and Shaw, did not want the OM. He and Eliot were the only writer-OMs to receive the Literature Prize; two other winners will be found in other chapters – Bertrand Russell and Winston Churchill.

Galsworthy's Prize was clearly linked to his best-known work. It was awarded 'for his distinguished art of narration which takes its highest form in *The Forsyte Saga*.' He gave the prize money to form a trust fund for the benefit of international PEN, the association of writers , of which he was the first President.

Galsworthy died on the last day of January 1933. The Dean of Westminster would not agree to Galsworthy's ashes being buried in the Abbey, although he conducted a memorial service for him. The assault on his reputation began as soon as he was dead. *The Times* spoke of his participation in the literary 'challenge to nearly all accepted values' at the turn of the century:

> The author of *Strife* and *Justice* began like his own Forsytes to 'date'... [His] social philosophy tends to eliminate responsibility from its humanitarian scale of values... he felt the menace of catastrophes which he knew no skill to avert.[61]

Galsworthy's plays are rarely produced now. As one recent critic wrote: 'His theatrical eclipse is total.'[62] He is not considered to have extended literary frontiers.

After Galsworthy's death in 1933, nearly 40 years passed before another novelist was appointed to the Order of Merit: **E. M. Forster**, on 1 January 1969, his ninetieth birthday. It was 46 years since the publication of his last novel, *A Passage to India*. It was not Forster's first state honour. He had been made a Companion of Honour in the New Year Honours of 1953, which coincided with his seventy-fourth birthday. There was comment both on how long he had waited for such an honour and on why it was not the Order of Merit anyway. 'These honours recognized that, second only to D. H. Lawrence, Forster was the most important British novelist of his generation.'[63] Three years earlier, Forster had declined a knighthood and he had to wait only three years for the more exclusive CH.

When Forster's OM was announced, the Palace emphasised that this personal award from the Queen was not part of the New Year Honours published on the same day; it just happened to be the recipient's ninetieth birthday.

(Edward) Morgan Forster – Morgan to his friends and EM to his readers – was the son of an architect, who died of consumption when the boy was nearly two. He was brought up by his mother and doting aunts. A legacy of £8,000 from a great-aunt (Marianne Thornton, whose biography he later wrote) paid for his education at Tonbridge and King's College, Cambridge and gave him independence to exist as a writer. He later described the products of Tonbridge and similar schools as having 'well-developed bodies, fairly developed minds and undeveloped hearts'.

King's was altogether different. 'They taught the perky boy that he was not everything and the limp boy that he might be something.'[64] Forster

30 E. M. Forster by Dora Carrington.

repaid his mental debt to one of his Cambridge mentors, G. Lowes Dickinson (the political scientist and Hellenophile), by writing his biography. He was elected to the elite society of the Apostles, came under the influence of the philosopher, G. E. Moore, and met the embryonic Bloomsbury set, from whom, however, he always maintained a certain detachment. He achieved no academic distinction at Cambridge but secured seconds (in classics and history) in both parts of the tripos.

After travelling in Greece and Italy, Forster began to write short stories, which were later gathered together in *The Celestial Omnibus* (1911) – in which his fantasy allowed a horse-bus driven by Dante and Sir Thomas Browne to ply between Surbiton and Heaven – and *The Eternal Moment* (1928), which were whimsical and dealt with the supernatural.

Forster quickly found, however, his true medium in the novel and he wrote four within five years. In the first, *Where Angels Fear to Tread* (1905), he explored prejudice versus passion and began his description of the sterility of the English middle class. Forster described his second novel, *The*

Longest Journey (1907), as about reality and the need for accepting it – of discovering what is 'really there' and what is illusory. It was Forster's own favourite.

Although *A Room with a View* (1908) was Forster's third novel, it was the first he had begun. It drew on his experiences in Italy and the final version has a happy ending. It showed his belief that in everyone, however snobbish or awful or ridiculous their appearance, there is some redeeming quality.

Howard's End (1910) consolidated Forster's reputation. The house of its title was based down to the smallest detail on 'Rooksnest', his childhood home. It has been described as

> Forster's symbol of England, an immemorial rural England resisting the 'red rust' of advancing suburbia and opposed to the impersonal flux of London.[65]

Howard's End contains the most famous of Forster's epigraphs – the maxim

> *Only connect* the prose and passion, and both will be exalted, and human love will be seen at its height. Live in fragments no longer.[66]

There came a long silence after *Howard's End*. (*Maurice*, although written in 1913, was not to be published until after Forster's death, nearly 60 years later.) In 1914, he thought he was on the edge of a literary abyss 'into which I dread to peer'.[67] Much later, he told Mark Boxer, the cartoonist (whom he reminded of an Edwardian tobacconist) that he disguised real people in his novels by changing their sex.[68]

With Forster, there has been no necessity – as with James, of an earlier age – to speculate about the nature of his homosexuality:

> Forster asked his biographer not to dissemble about his private life. He in no way resembled Oscar Wilde or sought the milieu of international homosexuals; he longed only for a loving and stable relationship with someone not of his own class. This was denied him until the 1930s when he achieved such a relationship, which endured with great happiness until his death.[69]

Forster found this happiness with a young married policeman, Bob Buckingham, and it was in their small suburban house in Coventry that he died on 7 June 1970. (As a humanist, he was cremated without religious ceremony.)

Maurice was originally written on the eve of the First World War and was extensively revised up to 1960. After his death in 1971, his literary co-executors found the last typescript with the note, 'Publishable – but worth it?'. They decided it was, along with *The Life to Come*, containing homosexual short stories long hidden from view. According to one biographer, the novel

> is not thinly-disguised autobiography or wish fulfilment but a created fictional world...[with a] presentation of the many aspects of homosexuality [that] is illuminating and moving.[70]

Forster spent most of the First World War in Alexandria, collecting information from the wounded as a search officer for the Red Cross. While there he wrote a history and guide to the city, a series of essays (under the name 'Pharos'). His time in Alexandria reinforced his love of the warm and more relaxed Mediterranean. It was an atmosphere in which he was able to pursue an affair with an Egyptian tram conductor, Mohammed el Adl, whose death a few years later greatly saddened him when he was completing *A Passage to India*.

Forster's association with India began in 1912 when he went there with Lowes Dickinson. During the visit, he drafted the first chapters of a novel on the country and there it rested for ten years – along with a never-completed novel, *Arctic Summer*. He returned to India in 1921 as private secretary to the Maharaja of Dewas (Senior Branch), a small Hindu state of 75,000 people. (He wrote about his experience in *The Hill of Devi* (1953).) This second spell in India gave new life to the novel, which he completed on his return to Britain. *A Passage to India* (1924) is generally considered to be his masterpiece, as well as the end of his short career as a novelist. The title came from Walt Whitman. The work was immediately acclaimed in Britain and America and Forster's reputation increased steadily thereafter.

When the critic, V. S. Pritchett, asked him why he had not written another novel, Forster replied: 'I have forgotten how.'[71] To another enquirer, he said that: 'the post war world was not one in which his imagination felt at home – too much had changed.'[72] Bernard Levin wondered whether he was simply sick of people asking him what his novels meant. Another critic's explanation was more blunt:

> Forster had not in fact dried up. But [if he] could not publish fiction as a homosexual, he would not publish it as if he were not one...He did not wish to pay whatever price frankness in his lifetime might involve.[73]

Recognition of *A Passage to India* was immediate and led to Forster's first fellowship at King's from 1927–33 and his delivery of the Clark Lectures in 1927. These were published as *Aspects of the Novel* and were his most substantial contribution to literary criticism.

In the 1930s, Forster dissected Oswald Mosley's 'personal magnetism' and the exploitation of

> the boredom which devastates people who are not quite sure they are gentlemen... the bank clerks and little typists who don't know how to enliven life.[74]

He became increasingly concerned with political and social questions and was twice president of the National Council for Civil Liberties (now known as Liberty). From this time came a statement which was later much used by traitors to justify their actions. Forster had written (and the first and last phrases were often conveniently omitted in quotation):

> I hate the idea of causes, and if I had to choose between betraying my country and betraying my friend, I hope I should have the guts to betray my country... Love and loyalty to an individual can run counter to the claims of the State. When they do – down with the State, say I, which means that the State would down me.[75]

In mid-life, Forster had lived with his mother in a house near Dorking. On his mother's death in 1945, he accepted an invitation to return to King's College, Cambridge where he occupied rooms as an honorary fellow. In 1951, he published essays, broadcasts and articles of the preceding 15 years, which elaborated on his tolerant personal creed under the title *Two Cheers for Democracy*. When his close friend, Kenneth Clark, told him 'One too many', he gave 'a sweet smile of agreement'.[76] He stayed with Clark for two weeks every year when King's College kitchens were closed. Clark summarised Forster's outlook as that of

> a man with a genuinely free mind. At Cambridge Lytton Strachey had called him the 'mole' because you never knew where he would come to the surface or by what invisible means he had got there. But he was really quite consistent. Even his most surprising remarks revealed the same state of mind. He believed in human beings and human relationships and thought nothing else mattered. He loved people, places and music. He disliked institutions, categories and hierarchies.[77]

Yet Forster realised his own worth. In 1951, when he was working with Eric Crozier on the libretto of Britten's opera *Billy Budd* and just before he and the much younger Britten began to accept honours such as the CH and OM, *The Observer* observed:

> In old age he has become sensitive of the respect which he feels is owed to him, although he is the least pompous of great men. He is conscious

of being England's premier novelist, and is quick to notice any slight to art or to himself in the great world of politics and affairs.[78]

In his *DNB* entry, Noel Annan (who had been Provost of King's for much of Forster's last years there) described the novelist as speaking

> for liberal humanism. No one wrote with greater simplicity or originality in defence of such well-worn concepts as liberty, democracy, and tolerance. He was unafraid of the contradictions in life which he believed liberals ought to face ... if a choice had to be made he would make it. 'If I had to betray my country or my friend, I hope I should have the guts to betray my country.' His works were full of aphorisms: 'panic and emptiness', 'the life of telegrams and anger', 'only connect'.
>
> He distrusted size, pomp, the Establishment, empires, politics, the upper classes, planners, institutions. He put his trust in individuals, small groups and insignificant people, the life of the heart and mind, personal relations ... he could be melancholy and low temperature – he once said, 'I have warmed both hands before the fire of life. And put it out'; his vitality went into the characters in his novels and his writing.[79]

There are two accounts of Forster's encounters with royal ladies and cakes. In one, the short-sighted novelist bows to the cake at Lord Harewood's wedding, mistaking it for Queen Mary. In the other, the inebriated novelist attempts to blow out Queen Elizabeth The Queen Mother, mistaking her for a birthday cake. There is probably only one incident, spawning two (?or more) versions.

As with Hardy and James, Forster's novels have become much better known by their dramatisations. Fearful of the effect of the cinema, he had refused offers in his lifetime for the filming of *A Passage to India*, but it was successfully produced by David Lean in 1984. Later, the partnership of Ismail Merchant and James Ivory filmed, with equal success, *A Room with a View*, *Maurice* and *Howard's End*. Finally, Derek Granger produced *Where Angels Fear to Tread*.

Forster's reputation has wonderfully survived the biographies, both of him and of others in which he is mentioned:

> 'Recent years have ... revealed the whole man, in a way that leaves him fully exposed but quite unsullied by exposure.
>
> In the last analysis, what Forster did is merely interesting; but what he stood for matters and matters as much today as when he first found words to describe it.[80]

31 J. B. Priestley by Howard Coster.

When **John Boynton Priestley** received the Order of Merit on 24 October 1977, he stole the headlines from the three other distinguished recipients: Oliver Franks, the outstanding administrator; Alexander Todd, Nobel chemistry laureate and President of the Royal Society; and Frederick Ashton, the founder-choreographer of the Royal Ballet. Yet they all had the titles and other honours consistently refused by 'Grumpy Jack': plain J. B. Priestley, dramatist and novelist.

Priestley, contrary to the usual conventions, made no secret of his refusals of what he described as

> those pats on the head and shoulder from the Establishment, meant for better or worse men, not for me.[81]

Later, he wrote of his 'lack of interest in Establishment honours, traditionally unwelcome in my profession.'[82] Priestley declined the offer of a peerage and the CH – twice – 'convinced that Lord Priestley would ill become a socialist with roots reaching far back into the past'.[83] The only honour which Priestley did not despise was the Order of Merit, as he made clear in his book, *The Edwardians* (1970):

> [Edward VII] helped to create an atmosphere in which the arts could flourish. And it was this 'arch-vulgarian' who early in his reign created an Order of Merit that really was – and still is – an order of merit, not just another title and ribbon.

The news of the award of the OM was announced by his delighted wife, Jacquetta Hawkes, to a weekend party that included John Bayley and Iris Murdoch, as well as Diana Collins, the campaigner against apartheid and nuclear weapons:

> That was truly a moment of emotional delight; we knew that the Order of Merit was the only honour that Jack had said that he would ever accept, as it was not political, being in the sole gift of the Queen and given only for genuine merit and special service to the country.[84]

Priestley was indeed delighted with the honour and bluntly defended his acceptance of it in a radio interview:

> I deserve it. Other people think I deserve it.[85]

He headed his writing paper 'JB Priestley OM' and declared it was 'nicer than any title'. On his death in 1984, his 'local' newspaper, *The Yorkshire Post*, wrote that:

> He settled, with Swan Arcade shrewdness, for the Order of Merit and its incomparable cultural distinctions, when many other honours must have been put before him.[86]

Priestley joined the Order of Merit just as it took on something of a collegiate life, with quinquennial gatherings as guests of the Queen:

> Jack enjoyed Buckingham Palace and subsequent lunches with his fellow OMs. Jacquetta, with her feeling for ancient history and mythology, had always believed in royalty. Jack, the egalitarian democrat, thought their existence added to the social silliness of the English, until that is, he watched a television documentary and realized that the royals were hard-working professionals, entitled to respect and understanding from another hard-working professional.[87]

John Priestley ('Boynton' appeared later) was the son of a Bradford elementary school headmaster, whom he described as 'the man socialists have in mind when they write about socialism'; his father's school was the first of its kind to serve meals to the pupils. He went to Belle Vue Grammar School in the city but left at 16 to work as a clerk in a wool firm until the outbreak of the First World War.

Bradford, the home of the Independent Labour Party, was sometimes called the 'Rome of Socialism'. The young Priestley enjoyed there what he later described as an idyllic life, 'belonging at heart to the pre-1914 North Country'. He went to the theatres, music halls, art galleries and concerts. He wrote poetry and articles for socialist weeklies.

The war proved, however, that Bradford or, indeed, the North Country would never be enough to satisfy Priestley. He seized the opportunity to enlist, served in the ranks and was twice wounded in Flanders. He was commissioned in the last year of the war. Like many others, he preferred to put the four grim years behind him, never collecting his medals and rarely writing on the subject. But he never forgot about it.

Priestley used an ex-serviceman's grant to go to Trinity Hall, Cambridge, wearing his uniform dyed blue. He obtained seconds in English and history, while remaining determined not to acquire 'a private income accent'. On leaving Cambridge, he was married and he settled with his wife in London. He led the life of a literary journalist, producing reviews, articles and essays, besides two novels and a biography of George Meredith.

What brought Priestley great popularity – and financial success – was his novel *The Good Companions* (1929), about an impoverished travelling theatrical troupe, the 'Dinky Doos'. It was dramatised in 1931 (with John Gielgud in the lead) and filmed in 1932. Although it opened up a new career for Priestley as a dramatist, he thought his London novel *Angel Pavement* (1930) was much better.

In the 1930s Priestley made the transition to playwright that earlier novelists, including Dickens and Henry James, had signally failed to do. His plays greatly increased his fame and wealth. The first play, *Dangerous Corner* (1932) was described by the leading critic, James Agate, as 'a piece of sustained ingenuity of the highest technical accomplishment'. *Eden End* (1934) evoked pre-1914 nostalgia. Drawn to the writings of the philosopher and inventor, J. W. Dunne (as well as to those of P. D. Ouspensky and Carl Jung), he became fascinated with the problem of Time and produced a succession of plays drawing in various ways on this theme: in 1937 *Time and the Conways* and *I Have Been Here Before*; in 1938 *When We Are Married* (a Yorkshire comedy); in 1939 *Johnson Over Jordan* (about life after death). A postscript to these was *An Inspector Calls*, which was performed first in Moscow in 1945 and subsequently in Britain; it was filmed and is still regularly staged. Priestley was convinced that the Past had not vanished; it still existed, not as a dim memory but in all its colour and hum.

Alongside his pre-war plays Priestley wrote *English Journey*, a record of travels through the country during the economic depression. He identified the whole industrial process as the real enemy of the working class, who would not benefit significantly from the taking of private industry into public ownership.

The idea of Priestley's famous broadcasts in the summer of 1940 came from a listener. Going out as *Postscripts* to Sunday evening news bulletins, their plain and practical gruffness made them very popular. A later Conservative prime minister, who remembered the Priestley talks from her youth, thought that he: 'had a unique gift of cloaking left-wing views as solid, down to earth, Northern homespun philosophy.'[88] The broadcasts remained a source of pride to Priestley.

Priestley stood unsuccessfully as an Independent in the 1945 election and made an official Labour election broadcast in 1950. He did not, however, fit easily into any organisation and resigned from the British committee to UNESCO and the boards of the National Theatre and the *New Statesman*. It was an article in that journal in 1957 that led directly to the Campaign for Nuclear Disarmament. He was briefly associated with the early marches to Aldermaston but quickly became disillusioned with what he saw as the left-wing takeover of the movement.

After the early death of his wife in 1925, he soon married a woman who had already borne his child. Twenty-five years (and many affairs) later, there was a notorious divorce case, involving Jacquetta Hawkes, the archaeologist daughter of an OM (Frederick Gowland Hopkins), who became his third wife. The case left him with a lasting sense of grievance against judges. He described the summing-up in his own case:

> I now come to the co-respondent. I am told he is a writer of fiction. And [wagging his empurpled jowls over his crimson and ermine] having heard him in the witness box, *I can well believe it.*[89]

Other parts of the Establishment fared little better. He said he always found it difficult to know where the Foreign Office ended and the MCC began.

Priestley did not settle easily into any sort of 'retirement'. He continued to write almost to his death. *Literature and Western Man* (1960) drew on his voracious reading over the years. There were novels of varying quality, such as *Festival at Farbridge* (1951), to coincide with the Festival of Britain, *Sir Michael and Sir George* (1964), reminiscent of an order he would never have accepted, *Lost Empires* (1965) about the old music halls, in a TV adaptation in which Laurence Olivier starred as a failed comedian, *The Image Men* (1968), an attack on mass advertising, and *Found, Lost, Found* (1976), a modern fairytale.

Priestley added two volumes of autobiography, *Margin Released* (1962) and *Instead of the Trees* (1977) to those he had written earlier: *Midnight on the Desert* (1937) and *Rain upon Godshill* (1939). He dabbled in history with a trilogy (1969–72) covering 1815–1910: *The Prince of Pleasure,*

Victoria's Heyday and *The Edwardians*, as well as an attempt to sum up his countrymen in *The English* (1973). He adapted Iris Murdoch's *A Severed Head* for a long West End run. In *Particular Pleasures* (1975), Priestley described the painters, musicians and actors, British and foreign, whom he especially admired.

On his own achievement, Priestley was realistic:

I am not a genius – although I do have a hell of a lot of talent.[90]

He thought that he was overvalued before the Second World War and undervalued after it. He once described his greatest achievement as being the first and perhaps only British playwright to demand successfully from the management a nightly cut from the receipts of the theatre bars.[91]

Priestley's eightieth birthday in 1974 was marked by the publication of a collection of short pieces, *Outcries and Asides* and of a travelogue, *A Visit to New Zealand*, where he discovered that hotel measures of whisky were like 'minute samples of poison'. He died on 14 August 1984, a month before his ninetieth birthday.

Priestley was never a 'writer's writer'. He was always vulnerable to criticism from his peers:

Graham Greene credited him with a crude mind, and no more depth than a holiday snapshot. He was, tittered Virginia Woolf, not a man of letters but a 'tradesman of letters'.[92]

Priestley's 'fellow' novelist, Anthony Powell, thought his mind was a 'stupefying banality'.[93] (Powell also thought that Graham Greene was 'seriously overrated' but, despite being tipped to 'succeed' him in the Order of Merit, he never did so. He stayed at the level of CH.) There were, however, those who spoke up for Priestley. Richard Church maintained that his literary gift was

not so ordinary as some superior critics have assumed it to be. As a verbal craftsman he is admirable, for he loves his medium of words and uses them ... [He] has skill and tenderness, a sensitiveness and a sense of solitude and privacy.[94]

T. S. Eliot told Priestley that he was one of the few contemporary dramatists whose plays he respected.[95] His publishers, Heinemann, called him the 'gasfire Dickens' and, indeed, he was the last serious English writer to command an audience of Dickensian proportions.

Unlike other OM novelist/playwrights, Priestley's reputation has not been helped in recent years by films and TV productions. A common question is 'Who reads Priestley now?' The answer is probably 'not many', except

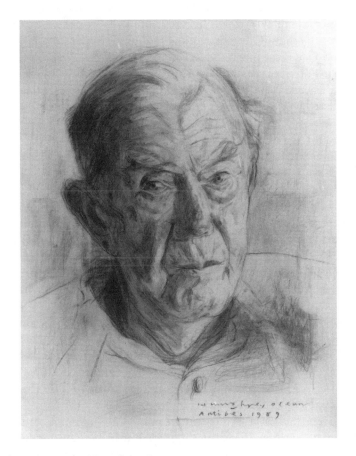

32 Graham Greene by Humphrey Ocean.

those studying *An Inspector Calls* at A Level. For many years, however, his plays have sustained theatre in the regions outside the pantomime season and they are the staple fare of amateur dramatic societies. His work overall scarcely arouses the same universal interest as Hardy, James and Forster. For someone who yearned so long for the Order of Merit, his reputation has not markedly enhanced its standing.

Eighteen months after Priestley's death in August 1984, **Graham Greene** was appointed to the Order of Merit on 11 February 1986. Like Priestley, he had refused a knighthood but, unlike his predecessor, he had not also shunned a CH, which he accepted in 1966. Frederic Raphael once said that the knighthood declined by Greene was 'the kind gained by services to the Garrick bar'.

The OM for Greene gave the press the usual difficulty in explaining the honour. Even the royal correspondent of *The Times* wrote that, 'although it does not bring a knighthood, the exclusivity guarantees that the suffix "OM" is just as highly prized'. 'Just as'? Surely, 'far more'.

Whenever Graham Greene's works are discussed, the only honour normally mentioned is the one he never received: the Nobel Prize for Literature. Its continued absence was highlighted by the appointment to the Order of Merit, at the same time, of Dr Frederick Sanger, the chemist who had won *two* Nobel Prizes. Even Greene's publisher and close friend, Max Reinhardt, said that he was

> immensely proud to have been awarded the Order of Merit in 1986, even if it was seen as some sort of consolation prize.[96]

Champions of English literature, finding it difficult to understand the Prize being awarded to writers in 'minority' languages, have often complained that neither Hardy nor Forster received the Prize. But then nor did Tolstoy or Gorky or Rilke. In its first century, the Nobel Prize was no more infallible than the Order of Merit.

(Henry) Graham Greene was born into the professional middle-class, with connections to the Greene King brewing family. His clergyman father was headmaster of Berkhamsted School and, as a pupil there, Graham felt 'like the son of a quisling in a country under occupation'.[97] His mother was a cousin of Robert Louis Stevenson. His fascinating early years are best told through his own words and the quotations that follow – until we reach the 1930s – are from his partial autobiography, *A Sort of Life* (but are not individually referenced in the Notes).

After Greene had briefly run away from school (and home) at the age of 16, his father sent him to stay with an analyst in London for 'what were perhaps the happiest six months of my life'. He read history in Kensington Gardens and had a daily session with the analyst, when he recounted the previous night's dream – or invented one if he could not remember it:

> Dreams have always had an importance for me...Two novels and several short stories have emerged from my dreams...

At Oxford, between drinking and amateur espionage, he wrote his only published poems and his first (unpublished) novel. He also obtained a moderate second in History. Greene, the spy, naturally fitted into his seedy fictional world of 'Greeneland'. While still at Oxford, he toyed with espionage: 'the idea of experiencing a little danger made me write to the German Embassy and offer my services as a propagandist.' The Germans gave him £100 to travel in the French-occupied zone of Germany, where he met a German whose task it was to kidnap Germans who collaborated with the French authorities and smuggle them into unoccupied Germany for trial for high treason. Later, he approached the French Embassy in London with the idea of becoming a double agent. An improvement in the international situation, however, brought an end to all his schemes – the Germans dispensed with his services. Greene had passed the interview for the Consular Service, with the idea of following James Elroy Flecker on the Golden Road to Samarkand, but he never sat the examination and so was lost to straightforward British diplomacy.

After two weeks with the British-American Tobacco Company (destined for China), Greene resigned. A short spell of private tutoring was followed by journalism, in which he had indulged at Oxford. With no 'apprenticeship' available in London, Greene began work on the *Nottingham Journal*. But Greene wanted – and needed – more money than he could earn in Nottingham and so he set out for the golden streets of London in 1926. Within a month, he was a sub-editor on *The Times*. Soon after he joined *The Times*, the General Strike was declared and it was the only paper that was published without interruption. During the Strike he became a special constable, patrolling Vauxhall Bridge.

Greene turned early to alcohol and also to sex, even if unrequited; and subsequently even to Russian roulette.

Greene met his wife, Vivienne, after she left a note for him at Balliol complaining of his use, in a film review, of the 'worship' Catholics gave to the Virgin Mary when he should have said 'hyperdulia'. Intrigued, he met her and, after their engagement, decided he ought to become a Catholic himself. Later, fearing that he had epilepsy, he stood on an Underground platform and tried to summon the will and the courage to jump: 'But suicide requires greater courage than Russian roulette.' He secured little comfort from a talk with a priest.

In the face of Catholic criticism of his novels – he received a stern lecture from the Cardinal Archbishop of Westminster on *The Power and the Glory* – he readily took comfort from what Pope Paul VI told him:

> Some parts of your books will always offend some Catholics. You should not worry about that.

With his wife, Greene went to live in a thatched cottage near Chipping Campden in the Cotswolds. He and Vivienne later separated, over 40 years before his death, but they never divorced.

Greene's first novel to reach the public, *The Man Within*, was published in 1929 by Heinemann. It led to a deal with the publisher – £600 a year for three years in return for three novels. His next two novels were failures. There was, however, the 'temporary popular success' of his first so-called 'entertainment', *Stamboul Train*, which was chosen by the Book Society, worth 10,000 copies. Nevertheless, Greene's stock, as a writer of originality and power, steadily rose during the 1930s. *It's A Battlefield* (1934) was followed by *England Made Me* (1935) and *Journey without Maps* (1936), an account of a visit to Liberia. *Brighton Rock* (1938) introduced a subject he was to pursue over the years: sin in a Catholic context, although he found it 'very difficult to believe in sin'. He intended, on the model of Eliot's *The Waste Land*, to attack the 'soulless, modern culture' of the mid-twentieth century; but he grew to like Brighton and the characters he created there.

In 1940, came what is regarded by many as his masterpiece, *The Power and the Glory*, set in Mexico during the struggle between church and state. 'Whisky priest' entered the language, much as 'Our Man in . . .' was to do later.

Greene's war service was in espionage – real espionage, working for MI6 in Sierra Leone, an experience he used in *The Heart of the Matter* (1948). A long-standing dislike of uniforms – bred in his school OTC days – led him to resist the cover of a naval commander or an air group captain and describe himself instead 'CID Special Branch'.

The End of the Affair (1951) was inspired by his long-running involvement with Catherine Walston, whose rich complaisant husband later became a Labour peer and minister. *The Quiet American* (1955), heavily satirical of US policy in South East Asia, was eerily prophetic of what was to happen ten years later in Vietnam. More politically-motivated novels were to follow: *Our Man in Havana* (1958), mocking the activities of his erstwhile employer, MI6; *The Comedians* (1966), set in Papa Doc Duvalier's Haiti; *The Honorary Consul* (1973), with a whisky-sodden pseudo-diplomat in a remote corner of the world; and *The Human Factor* (1978), about spying.

> His nose for the world's next trouble-spot became so uncannily efficient that dictators were said to turn pale when he set up his typewriter overlooking their capitals.[98]

Another 'Catholic' novel, *A Burnt-Out Case* (1961), was set in a leper colony in the Congo. At the end of the decade came a change of course, with the farcical *Travels With my Aunt* (1969), in which an outrageous aunt lures a stuffy bank official on extraordinary and mostly illegal adventures around the world.

Greene, unlike earlier novelists, wrote most of his books in the golden age of the cinema and nearly 20 of them have been filmed. *Stamboul Train* was screened only two years after its publication and *Brighton Rock* within ten years, giving Richard Attenborough one of his early leading screen roles. As with later films, such as *Our Man in Havana* and *The Comedians*, Greene wrote the screenplay. He wrote *The Third Man* as a film before it became a novel. *The End of the Affair* and *The Quiet American* have been filmed twice. Greene was a reviewer of films before a writer of them. He became the film critic of *The Spectator* in 1935.

Greene's left-wing 'credentials' were always obvious. At Oxford, he had been in the Communist Party – for a few weeks, in the hope of winning a free trip to Moscow. Much later, in 1968 (after he had accepted the CH), he wrote the introduction to the autobiography of the spy and defector, Kim Philby:

> It is far more gripping than any novel of espionage . . . a dignified statement of his beliefs and motives . . . who among us has not committed treason to something or someone more important than a country?[99]

Here were echoes of E. M. Forster. He saw Philby again in Moscow in 1987 but passed the exile's subsequent letters to him to MI6.

In all his travels, Greene was especially fond of Latin America. He thought that *The Honorary Consul* (1972), set on the Argentine–Paraguayan border, was his best novel. His friendship with Omar Torrijos, the Panamanian leader, was recounted in *Getting to Know the General* (1985); its writing delayed his twenty-sixth and last novel, *The Captain and the Enemy* (1988), which was set in Central America.

Like all writers, Greene was influenced by others. Henry James was his idol: 'to say he influenced me is a bit absurd – like saying a mountain influenced a mouse.'[100] He regretted Joseph Conrad's influence on his early unsuccessful novels but appointed a Conrad scholar, Norman Sherry, as his official biographer. He admired Evelyn Waugh: 'the best . . . One felt as if one's commanding officer were dead.'[101] He did not admire J. B. Priestley, who compelled him to alter the description of a character: a pompous, pipe-smoking, popular novelist in *Stamboul Train*.

Greene's prodigious writings to the press were gathered in a book, *Yours etc: Letters to the Press 1945–89*. He ranged widely: from 37 misprints on a single page of *The Times* to the Papacy under the conservative John Paul II. In a famous letter to *The Times* in 1967, he wrote that 'if I had to choose between life in the Soviet Union and life in the United States of America, I would certainly choose the Soviet Union.' He confessed that 'after a drink too many I'm always tempted to write a trivial letter to *The Times*'.[102]

For most of his later years, Greene lived in Antibes, on the French Riviera, where he told the redoubtable drinker, Jeffrey Bernard, that his doctors had limited him to one drink a day. Filling a large glass with vodka, he said: 'Here it is.' In the last year of his life, Green moved to Switzerland for health reasons and died there on 3 April 1991. With him was Father Leopoldo Duran, the close friend on whom he had modelled the *Monsignor Quixote* of his novel of 1982.

The obituaries and leading articles were unanimous in praise of Greene. According to *The Times*:

> [his] reputation must rest on his serious religious novels, the first to be written in England in this century. But he was versatile and his travel books, short stories, criticism and those lighter novels he called

'entertainments' were of high quality. He was an outstanding storyteller; he wrote plays and film-scripts as well as being an excellent critic . . . No other contemporary British writer enjoyed so high a reputation on the continent of Europe.[103]

He established in English literature a 'Greeneland', a peculiar no-man's land inhabited by gamblers, alcoholics, debtors – and spies. It is a world of seediness, especially the urban variety. Phrases such as 'worthy of a Graham Greene novel' or a 'Graham Greene quality' are now common in the language.

As is so common with writers and other artists, Greene's reputation sagged after his death. The question will continue to be debated whether, as some critics maintain, he is simply at the top of the second division of authors and whether his reputation is higher abroad than in Britain.

The sole living representative of Literature in the Order is the playwright, **Tom Stoppard**, who was appointed on 9 May 2000. Like Henry James and T. S. Eliot, he was born in a foreign country of foreign parents but, unlike them, the English language in which he has achieved his fame is not his mother tongue. Born in Czechoslovakia a year before the German invasion of 1938, Tomas Sträussler was taken to Singapore at the age of two by his parents, a doctor and nurse who worked for the Bata shoe company. His father died in the Japanese invasion and his mother escaped to India, where she married a British army officer, Major Stoppard. It was many years before the renamed Tom Stoppard learned of his Jewish origins and the deaths of many of his family in Nazi concentration camps.

Leaving school at 17, Tom Stoppard began work as a journalist in Bristol. After moving to London, he attracted considerable attention in 1966 with *Rosencrantz and Guildenstern are Dead*, in which two of Hamlet's courtiers are placed at the centre of a drama in which they are bewildered witnesses and predestined victims. It was when asked what the play was 'about' that he replied 'about to make me rich', a quick response that has trailed him.

There followed, in the early 1970s, *Jumpers*, a comedy about academic philosophy in which the central character is really G. E. Moore OM, and *Travesties*, an extravaganza in which Lenin, Joyce and the painter Tzara are engaged in a performance of *The Importance of Being Earnest* that produces a commentary on their own works and on the nature of the artist in general.

Among Tom Stoppard's many other plays or 'events' are *Indian Ink*, contrasting the India of the 1930s and 1980s, and *The Invention of Love*, contrasting the fates of two homosexual writers, Oscar Wilde and A. E. Housman. At one time, Tom Stoppard had four plays running in London at the same time. A recent work is the nine-hour trilogy, *The Coast of Utopia*, based on Isaiah Berlin's book of essays, *Russian Thinkers*, and

33 Sir Tom Stoppard by Daphne Todd.

written in the manner of Chekhov. He has had a *Cambridge Companion* devoted to him and his work and his papers already rest in an American university.

In 1998, Tom Stoppard had the distinction of being, by virtue of a change in French law, the first foreign playwright to see his work performed at the Comédie Francaise. It was *Arcadia* and its translator, the French playwright Jean-Marie Besset, observed:

Who would have thought that Tom Stoppard, master of verbal pyrotechnics, cerebral juggler of hyper-cultivated paradoxes, would one day give us *Arcadia*, a masterpiece of love drama against a metaphysical background, doubling up as a salon comedy? Written by a British author of Czech origin this is, so to speak, an almost French play.[104]

Tom Stoppard himself has commended the foreign regard for culture:

> When you go abroad, you feel that culture is integral, not a little treat
> for a day off. Here, we're always talking about art *and* society. Art *is*
> bloody society.[105]

Besides his stage work, Tom Stoppard has written many film scripts. These
include *The Russia House, Empire of the Sun, Cats* – the animated version of T. S. Eliot's verse for children – and *Enigma*. For his screenplay of
Shakespeare in Love, he won an Oscar.

Tom Stoppard's detractors argue that he is too clever by half, making his
audiences believe that *they* are more clever than they are. Some critics claim
he is a Tin Man, with brilliant language hiding the lack of any heart or core.
An exchange between two of his characters in *Travesties* is cited in evidence:

> Oh, what a lot of nonsense you talk. It may be nonsense, but at least it's
> clever nonsense.

Possibly, the critics are irritated at finding it difficult to penetrate the privacy
of a man who told one interviewer:

> A guy's writing a book about me at the moment and my inner desire is
> that his book should be as inaccurate as possible.[106]

The Times applauded Tom Stoppard's knighthood in 1997:

> [After recounting his family history] The combination of Central Europe
> and the British Empire has proved a potent one . . . he brought an intellec-
> tual intensity, anarchic wit and heightened linguistic consciousness to the
> British stage which had no precedent . . . [He] has kept his pre-eminent
> status while taking risks to explore new realms . . . the playwright is
> there to render mortality immortal and immortality mortal. We have
> no greater practitioner of that art than Sir Tom.[107]

As the best known of the four OMs named in May 2000, his name was
the headline to the reports of their appointment. A leading critic described
him on his sixty-fifth birthday in 2002 as

> undeniably the wittiest of British dramatists, the most verbally elegant,
> the most intellectually questing and taxing . . . also the most gloriously
> paradoxical . . . [who has] described his dramatic aim as 'achieving the
> perfect marriage between ideas and high comedy or farce' . . . [He] is a
> dramatist who delights in wordplay, puns, conceits, unexpected verbal
> connections, pastiche and parody . . . [108]

The poets

In 1924, after he had been Poet Laureate for 11 years, **Robert Bridges'** name was being mooted for the OM. His name came up again in 1928, when he was 84, but serious doubts were expressed as to whether a Poet Laureate had any automatic right to the honour. Frederic Kenyon thought that Bridges was

> since Thomas Hardy's death [earlier in 1928], the figure-head of English Literature and it would be regarded as natural that he should succeed to Hardy's place in the OM.[109]

Stamfordham went ahead with putting Bridges' name to the King, who approved the recommendation. It was as 'Poet Laureate. In recognition of his eminent position in the World of Literature' that he received the honour – with Galsworthy – in the Birthday Honours of 1929.

34 Robert Bridges.

Bridges dedicated his last poem, the long *Testament of Beauty*, to the King. It was published on the poet's eighty-fifth birthday in 1929. It was acclaimed and sold well. Bridges died the next year.

Robert Bridges came from a Kentish family that had progressed over three centuries from yeomen to gentlemen farmers to country gentry. He was one of nine children but, when his father died, the division of the family property meant he never needed to earn a living. His mother, the daughter of a clergyman-baronet, remarried, to a clergyman in Lancashire, which became Robert's home. At the age of ten (the year after his father's death) he went to Eton, where the surroundings and companionship

> fed and confirmed the inborn aesthetic sensibility and mental energy which distinguished him throughout his life.[110]

He was drawn towards 'Puseyite' High Church Anglican views but, according to his own record, he drifted fast away from such religious sympathies when he went to Oxford.

At Corpus Christi College, Bridges was a noted oarsman and took a second in Greats at the same time as his close friend, Gerard Manley Hopkins, took a first. They corresponded until the death in 1889 of Hopkins. Bridges was fascinated with Hopkins' experiments in sprung rhythm – the combination of traditional regularity of stresses with a varying number of syllables in each line, which greatly influenced later twentieth-century poetry. None of Hopkins' work was published in his lifetime but Bridges arranged its publication over the years, culminating in a complete edition in 1918.

Before embarking seriously on his own poetry, Bridges qualified as a doctor. He combined his studies with long periods spent in Germany, France and Italy and also travelled to the Middle East. He worked in London hospitals for seven years: in the casualty department of St Bartholomew's, at the Great Ormond Street Hospital for Sick Children and at the Great Northern Hospital in Holloway. Already writing verse, he intended to retire at the age of 40 but an almost fatal bout of pneumonia caused him to retire at 37.

After recovering, Bridges married, at the age of 40, the daughter of Alfred Waterhouse, the eminent architect. For over 20 years, the Bridges lived at Yattendon in Berkshire. He produced the *Yattendon Hymnal*, which helped to reform hymnody and revive the music of the sixteenth and seventeenth centuries. He was always interested in the musical settings of words and collaborated on four of Hubert Parry's works.

It was Bridges' golden period, in which he produced much of his best poetry: his one long narrative poem *Eros and Psyche*, as well as a number of dramas and semi-dramas. He wrote influential essays on *Milton's Prosody* and Keats. His four books of *Shorter Poems* and *The Growth of Love* established his reputation as a lyric poet. He declined to stand for election as

Professor of Poetry at Oxford in 1895. Among his admirers was the classicist and future OM, J. W. Mackail.

In 1907, Bridges moved to a house, Chilswell, isolated at the end of a long lane on Boar's Hill, overlooking Oxford. He took a cold bath every morning in the great hall before a roaring fire. He had a reputation for being shy and somewhat difficult in temper. A later OM, E. M. Forster, said of him:

> He was class-bound and all that, and oh dear how he lowered his voice before articulating the word passion.[111]

In 1913, Bridges was appointed Poet Laureate. He succeeded Alfred Austin; to most critics that was an easy act to follow. He was soon called on to compile an anthology, *The Spirit of Man*, to console the bereaved and entertain those serving at the Front. He set about making a book of *Beauty*, excluding sexual passion and mirth.

Bridges' poetry was too restrained for some. From a very different background, Richard Church wrote:

> a kind of English literary figure which changing social conditions tend to make more and more rare...The essence of his work is dignity...somewhat overbred in matters of literary taste...The beauty of his work, especially his shorter lyrics, is of chiselled marble...They have a morning-glory light about them, as though they were minted in the Golden Age before the smoke of Industrialism fogged the air we breathe...[Of *The Testament of Beauty*] he said much about the economic inequalities of society, but his views were picturesque, rather than deeply felt.[112]

When most of his works were reissued by Oxford University Press in 1953, the *Times Literary Supplement* described him as

> so withdrawn from the poetic preoccupations of the present day that it is easy to overlook him altogether...
>
> he was rash enough to be happy, balanced and modest...enough to imperil the reputation of a poet among his contemporaries...[113]

Bridges thought poetry should be appreciated for itself. He did not want any biography written of him. When one was published in 1992, the reviewers emphasised the decline in Bridges' reputation; they included Stephen Spender, who said he was a 'perfect example of a third person person...betraying no confidences in his poetry...the excision of the ugly from the beautiful in his work results in poems that have a curious

35 John Masefield by William Strang.

impersonality about them: a gelatinous transparency like the negatives of black-and-white photography.[114]

John Masefield had succeeded Robert Bridges as Poet Laureate in 1930 and, in due course, he also received the Order of Merit, thus appearing to create the precedent feared at the time of Bridges' appointment. Unlike Bridges, however, he was 57 not 84 when made an OM and held the honour for 32 years rather than ten months.

Masefield was being considered for the honour as early as 1924. Esher was bracketing him with Shaw, who

> in all probability, will in times to come, be better known than any of their contemporaries because of the high quality of their best achievements, and their bulk. I can imagine 'Reynard the Fox' becoming a classic for all time...I cannot see in the work of all these other men [Housman, Bridges, De la Mare, Davies and Newbolt] anything to compare with these [Masefield and Shaw] in the higher regions of literature.[115]

In the end, 'with the King's warm approval', Masefield was offered and accepted the post.[116] Perhaps it was the appeal of one old sea salt to another. Indeed, there were some who wondered about the adjustment to a courtly role of a man who had written so disparagingly (in *A Consecration*) of 'princes and prelates with periwigged charioteers' and 'the be-medalled Commander, beloved of the throne'.

In the Silver Jubilee Honours of 3 June 1935, Masefied was appointed to the Order of Merit in exactly the same terms as those used to describe Bridges six years earlier: 'Poet Laureate. In recognition of his eminent position in the World of Literature.'

John Masefield's life began in idyllic surroundings in Herefordshire; he used to claim that he had lived in Paradise. The idyll was shattered when he was six. His mother died and when he was 12, his father had a complete mental breakdown and died in hospital soon after. With his brothers and sisters, Masefield was brought up by an uncle and aunt. At 13, he went to the naval training ship *Conway* for three years. Thus began his association with and love of the sea that was to shape his life and colour much of his poetry.

He went to sea and 'served before the mast' in the classic fashion, although as an apprentice, rather than a seaman, he was not actually in the fo'c'sle, as legend would later have it. He sailed round the Horn to Chile, where he was taken seriously ill, a combination of sunstroke and some kind of nervous breakdown. A kindly captain ensured that he was sent home by steamship.

At the age of 17, Masefield began two years of working around America. He was a carpet factory hand, a longshoreman and a saloon porter. It was in New York that he discovered the great English poets and through them, a love of his homeland and its nature. Queen Victoria's Diamond Jubilee in 1897 turned an exile's thoughts to that homeland and Masefield returned from America.

At 19, Masefield was back in Britain, but in a pitiful state. He worked as a bank clerk for three years, began to write and pull himself out of bouts of depression. He was befriended by W. B. Yeats and Laurence Binyon. He developed a strong interest in art and became close to William Strang, who was to draw many of the portraits of OMs in the collection at Windsor (described in Chapter 25).

Supplementing his writing with journalism, Masefield published his first notable work in 1902: *Salt-water Ballads*, which he readily acknowledged owed something to Kipling's *Barrack-room Ballads*. It contained *Sea Fever* – 'I must down to the seas again' altered to the more familiar 'I must go down to the seas again' when set to music by John Ireland.

In 1910, Masefield's *Ballads and Poems* included *Cargoes*, in which he linked Britain, with its 'Dirty British coaster', to earlier seafaring empires, with their 'Quinquireme of Nineveh' and 'Stately Spanish galleon'. He shook his growing public in 1911 with *The Everlasting Mercy*. The inspiration for it came to him on a country walk: 'Now I will write a poem about a blackguard who becomes converted.' And with it, 'Masefield had achieved the impossible. He had made the great British public read contemporary poetry, an event which had not occurred since Tennyson.'[117]

There followed between 1912–13, two strong narrative poems: *The Widow in the Bye Street*, about a poor woman in Herefordshire whose only son is hanged for a crime of passion, and *Dauber*, the tale of a young artist (Masefield himself?) who rounds the awful Horn but avoids a nervous breakdown by gallantly climbing to the yardarm and falling to his death.

Masefield reached his zenith with *Reynard the Fox* (1919), the tale of a great chase seen through the eyes of the fleeing animal:

> No English poet since Chaucer had called up the vision of the English countryside so effectively as he did there, with his powers of honest and accurate observation and his mastery of material pattern and pace.[118]

When questioned about his motives, in the light of his compassionate nature,

> he claimed that hunting was the sport which brought all ranks of society together on terms of equality and good fellowship . . . 'I am not and never have been a fox-hunter but it is *the* passion of English country people, and into it they put the beauty and the fervour which the English put into all things when deeply roused.'[119]

He followed *Reynard* with *Right Royal*, a poetic dram of the steeplechase.

Regarded mainly as a poet, Masefield was also a prolific novelist, critic and playwright: writing over 100 works in all. The novels ranged from *Lost Endeavour* (1910), a racy story for boys, to *The Bird of Dawning* (1933), set on the old China clippers. One novel, *Odtaa* (1926), took its title from a remark made to him in America – 'One darned thing after another'. He wrote enchanting children's books, such as *The Box of Delights* (1935). His *William Shakespeare* (1911) was

> of such imaginative power as to make it appear that he had entered into Shakespeare's very thought processes.[120]

'I was never any good as a playwright' was Masefield's own verdict on his dramatic output. A couple reached the commercial stage but most were performed in the little theatre of his garden at Boars Hill. He was better at religious drama, such as *The Trial of Jesus* (1925).

Lecturing in neutral America – with some undercover work for the Foreign Office – was not his only contribution to the war effort. Rejected by the army because of ill health, he worked as a Red Cross orderly in France and the Dardanelles. From that experience came a history, *Gallipoli* (1916). Twenty-five years later, he was moved by the miracle of Dunkirk to write a short prose work, *The Nine Days Wonder* (1941).

In his long tenure of the office of Poet Laureate (only Tennyson held it longer), Masefield took his duties seriously. He meticulously composed verses for royal and national occasions, something Bridges had been reluctant to do. In the year of his appointment, Masefield presented illustrated copies of his poems to the King. Later, he credited his daughter, Judith, with the best illustrations.

In 1933, Masefield suggested the institution of an annual 'King's Poetry Medal', which has been awarded ever since. Recipients have included W. H. Auden, Robert Graves, Philip Larkin and John Betjeman. He undertook various literary offices: as President of the Society of Authors (following earlier OMs, Meredith, Hardy and Barrie), and as the President of the National Book League (now the Book Trust). When the Royal Society of Literature created the distinction of Companion of Literature (C Lit) in 1961, he was one of the first five recipients, along with fellow OMs, Churchill, G. M. Trevelyan and Eliot, and the CH, Somerset Maugham.

It has to be said, however, that Masefield's assiduity in his role as Laureate did his reputation no good. A critic, and admirer, Fraser Drew, thought his odes bore 'the unmistakable stamp of the duty done and the deadline met'; he observed that Masefield had included very few of them in his printed verse.[121]

In 1967, Masefield refused to rest to ease a painful leg. 'The surgeon said he must have it off or die. He said, "I'll die," and did.'[122] On Masefield's eightieth birthday, *The Times* had been predictably warm in its tribute, entitled 'Many Cargoes', with numerous nautical allusions to 'an old sailor . . . whose sails are still spread'. It thought that

> A reader who was proof against Mr Masefield's art in any of its many phases would be beyond hope of aesthetic redemption . . . At his touch even the drab and the vulgar are tinged with romance . . . he can still bring unaffected wetness to the eyes.

Such tributes were repeated on his death. Twelve years later, however, on the centenary of Masefield's birth and the publication of a selection of his poems, the tone had changed, as it so often tends to do:

> absolutely out of fashion now. He was over-valued in his own lifetime, so no doubt there is justice in this reaction . . . never really as revolutionary as he seemed to be . . . He *tried* to sound as though he was writing in his shirt sleeves.

Perhaps we are now far enough away from Masefield's official fame to recognise his genuine minor gifts...There is a case to be made that his best work was...simple, racy straightforward prose.[123]

One critic harshly compared Masefield's short unsuccessful time at sea with his much longer successful life writing about it:

In reality the mindless brutality of sea life had revolted him. But he blamed his own weakness, and, as an atonement, idolised the sea's beauty all his days. Failure fed romance, as it always does. Putting himself across in the poems as a lyrical old salt, he could fill a role for which life had proved him too delicate.[124]

The next two writers appointed to the Order of Merit were poets and they were considered alongside each other for many years before they received the honour – five years apart: **T. S. Eliot** in 1948 and **Walter de la Mare** in 1953. (The latter's name had been mentioned, in a tentative way, as early as 1924, when Esher had said he would not be surprised if in a few years, de la Mare would 'surpass them all', including Bridges and Masefield.)[125]

T. S. Eliot was suggested by Kenneth Clark in 1940 as

generally regarded as the most significant poet now writing in English...largely responsible for the younger school of poetry...representative figure...has also held a leading position as a critic and man of letters...would be acceptable to the bien-pensants because he is the author of *Murder in the Cathedral*...[126]

In 1947, Geoffrey Faber said that both de la Mare and Eliot ought to have priority for the Order. He followed this up with a tribute to de la Mare's

remarkably wide and even solid body of work...a solid man in himself. The whimsicality doesn't contradict the solidity. I wouldn't put him amongst the *absolute* top-notchers (as I most certainly put Eliot), but they are rare and if the OM were confined to them, it wouldn't be often awarded...no finer literary craftsman...And craftsmanship is worth a lot.[127]

Masefield, the only literary OM, gave his view:

I would put first Mr Walter de la Mare, as a poet of exquisite accomplishment, as a mind of the finest distinction and delicacy...[He] has

36 T. S. Eliot, plastercast of a bust by J. Epstein.

created an ideal world in which thousands have found delight . . . Next, I would put Mr TS Eliot . . . no doubt of his intellectual eminence, and of his very great influence upon young writers here. His poetical plays have almost restored poetical drama to the English theatre.[128]

Harold Nicolson thought that:

Eliot is not only the leading poet of our age but he has had more influence on poetry than anybody else . . . no hesitation at all in choosing him beyond anyone in England. De la Mare . . . admirable and deserving . . . [but] not in the same street as a creative writer.[129]

Lascelles noted on Nicolson's letter: 'David Cecil and others whose advice I have asked agree in supporting T. S. Eliot.'

37 Walter de la Mare, lithograph by Walter Tittle.

George VI approved the appointment of Eliot on 24 November 1947. The Secretary of the Order was stirred into commenting:

> I note among his literary work is one called *Practical Cats*, which I feel sure is quite a fresh intellectual field of knowledge to be rewarded with the Order of Merit![130]

Communication between the Palace and Number 10 must have slipped on this occasion because when the Prime Minister's recommendations for the New Year Honours arrived at the other end of the Mall, it was discovered that Eliot was being proposed for a CH. Following hasty telephone contact on 2 December, his name was withdrawn:

> [The Prime Minister] was, of course, unaware that it was the King's intention to offer the Order of Merit to Mr Eliot and would not at all wish to press him for a Companion of Honour as things stand . . . [131]

given that he had actually accepted the OM.

De la Mare was caught up in the slipstream of Eliot's OM, for which he had been a contender. As it was, de la Mare accepted a CH in the next Honours List in June 1948. It might have seemed that, at the age 75, he had 'missed' the OM, especially as the CH was not then the stepping stone which it has frequently been since. Only the three statesmen, Churchill, Smuts and Attlee, had made the jump before and de la Mare was the first of the 16 – all from the arts, learning, literature or science – who have subsequently achieved the 'double'. For, early in the new reign, in the Coronation Honours, he *did* receive the OM. De la Mare enjoyed his enhanced honour for only three years. Eliot, who was 15 years his junior, outlived de la Mare by nine years and obviously held the OM for much longer. Eliot was also the only poet in English to receive the German Order Pour le mérite – in 1959. In 1964, the year before his death, he was honoured by the land of his birth – with the Presidential Medal of Freedom, the highest civilian honour in the United States.

A few months after the OM, Eliot wore it to attend the Nobel ceremony where he was honoured with the Literature Prize for 1948. On his way to the ceremony, he answered a reporter's questions by saying he was getting the prize for his 'entire corpus'. 'When did you publish *that*?' asked the reporter. Later, Eliot said that 'The Entire Corpus' might make a good title for a mystery novel.

According to a biographer, the OM

> gratified him more than the Nobel, and certainly he seemed to enjoy wearing the medal and ribbon on ceremonial occasions.

Thomas Stearns Eliot was an American until he was 39, a little over half his life. Born in 1888, he was naturalised in 1927, having lived in Britain since 1914. He was born in St Louis, Missouri, into the family of a successful industrialist, whose wife had literary interests. After schooling in St Louis, he went to Harvard.

He planned to teach philosophy and, after a year at the Sorbonne, he returned to Harvard to write a doctoral dissertation on *Appearance and Reality* by the OM-philosopher, F. H. Bradley. One of his teachers was Bertrand Russell, who found him 'very well-dressed and polished . . . very silent'. With the aid of a travelling fellowship, he came to Bradley's college at Oxford, Merton, in October 1914. For a variety of reasons, he never finished the doctorate but 50 years later, almost at the end of his life, the dissertation was revised and published as *Knowledge and Experience in the Philosophy of F. H. Bradley*.

Eliot decided to stay in Britain and write poetry. He had written his first, *The Love Story of J Alfred Prufrock*, in 1910 and it was published in 1915, with the help of Ezra Pound, to whom Eliot remained close and faithful through all his fellow-American's later tribulations.

In the month that *Prufrock* was published, Eliot married, most unhappily as it proved. His English wife, Vivienne, became unstable and the marriage deteriorated. They formally separated in 1933, although he provided for her financially until her death in 1947, by which time she had been committed to an asylum. The exact nature of their relationship, and its effect on his poetry, has fascinated later critics. It was sufficiently interesting to be the subject of a play, *Tom and Viv*, in 1984, which was made into a film ten years later.

To return to 1915, Eliot was short of money and so taught for a year at Highgate Junior School in London. Teaching, however, took up too much of the time he needed for poetry. He joined Lloyds Bank in 1917. Rejected on medical grounds for military service when the United States entered the war in 1917, he stayed at the bank until 1925. Again, the strain of working and writing poetry told on him and he had a nervous breakdown in 1921. In 1922, he founded and edited a new quarterly review, *The Criterion*, which was taken over by Faber and Faber, the publishing firm that he joined in 1925. He increased their poetry list with the aim of losing as little money as possible.

In 1917, Eliot emerged on the poetic scene with *Prufrock and Other Observations*, the 1915 poem and two others. Eight years later, in rating it as one of the 'books of the century', an eminent critic wrote:

> This slim volume . . . transformed English poetry. For originality, it put even Wordsworth and Coleridge in the shade. Most contemporary readers were baffled, and rightly. Bafflement was Eliot's plan. His problem was to reconnect poetry to the intellect, rather than submerging it in the emotions as (he thought) the Victorians had done.[132]

Some of the supposedly small things have entered the language: 'I have measured out my life with coffee spoons.'

Five years later came *The Waste Land*, dedicated to Ezra Pound who had encouraged and helped Eliot (through the time of his nervous breakdown) to finalise the long poem on which he had been working for three years. It excited considerable interest on both sides of the Atlantic:

> Although many readers found it outrageous, it gave Eliot his central position in modern verse. The work brought poetry into the same atmosphere of innovation which characterized music and painting of the time . . . it broke with traditional structure . . . Eliot brought together various kinds of despair, for lost youth, lost love, lost friendship, lost value. Sombre and obscure . . . with all its mustering of past ages it spoke sharply to its own time.[133]

In 1925, Eliot's *The Hollow Men* concluded with two lines that are among the most quoted of any poet writing in English:

> This is the way the world ends
> Not with a bang but a whimper.

Nearly half-a-century later, the critic, Cyril Connolly, recalled the enormous impact Eliot had had on his generation; the early poetry was 'the great event of our youth'.[134]

In 1944, *The Four Quartets* brought together poems he had published between 1935–1942. Of the four, *East Coker* was the village in Somerset from which his ancestors had emigrated to America in the seventeenth century and to which his own ashes were to be taken. It was in this war-time poem that he was moved to observe that, 'Human kind cannot bear very much reality'. Of 1940 in particular he wrote: 'History is now and England.'

Eliot was a critic and playwright as well as a poet. From *The Sacred Wood* (1920) onwards, criticism flowed, on the place of tradition in literature as a changing entity and on the writer as a catalyst who joins the literary tradition to the language and experience of his own time. Such essays, as well as those on particular writers, ranging from the Elizabethan dramatists to contemporaries (Joyce, Pound and Lawrence) 'became focal points of modern criticism'.[135]

Eliot's plays were perhaps less enduring than his poetry or criticism. He made his mark with *Murder in the Cathedral* (1935), about the martyrdom of Thomas à Becket, which was followed over the next 25 years by a number of quasi-religious and moral poetic dramas: *The Family Reunion, The Cocktail Party, The Confidential Clerk* and *The Elder Statesman* (1958).

In the year of his naturalisation, 1927, Eliot was confirmed in the Church of England and it was at this time that he described himself as, '"classical in literature, royalist in politics, and anglo-catholic in religion". (He would later regret the phrasing, though not the stances.)'[136] Eliot had decided on naturalisation because

> I thought here I am, making a living, enjoying my friends here. I don't like being a squatter. I might as well take the full responsibility.[137]

The genial side of Eliot's nature appeared in *Old Possum's Book of Practical Cats* (1939), written for his godchildren and friends. The book was set to music by Alan Rawsthorne for a *Punch* revue in the 1950s and was subsequently recorded with Robert Donat as narrator. In 1981, however, Andrew Lloyd-Webber, who had picked up a copy of Eliot's book at Heathrow, wrote the musical *Cats*.

Eliot was able to mock his own reputation for melancholy with lines such as, 'How unpleasant to meet Mr Eliot...' and his lighter side would find outlet in remarks such as his reply when asked whether he thought all editors were just failed writers: 'Oh yes, but so are most writers.'

From the mid-1930s, Eliot's lifestyle became more ordered and increasingly stately. Shortly after the war he moved into a flat on the Chelsea Embankment, below the one in which Henry James had lived and died. In 1957, very privately and to the surprise of many friends and colleagues, he married Valerie Fletcher, 38 years his junior. She had been his secretary at Faber and Faber for eight years and was to be his wife for the remaining eight years of his life. 'Happy at Last' was the description of that period by his main biographer, Peter Ackroyd, who was forbidden by the Eliot estate to quote from the poet's published work, except for purposes of fair comment in a critical context. (Like many other famous men, Eliot had wanted no biography.) Valerie Eliot has remained the main guardian of the poet's memory and fame – as his literary executor. In 1988, she published the first volume of his letters (1896–1922) but there are obviously more to come.

Much has been made of Eliot's 'anti-Semitism', based on writings, both published and unpublished, in the 1920s. A biographer concludes:

> it was a period when his own personality threatened to break apart, and it seems likely that his distrust of Jews and women was the sign of an uneasy and vulnerable temperament in which aggression and insecurity were compounded. That is an explanation, however, and not a justification.[138]

When Eliot died on 4 January 1965, his obituaries were predictable:

> The most influential English poet of his time ... His works in verse and prose ... have been the subject of more books and articles than have ever been published about an author during his lifetime.[139]

The *DNB* described him at his height:

> With his plays on Broadway and in the West End, his best lines on every lip, his opinions cited on all manner of subjects, he was the man of letters *par excellence* of the English-speaking world.[140]

Eliot himself thought that the test of a great writer was that after him no one can write without being aware of him. It is a high standard against which to be judged. The literary gatekeepers are busy – in the *TLS* and the weekend review columns and on late-night TV arts programmes. One thing is certain – he is not forgotten. Books on him abound, maintaining what has been called 'the litigious state of Eliot criticism'. One recently, on the oblivion that has overtaken many twentieth-century poets, specifically excluded Eliot (and Hardy and Auden) from consideration because they seem already sure of literary immortality.

In writing of T. S. Eliot, I deliberately covered the subsequent award of the Order of Merit to Walter de la Mare because the two poets were considered in tandem for the honour for so long. I also referred to the CH which de la Mare received shortly after Eliot's OM. (He had twice declined a knighthood.) It can be clearly seen now that 'they' made the right decisions about the priority of these awards. Eliot is still a renowned figure in the world of twentieth-century poetry, which can scarcely be said of de la Mare.

Nevertheless, at the time of de la Mare's OM in the Coronation Honours List of 1953, it was still commended as: 'an outstanding and proper tribute to a great artist in poetry and prose.'[141] De la Mare told his friend, Joyce Grenfell, about his investiture by the Queen a month after the Coronation: 'I talked too much but she was so nice.'

Walter Delamare was born in 1873 in Charlton, then a Kentish suburb of London. His father was a Bank of England official, who had married a distant relative of Robert Browning. After attending St Paul's Cathedral choir school, he worked for nearly 20 years for the Anglo-American Oil Company in London. To emphasise his Huguenot descent, he changed the spelling of his name to de la Mare.

Encouraged by an indulgent employer, he had begun to write in his early twenties under the name of Walter Ramal, his surname spelt backwards. He was taken up by Henry Newbolt, poet and literary editor of the *Monthly Review*, who managed to persuade Asquith to provide him with first a grant and later a pension from the civil list. (He later benefited from Rupert Brooke's will.) De la Mare was able to leave the city and devote himself to writing. He moved on to being included in Edward Marsh's first volume of *Georgian Poets*.

De la Mare's early work included short stories in literary journals but his career proper began with *Songs of Childhood* (1902), quickly followed by a prose work *Henry Brocken* (1904), in which the hero encounters European writers from the past. Other prose work followed: *The Return* (1910), an eerie story of spirit possession which used fear because it most quickens the sense of the wonder of life; *The Three Mulla-Mulgars* (1910), in which an uncomprehending child describes the breakdown of his parents' marriage; and the self-explanatory *Memoirs of a Midget* (1921), choosing an odd point of view because everything was odd to her. He also wrote critical works on Rupert Brooke, Lewis Carroll and Christina Rossetti. It was, however, largely as a poet, especially for children, that de la Mare achieved fame in his lifetime. *The Listeners* (1912) brought him a wide public.

In 1947, when he was 73, came *The Traveller*:

a parable that lies at the heart of perhaps every poem that [he] wrote –
bore witness to his sense of the transitoriness of natural things and of

the ultimate reality. It is a poem that sums up the poet's inward grace of vision.[142]

In 1951, de la Mare published *The Winged Chariot*, which W. H. Auden called his most ambitious poem. By the 1940s, eminent critics were praising 'all the elfin loveliness [which retained] something of the serenity of a former age'.[143] Twenty years later, his *DNB* entry considered that:

> His was a mind, a personality, which loved dangerous living... Atomic fission was his daily practice... [He] was obsessed with the curiosity of what might happen if he should dissociate this material world from its physical coherence and set free the forces which so restrained it.[144]

In his last years, de la Mare came to know Sir Russell (later Lord) Brain, an eminent physician, who recorded much of their conversation in a small book.[145] De la Mare thought highly of Hardy's poetry (even the bad verse was good), of Henry James' ghost stories, of Bridges' lyrics and of Eliot's effective use of repetition ('O dark, dark, dark. They all go into the dark' in *East Coker*). He recalled meeting the Alice of Wonderland: 'an old woman, rather peevish... nothing of Alice left in her at all.' As regards there being a pattern in the life of Churchill, whom he knew, de la Mare 'thought the pattern-maker must have had a hard job, he could hardly have arranged the two world wars to give Churchill his opportunity'.

De la Mare died in 1956. His ashes were buried in the crypt of the cathedral where he had sung as a boy; at the later unveiling of a plaque, Siegfried Sassoon described him as the best-loved poet of his time, who could stimulate and heighten one's perceptiveness more than anyone else he knew.

The day after his death, the Poet Laureate, John Masefield, saluted de la Mare as the 'Angel of Words' and the 'Laureate of Dreamland'. And there were tributes from the 'modern' poets, Stephen Spender and W. H. Auden. A quarter of a century later (in 1982), Angela Carter wrote that while

> *Peacock Pie* and *Come Hither* remain beloved cornerstones of the middle-class nursery, his reputation as a poet and writer for adults has softly and silently vanished away since his death.[146]

In 1993, Peter Ackroyd wrote that de la Mare

> does not fit neatly into the pattern of literary history, he seems, as it were, to have slipped through the net... He is not much read now, but neither is he altogether forgotten...[147]

After Walter de la Mare's appointment to the Order in 1953, it was 45 years before another poet joined it: **Ted Hughes** in 1998, but, sadly, for

38 Ted Hughes by Bob Tulloch.

only two months. He had been Poet Laureate since 1984 and was the third of the six holders of that office to receive the Order since its institution in 1902. His only previous honour had been an OBE in the Jubilee Honours List in 1977. The press reports on Hughes' appointment as an OM made no mention of the cancer of which he was shortly to die. Only 12 days before his death on 28 October 1998, 'Mr Ted Hughes, Poet Laureate' was able to go to Buckingham Palace to receive the insignia of the Order from the Queen.

Among the memorials to Ted Hughes are two stained-glass windows, placed by the Prince of Wales, later also an OM, in a sanctuary in the grounds of Highgrove, the Prince's country house. The two men were friends who shot and fished together in Scotland and went on expeditions on Dartmoor, where Hughes lived. They shared a deep concern for conservation and the poet was a frequent visitor to Highgrove. The Prince referred to their friendship in an article about the need to maintain a coherent, chronological narrative:

> I am one of those people who was lucky enough to have known Ted Hughes...I much admire his poetry but that does not mean I would therefore never want to read Wordsworth or Milton, any more than my pleasure in the language of Tom Stoppard means that I no longer have a need of Shakespeare.[148]

There was some disbelief at Hughes' appointment as Poet Laureate in December 1984, after the post had been declined by Philip Larkin (who died a year later, after receiving a CH). The Literary Editor of *The Times* thought it was

> a bit like appointing a grim young crow to replace a cuddly old teddy bear [John Betjeman]...without doubt the most anti-Establishment, black and acerbic poet to have become a court official...a true poet, which is more than can be said for some of his predecessors...[149]

In his 14 years as Poet Laureate, Hughes was not prolific but nevertheless wrote to celebrate various royal occasions: the eightieth birthday of Queen Elizabeth The Queen Mother, the wedding of the Duke of York, the sixtieth birthday of the Queen and the fortieth anniversary of her accession. In 1992, a collection of his 'official' work was published as *Rain Charm for the Duchy and Other Laureate Poems*.

The poem for the Queen Mother, *The Dream of the Lion*, led to a significant friendship with her and an attribution to her of unifying powers within the fragmenting United Kingdom. He wrote to a literary friend:

> I have to keep out of the piece the general sense that the lion passes away with the Queen Mother. What is left after her is the breakdown of the federation...The pulls for home rule are signs of it. The country's falling to bits. Monarchs can only reign if they are created by the unity of the group.[150]

He did not live to see the passing away of the 'lion' but the 98-year-old Queen Mother, with the Prince of Wales, attended the memorial service for Hughes in 1999. Many literary figures, including his close friend and Nobel Laureate, Seamus Heaney, participated in that final tribute.

Edward James Hughes was the son of a Yorkshire carpenter, whose experiences in the First World War were to influence some of his son's poems of precarious survival. After the local grammar school and national service as an RAF wireless mechanic (when he read most of Shakespeare), he went to Pembroke College, Cambridge. He abandoned the 'disciplined sterility' of

English and took a degree instead in archaeology and anthropology. While writing his first poems, he had various jobs, including as a zookeeper.

Soon after leaving Cambridge, Hughes met at a party there, and quickly married, an American student, Sylvia Plath, who had been writing poems from the age of 15. They admired each other's writing but, although Sylvia told her mother of her deep love for Ted, she added: 'It can only lead to great hurt.' So it did.

The couple moved for a couple of years to the United States where both taught at universities in Massachusetts. Hughes' first book of poems, *The Hawk in the Rain*, in 1957, was enthusiastically received. By the time of their return to Britain in 1959, he was already regarded as one of the best young poets.

In 1960, Hughes' second book of poems *Lupercal* won the Hawthornden Prize. In 1963, however, came the event that was to overshadow the consideration of Hughes and his work for the rest of his life. Sylvia Plath committed suicide. Hughes wrote no poetry for a few years and devoted much of his time to the upbringing of the children. The daughter, Frieda, became a painter and poet.

Over the next 40 years, the Sylvia and Ted Show has run and run. As one American woman writer put it on his death:

> Hating Hughes became a cottage industry. Attacking him was practically a syllabus requirement in women's studies courses in the 1970s and '80s. His name was gouged out of Plath's tombstone ... The brazen heartlessness that according to his poems, he saw in nature could have been spotted just as easily in his shaving mirror. Worse yet, Hughes refused to defend himself ... frustratingly silent about Plath and their life together.[151]

There were press attacks and lawsuits and the media helped to fuel the controversy. As the *TLS* once put it: 'it's always either Sylvia Week or Ted Week.'[152]

After Plath's death, Hughes' next poems and stories were in *Wodwo* (1967) and one, *Thistles*, epitomised the long-running fight of nature with man. In 1969, Hughes' private life suffered a second shock. Assia Wevill, the mother of his second daughter, took not only her own life but also that of the child. In the following year, he married Carol Orchard. In 1970 Hughes published his bleak and savage poem, *Crow*, in which the bird was a symbol of the world's heart of darkness. By the end of the decade, however, he had published poems about Devon where he lived (*Moortown*) and Yorkshire where he had been brought up (*The Remains of Elmet*, the last British Kingdom to fall to the Angles). Of this period, however, *The Times* commented, in his obituary:

> In spite of his stature as one of the great poets of the century, Hughes was oddly neglected in Britain for most of his middle career. He was the recipient of no prize for a period of 30 years until he received the *Sunday Times* Award for Literary Excellence in 1995.[153]

Over his career, Hughes wrote a number of books for children, including *The Iron Man* (1968), lines from which have become as well known to a younger generation as those of Masefield and de la Mare were to its parents. There were also anthologies such as *The Rattle-Bag* (edited with Seamus Heaney in 1982), and *The School Bag* (1997).

In 1997, the prize-winning *Tales from Ovid* contained a selection of free verse translations from Ovid's *Metamorphoses*. It was only a few months before his death the following year, when his fatal illness was not generally known, that he produced his last major work: *Birthday Letters*. Its 88 poems, written over 25 years, recounted in snapshot detail his relationship with Sylvia Plath. Finally, he was speaking out. The book was dedicated to his and Plath's two children and the fiery dust jacket was painted by the daughter, Frieda. It had poetry, death and sex and was written by the royal laureate. It became an instant bestseller and prize-winner. Seamus Heaney described it as:

> the psychic equivalent of 'the bends'. It takes you down to levels of pressure where the undertruths of sadness and endurance leave you gasping . . . [154]

Hughes' successor as Poet Laureate, Andrew Motion, thought it was

> like a thunderbolt from the blue . . . this book will live. Even if it were possible to set aside its biographical value (and why should we do that?), its linguistic, technical and imaginative feats would guarantee its future. Hughes is one of the most important poets of the century, and this is his greatest book. It's as magnetic as Browning's poems for Elizabeth Barrett, as poignant as Hardy's *Poems 1912–13*.[155]

He is the last of the memorable British poets of the twentieth century. Only time will tell how he will fare alongside his predecessors in the Order of Merit, particularly Eliot.

13

THE SCHOLARS

Philosophers

1. 1924   F. H. BRADLEY
2. 1930   Samuel ALEXANDER
3. 1945   A. N. WHITEHEAD
4. 1949   Bertrand (Earl) RUSSELL
5. 1951   G. E. MOORE
6. 1963   Sarvepalli RADHAKRISHNAN (Honorary)
7. 1971   Sir Isaiah BERLIN

Classical scholars

8. 1905   Sir Richard JEBB
9. 1908   Henry JACKSON
10. 1925   Sir James FRAZER
11. 1928   Sir George GRIERSON
12. 1930   M. R. JAMES
13. 1935   J. W. MACKAIL
14. 1941   Gilbert MURRAY

Historians

15. 1902   John (Viscount) MORLEY
16. 1902   W. E. H. LECKY
17. 1907   James (Viscount) BRYCE
18. 1911   Sir G. O. TREVELYAN
19. 1930   G. M. TREVELYAN

20. 1937 H. A. L. FISHER
21. 1943 Sir William HOLDSWORTH
22. 1963 G. P. GOOCH
23. 1969 Dame Veronica (CV) WEDGWOOD
24. 1970 John BEAGLEHOLE
25. 1976 Kenneth (Lord) CLARK
26. 1976 Sir Ronald SYME
27. 1983 Rev Owen CHADWICK, KBE
28. 1988 Sir Ernst GOMBRICH

Preliminary

The 28 scholar-OMs have been divided for convenience into three groups: philosophers, classical scholars and historians. Of course, these are not watertight compartments and there is obvious overlapping. Isaiah Berlin was a historian and philosopher, while Gilbert Murray was a philosopher and classical scholar. Among the classical scholars, Frazer, Grierson and M. R. James did not fit neatly into the classical mould of Greece and Rome.

Within the historians are many varieties. Some painted with a broad brush, like H. A. L. Fisher, while others concentrated on a period of history (Syme on the Roman Empire and Wedgwood on the seventeenth century) or on a type of history (Holdsworth on legal, Gooch on diplomatic, Clark and Gombrich on art and Owen Chadwick on ecclesiastical) or even on an individual (Beaglehole on Captain Cook).

As far as titles are concerned, the scholars were relatively abstemious. Only ten of the 28 accepted a title in respect of their scholarly work and, even then, sometimes reluctantly (like Berlin) or without obvious effect (like Owen Chadwick, whose knighthood is masked by his clerical status).

What they all, bar one, had in common was fellowship of the British Academy – and four of them were President. The exception was Beaglehole, who lived overseas. Additionally, seven of them had the rare distinction of being also Fellows of the Royal Society.

The philosophers

The first philosopher appointed to the Order of Merit was **Francis Herbert Bradley** in 1924. In 1921–22, Haldane was strongly promoting Bradley's cause, at length in order to convince:

> A great man in philosophy and letters alike...doubt whether the PM [Lloyd George] has ever heard of him...highest stature...greatest Englishman in his domain...author of *Appearance and Reality* and much else...If his public is select, it extends all over the world...The

OM has never been given for philosophy [this from the 'philosopher' Haldane] . . . absurd that his name should escape attention . . .

And later:

> [one of] the greatest philosophical figures in the world . . . a noble English style which makes him a great man of letters. Philosophy has not been recognised in the Order as it should have been. The PM may or may not know about these things but I observe that the literary world is already beginning to suggest Bradley's name.[1]

Nothing more happened until it was almost too late. By mid-1924, Bradley was 78 and in continuing poor health and Haldane was back in office as Lord Chancellor. Stamfordham again made soundings. Asquith was keen on a 'very good suggestion':

> The Order has always been weak on the side of Philosophy – its only representative there being Haldane and A. J. Balfour, neither of whom is more than an amateur . . . [first class professionals] do not grow readily in English soil . . . Bradley . . . easily first in originality and real speculative power . . . pioneer in England of what used to be called the neo-Hegelian school and cleared the road for all the later developments . . . [2]

Given the support of Haldane and the Prime Minister (Ramsay MacDonald), Stamfordham felt able to recommend the appointment to George V and, on the latter's instructions, to offer it to Bradley

> In recognition of your great works on Philosophy and of your distinguished position as a Philosopher and Man of Letters.[3]

The appointment was announced in the Birthday Honours of 1924, along with that of Sherrington, the neurologist President of the Royal Society. Bradley was described simply as 'Fellow of Merton College, Oxford'. It was appropriate, as if to demonstrate the non-political nature of the Order, that such a conservative figure should be the first OM appointed during the short-lived Labour minority government of 1924. The praise in the press for the appointment indicates Bradley's high standing at the time. In a long leading article, 'A Philosopher Recognized', *The Times* described it as:

> The outstanding feature of the present list . . . by common consent the most influential of living English philosophers and it has been mainly through him that philosophy in England, and indeed in America too, is as vigorous and healthy as it is today.[4]

Bradley was summoned to an investiture on 9 July but he immediately pleaded ill health. His health did not improve, although he continued with his work until sudden symptoms of blood poisoning led to his removal to an Oxford nursing home where, after only a few days, he died on 18 September. He was 78. George V's Private Secretary telegraphed to his brother, A. C. Bradley:

> The King is grieved to hear of the death of your learned brother and the loss sustained thereby by the whole world of philosophy. It was a great satisfaction to the King to confer upon Mr Bradley the Order of Merit and his Majesty regrets that he has not been spared longer to be associated with the other distinguished members of that Order.[5]

F. H. Bradley was, by a second marriage, one of the 20 children of a tyrannical evangelical clergyman. Part of his schooling was at Marlborough, of which a half-brother was headmaster, before going up to University College, Oxford. Although he secured a first in classical moderations, he (like Newman and Curzon) managed only a second in Greats. Nevertheless, in 1870, he was elected to a fellowship at Merton College that was terminable only by marriage. He held it for 54 years and died unmarried.

Bradley's biographer, Richard Wollheim, had to admit that 'information about Bradley's life is scanty'.[6] Severe inflammation of the kidneys afflicted him for life and both cold and anxiety brought on severe illness, to which increasing age added deafness. As a result, aided by having no teaching or lecturing obligations, he led a quiet life in college and wintered abroad. The great friend of his life was Mrs Radcliffe ('E. R.'), an American living in France, to whom he dedicated all his books; it is said that his doctor dissuaded him from marrying her. Although she claimed never to have read a book and was not interested in philosophy, he 'sketched out his complete system of metaphysics in a series of letters to her, which she destroyed'.[7] According to his biographer:

> In political matters he was deeply conservative or reactionary. The mere mention of Gladstone's name enraged him and he tried to justify this by referring it to the Liberal party's 'betrayal' of Gordon in the Sudan . . . implacable enemy of all utilitarian or liberal teaching . . .[8]

Bradley's contribution to philosophy was embodied mainly in four books, published between 1876 and 1914: *Ethical Studies*, *The Principles of Logic*, *Appearance and Reality* and *Essays on Truth and Reality*, covering most fields except aesthetics. He had imbibed Kant as a schoolboy but, in maturity, Hegel was his inspiration, even though he diverged enough to disclaim the term Hegelian. He was an Idealist, who held that thought is inevitably artificial and the absolute – the totality of Being – is the only and ultimate reality; everything in the universe is composed of experiences. In 1994, a study was published called *James and Bradley: American Truth and British Reality*, reviewing the philosophies of the British academic and his American contemporary, William James, brother of that other OM, the novelist Henry. Interest therefore continues in philosophical circles even though his name is now scarcely known outside them.

In the Birthday Honours of 1930, **Samuel Alexander** was appointed an OM 'in recognition of his eminent position as a British Philosopher and for his services both as a writer and teacher'. He had retired in 1924 after 31 years as Professor of Philosophy at the University of Manchester. He was a rare example of an academic OM coming from outside the charmed triangle of Oxford, Cambridge and London, and that rarity may even have contributed to his selection for the Order.

Samuel Alexander was the posthumous son of an Australian saddler and his South African wife. After gaining all the distinctions open to him at school and university in Melbourne, he came to Britain in 1877, intent on

39 Samuel Alexander.

winning a scholarship at Oxford or Cambridge. Fearing that Balliol might be beyond his reach, he tried also for Lincoln; he succeeded at Balliol but not at Lincoln. After he had secured firsts in classical moderations and Greats, however, Lincoln elected him to a fellowship in 1882. Samuel Alexander was the first professing Jew to become a Fellow at either Oxford or Cambridge – as, later, he was to be the first Jew appointed to the Order of Merit.

Alexander stayed at Oxford for 11 years, except for a couple when he went away to study in Germany and to move in a wider world. He lectured at Toynbee Hall, the university settlement in the East End of London and tried to popularise academic subjects. After his move to Manchester, he became a legend of bachelor untidiness (aggravated by deafness), with an influence far beyond his academic role. Soon after leaving Oxford, he had produced a book, *Moral Order and Progress*, which

> ... in its day was widely believed to be the best systematic general treatise on evolutionary ethics in the English language.[9]

After that he was slow to write anything of substance, to the concern of his friends and admirers. There were presidential addresses to the Aristotelian Society, articles in *Mind* and the Gifford Lectures at Glasgow in 1917–18 entitled (and published in two substantial volumes as) *Space, Time and Deity*, for which *The Basis of Realism* (1914) had been a forerunner. According to the writer of Alexander's *DNB* entry:

> The value of the book has to be estimated by the vision, skill and res- olution with which it pursued its sweeping design. It is only accurate to say that, after Hobbes, no English philosopher, before Alexander, had built in accordance with so ambitious an architectural plan... In less than a decade the general opinion was that the book marked the end of an epoch rather than a fresh beginning and Alexander himself considered that the future was with A. N. Whitehead rather than with himself, so far as such a philosophy had a future... Alexander was a great philosophical architect whose skill and resourcefulness deserve abiding recognition.[10]

Philosophy had not done too well out of the Order of Merit. Bradley had had it for only three months and Alexander for only eight years. After his death in 1938, this branch of Learning had no representative in the Order. The philosophers decided to move but, by the time they did, their preferred candidate, **A. N. Whitehead**, was already 81 and had lived in the United States for nearly 20 years as Professor of Philosophy at Harvard. There were doubts about his nationality and his state of health.

The first approach was made formally (but mistakenly) to the Prime Minister in 1942 by Lord Samuel, the former Minister (and future OM) and Sir David Ross, Vice-Chancellor of Oxford University, on behalf of the British Institute of Philosophy. Downing Street passed the letter to the Palace where it was received rather coolly. Subsequently, Ross, with other members of the Philosophical Section of the British Academy, made a second, more detailed approach to the Prime Minister. It listed Whitehead's achievements:

1. The formulation of a universal algebra.
2. A critical examination of the principles and methods of mathematical disciplines.
3. ... a body of philosophical teaching ... classics in the field of philosophy.
4. ... semi-popular works that have made him a recognized teacher of educated thought in our time.[11]

Hardinge did no more but his successor, Lascelles, twice had Whitehead commended to him as 'pre-eminent'. Eventually, towards the end of 1944, Lascelles was persuaded by Morshead into recommending Whitehead – at last – for the OM. Lascelles admitted that the philosopher

> has got much the most impressive dossier in my file and is probably our outstanding British philosopher. But he is 83+, has published nothing since 1938 and has lived for years in Boston. I'm inclined to write him off as a bus-misser, though I do think he ought to have had it 10 years ago.[12]

The OM was offered to Whitehead 'in recognition of your outstanding services to philosophy' and promptly accepted. It was announced in the New Year Honours of 1945. The British Consul General in Boston presented the insignia to Whitehead at a ceremony in Harvard on 6 June 1945.

Whitehead was the son of a schoolmaster turned clergyman. After Sherborne, where he was head of school and captain of cricket and football, he embarked on the first of the three chapters of his life: Cambridge, which was followed by London and Harvard. He was a mathematician who was elected to a fellowship at Trinity College at the age of 24. His first major work, on algebra, did not appear for 13 years but it led to his election as FRS when he was 38. By then he had linked academically with a former pupil, Bertrand Russell; they wanted to try to settle the foundations of mathematics and concluded that it was a part of logic without a separate philosophy of its own. Their conclusions were published in 1910–13 in *Principia Mathematica*, three large volumes. This was described by the writer of the *DNB*'s entry on Whitehead as 'the greatest single contribution to logic that has appeared in the two thousand years since Aristotle'.

Whitehead suddenly put an end to his Cambridge mathematical career in 1910 to take what he called a 'bottle-washing' job at University College,

London. As the First World War began, Whitehead obtained the chair of applied mathematics at the Imperial College of Science and Technology. His work gradually acquired philosophical character and he published several works of that nature between 1915 and 1920. Whitehead was surprised by the offer, in 1924, of the chair of philosophy at Harvard. He retained the chair until 1937 but remained in Cambridge, Massachusetts, until his death ten years later. The *Dialogues* record Whitehead's views over a whole range of subjects. On Edward VII:

> He was very badly brought up. He couldn't get on with the Kaiser . . . It was Edward's *job* to get on with the Kaiser. That is what we paid him for, and paid him handsomely, jolly well too much. No, he was ill-bred.[13]

On the monarchy:

> The English never abolish anything. They put it in cold storage. That has its advantages. If they should want it again, there it is![14]

On Churchill (in 1944):

> He is an admirable leader to arouse the patriotism of his people in a desperate war; but he doesn't think sociologically in terms of a new epoch. I doubt if he would be so admirable in the making of the peace.[15]

Bertrand Russell's OM was a long time coming because of his unconventional behaviour, matrimonially and otherwise. He had been both fined and imprisoned in the First World War for anti-conscription and anti-American activities and, by 1949, the third of his four marriages was collapsing. Nevertheless, in the previous year, he had successfully inaugurated the Reith Lectures series on the BBC. By 1949, however, Whitehead had been in and out of the Order, having died at the end of 1947. The lack of a philosopher among its members was again being noticed. The responses to the 'usual soundings' by the Palace were uniformly positive. From Oxford came a reminder (from the President of Trinity College) that he had been elected an FRS 40 years earlier for his work on Mathematical Logic. (He was also an FBA since he moved in that world where mathematics meets philosophy.) He was endorsed by those with chairs:

> the most eminent living English philosopher [and] the greatest . . . since John Stuart Mill [Russell's secular godfather] and possibly since Hume . . . unquestionably a genius and his work and influence as far as I can judge will certainly be permanent.[16]

40 Bertrand Russell by Roger Fry.

From Cambridge came the important endorsement of the Master of that other Trinity College, G. M. Trevelyan:

> I was instrumental in bringing him back to this college from America ... proved a great success ... Though he is 76, his lectures, both the technical and the popular, are immensely appreciated by the young and all the older members of the University competent to judge regard his position in English philosophy as being of [a] very high order ... He has a touch of genius which I think the Order of Merit is meant to mark, though it has generally to fall back on industrious talent as in the case of ...
>
> Yours sincerely
> G. M. Trevelyan[17]

Russell's actual investiture, on 30 June 1949, was recorded by himself at some length, since he seems to have been intrigued at, what was for him (unlike his grandfather, the nineteenth-century Prime Minister), a rare meeting with royalty:

> The King was affable, but somewhat embarrassed at having to behave graciously to so queer a fellow, a convict to boot. He remarked. 'You have sometimes behaved in a way which would not do if generally adopted.' I have been glad ever since that I did not make the reply that sprang to my mind: 'Like your brother.' But he was thinking of things like my having been a conscientious objector and I did not feel that I could let this remark pass in silence, so I said: 'How a man should behave depends upon his profession. A postman, for instance, should knock at all the doors in a street at which he has letters to deliver but if anybody else knocked on all the doors, he would be considered a public nuisance.' The King abruptly changed the subject by asking me whether I knew who was the only man who had both the KG and the OM. I did not know and he graciously informed me that it was Lord Portal. I did not mention that he was my cousin.[18]

If Russell's memory was accurate, it is strange that George VI, who was so assiduous in honours matters, had forgotten that Halifax and Alanbrooke also had both orders at that time.

Bertrand Russell's supposed lack of 'respectability' was certainly not due to lack of 'birth'. He came from the Whig aristocracy, which had little regard for the Crown it supposedly served. His grandfather, a son of the Duke of Bedford, was Lord John Russell (the first Earl Russell), who was born during the French Revolution, 'won' a family rotten-borough parliamentary seat in 1813, piloted the Reform Act through the Commons in 1832 and ended his second term as Prime Minister in 1866, six years before Bertrand's birth.

Bertrand's radical parents died before he was four and he was brought up by his grandmother. Educated by tutors at home, Russell was crammed for Trinity College, Cambridge, where he read mathematics and natural sciences. He came under the influence of Whitehead and G. E. Moore; it was Moore who slowly weaned him from the Idealism of F. H. Bradley.

From the age of 15, when he 'began to have sexual passion, of almost unbearable intensity',[19] women and thoughts of them loomed very large in Russell's life. He was married for nearly 80 of his 98 years to four women, with virtually no interruption between divorces and re-marriage.

His family tried to stop his first marriage by having him appointed as an attaché in the British Embassy in Paris but he persisted and the marriage lasted for 27 years; although he had told his wife (Alys) he no longer loved her after eight years and they separated after 15. His second marriage to Dora lasted 14 years but she had children by another man. Eventually, it was she who unveiled the humanist memorial to Russell in Red Lion Square in London.

His third wife (Patricia or 'Peter') was the family governess and it was this marriage which was breaking down at the time of Russell's OM; it lasted 16 years. His fourth marriage, to an American (Edith) survived until his death; she shared his political activities, including his short imprisonment in 1961. On her death, in 1978, it was recalled that:

> She was well aware of the gossip that he had married her when 'past it'. Past it, indeed! He remained her lover until almost at the gates of death.[20]

Marriage was not enough for a 'lustful satyr', as one woman called him. The list of his (known) relationships is long and includes Evelyn Whitehead (wife of his collaborator, A. N. Whitehead), to whom he later gave money to pay her household bills, unknown to her husband; Vivienne, first wife of T. S. Eliot and the governess – 'I could not resist making love to Mademoiselle,' he told Dora.

Politics were always part of Russell's life. He failed, on a woman's suffrage ticket, to win a Commons seat in 1907. Russell found the First World War

> trivial for all its vastness. No great principle is at stake, no great human purpose is involved on either side. The supposed ideal ends for which it is being fought are merely part of the myth.[21]

Such views led him into a fine in 1916 and prison (and the temporary loss of his Trinity fellowship) in 1918. A. J. Balfour intervened to ensure that he was placed in the 'first division', which enabled him to write a book: *Introduction to Mathematical Philosophy*.

After having again failed to secure a Commons seat (in the Labour interest) in 1922 and 1923, the hereditary system enabled Russell to enter the House of Lords on succeeding his brother in the earldom in 1931. He was already teaching in the United States when the Second World War began. A post at the renowned Bryn Mawr enabled him to complete *A History of Western Philosophy*; this was his most popular work and it rescued him from his recurring serious financial difficulties.

At the end of the war, he returned to Trinity and his distinctive voice and appearance became well known to a wide public, not least because of the BBC Brains Trust. He became the first president of the Campaign for Nuclear Disarmament (CND) and later headed the more militant Committee of 100, on which J. B. Priestley joined him but Henry Moore did not.

His activities led him into prison again, for a week in 1961 (at the age of 89), after refusing to be bound over to keep the peace. Although other OMs have been in prison (Mandela and Tippett, for instance), Russell is the only one to have been there after gaining the honour. Russell's political activism, 'celebrity tours' (as they would now be called) and journalism led to his being derided as 'England's wisest fool' or condescendingly seen as in the long tradition of eccentric upper-class radicals. G. M. Trevelyan said

> He may be a genius in mathematics – as to that I am no judge; but about politics he is a perfect goose.[22]

Isaiah Berlin considered him the greatest logician since Leibniz, 200 years earlier, whose work was a great early influence on Russell. Apart from his collaboration with Whitehead on *Principia Mathematica*, already referred to, his works included *The Problems of Philosophy* (1912), *The Analysis of Mind* (1921), *The Analysis of Matter* (1927) and *An Inquiry into Meaning and Truth* (1940). He also wrote profusely on politics, morals and education, as well as a three-volume autobiography, towards the end of his life.

The Nobel Prize for Literature, awarded to him in 1950, was 'in recognition of his varied and significant writings in which he champions humanitarian ideals and freedom of thought'.

Russell was irrepressible. In nearly 98 years of flamboyant existence, he gave rise to many stories, which were often based on his considerable intellect and his self-absorption. One related to Patrick Blackett, the future OM and President of the Royal Society. Shortly after he had won the Nobel Prize for Physics, a mutual friend took him to meet Russell, who was reluctant to lift his eyes from a newspaper:

> I'm very sorry; I cannot pay attention to anybody. I am reading about myself.[23]

Russell died in 1970, aged 97. The Queen's message to his widow said that his 'distinguished contribution to twentieth-century thought is recognized throughout the world'. The Prime Minister (Harold Wilson) described him as

> the British Voltaire and, like Voltaire, his conversation was even more brilliant than his writing... unanimous admiration... for his contributions to the advance of scientific thought and to the advance of civilized ideals...[24]

Many obituaries repeated the paradox of the liar which Russell used: if a man says he is a liar, is he to be believed or not? If he's telling the truth when he says that, how do you know that isn't a lie as well. And if he's lying when he says he's a liar... Also resurrected was his epigram that the Ten Commandments should be headed like an examination paper: 'only six to be attempted'. It is fairly simple to name at least one that he never attempted.

Russell was a great pipe-smoker but, when asked whether he enjoyed smoking, he replied 'No, but I dislike non-smoking.' On one occasion this habit saved his life. He was aboard a flying-boat which crashed into a Norwegian fjord. The front end sank and the non-smokers in it were drowned. The rear-end, where Russell was puffing his pipe, floated long enough for him to escape through a window, the first time he had had to swim in an overcoat clutching an attaché case. Before he was rescued, he lost the case that contained his passport but seemed surprised that 'no one seems to doubt that I am me'.

Russell claimed that the incident proved that a philosopher could speak the truth without knowing it at the time, because he had told the stewardess before boarding: 'If I don't smoke, I shall die.' We shall never know whether on meeting God he did say, as Isaiah Berlin's version of an oft-quoted story goes:

> Why on earth didn't you give better evidence of your existence?[25]

Close on the heels of Russell in the Order of Merit came **G. E. Moore**, with whose name – and that of Wittgenstein – he is so closely linked in any discussion of British philosophy in the first half of the twentieth century. Moore was appointed to the Order in the Birthday Honours of 1951, less than six months after his name had been suggested by a 41-year-old Fellow of All Souls and Lecturer in Philosophy at New College, Oxford – Isaiah Berlin, 20 years before he himself received the honour.

Lord Brand, the banker, who had been a member of Milner's 'Kindergarten' in South Africa (the group of bright young officials whom he gathered around him) and a Fellow of All Souls, told his son-in-law, Edward Ford (then Assistant Private Secretary to the King and later the Secretary and Registrar of the Order of Merit) that he had not read Moore but went on to make some general and interesting observations:

> You can never tell about a philosopher till after his death and sometime after. For instance, I should imagine Isaiah B. and his friends would certainly now hold the view that F. H. Bradley was not worthy of an OM...I can't imagine that a philosopher like Moore can possibly or should mind whether he gets an OM or not, but you can never tell.[26]

From the Master of Trinity College, Cambridge and OM, G. M. Trevelyan, came unsurprising support:

> As a young man I heard an immense amount of philosophical discussion among them [Cambridge philosophers] and of course Moore himself, arising out of the *Principia Ethica*, which dethroned Hegelian philosophy in Cambridge...great reputation Moore got fifty years ago...has since never wavered...*as a philosopher*...fully on an equality with Bradley, Alexander, Whitehead and Russell.[27]

A couple of months elapsed and Isaiah Berlin returned to the charge, this time direct to the Palace. He described Moore as

> A deeply venerated figure...has not written a very great deal...has done more than any other human being to initiate the process whereby Anglo-Saxon philosophy has, in the last fifty years, entered into a period of fruitful development...The late Lord Keynes is perhaps the most notable example of a man whose life was deeply affected by Moore's friendship and teaching...a kind of moral genius which he appeared to radiate...his name will certainly rank as high as that of Russell – and very much higher than that of Whitehead...[28]

The OM was duly offered to Moore and he was the last to be invested by George VI – on 13 December 1951, a few weeks before the King died. Of that investiture, the ethereal Moore is supposed to have told the more worldly Berlin:

> The most extraordinary thing. When I mentioned Wittgenstein, the King didn't seem to know who he was.[29]

In 1951, I did not know who Moore was and that is why his appointment lodged in my mind. It came at the time when I was beginning to take a serious interest in the Order and I remember saying to the schoolmaster who influenced me so much (and to whom I paid tribute in the preface): 'What's the meaning of this honour if it's given to old professors at Cambridge who no one has heard of?' – meaning, of course, that I hadn't. Trenchard was appointed just before him and Attlee followed him: I had heard of them. At that time, I was probably the 'man in the street', without much knowledge of the intellectual fastnesses into which the Order tried to penetrate. An appointment like Moore's made the Order seem remote and rarefied. I have learned a lot since.

George Edward Moore was the son of a south London doctor and the grandson of a home-spun philosopher, who became the Dr Spock of Victorian England. He hated the name George, hence 'G. E.'; later, his wife and children called him 'Bill', although she sometimes referred to him as 'Moore'.

From Dulwich College, Moore went to Trinity College, Cambridge, where he first read classics, with future OMs as tutor (Henry Jackson) and examiner (Richard Jebb). After gaining a first in moral sciences, he was elected, at the second attempt, to a Trinity prize fellowship in 1898. When it expired after six years, he lived away from Cambridge on private means before returning there as a university lecturer in moral science from 1911–25 and Professor of Philosophy from 1925–39. For over 25 years (1921–47), Moore edited the philosophical journal *Mind*, which he 'used to train the young philosophers'.[30] Russell and Moore, two years his junior, had an immense influence on each other as what was described as the begetters of Anglo-American 'New Realism'. Russell wrote:

> On fundamental questions of philosophy, my position, in all its chief features, is derived from Mr G. E. Moore.

Moore wrote:

> I should say that I have certainly been more influenced by him [Russell] than by any other single philosopher.[31]

This did not mean they were close friends. 'Once Russell remarked to Moore, "You don't much like me, do you?" to which Moore, after serious consideration, answered "No", continuing cheerfully with the conversation and with the friendship'.[32] Both revolted against the Hegelianism they had imbibed at Cambridge, and Moore's philosophy was essentially one of 'back to common sense'. His contribution to *Contemporary British Philosophy* (1925) was entitled *A Defence of Common Sense*. Moore wrote relatively little. After his first and principal work, *Principia Ethica* in 1903 when he was 30, there were only three books: *Ethics* in 1912, *Collected Essays* in 1922 and *Lectures (from 1910–11)* in 1953. His influence, however, went far beyond what could be inferred from his published work. It began at Cambridge, where he was

> at his very best . . . not easy to imagine how lecturing could be done better than he did it.[33]

Moore died in Cambridge in 1958 and is buried there, a few steps from the grave of Wittgenstein. His reputation has paled besides those of Russell and Wittgenstein. Critics have written of his 'being eclipsed'[34] and of his influence having 'been great' but expressing 'doubt about how long lasting or deep it may prove to be'.[35]

The next philosopher to be honoured with the Order of Merit was not British and therefore became an Honorary Member. He was **Sarvepalli Radhakrishnan**, who was President of India in 1963 when he received the award, which is discussed in Chapter 17 on Honorary Members.

Just over a year after Bertrand Russell's death, the next – and, so far, last – British philosopher was appointed to the Order of Merit, on 28 May 1971. He was not, however, British by birth and he preferred to call himself a historian of ideas.

Isaiah Berlin was born a Russian subject in Riga (Latvia) but his Jewish businessman father brought the family to Britain after the Revolution. The son had a conventional British education at St Paul's School and Oxford,

41 Sir Isaiah Berlin by John Ward.

where he took firsts in Greats and 'Modern' Greats before election as the first Jewish Fellow of All Souls. The Warden of New College, H. A. L. Fisher (an OM late in life), was one of the first to recognise Berlin's outstanding gifts and a lectureship and fellowship there followed. He remained an Oxford man, in one form or another, all his life.

'The Reluctant Philosopher' was the title of an article by Bernard Williams, shortly after Berlin's death:

> he gave it up – philosophy that is to say, to use his words 'as it is taught in most English-speaking universities and as I believe it should be taught...'. I gradually came to the conclusion that I should prefer a field in which one could hope to know more at the end of one's life than when one had begun; and so I left philosophy for the history of ideas.

This conclusion had come to him after a nine-hour sleepless crossing of the Atlantic in an unpressurised aircraft, during which he 'had nothing to do except think', something which (he claimed) he 'always found exceedingly painful'.[36]

When the *Times Diary* set out in 1981 to find Britain's leading intellectual, the concensus of answers placed Berlin above everyone else. It was said that if you went for a walk on Hampstead Heath in the 1980s, you would probably meet Michael Foot walking his dog and Isaiah Berlin walking his brain. He was a man about whom stories abounded. He became a legend in his own lifetime, so that towards the end it was pardonable to be uncertain whether he was alive or dead.

The war took Berlin away to serve in the British Embassy in Washington under Lord Halifax, who developed a high regard for his judgement. The story of Berlin's reports from Washington, which Churchill so much admired, have become central to the legend of the man. Berlin was said to have delighted in the numerous versions of the story of *Irving* Berlin being invited to Number 10, especially the one which has Churchill saying, 'You know, it's strange – he writes so much better than he talks.' From Washington, he went to serve briefly at the British Embassy in Moscow. Berlin's reward for his war work was a CBE. When he was elected to the chair of Political Theory at Oxford in 1957, his 'vast erudition with such irresponsible gaiety' was singled out for comment:

> As a conversationalist alone, he is almost legendary . . . rapid, vivid, torrential cascades of rich, spontaneous, tumbling ideas and images. There is a theory that he . . . can suck in the contents of books, without actually opening them . . . [not so!]. He reads.[37]

His rapid speech (400 words a minute) was always a problem. When asked to speak more slowly if he wanted Americans to understand him, he replied, 'Yes, I know, I know, I know. But if I did, I should be quite a different person, quite a different person.'[38] Shortly after his election to the chair, Berlin was knighted:

> His first instinct was to turn it down. He felt, as he wrote to T. S. Eliot, that he was being asked to wear a funny hat. When he told his mother of his decision, her eyes filled with tears and he decided he must accept.[39]

Nevertheless, he felt that

> The Prime Minister [Harold Macmillan] is dispensing patronage to people who entertain or amuse him in one fashion or another. Which may indeed be true, for the reason for this 'elevation' is genuinely obscure to me as to others.[40]

He gave up his chair to become the first President of Iffley College, the post-graduate institution that was transformed by generous benefaction into Wolfson.

By his persistent and successful lobbying for the OM for G. E. Moore in 1951, the young Isaiah Berlin had, probably unwittingly, put himself into the OM frame. On being told that he was to receive the award, he reacted: 'Oh no, it's too much. I must emigrate.'[41] Since the practice of the inter-war years of publishing short citations for OM awards had been discontinued, it is difficult (without access to the Royal Archives of the time) to be absolutely certain why Berlin received the honour. It was probably best summed up by the *Oxford University Gazette* at the time of his death:

> in recognition of his public service, academic achievement, and multi-sided eminence.[42]

The response of other Oxford luminaries to his OM was mixed. William Hayter, the ex-diplomat Warden of New College, whose reaction to Berlin's knighthood had been 'I wonder why', now 'almost fainted'.[43] Exactly the same story is told of Maurice Bowra, the Warden of Wadham College[44] – so much for the Oxford rumour mill. Nevertheless:

> It cost Maurice much to write his letter of congratulation...The bile rose; but to give in to such a base emotion would be despicable...He told his friends how much Isaiah deserved it. But he could not suppress his joke. The OM, he said, was the rich man's CH.[45]

His own CH had come a few months earlier, in the New Year Honours.

In 1987, I wrote an article on the OM service that year, which the Secretary of the Order sent to all the Members. In a response, which I rated as Beta plus rather than Alpha minus, he commented on my description of him as 'the greatest Oxford philosopher of his day': 'I hope Freddie Ayer doesn't see this.'[46]

Berlin's 'intellectual impresario', Henry Hardy, who edited all his later works for publication, has told of the wealth of his correspondence, which is now also being edited. Strangely, when his friend, Lady Gore-Booth, had asked him whether his papers might eventually come to the Bodleian Library, Berlin had replied that he never thought of himself as possessing any. Two hundred and fifty boxes and several filing cabinets now rest in the Bodleian.[47] When questioned about the relative scarcity of his written work, he responded:

> I didn't feel I had enough to say. I've never felt that what I was thinking or feeling was so new and important that I couldn't be silent, that I must speak. That is why very nearly every single piece I've written has been

done to order. Fundamentally, I'm a taxi-cab: if I'm not summoned, I don't move.[48]

A year or so before his death, Berlin said

> I do not believe in a world after death . . . I see absolutely no evidence of it . . . It is just a comforting idea for people who can't face the possibility of total extinction . . . Let me add this . . . I wouldn't mind living on and on. I'm by nature an observer, not a man of action. I am filled with curiosity and long to know, what next?[49]

Berlin was a lifelong Zionist and champion of Israel: one of the most respected of free-thinking Jews in the Diaspora. Three weeks before he died, Berlin had dictated an appeal to the Israelis to accept a partition of the land with the Palestinians. His achievement was summarised at the outset of the obituary in *The Times*:

> Sir Isaiah Berlin was for many years one of the most influential figures in the intellectual life of the country, and also one of the most original. The part he played in the social and intellectual worlds of London and Oxford is very difficult to describe, because it was unique. It owed very little to any achieved position and status, but was due rather to the richness of his mind, his brilliance in conversation, his personal charm and to the generosity with which he put his famous abilities at the disposal of others, without stint or calculation.[50]

One of the most engaging of the many obituary tributes to Berlin was entitled *An ideal of Englishness*, by William Waldegrave, former minister and a Fellow of All Souls. In conclusion, he described how he would have shown the reader what he meant by its title:

> I would have taken you to see a Latvian, Jewish, Russian, German, Italian mixture of all the cultures of Europe. I would have taken you to see Isaiah Berlin.[51]

The classical scholars

All the classical scholars admitted to the Order of Merit were appointed in its first 40 years. There have been none in the following 60 years, when the study of the ancient world in Britain has decreased so greatly. The Classical Association was founded only a year after the Order of Merit but of the eight OMs who have been its President, only two have come from the ranks of the classical scholars: Murray (twice) and Mackail. The other six were men of affairs (Cromer and Samuel), a poet (Eliot), a historian (Bryce) and scientists (Geikie and Hinshelwood).

The first classical scholar appointed to the Order, on 30 June 1905, was **Richard Jebb**, who had been knighted in 1900 after having refused that honour in 1897. He came from a family of lawyers and clerics and began his long association with Trinity College, Cambridge at the age of 17. Five years later, after gaining all the highest classical prizes at Cambridge, he was elected (at the second attempt) to a fellowship at Trinity. For 12 years he combined his teaching duties with being Public Orator of the University and a leader-writer and reviewer for *The Times*, as well as writing the first four of his books.

The Regius Chair of Greek at Cambridge was occupied by Benjamin Hall Kennedy, whose *Latin Primer* and *Grammar* are familiar to many of us from our schooldays. Jebb was confident of succeeding Kennedy but, rather than wait in Cambridge, he accepted the chair of Greek at Glasgow in 1875. In his 14 years there, he began the great work of his life: an edition of *Sophocles*. Jebb's first volume appeared in 1883 and six more followed, at intervals of two to three years, until 1896. He also helped to start the Society for the Promotion of Hellenic Studies and was instrumental in the founding of the British School of Archaeology in Athens. Indeed, he was unusual among classicists of the time in knowing modern Greece and speaking modern Greek. He was a close friend of Tennyson, who dedicated a poem to him.

Kennedy retained the chair at Cambridge until he died in 1889, aged 85; Jebb was duly selected to succeed him. Soon after returning to Cambridge (where, in any case, he had lived every summer during his tenure at Glasgow), Jebb became the (Conservative) MP for the University. He pursued his parliamentary career with vigour and was active on various official commissions on education. At Cambridge, one of those Jebb encountered was the young mathematician, A. N. Whitehead, who was to follow him into the Order of Merit many years later. Of Jebb, he recalled:

> delightful fellow...rather a fiery temper which was carried off by the charm of Mrs Jebb. '*Lady* Jebb', Mrs Whitehead corrected him, 'Don't rob her ghost. She loved the title.'[52]

Jebb took a leading part in the foundation of the British Academy in 1902 and his duties as president of the education section of the British Association hastened his death. The Association met in Capetown in 1905 and the travelling and the business of the meeting overtaxed him. Shortly after returning to Britain, he fell ill and died, at the age of 64, only five months after receiving the OM. According to the *DNB*, Jebb

> was far more distinguished as a scholar and man of letters than as a politician and public speaker; and his reputation will depend chiefly upon his edition of *Sophocles*, which is the most completely satisfactory on a

classical author that has been written in the English language...Every part of the edition is good but best of all is the commentary...Jebb seems to wind his way into the very mind of Sophocles...Few men of Jebb's time had received as great gifts from nature as he and few worked as hard to exercise and improve them.[53]

More recently, there has been sterner criticism:

his knowledge of ancient Greece and its language was voluminous and exact...but he could produce nothing but generalities. That his career was markedly successful in spite of these shortcomings...sheds an interesting light on the character of late Victorian scholarship.[54]

Jebb had been dead for only a couple of years when his successor in the Chair of Greek at Cambridge, **Henry Jackson**, succeeded him also in the Order of Merit. He was appointed on 26 June 1908. Like Jebb, he was a

42 Henry Jackson by William Strang.

lifelong Trinity man and even more devoted to Cambridge, with few interests outside it. He went up to Trinity at the age of 19 in 1858 and stayed there until his death 63 years later. Elected a Fellow in 1862, he became Vice-Master in 1914; for three years (1918–1921) the college had both its Master (J. J. Thomson) and its Vice-Master in the Order of Merit.

Jackson published little: a series of articles on Plato's *Later Theory of Ideas*, maintaining that the philosopher criticised and modified his own views; and an edition of Aristotle's *Ethics Book V*, as well as translations, papers and articles. He also wrote a book, *About Edwin Drood*, on Dickens' last unfinished novel. Thackeray was his favourite author and, long before his death, he had read *Henry Esmond* 40 times. His lack of scholarly publications was discounted by the *DNB*:

> But all who knew Jackson felt his personality to be more wonderful than any printed book, and every one fell under the spell of it. The secret of this was an extraordinary power of sympathy ... such an interest in others that he remembered details about them forgotten by themselves ... he was constantly occupied with college and university business during the day. He would often sit up late talking with any visitor till three or four o'clock, then work at a lecture, go to bed sometimes as late as six, and lecture at ten.[55]

Noel Annan (the historian and university administrator) was disparaging, in a nice way, about Jackson's suitability for the Order:

> [Jackson] was made OM but that could hardly have been for his publications. No doubt it was for his geniality, his gift of making college and university business agreeable and harmonious, and he was on the side of reform. [His last appearance in public was to be carried to Senate House to vote for degrees for women.] Perhaps also because he had been tutor to many who rose in the world and remembered him with affection. These gifts, as well as publications, are welcome in a don but not in our days sufficient for the OM.[56]

James Frazer sits rather uneasily in this section. His undoubted scholarship could not be defined, or indeed confined, by the word 'classical', in which realm it had begun. He was a learned man but one, in his own time and now, of whom most educated people have heard but whom relatively few have read. He was strongly championed in 1922 by Lord Crawford and Balcarres:

> [A] really great figure ... *The Golden Bough* ... developed into a majestic series of volumes unique in British literature for constructive research and analysis ... quite unknown to the general public [but] his claim to

pre-eminence would be triumphantly acknowledged [in the universities of Europe]...has contributed much to the science of anthropology, to the elucidation of the mysterious problems of ethnology and inchoate religions, subjects which in a sense are obscure, but which subconsciously influence mankind to a phenomenal extent.

Frazer's name came up again in 1924. The Prime Minister (Ramsay MacDonald) passed to Stamfordham the views of several literary figures recommending him for his 'marvels of research, presented in a brilliant literary style'.[57] Stamfordham responded:

At the present moment there are only 15 members, for the reasons that the King, on the very best advice, has failed to find those who stand pre-eminent in science, art or literature...I cannot get anyone to say that [Frazer's] claims are unquestionable.[58]

Before the end of the year, Frederic Kenyon was renewing Frazer's claims:

the most learned and industrious writer alive on mythological and folk-lore subjects. His *Golden Bough* is an encyclopaedia of learning...a scholar of universally accepted eminence in his own field.[59]

He also referred in passing to Frazer's rather ferocious Alsatian wife, who had bullied him into marriage. She died a few hours after him, in 1941, causing the Fellows of Trinity to joke that she would not allow him even one day's peace by himself.

The growing support for Frazer persuaded Stamfordham: 'so I should not go wrong by choosing him.'[60] He also talked and wrote to the Archbishop of Canterbury, emphasising that he was 'trying my utmost to find two or three good candidates for the OM'; as well he might, with membership only just over half-full. Stamfordham was eventually able to put Frazer's name to the King as being recommended by not only the Archbishop but also by Lords Balfour, Crewe, Crawford and Balcarres, Ramsay MacDonald (now the ex-Prime Minister), Frederic Kenyon and Humphry Ward. The uncertainty as to quite where Frazer fitted is reflected in the offer being made to him 'in recognition of your eminent services in the world of literature, science and scholarship'.

Frazer came from Glasgow merchant families and, after school and university in that city, he won a scholarship to Trinity College, Cambridge. After coming second in the first class of the classical tripos, he was elected in 1879 to a fellowship of the college, which he held until his death 62 years later. A chair of social anthropology was created for him at Liverpool University in 1907 and he retained it until 1922. He spent little time there, greatly preferring his study at Cambridge. He was a prodigious

Victorian worker and H. N. Brailsford, the political journalist, is quoted as saying:

> The mere bulk . . . would compel respect but when one analyses a page of his writing, with its close-packed material drawn from a dozen sources in five or six languages, one asks by what miracle he fitted twenty-four months into his year.[61]

The name for his great work, *The Golden Bough*, came from Virgil's *Aeneid*, where Aeneas, wishing to visit the underworld, was told that its queen required a gift – a golden bough (the mistletoe) – plucked from a certain tree in the sacred Arician grove of Diana on the sylvan shores of Lake Nemi. The ritual grew of the annual slaughter of the grove's priest by his successor, to be slain in his turn.

Frazer's attempt to explain the rule of the priesthood led from question to question and ranged through such notions as superstition, totemism, taboo, vine-god, corn-mother and corn-maiden and scapegoat. The work grew so much that it was sometimes, with mixed admiration and humour, referred to as 'The Golden Banyan'. From the two volumes that appeared in 1890, it grew to 12 by 1915, with an abridgement in 1922 and a final supplement in 1936. He described the work as depicting

> the long evolution by which the thoughts and efforts of man have passed through the successive stages of Magic, Religion and Science.[62]

The *DNB* summed it up:

> Whatever may be the ultimate explanation of the strange rule of the Arician priesthood, in this vast survey and mighty synthesis of customs and beliefs of primitive man, Frazer has placed on record an array of facts, collected with infinite pains and accuracy, which is of unique value as a permanent contribution to knowledge.[63]

Frazer's claim to 'classical' scholarship rests on his four-volume edition in 1898 of Pausanias's *Description of Greece*. His translation and extensive commentary drew not only on writings in many European languages but also, in sharp contrast to *The Golden Bough*, on his own visits to Greece. Frazer went on to be a founding Fellow of the British Academy in 1902, a knight in 1914 and an FRS in 1920.

Around 1990, the centenary of *The Golden Bough* brought forth renewed interest in and evaluation of Frazer. There was a biography in 1988 by Robert Ackerman and in 1990 a book by Robert Fraser on *The Making of*

The Golden Bough. One review (of *The Making*) said:

> Frazer's prose is Gibbonian and grand, but his doctrine is almost more than Nietzschean . . . he said that 'I reject the Christian religion as utterly false.'

It concluded that the book

> rehabilitates a man who may be called the last great figure of the Scottish Enlightenment.[64]

The next scholastic recipient of the Order was an authority not on Greece or Rome but on India, especially its numerous languages and dialects. **George Grierson,** who was appointed in the Birthday Honours of 1928, had not seen India for 25 years. Earlier, however, he had spent 30 years there, in routine posts in the Indian Civil Service, culminating in the modest post of opium agent for Bihar. Grierson had always had a strong interest in the languages and folklore of India and, soon after his arrival in the country, he began his copious writings: articles, reviews, translations, books and dictionaries.

At the Oriental Congress in Vienna in 1886, Grierson introduced the project of a linguistic survey of India and, when this was sanctioned in 1898, he was designated its superintendent. Although he retired from India in 1903, he continued his work on the survey – with the aid of many correspondents in India – from a house he built in Camberley. Grierson was made a KCIE in 1912 and, in 1928, the survey was completed: 19 volumes, 8,000 pages, describing 179 languages and 544 dialects.

Today, George Grierson is among the least known of all OMs but he was not much better known when he was appointed to the Order. As if to explain the appointment, there is a memorandum in the Royal Archives:

> With regard to The Order of Merit for Sir George Grierson, the Prime Minister initiated the idea and consulted Sir Walter Lawrence [former private secretary to the Viceroy] about it and then spoke to Lord Stamfordham when the latter saw him at Downing Street.[65]

The memorandum summarised the initial misgivings of Stamfordham, who consulted, among others, Arthur Balfour, whose response was:

> admirable idea . . . has performed a unique work, which really adds to the World's knowledge and reflects honour upon British scholarship . . . the ordinary Englishman – and perhaps the ordinary Indian – will have it driven into him that to talk of India as a unity when its millions talk 190 different languages (or whatever the number is) must be done with caution.[66]

Lawrence had told Baldwin that the proposal was justified because it would

> be appreciated by foreign countries, who twit the English for their neglect of research in India ... often been said that Paris and Berlin have done much more for Oriental studies than has England, which holds the East in fee.

Baldwin had also told Stamfordham that the India Office were 'entirely in favour'.[67] The OM was therefore offered to Grierson and, in the 1928 Birthday Honours, the award was recorded as 'in recognition of his eminent position as an Oriental Scholar and of the value to the Empire of his work on Indian Languages and Dialects'. What the appointment demonstrates is the importance of India to Britain ('England') at that time and the relative ignorance in the British establishment of the 'inner' India they were governing. Grierson mattered when India mattered.

Grierson died at the age of 90 in 1941, and there is a touching description of a visit to him in old age by his nephew, Maurice Collis, the historical writer, who had also been in the ICS:

> He was much liked by Indians of all classes. When the Maharajahs came to London on a visit they used to call on him, bringing presents ... a wonderful sight, propped on his pillows ... a gold-embroidered cap on his head (This was a present from the Gaekwar of Baroda.) ... He looked like a pastoral King, noble and benign.[68]

Like Grierson, the next 'classical' scholar appointed to the Order of Merit was not in the Greek or Roman mould. From grounding in that world, he had moved on to medieval studies. He was **Montague Rhodes James**, the Provost of Eton and former Provost of King's College, Cambridge and he was well known to the court.

When looking at literary candidates in 1928, Morshead told Stamfordham that he had thought of tackling James but did not because he seemed to be a candidate himself: 'Though I reluctantly place him just out of the running.'[69] Stamfordham did not feel similarly inhibited and did consult James. (Incidentally, Morshead owed his post largely to James, who recorded, in May 1927: 'The King was full of gratitude to me for having procured him such a nice new Librarian.'[70])

Within a couple of years, James had come into the running and his name appeared in the Birthday Honours of 1930, alongside two other scholars: Alexander, the philosopher, and G. M. Trevelyan, the historian. The award was 'in recognition of his scholarship and of his eminent contributions to Medieval Learning'. James might have sensed some impending sign of royal favour:

> Both King George and Queen Mary seem to have come to feel a personal
> fondness for M. R. J. . . . Both showed an exceptional willingness to visit
> Eton, indeed with a regularity that was almost burdensome.[71]

James had rewritten one of his famous ghost stories to be *The Haunted Doll's House* for inclusion in Queen Mary's dolls' house at Windsor Castle.

Eton was naturally to the fore in congratulating its Provost on his high honour. A telegram (in Latin) came from 'One Hundred and Twenty-Two Etonian Members of the Athenaeum'. A. E. Housman, who had declined the OM a year earlier, wrote

> I do not grudge this cruelly expensive postcard [from Paris] as a vehicle
> of congratulation, nor do I grudge the letters OM, which you ought to
> have had before.[72]

The Bishop of Ely offered to sell James his car, with its number OM1. (Over 50 years later, I saw that number on a car on the M1.)

'Monty' James, son of an evangelical clergyman, was a brilliant linguist, biblical scholar, medievalist and palaeographer. A lifelong bachelor with a host of friends, he spent much of his life at Henry VI's twin foundations: Eton (which he called the 'hub of the universe') and King's College, Cambridge. His immersion in, and devotion to, both institutions was evident in his memoirs, entitled simply *Eton and King's*.

After firsts in both parts of the classical tripos, James was set for an academic career as a Fellow of King's and assistant director of the Fitzwilliam Museum. He chose biblical over classical studies and built on a schoolboy interest by visiting all but two of the 143 cathedrals in France. He became director of the Fitzwilliam in 1893 but gave up the post after being elected Provost of King's. His successor, Sydney Cockerell, said of James:

> He had an enormous knowledge of medieval Latin. He'd smell a page
> of a manuscript and say, 'St Augustine' – and it *was* St Augustine![73]

James produced an immense quantity of learned work, while leading an active social life. When Lord Acton, the historian, asked one of James' friends how he managed to combine such a life with being third or fourth in Europe in his knowledge of manuscripts, he was told, 'We have not yet found out.'[74]

James spoke eight languages, with a modicum of others. He travelled widely, often by bicycle, in France and Scandinavia and rather less in Germany. He was particularly fond of Denmark. Danish folklore engrossed him and he used it in some of his ghost stories. He translated many of Hans Christian Andersen's stories.

James' work on manuscripts placed him in the front rank of palaeographers. He catalogued not only those at Eton, Lambeth Palace and Westminster Abbey but also many in leading libraries and in private collections. He was the first English scholar to specialise in Apocryphal literature and his *Apocryphal New Testament*, which he wrote in three months in 1924, crowned his achievement in this field.

James became the first lay Provost of Eton for 300 years, in 1918. He was also the first Provost ever to move between King's and Eton in either direction. He had been Provost of King's since 1905 and he was Vice-Chancellor of Cambridge from 1913–1915. He opposed full membership of the university for women and the abolition of Greek as an entry requirement. When he accepted the Crown's offer of the Eton post, many at Cambridge lamented it but his fellow classicist OM, Henry Jackson, commented that the right man would now be in the right place. James himself thought he had come home and he stayed at Eton until his death in 1936. As his biographer commented, it was

> the ghost stories of M. R. James, which made his name known to a wide reading public that was, and has remained, largely unaware of the extent and distinction of his other activities.[75]

There followed three more volumes, in 1911, 1919 and 1925 and they have continued to be regularly reprinted and produced on the radio. Anthony Quinton said that

> M. R. James was, first of all, for that is how he is known and admired by the largest number of people, just about the best writer of ghost stories of the last hundred years. His only serious competitor in this line is Walter de la Mare, who was a better, altogether more serious writer, as M. R. James would probably not have disputed, but a little too indefinite and whimsical. In de la Mare something a little funny is going on, or so it might seem, but perhaps it is only an effect of the lobster or the hot afternoon sun; in James there really is a yellowish face looking at one through the gap in the curtain, with tatters of blackened flesh on it and long, greasy strands of something very like hair.[76]

John William Mackail was appointed to the Order of Merit in the New Year Honours of 1935; 'Monty' James, Grierson and Frazer were still alive. He had been considered ten years earlier. In a round of consultation in late 1924, Mackail was placed by Frederic Kenyon (Director of the British Museum) after Murray and Housman but still worth considering as

> One of the best exponents of classical literature. He has been Professor of Poetry at Oxford and President of the Classical Association, and is a

Fellow of the British Academy. (So, of course, is Murray, and Housman could have been, but refused it.) He has written several volumes of lectures and addresses on classical and English literature.[77]

The Prime Minister, Stanley Baldwin, thought that Mackail (his cousin by marriage) was better than Murray. An earlier Prime Minister (and OM), Balfour, rated Mackail's ability very highly and thought there was not much to choose between him and Murray.[78]

Mackail was in the long line of Scottish scholars who came south to Oxford and Cambridge and never returned. A son of the manse, he won a scholarship from Edinburgh University (which he entered at 15) to Balliol College, Oxford, during the legendary mastership of Benjamin Jowett. Among his contemporaries there were his predecessor in the Order of Merit, Samuel Alexander, and George Nathaniel Curzon. The young Scotsman was 'without question the most brilliant undergraduate scholar of his time',[79] gaining not only a double first in Greats but also the Hertford, Ireland, Craven and Derby Scholarships, as well as the Newdigate Prize. A fellowship at Balliol naturally followed but, like his fellow-OM Grierson, Mackail combined his scholastic work with a career as a civil servant, rather than as an academic.

In Mackail's case, it was the Home, rather than the Indian, Civil Service. For 35 years (1884–1919), he served in the office that became the Board of Education and was active in the work to establish a secondary education system under the Act of 1902. H. A. L. Fisher, the historian who was shortly to join Mackail in the Order, recorded a glowing view of him:

> In my time [as President of the Board of Education] literary scholarship was brilliantly represented by J. W. Mackail ... [who], while discharging to the full his duties as a public servant, found time to achieve fame in the world of learning and letters.[80]

Mackail devoted his scholarly energies to classical poetry, to poetry generally and to biography. His main interest was Virgil, of whose work he published translations both early and late in life: in 1885 and 1930. In his *Latin Literature*, he covered its whole range from early poets to Christian writers. He also wrote on Greek literature: a three-volume translation of the *Odyssey*, lectures on poetry and an edition of epigrams, which Cyril Connolly called 'one of the sacred books of the inner culture' at Eton, which 'exhaled pessimism and despair'.[81] His biographical subjects included George Wyndham and William Morris.

During his five-year tenure of the Chair of Poetry at Oxford (1906–11), Mackail ranged beyond classical poetry to English (Chaucer, Shakespeare,

Spencer and Milton), Italian (Dante) and Arabic. He believed that

> Poetry is at once the interpretation and the pattern of life. Behind all the volumes lies a wealth of learning often concealed in order to expound a broad interpretation, and a deep love of poetry, which it was his life's work to awaken in others.[82]

Academic honours came to Mackail in abundance and he was, at various times, president of the Classical Association, the English Association, the Virgil Society and the British Academy; he held the last appointment at the time of his appointment as an OM. It is said that he turned down the Mastership of Balliol. Mackail married the only daughter of the painter, Sir Edward Burne-Jones.

Gilbert Murray, through no fault of his own, created more paper in the archives of the Order of Merit than any other recipient in the first 50 years of its existence. (I have already explained that I cannot speak for the second

43 Gilbert Murray by Francis Dodd.

50 years.) The story of the offer that was never made (in 1921) has been told in Chapter 5 because it is more relevant to the account there of the delicate relationship between the Sovereign and the Prime Minister than it is to Murray's own qualifications.

The decision, in the face of Lloyd George's objections, not to offer the OM was a monstrous setback to a distinguished scholar. It is puzzling that his candidature was not immediately proceeded with once Lloyd George was no longer Prime Minister. Murray's scholastic qualifications for the Order were obviously not in doubt when the King proposed to appoint him. Instead, however, he seems to have slipped to the back of the queue, to be considered virtually de novo and it is not therefore surprising that the rats began to get at the case for him. He had to wait 20 years, although his name came up intermittently. In 1924, Frederic Kenyon wrote to Stamfordham:

> Murray is the one with the wider appeal [as compared with Housman], with imagination and a power of giving life and modern interest to all that he writes about the ancient world... [83]

In reply, Stamfordham was somewhat disingenuous:

> [His] name was brought forward sometime ago and objections were raised on account of his Liberal views. His Majesty entirely disregards the question of the political opinions of anyone who may be suitable for the honour... Balfour was certainly in favour... [84]

The rub is that George V did not 'entirely disregard' Murray's political opinions.

Balfour himself renewed his plea for Murray but somewhat half-heartedly. Stamfordham, having burned his fingers, seemed curiously reluctant to move again on Murray. Time moved on. Stamfordham died on 31 March 1931, but when the new Private Secretary (Sir Clive Wigram) looked again at Murray's candidature, the notion was torpedoed by Frederic Kenyon, who reported that there was dissatisfaction at Oxford over the way in which he had subordinated his classical work to active interest in the League of Nations; Kenyon was told that Murray's name had been taken off the OM list. [85]

Murray, however, was too good a man to hold down. In the mid-1930s, he again received support from people who counted, including two OMs. The first was from Stanley Baldwin (Prime Minister again). And Geoffrey Dawson (editor of *The Times*) told the Private Secretary:

> I have always been slightly in favour of including Gilbert Murray, as the man who really brought Greek literature into the home. [86]

Finally, John Masefield, the Poet Laureate, described Murray as

> one of the great men of Oxford University, expounder of Greek thought, illuminator of Greek Drama, a fresh and living influence on poetical drama everywhere, as well as an untiring champion of the League of Nations and of every noble and difficult cause everywhere. His influence for good in all these ways and causes can never be told.[87]

Fortunately, when Murray's name again came forward for actual appointment, his political attitudes proved a positive plus. Winston Churchill, the Prime Minister, was consulted by the King's Private Secretary in 1940 and was enthusiastic:

> I think Professor Gilbert Murray would be an admirable recipient of the OM. In the months preceding the war, he and I were in very close sympathy, and I have no reason to suppose that he has changed his purpose in any way. I should therefore be in no way embarrassed if the King decided to confer this high honour upon him.[88]

The offer was made and Murray accepted, 'deeply sensible of the honour'. According to Murray's biographer, 'congratulations poured in from all manner of men: from Lloyd George...'[89] An interesting end to one of the most significant OM tales.

What of George Gilbert Aimé Murray himself? He was born in Sydney but left for Britain with his widowed Protestant mother at the age of 11. His knighted, easy-going, Catholic father had been a rich stock-farmer, who was both Speaker of the Lower House and President of the Upper House in New South Wales. Melancholy, extravagance and alcoholism combined to kill him when the boy was only seven.

When mother and son arrived in Britain, her cousin, W. S. Gilbert, was working on *HMS Pinafore*; it was from him that the boy derived the name by which he became known. At first Murray had no Christian name, because of his parents' mixed religious marriage; at three he was christened in the Catholic faith but he became an agnostic.

At Oxford, Murray secured 'a full bag of academic honours': the Hertford and Ireland scholarships and a first in Greats. The monumental Master of Balliol, Benjamin Jowett, described him as 'the most distinguished undergraduate of his time'.[90]

Gilbert Murray was a precocious Greek scholar, arousing early comment from two men who were to precede him in the Order of Merit. Jebb, whom he succeeded as Professor of Greek at Glasgow University at the age of 23, described him as, 'the most accomplished Greek scholar of the day'. Jackson was less complimentary, writing in the margin of an early book by Murray, *A History of Ancient Greek Literature*, 'insolent puppy'.[91]

Murray himself had wanted to study in Göttingen because 'Germans are like a superior race to scholars' imaginations'.[92] The need to secure a well-paid academic post, in order to marry, drew him instead to Glasgow. His fiancée was Lady Mary Howard, daughter of the Earl of Carlisle whose wife, much later, was described by Balfour, as

> that odious woman... recently deceased; but no man should be made to suffer for the sins of his mother-in-law.[93]

His students' poor Greek forced Murray into translation of Greek classics, particularly those of Euripides, such as *The Trojan Women*, *Medea* and *Electra*. They were performed at the Court Theatre in London from 1902 and Bernard Shaw, drama critic, wrote that they 'came into our dramatic literature with all the impulsive power of an original work'. In Murray's lifetime, the translations sold 400,000 copies.

Murray also ventured into modern fiction: a novel about a lost Greek tribe discovered on the other side of Tibet and a play (produced by Mrs Patrick Campbell and running for only a fortnight) about an ex-Indian Governor trying to prevent discovery of his having poisoned native wells but dying of poison himself on stage.

Teaching at Glasgow put a great strain on Murray and he resigned after ten years. Later, he was lured back to New College and, in 1908, he was appointed Regius Professor of Greek at Oxford, a chair he held for 28 years. He also undertook psychical research, where his demonstrations of telepathy achieved a high success rate, and the reform of English spelling. His overwhelming 'outside' interest was international affairs and the promotion of peace. This grew to an extent that attracted criticism in Oxford and damaged his prospects of the OM in the early 1930s. He was a founder of the League of Nations Union and was its chairman from 1923–38. His friendship with Smuts led to his being a member of the South African delegation to the League for a few years.

In 1929, it was rumoured that Ramsay MacDonald would appoint him as Ambassador in Washington so as to interest the Americans in the League they had not joined. He thought he could do the job:

> it is after all a one-man job... most of the elderly diplomats who occupy embassies are not such hard workers as to make it difficult for me to keep up with them.

Murray did not, however, really want the job and did not go.

I have already referred to Murray's refusals of honours in 1917. Earlier (in 1912), he had refused a knighthood because 'he was fairly, but not totally, indifferent to such honours'.[94] In 1917, he was initially inclined to accept the newly-instituted CH, 'but decided finally that, if he did so, he would be considered to have 'other companions besides Honour'.[95] The knighthood offered at the end of 1917 he refused 'without any hesitation'.[96]

The Second World War shattered the dreams of Murray – and many others. Undaunted, in 1945, he became the first president of the United Nations Association and remained so until his death. His ashes were buried in Westminster Abbey under a stone tablet with a Latin inscription to commemorate the great Greek scholar.

The historians

There were two historians among the original seven civil Members of the Order of Merit: **John Morley** and **W. E. H. Lecky**, who were also political figures. Lecky enjoyed the honour for only a year but Morley lived for another 20 years and was an influential voice in early appointments to the Order, such as Meredith, Bryce and G. O. Trevelyan. The two last-named were the next historians to become OMs.

James Bryce might possibly have been included in Chapter 14 on 'The Men of Affairs'. Before receiving the OM, he had been an MP for 26 years

44 Viscount Bryce.

and a cabinet minister for four and, after the award, he was an ambassador for six and a peer for eight; he rendered considerable public service. He was, however, also a professor at Oxford for 23 years and the author of two of the most respected historical works of his time. Marginally, I think he was appointed more as a historian than as a public man but I think both aspects of his life are needed to justify his inclusion in the Order.

The offer of the Order was made to Bryce by his political chief, the Prime Minister, Henry Campbell-Bannerman. The award greatly pleased his fellow Cabinet member, the Secretary of State for India, John Morley, who had received the OM in the first list for broadly similar achievements. An enthusiastic recommendation was made by Lord Esher, who thought the Order

> would be best bestowed upon James Bryce [for his] *The Holy Roman Empire* and *The American Commonwealth*. His appointment would be very well received here and would be enormously popular in the United States.[97]

James Bryce was an Ulsterman, the son and nephew of schoolmasters. He was educated partly in Glasgow, where his father taught, and partly in Belfast, where his uncle was headmaster of the Academy. He was already asking questions on the British constitution at the age of eight.

It was in the vacations from Glasgow University that Bryce acquired a love of mountain climbing that endured into old age. From Glasgow, Bryce won a scholarship to Trinity College, Oxford. He swept the academic board in the 1860s: firsts in Greats and in law and modern history; university prizes and scholarships. He was President of the Union and held a fellowship at Oriel College from 1862 until his marriage, at the age of 51, in 1889.

Bryce was called to the Bar by Lincoln's Inn and practised on the Northern Circuit but gave it up after 15 years because it interfered with his other activities (at Oxford and in Parliament) and with his love of travel. Before he embarked on his parliamentary career, Bryce had already made his mark as an academic. Like so many of his generation, he studied in Germany (at Heidelberg) and, at the same time, his Oxford essay prize on the *Holy Roman Empire* was expanded into the published book that established his reputation (official German recognition came with the Order Pour le Mérite in 1908, the year after his OM). His appointment as Regius Professor of Civil Law at Oxford, at the age of 32, revived the study of Roman law in the university.

Bryce was already being drawn into politics, however, largely because of a consuming interest in the 'Eastern Question'. His official entry into politics came with his election in 1880 as Liberal MP for Tower Hamlets, a working-class district of East London, in which he addressed the German sugar-bakers in their own language. He moved to the constituency of South Aberdeen in

1885 and retained it until 1906. Bryce achieved ministerial office briefly in 1886 and, more substantially, when Gladstone returned to office in 1892. As Chancellor of the Duchy of Lancaster, he was involved in the preparation of the Irish Home Rule Bill and, within the Duchy, he appointed some of the first working-class magistrates. He moved into the Cabinet as president of the Board of Trade.

Bryce's significant political contribution, however, was as chairman of the Royal Commission on Secondary Education (1894–95), which concluded that there should be a state system at that level. Queen Victoria liked him, and not only because he could, when required, speak to her in fluent German. She found him

> one of the best-informed men on all subjects I ever met, and has a very agreeable way of imparting what he knows. His knowledge is wonderful, and he seems to me to be an impartial and certainly not violent politician...[98]

She took the precaution, however, of pointing out to Bryce 'the great danger of over-education'.[99]

Bryce's interest in the United States, with which his name is so closely associated, was aroused by three extensive visits there, in 1870, 1881 and 1883. On his return, he began writing *The American Commonwealth*, which was published in 1888 and ran into several editions. His aim was to portray

> the whole political system of the country in its practice as well as its theory [to explain] not only the National Government, but the State Governments, not only the constitution, but the party system, not only the party system, but the ideas, temper, habits of the sovereign people.[100]

It became a standard authority in the United States and was used as a textbook for many years. In many ways, it marked the beginning of American studies in Britain.

Bryce returned to office in the Liberal Government at the end of 1905, as Chief Secretary for Ireland. At the end of 1906, he was appointed Ambassador in Washington, largely because he

> would be greatly appreciated in America as knowing far more of the history and Constitution of America than most Americans. He also had the quality of liking to make long and rather dull speeches on commonplace subjects, which I knew to be a trait that would be popular with the American masses.[101]

Not surprisingly, some career diplomats were unenthusiastic:

> I suppose the Yanks will be charmed, as what they want is to feel that we recognise that an ordinary 'dip' is not good enough for Washington because it is the most important post of all, and that we must send them a celebrity, I think *any* celebrity would suit, as long as his name was really well known to them.[102]

The notion of 'celebrity' appears to predate television.

Bryce spent six years in Washington and he travelled widely throughout the country. At that time, in the absence of a Canadian diplomatic service, Bryce knew that:

> Everything which a Canadian ambassador would do for his country, the British ambassador acting for Canada should be prepared to undertake.[103]

This involved negotiating with the Americans over such matters as the equal division of the waters of the boundary streams with Canada and Canadian fishing rights in the North Atlantic and sealing rights in the North Pacific.

On his return from Washington, Bryce embarked on the last, short phase of his career – in the House of Lords, having finally accepted the peerage he had declined in 1906 and again in 1910. He continued his public service: in 1914, as chairman of a commission on alleged German atrocities in Belgium; in 1917, by forwarding to the government a memorandum outlining the structure of a future League of Nations and; in 1918, as chairman of a parliamentary conference which failed to agree on reform of the House of Lords. In the New Year Honours of 1918, he was made a GCVO and his closeness to George V was shown by the King's message later to the widowed Lady Bryce:

> I regarded Viscount Bryce as an old friend and trusted counsellor to whom I could always turn, confident in the strength and wisdom of his advice...[104]

In 1921, he published his last work *Modern Democracies*, which compared the United States with other democratic countries.

Bryce died in January 1922, while his fellow-OM, Balfour, was leading the British delegation to the Naval Conference in Washington. In response to warm tributes to Bryce from the American delegates, Balfour 'rose splendidly to the occasion and spoke of Bryce with all his usual elegance'. Hankey (the Secretary to the Cabinet) realised he had completely failed to inform, let alone brief, Balfour about the event and was puzzled at his polished reaction: 'Oh! It was all right! Sarah told me.' Sarah was the cook at the British Embassy.[105]

Later in the year, a bust of Bryce was placed in the United States Capitol building with the inscription:

> Friend and Ambassador to the American People and Interpreter of their Institutions.

In accepting it, Chief Justice William Howard Taft (who had been President for most of Bryce's time as Ambassador) said:

> He knew us better than we knew ourselves, and he went about and among us and gave us the boon of his illuminating wisdom derived from the lessons of the past.[106]

Before Edward VII's reign was over, Morley was commending G. O. **Trevelyan** to the King's Private Secretary, in 1909:

> [Trevelyan] would be *excellent* . . . a brilliant scholar, a diligent historian and the author of one of the most admirable biographies [of Macaulay] in the history of literature . . . His *time is getting on* for he was born in the same year as Bryce and myself [1838].[107]

Asquith agreed that, 'Trevelyan has undoubtedly good claims'.[108] Trevelyan accepted the offer with:

> much gratitude . . . the value of the honour is greatly enhanced by the deep personal respect which I entertain for His Majesty.[109]

His son, G. M. Trevelyan, who was to follow him into the Order, wrote that it was, 'an honour he greatly appreciated'. G. M. Trevelyan was equally delighted for his father because he thought, 'that it publicly recognised "literary history in the Macaulay tradition"'.[110]

George Otto Trevelyan had inherited in 1886 the baronetcy conferred 12 years earlier on his father, Charles Edward, for services in India and Britain. G. O.'s mother was a sister of Lord Macaulay, the bachelor historian, who treated the Trevelyans' home in Clapham as almost a second home.

From Harrow, G. O. went to Trinity College, Cambridge, where his success lay not only in academic success but also in his intellectual high spirits: articles and a book satirising the contemporary university. The Master of Trinity, in 1862, 'considered the author lacking in deference'.[111] Not surprisingly, G. O. failed to secure a fellowship at the college. Instead of trying again for a fellowship, he spent a year in India as private secretary to his father. The experience resulted in two books: *The Competition Wallah*, about the life of British administrators in India after the Mutiny, and *Cawnpore*, dealing with one of the most vivid events of the Mutiny itself.

Shortly after his return to Britain, G. O. Trevelyan entered Parliament as a Liberal and, an enthusiastic supporter of Cardwell's army reforms, he was made Civil Lord of the Admiralty in 1868. He resigned in 1870 over the decision to increase the grant to Church schools and his political career was never as bright again. It was while out of office that he wrote, anonymously, a pamphlet entitled *What Does She Do With It?* It enjoyed a wide circulation and was an attack on the Civil List expenditure of Queen Victoria, alleging that, in her seclusion at Windsor, she

> was hoarding treasure in a miserly and eccentric way.[112]

G. O. Trevelyan's writing career began in earnest in the 1870s with the publication of the *Life and Letters* of his uncle, Lord Macaulay, and the *Early History of Charles James Fox*.

When Gladstone returned to office in 1880, Trevelyan was initially left out but, later, he became Chief Secretary for Ireland and, on promotion to the Cabinet, Chancellor of the Duchy of Lancaster and then Secretary for Scotland. He resigned again, however, in 1886, over Gladstone's introduction of a Home Rule Bill for Ireland. In the subsequent election he was defeated, but finding life with the Conservatives uncongenial, he rejoined the Liberals and won a seat. He served again as Secretary for Scotland from 1892–95, before retiring from public life in 1897. He declined Asquith's offer to return to it, with a peerage, in 1908.

The last 30 years of G. O. Trevelyan's life were spent mostly at his country home in Northumberland, where he wrote a six-volume *History of the American Revolution*, which was published between 1899–1914. According to his son, G. M., the book

> had a great effect in the United States, where its chief sale has always been. It did much to help the movement over there for a better understanding of England.[113]

It certainly brought him many American friendships, especially among the intellectual and social élites of the East Coast.

G. M. Trevelyan's entry into the Order of Merit came speedily and at a young age, by OM standards. In 1924, while his father was still alive, he was being compared alongside the Regius Professors of History at Oxford, C. H. Firth and, at Cambridge, J. B. Bury, whom he was to succeed in 1927:

> ... younger than these, but the best writer of them all.[114]

Trevelyan's father died in August 1928 and his own name was quickly being canvassed. Kipling was clear that Trevelyan

> would be the best choice. The crab . . . is that it looks as if he succeeded his father . . . son is, in every way, a more important man than he, as an historian, and his popular appeal is vastly greater [the *History of England*, published in 1926, had sold 50,000 copies and was to sell another quarter of a million in the next 30 years] . . . appointment might be made to signify that the Order kept a place for the most eminent historian of Great Britain. In other words, that there was, as one might say, a Chair for History, as there is for Literature, Science, Art and Music.[115]

Balfour thought that perhaps Trevelyan might wait but not for fear of the 'inheritance' criticism:

> I would never think of excluding George Trevelyan on an hereditary ground. But my impression is that we have not yet seen his greatest work. Is that a reason for waiting? I am not sure.[116]

Balfour's instinct was right. Many critics would say that Trevelyan's greatest work was his *English Social History*, which was not published until 1944, when it met with considerable acclaim and good sales: 400,000 copies within five years. Trevelyan certainly did not have to wait until then for the OM. He received it in the Birthday Honours of 1930, less than two years after his father's death. From a number of sources, it is clear that he was overjoyed with this particular honour: 'the OM . . . was the only honour seriously worth having.'[117]

> one yet smaller club to which Trevelyan belonged was the Order of Merit . . . From the time of its inception, Trevelyan regarded it as 'the highest honour in the state' and, when Sir George Otto became an OM in 1911, his son's delight knew no bounds. 'The appointment,' he told his father, 'stamps your life as a recognized success as well as a real one.' 'It was,' he went on, 'a very great honour, and the only very great honour.'[118]

Inevitably, as can be seen elsewhere in this book, G. M. Trevelyan gained increasing influence over appointments to the Order.

It was percipient of G. O. Trevelyan to give the second name Macaulay to his youngest son, George, who was to become, in the words of G. M. Trevelyan's biographer, David Cannadine

> the most famous, the most honoured, the most influential and the most widely read historian of his generation.[119]

Quite apart from ancestry, his interest in history had been aroused by the same master at Harrow who taught Churchill, a year senior to Trevelyan. From Harrow, G. M. went to Trinity College, Cambridge where, after gaining a First in History (and speaking once at the Union, in defence of Dreyfus), he won a fellowship, the dissertation for which became *England in the Age of Wycliffe*. He tired of Cambridge, however, and had enough money to pursue his historical studies in London. He did not return to Cambridge until after the publication of his popular *History of England* in 1926 had led to the offer of the Regius Chair in the following year. In the meantime, G. M. had expanded his philosophy of history in *Clio A Muse*. His biographer wrote:

> Trevelyan insisted that history was a science and an art, and judged by the standards of his time, his history was as 'scientific' as anyone else's. But his particular, self-appointed task was ... to write 'scholarly but readable history'.[120]

Owen Chadwick (in his inaugural lecture as Regius Professor) described how

> for Trevelyan, history was 'a magic mirror' in which you could see figures moving mistily, and the poetry lay in conjuring up the living though they were dead.[121]

For G. M., poetry was a life-long love. When young, he wrote *The Poetry and Philosophy of George Meredith*, whom he knew. When old, he was President of the English Association and lectured on *A Layman's Love of Letters*.

G. M.'s attachment to Italy was long and strong, in peace and war. It led him to walk and cycle through the country before producing the trilogy on Garibaldi and Italian unification that established his reputation. When the First World War came and his poor eyesight debarred him from active service, he raised and commanded a British Red Cross ambulance unit in Italy for three years. This earned him his first decorations: a CBE and the Italian Silver Medal for Valour.

G. M.'s love of Northumbria, where he led a spartan life indoors and outdoors, was reflected in the biography he wrote of his neighbour, Edward Grey (of Fallodon), whom he considered to be

> in his grand simplicity, the finest human being I ever came across.[122]

With one or two exceptions (such as Keynes and Leonard Woolf), G. M. never warmed to the Bloomsbury set – nor they to him. Others did not find him easy. Beatrice Webb's comment on him, at 19, was, ' [A] youth of great promise ... He is bringing himself up to be a great man ... ' Later, she thought him 'a consummate prig', a view with which he came to agree.

The British Academy enjoyed scarcely more favour with G. M. than the Bloomsbury set, despite having as its president his great friend, H. A. L. Fisher, whom he asked not to put his name forward to join 'the fatuous dons' who composed it. Eventually he did become a Fellow but

> sternly declined to be president, on the grounds that he had better things to do with his time and his talents.[123]

He was proud, however, to be the first historian elected FRS.

G. M. Trevelyan was president of the Historical Association and a founding father of the magazine *History Today*. The leading article in *The Times* on his death was headed 'History Made Readable'. His activities, however, went far beyond the study of history. He served on the important Royal Commission on Oxford and Cambridge (1922) and was a Trustee of the British Museum and the National Portrait Gallery. As a dedicated walker and hill-climber, he was president of the Youth Hostels Association. He was both active in, and generous to, the National Trust.

By the time of his OM, G. M. Trevelyan was 'a firm and fervent monarchist'. His father's anti-royalist pamphlet was 60 years earlier and as G. M. himself had written: 'Monarchy in the reign of George III was very different from monarchy in the reign of George V.'[124] As 'Historian Laureate', he wrote not only the lead article for *The Times* Silver Jubilee commemorative edition but also George V's speech to both Houses of Parliament in Westminster Hall. Later, he was instrumental in the choice of Harold Nicolson as the King's official biographer. He believed that, 'the new English democracy is in love with the Crown', 'radicalism has withered away', 'the modern Labour Party has no quarrel with the English monarchy' and 'the Crown is the one symbol that all classes and parties can without reservation accept'.[125]

It was to the Crown that G. M. Trevelyan owed the three most important appointments of his life: the Regius Chair of Modern History at Cambridge in 1927, the OM in 1930 and the Mastership of Trinity College, Cambridge in 1940. Staunch royalist though he was, G. M. could not be prevailed on to accept the title that customarily went with the Trinity post. His wife did not want to be Lady Trevelyan and, of another historian's knighthood, he himself remarked, 'What an awful thought'. As to a peerage, his biographer regards the evidence as inconclusive, despite a Trevelyan tradition that he did turn one down.

G. M. Trevelyan could also not be persuaded to let his name go forward to represent the Crown overseas. When sounded in 1945 by Vincent Massey, the Canadian High Commissioner, about the Governor-Generalship, he responded, 'I'm no John Buchan!'

Trevelyan's end was slow and, after his wife's death, lonely. Shortly before he died, he was visited by a young cousin, Humphrey, a diplomat who was to become not only a peer but one of the very few in that career to receive the Garter. He recorded that the old man said, ' "I am 86; it is time I was off." It is related that as he lay dying he was asked the date of the battle of Preston Pans, and that he gave the right answer and died. True or not, it is a story which he would have enjoyed.'[126]

There are many memorials to Trevelyan, which bear his name: scholarships at Oxford and Cambridge; a lectureship at Cambridge, the appeal for which was led by Churchill; the History Faculty Building at Cambridge; a college at Durham University, of which he was Chancellor. G. M.'s biographer, David Cannadine, summed up his subject as

> a great historian who was also a great man ... an authentic phenomenon. There never has been anyone in British public life quite like him since ... No historian since his time has been so well connected, or wielded such unchallenged cultural authority.[127]

Above all, in the context of this book, G. M. Trevelyan was an OM to his fingertips – the quintessential recipient.

G. M. Trevelyan had been made an OM at the young age of 54 and was to hold the Order for 32 years. The next historian was nearly 72 when he received it and was fated to have it for only three years. By 1936, after the publication of his *History of Europe*, H. A. L. Fisher had strong backers. Geoffrey Dawson, editor of *The Times*, was

> strongly in favour ... peculiarly timely just after the completion of the great work of his life.[128]

Matters hung fire, however, because the abdication of Edward VIII caused the New Year Honours of 1937, the first in the reign of George VI, to be deferred from 1 January to 1 February. When the delayed offer was made to Fisher, he replied that it was 'far beyond anything of which I have dreamed'.[129] The appointment was announced as being to the 'Warden of New College, Oxford. In recognition of his eminent position as an Historian and of his services to Literature'. Fisher's biographer wrote of the award:

> This honour has been so carefully guarded that its award is recognised as the clearest possible evidence of exceptional distinction in science, in arts or in letters, and the many-sided achievements of Fisher made him a specially worthy recipient of the Order.[130]

Herbert Albert Laurens Fisher was the son of a barrister, who was tutor and later private secretary to the founder of the Order of Merit – Edward VII, while Prince of Wales. As a godson of the Prince, Fisher was probably unique among OMs. His mother had modelled for G. F. Watts, the first painter-OM, who also painted Fisher himself as a young man.

Fisher went from Winchester to New College, taking first classes in classical moderations and Greats before election as a fellow in 1888, along with Gilbert Murray. From the classics, he turned to modern history, which he studied in Paris and Göttingen. Over the next 20 years, Fisher wrote books on French and German history, especially the civil side of the Napoleonic system, and including a short life of Napoleon in the *Home University Library* series, which he edited. He also wrote a biography and edited the papers of his brother-in-law, the distinguished legal historian, F. W. Maitland.

Just before the First World War, Fisher entered the field of administration, first as a member (from 1912–16) of the Royal Commission on the Public Service in India and (in early 1914) as Vice-Chancellor of the University of Sheffield. In the middle of the war, Fisher suddenly moved from the academic world into politics. At Lloyd George's invitation, he was President of the Board of Education from 1916–22. He was found a Commons seat and remained in the House until 1926. He was a reforming education minister and adjusted rapidly to parliamentary procedures, although the veteran John Burns (who had resigned from the Cabinet along with John Morley in 1914) advised him to change his tactics in committee:

> You don't know how to get a Bill through. You try to make your speeches interesting. Send them to sleep, Mr Fisher, send them to sleep.[131]

Fisher's monument was the 1918 Education ('Fisher') and Teachers' Superannuation Acts, essential forerunners of R. A. Butler's 1944 Act, at the end of the next great war. Fisher introduced state scholarships to universities, replaced 55 separate entrance examinations with the single School Certificate and vastly improved the pay and pensions of teachers.

Fisher added to his education portfolio, from 1920–22, membership of the British delegation to the League of Nations. He twice declined approaches to become Chief Secretary for Ireland, doubting his adequacy for the post. After leaving office, he declined a chair of history because he thought his reading was not up to date but, in 1925, he accepted the wardenship of New College; he had come a full Wykehamist circle.

Fisher began to write again: on *The Whig Historians* and *Our New Religion*, an urbane criticism of Christian Science and its founder. He wrote the official biography of James Bryce. His last and largest work was reckoned by most critics to be his best: the three-volume *History of Europe*, published in 1935, which did much to precipitate his OM shortly afterwards. Richard Church described it as, 'notable for its fine sense of proportion, its well-tempered criticism, and its quiet dignity of style . . . He believed in reason rather than revelation.'[132] For instance, he considered that the Christian religion would not have conquered Europe, unless it had accorded with the Greek philosophical thought and popular notions prevailing in the Eastern Mediterranean at the time.

Fisher died on 18 April 1940, a few days after being knocked down in the street. His ashes were placed in the cloisters of New College with a memorial tablet recording his services to learning, to education and to the state and his OM: 'in ordinem de republicae optime meritorum ascripto.' He may even have continued to help the war effort after his death. According to good New College sources, his underwear was on the body of Major Martin – *The Man Who Never Was* used as a decoy to deceive the Germans – when it was washed ashore on the coast of Spain.[133]

Fisher's reputation, which stood so very high in the post-Victorian atmosphere of the early years of the twentieth century, has not survived. Indeed, when a later historian, John Grigg, gave a lecture on him for the London Library (of which he was chairman from 1930 until his death), the title was 'The Curious Eclipse of H. A. L. Fisher'. Grigg thought it curious that he – and particularly his *History of Europe* – had been seriously underestimated by later generations.

When G. M. Trevelyan was consulted by the Prime Minister (Stanley Baldwin) in 1936, he included among the names he suggested for the Order of Merit **William Holdsworth**, 'for his great *History of English Law* – a work *aere perennius*' [longer lasting than bronze].[134]

Later, in 1941, Morshead was assembling OM candidates to pass to Hardinge. As Holdsworth was Vinerian Professor of English Law at Oxford, he wrote deliberately to Cambridge to secure an unbiased view – from Henry Hollond, Reader in English Law. He asked whether Holdsworth was

> of the heroic stature that the Order has hitherto been able to maintain. The true criterion is whether the Order would be strengthened by the inclusion of a given recruit rather than whether or not the candidate has merited it by his devotion to scholarship or for any other reason.[135]

Hollond's reply (strongly endorsed by G. M. Trevelyan, by then Master of Trinity College) was enthusiastic:

> I regard his works as of a monumental character . . . *History of English Law* . . . is a treasure-house of scholarship . . . some affinities with Frazer. Both men have not only enriched their subjects with distinguished original work, but have also assembled material on a scale which few men in any generation have the ability, industry and health to attempt . . . an injustice will have been done if Holdsworth dies without having been included in the Order.[136]

Morshead was delighted with this reply and passed it on to Hardinge as: 'a good "dark horse"; and dark horses are always particularly pleasing in this stable.'[137] Hardinge indulged in a little 'put-down': 'He has been on my list for a few years [recalling the 1936 consideration]. I think he is probably the safest choice of all.'[138] The OM was offered to Holdsworth and the award was announced in the New Year Honours of 1943.

Holdsworth had a legal background. Son of a suburban solicitor, he went from Dulwich College to New College, Oxford, where he obtained firsts in history and jurisprudence but only a second in the Bachelor of Civil Law examination. He was called to the Bar but pursued an academic career from 1897, when he was elected to a fellowship at St John's College, Oxford. Over the next 25 years, he taught not only at Oxford but also at University College, London, as well as playing an active role in the Inns of Court; he became a KC in 1920 and was knighted in 1929.

In 1922, Holdsworth became Vinerian Professor of English Law at Oxford, with a fellowship of All Souls. He sat on government committees and frequently lectured abroad, while continuing to work on his mammoth *History of English Law*, stretching from the earliest times to the great Judicature Act of 1873. Twelve volumes were published in his lifetime and the final two were edited for publication after his death by distinguished Oxford lawyers (from whom I learned a great deal): A. L. Goodhart, Master of University College, and H. G. Hanbury, Holdsworth's successor as Vinerian Professor.

A human gloss was put on the *History of English Law* by A. L. Rowse, when bemoaning the fate of the Junior Fellow of All Souls who had to sit at table until the Senior Fellows had finished their port:

> It was intolerable. Old Holdsworth was the worst offender, soaking up glass after glass of the college port; with the constitution of an ox, he would then go away and write solidly at his immense book until midnight. I used to think the *History of English Law* must be solidified All Souls port. But his sensibilities were such that he couldn't tell whether it was port or claret, or the two mixed.[139]

Despite its reputation as a heavyweight work, the *History of English Law* was described by Hanbury as capable of being 'read by students with pleasure as well as with great profit'.[140]

Holdsworth died on 2 January 1944. By that time, he was widely acknowledged as the greatest Oxford jurist since Sir William Blackstone in the eighteenth century.

George Peabody Gooch waited a long time for the OM. The press certainly lamented the lateness of the award. *The Times* commented that Gooch, 'now only two months short of ninety' belonged 'to a native tradition of liberty and intellectual integrity'. He was

> a link with names like Acton and Treitschke...as much at home in eighteenth-century France and Germany as in the complexities of contemporary diplomacy to which he has devoted so much of his attention. No historian has spent more time among documents or written more affectionately about men and women.[141]

The Guardian wrote of 'Merit honoured – not before time' and commented:

> Dr Gooch is a splendid representative – perhaps the last – of the school of liberal historians who learned much of their scholarly method and industry from the great nineteenth-century German historians but who were not deceived by the murkier versions of nineteenth-century German idealism...his most notable books...are a kind no longer fashionable. Yet historians with Dr Gooch's grasp of the 'matter of Europe' are surely beyond fashion.[142]

The Queen herself also commented on the delay, according to the detailed note left by Gooch of his audience to receive the insignia of the Order:

> I began by expressing my gratitude for the honour, and she replied: 'You had to wait a long time for it.' I told her of my previous visit in 1940 when her father had made me a Companion of Honour. I never looked into kinder eyes, I told her, and she replied: 'Yes, he was a very kind man.' Then I said: 'I used to tell my friends that George VI was the most beloved of our sovereigns since Alfred the Great. Queen Victoria was immensely respected but not beloved.'... 'What,' asked the Queen, 'has struck you most in your long life?' I rather expected she would ask such a question and I gave her three replies:...the transformation of our Empire into a Commonwealth,...the creation at home of the welfare state [the foundation of which he recalled had been laid during the Liberal Parliament of 1906 in which he had sat] and...the emergence of the coloured peoples in Asia and Africa...Our talk was entirely frank and without the slightest sentiment of strain on either side. We met as two human beings who had seen a good deal of life. I was deeply impressed by her friendliness, her perfect simplicity and absolute lack of formality.[143]

Gooch had always had a strong admiration for the monarchy. He paid a warm obituary tribute to George VI in the *Contemporary Review*, the monthly foreign affairs journal, which he edited from 1911–60.

Gooch was the son of a rich merchant who became a partner of George Peabody, the American banker and philanthropist after whom the boy was named. He moved from Eton at the age of 15, because he disliked it. After three years at King's College, Cambridge, he gained a first in modern history but failed to secure a fellowship.

A rich man, G. P. Gooch was able to become 'almost the last gentleman historian', as *The Guardian* described him on his death (in 1968). He came under the influence of Lord Acton and shifted his historical basis from the ecclesiastical to the political and diplomatic. His teaching was done at Toynbee Hall and other centres for working-class education and improvement. He was briefly in politics, as a Liberal MP from 1906–10 and was one of the last survivors of that reforming parliament. He became parliamentary private secretary to James Bryce, Chief Secretary for Ireland, and was disappointed not to be appointed to the junior ministerial post in the Foreign Office. After losing his seat and failing twice to secure re-election, he concentrated his public activity on the *Contemporary Review* and the Royal Institute of International Affairs (Chatham House). His main effort, however, was directed into his writing: contributions to the *Cambridge Modern History*, a bestselling *History of Our Time* in H. A. L. Fisher's Home University Library and *History and Historians in the Nineteenth Century*.

Gooch's long love affair with Germany, its history and its scholarship, began with three months of study in Berlin. Later, he married a German Catholic. Much of his writing concerned Germany: *Germany and the French Revolution*, the editorship (with Harold Temperley) of the 13 volumes of *British Documents on the Origins of the War* (published between 1926–38) and *Before the War: Studies in Diplomacy*. From an original view that Grey's pre-war policy had tended to make war more probable, while ensuring that Britain would not be isolated in the event of a conflict, Gooch moved to believing that Grey had had fewer options than had been imagined and that he had tried to do more good than it would have been prudent for him to make public at the time.

For a man with Gooch's sympathies and connections, the two wars with Germany were especially tragic. Between them, he saw the Weimar republic as the truest expression of the liberal German spirit but gave warning of the Nazi menace and stood up for the victims of its terror.

After the Second World War, came Gooch's *Studies in German History* and *Frederick the Great*. Appropriately, in 1954, he was the first British recipient since 1912 of the order Frederick had originally founded in 1740: Pour le mérite, the model for the OM that he was to receive a decade later. In 1958, his old friend, Professor Theodor Heuss, paid the first state visit to Britain by a German head of state since 1907 and there was an emotional meeting between the two men.

In that same year, 1958, Gooch published his memoirs, *Under Six Reigns*, which demonstrated a wide range of contacts, especially during his active political years. On Gooch's ninetieth birthday in 1963, President Kennedy, only a month before his assassination, paid tribute:

> For more than half a century, as historian and as editor, Dr Gooch has maintained the noble traditions and high standards of liberal scholarship. He has seen history both as a reconstruction of the past and as an illumination of the present.[144]

On Gooch's death, the tributes were fulsome to a man who had

> carried forward into our own day the scholarly conscience, the immense learning and the enlightened liberalism of his master, Acton...He was perhaps as well versed as any Englishman in the cultural tradition and political development of modern Germany. In an age that was haunted by the still unresolved menace of the German problem, Gooch proved a conspicuously discerning and impartial guide and witness.[145]

An aspect of his character that attracted comment was that

> he dreaded the responsibility which participation in practical affairs involved...Even in history, Gooch disliked responsibility and preferred to direct the reader to the verdicts of others.[146]

Within a year of Gooch's death in 1968, another historian was appointed to the Order of Merit – on 14 July 1969 – to her own and others' surprise. Much was made of the fact that C. V. (Veronica) Wedgwood was only the third woman, after Florence Nightingale and Dorothy Hodgkin, to be included in the Order. It was only a year since she had been made a DBE, although it was to be another six years before she was elected FBA.

Wedgwood's own surprise stemmed as much as anything from her own innate modesty:

> when I got the letter I was completely bowled over. Fortunately there was a chair behind me. It is a great honour but I don't think I deserve it.[147]

Others expressed surprise, especially her unhonoured former tutor, A. L. Rowse:

> He regarded the OM, particularly that bestowed on Veronica Wedgwood, as his by right... 'My OM!' as he grew, with resentful jealousy, accustomed to exclaim. He sent her a telegram: 'Warmest congratulations, but isn't it *un peu exaggéré?*' She replied by postcard: 'It is no doubt excessive but it's certainly nice'.[148]

In correspondence with someone he hardly knew, Rowse could be more extreme:

> Certainly it was absurd that my pupil Veronica Wedgwood should have had an OM. She herself thought it 'excessive'. Trevelyan wrote to me, 'You and I know that Veronica is an historian of the second rank.' Toynbee was infuriated by it.[149]

He had similar trenchant views about other OM historians, such as Gooch and Beaglehole:

> It shows that they have *no* idea of who is who or what is what in the field of history and literature.[150]

Wedgwood came from the pottery family – Josiah was her great-great-great grandfather. Her father, after a career with the London and North Eastern Railway, was made a baronet for having chaired the Railway Executive Committee in the early years of the Second World War

Wedgwood was educated privately before going to Oxford, where she gained a First in History. Before the age of 30, she had written two notable books: a biography of *Strafford* and an account of the *Thirty Years War*. They were followed before long by a short biography of *Oliver Cromwell* and a longer one of *William the Silent*, for which she was honoured by the Netherlands.

In the 1950s, she moved on to her major work: a trilogy on *The Great Rebellion*. Only two parts were completed: *The King's Peace* (1637–41) and *The King's War* (1642–47); although she did write a short volume on *The Trial of Charles I*. She spent a good deal of time at this period at the Institute of Advanced Studies at Princeton, the American 'All Souls'.

Among Wedgwood's other works were translations, the most notable of which (in 1946) was Elias Canetti's *Auto da Fë*. It was largely for this work that the Bulgarian/Austrian/Jewish novelist (with British citizenship) received the Nobel Prize for Literature in 1981.

In his obituary of her in *The Independent* in March 1997, A. L. Rowse was rather more charitable than in his private letters:

> At a time when women were coming to the fore in so many walks of life, Veronica Wedgwood may be regarded as something of a front-runner. As such she was phenomenally rewarded... eventually (though early – she was still in her fifties) the Order of Merit... her awards were well earned, for public work as much as for her writing, which was as prolific as it was of high quality.[151]

Wedgwood had expressed her own attitude to history in a broadcast she made in 1949:

> Reading the letters and diaries of people long dead, looking over the shoulders of the dead, for that is what it is – does not make me think of mortality. It makes me think rather of immortality, of the astonishing persistence and compassion of the human spirit in the face of obstacles.[152]

The next historian to receive the Order was, and remains, relatively unknown in Britain. He was **John Cawte Beaglehole**, the accepted world authority on Captain James Cook, 'the prince of navigators'. The Queen conferred the honour on him at Government House in Wellington on 20 March 1970, during the tour she made of Australasia that year to commemorate the bicentenary of Cook's landing in Australia.

According to the New Zealand press, Beaglehole thought that the OM was 'too high an honour' and the Governor-General, Sir Arthur Porritt, had to work hard to persuade him to accept. There had been some adverse comment, particularly from fellow academics, about his omission from the New Year Honours at the beginning of the Cook bicentenary year. He had been made a CMG in 1958 and it was probably a knighthood that they thought he deserved.

The press used the old mantra about the Order 'being designed as a special distinction for eminent men and women without conferring a knighthood' and emphasised that only one New Zealander – Rutherford – had previously received it. Its international standing was recognised:

> The order has established itself as the most exclusive of the orders of chivalry because almost all its members have won admission by exceptional achievement that has brought them international renown.[153]

Beaglehole had discovered his vocation, as a schoolboy at the end of the First World War, through H. G. Wells:

> Bliss was in that dawn to be alive, to be young, to be reading the *Outline of History* in weekly parts.[154]

Beaglehole graduated in, and then taught, history at the Victoria University of Wellington before coming to London on a scholarship in 1926. He studied under the left-wing Harold Laski. His first published research was on early colonial governors of New Zealand. He lost his post as a lecturer at Auckland University during the depression. He described the next stage of his career as 'unemployed and odd jobs, 1933–35'. From 1936, he had various teaching and research posts at Victoria University, culminating in the chair of Commonwealth History from 1963–66.

It was Beaglehole's praised book, *The Exploration of the Pacific*, in 1934 that set him on the exploration of Cook that was to be his lifework. First, however, he was to write *New Zealand*, *The Discovery of New Zealand* (his contribution to the centennial celebrations of 1940) and *New Zealand and the Statute of Westminster*.

Only after the Second World War was he able to visit Britain again to discover how thoroughly 'messed up' Cook's journals had become. The venerable Hakluyt Society, with generous financial assistance from the New Zealand government, commissioned him to edit those journals. Four massive volumes appeared between 1955 and 1967, with a large supplementary volume on the journal of Joseph Banks, the naturalist accompanying Cook. The undertaking

> earned for him a world-wide reputation as the foremost Cook and Banks scholar. Beaglehole's volumes have been hailed as the greatest works of scholarship to emerge from the Antipodes.[155]

Beaglehole enjoyed the OM for only 18 months and wore the insignia only once. There was however just enough time for him to complete his biography of Cook, which he observed had ironically been delayed by the author's heavy involvement in the bicentenary celebrations. The book was a fitting end to his career:

> 'The study of Cook is the illumination of all discovery,' he once said, and the studies of Dr Beaglehole have illuminated the work of Cook in a way no one else has done.[156]

Beaglehole's reputation has not diminished with the years. His work has remained the cornerstone of any research on Cook and the exploration of the Pacific.

Kenneth Clark was an administrator as well as a historian of art. His rise in both fields was meteoric: Keeper of Fine Art at the Ashmolean Museum in Oxford at the age of 28, Director of the National Gallery and Surveyor of the King's Pictures at 31 and a KCB at 35. He himself described those years as, 'the Great Clark Boom':

> mysterious [but] unquestionable... borne along on the crest of a social wave... asked everywhere, and almost everyone of note came for lunch or dinner.[157]

Among those he met, Ramsay MacDonald made a particular impression:

> He was kind to me. 'Never let the Tories get ye, Kenneth,' he would say, as Lady Londonderry offered him a Tranquillising pill, and I never have.[158]

An obituary tribute aptly summarised Clark's place in the British art world in the middle of the twentieth century:

> the most gifted and influential art historian of the thirties, the most important public figure in the arts during the forties and the fifties and one of the most informative and entertaining television personalities in the sixties.[159]

It was, however, only in 1976, at the age of 76, that he received the Order of Merit. His honours had been steadily mounting. After that early knighthood, he had been made a CH in 1959 and a life peer ten years later.

Clark was born in a house on the side of Grosvenor Square now occupied by the American Embassy. His family were rich from Paisley thread manufacture and it was not so much earlier that, as his politician son Alan would have put it, they had to buy their own antiques. He was an only child and his father devoted himself to shooting, yachting, gambling and drinking, although his remarkably good mind (and perhaps some time he spent in New Zealand) made Clark later see in him some similarity to Ernest Rutherford. The loneliness of Clark's childhood is illustrated by the fact that his only friend in Monte Carlo (where his father frequently broke the bank) was the 80-year-old Empress Eugenie, widow of Napoleon III.

From Winchester, Clark went to Oxford, where an increasing interest in art contributed to his securing a Second, rather than the expected First, in Modern History. He immediately went to Florence to assist the rich art critic and historian, Bernard Berenson, in preparing a new edition of his *Florentine Drawings*. Early appreciation of the opportunity – 'the most golden egg that the world of art had to offer' – dimmed, however, and Clark's final verdict was that Berenson

> was perched on the pinnacle of a mountain of corruption. The air was purer up there.[160]

Clark produced his first book, *The Gothic Revival*, in 1928, at the age of 25. He was asked to catalogue the great collection of Leonardo da Vinci in the Royal Library by Owen Morshead, the librarian who gave much advice on the appointments to the Order of Merit. Clark considered the catalogue to be his 'only claim to be considered a scholar'.[161]

The offer of the directorship of the National Gallery came to Clark as he neared his thirty-first birthday:

> I was flattered. But on reflecting I saw that this apparent stroke of luck had come to me too early. I had no administrative experience.[162]

While he acquired many masterpieces for the Gallery, he alienated its senior staff and there were damaging public controversies.

Later in 1934 another offer came. Morshead had recommended him to be Surveyor of the King's Pictures but, believing he had enough on his hands with the National Gallery to take on also an enormous and neglected royal collection, he refused. George V, who had a high regard for Morshead's judgement, would not be baulked and decided to visit the National Gallery, the first reigning monarch to do so. He tackled Clark:

HM: Why won't you come and work for me?
Clark: Because I wouldn't have time to do the job properly.
HM: What is there to do?
Clark: Well, sir, the pictures need looking after.
HM: There's nothing wrong with them.
Clark: And people write letters asking for information about them.
HM: Don't answer 'em. – I want you to take the job.[163]

Clark accepted. There was an amusing postscript to his royal service:

Next to his people, King George V loved postage stamps. [He sent for me] 'I want you to make me a promise. Never allow them to make all those fancy issues of stamps like some ridiculous place like San Marino!'

Clark honoured his promise 30 years later by resigning from the chairmanship of the Postage Stamp Committee when the Postmaster General, Tony Benn, announced his intention to make frequent issues of illustrative stamps.[164]

The Second World War brought great variety into Clark's life. Having put most of the pictures from the National Gallery and the Royal Collection into safe storage in the caves of North Wales, he worked for a couple of years at the Ministry of Information, initially as Director of the Film Division:

an inexplicable choice, commonly attributed to the fact that in those days films were spoken of as 'pictures' and I was believed to be an authority on pictures.[165]

He believed his most lasting achievement at the Ministry was to tell John Betjeman that in the canteen was 'a most ravishing girl – she's called Miss Joan Hunter Dunn'.[166]

At the Gallery, Clark facilitated the concerts of Myra Hess that have become part of the folklore of the war. Beyond, he was chairman of the committee that commissioned artists to record the war; they included, as already noted, the future OMs, Henry Moore and Graham Sutherland, as well as others such as John Piper and Stanley Spencer.

Clark featured on the popular radio programme Brains Trust and was sent to neutral Sweden (just after T. S. Eliot) 'as a sort of advertisement for English culture' – and as a courier in connection with the securing of vitally-needed ball bearings. He was even sent by Churchill to discuss the Irish Atlantic ports with Eamon de Valera. He was involved with the establishment of the Council for the Encouragement of Music and the Arts, of which, as the Arts Council, he was later chairman.

As the war ended, Clark turned to lecturing and writing. He gave up his royal post in 1944 and was succeeded by Anthony Blunt. In 1945, he also resigned from the National Gallery: 'I was not really cut out for an administrative post.'[167] The next year, he became Slade Professor of Fine Art at Oxford, a post he held until 1950 and again from 1961–62. He produced *Landscape into Art*, *Piero della Francesca* and *The Nude* (probably the most popular and most often quoted of his books), mostly based on lectures given in the post-war period.

Clark did not return to administration until his chairmanship of the Arts Council (1953–60) and of the new Independent Television Authority (1954–57). He accepted the second post with some hesitation because

> like all pseudo-intellectuals I had at first been hostile to the idea of television. It seemed to threaten the humanising predominance of books, which was the background of our lives.

Nevertheless, he thought the Authority

> could intervene and prevent the vulgarity of commercialism from having things all its own way.[168]

After leaving the ITA, he presented nearly 50 art programmes for ATV, which 'were probably more widely seen by the British people than 'Civilisation' and had more influence in England'.[169] It was, however, the 13-programme BBC series on *Civilisation* in 1969 which brought him fame and 'the happiest years of my life'. He claimed to have had nothing in mind at all except to give the viewer a pleasant 50 minutes. He ranged around sites in Europe and America and each programme unashamedly had a 'hero', such as Charlemagne, Erasmus, Voltaire and Brunel. Clark was amazed and puzzled by the success of the series. He attributed it to

> the average man ... [acknowledging] there is no such man ... being pleased when someone spoke to him in a friendly, natural manner about things that he had always assumed were out of his reach.

He knew that the programmes had particularly annoyed

> intellectuals of the left, who believed they had a prescriptive right to speak to the working classes ... [and] academics [who] were furious at the simplification of their labours ...[170]

Clark's peerage in 1969 enabled the media to dub him 'Lord Civilisation' and the series played its part in paving his way to the Order of Merit. Clark's wealth, inherited and made, enabled him to become a notable collector. After his death in 1983, his estate was valued at over £ 5 million. Beyond that, at auction, there were record prices for a number of artists. After family legal disputes, the prize sale was Turner's *Seascape: Folkestone*, which went to the Thomson newspaper family in Canada for a record £7.3 million. His art archive went to the Tate Gallery in lieu of tax. An appeal resulted in a memorial lecture room at the Courtauld Institute in Somerset House.

Appointed to the Order of Merit with Kenneth Clark in 1976 was another historian from Trinity College, Oxford: **Ronald Syme**, who had already been described as

> perhaps the most esteemed scholar to emerge from New Zealand... Widely regarded as the world's leading authority on ancient Roman history.[171]

Syme lived to be, after Rutherford and Beaglehole, the third New Zealander to become an OM. The award was variously described in his obituaries as being the 'crowning honour' and a 'fitting crown' to his career and a 'splendid recognition of his unique scholarly standing', since it was 'Britain's most coveted civil distinction'.

Syme's solicitor father filled their house, in a small town on the North Island, with books and had academic inclinations himself. The young Ronald found history at school 'frightfully dull' and New Zealand itself 'very, very boring' until around 1960.[172] A first-class Latin teacher encouraged him and he won a university scholarship when he was too young to take it up. When old enough, however, he topped the scholarship list for the whole country. At Victoria University in Wellington, he added Greek to Latin before moving to Auckland University where he was a lecturer and acting professor. In 1925, Syme came to Oriel College, Oxford, on a scholarship and

> created one of the greatest academic sensations Oriel has known during this century, when one morning...it was announced that he (a commoner of the college at that) had won, not merely one of the University's great classical prizes, but all four.[173]

After taking a First in Greats and starting on his research work, Syme was elected in 1929 as a Fellow of Trinity College, Oxford, where he remained for 20 years.

Ten years later, on the outbreak of war in 1939, Syme produced his first and probably greatest book, *The Roman Revolution*, which revolutionised the view of ancient Rome by demonstrating that apparently noble men were actuated by a desire for power and money. He was anxious to see it published before the impending conflict. The book was notable for using the relatively new group-biographical approach of prosopography, fashioned in Germany, which analysed the social and political factions behind the fall of the Republic and the inauguration of the Augustan Principate. It was judged to be the most remarkable work in its field since the German nineteenth-century giant, Theodor Mommsen. Syme himself explained

> [oligarchy] really is the subject of *The Roman Revolution* – the inevitability of oligarchy ... a minority of people who are running things, or perhaps a hierarchy of groups. And so the origin, composition and continuity of these groups is a very, very exciting subject.[174]

Twenty-one years later *The Roman Revolution* was the first paperback issued by the Oxford University Press.

Like many other academics, Syme's specialised talents were soon utilised in the war. A knowledge of Serbo-Croat, acquired during his work on the Danube as a frontier of the Roman Empire, led to his appointment as Press Attaché at the British Legation in Belgrade. After the fall of Yugoslavia, he moved to the Embassy in Istanbul, before becoming Professor of Classical Philology at the university there.

It was not long after returning to Oxford at the end of the war that Syme became Camden Professor of Ancient History, a chair he held from 1949–70. It entailed a move to Brasenose College.

In 1958, Syme produced his second major work and a lesser one: *Tacitus* was about the man it was said he 'feels he knows and belongs to'; *Colonial Elites* was a slim volume of lectures, comparing the Romans in Spain with the Spanish in South America and the English in North America and the West Indies. Syme was knighted in 1959.

Fluent in German, French and Italian, Syme pursued his love of travel, especially in his capacity as Secretary-General of the International Philosophical and Humanities section of UNESCO. As he approached retirement, he became concerned with the dating and authorship of an early biographical compilation, the *Historia Augusta*, and he wrote prolifically about it over 15 years or so.

In retirement, Wolfson College, Oxford, provided Syme for 20 years with a fellowship and a penthouse home, from which his output was undiminished and included five volumes of *Roman Papers*, *History in Ovid* and, only two years before his death at the age of 86, his swansong, *The Augustan Aristocracy*. He published nearly 50 articles after the age of 80.

A bachelor, Syme was a reserved and self-contained (almost secretive) man: 'an unsuitable subject for prosopographical study by future historians.'[175] Yet he had many friends, not least among the younger academics in Oxford (and their families): his 'scholarly progeny', whom he did not treat as 'disciples'.

Syme's death came on 4 September 1989, four days before a planned party to celebrate the fiftieth anniversary of *The Roman Revolution*. *The Oxford Magazine*, the house journal of his academic world, wrote that

> Even the phenomenal output of Ronald Syme, surely unequalled in any field of the humanities in this century was rooted...in a life of constant travel, international activities (UNESCO), and adventures which sometimes read like a novel of Balkan espionage, to say nothing of the (presumably) less dramatic world of Trinity.[176]

The Guardian obituary concluded:

> As a writer of history, it is not too much to say that Syme belongs with Gibbon and Macaulay. The last sentence of his *Tacitus* may serve as his own epitaph: 'Men and dynasties pass but style abides.'[177]

Professor **Owen Chadwick**, a living historian in the Order of Merit, scored a 'double first' on his appointment in 1983. He was the first Member to be an ordained clergyman and the first who, while a British citizen holding a British knighthood, did not use the title 'Sir'. His knighthood had come only a year before the OM.

Press reports concentrated on the prestigious appointments Chadwick had recently held: Master of Selwyn College, Cambridge (1956–83), Regius Professor of Modern History at that university (1968–83) and, still, President of the British Academy (since 1981). There was, however, some mention of the real reason for his inclusion in the Order – his eminence as an ecclesiastical historian.

Son of a barrister, Owen Chadwick went from Tonbridge School to St John's College, Cambridge. He played rugby against Oxford, took holy orders and, in 1947, became a Fellow of Trinity Hall, Cambridge, at the age of 31. From Trinity Hall, he moved on to the posts already mentioned, as Master of Selwyn and as a Regius Professor; before appointment to that chair, he was Dixie Professor of Ecclesiastical History from 1958–68. Beyond these duties, he chaired the Archbishops' Commission on Church and State (1966–70), which recommended important changes in the system of episcopal appointments and was Vice-Chancellor of the University (1969–71). Among many activities after retiring from his Cambridge duties was the Chancellorship of the neighbouring University of East Anglia (1985–94).

At a lecture on 'Civilization and Religion', which he gave in 1985, he contrasted the approaches to the Second World War of two OMs: Halifax, for whom the centre of the whole struggle was the anti-Christian character of Nazism, and Priestley, for whom it was not but who nevertheless thought that the fundamental values of the post-war society must be spiritual and therefore religious. He quoted a third OM, Churchill, as saying that upon the Battle of Britain 'depends the survival of Christian civilization.'[178]

Professor Chadwick's KBE in the New Year Honours of 1982 – the knighthood without the 'Sir' – confused many people. He himself was not confused but he remained puzzled by the official practice, at least in Britain, of denying the accolade and therefore the title 'Sir' to ordained clerics of the two established churches – of England and of Scotland. This is a complicated subject, on which I have already written an article.[179] Owen Chadwick, after much research and correspondence with the official authorities, wrote a much fuller (unpublished) paper on the matter, of which he sent me a copy. As a good subject of the Queen, and armed anyway with the incomparably higher honour of the OM, he conforms to the 'practice', as it has been propounded to him, although whether it amounts to a 'rule' is questionable.

Both during and since his active teaching time at Cambridge, historical works have flowed from Owen Chadwick. They have ranged widely over the whole field of church history. He was general editor of the *Penguin History of the Church* and wrote two of the seven volumes himself, *The Reformation* and *The Christian Church in the Cold War*.

The Papacy has naturally figured greatly in much of his work. More specifically, however, he has written *The Popes and the European Revolution* and *A History of the Popes, 1830–1914*. A more limited book about the Papacy – *Britain and the Vatican in the Second World War* – is an intriguing glimpse of an unusual piece of diplomatic history. In 1990, he produced the authorised biography of Michael Ramsey, the academic who did reluctantly accept preferment as, successively, Bishop of Durham, Archbishop of York and the one-hundredth Archbishop of Canterbury and who died wearing the episcopal ring given to him by Pope Paul VI.

It is said that Owen Chadwick relishes the challenge of a towering theme. He certainly had that in *A History of Christianity*, a late work in which he concludes

> that Christianity has never been a static but a kaleidoscopic and evolving faith. It has slowly shed some of its past beliefs . . . it has to a varying degree come to terms with the findings of modern science, and of literary and historical criticism . . . [He] foresees the greater activity of women as deacons, priests and bishops, and the concentration of Christians into house churches and small groups . . . [and] at the end, he returns to the Bible as the fount of belief and to its teaching of 'absolute rules of right and wrong', Christian life illuminated by a 'sense of eternity, the conviction of ultimate order and purpose in the universe'.[180]

Another historian to be appointed to the Order of Merit was, like Kenneth Clark, a specialist in art: **Ernst Gombrich**, in 1988. His reaction was one of bewilderment. On 'Desert Island Discs' a few years later, he said:

> I am still staggered that the Queen decided to award me the Order of
> Merit. But I would be deceiving myself if I thought that made me an
> Englishman.

He said he remained a Central European – 'hear my accent'; he thought he
was British but not English.[181] He was an outstanding member of the group
of Central European exiles from the tyranny of Nazism in the 1930s:

> one of those greatly gifted refugee immigrants to this country whose
> impact on cultural, scientific and social life has been out of all proportion
> to their numbers.[182]

Gombrich had been born into a middle-class Viennese Jewish family,
which had converted to Protestantism. His father was a lawyer and his
mother a pianist and pupil of Bruckner; the family had a typically high
regard for 'Bildung' – culture in a general sense. Despite this background,
the conditions in Vienna after the First World War meant that the young
and undernourished Ernst was sent by Save the Children to Sweden. On his
return to Vienna, he went to the same school and university as the refugee
molecular biologist, Max Perutz, who was appointed to the Order on the
same day.

In 1933, the Warburg Library (60,000 books packed in 600 cases) was
transplanted from Hamburg to London. Three years later, the 27-year-old
Gombrich was invited to join the newly-founded Warburg Institute as a
research assistant, to edit the papers of its founder, Aby Warburg, whose
biography he was eventually to write. He had just written, in six weeks, a
child's history of the world, which proved very successful. When the Warburg lost its premises in 1938, Gombrich taught at the Courtauld Institute
for a year.

Following the outbreak of war in September 1939, Gombrich was
recruited by the BBC Monitoring Service, which he described as a 'very
cosmopolitan society'. It was appropriately a movement from a Bruckner
symphony, written to mark the death of Wagner, which alerted Gombrich
to an important announcement about to be made by German radio at the end
of April 1945. He jotted various possibilities on bits of paper and pointed
to the correct one, 'Hitler is dead', when the announcement was made. The
news was telephoned to Churchill in London.

After the war, Gombrich returned to the Warburg Institute, which had
become part of London University. He rose steadily from Senior Research
Fellow to Director, and Professor of the History of the Classical Tradition;
posts he held from 1959–76. His progression at the Warburg and his growing
reputation were marked by election as FBA in 1960, a CBE in 1966 and

a knighthood in 1972. Other distinctions and prizes poured on him from British and foreign institutions. He received both the German Order Pour le mérite (in 1977) and its Austrian equivalent, Ehrenzeichen für Wissenschaft und Kunst (in 1984).

Shortly after the publication of *The Story of Art* in 1950, Gombrich was elected to succeed Kenneth Clark as Slade Professor of Fine Art at Oxford, an experience he enjoyed less than holding the parallel chair at Cambridge a decade later. In his *Topic of Our Time* (1991), he thought that he

> never became a proper art historian . . . My main interest has always been in more general types of explanation, which meant a certain kinship with science.[183]

The Story of Art was Gombrich's first classic work and so great did its reputation become that, to his irritation, it was sometimes thought to have been his only book. It became the best-selling art book of all time: 16 editions; two or six million copies sold; translated into 23 or 30 languages (the figures depend on which article or obituary one reads). It has been widely used in schools and universities as a clear and ordered introduction to the complex subject of Western art. He himself later summed up its value:

> It crystallises the attitude of a vanished epoch for which art was not a subject of specialised knowledge, let alone of sensational auction prices, but still part of the mental furniture of civilised men and women.[184]

After *The Story of Art* came *Art and Illusion* (1960), an ambitious, and some think his greatest work, and *Meditations on a Hobby Horse* (1963). They

> confirmed the arrival in the world of art history of an intelligence of the very first rank . . . [He did not aim] to make qualitative judgments – he believed those emerged as the historical consensus of the well-informed – but to discover new facts and to squeeze from them new knowledge, 'We must feed on fact, and on observation,' he said.[185]

In *Tributes* (1984), Gombrich wrote about individual cultural historians so as to make more people aware of 'what is actually going on in the minds' of those historians and to emphasise the value, and fragility, of tradition.[186] He believed that no work of art could exist outside a tradition and that each artist should be seen building on or modifying the efforts of his predecessors. In discussing *A Lifelong Interest* (1993), he said:

> We can't predict. The best artist who ever lived may be in a garret in Wolverhampton at this very minute.[187]

Gombrich's transmission of knowledge and appreciation to a wide audience was not always popular. At a crowded Royal Academy exhibition, an offended member of the elite told him, 'This is all your fault.' He collected little art and was not very interested in connoisseurship, the attribution of particular works to particular artists.

Gombrich worked right up to his death on 3 November 2001, at the age of 92. Typical of the tributes was one in *The Independent*:

> the most famous art historian in the world...A brilliant lecturer, for whom the greatest sin was to exceed the time-limit...always claimed a particular debt, in his handling of historical evidence, to his great friend Karl Popper...Gombrich will be remembered above all for extending the frontiers of his subject and for his opposition to the more speculative and subjective flights of his colleagues.[188]

14

THE MEN OF AFFAIRS

Political figures (and sometimes also scholars)

1. 1915 Richard (Viscount) HALDANE
2. 1916 Arthur (Earl of) BALFOUR
3. 1919 David (Earl) LLOYD GEORGE
4. 1944 Sidney (WEBB, Lord) PASSFIELD
5. 1946 Sir Winston CHURCHILL
6. 1946 Edward (Earl of) HALIFAX
7. 1947 Jan SMUTS
8. 1947 J. G. WINANT (Honorary)
9. 1947 William MACKENZIE KING
10. 1951 Clement (Earl) ATTLEE
11. 1958 Herbert (Viscount) SAMUEL
12. 1971 Lester PEARSON
13. 1976 Harold (MACMILLAN, Earl of) STOCKTON
14. 1990 Margaret (Baroness) THATCHER
15. 1993 Roy (Lord) JENKINS
16. 1995 Nelson MANDELA (Honorary)

Administrators

17. 1906 Evelyn (Earl of) CROMER
18. 1951 Sir Alexander CADOGAN
19. 1956 Malcolm (Lord) HAILEY
20. 1957 John (ANDERSON, Viscount) WAVERLEY
21. 1963 Sir Owen DIXON

22. 1968 The Prince Philip, Duke of EDINBURGH
23. 1969 Malcolm MACDONALD
24. 1977 Oliver (Lord) FRANKS
25. 1997 Alfred (Lord) DENNING
26. 2002 The Prince Charles, Prince of WALES
27. 2002 Jacob, (Fourth Lord) ROTHSCHILD

Preliminary

The conferment of the Order of Merit on political figures has been the most difficult category to justify within the statutes, until they were amended to be all embracing in 1987. Doubts may well have been expressed as to whether a particular Member *deserved* the honour but there were no doubts that he or she was *qualified* under the statutes. Scientists, scholars, writers and artists all clearly came within their ambit. Politicians did not.

Although the Order was not conceived as an honour for political service, five of the first 20 civil recipients were MPs, of whom four were privy counsellors and three former cabinet ministers. They were, however, something more: four (Morley, Lecky, Bryce and G. O. Trevelyan) were historians and the fifth (Jebb) was a classical scholar.

Balfour was the first political figure to express concern about such appointments when reluctantly accepting the Order himself in 1916. He urged on the King's Private Secretary:

> ...the more general considerations which I laid before you at our interview. I am certain that there is a real danger lest the Order should be regarded as another reward open to Party Statesmen who combine literary or other interests with their political work. [He had looked through the list of civil Members]...I think you will admit it to be a most extraordinary coincidence that out of 13 gentlemen chosen *purely* for their eminence in literature, science, or art, no less than five should be Privy Councillors and ex Cabinet Ministers!...I am confident that the *general* argument which I developed this morning...is one which ought most carefully to be kept in mind, if the Order of Merit is to maintain all the consideration which is its due.[1]

In his reply, Stamfordham assured Balfour that:

> His Majesty fully appreciates the note of warning...lest the Order of Merit come to be regarded as a possible reward for political services; at the same time His Majesty does not consider that a political career should be a disqualification for admission to the Order.[2]

In 1919, there was the plain political appointment of Lloyd George to the Order, since it was the only honour he would accept in recognition of his services as wartime Prime Minister. I shall discuss this later in the chapter.

In 1921, when (as explained in Chapter 5) Lloyd George 'vetoed' the admission to the Order of Gilbert Murray, the question of 'political' appointments again came under review. In seeking the advice of the Secretary of the Order about Edward VII's original intentions, George V's Keeper of the Privy Purse conveyed his master's views, which had shifted somewhat since 1916:

> The King himself is very strongly opposed to this cherished Order being bestowed on politicians at all, as His Majesty thinks it will become ridiculous if Cabinet Ministers all wear it.[3]

In reply, the Secretary of the Order confirmed that the existing statute

> closes the door to Politicians unless the decoration is given for one of the qualifications enumerated [i.e. science, literature, art]. I agree that it would be a thousand pities to make any alteration and doing so must tend to lower the status of the Order, which is at present 'a thing by itself'. I feel sure King Edward never intended to make any alteration and never mentioned it.[4]

A relieved Keeper wrote:

> Lloyd George was to be treated as an exceptional case but if all politicians in future are to be given the OM there would be no particular honour in having given it to the Prime Minister. His Majesty says he means to firmly resist any politicians being added in future but, when it comes to who should get the Order, it is a matter of great difficulty. I understand that the Prime Minister thinks that however eminent a man may be, he must be a supporter of the Government before he is considered for this Order. The King, on the other hand, thinks that politicians should play no part in it at all and that men should be given the Order merely on account of eminence in literature, art or science.[5]

In 1930, the King's Private Secretary felt obliged to put down a private marker with the editor of *The Times* about the *in*eligibility of political figures for the Order. In commending the appointment of Samuel Alexander, G. M. Trevelyan and M. R. James, an article had said, 'the honour may befall any man deemed by the Sovereign to be worthy, in <u>statesmanship</u>,

the Services, science, art and letters'. Stamfordham had underlined the word
'statesmanship' and gone on to show, by quoting the relevant statute, that
this was incorrect. He continued:

> I think you will agree that, if Statesmen were to be admitted into the
> category, we should be up against all sort of political difficulties whereas,
> with the exception of Lloyd George, the honour has never been conferred
> upon any statesman, as such. I agree in thinking that the Statutes might
> have been worded so as to admit into the Order those who have rendered
> eminent services to the State, such as the [unidentified] man whose name
> you mentioned the other day: but that would include Lloyd George or
> any other distinguished Minister.[6]

Dawson was quick to apologise:

> I am so sorry about that slip…entirely agree that what are called
> 'Statesmen' are better on the whole excluded![7]

So, by 1930, the combined views of monarch, private secretary and influential editor seem firmly set against 'political' appointments to the Order and
no Prime Minister after Lloyd George was inclined to challenge the embargo.

Of the 14 political figures who have received the Order of Merit, nine
were Prime Ministers: six of the United Kingdom (Balfour, Lloyd George,
Churchill, Attlee, Macmillan and Margaret Thatcher), two of Canada
(Mackenzie King and Pearson) and one of South Africa (Smuts). The Prime
Ministers of Australia and New Zealand had to be content with the CH, to
the extent that so many of them were recipients, it became virtually a 'badge
of office'.

Of the five politicians who were not Prime Ministers, two (Halifax and
Jenkins) were potential holders of that office, while the other three were
honoured not only for holding a distinguished place in political life but also
for additional achievement: Haldane and Samuel in philosophy and Passfield
in social history and reform. (Of course, Jenkins was a notable biographer
beyond his political career.)

Of the six British Prime Ministers, four received it while in the office or
shortly after relinquishing it, especially because, at the time of conferment,
no other honour was appropriate or, indeed, acceptable to the recipient. Of
the two who waited, Balfour was not particularly interested in receiving it,
while Macmillan was only too interested. Otherwise, apart from peerages,
the Garter (or Thistle) has been the undoubted right of a former British
Prime Minister, both when those orders were on the recommendation of a
successor and, since 1946, in the personal gift of the monarch.

Every British cabinet from 1902 until 1963 had one or more present
or future OM in it; albeit after 1945 only the Prime Minister himself

or a successor. The most at one time was in 1940, when Churchill's government included, besides himself, Halifax, Anderson, Attlee and Malcolm MacDonald. Even Asquith's famous administration had only four: Haldane, Lloyd George, Churchill and Samuel. After 1963, the Wilson government of 1964–70 included Roy Jenkins and, of course, that of Margaret Thatcher from 1979–90 had herself.

The embargo on political figures broke down at the end of the Second World War, as it had with Lloyd George at the end of the First. I shall discuss this when I write about Churchill later in this chapter.

The political figures

Unlike peerages and knighthoods and, to some extent, the CH, the Order of Merit was never envisaged as compensation for loss of political office. Its first and only use plainly as such was when George V conferred it on **Richard Burdon Haldane** on 26 May 1915, to soften the blow of his removal from the government.

In 1915, Asquith had been obliged to bring the Conservatives into a coalition with the Liberal administration that had been in power since 1905 and which he had led since 1908. The price of Conservative participation in the coalition was the removal of Haldane as Lord Chancellor and the demotion of Churchill from First Lord of the Admiralty. Haldane's undisguised regard for Germany and its culture had brought about his political downfall. A brief manuscript note in the Central Chancery records:

> The King conferred the OM on Lord Haldane for 'his attainments in Science and Philosophy'.[8]

The announcement in the *London Gazette* on the day of the conferment, however, gave no description of Haldane or the reason for the award. At the time, Haldane was crestfallen, as one of his biographers records: 'the order of merit . . . was cold comfort.' In his own autobiography published in 1929, a year after his death, Haldane was more philosophical:

> Asquith wrote an admirable letter which was read out [at a dinner at the National Liberal Club]. He did more, for without my knowledge he and the King arranged that I should have the Order of Merit. I had not thought of such a thing and I was a little doubtful about accepting it. It seemed to me then that this Order of Merit was not meant for just such a case as mine, a case which had been made the occasion of violent controversy. However, the Sovereign and the Prime Minister had come to their conclusion without consulting me, and I let the matter go.[9]

At least the recipient was under no illusion about the figleaf. Nor indeed was Lord Rosebery, the former Prime Minister who had been consulted about the inception of the Order. At the time of the fuss in 1921 over Lloyd George's intervention in the proposed appointment of Gilbert Murray, he wrote to the King's Private Secretary:

> the late King never allowed anybody to interfere with the OM, which I think is wise. The present King was overborne in Haldane's appointment, which was political and therefore was so damaging to the Order.[10]

Haldane sensed that it might not be too long before the knives came out for Asquith also and when that did happen, 18 months later, there was no compensatory OM for a prime minister of eight years standing.

Haldane was the son of an Edinburgh lawyer, with family lines that were distinguished on both sides. On one side of the family were admirals and generals; on the other were lawyers, most notably his great-great uncles, the nineteenth-century brothers Lords Eldon and Stowell. On both sides of the family, there had developed a strong evangelical piety. The family distinction extended beyond him in his own generation. His sister, Elizabeth, and brother John, were both CHs.

Haldane's fiancée broke off the engagement just before the marriage. He never married but remained very close to his mother, to whom he wrote every day until her death, at the age of 100, only three years before his own. Asquith's daughter regarded him as, 'intensely human [but] in a sense impersonal . . . immune from passion'.[11]

From day school in Edinburgh, Haldane went on to the university there at the age of 16. After completing his studies at Edinburgh with a First in Philosophy, he came to London, was called by Lincoln's Inn and began a practice at the English bar. He now had two passions: philosophy and the law and the combination led to his specialising in cases involving the consideration of legal principles.

Within a few years, Haldane entered politics as the Liberal member for East Lothian in 1880 and represented it until he went to the Lords in 1911. As a young MP, after ten years at the Bar, he became a QC.

Like many other Liberals, Haldane's opportunity for high office came with that party's return to office in 1905. The new Prime Minister, Campbell-Bannerman made him Secretary of State for War, with the remark: 'We shall now see how Schopenhauer gets on in the kailyard.'[12]

The King was inclined to make fun of Haldane as 'a damned radical lawyer and a German professor.[13] Pointing to him in an unsuitable shabby soft hat at a garden party, he exclaimed:

> See my War Minister approach in the hat which he inherited from Goethe![14]

What Haldane is generally credited with, and certainly took credit for, was the reorganisation of the Army and its reserve forces. F. E. Smith (Lord Birkenhead) later summarised Haldane's work:

> He conceived and perfected our Expeditionary Force...re-organised, if he did not wholly create, the General Staff...brought into being those Officers' Training Corps without which the war could not have been won; he called into existence that indomitable Territorial Force, which...made a superb contribution to the strength of British arms in France.[15]

However, the verdict of later and more detached historians is more critical. The distinguished military historian, Michael Howard, later concluded:

> Haldane had done his best; but the idea he had conceived as a philosopher demanded more dynamic politics and more daemonic leadership to bring it to fruition. He had certainly served his country well, but not perhaps quite so well as he subsequently claimed.[16]

Howard later added:

> In any competition for the title of 'Most Boring British Statesman of the Twentieth Century', Haldane would certainly be among the top seeds, even if he was defeated in the finals by say, Kingsley Wood [Chancellor of the Exchequer, 1940–43].[17]

On his performance in Parliament, Howard wrote:

> When he sat down...they stampeded into the lobbies to vote on the issue, for fear that he should say something more.[18]

Haldane had declined a peerage, either to take over the India Office or the viceroyalty of India but, in 1911, he was persuaded by Asquith to take a viscounty (while retaining the War Office). The following year, he achieved his ambition to sit on the woolsack once occupied by his great-great uncle, Eldon.

To return to the phrase that haunted Haldane's life: Germany was his 'spiritual home'. In his autobiography, he avoids admitting using the phrase himself, simply saying:

> I had gone to Germany too often and had read her literature too much, not to give ground to narrow-minded people to say that Germany was my 'spiritual home'.[19]

Whatever the truth, Haldane himself knew that 'in August 1914 a formidable section of the public here had turned against me'. Prince Louis of Battenberg was driven from his post as First Sea Lord and Haldane told Asquith that perhaps he should also go. He concluded:

> If my full story could have been made public, I think that the attacks would have been destroyed. But both Asquith and Grey were averse to making public the details of previous negotiations with Germany while the War was going on. I had therefore to remain unshielded.[20]

After losing office in 1915, Haldane was still in official demand. In 1916, against the possibility that Bonar Law might seek a parliamentary dissolution as a condition of accepting the premiership, the Palace sought Haldane's opinion. He was quite clear that such a bargain was inadmissible; only a Prime Minister in office could advise on a dissolution.[21]

In 1917–18, Haldane chaired a committee on the machinery of government, which made far-reaching recommendations and he took a great interest in the establishment of the Department of Scientific and Industrial Research. When the Institute of Public Administration was founded in 1922, he was an obvious choice as its first president.

In 1918, Haldane's part in the allied victory was belatedly acknowledged (as it was much later by the military historian, Liddell Hart[22]). George V's Private Secretary told Haldane:

> how deeply [the King] appreciates all you have done to make our victory possible and how silly he thought the outcry against you.[23]

The most touching tribute, however, came from Douglas Haig. On the night of the victory parade in London on 19 July 1919, Haig called on the lonely Haldane and left him a volume of his recently printed war despatches. It was inscribed:

> To Viscount Haldane of Cloan – the greatest Secretary of State for War England has ever had. In grateful remembrance of his successful efforts in organising the Military Forces for a war on the Continent, notwithstanding much opposition from the Army Council and the half-hearted support of his Parliamentary friends. HAIG, FM.[24]

Haldane returned to government in 1924 – in the short-lived first Labour administration, which needed a number of peers but was reluctant to create them, especially if they had heirs. Haldane, who had grown distant from the Liberals and what he saw as their lack of interest in education, accepted Ramsay MacDonald's invitation to join him. He declined the education post but agreed to become Lord Chancellor again.

Throughout his life, Haldane was immensely interested in higher and adult education and its administration. As a young lawyer, he lectured at the Working Men's College and was later active in the Workers' Educational Association. He took a leading part in the University of London Act 1898. He was one of the founders, with Sidney and Beatrice Webb, of the London School of Economics in 1895 and for the last ten years of his life he presided over Birkbeck College.

At various times, Haldane chaired committees to look into university education in London, in Wales, in the North of England and into the constitution of the Imperial College of Science and Technology. The University Grants Committee, which advised the government for so much of the twentieth century on the allocation of public money to higher institutions, resulted from a committee he chaired. Much of this work was done while he was a minister from 1906–15, although he never held the education portfolio. He was a large part of the inspiration behind Fisher's Education Act of 1918.

Haldane was Chancellor of Bristol University from 1912 and in 1928, shortly before his death, he was elected (in succession to Haig) Chancellor of St Andrews University, where he had much earlier declined the Chair of Moral Philosophy. He was both FRS and FBA.

What of Haldane's philosophical work, on which the award of the OM was supposedly (but not publicly) based? It was, of course, rooted in the Germans. He translated Schopenhauer and contributed to a volume of *Essays in Philosophical Criticism* in 1883. The *Pathway to Reality* (based on lectures given at St Andrews in 1902–03) was the most comprehensive of his works. As the *DNB* put it:

> To him philosophy gave back what science threatened to take away, namely faith in the reality of the spiritual world... [Hegel's abstract thought] tended to make Haldane's exposition of his philosophical views difficult and obscure.

He recognised that the poet, artist or simple religious person could reach

> the highest result of speculative thinking. 'Abstract reasoning has no monopoly of the means of access to reality, although I hold it to be the only competent guardian of the pathway.'[25]

There was scepticism about Haldane's standing as a 'philosopher'. Only a month after his death, Esher (in writing to Stamfordham about possible candidates for the Order) commented:

> A. J. B[alfour] and Haldane received the Order. What for? 'Science, literature or art?' One qualified, I suppose, by his work on philosophic doubt: the other [Haldane] for his Kantian discourses.[26]

On his death in 1928, *The Times* had little doubt where Haldane's true reputation lay:

> Alongside his political name, Lord Haldane built up a more than national reputation as a philosopher of great devotion. He will not, perhaps, be accorded a place in the front rank of original thinkers . . . But it is likely to prove a just instinct among his contemporaries that chooses without hesitation for his monument the incomparable service which he did for his country during seven years – the most tempestuous and bitterly contested period . . . of his public career . . . [as] Secretary of State for War.[27]

Nevertheless, Haldane's membership of the Order of Merit probably owes most to the special circumstances of his removal from government in 1915.

Arthur James Balfour has already featured frequently in this book: as Prime Minister (of only a few days' standing) on the institution of the Order of Merit; as a frequent tenderer of advice on appointments to it; and as a reluctant recipient himself. His appointment in the King's Birthday Honours List of 3 June 1916 came to him, then First Lord of the Admiralty in Asquith's coalition government, in a letter from the Palace:

> in recognition of your eminent services in the field of philosophy, theology and scientific research.[28]

Balfour accepted reluctantly. As he later explained:

> I was a little reluctant to accept the Order in 1916, not (need I say?) because I underrated the honour but because I greatly feared that it was already becoming too political in character and that its original characteristics were being somewhat blurred as time went on.[29]

What of the philosophy that was the supposed ground of his appointment to the Order of Merit? His views were set out in two main works: *A Defence of Philosophic Doubt* in 1879 and *Foundations of Belief* in 1895:

> His strong conflict was with naturalism; his contention, that the foundations of natural science are no firmer than those of theology and even perhaps not so firm; his thesis, that Theism clears, instead of confusing counsel.[30]

Balfour's intellectual standing at the time was recognised by Presidency of the British Association for the Advancement of Science in 1904 (while Prime Minister), of the British Academy in 1922 and, possibly (had he not declined to be put forward), of the Royal Society in 1920. He was Chancellor of Cambridge and Edinburgh Universities and, earlier, Lord Rector of St Andrews. Balfour, the reluctant OM, was not especially keen on the later honours that came to him: the Garter and an earldom. On the man himself, F. E. Smith warned:

> It requires some audacity to attempt to write of Lord Balfour's career or to portray his character in a brief space. It is indeed like sketching a chameleon upon a postage stamp.[31]

Balfour certainly lent himself to anecdote and quotation; Piers Brendon provides proof of that in the amusing but hardly flattering vignette of Balfour in *Eminent Edwardians*: nearly 200 in 60 pages. (I have taken the liberty of borrowing a few.) Brendon also cites the 16 nicknames given to Balfour over his long career as 'the clearest tribute to his enigmatic character'. Churchill had employed a similar tactic – 'a few blades from my sheaf of Balfouriana' – in the essay on A. J. Balfour in his *Great Contemporaries*. To begin at the end: in 1930, Ramsay MacDonald, paying his Prime Ministerial tribute to Balfour, said that

> He saw a great deal of life from afar.

From a life of struggle himself, MacDonald

> could not but regard with admiring disdain the long, tranquil, Olympian career of his fortunate yet defeated predecessor.[32]

The *DNB* entry, written by Balfour's cousin, Algernon Cecil, was more prosaic:

> for all his long lifetime of service, his personality never quite captured the public imagination. His appeal was essentially to the few and not the many, to the salon and to the senate rather than to the street: and on more than one critical occasion he showed a lack of what goes by the name of the 'common touch'.[33]

These judgements could largely be explained by his upbringing. Balfour inherited £4 million at the age of eight in 1856, when his father died prematurely after fathering nine children. The family money had been made in commerce in India but was secured socially by marriage into the Cecil family. Balfour's mother was the sister of Robert, third Marquess of Salisbury, who succeeded Disraeli as leader of the Conservative Party in opposition in 1881.

An unsympathetic Eton was followed by a more congenial Trinity College, Cambridge. He gained a Second in Moral Sciences and began a lifelong interest in philosophy and in scientific development.

Salisbury found a safe family seat for his nephew in 1874. In his uncle's first government in 1885, Balfour was made President of the Local Government Board and then Secretary for Scotland. His preferment, in 1887, to the exacting and dangerous post of Chief Secretary for Ireland was explicable to many only because 'Bob's your uncle' – a phrase which has stayed in the language. He survived four years in Ireland and it was the political making of him – but it turned his hair prematurely grey.

On the death of W. H. Smith, in 1891, Balfour became leader of the House of Commons and First Lord of the Treasury; he was the last man to hold that post without also being Prime Minister. He was to hold the two positions again from 1895–1902, after having led the Opposition in the House of Commons during the Liberal governments of 1892–95. When Salisbury retired in July 1902, Balfour effortlessly succeeded to the premiership, retaining the office of First Lord of the Treasury, a link that has never since been broken. Shortly before leaving office in 1905, Balfour established constitutional recognition of, and high formal precedence for, the hitherto 'unofficial' office of Prime Minister.

Prime Minister for three years, Balfour's government is remembered chiefly for the intense controversy within the Conservative Party between the tariff-reformers and the free traders. With the spectre of Peel behind him, Balfour strove to keep the party united.

In foreign affairs, Balfour created the Committee of Imperial Defence and made defence very much the Prime Minister's own subject, which it has remained. He secured the entente with France and a new treaty with Japan. His relations with Edward VII were correct but not cordial. Their tastes differed and the King may have thought Balfour condescended to him or been piqued that he came to call in a motorcar and wearing a homburg hat. Balfour was later

> at pains to scotch the widespread belief that King Edward had been responsible for the 'entente cordiale' with France and he wrote [in 1915] to ask Lansdowne [Foreign Secretary in 1903] to confirm his recollection that 'during the years you and I were his Ministers, he never made an important suggestion of any sort on large questions of policy.' That was true . . . [34]

Balfour resigned in December 1905 and the next month lost his own seat in the disastrous electoral defeat of the Conservatives. He quickly found a safe seat and led the Opposition until 1911. Not for the first time, however, there were cries within a heavily defeated party for a more forceful leader, one who might regain power for the 'natural' rulers of the country. Balfour's nonchalance bordered on flippancy and encouraged the 'Pretty Fanny' image; he very rarely rose before lunch. Even years before, his apparent boredom on the front bench had led journalists to wonder 'if he was born tired like the man who couldn't eat roast beef so exhausted did it make him to reach for the mustard'. In his own party, there were those who saw some force in the humiliating savaging of him by the new Prime Minister, Campbell-Bannerman:

> The right honourable gentleman is like the Bourbons. He has learned nothing. He comes back...with the same airy graces...the same light and frivolous way of dealing with great questions...I say, enough of this foolery!

Although Balfour insisted that he would rather take advice on policy from his valet than from a Tory party conference, he kept his hold on the leadership until November 1911, when he resigned on the grounds that he did not have the vigour again to conduct a ministry.[35]

The demise of Balfour as a politician seemed to mark his birth as a statesman and an active one at that. On the outbreak of war in 1914, he was invited to sit again on his own creation, the Committee of Imperial Defence, and, when the coalition government was formed in 1915, he displaced Churchill as First Lord of the Admiralty. Thereafter, he remained in office for all but four of the remaining 15 years of his life.

Although he played no active part in the plotting to remove Asquith, he benefited from it, emerging as Foreign Secretary in the Lloyd George coalition. As Foreign Secretary, Balfour was in the shadow of the wartime leader, Lloyd George, but he lent an old-fashioned dignity to the government. In 1917, he visited the new ally, the United States, and was the first Briton to address Congress. He attended the Peace Conference in Paris in 1919 but, on its conclusion, he resigned as Foreign Secretary (he was then 71) but remained as Lord President of the Council until 1922 – and resumed that post under Baldwin from 1925–29.

A future OM, Smuts, was bitterly critical of Balfour's performance at the Peace Conference: 'a tragedy, a mere dilettante, without force or guidance, when a strong British Foreign Minister might have saved the whole situation.' If Balfour ever heard the comments on him by his successor at the Foreign Office, George Curzon – 'disaster...sheer intellectual indolence...instinctive love of compromise' – he certainly got his own back, by deploying forceful constitutional arguments when the time came. In 1923, George V had to choose a successor to the mortally ill Prime Minister, Bonar Law:

> No man played a more decisive part than Balfour in clarifying the King's mind. During his two interviews with Stamfordham on 21 May, he dwelt

on the problem that would face a Prime Minister who sat in the House of Lords.[36]

On returning home, friends asked him:

> 'And will dear George be chosen?' 'No,' he replied placidly, 'dear George will not.'[37]

In Balfour's 'statesman' years, three important statements on overseas policy acquired his name. The implications of the first are still with us. The Balfour Declaration of 1917 stated that the British Government

> view with favour the establishment in Palestine of a national home for the Jewish people . . . it being clearly understood that nothing shall be done which may prejudice the civil and religious rights of existing non-Jewish communities in Palestine . . .

Few such statements have been subjected to so much differing criticism and interpretation. It made Balfour a hero of Zionism. The Balfour Note of 1922 recommended a general cancellation of war debts as part of a general settlement. In 1926, the Balfour Definition explained that the United Kingdom and the Dominions were

> equal in status, in no way subordinate one to another in any aspect of their domestic or internal affairs, though united by a common allegiance to the Crown and freely associated as members of the British Commonwealth of Nations.

It was the informal prelude to the legal framework of the Statute of Westminster in 1931 and was the constitutional basis of the Commonwealth until the declaration of 1949 that took account of the forthcoming Indian republic.

There is a photograph of Lloyd George and Churchill talking after the memorial service for Balfour. Perhaps those two OMs were exchanging views about the third: Lloyd George that Balfour's impact on history would be no more than 'the whiff of scent on a lady's pocket handkerchief' and that he was not a man but a mannerism; or Churchill that, 'if you wanted nothing done, A. J. B. was undoubtedly the best man for the task. There was no one to equal him.'

Balfour, from the grave, might have recalled what he said about them: generously of Lloyd George when defending him against charges of being a dictator: 'Let him be. If he thinks he can win the war, I'm all for his having a try.' Less generously he remarked of Churchill's *The World Crisis*: 'I am immersed in Winston's brilliant autobiography, disguised as a history of the universe.'[38]

45 David Lloyd George by Sir William Orpen.

After the appointment of the 'statesmen-philosophers', Haldane and Balfour, came a purely political nominee, **David Lloyd George**, the first of the two outstanding British war leaders of the twentieth century.

In mid-1919, the War was over and the Peace was nearly concluded. Honours were descending on the military leaders: peerages, baronetcies, knighthoods and for the top two, Haig and Beatty, the Order of Merit. It was entirely natural to think of honouring the Prime Minister who had led the country through the last two dangerous years, won a 'khaki' election and was soon to return from the peace conference in Versailles. According to one of Lloyd George's children, the question of an honour was raised when the King and Queen entertained his parents to dinner on the evening of the triumphal return from Paris. The King

> intimated his desire to confer some honour on [Lloyd George]. Forestalling my father's shying at this, His Majesty very cunningly mentioned that England, Scotland and Ireland had their own Orders... Wales had nothing. He wished to create a new Order of St David... [and] my father to be the first recipient. Very wily! My father was on the horns of a dilemma. Here was a chance indeed to do something for Wales – but, like his great old chief Gladstone, he had determined to remain a commoner. It was a sad pity in many ways the project was laid aside.[39]

Lloyd George refused the peerage which the King offered but, when asked whether he would take the Order of Merit, answered simply 'Yes, sir.'[40]

It was Bonar Law, leader of the (Conservative) Unionist Party and Lord Privy Seal in Lloyd George's coalition government, who pressed the idea of the OM on George V, even after the King's objection that such an award would be outside the statutes of the Order. I have already referred to the scholarly cover provided for previous appointments of political figures. Bonar Law conveyed his final argument to the King's Private Secretary on 5 August:

> agree with you that the wording of the Statutes makes this decision a difficult one for His Majesty. At the same time I am sure that the instinct of the King that he ought to show some special mark of appreciation of the work of the Prime Minister in connection with the War is sound and would be approved by his people. The War has created a situation so different from anything which could have been foreseen that an exception might I think well be made and the fact that it is an exception would enhance the value of the distinction. This order is I think the only one which it is understood is bestowed by the King without any consultation with his Ministers and so far as I can judge the bestowal of it on the Prime Minister would be approved by the nation.[41]

The King was convinced and wrote immediately to the Prime Minister:

> The Honours and rewards to the Officers of the Navy, Army and Air Force having now been submitted to Parliament, I feel that my people will share with me the regret that it is not possible to express the Nation's grateful recognition of the pre-eminent services rendered by the Prime Minister both in carrying the War to a victorious end, and in securing an honourable Peace. To rectify somewhat this omission and personally to mark my high appreciation of these services, it gives me great pleasure to confer upon you the Order of Merit.[42]

The text of the letter was sent to *The Times* and leading news agencies and the King invested his Prime Minister with the insignia at the Palace a week later. Unusually, the wording of the confirmatory notice in the *London Gazette* was cleared with the King, who approved the description 'Prime Minister and First Lord of the Treasury'. There was to be no pretence of intellectual achievement. It was plainly for national leadership in time of war – a clear exception to the Statutes of the Order and therefore, as Bonar Law had observed, all the more valued.

On 5 May 1919, Lloyd George's right-hand man, the 42-year-old Secretary of the Cabinet, Maurice Hankey, had told his master that, 'he would like an OM but realised they were usually given to old buffers'.[43] I am sure that, nevertheless, he was able to congratulate the 56-year-old buffer on 5 August.

The 'Welsh Wizard' was born in Manchester of Welsh parents but, after the death of his father when he was only one, his mother took him to live in North Wales with her brother, a master-shoemaker in the village of Llanystumdwy, near Criccieth. The uncle was a powerful radical influence on the young Lloyd George and the boy added his name of Lloyd to his own of George. He bore throughout life the hostility to English privilege and domination that was bred in the schools and chapels of North Wales.

After local schooling, Lloyd George qualified as a solicitor. In 1890, at the age of 27, he defeated the local squire to become Liberal MP for the Carnarvon Boroughs, a seat he retained until his elevation to the peerage in 1945. He went straight from the back benches into Campbell-Bannerman's Liberal cabinet of 1905 as President of the Board of Trade.

By 1909, Lloyd George was Chancellor of the Exchequer and in April that year introduced his 'People's Budget', probably the most notable financial statement ever made to Parliament. His intemperate language, in response to Unionist attacks, again angered the King:

> Lloyd George quickly focused his insults on 'the Dukes' whom he described as 'the first of the litter'... 'a fully-equipped Duke costs as much to keep up as two dreadnoughts' and was less easy to scrap.[44]

Lloyd George continued at the Treasury through the constitutional crises over the initial rejection by the Lords of his budget, the two elections of 1910 and the reduction of the powers of the Upper House by the Parliament Act 1911. In that year, he introduced a revolutionary scheme of health and unemployment insurance. He was rocked politically in 1912–13 by the Marconi scandal, in which, although he was cleared of personal dishonesty, he had to apologise to Parliament.

Lloyd George was initially hesitant about British participation in the First World War but the German invasion of Belgium convinced him. When Asquith formed a coalition government in 1915, he moved from the Treasury to be the first Minister of Munitions, with the aim of ensuring a vastly increased output of guns and shells. In July 1916, he succeeded Kitchener as Secretary of State for War. The conflict was at a desperate stage and he came to believe Asquith was no longer capable of pursuing it effectively. In December, he resigned and precipitated the resignation of Asquith also. As Churchill put it bluntly in his obituary tribute to Lloyd George in the House of Commons in 1945, he then

> seized the main power in the State and the leadership of the Government. (Hon Members: 'Seized?') Seized.[45]

Churchill went on to describe Lloyd George's leadership over the following two years:

> He imparted immediately a new surge of strength, of impulse, far stronger than anything that had been known up to that time and extending over the whole field of war-time Government ... the adoption of the convoy system ... the unified command which gave Marshal Foch the power to lead us all to victory; and in many other matters ...[46]

After the war Lloyd George embarked on another four years at Number 10. In the 'khaki' (or 'coupon') election, his 'demagogic conduct did his reputation permanent harm'[47] and in the coalition's immense majority, the Unionists outnumbered his Liberals by three to one. At home, he had pledged to build 'homes fit for heroes' and abroad he had much to do on the continent. Supposedly, he had problems with geography: 'Is it Upper or Lower Silesia we are giving away this afternoon?' Lloyd George was heavily involved in the tortuous peace negotiations at a series of conferences to pacify and restore the economy of Europe.

Apart from Great Britain and the continent, there was Ireland. Basically a Home Ruler himself, he had to contend with the fierce civil war that broke out:

> The Irish 'treaty' which finally resulted [in December 1921] was achieved mainly by Lloyd George's patience and negotiating skill.[48]

As Lloyd George left the King's service for the last time, in 1922, it is interesting to look at his relationship with the monarch who gave him such a personal honour. It varied but, on the whole, was not good:

> Lloyd George displayed a nonchalance not far removed from contempt. Over the years the King had not troubled to conceal his dislike of Lloyd George, now the Prime Minister seemed to be taking a spiteful revenge. He left letters unanswered, ignored a summons to a Privy Council without explanation or apology, gleefully admitted to his secretary that he had treated the King 'abominably' and claimed that Balfour had once asked him, 'Whatever would you do if you had a ruler with brains?'[49]

Honours were a particular bone of contention. The King was disturbed by

> the failure of the Prime Minister to consult him before promising titles to certain political or financial supporters; the number of honours recommended by the Prime Minister; the character of the recipients; and the use of go-betweens to sell the royal prerogative in the market-place.[50]

On the question of honours, Lloyd George, like other Prime Ministers apparently disdainful of rewards for themselves, was lavish in distributing them to others. This probably accounts for some of the rather dubious early appointments to the two orders instituted in his premiership: the British Empire and the Companions of Honour. Lloyd George did the honours system no favours and it took some time for it to escape from the cloud he had cast over it.

Lloyd George was out but not down, although he never held office again. He briefly reunited forces with Asquith and they supported the Labour minority government in 1924. Then they split again and for the next 20 or more years the Liberals were riven by division. In early 1931, MacDonald made overtures to Lloyd George about a possible coalition but after the formation later that year of the National Government and the subsequent election, which left Lloyd George with few supporters, he bowed out of the party leadership.

In the early 1930s, Lloyd George was busy writing his seven-volume *War Memoirs* and *The Truth about the Peace Treaties*, recounting his serious difficulties with the generals, particularly Haig. Margot Asquith cynically observed:

> I always knew L. G. had won the war but until I read his *Memoirs* I did not know he had won it singlehanded.[51]

On the formation of the coalition government in 1940, Lloyd George was 77 but Churchill was anxious to enlist his services. According to the *DNB* account, poor health led Lloyd George to refuse offers of a Cabinet post in June and the ambassadorship in Washington in December.

The two leading women in the life of 'the Goat' were honoured with the Order of the British Empire when it was new and somewhat mocked. Margaret, long-suffering wife and mother of his five legitimate children, was made a GBE in August 1920, a year after his OM. To the end of her life in 1941, they remained *Mr* David and *Dame* Margaret Lloyd George. Her death enabled him to marry, in 1943, Frances Stevenson although, as she put it:

> '...our real marriage had taken place 30 years before.' From the start, however, he made no bones about wanting her as mistress and secretary...not as wife.[52]

By the end of 1944, victory was in sight but Lloyd George was in no state to fight the anticipated election. He had cancer and, since an unopposed contest could not be assured, the old enemy of the Lords accepted a peerage. His earldom was announced in the New Year Honours of 1945 and later gazetted as 'Lloyd George of Dwyfor'. He did not live long enough to sit or speak in the Lords, if that had been his intention. Indeed, he did not live to see peace. He died on 26 March 1945.

The Times tribute, while blaming his political fall on the way he had himself exploited so quickly the victory in 1918, took a nobler long-term view:

> Among British statesmen since Gladstone, none had been more familiar to his own or other peoples, none had lived more vividly in their comprehension, whether by force of sympathy or of antipathy... He was, in short, a great War Minister... the greatest... since Chatham.[53]

In the Commons, the main tribute naturally came from Churchill, one of Lloyd George's adjutants in the First World War, who had led the country for most of the Second:

> As a man of action, resource and creative energy, he stood, when at his zenith, without a rival. His name is a household word... He was the greatest Welshman which that unconquerable race has produced since the age of the Tudors. Much of his work abides, some of it will grow greatly in the future, and those who come after us will find the pillars of his life's toil upstanding, massive and indestructible.[54]

John Grigg in his uncompleted biography had no doubt that, next to Churchill, Lloyd George was the most important British politician of the twentieth century.

It was 25 years before another politician was appointed to the Order of Merit, but in his case there was also a background of scholarship and work beyond the strictly political sphere. It was Attlee who suggested **Lord Passfield (Sidney Webb)** for the Order in April 1944. He minuted to Churchill that

> it would... be a fitting recognition of the outstanding contribution to social and political science made by the Webbs if the surviving member of a remarkable partnership were thus honoured. Further, the Order does not... include anyone who is distinguished in this field of human endeavour.[55]

There was some discussion of muddying the Order with politics. The Private Secretary concluded that Passfield's

> 'political' career was surely incidental to his life-work, which was pioneering what for want of a better word one may call the New Deal in England, which has been evolving since we were boys... the science of Politics in its better sense... I really don't think the 'non-political' essence of the OM is contaminated by this.[56]

Passfield was therefore offered the OM 'in recognition of your eminent services to Social and Political Science'. The award was announced in the Birthday Honours of 1944, alongside those to Henry Dale, the pharmacologist and Giles Gilbert Scott, the architect. *The Times* commended all three, but especially

> Lord Passfield's long years in Whitehall as civil servant and Minister [which] represent an honourable record of State service but his fame chiefly rests upon the long series of books written in the remarkable partnership with his wife as joint author and investigator when they were better known as Mr and Mrs Sidney Webb.[57]

The 'remarkable partnership' referred to by *The Times* was certainly how Passfield himself saw the honour. In reply to congratulations from Lloyd George, he wrote:

> My one impression is one of vexation at my wife not being included in the presentation. Will you please say that the award has no political significance; 'services to social and political science'.[58]

Sidney Webb's father was a modest public accountant and the family was mainly supported by his mother's hairdressing business. After schooling in Switzerland and Germany, he became a clerk in the City. Soon, however, he moved into public service and progressed (by examination) to be a first division clerk in the Colonial Office in 1881. He was also called to the Bar and took a law degree.

Webb's affiliation with socialism began in 1885 when Bernard Shaw introduced him to the Fabian Society, for which he began to write pamphlets. A decisive year in Webb's life was 1892. He had just left the civil service and so freed himself to enter politics, by serving on the newly-formed London County Council until 1910. Also, he married Beatrice Potter and theirs was one of the most unusual marriages in British public life in the twentieth century. They were in their early thirties but from very different backgrounds. She came from the rich mercantile class. Her father was a railway magnate and both her grandfathers were self-made Liberal MPs. One of nine sisters, she had an annual income of £1,000. Her interest in social work arose from collecting her father's rents in the East End of London and she was already well known from her writings and public appearances.

I have alluded to the wives of most other OMs only briefly, if at all. They provided the support (taken for granted for much of the twentieth century), which enabled their husbands to pursue careers which culminated in the OM. Few would be regarded as having a more or less equal claim to the Order as their husbands but this particular OM was seen by many (not least by Sidney himself) as a 'joint' award. As the joint *DNB* entry on the Webbs observed: 'it is impossible to treat their lives separately.' After their deaths, Bertrand Russell called them

> the most completely married couple I have ever known...[although she] would remark at intervals, 'As Sidney always says, marriage is the waste-paper basket of the emotions.' Their collaboration was quite dove-tailed...they decided to devote their lives to research and to the higher branches of propaganda.[59]

Beatrice called their marriage 'the firm of Webb'. To her diary, she candidly confided:

> We are both of us second-rate minds; but we are curiously combined. I am the investigator...A considerable work should be the result if we use our combined talents with a deliberate and persistent purpose.[60]

When John Burns, the socialist MP who became a Liberal minister, was asked what he thought the result of the marriage would be, he replied: 'A great big blue book.'[61] He was right, because they speedily produced hefty tomes on *The History of Trade Unionism* in 1894, *Industrial Democracy* in 1897 and *English Local Government* in nine volumes from 1906–29. He was extraordinarily industrious and seemed to prove, as one critic put it, 'that a good filing system lasts longer than sex'. (It was she, however, who was eventually elected FBA in 1931.)

In 1895, the Webbs launched the idea that led to the establishment of the London School of Economics and Political Science as a powerful social-sciences think tank. He was an honorary professor of public administration there from 1912–27. He served on the Royal Commission on the Review of Trade Union Law and she on the Royal Commission on the Poor Laws. She wrote the minority report, which was published as a Fabian paper and was one of the seeds of the welfare state. He was the first chairman of the board of the *New Statesman* in 1913.

The Webbs drew closer to the developing Labour Party as the most practical way forward for the social reforms they wanted. He was a member of the national executive from 1915–25 and drafted the policy statement in 1918 that included the memorable (and eventually controversial) Clause IV, calling for 'the common ownership of the means of production, distribution and exchange'.

After an unsuccessful attempt in 1918, Sidney was elected to the Commons in 1922 for the mining constituency of Seaham, in Durham. In the brief minority Labour government of 1924, he became President of the Board of Trade, which suited his administrative talents.

Although Sidney had decided to leave the Commons, he was persuaded by Ramsay MacDonald to enter the second Labour government in 1929 as

Secretary of State for the Dominions and Colonies. The price paid for these cabinet posts from 1929–31 was a peerage. He took the title of Lord Passfield from the house they had recently bought in Hampshire. She continued to call herself Mrs *Sidney* Webb, partly to avoid onerous social obligations and partly because (as she put it)

> by merely passing over my right to use a title, I help to undermine the foundation of British snobbishness.

In 1931, the Webbs parted company with MacDonald and embarked on a love affair with the Soviet Union. After meticulous preparatory reading, they made what amounted to a pilgrimage to that country and alienated many of their circle by apparently abandoning 'gradualism' in their adulatory *Soviet Communism: A New Civilisation?*, which was published in two volumes in 1935. (The question mark was removed in the Russian translation.) Over 20 years later, Attlee commented that it was a

> failure to understand the importance of the human factor in society as against the mechanics that led these two highly intelligent people to mis-understand so gravely the nature of the Russian Communist regime.[62]

It is often forgotten now the powerful influence which Soviet-style dicta-torships exerted on many Western intellectuals, who believed that 'liberty' was illusory and the 'freedom' that really mattered was about bread, jobs, schools, hospitals and the like.

In 1939, Sidney suffered a stroke and nursing him took its toll on Beatrice, who died in 1943, after a short illness. He died in October 1947 and two months later his ashes were united with those of Beatrice. They became the first husband and wife to be buried in Westminster Abbey. Within only a few years of their deaths, the *DNB* recorded that:

> Judgement on the large body of the Webbs' written work is not now as favourable as when it was first published. The combined literary style is heavy... but they broke fresh ground... influence on social study and social method has been immense.[63]

By the time of a biography of Beatrice in 1992, reviewers could write:

> [They] have a mixed press today... The years have not been kind to the memories of either... From being the first lady of British socialism, she had come close to qualifying as its Aunt Sally... In an earlier age, she would have made a marvellous abbess and, in a later one, a splendid Whitehall permanent secretary.[64]

The first volume (up to 1905) of the authorised biography of the Webbs, by Royden Harrison, appeared in 2000, after 30 years' gestation. Following the appearance of the second volume, to be written by others since Harrison died in 2002, perhaps a thorough re-evaluation of this memorable couple will be possible. They may even escape from the description of being

> singularly grim and unappealing . . . the driest of statistical collectivists, the proponents of socialism by filing cabinet.[65]

The next 'man of affairs' appointed to the Order was **Winston Churchill**. How can one make a character like Churchill come to life, when he is already so much larger than life? As a work of fiction, his life would be a bestseller. Each episode in it could be (and has been) a book in itself. He always said that history would be kind to him because he would write it. And he did.

Winston Churchill was supremely the OM who added more to the Order than it gave to him. Churchill's name had been mentioned for the OM long before the Second World War – for his work as a historian. The Nobel Prize awarded to him in 1953 was that for Literature: 'for his mastery of historical and biographical description as well as for brilliant oratory in defending exalted human values.'

The first time Churchill's name appears in the Royal Archives as a candidate for the OM is in 1928, when Lord Esher described him as 'another

46 Winston Churchill and Clement Attlee.

generation. Plenty of time'[66] – adding shortly afterwards, 'In due course I feel sure that Winston will be recognized as possessing *genius*'.[67] When consulted about 'living men of letters' in 1938, Masefield put Churchill first, as the 'best living historian'.[68] By 1941, the Private Secretary recorded robust views:

> I am one of those who look on him as about the greatest living historian and wanted him to have the OM a long time ago; but he was in violent opposition to the Government and an honour from The King might have been misunderstood [adding in manuscript] His time will no doubt come![69]

Of course, his time did come and his successor as Prime Minister, Attlee, told the Private Secretary that he thought an OM for Churchill was 'a very good idea'.[70]

Churchill, as is well known, had declined the Garter when George VI offered it to him on his resignation after his defeat in the 1945 General Election. For one thing, the Garter was still conferred (and would be for another year) on ministerial advice, although plainly the King was making the offer personally; for another, Churchill had just received the Order of the Boot from the electorate. As he put it to the King's Private Secretary: 'I felt that the times were too sad for honours or rewards.'[71] To avoid embarrassing Churchill by compelling him to decline in writing a second honour from the King, the offer was made in person by the Private Secretary, who recorded:

> I saw Mr Churchill this evening at his house in Hyde Park Gate and, by The King's direction, asked him if he would accept the OM at the New Year. Mr Churchill told me that he would be very glad to do so.[72]

Churchill subsequently wrote:

> The OM comes from the King alone and is not given on the advice of Ministers. This renders it more attractive to me.[73]

On his way to the OM, Churchill had acquired one other state honour: the CH, which he accepted in Lloyd George's resignation honours list in October 1922. He was one of the first politicians to take it as something which did not change their title, set them apart slightly from the ordinary run of politicians, gave them a pleasing neck adornment and kept them going until they decided whether to go to the House of Lords. He summed it up, when trying (unsuccessfully) to persuade Ernest Bevin to accept it in 1945, as 'something which has never done me any harm'.

After the OM, one further honour lay ahead: the Garter. The Palace made a private secretary approach to Number 10 and the Churchills were consulted without being told that the offer was likely to be remade. According to Sir Norman Brook (Secretary of the Cabinet), the decision to accept was not easy for Churchill:

> Though he had always been avid for medals, he was not interested in titles. This was why he was reluctant for so long...During the long period when he was struggling with this dilemma, he once said to me: 'I don't see why I should not have the Garter but continue to be known as Mr Churchill. After all, my father was known as Lord Randolph Churchill, but he was not a Lord. That was only a courtesy title. Why should not I continue to be called Mr Churchill as a discourtesy title?'[74]

So, he accepted the offer when it was made because, as he told friends:

> [in 1945] the Prime Minister had a say in it, now only the Queen decides. I took it because it was the Queen's wish.[75]

The appointment was announced on St George's Day 1953. In fact, however, Churchill was quick to recognise the disappointments inherent in any honours system:

> 'A medal glitters,' he told the House of Commons, 'but it also casts a shadow. For the one hungry sheep that is fed, a hundred look up in vain.'[76]

Two years later, with some reluctance, Churchill retired. He declined a dukedom. The story is that the royal offer was couched in terms of 'a dukedom or something like that'. He declined – just – and told Colville on his return to Number 10 from his farewell audience:

> I very nearly accepted, I was so moved by her beauty and her charm...for a moment I thought of accepting. But finally I remembered that I must die as I have always been...it's an odd thing, but she seemed almost relieved.[77]

Winston Churchill was quoted as saying that at Blenheim Palace he took two important decisions: to be born and to marry and he was equally content with both decisions. He was the son of a younger son of a duke but had largely to make his own way in the world. He was desperately proud of his descent from the first Duke of Marlborough, who (in G. M. Trevelyan's view)

> as a military strategist and a tactician, as a war statesman and war diplomatist, stands second to no Englishman in history.[78]

Winston was in awe of his father, Lord Randolph Churchill, whose early death, when the son was only 20, made the young man captain of his own destiny. He followed his father into politics and wrote his biography. He was, in the style of his class and time, closer to his nurse than his (American) mother:

> An indifferent schoolboy, he was indifferent at nothing else which he attempted.[79]

His subsequent achievements have been a perpetual encouragement to under-achievers at school. He was sorry not to have paid more attention at Harrow but later said he imbibed a great sense of history.

In 1895, Churchill was commissioned into a cavalry regiment and for five years he chased around the world – Cuba, the North-West Frontier of India, Sudan, South Africa. Sometimes he was on military duty, sometimes he was pursuing journalistic or writing trails. Always, he was in search of adventure, fame – and medals. From the Frontier emerged his first published book, *The Malakand Field Force*. From the Sudan came *The River War* and from South Africa (where he had been captured and nearly shot by the Boers, before escaping) came *London to Ladysmith, via Pretoria*. At 26, he was a national hero, had left the Army and was worth £10,000.

Churchill entered the House of Commons, at his second attempt, in 1900, against a background of furious self-education. In India particularly, he had read voraciously: Gibbon, Macaulay, Lecky (one of the original OMs) and back to Plato and Aristotle. He had, however, joined the wrong party, the Conservatives, and his free-trade beliefs led him in 1904 to cross the floor to join the Liberals. When the Liberals came into office in 1905, he became Parliamentary Under-secretary for the Colonies. Over the next 50 years, he was in office for 30, in the Cabinet for 27 and Prime Minister for nine. He endured, however, four periods in the wilderness: 20 years in all. His activity during those times, especially in the 1930s, was a formidable part of his political story. The breadth of his experience in Cabinet was extraordinary: Board of Trade (1908–11), Home office (1910–11), Admiralty (1911–15 and 1939–40), Ministry of Munitions (1917–19), War and Air (1919–21), Colonies (1921–22), Exchequer (1924–29) and Prime Minister (1940–45 and 1951–55). Only the Foreign Office eluded him, although he often took charge of it during his premierships when Eden was absent or ill.

The highlights of those many years in office are well-known: the Sidney Street siege, the Tonypandy miners, Antwerp, the Dardanelles, the Gold Standard and, above all, the Second World War.

Churchill always made the most of his periods in the political wilderness. For a few months in 1915–16, he served on the Western front as a battalion commander. At the end of 1922, Churchill entered on his second period in the political wilderness but this time he was out of Parliament. He was defeated at Dundee and

> in a twinkling of an eye I found myself without an office, without a seat, without a party and without an appendix.[80]

Churchill's third and longest wilderness period, from 1929–39, is the most famous. He wrote a monumental four-volume biography of the great Marlborough. And, of course, he railed against the German threat and the 'gathering storm'. After the Munich agreement, he told the government: 'You were given the choice between war and dishonour. You chose dishonour and you will have war.'

Entering on his fourth political wilderness after losing the 1945 General Election, Churchill appeared to relax, painting and writing. He left a lot of the leading of the Opposition to Eden and others. He went to the Riviera, celebrating his fortieth wedding anniversary with the Windsors. Once, at a Monte Carlo hotel, he asked the orchestra to play 'Lili Marlene' but next day told them:

> Please never play it again – it made me dream of Rommel all night.[81]

> Churchill began the writing of his six-volume *History of the Second World War* (1948–54), prefaced by the moral which he had originally suggested (unsuccessfully) for a French war memorial: 'In war: resolution; in defeat: defiance; in victory: magnanimity; in peace: goodwill.' It was the bulk of this work that immediately preceded the Nobel Prize for Literature in 1953. He made speeches, most notably in Fulton, Missouri, in March 1946 when he spoke of 'an iron curtain' descending across the continent of Europe. It was during that visit that the Communist Party of America put about a joke that Churchill much appreciated: 'Why did the sun never set on the British Empire? Because God didn't trust Winston Churchill in the dark.' [82]

Churchill's relationship with the monarchy was uneven. With Edward VII, his relations were initially good. George V, like his father

> recognized Churchill's zeal and energy [but] generally thought him 'irresponsible and unreliable' [and] 'a bull in a china shop'.[83]

After the First World War, the relations between George V and Churchill improved. The King came to appreciate an old friend who, by the mid-1920s, had returned to the Conservative fold. Churchill sensed British good fortune in retaining a monarchy that symbolised stability, compared with the unrest and chaos that had followed the fall of so many continental monarchies. He concluded:

> King George V brought about a resplendent rebirth of the great office which fell to his lot.[84]

Like many others who knew Edward VIII, Churchill had high hopes, despite an awareness of the new King's faults. His dogged support, throughout and beyond the abdication, damaged Churchill's standing, not least with the new monarch. The relationship with George VI thus began with much mutual suspicion but ended in a blaze of reciprocal adoration. In 1940, the King was not alone in preferring Halifax to succeed Chamberlain. Churchill, the adventurous mountebank, who had so publicly supported Edward VIII, was not much to his successor's liking. The war quickly changed all that. When the unexpected parting of their official ways came after the 1945 election, George VI made no secret of his dismay. The King kept in more than usual close touch with the new Leader of the Opposition. And when George VI died, Churchill, by then Prime Minister again, wept and pushed his papers aside, remarking: 'How unimportant these matters seem now,'[85] and described him as 'a spirit undaunted' during 'the hardest reign of modern times'.

With the new young Queen, he enjoyed playing John Churchill to her Queen Anne or even more, Melbourne to her Queen Victoria. He relished his lengthening audiences with her and his romanticism was fully fed by his Garter and her Coronation and subsequent six-month Commonwealth tour – the 'royal pilgrimage' as he called it. He steadfastly opposed 'Mountbatten' displacing 'Windsor' as the name of the royal house but, just before his resignation, suggested that the royal consort should be created a prince of the United Kingdom, a proposal carried into effect by Macmillan a couple of years later. The Queen was most solicitous when Churchill had a stroke (shortly after the Coronation), which was kept from the public.

Churchill bowed out politically on a royal note, entertaining the Queen and the Duke of Edinburgh to dinner at 10 Downing Street on the eve of his resignation. At his state funeral (described later), the Queen's wreath bore the handwritten inscription, 'In grateful remembrance'.

Churchill had a well-known and childlike delight in dressing up. His uniforms, and especially his hats, became the object of fond mockery. During the war, the service chief manqué in him led to frequent wearing of uniform.

There were accusations (by Hitler) and enquiries (by Roosevelt) about Churchill and drink. He certainly enjoyed a daily diet of champagne, brandy and whisky (and cigars) and it must be a great encouragement to many of us that he lived to be 90. He told his wife to remember that, 'I have taken more out of alcohol than alcohol has taken out of me.' Accounts of his drinking habits varied. Some described a bottle of champagne, or three ports and three brandies, for lunch. His secretaries – who were with him more constantly – talked of very weak whisky and sodas being symbols more than anything else. Whether drunk on liquor, Churchill was certainly drunk on words. It was in the Second World War, and especially in 1940, that he made the speeches, phrases from which have entered the vocabulary and consciousness of the British nation. He dragged the English language into battle and made it work for him in the frontline. Much later, I learned vicariously from his son-in-law, Duncan Sandys, what it was like to work for a man of dots and commas. On one occasion during Churchill's second premiership, he corrected a mis-spelt geographical name in a memorandum. An experienced official commented:

> Ramsay MacDonald would never have noticed. Baldwin would have noticed but just been bored; Chamberlain would have noticed, said nothing, but never forgiven the lapse; Attlee would have noticed but decided to say nothing out of kindness.[86]

While working hard and meticulously himself, Churchill drove others hard. His long-time secretary, Grace Hamblin, recalled leaving Chartwell at one o'clock in the morning and being told:

> There is no need to hurry in, in the morning. Eight o'clock will be quite all right.[87]

Once, when urged by Halifax to go on holiday, he replied:

> My dear Edward, my life is a perpetual holiday.[88]

Painting provided Churchill with his most pleasurable distraction from public life. He discovered it when he had to move from the busy Admiralty post to a sinecure in 1915; he concluded:

> Painting is complete as a distraction. I know of nothing which, without exhausting the body, more entirely absorbs the mind.[89]

He was elected, uniquely, an Honorary Royal Academician Extraordinary in 1949.

After his final resignation, Churchill went into his fifth and last wilderness, into God's Waiting Room – for ten years. It was, however, a wilderness full of respect and honour. When he retired from the House, only six months before his death, he was described as:

> The greatest member of Parliament of this or any other age ... The oldest among us can recall nothing to compare with his life and the younger ones among you, no matter however long you live, will never see the like again.[90]

Churchill's 'other' country went out of its way to honour him. In 1963, he was proclaimed an honorary citizen of the United States and his ninetieth birthday in 1964 was declared 'Sir Winston Churchill Day'.

The end was near, however, and, ten days after a cerebral thrombosis, he died on 24 January 1965. Britain, and the rest of the world, had had plenty of time to prepare for the event and there was an eruption of praise. *The Times*, which had still not put news on its front page, ingeniously wrapped its basic edition in a four-page outer obituary headed *Sir Winston Churchill Dies: The Greatest Englishman of His Time* and included in its summary of his life:

> [Churchill] led Great Britain from the peril of subjugation by the Nazi tyranny to victory ... In character, intellect and talent he had the attributes of greatness ... Leader of men and multitudes, strategist, statesman of high authority in the councils of nations, orator with a command of language that matched the grandeur of his themes, able parliamentary tactician, master of historical narrative, his renown is assured so long as the story of these lands is told.[91]

Churchill's passing was like that of a monarch. There was a state funeral, the first for a subject since Wellington's over a century earlier. The Queen and many other heads of state attended the service in St Paul's Cathedral, which was followed by private interment, alongside his parents in the graveyard of a country church near Blenheim. It was not what he had envisaged 70 years earlier. Discussing the arrangements for his father's funeral, he said:

> When I die I'm going to be buried in Westminster Abbey.[92]

He is not buried there but a large memorial stone near the grave of the Unknown Warrior enjoins the onlooker to 'Remember Winston Churchill'.

Memorials to Churchill proliferate. There are the thousands of books to which I referred earlier, including (according to the *Guinness Book of Records*) the longest biography ever written, mainly by Martin Gilbert. His entry in the *DNB* runs to 23 pages, far more than any of his contemporaries. There are statues, busts and memorial stones, indoors and outdoors. The most famous, in Parliament Square in London, is inscribed simply 'Churchill' – no other names or dates; it is confidently assumed that succeeding generations will know who he was, when he lived and what he did.

Churchill College at Cambridge was built and opened in his lifetime and it now includes the impressive Churchill Archive, housing his and contemporaries' papers. A memorial trust has 100 or more travelling fellowships a year. The Cabinet War Rooms in Whitehall, where Churchill did much of his business, have been restored and a Churchill Museum was opened there in 2005.

In conclusion, I shall quote the last sentence of the most recent significant biography, by another OM 'man of affairs', Roy Jenkins, who had originally thought that Gladstone, of whom he also wrote a biography, was the greater man:

> I now put Churchill, with all his idiosyncracies, his indulgences, his occasional childishness, but also his genius, his tenacity and his persistent ability, right or wrong, successful or unsuccessful, to be larger than life, as the greatest human being ever to occupy 10 Downing Street.[93]

Edward Halifax was very well known to the King and his Private Secretary. He had been Viceroy of India, Foreign Secretary, almost Prime Minister (preferred by the King over Churchill) and, in 1946, he had just returned from over five crucial years as Ambassador in Washington. The offer of the OM was made in May 1946. Halifax was a good friend of George VI and Lady Halifax was one of Queen Elizabeth's ladies-in-waiting. While Foreign Secretary, he was allowed to walk through the gardens of Buckingham Palace on his way from Eaton Square to the Foreign Office.

Edward Wood, later Lord Irwin, Viscount Halifax and Earl of Halifax was among the most aristocratic of OMs. His father was the second Viscount Halifax, a fanatical High Anglican, who owned large estates in Yorkshire. Edward was born with an atrophied left arm which had no hand (a disability he overcame with remarkable dexterity), he was the runt of the litter but, before he was ten, three older brothers had died and he was the heir to title and lands.

Halifax (as I shall call him, although he did not acquire that name until the death of his father in 1934) excelled as a scholar and, after Eton and a First in History at Oxford, he was elected to a fellowship at All Souls. His father's ambition was for him to become Prime Minister and reunite the United Kingdom with the Holy See. The nickname of Holy Fox, fostered by the Churchill family and later used by Andrew Roberts as the title of his biography of Halifax, was a pun, playing not only on his name but also on his twin loves of the High Church and fox-hunting and not overlooking his wiliness. His political start, however, was relatively slow. He was nearly 29 and married before he was elected Conservative MP for the safe Yorkshire seat of Ripon, which he held unopposed until he became a peer 15 years later.

In the First World War, despite his disability, Halifax served (mostly behind the lines) with his Yorkshire yeomanry regiment. In 1917, he came home to a dull administrative post in the Ministry of National Service. The position of Under-secretary for the Colonies came to Halifax in 1921. He benefited by promotion into Bonar Law's and Baldwin's cabinets: President of the Board of Education (1922–24) and as Minister of Agriculture (1924–25). He was equally ineffective in both. It was therefore a surprise all round when, at the suggestion of George V, he was appointed Viceroy of India in October 1925. The King was attracted by his unquestionable personality and charming wife (whose father had been Governor-General of New Zealand). Soon after his arrival in 1926 Halifax declared his aim to be

to keep a contented India in the Commonwealth 25 years hence.[94]

In 1951, a newly republican India was still in the Commonwealth. In 1929, Halifax proposed a Round Table conference of all British and Indian interested parties, coupled with a declaration 'that the natural issue of India's constitutional progress was the attainment of dominion status'. In 1931, Halifax and Gandhi, after a series of meetings, concluded the Irwin–Gandhi (or Delhi) Pact for future co-operation in Round Table conferences.

A biographer described both the inherent loneliness of the Viceroy and his main source of advice:

One man, Sir Malcolm Hailey, stood alone in his influence upon the Viceroy's mind. This great public servant [whom some thought] would himself have made a worthy Viceroy . . . his brilliant mind and profound knowledge of India caused Irwin from the first to place a particular reliance on his judgement.[95]

Halifax lived to see the aged Hailey join him in the Order of Merit in 1956.

The first and only Indian Governor-General (from 1948–50) of the short-lived Dominion of India, Chakravarti Rajagopalachari, described Halifax as

the most Christian and most gentlemanly Viceroy of them all.[96]

Halifax accepted the Garter from the King when he and his wife lunched at Windsor Castle on the day of their arrival back in Britain in May 1931. Out of filial respect, however, he declined an earldom, because it would have given him a higher rank than his viscount father. In 1932, he returned to the Ministry of Education. His real service in that MacDonald government was to help in the preparation of the immense Government of India Act 1935. He was glad to move away from education and India in 1935 to become Secretary of State for War (briefly), Lord Privy Seal and Lord President of the Council. He took an interest in foreign affairs and formed a good relationship with the Foreign Secretary, Anthony Eden. Both knew the military weakness of Britain and France but they differed over how to tackle an increasingly belligerent Germany. Like others before him, such as Lloyd George, he found Hitler 'very sincere'. This was after he had first mistaken the Führer for a footman and (until hastily checked) nearly handed him his hat and coat.[97]

On Eden's resignation in February 1938, Halifax succeeded him. Within weeks, Hitler embarked on the incorporation of Austria and the dismemberment of Czechoslovakia. British foreign policy over the following 18 months was conducted more by Chamberlain than by his Foreign Secretary, but Halifax did intervene to secure a short breathing space for the Czechs in meeting Hitler's demands. He also successfully warned Chamberlain against holding a general election to take advantage of the widespread relief at 'peace in our time'.

When war came, Halifax continued as Foreign Secretary, but the crucial moment in his life came in May 1940, when Chamberlain decided he had to resign after what amounted to an adverse vote in the Commons on the conduct of the war. The succession lay between Halifax, favoured by Chamberlain himself, the King and the majority of Conservative backbenchers and Churchill, the unpredictable maverick, who had returned to office as First Lord of the Admiralty on the outbreak of war but was still mistrusted by many in his own party and beyond. His latest biographer concludes:

> Halifax's natural modesty and shrewd political instinct told him that his 'inability to say the stirring thing' meant that he must rule himself out. He had no wish to become the Asquith to Churchill's Lloyd George, marginalized by his lack of military expertise until finally disposable. Instead, like Bonar Law in December 1916, he stood aside for the Man of Destiny. Where Churchill relished the opportunity of at last running the war, it gave Halifax a stomach-ache.[98]

Soon afterwards, in nine vital cabinet meetings held over three days (26, 27 and 28 May), Halifax was attracted to the possibility of a negotiated peace whereby Britain was left alone, while Germany went on to dominate continental Europe. A more robust line prevailed among his colleagues.

Halifax had not wanted to be Prime Minister. Nor did he want to be Ambassador in Washington, when Lord Lothian died in December 1940. Duty, however, was always Halifax's watchword and so, in January 1941, he came to live for the second time in a 'palace' designed by the architect-OM, Lutyens: the ambassadorial residence in Washington. He had been the first occupant of Lutyens' Viceroy's House in New Delhi. On arriving in the US, he was, unusually, greeted personally by President Roosevelt in Chesapeake Bay. Initially, his task was to keep American neutrality firmly steered in the direction of Britain. Halifax established very good relations with Harry

Hopkins, Roosevelt's close adviser, thereby gaining unprecedented access to the President. When the US came into the war in December 1941, Halifax's role changed. His staff expanded to ensure the closest co-operation with all arms of the American administration. In July 1944, he was rewarded by promotion to an earldom. In his last couple of years in Washington, Halifax was involved in many important meetings: the conferences at Dumbarton Oaks in 1944 and San Francisco in 1945 and the vital negotiation, at the end of the war, of an American loan to replace the abruptly-terminated lend-lease agreement.

Replete with earldom, Garter and OM, Halifax declined a place in Churchill's shadow cabinet, particularly because he had so recently served the Labour government. He settled down to a retirement that was to last until his death in 1959. He attended more assiduously to his duties as Chancellor of Oxford University, a post to which he had been elected unopposed in 1933. He spent more time in Yorkshire and became Chancellor also of Sheffield University. He wrote what the *DNB* called 'a gently evasive volume of memoirs', *Fulness of Days*, in 1957.

Even more official honours came to Halifax. As Chancellor of the Order of the Garter, he took a keen interest in appointments, particularly as they had reverted to the personal gift of the Sovereign. Belatedly, and briefly, he was Grand Master of the Order of St Michael and St George from 1957–59.

On Halifax's death, the main political tribute came from Lord Home, as Leader of the House of Lords. Home came from a similar background but was markedly less detached and intellectual. I recall, as a Private Secretary, the effort he put into the tribute:

> however great the post, it gained in dignity and authority by reason of his association with it...that is not to say that his actions were always approved by the public – indeed, he found himself a figure of controversy...The historians will weigh the evidence and will seek a judgement...his actions were always guided by what his religion, his very fine intellect and his true character told him to be the truth.[99]

The press obituaries varied, torn between descriptions of a distinguished Viceroy, a questionable Foreign Secretary and a solid Ambassador. Halifax himself would have been unperturbed. When told by the historian, John Wheeler-Bennett, that he was about to write a book on Munich, Halifax asked:

Will I have to stand in a white sheet in the judgement of History?

On being told he probably would, he commented, with his slight lisp:

My wivvers are quite unwung.[100]

Like Churchill, **Jan Smuts** was already a CH when he became an OM. Indeed, he headed the first list issued when that order was founded on 4 June 1917 and is probably now the only name remembered from it. The CH rewarded him for the many roles he had played: in reconciling the Boer and British peoples after the war of 1899–1902; in the formation of the Union of South Africa in 1910; in commanding the troops in the East African campaign in 1916–17; and, more immediately, as a member of the Imperial War Cabinet in London.

In the Second World War, Smuts' leadership of a country which had only narrowly entered the conflict but whose troops were now heavily engaged in the Middle East was recognised by his promotion to the rank of Field Marshal in 1941. He was the first holder from a Commonwealth country other than Britain. Nevertheless, he preferred to continue being called 'general', the rank he had earned originally fighting *against* the British.

In 1946, the idea came up of offering the OM to Smuts in connection with the forthcoming royal visit to South Africa. It was offered in October, 'in recognition of your outstanding services to the British Commonwealth and Empire and to humanity at large'. The honour was announced in the New Year Honours of 1947 and his formal telegram to the Palace associated his country with the honour:

> Please convey to His Majesty my most sincere thanks for high honour conferred on me and on South Africa. All South Africa thanks His Majesty for this signal and gracious favour.[101]

The actual investiture was one of the strangest in the history of the Order. It was before a large audience, rare enough in itself, but it ought to have been even larger. The two Houses of the South African Parliament had gathered in the dining room of Government House in Cape Town to present addresses of welcome to King George VI on the first day of his visit to the Union with Queen Elizabeth and the two Princesses. Absent, however, were most of the members of the Opposition Nationalist Party. Smuts had long enjoyed warm relations with the Royal Family and he had been particularly happy to invite them to South Africa so that they could enjoy a well-deserved postwar holiday as well as pay tribute to that country's contribution to the war effort. In fact, he thought the eventual itinerary had been too strenuous. His relations with the King's parents had also been close. During the war, he had sent food parcels to Queen Mary, who always wrote to Mrs Smuts as 'Dear Ouma' ('Granny').

Jan Smuts was born in 1870 on the birthday of his monarch, Queen Victoria: 24 May, celebrated for many years as Empire Day. His family had been in the Cape for 200 years and his father was a successful Boer farmer and MP in the Cape Colony Parliament. Smuts himself was a British subject until he was 28.

His formal schooling did not begin until he was 12 but only four years later he was at Stellenbosch University, from where he graduated in science and literature. A scholarship took him on to Christ's College, Cambridge. There he took a First in law and was considered by the great F. W. Maitland to be the best pupil he had ever taught. He was called to the English bar but, after declining a teaching post at Cambridge, returned to practise at the Cape bar.

At this stage, Smuts was a supporter of Cecil Rhodes but, after the latter's inspiration of the ill-fated Jameson Raid into the Transvaal, he moved to Johannesburg to practise there. In 1898, he became state attorney of the Transvaal and renounced his British nationality. He worked hard for peace in the Anglo–Boer negotiations, but after war came in 1899 and turned into guerrilla fighting the following year, Smuts became a soldier. In 1901, with the rank of general, he commanded a raiding commando sent into Cape Colony for eight months to stir up rebellion. His wife was put into a concentration camp, where her firstborn child died. He took part in the Vereeniging conference that ended the war and was instrumental in persuading the Boer leaders to accept the peace terms. As the representative of Het Volk (the People's Party), Smuts was sent to London in 1906 to negotiate with the new Liberal government. He met Campbell-Bannerman, on whom he made a great impression and whom he always credited with wreaking the 'miracle' whereby responsible government was granted to the Transvaal in 1906 and the Orange River Colony in 1907.

In Louis Botha's first Transvaal Government, Smuts was Colonial Secretary and Minister of Education. He worked for the formation of the Union of South Africa as a dominion in 1910 and became Minister of Mines, Defence and Interior in the cabinet of Botha. Shortly after the outbreak of war in 1914, the South African Defence Force, which Smuts had built up, was able to put down a rebellion led by some of his former Boer comrades-in-arms. In 1915, he supported Botha in defeating the enemy forces in German South West Africa (now Namibia). In 1916, as a lieutenant-general in the British Army, he took command of all imperial forces in East Africa that defeated the Germans in their colony that later became Tanganyika.

Early in 1917, Smuts was sent to London to represent the Union at the Imperial Conference and in the Imperial War Cabinet. He expected to stay for a month or so but, in fact, he remained in Europe for two and a half years. His counsel proved so valuable that Lloyd George invited him to join the British War Cabinet. He became, in effect, an additional unpaid member of the British government. It was a highly anomalous position for the minister of another country, possible only in an emergency wartime situation. He was a privy counsellor and, as we have seen, the CH soon followed. Much of his activity was, as envisaged, connected with the war effort. He also became involved more widely. At a dinner in the House of Lords, chaired by a Boer War adversary (Lord French, the first OM of the First World

War), he propounded a blueprint for the developing Commonwealth that foreshadowed the Balfour definition of 1926. His speeches earned him the title 'Orator for the Empire'. Smuts chaired a committee on air defence, the report of which led to the establishment of the RAF and another to deal with the question of demobilisation.

Smuts resigned from the War Cabinet at the end of 1918 in order to concentrate, with Botha, on representing South Africa at the Peace Conference. He published a pamphlet called *The League of Nations: A Practical Suggestion* and was the principal member of the committee, under President Wilson, which drafted the covenant of the League. Like Keynes, to whom he was close but whom he did not join in denouncing the Versailles treaty, Smuts was unhappy with it. He remembered the generosity of Veereeniging and thought Versailles was too much of a 'Carthaginian peace'.

A month after the signature of the Versailles treaty, Botha died and Smuts succeeded him as Prime Minister. It was not easy because he had been away from 'small' South Africa in the 'big' world of Europe for nearly three years. He narrowly won an election in 1920 but, two years later, he faced serious unrest on the Rand. He had to declare martial law and 150 people were killed. For the next 20 years, his political career was linked with that of General Hertzog, the alternative political leader. Smuts was Prime Minister from 1920–24 and Hertzog from 1924–33. Between 1933 and 1939 there was an uneasy alliance, with Hertzog as Prime Minister and Smuts as his Deputy.

Smuts used his period in opposition from 1924–33 to pursue his intellectual side. In 1926, he published *Holism and Evolution*, in which he drew inspiration from one OM, A. N. Whitehead, and another OM, Robert Bridges, and declared that his *Testament of Beauty* was a poetical version of the same thesis.

He gave the Rhodes lecture at Oxford and, indeed, his unsuccessful attempt to persuade the people of Southern Rhodesia to join the Union had led to his being labelled the 'renewed Rhodes'. He presided at the centenary meeting of the British Association for the Advancement of Science in 1931.

When war came in 1939, the 'uneasy alliance' foundered. Hertzog, who was of German stock, wanted neutrality. Smuts, the British-born Boer, who had become so British, wanted to support Britain. After a narrow parliamentary defeat, Hertzog resigned and Smuts became Prime Minister again. For the second time, he was a counsellor in the British war effort but from a greater distance.

At the end of the war, Smuts helped, at San Francisco, with the creation of the United Nations. He was the only major player there from the first attempt in 1919 to provide the world with an organisation aimed at maintaining peace and security.

Smuts was defeated in the general election of 1948 by the National Party, dedicated to the introduction of separate development of the races: apartheid. He led the Opposition until his death in 1950 and for those last two years was also Chancellor of his old university, Cambridge. The major British memorial to him was the founding there of a chair of Commonwealth studies, an appropriate tribute to a man whom many regarded as the principal architect and philosopher of that Commonwealth.

On Smuts' death, the obituaries were full and fulsome. At a time when *The Times* still carried no news on its front page, he was honoured with a note on its masthead, 'General Smuts: Special Memoir'; he was 'A Great Imperial Statesman'. To the radical *Manchester Guardian*, he was a 'Great Commonwealth Statesman'. To the *Daily Telegraph* he was both 'Empire Soldier and Statesman' and 'A Great Son of the British Commonwealth of Nations'. Churchill said:

> He fought for his own country; he thought for the whole world.

The *DNB* summarised his achievements but wondered about his character:

> In realizing his objects, he had often been a lone figure unable to suffer fools gladly or to make contact with the common man on the vulgar plane. 'The dogs may bark,' he would say, 'but the caravan moves on.' In these traits lay his strength and his weakness. It was said by some that he was a great tree under which too little else could grow.[102]

Smuts died when his fame and reputation stood high and his OM was amply justified. He and Abraham Lincoln are the only overseas figures with statues in Parliament Square.

William Lyon Mackenzie King's first three names were those of his maternal grandfather, an MP and first Mayor of Toronto, whose rebellion at the head of the 'mechanics and freeholders of Upper Canada' had failed in 1837 and who had spent some years of exile (and imprisonment) in the US. His paternal grandfather was an Army officer, who had helped to put down the rebellion.

Mackenzie King did not come unadorned to the Order of Merit, despite the fact that Canada had not taken British honours since 1919, except for a brief (politically divisive) period in the early 1930s and during the Second World War. As a very bright 31-year-old civil servant, Mackenzie King had caught the eye of the Governor-General (Lord Grey). In 1908, he was in Parliament, on the way to his record premiership.

Grey had certainly taken a shine to the young Mackenzie King, whom he introduced to Evelyn Wrench (the founder of the Royal Over-Seas League and the English-Speaking Union) as 'my friend, the future Prime Minister of Canada'.[103]

By 1947, Mackenzie King was, rather self-consciously, coming up to breaking two prime ministerial records: of Sir Wilfred Laurier, of Canada

and of Sir Robert Walpole, of any country in what was now the Commonwealth. Aware of this, the Palace (with the OM in mind) consulted Lord
Salisbury, who had been Dominions Secretary in the wartime coalition and
was now Leader of the Opposition peers. He was in favour, but wondered
about Mackenzie King's qualifications for the OM from which he thought
'politicians were specifically excluded', unless, like Churchill and Smuts, they
had other accomplishments. That aside, however, 'so great an honour to him
would be regarded as an honour to the Commonwealth as a whole'.[104]

At the same time, the British High Commissioner in Ottawa suggested to
the Dominions Office in London that Mackenzie King should be considered
for an OM. In forwarding his letter to the Palace, the Dominions Office
commented that it

> confirms the view that this particular proposal would be most apposite
> and also that this is the right time to take it up.[105]

So the offer was made. Mackenzie King, who had opposed honours all his
political life, was in a quandary. Would his acceptance be misunderstood
and made play of by his Tory opponents? On the other hand, he did not
want to appear churlish to the King and Queen (whom he had accompanied
on their visit to Canada and the United States in 1939). Finally, he persuaded
himself that:

> It is perhaps the most distinguished of all the Honours in the British
> Empire... It is not an honour that brings one into the category of aris-
> tocracy, except to be in the aristocracy of knowledge, but what is finer,
> it is the aristocracy of public service...[106]

Mackenzie King received the insignia from the King when he came to
London for the wedding of Princess Elizabeth in November 1947. After
referring to Churchill and Smuts having the Order, the King

> said something about the three of us being outstanding in the Common-
> wealth in the service we had rendered.[107]

Before and over lunch the King gave Mackenzie King a lesson in the history
of, and proper way of wearing, the Order, that is, 'For Merit' should appear
in front. Smuts had worn it the wrong way round and to help Mackenzie
King avoid this solecism, the King took the Badge out of its box and hung it
round his neck. The King also explained that there was no miniature to be
worn on any lapel (unlike the foreign orders Mackenzie King was beginning
to acquire). The British have always been determined not to let honours
recipients display their awards in everyday dress but this 'foreign' habit has
been adopted by countries, like Canada, Australia and New Zealand, with

a strong British tradition. The custom of restricting any honours display to formal dress denies that opportunity to the vast majority of recipients who never wear such dress.

Smuts, when he called to congratulate Mackenzie King, remarked on how wise the King was to extend membership of the Order. 'They have been keeping these things too much in their own little circle here.'[108]

Years later, Mackenzie King's decision to accept the OM was still a source of comment in Canada. Vincent Massey, the first indigenous Governor-General, who was a CH and held the Royal Victorian Chain, remarked:

> after years of effort to eliminate honours from Canadian life, he was prepared to accept the Order of Merit . . . and the highest decorations of a number of Allied powers.[109]

Mackenzie King graduated in political science and law from Toronto University and did postgraduate work at Chicago and Harvard. He lived at Hull House, the 'Toynbee Hall' of Chicago and wrote about the sweatshop conditions he discovered there and in his native Toronto. At Harvard he worked on a PhD on oriental immigration into Canada. He came to the notice of the new Liberal government in Canada and accepted the post of Deputy Minister, or Permanent Secretary, of the new Department of Labour. His success was clear, in labour conciliation at home and international negotiations over immigration.

Mackenzie King's first foray into politics was short. Elected to Parliament in 1908, he was defeated in 1911 but for two of those years he was back in his old department as Minister of Labour. In 1914, he accepted a post with the Rockefeller Foundation in the US. But he still spent time in Canada and, when the leadership of the Liberal Party became vacant in 1919, he was elected leader and, after securing a seat, he became leader of the parliamentary opposition.

In December 1921, Mackenzie King became Prime Minister for the first time as the leader of the party with most seats but annoyingly dependent on the votes of another, the Progressives. He was to be Prime Minister (and for most of the time also Minister of External Affairs) for all but five of the next 27 years. It is hardly surprising that he is regarded as the dominant figure in the politics of Canada and the development of its nationhood during the first half of the twentieth century.

Mackenzie King made it clear to Lloyd George that Britain could not take Canada for granted over such matters as the provision of troops in times of international crisis. He resisted Smuts' efforts to achieve a Commonwealth that acted as a single unit internationally. He began to have treaties with the US signed by Canadian, rather than British, ministers. Later, he appointed the first Canadian diplomatic representative abroad – Vincent Massey, as Minister to the US.

In 1926, Mackenzie King ran into a constitutional crisis too intricate to set out in full detail here. In the election the previous year, the Conservatives had won most seats but with the continued support of the Progressives, Mackenzie King's Liberals were able to stay in office. He gave an undertaking, which the Governor-General (Lord Byng of Vimy, the British general who had commanded Canadian troops in the war) took to mean that he would resign if defeated in Parliament. To avoid that happening some months later, Mackenzie King asked for a dissolution of Parliament, claiming that the Conservatives would not be able to govern. The Governor-General refused his request and the Conservatives, under Arthur Meighen, took office on a tenuous basis until defeated only a week later. Meighen was then granted the dissolution refused to Mackenzie King, who won an outright majority in the ensuing election.

Much has been written about this episode, centring on the circumstances in which the Crown may properly refuse a request for dissolution. What is clear, however, is that Mackenzie King

> was enabled to present himself to the country simultaneously as the champion of Canadian independence whose advice as an undefeated prime minister had been refused by the unwarranted interference in Canadian politics of the British governor-general; and as the saviour of the British constitutional method endangered by an illegal Government.[110]

Soon after the onset of the Depression, the Liberals suffered (in 1930) their only defeat under Mackenzie King's leadership. It was during and after his years in opposition from 1930–35 that

> his strong sense of the personal survival of those near to him developed... into a spiritualistic belief in communication which was especially strong in connexion with his mother [who had died in 1917]. Mediums whom he consulted agree, however, that he never sought other-world advice on questions of State and his interest was kept very strictly secret.[111]

Mackenzie King was a bachelor who seemed never to allow himself to form a deep friendship after the death of a fellow student and civil servant, Henry Harper, who was drowned in 1901 while attempting to save the life of a woman. In his memory, Mackenzie King published *The Secret of Heroism* in 1906.

The Conservative government, led by R. B. Bennett, was defeated in 1935. Mackenzie King now embarked on 13 unbroken years as Prime Minister. He attended the coronation of George VI in 1937 and went on to visit Hitler when, according to the *DNB*,

> he told the Führer that Canada would fight along with Britain should Germany provoke a war. He would seem, however, to have come away with the impression that Hitler was no danger to world peace.[112]

Like many others, Mackenzie King did not give up hope of peace with Germany until war came.

Before war came, however, King George VI and Queen Elizabeth paid an historic visit to Canada and the US, the first by a reigning British Sovereign to either country. Mackenzie King hoped the visit, which he had stimulated and in which he played a prominent role, would cement Canadian unity and reinforce Canadian loyalty following the abdication of Edward VIII, who had had special links with Canada:

> For the royal couple it was to provide an opportunity of establishing themselves on the international stage; two years later, the Queen was to tell [Mackenzie King] 'that tour made us', speaking of it as 'coming at just the right time for us'.[113]

In Canada, there was little doubt about the decision to go to war; but it took a week to reach the decision. This not only underlined Canadian independence from Britain but also enabled US supplies to be rushed to a 'neutral' country. Mackenzie King was determined that Canadian involvement in the war effort should be on a more equal footing than in the previous conflict. He kept control over the Empire Air Training Scheme in Canada and over Canadian forces overseas. He opposed the idea of an Imperial War Cabinet on 1917–18 lines and concentrated on the tripartite relationship between Canada, Britain and the US. He developed close links with Roosevelt and helped in removing misunderstandings between the President and Churchill. There was co-operation between the three countries on the atomic bomb.

Like Churchill, Mackenzie King went to the electorate in mid-1945 but, unlike Churchill, he won the election but lost his own seat, before quickly finding another. His strength was taxed by work in international affairs in London, San Francisco (the United Nations conference) and Washington and he resigned the external affairs portfolio in 1946. He remained Prime Minister for another two years and was particularly proud of becoming the first 'Canadian citizen' under the Citizenship Act of 1946. That, with the increased powers of constitutional amendment (in 1949, shortly after his resignation), completed his long work for Canadian autonomy.

After attending Princess Elizabeth's wedding and receiving the OM (as already recounted), Mackenzie King moved somewhat slowly off the scene. On 20 April 1948, he completed 7,621 days as Prime Minister and so passed Walpole's record.

Mackenzie King resigned as party leader in August 1948 but did not relinquish the premiership until November. He had less than two years of retirement, dying on 22 July 1950, at the age of 75. The obituaries concentrated on the 'flowering of Canadian nationhood' under his leadership. His greatest service was that

> as a reward of wise and understanding policy, he brought a united Canada into the war, and in spite of the strains imposed on her, continued to preserve her unity.[114]

The *DNB* described him as

> respected as an elder statesman of international stature...[who] had for long been admired as a superb party leader...The most durable, certainly the most successful, if not the most lovable of Canadian statesmen, Mackenzie King was the rock upon which many broke but upon which modern Canada was built.[115]

It was not long before inquisitive biographies began to appear. One concluded by describing the crowds at Mackenzie King's lying-in-state and funeral:

> They did not weep, for they had not loved this man. They were respectful, they glimpsed King's greatness even if they had seen in life only his self-made caricature, but they were puzzled because King reflected them as in a true glass, and the Canadian people did not understand themselves.[116]

In 1976, the 30-year rule enabled an eminent Canadian historian, C. P. Stacey, to use Mackenzie King's wartime diaries to write a 'hard-hitting and revelatory biography...[which] became a best-seller in Canada'. This was hardly surprising since:

> It revealed details of the bachelor prime minister's sexual fantasies; his habit of visiting prostitutes; his belief in the occult and his participation in séances.[117]

The next political figure to be appointed to the Order of Merit was another Prime Minister: **Clement Attlee**, on 6 November 1951, within days of resigning as head of the first British Labour government with an overall majority. Only a week after his resignation, Attlee received a letter from George VI:

> I am writing to tell you how grateful I am for the help that you have always given me in our personal relationship throughout these most

difficult years. It would give me much pleasure if you would accept from me the Order of Merit.

I hope this offer will be agreeable to you, for I should much like to mark in this way my appreciation of your services to the country and to myself during the years that you have held office as one of my Ministers – for six of them, as my Prime Minister.[118]

He received the insignia from the King on 5 November. Attlee had a great respect for the monarchy, besides which he

and George VI had grown fond of each other. Michael Foot writes that the King's death was the only event which he ever knew to affect Clem emotionally, in public. He could speak calmly even of the death of Ernie Bevin 'but when he spoke of George VI's death, tears were in his eyes and voice'.

Attlee's appointment was greeted with widespread approval. The broadsheets on 6 November gave it leading articles. *The Times* wrote:

The award...has given pleasure to all parties...it can be taken for granted that he will not be one of the forgotten Prime Ministers...[his] reputation has risen steadily from the moment he took office as Prime Minister...He is acutely aware of the practical in politics, yet, as his action over India proved, he has some of the daring and vision which distinguish the statesman from the politician. He has great personal and political integrity...moral dignity...profound belief in the worth of ordinary people and a selfless interest in their welfare.

In the House of Commons, Churchill, now Prime Minister again, was quick to congratulate Attlee, the news being 'especially gratifying to those who had served with him in the hard days of war'. Perhaps this typifies the real relationship between the two men more than the old stories of Churchill saying that when an empty taxi drew up, it was Attlee who got out or that when Attlee asked him for 2d to telephone 'a friend', Churchill gave him 4d so that he could ring 'the other one as well'.

In his letter of acceptance, Attlee had also expressed his hope that the King's health would improve (after the serious operation he had undergone in September). It did not. George VI died three months later, on 6 February 1952. Attlee's was his last appointment to the Order of Merit. It is therefore the last to which I have had access to the confidential papers in the Royal Archives.

The OM was not Attlee's first honour. He had been made a privy counsellor in George V's Silver Jubilee Honours List in June 1935. Like Churchill, Attlee had been made a CH but without such a long gap between that and the OM. The CH came in 1945, when the wartime coalition broke up. Attlee was not averse to honours. When it came to the customary earldom for former Prime Ministers, Attlee took the precaution of consulting the Parliamentary Labour Party:

'I'm resigning. Shall I take an earldom? It's up to you.' They said: 'Of course you must, Clem.'[119]

In June 1956, Attlee greatly enjoyed his installation as a Knight of the Garter. He had played a significant part in the development of that order ten years earlier. George VI had long wanted to redeem it from the influence of politics and so he

spoke to Attlee about the future KGs. His people are against accepting honours and most recipients would have to be of the other party. I want it non-political and in my gift. Naturally I would tell him my ideas.

He happily told Queen Mary:

after a talk with the PM and Winston I have arranged for the Garter and Thistle appts. to be in my hands like those of the Order of Merit.[120]

Attlee's honours were now complete. As Roy Jenkins, the future OM, said:

He collected great honours like a fly-paper collects flies. No other Prime Minister except Mr Balfour has had an earldom, a Garter and an Order of Merit.[121]

Clement Richard Attlee was the son of a solicitor in the City of London, with houses in Putney and Essex. He went to Haileybury and remained devoted to it. In 1901, he went up to University College, Oxford, at a time when, as he once told me, 'one had breakfast in one's room and there were horse trams in the High'. He secured a half-blue for billiards and a Second in history. He told me (in 1957) of his pride that there had been a Univ man in every government since 1841 and that he and another Univ man had been the first Labour MPs educated at Oxford. He followed closely the appointment of Univ men to the episcopal bench.

Attlee was called to the Bar by Inner Temple, although his 'interest in the law was, to put it mildly, very tepid'. As it was, he took a 'decisive step' in his life by visiting the Haileybury club in Stepney. His increasing involvement led to his becoming its manager. He immersed himself in the East End and made his home there for the next 14 years; a legacy of £400 from his father enabled him to live adequately there, without having to pursue a profession. He joined the Fabians and the Independent Labour Party and became secretary of Toynbee Hall. Besides the Webbs, he had read Ruskin and Morris. One author eluded him. Years later, he asked the British Ambassador in Moscow whether he had ever read Marx and received the nervous diplomatic reply: 'Only the potted version supplied to us by the Foreign Office.' Attlee commented: 'Haven't read a word of it myself.'[122] Attlee recorded his conversion to Socialism in typically undramatic terms:

> I soon began to learn many things which had hitherto been unrevealed...These people were not poor through their lack of fine qualities. The slums were not filled with the dregs of society...From this it was only a step to examining the whole basis of our social and economic system...I got to know what slum landlordism and sweating meant. I learned also why there were rebels.[123]

When war came in 1914, Attlee became a lieutenant in the South Lancashire Regiment. He served in Gallipoli and was badly wounded in Mesopotamia (Iraq) but recovered in time to serve in France in the closing months of the war. After the war, 'Major Attlee' as he was mostly known for the next 20 years, returned to the East End and a fuller political life. He was co-opted as Mayor of Stepney in 1919 and elected as MP for Limehouse in 1922, the year also in which he married (at the age of 38) and settled down to a predominantly suburban existence. Ramsay MacDonald made him one of his Parliamentary Private Secretaries and, in the short-lived Labour minority government of 1924, he was Under-Secretary of State for War. He served from 1927–30 as one of the Opposition nominees on the Simon Commission to consider the future government of India.

When Labour did return to office in 1929, Attlee was initially overlooked but he became Chancellor of the Duchy of Lancaster in 1930 and Postmaster-General in 1931. In the electoral slaughter of 1931, Attlee retained his 'safe' Labour seat by only 551 votes. The 52 surviving Labour MPs elected the only ex-cabinet minister, George Lansbury, as their leader and Attlee as his deputy. After the defeat of Lansbury at the party conference in 1935, Attlee's election as his successor was seen by many as only an 'interim appointment'. The interim lasted 20 years.

At the outbreak of the Second World War, Attlee was ill but had recovered by the time the future of the Chamberlain Government came into question in May 1940. After consulting his colleagues, Attlee told Chamberlain that they would serve in a coalition, provided it was led by someone else. As soon as Churchill emerged as Prime Minister, Attlee collaborated with him in forming a new government. It was a fruitful partnership, with Attlee as Deputy Prime Minister in effect for the rest of the war but in title only from 1942. He was successively Lord Privy Seal (1940–42), Dominions Secretary (1942–43) and Lord President of the Council (1943–45).

Attlee relieved Churchill of much of the burden in the domestic field. He saw clear advantage to the Labour Party in gaining general acceptance by the coalition of many Socialist objectives in planning for a post-war Britain. He was utterly loyal to Churchill, whom he once described in terms that might be applied to himself: 'History set him the job that he was the ideal man to do.'[124]Nevertheless, there was no real friendship between these two very different men. Churchill thought Attlee was 'an admirable character but not a man with whom it is agreeable to dine'.[125]

Attlee emerged from the war less well known to the public than his party colleagues, Ernest Bevin and Herbert Morrison, who had been more prominent figures on the Home Front. The 1945 election produced a landslide victory for Labour. The plotting began again, on the basis that the new Parliamentary Labour Party (with many new MPs unfamiliar with Attlee's qualities) ought to elect a leader who would then form a government. Attlee would have none of it:

> If you're invited by the King to form a Government you don't say you can't reply for forty-eight hours. You accept the commission and you either bring it off successfully or you don't, and if you don't you go back and say you can't and advise the King to send for someone else.[126]

Attlee skilfully managed a very able but difficult team. The new confident Labour Government pressed on with what Attlee himself considered an extraordinarily quiet and peaceful revolution: nationalisation of key industries and the transition to a mixed economy; reforms creating a 'welfare state'; transition of Empire to Commonwealth; and support for a strong NATO – and (secretly) development of an independent nuclear capacity. The Labour Government's measures set the political agenda for the third quarter of the twentieth century. Attlee also associated himself particularly with the speedy granting of independence to India, Pakistan, Ceylon and Burma.

Attlee had little time for newspapers: 'Suppose they've got to say something.' He used *The Times* for its age-old purpose, as the tribal noticeboard – and for the cricket reports. It was only the prospect of receiving the latest cricket scores hourly that persuaded him to have a tickertape machine installed in Number 10. He was once discovered looking at a similar machine in the House of Commons and saying, '*that's* news, *that's* really news' as the tape showed 'Brisbane Test. Australia 35 for 3.'[127]

By 1950 (after ten years in office), the Labour leaders were tired and, in some cases, ill. In the election that year, the Labour majority collapsed to ten. Nevertheless, the government lasted for nearly two years. In October 1951, Labour lost the election. The Order of Merit for Attlee followed within days.

By 1951, Attlee was past his political peak and the next four years in opposition were an anti-climax. In 1954, he published a relatively short autobiography, with the throw-away and self-deprecatory title, *As It Happened*. He became increasingly out of touch and in the 1955 election he again lost. He delayed his retirement until the end of the year, which helped to ensure that it was Gaitskell and not Morrison who was elected to succeed him.

Following his retirement, Attlee led a busy life, lecturing and writing newspaper articles. He travelled extensively promoting the cause of World Government. He was lukewarm on Britain in a united Europe.

I met Clement Attlee in 1957. As an undergraduate at his college and a student of his inn of court, I decided to chance my arm by asking him to speak to the Oxford University Law Society. I received a speedy refusal. In a spidery hand that crept unevenly across the sheet, he told me he would 'find it difficult to say anything worth while . . . mere anecdotage is about all that I could manage.' I persisted and he gave in – 'if we can find a suitable subject'. He agreed to talk on 'The Office of Prime Minister', with emphasis on the practice and conventions of the constitution.

Before dinner, he reminisced about Oxford and politics in a style that was as crisp in private as in public. He was quite clear as to what he wished his government to be remembered for: Indian independence and the abolition of the last vestiges of the Poor Law. The talk itself was extempore and, as Attlee had to tell many enquirers, the best account was that in *The Times* on 15 June 1957. It ranged, in reported speech and quotations, through the varied aspects of the Prime Minister's role – as perceived over 50 years ago:

> . . . the first necessity of a Prime Minister was a sense of priorities. 'In Cabinet the important thing is to stop people from talking' . . . The Prime Minister must be a good House of Commons man . . . [and] should not act as his own foreign representative except on very rare occasions . . . He had an absolute duty to be ruthless in making appointments and in sacking those who, for one reason or another, should be relieved of their jobs, either for incompetence or because a younger man should have the job . . . 'a most unpleasant task' . . . he disliked broadcasting but felt it essential to keep in touch with 'the ordinary people' . . . The Prime Minister was a servant of the monarch. 'King George VI was always remarkably well informed' . . . 'A conscientious, constitutional monarch is a strong element of stability and continuity in our Constitution.'

The talk attracted considerable attention in other parts of the press. As the *Manchester Guardian* said:

> it is also the first time that a former Prime Minister has talked in this unbuttoned fashion of how the job is best held down.

Attlee insisted on attending Churchill's funeral in 1965 but, in poor health himself, he had to sit on a chair on the steps of St Paul's as the coffin left. By the time of his death in October 1967, Attlee's stock had already begun to rise again. *The Guardian*'s obituary thought that:

> If he had not the touch of genius that belonged to Lloyd George or Churchill, or the intellectual power of Asquith, he had gifts that providentially matched the needs of his day ... He was a wise Prime Minister given to England at a moment when steady wisdom was needed rather than genius, which would not be genius if it were not sometimes erratic.[128]

His ashes were buried in Westminster Abbey.

Attlee left only £6,700, although his wife (whom he had expected to die before him) had left over £50,000 three years earlier. A will published on the same day as Attlee's was that of a much younger man, Brian Epstein, who left £266,000 – but he had managed the Beatles for six years.

His main memorial was the Attlee Foundation, based next to Toynbee Hall in the East End. Opened by the Queen in 1971, Attlee House was built from £500,000 raised by public subscription; India contributed extensively to its furnishing. The Foundation (of which I was a trustee for some years) aims to provide recreational facilities to young people, help the poor and disabled, fund prizes and scholarships and promote research in the social welfare field. When Attlee himself was told about the projected scheme, he commented: 'Quite.'

In 1983, the centenary of Attlee's birth was the occasion for further revision – upwards – of his reputation. Harold Macmillan wrote of him:

> The key to his authority perhaps lay in his absolute integrity and sincerity. He was a good man as well as a good politician.[129]

To this, a decade later, another Conservative Prime Minister-OM, Margaret Thatcher, was to add her tribute:

> I was an admirer of Clement Attlee. He was a serious man and a patriot. Contrary to the general tendency of politicians in the 1990s, he was all substance and no show ... Moreover, his was a genuinely radical and reforming government.[130]

The record of the Attlee government of 1945–51 is naturally under constant historical review. On the one hand, Peter Hennessy has written sympathetically of the period in books such as *Mr Attlee's Engine Room* (about the machinery of government of 'perhaps the most efficient' of post-war prime ministers). On the other hand, Corelli Barnett has strongly attacked the Attlee government of 1945–50, in *Lost Victory*, for giving the welfare state priority over industrial reconstruction and continuing to behave as though Britain were a first-class world power.

Attlee was the least flamboyant and yet one of the strongest political leaders of the twentieth century. He never worked on his 'image', although he enjoyed the way his reputation developed, even in his own lifetime. On Attlee's centenary, Roy Jenkins wrote that he had 'enjoyed being just a little of a caricature of himself'.[131] Peter Hennessy has described him as a 'Captain Mainwaring, in excelsis'. Yet he is still almost a 'household god' within the Labour Party.

Most observers would now think that the judgement of George VI, in conferring the Order of Merit so promptly on Clement Attlee when he left office, has been amply justified.

After a routine privy council on 21 November 1958, the Queen invested **Viscount Samuel**, aged 88, with the Order of Merit. It was 50 years to the day after he had joined her great-grandfather's council. Although he had been Leader of the Liberals in the Lords until 1955, he had been out of truly active politics for 20 years. He had last held office (briefly) 25 years earlier. He represented a vanished part of British politics – the high water mark of Liberalism in the early years of the century. He was a philosopher to boot. It all added up to honouring an aged man who had long ago had a peerage and two grand crosses and was moreover, by reason of his religion, ineligible for the Garter. *The Times* welcomed the award of the OM to a 'sage councillor' for his 'great services':

> It has been his fate as a resolute member of a party in decline to spend most of his public life in the political desert. But the desert rejoiced and blossomed as a rose . . . Though undoubtedly he is a party politician . . . he is not commonly reckoned as one. His principles are nurtured in philosophy, not politics. Like A. J. Balfour, he has managed in the course of a strenuous public life to keep a place for himself in the increasingly academic subject of philosophy.[132]

Herbert Samuel was born into a rich orthodox Jewish family, with origins in Poland. His father (who died when he was seven) and uncle (later Lord Swaythling) founded the banking firm of Samuel Montagu. He went to Balliol College, Oxford, in 1889 and left with a First in History. He was elected Visitor of his college in 1949. One memory he brought away from Oxford was of attending the ceremony at which H. M. Stanley had received an honorary doctorate and, in a moment of silence, a voice came from the gallery: '*Doctor* Stanley, I presume.'[133]

Like Attlee, Samuel undertook social and political work in the East End of London, where he was similarly shocked by the living conditions of the poor. It did not, as with Attlee, convert him from conservatism to socialism – he was a Liberal at Oxford and remained so – but the radical aspect of his politics was strengthened. He set out his views in 1902 in *Liberalism: its Principles and Proposals*, to which Asquith provided an introduction.

Meanwhile, Samuel's first attempts to enter the House of Commons had narrowly failed, in the elections of 1895 and 1900. In 1902, however, he won a by-election to the Yorkshire seat of Cleveland. The long period of Liberal government after 1905 ensured office for someone like Samuel. As Under-Secretary at the Home Office, he was largely responsible for the Children Act 1908, which introduced juvenile courts and the probation system and changed reformatory schools into 'borstals'. He extended the scope of workmen's compensation. When Asquith became Prime Minister in 1908, Samuel asked to continue his work at the Home Office but was made a privy counsellor.

Promotion did come the following year when Samuel became the first practising Jew to sit in a British cabinet, as Chancellor of the Duchy of Lancaster. Within a year, Samuel moved to become Postmaster-General, a post he retained for four years. During this period, Samuel played his part in helping to steer other government measures through the Commons:

> On one occasion in 1911, 'very flushed and unsteady in gait' [Asquith] flopped on to the front bench and went to sleep while two of his ministers, Herbert Samuel and Rufus Isaacs, defended the Welsh Church Bill – a scene which prompted Arthur Balfour, the Tory leader, to complain that the church's fate was 'in the hands of two Jews who are entirely sober and one Christian who is very patently drunk.'[134]

At the beginning of 1914, Samuel moved to be President of the Local Government Board. As with others, notably Lloyd George, it was the German invasion of Belgium that decided Samuel that it was right to go to war. When Asquith formed his coalition with the Conservatives in 1915, Samuel moved back to the Post Office but lost his seat in the Cabinet. He did regain it and, for the whole of 1916, was Home Secretary as well as being responsible for Irish affairs over the crucial period that included the Easter rebellion in Dublin and the arrest of Roger Casement after landing from a German submarine.

In the formation of a new coalition by Lloyd George in December 1916, Samuel could have stayed on as Home Secretary but he chose to go with Asquith. Declining a peerage, he sat on the backbenches until defeated by a supporter of the continuing coalition in the 1918 election.

Although Samuel was not a Zionist, he sympathised with their objectives. In 1920, he was asked by Lloyd George to be the first High Commissioner of Palestine, which had just become a British mandate. He hesitated but, after consulting Zionist leaders, accepted. It was not an easy five years for

Samuel. There were personal and political dangers. Although he faithfully pursued the official policy of aiming at a multi-national country, there were those who could never forget he was a Jew: Arabs, who thought he favoured his own race too much, and Jews, who considered he did not do enough for them. Samuel recorded his belief that a National Home for the Jews, as promised in the Balfour Declaration, did not mean 'subordination, possibly spoliation, for the Arabs'.

Perhaps it was Samuel's reputation in Cabinet that ruined his retirement plans. He wanted to stay in Palestine and study philosophy. His successor objected and so he decided to live in Italy. At the request, however, of Stanley Baldwin, the Prime Minister, he accepted the chairmanship of a royal commission on the coal industry. After a strenuous six months, its recommendations, such as removing the subsidy for the industry and reducing miners' wages, pleased neither the owners nor the workers. When the subsidy ended, the owners declared a lock-out and the TUC supported the miners by calling a general strike. Later in 1926, Samuel was made a GCB, having refused a peerage for the third time.

The events of 1925–26 drew Samuel back into politics. Following Asquith's retirement from the scene, Samuel agreed to co-operate with Lloyd George in trying to restore the Liberal fortunes. He narrowly managed to return to Parliament in the 1929 election. When the financial crisis came in 1931, Lloyd George was ill and it was Samuel, as acting leader of the Liberals, who was consulted by George V. Like Baldwin, the Conservative leader, he advised the formation of a 'national' government with the Labour leader, Ramsay MacDonald, continuing as Prime Minister. So it happened and Samuel became Home Secretary again but for only a year. After the ensuing election, which reduced and split the Liberals still further, the National Government proceeded in 1932 with the Ottawa agreements, including imperial preferences. The Liberal ministers stuck to their anti-protectionist principles and resigned; Samuel was never to hold office again. It may have been around the period of great difficulty for the Liberals in the 1930s that Samuel fell sufficiently foul of Lloyd George for the latter allegedly to remark: 'When he was circumcised, they threw away the wrong bit.'[135]

Samuel's defeat in the election of 1935 effectively ended his real political career. He recognised this by accepting a viscounty in the Coronation Honours of 1937. Increasingly, he devoted himself to philosophical studies and cultural pursuits. He produced books such as *Belief and Action* (1937) and *Creative Man*, mainly the text of his Romanes Lecture at Oxford in 1947:

> He believed that the future could be moulded by man's efforts, and conscious evolution could be accepted as the underlying principle of action. He called himself a 'meliorist', and believed that free will was the essential basis of ethical behaviour.[136]

Samuel collaborated with two other OMs, H. A. L. Fisher and Gilbert Murray, in production of a series, the *Home University Library*, and he was President of the British Institute of Philosophy. In 1951, he made the first party political broadcast on radio.

The publication of a biography in 1992 provided opportunities for reassessment of Samuel's character and contribution to British life. He did not fare particularly well. Much was made of the long antipathy between him and the stronger Lloyd George. One experienced commentator wrote:

> If he is remembered at all today, it is probably for leaving behind him a pile of reforming acts of parliament... never quite able to raise his eyes above the level of being a social engineer. He lacked the one attribute necessary to any successful radical politician, a sense of outrage.[137]

Herbert Samuel emerges, at this distance, as definitely worthy – but rather doubtfully worthy of the OM.

When the first Canadian Prime Minister-OM, Mackenzie King, left office in November 1948, the second, **Lester Pearson**, had been in his cabinet for just two months as Secretary of State for External Affairs. The OM for Pearson was announced on 28 May 1971 and he received it from the Queen on 8 June 1972, only six months before his death.

Almost exactly four years after the award, shortly after Pearson's death, the question of Pearson's OM was indirectly raised in the Canadian Parliament by John Diefenbaker, the former Conservative Prime Minister, who asked about the conferment of 'royal' honours on Canadians. Pierre Trudeau, Pearson's successor as Prime Minister, replied:

> only one such honour was accorded during the time I have been Prime Minister, namely, the one accorded to the Right Honourable Lester B. Pearson. I confirm... that I was informed of that in advance but not consulted.[138]

The award to Pearson was given pride of place in *The Times*, above the two announced with his, to Isaiah Berlin, the philosopher, and George Edwards, the aeronautical engineer. It was the 'OM for a pioneer of the United Nations' that caught the headlines. What was highlighted was that Pearson was

> the first Prime Minister who was not a war leader to receive the award, which has previously been given to such leaders as Lloyd George, Smuts, Churchill, Attlee and Mackenzie King. An interpretation of the award could therefore be that it is in recognition of his position as a world statesman and of his work for international organization as much as for the fact that he was Prime Minister of Canada.[139]

We also know authoritatively from Pearson himself that he had been flattered

> when Sir Michael [Adeane, Private Secretary to the Queen] told me that
> the Queen had come to consider me not only as a most experienced
> prime ministerial adviser, but as a close friend and valued friend.[140]

Lester Bowles Pearson, known as 'Mike', was the son of a Methodist minister in Ontario, whose family was predominantly Irish. After high schools, he went to the University of Toronto but, in 1915, when he was 18, he joined the Canadian Army Medical Corps and served in the ranks at a hospital in Salonika. Later, Pearson was commissioned and transferred to the Royal Flying Corps. After being hit in the blackout by a London bus, he was returned to Canada in 1918.

Pearson graduated in history from Toronto and, after false starts in business and law, he turned to an academic career. He spent two years on a Massey scholarship at St John's College, Oxford. After his return to Canada in 1923, he lectured for five years at his old university. In 1928, he changed course and passed first into the new Canadian diplomatic service. In 1935, he received the OBE during the short-lived revival of British honours for Canadians. That same year, he went to the High Commission in London and stayed for six years. Pearson's time in London ended during the blitz. After a brief spell in Ottawa, he went to Washington as minister-counsellor from 1942–45 and ambassador from 1945–46. At the end of the war, he was closely involved in the preparatory work for establishing the United Nations.

When Pearson went back to Ottawa, it was as Deputy Minister (or Permanent Secretary) to Louis St Laurent, the first separate Secretary of State for External Affairs after the post had been relinquished by the Prime Minister, Mackenzie King. When St Laurent succeeded Mackenzie King as Liberal Party leader and (later) Prime Minister, he offered his old post to Pearson.

Pearson's nine years as foreign minister were those of Canadian emergence as a 'middle power', anxious to exercise an influential role in world affairs. He became a notable player on the international scene. He was the first choice for Secretary-General of the newly established NATO. He felt, however, he owed it to St Laurent to stay in Canada. He represented Canada at the significant meeting of Prime Ministers in London to consider the Indian wish to become a republic but remain in the Commonwealth. He played a key role at and away from the table, which evolved the formula of 'Head of the Commonwealth'. During the meeting Pearson had tea with Princess Elizabeth and her family. He was able to make baby Prince Charles smile and thought

> [the Princess is] obviously conditioned to her job by long years of training, and very sincere in her desire to do well what she is destined to do. He [the Duke of Edinburgh] seems to be a high-spirited lad,

intelligent and attractive, but will no doubt settle down to the business of royalty.[141]

It was in the United Nations that Pearson shone most brightly. He was involved in negotiations over the future of Palestine and in the ending of the war in Korea. By a large majority, with only Soviet bloc votes against, he was elected President of the General Assembly in 1952 and made a reputation for cutting short interminable points of order. In 1953, the Soviet Union refused to accept him as Secretary-General of the UN, as they had done in 1945.

The Suez crisis in 1956 tested the loyalty of Canada to its two mother countries when they invaded Egypt. Pearson strove

> through the United Nations, to contain the damage. By a prodigious display of energy and patience, he succeeded in securing agreement on a cease-fire, the withdrawal of invading forces, and the dispatch to the area of a United Nations peace-keeping force. His efforts were recognised by the award of the Nobel Peace Prize in 1957.[142]

After the election of 1957 had ended 22 years of Liberal rule, St Laurent resigned as leader and Pearson was elected to succeed him. Unlike the new Prime Minister, John Diefenbaker, he was no campaigner. He performed badly as Leader of the Opposition and the Conservatives were soon able to go back to the electorate for an overall majority. The Liberals were in opposition from 1957–63. They won the elections of 1963 and 1965 but without achieving an overall majority. Under that disability, Pearson was Prime Minister from 1963–68. It was in the field of improving the balance between English and French Canada that he had what he considered to be his most important achievement. Against bitter opposition, Pearson was able to introduce a new national flag, which had neither the Union Jack (embodied in the old Red Ensign flag) nor the French fleur-de-lys.

It is appropriate to describe here how an OM had the opportunity to create an order; the only other Member to do so was Lloyd George in 1917 when the Orders of the British Empire and of the Companions of Honour were established. The germ of the idea for the Order of Canada came to Pearson in June 1943. Along with many other Canadians, he was surprised at a list of honours published in Ottawa. Pearson noticed one richly deserved award to a colleague in Washington and another not so worthy. He made a point of noting:

> This is the sort of thing that makes a joke of Honours Lists. There is another defect in the list. Owing to the decision, a right one, not to permit titles, only junior decorations are available for those Canadians on the

list who, if they were in England, would have received the most senior ones... The only way to avoid this is to establish our own Canadian Order.[143]

He could scarcely have imagined that one day he would be able to implement his idea. So, as Prime Minister, he brought the proposal to his Cabinet. They agreed there ought to be a federal system, including an Order of Canada. In April 1967, Pearson was able to announce the establishment of such a system:

> ...as a means of recognizing merit, gallantry, and distinguished public service. As I told the House, 'I believe that recognition of this kind can strengthen national pride and the appreciation of national service.'[144]

The centenary of Canadian confederation as the first British dominion was celebrated in 1967. Among the events was an EXPO in Montreal and visits by the Queen and General de Gaulle. The first recalled a visit by Her Majesty in 1964, which had also included Quebec. On that occasion, there were security fears that prompted Pearson to suggest he might ride with her and

> even throw my body in front of her, if necessary. In fact, I became quite fascinated by a Walter Mitty phantasy of thus assuring my place in history. But the managers would have none of it, and the Queen preferred Prince Philip as a travelling companion in danger.

In 1968, Pearson retired and left Parliament. He was active in his short retirement, chairing a World Bank commission on development problems and giving the BBC Reith lectures on 'Peace in the Family of Man'. Before his death in December 1972, he had finished the first volume of his memoirs and left enough material for the other two to be completed by others. He would have been proud that, since 1996, there has been a Lester B. Pearson Professor of International Relations at Oxford.

The next political figure to receive the Order of Merit, on 2 April 1976, was **Harold Macmillan**, who delighted to dispense honours but was reluctant to take them himself. During nearly seven years as Prime Minister, from 1957–63, he had been every bit as lavish with honours as many of his predecessors:

> I rather enjoy patronage. I take a lot of trouble over it. At least it makes all those years of reading Trollope worthwhile.[145]

According to his intimate friend, Eileen O'Casey (widow of Sean, the playwright), she was instrumental in dissuading Macmillan from succumbing to a title:

> On one occasion she recalled being at a lunch when Lord Home had tried
> to persuade Macmillan to accept a peerage . . . Harold turned to me and
> said, 'What about that, Eileen?' I told him I thought it nicer to keep
> the name Harold Macmillan to the end of his days and said, 'Titles are
> two-a-penny these days. Butchers and Bakers and Candlestickmakers
> are all getting them . . . ' I got the impression that Alex Home was a bit
> annoyed with me . . . [146]

The confirmation (by Buckingham Palace) of his refusal appeared in the press
in April 1964:

> Mr Macmillan . . . has been asked by the Queen to accept an earldom and
> a Knighthood of the Order of the Garter . . . He has begged the Queen
> that he may be allowed to decline both offers . . . [147]

It was some years before Macmillan did comment on his refusal to take a
peerage, in answer to questions in an American TV interview:

> I was 40 years in the House of Commons. A lot of people go into a
> mausoleum, but there's no need to go in prematurely.[148]

Interviewed in 1973, shortly before the publication of the last volume of
his memoirs, Macmillan said:

> It's one thing being the 14th earl, quite another being the first. When
> the curtain falls on the last performance, it is more artistic to withdraw.
> *E finita la commedia.*[149]

As to the Garter, Macmillan's letter to the Queen in March 1964, 'implied
that he felt it should be awarded only for service in a period of national crisis
(as per Churchill).'[150]

Earldom and Garter put to one side, Macmillan was clear what he *did*
want:

> The only honour that appealed to me was the OM, which remains the
> Sovereign's personal gift.[151]

Macmillan's official biographer commented that the OM was 'the one honour
he ever truly coveted'[152] and 'he always prized [it] above all other distinctions'.[153] Not surprisingly, the 13-year delay in his receiving the Order led
to suggestions that the Queen had kept him waiting because of pique over
his having refused the Garter, which had been good enough for Churchill.

The biographer states that this is not corroborated by the Royal Archives. Nevertheless, his relieved response when he eventually received the OM was:

Thank you, ma'am, for making an o̲ld m̲an happy.[154]

Macmillan's appointment, on 2 April 1976, was reported by the broadsheets on their front pages. The *Daily Telegraph* noted that 'the coveted award' had been made to only four other British prime ministers; it concluded that he 'surely deserves the OM as our most stylish Prime Minister since Palmerston'.[155]

On his ninetieth birthday (10 February 1984), Macmillan accepted an earldom. This eventual change of mind was explained by his biographer, Alistair Horne:

Perhaps the most compelling reason of all was that he felt he still had important things to say and he needed a more prominent platform than the common rooms of Oxford [of which he was Chancellor] from which to say them.[156]

When it came to Macmillan's titles, Bromley, which had rescued him from the political wilderness after his defeat in 1945 and which he represented for 18 unbroken years, might have hoped to share in his honour but it was overlooked, even as a second title. Instead, he chose his first political love, Stockton, which elected him thrice but rejected him twice and which he represented for two periods totalling only the same length of time. The Labour mayor said the town would be quite honoured but 'half the people are more concerned with unemployment than earldoms'.[157] Not much had changed in Stockton in half a century.

(Maurice) Harold Macmillan came from a Scottish crofting family, as he was fond of emphasising as he grew older. In fact, it was his great-grandfather who was a crofter and his grandfather who left Scotland and founded the successful eponymous publishing firm. Harold himself was born in Belgravia and went to Eton and Balliol College, Oxford, before serving in the Grenadier Guards in the First World War. Like Churchill, he had an obsessive American mother, who was highly ambitious for him. At Oxford, he gained a First in classical moderations and was active in the Union. He remembered the visit to Oxford of Lloyd George: 'A tremendously dynamic figure', who was later to be the hero of *The Past Masters* (1975), in which Macmillan reflected on policies and politicians between 1906 and 1939.

Macmillan was 20 when war broke out and he went to France the following year. Like many others, he was affected both physically and mentally. He was wounded three times and emerged with a limp handshake, a shuffling walk and sporadic pain. He gained a strong sympathy for the working-class men he commanded. He would sometimes carry his affinity with the working class to laughable limits. When a Labour MP boasted that he was a miner's son, Macmillan responded: 'Yes, so was I – until he sold the mine.'

Although Macmillan was able to join the publishing firm after the war, his mother arranged for him to become ADC to the Governor-General of Canada, the Duke of Devonshire. He married the Duke's daughter, Lady Dorothy Cavendish, whose mother had intended to marry her off to another duke. The ceremony at St Margaret's, Westminster, had a bride's side filled with the Cavendishes' royal and aristocratic friends, while the groom's side had many authors published by Macmillan, including six OMs. John Morley whispered loudly:

Which weighs most, three OMs or one duke?[158]

Encouraged again by his mother, Macmillan embarked on a political career and, because the Liberals were on their way out, he opted for the Conservatives. He was elected as MP for Stockton-on-Tees in 1924 but made little impression on the House of Commons and lost his seat in 1929.

After a serious nervous breakdown, Macmillan regained the Stockton seat in 1931 and retained it in 1935. He was significantly on the left wing of the Conservatives and wrote *The Middle Way* in 1938. Attlee said: 'He demanded proper treatment for the unemployed in the thirties; didn't make him popular with his party.'[159] On foreign affairs, he opposed appeasement and resigned the party whip for a year when the sanctions against Mussolini's Italy were lifted.

The advent of Churchill to the premiership in 1940 brought Macmillan into office for the first time. He was Parliamentary Under-Secretary in the Ministry of Supply and for a few months in 1942 he had the junior ministerial post in the Colonial Office. He was also made a privy counsellor, an unusual honour for such a new junior minister.

Macmillan's great opportunity, which he seized successfully, was appointment as Minister Resident (with cabinet rank) at Allied Headquarters in Algiers. In his dealings with Eisenhower and the French authorities, he was helped by his American ancestry and fluent French, a language his mother knew and had insisted on his learning. When he was badly burned in an air crash, he was irritated by a hatless French admiral bemoaning: 'J'ai perdu ma casquette.' Macmillan snapped: 'I've perdued my bloody face, so shut up!'[160]

In May 1945, Macmillan returned to Britain and was briefly Secretary of State for Air in Churchill's caretaker government. In the election, however, he was defeated in Stockton. When the member for the safe seat in my home town, Bromley, died soon after the election, Macmillan was elected in his place. During the six years of opposition, he divided his time between the front bench and his publishing interests. His views remained what some of his colleagues regarded as 'neo-socialist'.

A domestic political challenge came in 1951, when Macmillan reluctantly accepted Churchill's invitation to be Minister of Housing and Local Government. The Conservatives had committed themselves, rashly many thought, to building 300,000 houses a year: 50 per cent more than the Labour Government had achieved. Macmillan achieved it in 1953, with great help from (among others) Ernest Marples, his junior minister. Later, he said: 'Marples made me PM: I was never heard of before housing.'[161]

Macmillan was moved on, in quick succession, to three senior ministerial posts in 1954–56. At Defence, he had the aged Churchill breathing down his neck. At the Foreign Office, he had Churchill's successor (Eden) doing likewise. At the Treasury, Eden could also not let him alone and his one budget is remembered only for the introduction of premium bonds.

The Suez affair in 1956 was described by Macmillan himself as 'a very bad episode in my life'. At first in favour of the enterprise, he helped to mislead Eden into believing that Eisenhower would support British military action and he failed to amass reserves against the ensuing run on the pound. In a state of panic, he argued for withdrawal from Egypt. Harold Wilson accused him of being 'First in, First out'.[162] He later told his biographer, Alastair Horne, that, at Eden's request, he had destroyed the pages of his diary dealing with the final stages of the crisis.[163]

Nevertheless, the episode turned to his advantage when, on Eden's resignation in January 1957, he emerged as his successor. He supposedly told the Queen he might last for only six weeks. In fact, he was Prime Minister for well over six years. The odds looked stacked against him but, in just over two years, his confidence won back the electorate and in the election of 1959, he doubled the Conservative majority.

Macmillan's economic policy owed a good deal to his 'middle way' philosophy. He was horrified, however, by the doubling of unemployment. Overseas, he fared better. He realistically accelerated the withdrawal from empire and famously used, even if he did not write, the phrase 'wind of change' to denote particularly the transition to black rule in Africa.

Macmillan fostered furiously the British relationship with the US, using his own American ancestry and playing son to Eisenhower and father to Kennedy. Macmillan had been able to recover the old agreement on Anglo–American nuclear collaboration, play a major part in negotiating the Atmospheric Test Ban Treaty with the USSR and, in December 1962, he acquired the American Polaris missile. The Polaris agreement precipitated the veto by de Gaulle in January 1963 of the British application to join the European Economic Community. Macmillan wrote in his diary: 'All our policies at home and abroad are ruined.'[164]

The security scandals of an Admiralty clerk (Vassall) and of the Secretary of State for War (John Profumo) in 1962–63 badly shook both Macmillan personally, who appeared to be out of touch, and his government. 'Never glad confident morning again': Nigel Birch's quote from Browning's *The*

Lost Leader hit home and was long-remembered. Perhaps it was the memory of that time which led Macmillan to tell a questioner later that what did for governments was 'Events, dear boy, events'. Nevertheless, Macmillan might have weathered the political storms and survived had he not, to his everlasting regret, misread his own health (believing a prostate condition to be malignant) and panicked himself into resignation in October 1963. (He lived for another 23 years.)

Macmillan's laid-back manner in office was not entirely a pose. When a visitor suggested that the Prime Minister might be too busy to see him, Macmillan's Private Secretary responded:

Busy! He isn't busy. He is sitting in there doing *The Times* crossword.[165]

In retirement, Macmillan laboured for eight years to produce six volumes of memoirs: two-and-a-quarter million words in all. As his son told Enoch Powell, however: 'Sensitive matter was deliberately censored out.'[166] In lighter style were his subsequent *The Past Masters* and *War Diaries*. He took great delight in the Chancellorship of Oxford University, to which he had been elected while Prime Minister, narrowly defeating Oliver Franks, whom he later also narrowly beat to the OM – by a year.

Macmillan's last speech was to the Tory Reform Group in November 1986, only a month before his death: 'Selling the family silver', even if not strictly accurate, was a telling phrase, not much to the liking of the Thatcher government, against whose policy of privatisation it was directed.

A few weeks short of 93 on his death at the end of 1986, Macmillan had lived longer than any other Prime Minister, although Callaghan was to capture that record later.

Harold Macmillan waited 13 years after giving up the premiership before he received the Order of Merit. **Margaret Thatcher** waited nine days, one day less than Clement Attlee, with whose appointment hers must obviously be compared. Both headed radical governments whose policies changed Britain. After their administrations, the clock could never be completely put back.

After 11.5 years as Prime Minister and winning a record three general elections (and one war), she had lost the confidence of the Conservative MPs, although almost certainly not of the party in the country. Those close to Margaret Thatcher knew that, in the aftermath of her downfall, the special royal distinction of the OM would do something to lift her spirits. The suggestion was favourably received at the Palace. Apart from being the first British woman Prime Minister, Margaret Thatcher had held the office longer than anyone since the Reform Act of 1832. Although resigning as Prime Minister, she was not yet ready to resign from the Commons and go to the Lords. That transition was to come two years later, when she did not stand in the general election of 1992.

Both in anticipation of the award and after it had actually been announced, the press appreciated that the OM would, 'place her among the world's elite' and 'place her name alongside that of her hero Sir Winston Churchill and dozens of renowned figures who have dominated the social, cultural and scientific history of the 20th century.' It was 'a recognition that outranks all others in Britain' and 'the highest accolade for achievement [the Queen] can offer' and so on. The Palace was quoted as saying that:

> The conferment of such an exclusive and prized award on Mrs Thatcher was in recognition of her outstanding service as prime minister for more than 11 years.

The Garter – the perquisite of every prime minister – came to Margaret Thatcher in 1995. Non-royal women had been eligible for it only since 1987.

Margaret Hilda Roberts was born in Grantham, Lincolnshire. Her father was a prominent grocer, a lay Methodist preacher, an alderman and mayor of the town. His influence is one she has constantly acknowledged and it helped to imbue in her the self-confidence for which she became so notable. From her local high school, she went to Somerville College, Oxford, during the Second World War to read chemistry, in which she also took a second degree. Her tutor was a woman she was later to join in the Order of Merit: the Nobel laureate, Dorothy Hodgkin. She began a career as a research chemist in industry and was the first Prime Minister to have had a scientific training and career.

Margaret Thatcher quickly determined on a political career but was defeated twice in the safe Labour seat of Dartford. Marriage to an older businessman of means, Denis Thatcher, in 1951, gave her financial security. She was enabled to study for the Bar, to which she was called in 1954, and to engage help with the care of her twin children.

She entered the Commons at the age of 33, in 1959 as the member for Finchley, a seat she retained until her retirement 33 years later. Her potential was quickly recognised and, after only two years, Macmillan appointed her to a junior ministerial post in the Ministry of Pensions and National Insurance. After eight years in Parliament, Thatcher was in the shadow cabinet and, on the Conservative victory in 1970, Edward Heath made her Secretary of State for Education and Science, a post she held for the four years of that government. It was the only cabinet post she was to hold before becoming Prime Minister.

In the inevitable post-mortem after the two Conservative electoral defeats in 1974, she emerged the following year – from the position of Shadow Chancellor – to become the unexpected successor to Edward Heath as Leader of the Party and, consequently, as Leader of the Opposition. The Conservatives won the 1979 election with a majority of 43. They were to stay in power for 18 years. The record of Margaret Thatcher's political leadership throughout the 1980s is too recent to require much reiteration. Few people were neutral. Her 'not for turning' brand of conviction politics ensured that she was worshipped or vilified by most people. The worshippers of 'The Blessed Margaret' came up against those to whom she was 'Attila the Hen', 'Pétain in Petticoats' and 'The Immaculate Misconception'. One particular jibe came most frequently from Tories who thought she had deprived them of their divine right to rule the party and, indeed, the country. To them, she was the 'grocer's daughter'. One grandee supposedly likened the party to 'a cavalry regiment led by a corporal in the Women's Royal Army Corps'. She was the first British Prime Minister to give birth – either naturally, to children, or politically, to an 'ism'. In 1985, she said that the 'Thatcherism' derided by her opponents would come to be seen as a compliment.

In her first government, from 1979–83, she embarked on curbing inflation, with a steep rise in unemployment and a reduction in manufacturing industry. The successful Falklands conflict of 1982, in which her political reputation was obviously at stake, ensured her re-election in 1983, with a greatly increased majority. Her second government, from 1983–87, was a time of right-wing consolidation, of rolling back the frontiers of the state and emphasising the market economy with a programme of considerable privatisation in fields such as airlines and telecommunications. The power of the trade unions was severely limited by legislation.

By the end of Margaret Thatcher's second term in office, her intransigence and authoritarian attitude was beginning to tell on her colleagues. Nevertheless, she achieved a record third term in 1987, with a majority of still over 100. She was not to survive until the end of that term, although in 1988 she surpassed Asquith's record time for a twentieth-century premiership.

In international affairs, she formed a close but frank relationship with President Ronald Reagan, whose discreet help in the Falklands conflict in 1983 was repaid with agreement for British air bases to be used for an attack on Libya in 1986. She famously described Mikhail Gorbachev as 'a man I could do business with'. The collapse of Communism was very much to her liking but one of its immediate consequences – the reunification of Germany – was not. It was said that she loved Germany so much, she thought there should be two of them. Francois Mitterand, who was French President for most of her period in office, spoke of her as having 'the eyes of Caligula but the mouth of Marilyn Monroe'.[167]

There was frequent speculation about a new phenomenon in British politics: the relationship between a female head of state and a female head of government. According to a recent account, Margaret Thatcher was adamant that their common gender was irrelevant:

> The Queen was the monarch and it happens that she was a perfect lady. I was a prime minister, it happened that I was a woman. But it was the monarch talking to the Prime Minister, and therefore it was the

same constitutional relationship as any monarch talking to any prime minister.[168]

It was on Thatcher's tenth anniversary in office that Roy Jenkins, the politician who was to follow her into the Order of Merit, wrote that she resembled an earlier Member, Lloyd George

> in having captured the establishment without herself being captured by it, in having a restless innovative capacity and in her ability to dominate even her senior ministers.[169]

Such senior ministers could not, however, be dominated forever. Not many Prime Ministers could survive the resignations, on questions of policy, of a Chancellor of the Exchequer (Nigel Lawson) and a Deputy Prime Minister (Geoffrey Howe), who had been both Chancellor and Foreign Secretary. Margaret Thatcher was no exception. Her leadership was quickly challenged and after only narrowly defeating Michael Heseltine (who had returned with a vengeance) in the first round of the contest, she withdrew – and resigned as Prime Minister. She was succeeded by her preferred candidate, John Major.

In retirement, she turned not to the city directorships favoured by most of her male Conservative colleagues but to the even more lucrative lecture circuit, particularly in the US. She also launched the Thatcher Foundation to promote the ideals of democracy and free enterprise, especially in post-Communist Eastern Europe, where she is still better known than any of her countrymen. One of the few offices she accepted was that of Chancellor of the University of Buckingham.

She wrote her memoirs about *The Downing Street Years 1979–90* in 1993, followed by an account of her earlier life, *The Path to Power*, in 1995. In 2002, there appeared *Statecraft: Strategies for a Changing World*, the blurb for which described her as playing 'a continuing role in British political affairs'. She is one of the few retired politicians who can still command the front pages of the newspapers – and not just by dying. For much of the 1990s, she showed that there was little sign of the 'Iron Lady' going rusty.

Minor strokes have recently limited Margaret Thatcher's activities, with doctors even trying to stop her making speeches. Denis Thatcher had the last word on that:

> You can't have been paying attention for the past 30 years.

Roy Jenkins was another recent British political figure to be appointed to the Order of Merit – on 6 December 1993. It is reasonable to assume, however, that he did not secure the honour on grounds of politics alone, as one of the small group of 'best Prime Ministers we never had'. On that score, he would probably have been recruited to the Order of the Garter, as was R. A. Butler. It was the literary dimension to his life that, like Bryce Balfour and Samuel, brought Jenkins within the ambit of the more intellectual order. Moreover, he was Chancellor of the University of Oxford, whose two predecessors, Macmillan and Halifax, had been OMs. The various facets of his notable career seemed to add up to the Order.

It was certainly an order for which the new recipient had great regard. In his autobiography, Jenkins scrupulously appended 'OM' to those Members to whom he referred, such as Zuckerman, Berlin and Dorothy Hodgkin; he carefully included the last two among the Oxford figures on whom he conferred honorary degrees after becoming Chancellor of the University.

After receiving the honour himself, Jenkins used it to try (unsuccessfully) to persuade John Mortimer to yield pride of speaking place at a literary lunch:

> 'When you are an OM and chancellor of Oxford University, you will be able to speak last ... but till that time comes, I claim the wight' ... [and later Mortimer is] left with the vague feeling that I have shown some sort of disrespect for Oxford, the Privy Council and the Order of Merit.[170]

Roy Harris Jenkins came from the 'purple' of the Labour Party. He was the only child of a South Wales miner who moved away from the pit, being ambitious for himself and his son. After a spell in prison during a miners' lock-out (an occurrence hidden from the son for many years), Arthur Jenkins became a JP, councillor and Labour MP. He was Parliamentary Private Secretary to Clement Attlee during the Second World War and a junior minister in the Labour government until his death in 1946. The young Roy remembered being 'brought up to be the son of a leader of the local community, part of a family that was looked up to.'

Arthur's ambitions for his son were realised when Roy went from his local secondary school to Balliol College, Oxford, where he obtained a First in Philosophy, Politics and Economics. From Oxford he went into the Army in 1942, serving in the artillery and in intelligence – at the Bletchley Park decoding centre. It was there that he began the reading of what he called the 'tombstone' political biographies, including those by OMs he was to emulate, such as John Morley and G. M. Trevelyan:

> I read all day, apart from getting up for a few minutes every one and a half hours or so and playing a ball game with arcane rules of my own devising against a wall of my solitary room.[171]

In 1945, Jenkins married Jennifer Parker, the daughter of a distinguished public servant. Having failed, even in the Labour landslide of 1945, to secure a seat, Roy Jenkins entered Parliament at a by-election in 1948. After the prospect of office disappeared with the defeat of Labour in 1951, he turned to writing and journalism. During the 13 years of Labour opposition, he was a conscientious but, to use his own words, 'semi-detached' MP; nevertheless, he chaired the Fabian Society for a year.

In 1948, Roy Jenkins had attempted the impossible – a biography, albeit 'interim', of a living man, who was to boot Prime Minister at the time: Attlee. In the long years of opposition, he went on to more substantial work, which laid the foundations of his literary reputation. In 1954, there was *Mr Balfour's Poodle*, an account of the 1909–11 constitutional crisis over the House of Lords; in 1958, *Sir Charles Dilke: A Victorian Tragedy*; and in 1964, *Asquith*, the success of which enabled him to buy a country home in which to expand his life.

When Labour returned to power in 1964, Jenkins became Minister of Aviation, outside the Cabinet. In 1965, he became Home Secretary. He is one of the few politicians to have enhanced his reputation at the Home Office. He introduced the parole board and majority verdicts in criminal trials and supported private members' legislation to legalise abortion and homosexual relations between consenting adults.

On the reshuffle that followed the devaluation of the pound in 1967, Roy Jenkins changed places with James Callaghan and became Chancellor of the Exchequer. He raised taxes and cut public expenditure and by 1970 the economy had improved. Nevertheless, to some surprise, Labour lost the election that year, after which he was elected its Deputy Leader. After five years as a successful senior minister, his stock stood high and he probably never stood closer to the premier post.

The European issue now emerged again on the British political scene. As a convinced European, Roy Jenkins found difficulty in following the Labour Party line of opposing entry into the European Economic Community. After defying that line in a crucial vote in 1971, he resigned as Deputy Leader in the following year in protest against the party's equivocation on the European issue. Nevertheless, he returned to government in 1974 as Home Secretary for an uneventful second term.

Jenkins' poor showing in the 1976 Labour leadership and subsequent failure to secure the Foreign Office in the Callaghan government decided him to go to Brussels as the first (and, so far, only) British President of the European Commission. He was later to write an account of this period in *European Diary 1977–81* (1989).

For a man so apparently rooted in the past, it is surprising that Jenkins was forward-looking enough to take the lead in founding a new political party, designed to 'break the mould' of British politics. He was still in his European post when he began the move towards the foundation of the Social

Democratic Party. On returning from Brussels in 1981, he joined three other leading Labour dissidents – Shirley Williams, David Owen and William Rodgers – to issue the *Limehouse Declaration*, the foundation document of the new SDP. The best known of the Gang of Four, he made (unsuccessfully) the first SDP attempt to enter Parliament, in 1981. At a by-election in the Hillhead division of Glasgow in 1982, he succeeded and held the seat for five years. In the same year, he became the first Leader of the SDP. In coalition with the Liberals, the two parties won 25 per cent of the votes in the 1983 election. The mould of British politics had been seriously fractured, if not actually broken. Under threat from Owen, Jenkins resigned the leadership of the SDP after the election and, despite illness, found time to publish two more political biographies: of Truman (1986) and Baldwin (1987). In the 1987 election, he was defeated and subsequently accepted a life peerage.

Jenkins never disguised his love of good wine, especially claret, nor did he artificially disdain aristocratic company. His difficulty in pronouncing the letter 'r' ('sort of semi-physical deficiency' he called it) was deemed to be another of 'Woy's' aristocratic traits. His mannered speech, especially after becoming Chancellor of Oxford, led increasingly to his being called a 'grandee'. He was eminently 'clubbable' and belonged to six, ranging from the learned Athenaeum to the socially selective Pratt's. It was at Brooks's that there was a dinner to celebrate his OM.

Jenkins' almost obsessive fascination with keeping lists – how many words he wrote, how many minutes he walked – intrigued those around him. One of his former civil servants says he was the only minister he worked for who knew exactly how long it took for the main traffic lights to change in every major city in Britain.[172]

Roy Jenkins led the (now united) Liberal Democrats in the House of Lords from 1987–97. While combining that with the Oxford Chancellorship and an active social life, he embarked (in his seventies) on a notable writing period. His autobiography, *A Life at the Centre*, appeared in 1991. It was after receiving the OM that he wrote two of his most substantial historical works: biographies of two great British Prime Ministers – Gladstone (1995) and Churchill (2001).

The Chancellors (1998) obviously benefited from being written by a former holder of the office. Jenkins' personal experience was also deployed in 2002 in *Twelve Cities*, those in Britain, continental Europe and America which had been significant in his life and which had pleasing architecture and interesting history. Appropriately, he was President of the Royal Society of Literature from 1988.

In maturity, Jenkins became what was often described as a mentor to the 'New Labour' government of 1997, particularly of Tony Blair himself, whom he described in 1994 as 'the most exciting Labour choice since Gaitskell in 1955'.[173] He provided the new leader with a first-hand background of the

Labour Party – and its problems – of the previous 50 years. His actual influence, however, is perhaps more doubtful. The report of the Commission on Electoral Reform in 1998 came to nothing, although he left a proportional voting system for the election of his successor as Chancellor of Oxford University. The reform of the House of Lords has been less speedy and radical than he might have hoped.

Lord Jenkins of Hillhead died on 5 January 2003.

The administrators

Many of the political figures were household names in their day and some remain so. Most of the administrators, however, have never been well known, even at the height of their activity. Their renown has been within their own spheres and occasionally, for a time, further afield. An obvious exception is Prince Philip, but is he an 'administrator'? Not in the ordinary sense of the word but nor are some others in this somewhat artificial category. 'Public servant' could be an equally suitable label for those who, outside the scientific, artistic and humanitarian fields, have rendered 'exceptional service' to the democratic societies in which they lived.

The 11 men described in this section divide into six in the civil service (home, colonial or diplomatic): Cromer, Cadogan, Hailey, Waverley, MacDonald and Franks; two judges: Dixon and Denning; and Prince Philip, not only consort and helpmeet of the Sovereign of the Order of Merit but also a major contributor in his own right to the life of the nation. Also included in this category are recent inductees Prince Charles and Lord Rothschild.

The appointment of **Evelyn Baring, the First Earl of Cromer** to the Order on 29 June 1906 broke new ground and he can be reckoned as the first recipient 'for public service', which was not then provided for in the Statutes. The background to the appointment is set out in the biography of the man who suggested it, the First Lord Hardinge of Penshurst. Hardinge, although a civil servant as Permanent Under-Secretary of the Foreign Office, attended Edward VII as 'Minister in Attendance' on a cruise of the Mediterranean. The Khedive of Egypt knew that the King did not like Cromer (because of alleged discourtesy to him when Prince of Wales) and hoped for the recall of the 'grand' governor. Hardinge impressed on the King 'the absolute necessity of supporting Lord Cromer at all costs' and said that a letter to Cromer expressing the King's confidence would not suffice because the Khedive would not see it. It was therefore

> absolutely necessary to show to him a signal mark of favour which would convince the Khedive of the futility of his efforts to get rid of him and I suggested that he should bestow upon him the Order of Merit, remarking that Lord Cromer would not be the least worthy of those already enjoying that honour. The King at first objected that the order

47 Earl of Cromer.

had been given only to soldiers, sailors, and people of literary or artistic merit. To which I replied that it would be very invidious to exclude the Diplomatic Service from the possibility of receiving this high decoration. The King agreed and finally accepted the idea in a very kindly manner, and the Order of Merit was shortly bestowed on Lord Cromer.[174]

Evelyn Baring, son of an MP from the banking family, had started in the army with a posting to the (then British) Ionian Islands, where he acquired a deeper knowledge of Greek, an acquaintance with diplomacy (as ADC to the High Commissioner) and a wife. At the age of 30, however, he decided on a civil rather than military career when he accepted an offer in 1872 to accompany his cousin, the new Viceroy (Lord Northbrook) to India, as his private secretary.

Shortly after returning from India, Baring was chosen to be the British commissioner to oversee the finances of Egypt, following the extravagances of Khedive Ismail. After a couple of years, when the creditor foreign powers did not intervene to support him, he resigned, but was persuaded to return as controller with increased authority. His reputation in both India and Egypt took him back to India as Finance Member of the Viceroy's Council in 1880.

Meanwhile, Egypt had erupted. Someone was needed to take over the civil administration. Cromer was sent there and remained for the next 24 years. He dominated everyone in Egypt and

> his own personal authority, backed by the small army of occupation, was the one effective power in the country ... 'I had not to govern Egypt but to assist in the government [by the Khedive] without the appearance of doing so and without any legitimate authority over the agents with whom I had to deal.'[175]

Baring enjoyed the unassuming title of Agent and Consul-General in Egypt, which was (formally) within the Ottoman rather than the British Empire. His task was to safeguard the British investment in the Suez Canal, the newly-forged route to India, the Jewel of the British Empire. He was amply rewarded for his services: a barony in 1892, a viscounty in 1899 and an earldom (the Prime Minister's Prize) in 1901, quite apart from a GCB and a GCMG.

Early in life, Baring had acquired nicknames which played on his name, such as 'Overbaring' or 'Le Grand Ours' [bear] and this side of his nature was later highlighted by *The Times* when it compared the new President 'Teddy' Roosevelt of 1901 with the 'Evelyn Baring of 1882':

> both are of Dutch origin, the one of British and aristocratic or Whiggish growth, the other though equally well-born, of American and demo-cratic growth; the one of official development, the other of free national development; and making allowances for these differences (no one ever called Lord Cromer 'Teddy'), you see the same type.[176]

By the time of his appointment as an OM, Cromer was tired and in ill health:

> The King suggested the bestowal of the Garter ... but Cromer, who already had half a dozen Orders, expressed a preference for a grant of money, in which the King concurred. The government now suggested a sum of £50,000 and the King's comment ran: 'The government had better settle the matter. They know my views.' Two months later the gov-ernment did 'settle the matter' in accordance with the King's somewhat uncompromising hint.[177]

One of the causes to which the new OM devoted his energies in retirement was the Anti-Suffrage League. Cromer also wrote *Modern Egypt* and *Ancient and Modern Imperialism*. His last public service was to chair the commission of enquiry into the Dardanelles campaign. He died in January 1917, before it completed its deliberations. The memorial plaque to him in Westminster Abbey is inscribed 'Regenerator of Egypt'.

Forty years after Cromer's appointment, the next 'administrator' was offered and accepted the Order of Merit but he died before the award could be announced or the insignia bestowed. He was **John Maynard Keynes**, a key figure in the Treasury from 1915–19, for which he was made a CB. He resigned in 1919 from his post as the principal Treasury representative at the Peace Conference in protest at its provisions and set out his views in *The Economic Consequences of the Peace*. Between the wars, he was a fellow of King's College, Cambridge, and, as its bursar, he made a lot of money for it and himself. He explained his revolutionary theories for public investment in time of recession in books such as *The General Theory of Employment, Interest and Money* (1936) and the word 'Keynesian' entered the language.

Keynes' activities extended beyond economics. A member of the Blooms-bury set, he had always had a great interest in the arts and was married to Lydia Lopokova, the noted ballerina from Diaghilev's Ballet Russe. In addition to being Chairman of CEMA (the Council for the Encouragement of Music and the Arts, the forerunner of the British Council), Keynes was also Chairman of Covent Garden.

On 3 April 1946, the King approved Keynes' appointment to the Order of Merit, to be announced in the Birthday Honours. He responded that he 'could not have received a more honourable or agreeable proposal'.[178] Two weeks later, Keynes died of a heart attack, aged 62. A day or so afterwards, the Palace asked Louis Wulff (the Court Correspondent of the Press Association) to: 'let it be known unofficially that the King offered Lord Keynes the OM a few weeks before he died and that he accepted it.'[179] This seems to me to have been an unimaginative and bureaucratic response to the death of someone who was clearly intended to be a Member of the Order. If it had been a knighthood, which the King had formally approved, it would have been announced in the List, with a note of the date of death. A recipient's membership of the Order should be deemed to be effective from the time he or she accepts the Sovereign's offer and, if death intervenes, the appointment should be announced as being effective from the date of acceptance.

In the lists which I have kept of OMs, Keynes has always figured as Number 85A, after Alanbrooke and Cunningham. Since, however, I must abide by the rules as they are and not as I think they should be, he does not appear in the List of Members (Appendix C), although that is where he rightly belongs.

Towards the end of 1950, over 30 years after the death of the Earl of Cromer, the Order of Merit was again offered to a civil servant. Although

Alexander Cadogan was not an earl himself, he was the son of one (who was Viceroy of Ireland) and both his mother and wife were daughters of earls. Cadogan had recently retired from being the first British Permanent Representative to the United Nations, before which he had been Permanent Under-Secretary of State at the Foreign Office from 1938–46. No Cabinet Minister or Chief of Staff served before, throughout and after the Second World War. Cadogan's response to the choice put before him in 1950 by the King's Private Secretary was quite clear:

> I am very proud that the King should wish so to reward my services . . . A Peerage would be a special mark of honour, but if, as an alternative, I am offered the Order of Merit, I should choose the latter. That it is conferred by the King on his own initiative seems to me to give it all more value.[180]

Eden, the wartime Foreign Secretary, wrote:

> This is indeed splendid news. The most gratifying of all honours, and in every way appropriate.

'Alec' Cadogan's career had followed a traditional route. From Eton he went to Balliol College, Oxford, where he was disappointed to gain only a Second in history. After two years studying languages, he passed top into the Diplomatic Service in 1908. His first two postings were to Constantinople and Vienna. He did not serve abroad again for 20 years and for ten of those (1923–33), he headed the League of Nations section of the Foreign Office. While still a First Secretary, he was made a CMG and, after his promotion to Counsellor, a CB followed. Described by the then Permanent Under-Secretary as 'the best man in the Office', he worked hard to make a success of the League and of disarmament proposals. It was with some relief that he travelled 11,000 miles to become Minister to China in 1934 – with a KCMG. His legation became an embassy in the following year.

In 1936, however, Cadogan returned to the Foreign Office for ten eventful years: two as a Deputy Under-Secretary of State and eight as Permanent Under-Secretary. In those years, he enjoyed the confidence of successive Foreign Secretaries: Eden (who had manoeuvred him into the position), Halifax (whose background was similar to his own), Eden again and Bevin (from a very different background but for whose ability and firmness he quickly formed considerable respect). Of the Prime Ministers of the period, he had a higher regard for (and sympathy with) Chamberlain than most other observers, he developed the usual irritated admiration and respect for Churchill and he found Attlee, at least initially, very insignificant, especially by comparison with Bevin.

Like many others, his opinion of Churchill in the full flush of victory differed from the view he took of him at times during the struggle. The diaries were his safety valve in which he could vent his frustrations, while maintaining publicly his legendary imperturbability. After a Cabinet meeting which had 'rambled incoherently till 8.45', he wrote:

> Our charlady, who was to have come back today, will be another week, which gives T[heodosia, his wife] all the housework. I wish Winston could realise this. Of course *he* can stroll over to the Annexe at 9 or 10 o'clock and at a nod a dozen Marines spring to attention and produce dinner – *and* old Brandy. I wonder has he the least idea of the difficulties of life for the ordinary British subject?[181]

The diaries served to record (as Alanbrooke's did) both his own sense of over-work and his candid views on other people, particularly of Samuel Hoare, the former Foreign Secretary, who was going to Spain as Ambassador in 1940:

> Dirty little dog has got the wind up and wants to get out of this country! ... little blighter ... determined to fly out of this country as soon as he can get a plane ... he's frightened ... He's the first rat to leave the ship.[182]

Cadogan travelled to all the wartime conferences: Atlantic Charter ('Thank God I brought you with me,' said Churchill), Quebec, Tehran, Yalta and Potsdam. Cadogan's standing was summed up by the editor of his diaries and endorsed by the writer of his *DNB* entry:

> No one else occupied a position in the British Government comparable with Cadogan's in the years 1938 to 1950. Others stood nearer to this or that Minister for shorter periods but none – unless it be Sir Edward Bridges – stood so close to the centre of power for so long.[183]

An American once said that Cadogan 'kept his soul in the refrigerator'[184] and he was often thought to have neither temper nor sense of humour – but a combination of both came through in his nightly communing with the diary. He pitied most journalists and despised many politicians:

> How I *hate* Members of Parliament! They embody everything that my training has taught me to eschew – ambition, prejudice, dishonesty, self-seeking, light-hearted irresponsibility, black-hearted mendacity.[185]

Cadogan was flippant about honours, which were frequent for senior British diplomats. He was promoted to GCMG in the New Year Honours of 1939. Two years later, he was promoted to KCB. When it was suggested that he should go to the UN preparatory conference in San Francisco in 1945 in some undefined capacity, he rebelled:

> If necessary – like Van[sittart] – I shall claim a GCB, a Privy Councillorship, a Peerage and retirement![186]

The OM was not within his bureaucratic sights.

In his period as Permanent Under-Secretary, Cadogan had supervised the wartime amalgamation of the Foreign Office, the Diplomatic Service and the various Consular Services into one unified Foreign Service. He became its first Head. After the war, disappointed at not being appointed to Washington, he became the first British Permanent Representative to the United Nations. Some critics said that

> his quiet voice would not be heard amid the volleys and thunders at Lake Success. This impression quickly proved mistaken.[187]

Cadogan's firmness once included observing to a sneering Soviet delegate that Britain was the only country to have fought through every day of both world wars.[188] Because he was a veteran of the League of Nations, his advice was repeatedly sought by other delegates and the Secretary-General himself.

Cadogan's last two public offices involved him in the Suez affair of 1956. From 1950–57, he was the Government Director of the Suez Canal Company. In 1952, he was invited by Churchill to become Chairman of the Board of Governors of the BBC and held the post until 1957, after which he retired from public life.

Cadogan died in 1968, at the age of 83. If one excludes Cromer and MacDonald, both of whose diplomatic careers were unusual, he remains the only straightforward, mainstream diplomat to receive the OM.

In November 1941, George VI was briefed by his Private Secretary (whose father had been Viceroy) to raise with the Prime Minister the idea of conferring the OM on **Lord Hailey**, the acknowledged doyen of the Indian Civil Service, from which he had retired in 1934, as Governor of the United Provinces. Since then, he had conducted a magisterial *Survey of Africa*. The 1935 amendment to the Statutes had opened the Order to the Civil Service. But Churchill told the King, 'that the inclusion of H. would lower the standard.'[189]

Fifteen years later, however, Churchill's second premiership had ended and he was no longer in a position to object to the appointment of Hailey as an OM in the Birthday Honours of 1956 – the one hundredth Member. He was 84.

The Times devoted a leading article to 'Lord Hailey, OM', in which it said that the award

> will be welcomed throughout the British Commonwealth . . . particularly in those territories of Asia, now independent, where he once ruled, and in those territories of Africa, one day to be independent, whose natural resources and administrative organization he has chronicled with such encyclopaedic thoroughness . . . one of the outstanding proconsuls of his time . . . singular contribution to the colonial empire in two ways. First, he has been able . . . to apply all his acquired knowledge in the dispassionate study of colonial affairs . . . Secondly, he has been able to apply the knowledge and experience gained in the older, more settled imperial regime of India to the new and almost uncharted problems of African development . . . The Order of Merit is indeed enriched by his accession to it.[190]

A 300-page biography (published in 1992)[191] makes no mention, however, of this final supreme award, although it does record his first honour, CIE; his first knighthood, KCSI ('Sir Malcolm at last'); and his peerage. The omission is a salutary reminder that the OM can still be overlooked by serious writers, particularly if they follow the North American habit of being more impressed by titles than by honours as such.

Malcolm Hailey was the son of a doctor from Newport Pagnell in Buckinghamshire. After taking a classical double first at Oxford, he passed third into the Indian Civil Service (ICS) in 1894 and was posted to the Punjab. In 1912, the Viceroy, Lord Hardinge of Penshurst, picked Hailey out to be the first Chief Commissioner of the new capital of Delhi. Hailey's career in India continued to flourish. He became Finance Member of the Viceroy's Council at a time of difficulty for the rupee; it was the job he found least congenial. He was glad to be moved on, in succession, to the post of Home Member, in which he had to lead the Legislative Assembly; to the governorship of the Punjab (1924–28), where the overwhelming danger was that party divisions would coincide with the religious ones between Hindu, Sikh and Muslim; and, finally, to the governorship of the United Provinces (1928–34), where the cities were predominantly Muslim and the countryside Hindu and he found difficulty in educating the people in democracy. His second governorship was interrupted by recall to London in 1930–31 for the Round Table Conference, at which he liaised between the Indian and British delegates.

When Hailey retired at the end of 1934, the viceroyalty of Lord Willingdon was coming to an end. In India, the possibility was widely discussed of Hailey becoming the first member of the ICS since John Lawrence (1864–69) to achieve the supreme post. His wife's health weighed against it. Instead, he became the British representative on the League of Nations Permanent Mandates Commission. He subsequently accepted the directorship of the new Survey of Africa, a task by which he was to be remembered as much if not more than for his achievements in India. Indeed, when Hailey died over 30 years later, the two main obituaries were headed: 'Influential figure in the shaping of post-colonial Africa' (*The Times*) and 'Expert on Africa' (*Daily Telegraph*).

A survey of Africa had been suggested by Jan Smuts in 1929 and it got underway a few years later, under the auspices of Chatham House, with funds from the Carnegie and Rhodes Trusts. Hailey travelled 22,000 miles, mainly by car, from South Africa to the Sahara, talking to everyone he could, from governors to village headmen. One of his obituaries observed of the 'Survey':

> Everything was submitted to his own detailed and scholarly examination and was eventually translated into his own stately and measured prose. His conclusions on a long array of carefully marshalled facts are always judicial in spirit; all reasonable views are taken into account and a judgement delivered.[192]

The outcome, published in 1938, was a million words over 2,000 pages, which influenced Colonial Office thinking and policy for the next 15 years. Hailey's reward was a GCMG, to add to his GCSI and GCIE.

The 'Survey' was far from the end of a career. In 1939, the Colonial Secretary, Malcolm MacDonald, asked Hailey to visit African colonies at the outbreak of war and he produced the radical proposition that Africans should be appointed to the Colonial Administrative Service. In 1940, Hailey headed an economic mission to the Belgian Congo to secure its contribution to the war effort, particularly uranium. In 1943, he became Chairman of the Colonial Research Fund, founded on the basis of a recommendation in the 'Survey'.

Hailey travelled, lectured and wrote furiously: a survey in four volumes of native administration in British African territories; a revised edition of *An African Survey*, which 'was marked by the same judicial balance, the same minute scholarship as the first version';[193] and *The Republic of South Africa and the High Commission Territories*, published in 1963, when he was 91. His biographer ventured an assessment of his subject's personality:

> [He] was what psychologists term an obsessive-compulsive personality – a man driven to master, dominate and control. He was the embodiment of the so-called Protestant work ethic. Brilliant, quick, with a mind able to go to the heart of complex problems while keeping in touch with massive amounts of detail, as a worker he was phenomenal.[194]

Hailey lived long enough to become the oldest member of the House of Lords, an achievement in which he was succeeded by another OM, Bertrand Russell. After Hailey's death in 1969, at the age of 97, his ashes were taken to be buried in Simla (the old summer capital of British India), alongside those of his Italian wife, who had died in 1939, in the grave of his teenage daughter, buried there in 1922. The conclusion of Philip Mason, the historian of British India, in his *DNB* entry on Hailey was:

> Few men contributed so much to the transition from bureaucratic rule to democracy in India; few so much to the peaceful transfer of power in Africa. But he outlived his own achievement by ten years and the men he had influenced were already out of office when he died.[195]

Hailey is commemorated in Westminster Abbey with a wall tablet, unveiled by Lord Mountbatten, in the cloisters near to the Indian Civil Service Memorial.

The next administrator appointed to the Order of Merit was **John Anderson**, who was Viscount Waverley for the last six of his 75 years. He owed his OM to Harold Macmillan. For convenience, I shall refer to him throughout as Anderson. The story of his four-week membership of the Order is set out in detail in the authorised biography by John Wheeler-Bennett.[196]

Macmillan, an old friend, wrote to Anderson on 15 November 1958 (the day on which he was admitted to hospital with pneumonia and in a state of delirium) to say that the Queen wished to confer the Order of Merit on him:

> I hope very much that you will feel able to accept this, for it will be a tribute to your long service to the nation in many fields and will I think give especial pleasure to the Civil Service, with which you have been so long connected and which you served so well.

Ten days later, the Queen's Private Secretary (Sir Michael Adeane) conveyed the formal offer, adding that 'it is not often that a recipient qualifies under both headings as you do', that is, by service to the Crown and to the Arts, Learning Literature and Science. Wheeler-Bennett observed that it was

> an interesting example of the minds of the Queen and her Minister working along parallel lines. Her Majesty, as is her right, consulted Mr Macmillan and both were agreed upon the eminent suitability of Lord Waverley as a recipient of the Order.

Anderson accepted the offer on 2 December and the award was to be announced in the New Year Honours of 1958.

Anderson's condition, however, deteriorated fast and, to enable him to enjoy the actual honour, the family agreed to his receiving the necessary transfusion. After Macmillan had told Adeane on 8 December that Anderson might not live for another 48 hours, the Queen instructed Adeane to present the insignia to him at the hospital that afternoon.

The honour was greeted with respectful enthusiasm. *The Times* had a leading article, 'Viscount Waverley OM', describing it as

> one of those entirely appropriate yet imaginative acts which give dignity and colour to British public life. Few men have served Crown and people in more ways than John Anderson ... For years he was commonly acknowledged to be the greatest administrator of his time.[197]

Anderson was the son of a fancy stationer in Edinburgh – 'a shrewd man who had made his own hard way up from virtual poverty to a very comfortable competence.'[198] The son had an outstanding school and university career in the sciences in Edinburgh and, significantly for the future, a year at Leipzig University studying uranium.

Anderson's brilliant bureaucratic career began when he passed top into the Civil Service in 1905, entering the Colonial Office. Within 15 years, he was Joint Under-Secretary for Ireland and a KCB, having already been Chairman of the Board of Inland Revenue at the age of 37. He returned to London at the age of 40 as Permanent Secretary at the Home Office. He was promoted to GCB the following year. He was closely involved with the Government's preparation for, and actual handling of, the General Strike in 1926.

Anderson's rapid rise showed that he had impressed his seniors but his effect on his peers was often less impressive. His instinctive assumption of authority led to comments such as, 'If that's the kind of man they have in the Civil Service I am afraid I have come into the wrong profession.' He acquired the nickname of 'Pompous John', which stayed with him for a long time.[199]

After ten years at the Home Office and when still only 50, Anderson's career took an unusual turn. He became the first civil servant to be appointed Governor of one of the three Indian Presidencies – in this case, Bengal. They were posts that invariably went to British aristocrats or political figures. It was a time of intense unrest in India, especially in Bengal, and twice there were attempts on his life.

On Anderson's return to Britain, with the GCIE and GCSI customary for a Presidency Governor, he was made a Privy Counsellor. He secured some directorships and entered Parliament in 1938 as the National MP for the Scottish Universities in succession to Ramsay MacDonald. With war approaching, however, his services were soon required in the public field, but as a Minister. From 1938–45, Anderson was successively Lord Privy Seal, Home Secretary and Minister of Home Security, Lord President of the Council and Chancellor of the Exchequer.

In the first office, he was responsible for civil defence, including commissioning the outdoor shelter known as the 'Anderson'. In the second office, he supervised the arrangements for transition from peace to war, such as evacuation and the internment of aliens. In the third office (when he joined the small War Cabinet), he co-ordinated the country's civil administration and became very concerned with the secret work on the atomic bomb. In the fourth office, the Permanent Secretary of the Treasury paid him a remarkable tribute:

> Each [Chancellor I served] had had a different approach when confronted with the taking of a decision...John Anderson was different from all the rest. He was the only one who was always searching for the right answer. There could be no finer testimony to a great administrator.[200]

Anderson's standing in the wartime government was such that Churchill recommended to George VI in early 1945 that, if he and Eden were killed on their journey to the Yalta conference, the King should send for Anderson to form a government. Anderson's ministerial career ended when the war did. Attlee twice offered him a peerage but he preferred to believe that the Conservatives would honour their promise to restore the University seats. They did not and so, in the first honours list after Churchill's return to power, he received a viscounty and took the title of Waverley from his native Edinburgh. Remarkably for a man of such achievement, he seemed to stand in some awe of the old Scottish aristocracy:

> Indeed, when there were those who coveted the Thistle for him, he would say that he was not eligible and that this Order was for great landowners of ancient lineage or those whose services had been particularly associated with Scotland.[201]

Now that, to a large extent, selection for the Thistle (and the Garter) has become more meritocratic, Anderson would be an exceptionally strong candidate today.

Anderson's image as 'Pooh-Bah' was well illustrated during a visit by a delegation from a totalitarian country in the early 1950s. Within two days, they met the Chairman of the Port of London Authority, of the UK Advisory Council on Atomic Energy, of the Board of the Royal Opera House and of an official enquiry into East Anglian coastal flooding, as well as a distinguished privy counsellor at a Buckingham Palace reception. They reported home:

> Britain is not, as we thought, a democracy; it is an autocracy run by a man called Waverley.[202]

All this chairmanship was summed up by Kenneth Clark, whose later OM was for his administrative skills as well as his eminence as an art historian:

> Whether or not one knows anything about a subject, to be a chairman is a métier in itself; and John Anderson was a wonderful chairman.[203]

When Anderson died on 4 January 1958, a notable tribute came from the Marquess of Salisbury, a wartime colleague and grandson of the Prime Minister when the Order was founded:

> Her Majesty conferred on him perhaps the greatest of all honours which it is in her power to bestow. On the insignia are inscribed two words only: 'For Merit'. They may well stand as his epitaph.[204]

Another outstanding public servant, Lord Salter, wrote in the *DNB*:

> The range of Waverley's career – official, proconsular, ministerial – was perhaps unique. He was great both as an administrator and as a minister, but it was his quality as an administrator which was dominant. He was, in the general judgement of Whitehall, the greatest administrator of his time, perhaps of any time in the country's history.[205]

On 29 May 1963, the Chief Justice of Australia, **Owen Dixon**, was appointed to the Order of Merit, the announcement being made simultaneously from Buckingham Palace and Government House, Canberra. He was the first judge, the second jurist (after Holdsworth) and the fourth Australian (after Samuel Alexander, Murray and Burnet) to be admitted to the Order; only Burnet and he, however, were living in Australia when appointed.

The Australian press greeted the announcement with reports of the Order that were almost accurate and with comments such as 'OM for a great Australian' and 'Honor for great jurist'. The leading articles spoke of the OM being

> predominantly a splendid recognition of his work as a member of the High Court Bench for a generation and as its Chief Justice since 1952…he has achieved the impossible by becoming a legend in his own lifetime. As the Queen has honoured him, so has he honoured Australia.[206]

and of the Queen doing 'honour to our leading jurist and a man of great intellectual distinction'[207] and of the award being 'a signal and richly deserved tribute to a great Australian'.[208] Most of the press reports referred also to Dixon's work as a diplomat and Kashmir mediator and also to the very high opinion of him held and voiced by his first pupil at the Bar, Robert Menzies, the newly-knighted Prime Minister of Australia. Only a few days earlier, he had described Dixon as:

the greatest of contemporary lawyers . . . I never expect to hear a better legal advocate.[209]

Menzies later concluded:

I have no doubt that it was by reason of his acknowledged eminence in that [legal] field that his career was crowned by the rare award of the Order of Merit by Her Majesty the Queen.[210]

I was living in Australia at the time and, armed with a letter of introduction, I called on the Chief Justice who received the young British diplomat most kindly. When I wrote to congratulate him on the OM a couple of months later, he responded:

I am so glad to be reminded of the fact, which I had forgotten, that Sir William Holdsworth was a member of the Order of Merit. Would you believe it that I actually met him at All Souls.[211]

The insignia of the Order were sent to Canberra in February 1964 for presentation by the Governor-General.

Owen Dixon was the son of a Melbourne lawyer. He was 24 when called to the Bar. He quickly gained a high reputation and became a KC at the age of 36; at 39, he was an acting judge of the Supreme Court of Victoria. At 42, however, he was appointed to the High Court of Australia, the country's highest judicial body, which is charged with the interpretation of the federal constitution. He helped to make the constitution a guarantee of freedom of trade and commerce between the Australian states. In 1952, he became Chief Justice, at the invitation of his former pupil. He had been made a KCMG in 1941 and was promoted to GCMG in 1954.

Twice, Dixon was given leave from the High Court. During the Second World War, he combined legal and administrative ability as chairman of Government wool and shipping boards from 1940–42 and as Minister in Washington from 1942–44. Separate Australian diplomatic representation was in its infancy and Dixon helped to build, at a crucial time, the foundations of an outstanding diplomatic service. In 1950, he was appointed the United Nations mediator in the Kashmir dispute. He did not solve it but, over 50 years later, nor has anyone else.

Dixon retired from the High Court in April 1964, at the age of 78, when he adjudged himself 'no longer fit for the office'. Menzies, nearing the end of his 17-year premiership, came to the court on Dixon's final day to bid him farewell on what he said 'marked the close of the most brilliant chapter in the history of the Australian Bench'.

When Dixon died in 1972, there was little new left to say. *The Times* (of London) recounted much of the praise set out above but it also referred to his 'remoteness':

> Outside his position as Chief Justice he was little known to the Australian public . . . But his remoteness was of policy as well as of choice: 'The law must have a certain mysticism,' he once said. 'The men who administer the law in its higher reaches must not be visible like other men.'[212]

As we shall see, this was not a view shared by the second of the two judicial OMs: Alfred ('Tom') Denning.

In 1968, an appointment was made to the Order of Merit that was a first in its history – **The Prince Philip, Duke of Edinburgh** received it on his forty-seventh birthday on 10 June. No member of the Royal Family had

48 The Prince Philip, Duke of Edinburgh by Peter Grugeon.

previously been awarded it – and the Prince of Wales was awarded it on the centenary of the Order in June 2002. He remains also the youngest recipient ever. Significantly, but not surprisingly, he received the civil badge.

In the nineteenth and first half of the twentieth centuries, honours had come lavishly to royal males. Queen Victoria's husband and sons were showered with honours, as were George V, Edward VIII and George VI before their accessions. When the Queen acceded in 1952, the Duke of Edinburgh was a Privy Counsellor and had the Order of the Garter. He received the Thistle on Her Majesty's actual birthday that year and in 1953, he succeeded Queen Mary as Grand Master of the Order of the British Empire. The Order of Merit is the only British honour he has received since the early days of this reign, although it was strangely omitted from those listed in the '50 Facts' about him issued at the time of the Golden Jubilee. It could be argued that the title of 'Prince of the United Kingdom of Great Britain and Northern Ireland', conferred on him at the conclusion of his long Commonwealth tour in 1957, was an 'honour' but it was essentially the rectification of an anomaly that had existed since his marriage ten years earlier. He had been born a Prince of Greece (and Denmark) and remained so until he relinquished Greek nationality on his naturalisation as a British subject in February 1947.

Despite his technically alien status, he had – after schooling at Gordonstoun, where he was head boy – gone through the Royal Naval College at Dartmouth, winning the King's Dirk as the best all-round cadet of his term. He served in the Royal Navy throughout the Second World War, saw active service in the Mediterranean and was mentioned in despatches by Admiral Cunningham (the future OM) for his performance as a midshipman at the Battle of Cape Matapan in 1941. He moved to the Pacific in 1944 and was present at the Japanese surrender in Tokyo Bay the following year.

After his engagement to Princess Elizabeth in July 1947, Prince Philip's honours progression was unusual. On 19 November, he was created a Royal Highness and appointed a Knight of the Garter, deliberately a few days after the Princess's admission to that order. For a few hours he was therefore Lieutenant HRH Sir Philip Mountbatten, KG, RN. On the morning of the marriage, on 20 November, he was created Duke of Edinburgh, Earl of Merioneth and Baron Greenwich. He was not, however, made a *British* Prince and, since he had not been born one and had ceased to be a Greek one, he was formally HRH Philip, Duke of Edinburgh. Despite repeated speculation, he has never been made 'Prince Consort' and has presumably never sought a title so historically linked to Prince Albert.

The Duke of Edinburgh's naval career, in which he attained command of a frigate, was ended by George VI's deteriorating health, shortly before the Queen's accession. Following an interim promotion to commander, he was within a year promoted to Admiral of the Fleet, a rank that was no longer within his reach in the normal professional manner. His promotion to the highest naval rank was accompanied by appointment as Field Marshal and

Marshal of the Royal Air Force. He was the first MRAF to qualify as a pilot while holding that exalted rank, after which he flew nearly 6,000 hours (in 59 types of aircraft) until 1997. Additionally, he holds some 40 other service appointments, including those of Captain-General of the Royal Marines and Colonel of the Grenadier Guards.

Prince Philip has the civil badge of the OM because, despite helping to maintain the traditional strong links of the Crown with the armed services, his greatest contribution to the life of Britain and other Commonwealth countries has been in the general or civilian sphere. He has defined his place within the Royal Family as that of

> co-chairman...the whole thing's run on a committee basis really.[213]

His importance to the Queen, in her role as head of state, was summed up by Her Majesty at their golden wedding in 1997:

> ...he has, quite simply, been my strength and stay all these years and I...owe him a debt greater than he would ever claim or we shall ever know.[214]

Nevertheless, Prince Philip has been known to express some frustration at his ill-defined support role:

> Because she's the Sovereign everyone turns to her. If you have a King and Queen, there are certain things people automatically go to the Queen about. But if the Queen is also the *Queen,* they go to her about everything.[215]

Prince Philip's most abiding memorial will probably be 'The Duke of Edinburgh's Award Scheme', which he launched in 1956 with the aid of Sir John Hunt, the leader of the successful Everest expedition of 1953. It is designed to introduce young people to new experiences, including physical, skills-based and community challenges. Over four million young people from 90 countries have participated and it has complemented and reinforced the work done by the increasingly unfashionable uniformed youth organisations, such as the Scouts and Guides.

At a still young, but more senior, level, Prince Philip inaugurated a series of study conferences to examine the human problems in the rapidly growing industrial communities within the Commonwealth. They have been held at six-yearly intervals since 1956.

Although not a graduate (except of what Ernest Bevin called the University of Life – the 'edgerows of experience'), Prince Philip has forged close associations with many universities, particularly those of which he has been

Chancellor: Edinburgh, very appropriately, since 1952, Wales from 1948–76, Salford from 1967–90 and Cambridge since 1977, when he succeeded another OM, Lord Adrian.

In addition, Prince Philip has taken an active hands-on interest in a number of academic and educational bodies: as a Fellow of the Royal Society since 1951, President of the City and Guilds Institute since 1951, of the Royal Society of Arts since 1952 and of the English-Speaking Union since 1952. He has been Patron of the Industrial Society since 1952 and in 1976 he initiated the Fellowship of Engineering, which later become the Royal Academy of Engineering. He has taken a special interest in design and, under the aegis of the Design Council, an annual Prince Philip's Designer Prize is awarded. From 1952–99, he was Chairman of the Royal Mint advisory committee on the design of seals, coins and medals.

In his wide-ranging and persistent interest in science and technology, with due allowance for the passage of time, Prince Philip has followed in the steps of Prince Albert, notably in the connections with the Royal Society, the Royal Society of Arts and Cambridge University.

Prince Philip's long-held interest in caring for the environment found practical expression in 1961 when he was the first President of the UK branch of WWF (World Wildlife Fund International), whose prime concern was to preserve endangered species and habitats. He was International President from 1981–96, overseeing its change of name in 1988 to World Wide Fund for Nature (still WWF).

The Prince has always maintained close links with service veterans, particularly as Grand President of the British Commonwealth Ex-Services League. He has been an active supporter of many deserving charities, such as the Federation of London Youth Clubs, the National Playing Fields Association, the Outward Bound Trust and the Variety Club of Great Britain.

Prince Philip has always been a keen sportsman: yachting, cricket, polo and, more recently, four-in-hand driving. He was President of the International Equestrian Federation for 22 years and of the Commonwealth Games Federation for 35 years, during which time he opened and/or closed many of the Games.

Anecdotes about Prince Philip are not hard to come by. The media are happy to provide us with a story every other day, some based tenuously on fact. I suspect the majority of the British public would not have him otherwise:

> He is a national treasure. And his sayings add to the gaiety of language.[216]

The Prince undertakes an enormously wide range of activities, matched now by few other men in their mid-eighties. In Golden Jubilee year, 2002, he undertook more official engagements than any other member of the Royal

Family – nearly 600. In all, he has fulfilled nearly 20,000 engagements and made nearly 5,000 speeches, many of which have been published in collected form, along with books on subjects such as the preservation of wildlife, the Christian attitude to the environment and birdlife as observed on voyages on the royal yacht, *Britannia*. He presented a television programme in 1957 on his lengthy tour of the Commonwealth and in 1961 he became the first member of the Royal Family to be interviewed on that medium. He has naturally been freer than the Queen, or even a queen consort, to speak his mind, while steering clear of party political controversy. He certainly talks with knowledge about royal visits. Apart from those around the United Kingdom, he has paid nearly 600 overseas visits, in addition to accompanying the Queen on all her 259 official visits abroad. In some cases, his solo visit (to Russia, for instance) has been a careful prelude to the ultimate state visit by the Queen and himself.

The Second World War changed John Anderson from an outstanding civil servant into a minister and **Malcolm MacDonald** from a minister into an extraordinary civil servant. He summed up his own varied career:

> My successive posts have been very higgledy-piggledy. Starting with my unexpected appointment as a member of the British Cabinet in 1935, I have been in turn one Minister, two Secretaries of State, three High Commissioners, an Ambassador Extraordinary, three Governors-General, one Commissioner-General, a Governor, two Special Representatives, a couple of Special Envoys, and occasionally other highfalutin' potentates as well. It has all been very unplanned, very odd, and very enjoyable.[217]

The style befits the man. He enjoyed the power and influence but had little time for the accompanying ceremonial.

The second son of Ramsay MacDonald, the first Labour Prime Minister, Malcolm MacDonald shared not only his father's political views but also his dislike of honours and titles. His paternal grandfather was a ploughman, who did not marry his paternal grandmother, a farm worker. His maternal grandfather was a FRS and a nephew of Kelvin, one of the first OMs.

After Bedales and Oxford, Malcolm became a Labour MP in 1929 and when his father formed the National Government in 1931, he followed him and secured office as Parliamentary Under-Secretary for the Dominions. In that capacity, he moved the third reading in 1931 of the Statute of Westminster that set the legal framework for transition from Empire to Commonwealth, with which he was to be more continuously connected than any other man over the next 40 years.

On Ramsay MacDonald's retirement from the premiership in 1935, the way was clear for Malcolm's promotion to the Cabinet and he was Secretary of State for the Colonies and/or the Dominions until 1940. Ramsay remained in Baldwin's cabinet as Lord President of the Council and, apart from Joseph and Austen Chamberlain, he and Malcolm were the only father and son to sit in the same cabinet in the twentieth century.

Malcolm MacDonald played a significant role in the Abdication crisis of 1936 by reminding Baldwin of the need to consult the independent countries overseas of which the King was Sovereign. Malcolm regarded one episode in the crisis as unlikely to be repeated. Called from his bath by a telephone call from the King, who wanted to suggest an amendment to a message that was going to the Dominion Prime Ministers, he was

> inclined to think it was the only occasion in Britain's long and glorious history when a King was formally advised on high State affairs by one of his Ministers standing stark-naked except for a dressing gown thrown loosely round his person whilst his feet splashed in a puddle of bath-water dripping from his sopping-wet body.[218]

When Churchill formed his government in 1940, Malcolm MacDonald was moved away from overseas affairs to be Minister of Health. Even during his year at the Ministry of Health, Malcolm was employed by Churchill on a delicate mission: to persuade de Valera to bring the Irish Free State (or Eire, as it had become) into the war. He was impressed – but Churchill was not – by de Valera's argument that a belligerent but weak Eire would be quickly overrun by Germany as a stepping stone to an invasion of Britain across the narrow Irish Sea, whereas a neutral Eire was an area of protection on Britain's flank.[219]

In 1941, Malcolm MacDonald returned to the overseas field when he was appointed by Churchill to be High Commissioner to Canada, a post that had become particularly important in the light of that country's contribution to the war effort. One of his most colourful visitors was Lydia Lopokova, the wife of Maynard Keynes, who came to Ottawa for financial discussions. On her arrival, she startled MacDonald (whom she had never met) and the Canadian Minister of Finance by declaring:

> Oh, my dear High Commissioner, how are you? Last night, I dreamed zat I was lying in bed, and zat you were lying in my arms.

Later (wearing only a short white chemise), she revealed to Keynes and Mac-Donald that the key to her husband's official red box (for which an anguished search had been made) was 'hid for safety between my little bosoms'. As she lifted the key from its hiding place, MacDonald was obliged to notice that 'her breasts . . . were not quite so small as she suggested'.[220]

It was on his return from Canada that MacDonald refused, not for the last time, a high honour. Churchill wanted to recommend him for a GCMG. According to the *DNB*, he refused a peerage too.[221] It seems very likely that, as a former politician, a CH would also have been tried out on him. He was immune to all offers, except the Order of Merit on his eventual retirement in 1969.

Malcolm MacDonald refused Atlee's offer of a post in the post-war Labour Government and embarked on a high-level diplomatic career. From 1946–48, he was Governor-General of the Malayan Union and Singapore, one of those grand imperial concepts that was destined to founder. He moved on in 1948 to become Commissioner-General for South East Asia, with an oversight of British colonial and foreign interests in the area. In 1955, he transferred to a major independent and clearly defined post of his own – as High Commissioner to India, where he established a close rapport with Jawaharlal Nehru: once, he walked on his hands while Nehru stood on his head. He was impressed with Nehru's decision to resist his Congress Party colleagues' pressure to remove the portraits of the British Viceroys from the walls of the President's Palace in Delhi: 'You can't change history by taking a lot of pictures off walls.'[222]

Malcolm MacDonald disagreed firmly with the Franco–British operation at Suez. He stayed in Delhi until 1960 trying to restore the damage that had been done to Indo–British relations by the Suez episode. On his return to London, he was received by the Queen 'on retirement from the Public Service', but received no honour. Within a year, he led the British delegation to the international conference on the future of Laos. In 1963, although he knew almost nothing about Africa, he was prevailed on to accept the Governorship of Kenya by the 'characteristic stubbornness' of Duncan Sandys, the Commonwealth and Colonial Secretary, a characteristic with which I became very familiar during two years as a private secretary to that minister.

In Kenya, Malcolm MacDonald brought Jomo Kenyatta, the 'leader to darkness and death' of the 1950s, into government and it was the mutual respect that developed which led to his being invited to stay on as Governor-General on independence. When the country became a republic in 1964, he was transformed into the British High Commissioner, the only example of such a transition. On concluding his trilogy of positions in Kenya, MacDonald was appointed British Special Representative in East and Central Africa. This proved to be one of the hottest of his assignments, since it coincided with the quarrel between Southern Rhodesia (after its unilateral declaration of independence) and the emergent African nations around it. It was on his retirement from this post, and finally from public service, that he accepted his only official honour: the Order of Merit, on 14 July 1969.

In a decade of real retirement from official service, Malcolm MacDonald devoted himself to a number of voluntary bodies, mostly connected with the Commonwealth. On his death in 1981, the Commonwealth Secretary-General, Sir Shridath Ramphal, said that

> his life's work was to make imperial rule a thing of yesterday . . . The supreme interlocutor, interpreting Britain to the leaders of the new

countries; but, as important, interpreting them . . . to Britain and always with sensitivity and compassion and a keen pragmatic political judgement, bringing to his representational work the higher quality of intermediation.[223]

The Order of Merit caught up with the next administrator on 24 October 1977, when he was 72. Given the eminence of **Oliver Franks** in a number of different fields, it is strange that he received the honour above rather than below the average age of bestowal. Possibly, it was because he was not renowned for one clearly defined activity or achievement. He was simply 'Establishment Man', the captain of 'the great and the good', the team of disinterested people to whom successive British governments of all complexions turned for advice for so much of the twentieth century. Indeed, his standing was such that it was said of him:

> If Britain was a republic, Oliver Franks would have to be president. No one else would do.[224]

49 Lord Franks by Elliot and Fry.

Oliver Franks' career was divided between Oxford, the civil service (at home and overseas) and banking, with a good deal of inquisitorial work in between. It was the sheer multiplicity of his distinction that made him such a strong candidate for the OM.

Oxford was where Franks belonged. He left it many times but always came back, and died there nearly 70 years after his first arrival. From a noncomformist background, he gained an open scholarship in classics from Bristol Grammar School to The Queen's College in 1923. Four years later, after a double First, he was elected a Fellow in Philosophy at the college, aged 22. He spent ten years there, except for a year as a visiting professor in Chicago, before moving on to the chair of moral philosophy at Glasgow in 1937. After the disruption to his academic career of the Second World War, he returned to Oxford in 1946 as Provost of his old college, Queen's: 'the only job I'd ever faintly hoped for.' Franks looked set for an established Oxford career, with occasional traditional calls to serve on government committees.

In fact, Franks was almost immediately detached to head the British team at a conference in Paris in 1947 to consider the response to the American proposals for what became 'Marshall Aid'. It was very hot in Paris and

> a perspiring American diplomat watched fascinated as a bead of sweat formed on [Franks'] temple, divided neatly down both cheeks and then met once more under his chin. 'I take my hat off to that guy. He even sweats symmetrically.'[225]

Soon after, he was off to Washington in 1948 as Ambassador. He did not return to Oxford until 1962, when (with a newly-conferred life peerage) he was elected Provost of Worcester College, where he stayed until 1976. It is rare for a man to head two colleges at either Oxford or Cambridge. He had also chaired the important Oxford Historic Buildings Appeal in 1957. His presence in Oxford make him the obvious chairman of a commission set up by the university in 1964, partly to pre-empt outside investigation. Its remit was to take a 'long hard look' at the university and its place in the higher education of the country.

Franks' academic career was interrupted for the first time on the second day of the war when he was drafted into a low-level job in the Ministry of Supply. By the end of the conflict, his exceptional administrative talents had brought him a CBE, promotion to what he modestly called 'temporary permanent secretary' and the first of his three knighthoods, a KCB. His reputation for intellectual power in administration and negotiation was firmly established.

Franks was not the obvious candidate for the embassy in Washington in 1948. He was not a career diplomat, he had very little overseas experience and he had no known Labour sympathies. Attlee, however, simply thought he was 'the best man for the job'. Both he and Bevin had been impressed by

Franks' terse matter-of-fact command of matters during the Marshall Aid talks.

Franks' true achievement was in the impact he made on the American government rather than the public. An oft-repeated story, which differs slightly each time of telling, is of a Christmas radio broadcast in Washington. Various ambassadors were asked what they wanted for the festive season. The Frenchman said 'peace throughout the world', the Russian sought 'freedom for all the peoples enslaved by imperialism', the German wanted 'greater sharing of the wealth of the world', while Franks asked for 'a small box of crystallised fruit'.

On the official plane, Franks formed an especially close rapport with Dean Acheson, the Secretary of State. Sir Nicholas Henderson, a second secretary on Franks' staff and later Ambassador himself, relates how his master operated in the discussions leading to the formation of NATO:

> [he] possessed capacities of intellect and exposition which none of his colleagues could equal or ignore... He would sow doubts here and there and when they had taken root he would scatter seeds of his own persuasion in such a plausible way that the other representatives soon felt there was no alternative but to gather round and nourish them.[226]

Franks came home from Washington in 1952 with his second knighthood, a GCMG; he had been made a privy counsellor in 1949. Years later, when he received the Order of Merit, he was naturally conscious that he followed in it two of his predecessors in Washington, Bryce and Halifax, but he was glad to be reminded that the honour had also been held briefly by the American wartime Ambassador in London, J. G. Winant.[227]

Following Washington, Franks was never again a full-time public servant, although he rendered much more public service. Spreading though all his varied fields of activity was the role of Grand Inquirer, or even Grand Inquisitor. In addition to the enquiries he conducted at Oxford, there were many more. In 1956, he chaired a government committee to look into the proliferating administrative tribunals, which recommended their constant review by standing councils that exist broadly today. In 1972, it was the Official Secrets Act that claimed his attention, while in 1976 it was ministerial memoirs. Finally, in 1982 (at the age of 77), he chaired the Falkland Islands enquiry.

At various times, he was Chairman of the Political Honours Scrutiny Committee and of the Wellcome Trust (the country's largest charity). He also earned a third knighthood (KCVO) as Lord Warden of the Stannaries, a key figure in the administration of the Duchy of Cornwall. He thus had the unusual distinction nowadays of being a member of all four 'routine' orders: Bath, St Michael and St George, Royal Victorian and British Empire. Other worthy bodies such as the Rhodes Trust, the Pilgrim Trust and the Rockefeller Foundation also claimed his time. In 1954, he became Chairman of Lloyds Bank, a post he held for eight years, until he returned to Oxford.

Franks did not have a reputation, at least in his early years, for warm sociability. One acquaintance observed:

> One always has to break the ice and when one does one finds a lot of very cold water beneath.[228]

I remember, as a law student, watching Franks stretch out his legs under the table and carefully place his fingertips together as he grilled a permanent secretary during a sitting of the committee on administrative tribunals. I did not envy the civil servant. An Oxford don, after a similar grilling at the commission of inquiry into the working of the university, commented:

> I now know what the day of judgement will be like, only I expect God to be more human.[229]

I can make only a small personal observation. Once, I invited him to speak to a university student society. He was chairing both Lloyds Bank and the committee on tribunals; he was very busy and could have declined the invitation in a few lines. Instead, he courteously explained in some detail the precise reasons why he could not accept. There was nothing cold about his response.[230]

On Franks' death in 1992, he was described simply as 'the supreme administrator'. *The Times*, in a leading article entitled 'Last of the Spartans', wrote:

> Take him for all in all, we shall not look upon his like again ... The increased activity of public life has destroyed the traditional breeding grounds of the Great and Good. Britain did not need them all quite as much as many of them thought it did. But it will always need men of the stature of Lord Franks.[231]

At the time of the Falklands enquiry, Oliver Franks was once described as the 'Tom Denning of diplomacy'. He was being bracketed with the Grand Old Man of English law.

If Franks' OM seemed to have come rather late in life, it was positively premature compared to the award to **Alfred Thompson Denning**, who was 98. He was a superior court judge for nearly 40 years and by 1997, he had been retired for over 15. It may be that there were persuasive voices against his inclusion that were not stilled by death or senility until it was almost too late for him. As *The Times* discreetly commented:

> given his eminence, it was somewhat surprising that he had to wait until 1997 to be appointed to the Order of Merit.[232]

Denning's OM was well reported and he stole the limelight from his two co-appointees: Norman Foster and Denis Rooke. One headline was 'Queen judges Denning worthy of Merit' and his long life and career was set out at length.

Strangely, even at the age of 98, the OM was not Denning's last honour. Along with some 300 other surviving British veterans of the First World War, he was made a chevalier of the Légion d'Honneur in 1998, on the eightieth anniversary of the end of that conflict.

Denning was the fourth of five sons of the well-read draper in the small town of Whitchurch. Two of the brothers died in the First World War. A third became a lieutenant-general. A fourth became a vice-admiral. The fifth son became Master of the Rolls, the second most senior judge in England and Wales. He told the tale of his remarkable family in his autobiography, *The Family Story*.[233]

From his local grammar school, he won a £30 exhibition to Magdalen College, Oxford. Too young for the army, Denning took a First in Mathematics Moderations in 1917 before serving as an officer in the Royal Engineers. After returning from active service early in 1919, he completed his mathematics course with a First in Finals in 1920. He then went off to teach the subject at Winchester.

A day at the local assizes, however, re-awakened an early interest in the law. So Denning returned to Magdalen in 1921, gained a First in Law the next year, and was called to the Bar by Lincoln's Inn a year later. Denning's rise through the legal ranks was rapid. He became a KC at 39 and a High Court judge at 45, well below the age then prevailing. He was already acquiring the reputation of a judge who thought more highly of justice than of the strict law. He added to this when giving the first Hamlyn Lecture in 1949 on 'Freedom Under the Law'. He became a prolific lecturer in Britain and overseas and no judge was more highly regarded in the overseas Commonwealth. He had a lot of time for students. He became by far the most active of the Vice-Presidents of the Oxford University Law Society and, when I had a term as its President, I found that he took a much closer interest in its activities than could reasonably be expected of such a busy appeal judge. Years later, he told me: 'I always enjoyed coming down to Oxford and meeting all the students.'[234]

Denning had been promoted to the Court of Appeal in 1948 – still under 50 – and the inevitable move up to the House of Lords came in 1957. He was to be disappointed in his hopes of the highest court in the land as the place where the law could be remedied or changed where necessary. He was therefore only too ready to return in 1962 to the Royal Courts of Justice in the Strand, where he had spent most of his career. He did so as Master of the Rolls, the president of the Court of Appeal.

Soon after assuming his new position, Denning came to public fame as the one-man investigator, prosecutor and judge in the Profumo Affair, which had done so much in 1963 to damage the reputation of the dying Macmillan government. His report, with chapter headings such as 'The Slashing and the Shooting' and 'The Man in the Mask', was an instant bestseller (100,000 in the first three days) and acquired a reputation as 'the raciest and most readable Blue Book ever published'. Denning had become a name in households far beyond the legal world.

In Denning's eighties, an apparent need to consolidate both his personal history and his legal career brought forth for what, in a sitting judge, was a rush of books. Following *The Discipline of Law* came not only *The Family Story* but also *The Due Process of Law*. It was a fourth book, *What Next in the Law*, published in 1982, which precipitated his resignation. In it he seemed to imply that some immigrants were not suitable to serve on juries as they did not have the same standard of conduct as English whites. According to Denning, *The Times* then lived up to its name 'The Thunderer'. On 24 May 1982, a leading article entitled 'A Judgment Too Far' declaimed:

> for all his greatness as a judge, he has gone too far as a campaigner and commentator when out of court.[235]

Two days later, the book was temporarily withdrawn following the threat of a libel action from two black jurors. Three days after that, Denning announced his retirement because of the controversy.

A successor as Master of the Rolls, Lord Woolf (later Lord Chief Justice), said:

> Many of [Denning's] decisions were ahead of his day and only years later became accepted as representing the law...He put the Court of Appeal's civil division on the map. Until his time, on the whole it was the great criminal cases that caught the public imagination. With him, for the first time, it was civil cases, because he was protecting the little man against the big battalions.[236]

In retirement, Denning was active in both the public and private legal spheres and, at 90, he was still no stranger to public controversy. He continued to give unsolicited advice to the senior judiciary and, in an interview in *The Spectator*, he said the 'Guildford Four' were 'probably guilty' and that, if the 'Birmingham Six' had been hanged 'we shouldn't have all these campaigns to get them released'. All this controversy, allied to the circumstances of his retirement, may go some way to explaining the very long time he waited for his OM.

On Denning's one-hundredth birthday, *The Times* legal correspondent wrote:

> If judges had popularity ratings, Lord Denning would top the poll. He is the student's judge, the lawyer's judge and, above all, the people's judge. Litigants in person loved him and he was a gift to the media.[237]

Denning died on 5 March 1999, only six weeks after his one-hundredth birthday. His death commanded news items on front pages as well as lengthy obituaries. The headlines stressed his place in our legal history: 'the century's greatest judge', 'a benchmark of British justice' and 'legal legend'. Some emphasised the popular side of his reputation: 'champion of the little man', 'great judge who spoke for everyman', 'controversial "people's judge"' and 'defender of justice and liberty'.

The Prime Minister, Tony Blair (who appeared as a young barrister before Denning), described him as

> one of the great men of his age. His judgements were a model of lucidity. He was prepared to use the law for its true purpose – in the interests of fairness and justice. He had a tremendous feel for ordinary people.

A former Prime Minister, Margaret Thatcher, also a barrister, called Denning

> probably the greatest English judge of modern times. He combined a love of liberty with a passion for justice. His life and work will provide inspiration for generations to come.

Another successor as Master of the Rolls, Lord Bingham of Cornhill (then Lord Chief Justice), thought he

> was the best known and best-loved judge of this, or perhaps any generation ... He was a legend in his own lifetime.[238]

On the day after the Order reached its centenary, there was appointed to it the first lineal descendant of its founder, Edward VII: his great-great-grandson, **Charles, Prince of Wales**. He was the second 'Royal Highness' to receive this very personal mark of royal favour that is not normally conferred on royalty. His father, Prince Philip, had preceded him into the Order 34 years earlier.

The high status of senior members of the Royal Family and the respect they traditionally attract gives them an advantage in their public endeavours. Nevertheless, vastly increased media attention (often with little of the usual respect) has made their task much more difficult. They have to work very hard to gain and retain a truly respected place in the life of the nation. In the case of the Prince of Wales, the often-frenzied media interest in his life, his two marriages and his sons has fostered an inordinate amount of public attention.

As noted earlier, the honours bestowed in the past on royal figures have been much less frequent in the present reign. As heir apparent, however, Prince Charles had received the three highest possible honours before he was 30. He became a Knight of the Garter automatically on being created Prince of Wales at the age of nine, although he was not formally introduced into the Order until he was 19. He was made Great Master of the Order of the Bath when he was 26 and the Order of the Thistle (and membership of the Privy Council) followed at 28. Australian and New Zealand honours came later.

The Order of Merit, however, did not attach in any automatic way to Prince Charles' royal position and, indeed, he was 53 when he received it – young for an OM but reflecting that his royal status had involved him prominently in public life for longer than others of his age. The award must be seen as a clear demonstration of the Sovereign's regard for what her heir has done over a whole range of public service, the arts and science to stimulate the life of the nation. The Prince himself displays his pride in the award by wearing it in the place of his (technically higher) Bath neck badge on most occasions, including uniformed ones.

Prince Charles' early career followed that normal for an heir to the throne. Schooling at Gordonstoun (which seems to have left few fond memories) and university at Trinity College, Cambridge (that bastion of OMs) was followed by a few years in the Royal Navy. Before leaving the Royal Navy in 1976, he had commanded a minehunter, *HMS Bronington*, and secured RAF pilot's wings.

It was time for Prince Charles to devote more time to the public duties that necessarily fall to the heir. He has represented the Queen at events in the United Kingdom and overseas, particularly in other Commonwealth countries. He is her main alternate at investitures, especially since the virtual abolition of the British Empire Medal increased the numbers attending those ceremonies. More than any other person, he confers the accolade of knighthood on behalf of the Sovereign, by virtue of a special royal warrant issued for each occasion.

Apart from ceremonial events, Prince Charles has not been content merely to assume the usual honorary military and civil appointments and to give his patronage to a great number of charitable bodies. He has gone out into the field himself, notably in founding The Prince's Trust in 1976 with his severance pay from the Royal Navy. It helps 14–30 year olds to realise their potential, especially those who have struggled at school, been in care or in trouble with the law or are long-term unemployed. It offers training, mentoring and financial assistance.

From that initial trust, Prince Charles has developed a distinctive role as a charitable entrepreneur. The Prince's charities now comprise 16 distinct organisations focusing on areas that are central to how people live: homes and communities, health, education, work, the environment and the arts. They seek to address areas of previously unmet need and are now the largest multi-cause charitable enterprise in the country, raising over £100 million annually. Their names are now familiar and include Youth Business Trust, Business in the Community, Arts and Kids Foundation and Foundation for the Built Environment. Prince Charles devotes much of his time to directing in a hands-on manner the work of these charities. They have made an enormous difference to the lives of many ordinary people.

Apart from his 'own' charities, Prince Charles is president or patron of over 350 other charities. He has concentrated his public endeavours in a far wider and yet more focused way than any of his predecessors. The Prince's developing interest in the fields covered by his charities has led to his expressing firm views that have not always been welcomed by workers in those fields: education, health, architecture and the environment, for example. He has displayed an awareness of the need to understand the Islamic world – well before it became fashionable, or necessary.

Prince Charles gives a lot of time and energy to the careful management and development of his birthright, the Duchy of Cornwall, which has been vested automatically in the heir apparent since 1337. Although he therefore became Duke of Cornwall at the age of three, at the moment of his mother's accession, he was naturally not involved in the affairs of the Duchy until he came of age. The estate (much of it outside Cornwall) is managed with strict regard for the Prince's strong views on ecology and the environment generally. Many of its organic products (the 'Duchy Originals') are now familiar sights in shops throughout the world and profits from them go to the Prince's charities.

The founder of the Order of Merit waited almost 60 years to become King. So far, the new recipient of the Order of Merit has waited almost as long. In Edward VII, the frustrations were evident and well documented. It is generally accepted, even by Prince Charles' critics, that it is probably not easy to be 'King-in-Waiting' for so many years.

When he does become King, the Prince will be the first of the six Sovereigns of the Order of Merit to have held it in his own right. At the five-yearly reunions of the Order, its Sovereign will have no inhibitions about wearing the Badge. A small question is whether the new Sovereign will continue to count against the strict limit of 24 Members or whether his accession will create a vacancy. In that case, for the first time, the Order will have 25 Members, including its own Sovereign.

The Order of Merit has never gone to a man simply for being very rich. Indeed, few of its Members over the years would qualify under that heading. One who certainly does is **Jacob, Fourth Lord Rothschild** but his admission to the Order in October 2002 recognised not his wealth but what he had chosen to do with it and the influence it had brought him.

Since the term 'philanthropist' was vetoed by George V in 1935, on the grounds that it smacked of a 'cash order', those who might be seen in that light have had to be categorised as 'humanitarians' or 'men of affairs'. Jacob Rothschild is undoubtedly a 'man of affairs', an 'administrator' rather than a 'political figure'. He therefore sits, if a little uneasily, in this section. His 'administration' has taken two forms: that of his own inherited fortune, which he has considerably enhanced; and that of the affairs of numerous public and charitable bodies, to which he has contributed much time as well as money.

Jacob Rothschild's wealth is part of the vast fortune of the family of Rothschild – meaning 'Red Shield', from the sign outside their house in the Frankfurt ghetto. Bankers in that city since the fifteenth century, the 'modern' house was founded by Mayer Amschel in the late eighteenth century. Like other Frankfurt bankers (such as the Oppenheimers and Goldsmiths), he sent his sons to found branches in the major cities of Europe. The son who came to Britain, Nathan Mayer (sometimes called 'The Ruler of England'), financed the Battle of Waterloo and, in so doing, enriched himself. The family has provided the first Jew to sit in the House of Commons and the first Jewish peer. Nathaniel Mayer, on whom that peerage was conferred in 1885, had lent the money to build the Suez Canal; Disraeli said that, whenever he wanted to know an historic fact, he always asked 'Natty'. He was a good friend of Edward VII, who rewarded him with a GVCO and a privy counsellorship.

Victor, Third Lord Rothschild (Jacob's father) was only part-banker. He was more interested in science (a FRS), in music and in public affairs, ranging from service with MI5 in the Second World War to advising the government over a wide field in the 1970s. During the war, he was awarded the George Medal for dismantling a bomb concealed in a crate of Spanish onions on a ship.

Jacob, educated at Eton and Oxford (where he took a First in History), succeeded to the peerage in 1990, at the age of 53. By that time, he had already established himself in banking and the arts. He was an energetic head of the corporate finance department of the bank, N. M. Rothschild, taking it into the fierce world of takeover battles. Control of the bank had passed, however, to a cadet branch of the family, headed by Sir Evelyn. Jacob therefore founded his own financial house (now Five Arrows) in 1980; he is also chairman of RIT Capital Partners and deputy chairman of BskyB.

In 1985, Jacob Rothschild became chairman of the Board of Trustees of the National Gallery, heading the acquisition of funds for the new Sainsbury Wing. After relinquishing that post in 1991, he was for six years chairman of the National Heritage Memorial Fund, administering the Heritage Lottery Fund for the last three of those years. These positions gave him great influence in the world of the arts. He is also now chairman of the independent specialist committee that advises the government on honours in the fields of the arts and media.

In his own right, through the Rothschild Foundation and the Mentmore Trust, Jacob has contributed greatly to a wide range of activities, including the renovation of Somerset House and the bringing together in that splendid setting of such treasures as the Gilbert Collection. As the owner of the long lease on Spencer House, London's finest surviving eighteenth-century town house (a 'private palace'), he has restored the elaborately-decorated state rooms.

Jacob Rothschild's family trust has given Israel the buildings for its parliament and supreme court and its open university, which have been recognised by the city and university of Jerusalem. Yet (like his father) he is married to a Gentile, who has not converted to Judaism. He has been painted by his fellow-OM, Lucian Freud, although his wife does not like the result.

Jacob Rothschild's importance in the arts world has been recognised in many ways: he is an Honorary Fellow of the British Academy, the Royal Institute of British Architects and the Royal Academy of Music. When he received an honorary degree at Oxford in 2002, he was described as:

> the Maecenas of the age, an arbiter of taste and a promoter of the arts, who has done more than anyone else to elevate and educate the public.

Ineligible for the Order of the Garter, by virtue of his religion, Jacob Rothschild was first publicly honoured with a GBE in 1998 (20 or so years after his father). The OM in 2002 provided a more significant recognition of his outstanding contribution to the artistic and cultural life of Britain.

15

THE HUMANITARIANS

1. 1907 Florence NIGHTINGALE
2. 1937 Lord BADEN-POWELL
3. 1955 Albert SCHWEITZER (Honorary)
4. 1981 Lord CHESHIRE
5. 1983 Mother TERESA (Honorary)
6. 1989 Dame Cecily SAUNDERS
7. 1999 Cardinal Basil HUME

Nowhere does the word 'humanitarian' appear in even the latest Statutes of the Order of Merit and, at the beginning, it was not envisaged as one of the fields in which the Order could be earned. When Florence Nightingale was given it by a reluctant Edward VII in 1907, it was after considerable doubt had been cast on her eligibility within the Statutes, as I shall describe in the next chapter about the women recipients of the Order. *The Times* was quite certain in resisting such doubts:

> It is good that this high mark of the Sovereign's and the country's recognition is not to be denied to women...and to the lady who had done such inestimable service to her country and to humanity.[1]

After that first brush with 'humanity', the official British reluctance to honour services in this field limited this aspect of the Order's development. We have seen that when, in 1935, the Statutes were formally extended to include Air Force officers and incorporate 'Learning' the inclusion of 'Philanthropy' was vetoed by George V. Once the financial idea of donations was excluded, the word seemed to embody an intangible, difficult and therefore dangerous concept to introduce into the Order. The name actually cited in those papers, in favour of incorporating 'Philanthropy', had been that of

Robert Baden-Powell, the founder of the Boy Scout and Girl Guide Movements. Soon afterwards, in the Coronation Honours of 1937, Baden-Powell did indeed receive the OM. This was demonstrably for an outstanding contribution to the civilian life of the nation, the Empire and the world. Nevertheless, the badge he received was the military version.[2]

Owen Morshead, the Royal Librarian, suggested Baden-Powell's name a few years earlier:

> Baden-Powell . . . has done as much as any man now living to make our name honoured throughout the world.

Morshead acknowledged that Baden-Powell had got his peerage (and, indeed, he had also received a baronetcy, GCMG and GCVO for his scouting work) but the OM was

> a thing apart, a crown of laurel which no one . . . has done so much to earn.[3]

Geoffrey Dawson, the editor of *The Times*, had been urging, as far back as 1928, the claims of Baden-Powell: 'who seems to me to have done one of the biggest things of his generation.'[4] Baden-Powell's achievement had certainly been impressive. From a camp of 20 boys on Brownsea Island in Poole Harbour in 1907, his movement had grown worldwide by 1937 to nearly two and a half million Boy Scouts and some one and a quarter million Girl Guides and Scouts. To the man himself it came

> as a bolt from the blue. I had never dreamed of such an honour . . . [It] is proof of His Majesty's appreciation of the work done by the Scout officers and Scouts throughout the Empire, and as such will have a most inspiring effect upon them.[5]

The other five awards of the OM for 'humanitarian' services have been in the present reign. The two to foreigners, the universal icons, Albert Schweitzer and Mother Teresa are dealt with in Chapter 17 on honorary appointments. The remaining three have been in the last 20 years: Leonard Cheshire, Cicely Saunders and Basil Hume.

When **Leonard Cheshire** was made an OM in 1981, he received the civil badge. No one thought that this retired group captain, with a VC, DSO and DFC, was being honoured for military services. Those outstanding services had ended in personal glory for him at the close of the Second World War. Son of an Oxford law professor, he had a permanent commission in the RAF throughout the war. His VC was awarded in 1944 not, as is usual, for a single act of valour but for four years of flying bombers, completing over 100 missions, when most aircrew thought themselves lucky to survive five. He had already earned a DSO and two Bars and a DFC. Cheshire's last wartime assignment was as one of the two British observers on board the American aircraft that dropped the atomic bomb on Nagasaki in August 1945. (The other was a physicist, William Penney, also to become an OM.) He was quick to admit that this experience changed his life.

Cheshire resigned from the RAF and, after various travails and a conversion to Roman Catholicism, he founded the Cheshire Foundation Homes for disabled people. In due course, this was to be paralleled by his wife's, the Sue Ryder Foundation. They have grown and spread worldwide – for the relief of suffering.

Cheshire became an obvious candidate for honours but he declined a knighthood and a CH. Finally, 'because it was in the Queen's gift – he was always an ardent royalist'[6] he accepted the OM in 1981 and became the fourth VC to have this very unusual combination of initials. Barely a year before he died in 1992, Cheshire did accept a life peerage: a titular honour but with the opportunity (which he was briefly able to use) to speak in the House of Lords on matters affecting the disabled. He even made time to found the World Memorial Fund for Disaster Relief, which spawned the idea of a National Memorial Arboretum, in Staffordshire.

The opening paragraph of *The Times* obituary summed up Cheshire's life – military and civil – in the context of his honours:

> Leonard Cheshire held the two highest awards, for valour and for merit, which are in the gift of a British Sovereign. He won the Victoria Cross in 1944 as an RAF pilot with 'a record second to none in Bomber Command... placing himself, invariably in the forefront of the battle.' The Order of Merit, with which he was invested in 1981, marked the many years he spent in peacetime devoted, with religious fervour, to the welfare of disabled people.[7]

In her 1992 Christmas broadcast at the end of her 'annus horribilis', the Queen paid Cheshire a remarkable tribute, devoting nearly half her speech to him and his example:

> Curiously enough, it was a sad event which did as much as anything in 1992 to help me put my own worries into perspective. Just before he died, Leonard Cheshire came to see us with his fellow members of the Order of Merit. By then he was suffering from a long drawn-out and terminal illness. [...] he made no reference to his own illness but only to his hopes and plans to make life better for others ... [a] determination to put Christ's teaching to practical effect ... Perhaps this shining example of what a human being can achieve in a lifetime of dedication can inspire in the rest of us a belief in our own capacity to help others.[8]

The Queen's lunch for OMs was on 10 July; Cheshire died on 31 July.

In 1989, the pioneer of the modern hospice movement, **Cicely Saunders**, became the fifth woman recipient of the OM. Having once been a Nightingale Nurse, she wrote that

> it is particularly gratifying to join her. We heard a great deal about Miss Nightingale during our training in the War.[9]

At the relatively late age of 39, Saunders qualified as a doctor and turned her energies to palliative care. From small beginnings as a charity in 1961 and as a hospice from 1967, St Christopher's in Sydenham, South London has become what she described as 'a catalyst for other hospices', which have grown rapidly throughout the country. As Medical Director of St Christopher's from 1967–85 and Chairman from 1985 until her death in 2005, she concentrated on techniques to eliminate pain and raise the morale of terminal patients by high standards of nursing care and, especially, by the staff giving time to patients and their relatives: 'There is no parking meter at the bedside.'

Saunders was not only made a DBE in 1980 but also received two of the world's most prestigious, and (for the Hospice) financially rewarding prizes: the Templeton in 1981 and the Conrad N. Hilton Humanitarian in 2001.

Cicely Saunders had a self-confessed penchant for Poles: one, from the Warsaw Ghetto, who left her £500 and whom she considered to be the real founder of the Hospice; another whom she loved and whose death left her very sad, and a third, a painter, whom she married and who supported her in her work, not least by being artist-in-residence at the Hospice until his death.

Cicely Saunders died in 2005.

When the appointment as an OM of **Cardinal Basil Hume**, Archbishop of Westminster since 1976, was announced on 25 May 1999, it was hailed not only as highly deserved in personal terms – he was later described as 'arguably Britain's most eminent spiritual leader this century'[10] – but also as the first time the Order had gone to a Roman Catholic bishop. In fact, it was more significant. The Order had never been given to any bishop, of any faith or persuasion. Indeed, the only cleric to have received it was Owen Chadwick, for his eminence as an ecclesiastical historian. No leader of any faith had become an OM.

Hume had announced only two months before being made OM that he was suffering from inoperable cancer and it was only with great effort that he went to the Palace to receive the award. He managed to get out of his wheelchair, discard his stick and advance to receive the Badge from the Queen before sitting again. He died a few days later.

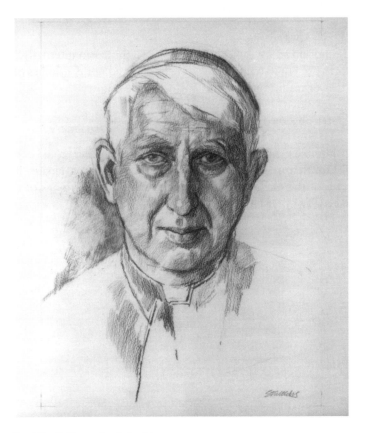

50 Cardinal Basil Hume by J. Stultiens.

It was said that the Queen had the greatest difficulty in persuading Hume to accept the Order.[11] He nevertheless acknowledged it generously:

> I would like to think that it was a recognition of the part played by Her Majesty's loyal Catholic subjects – laity, clergy and bishops – in the life of the nation.[12]

Press comment went along with this. On Hume's death, *The Times* said his

> great achievement [had been] that he enabled the Roman Catholic Church in England to find a place of full acceptance in the life of the nation.[13]

The experienced religious writer, Clifford Longley, pointed out, however, that

> he did not do so by somehow changing Catholicism internally, to make it worthy of equal treatment . . . [He had] cured non-Catholics of the last vestiges of traditional English anti-Catholic bigotry.[14]

Longley later observed that the Cardinal's

> mere humble membership of the Order of St Benedict would count more with him than the supreme honour and tribute contained in his membership of the Order of Merit . . . he always put the things of the spirit above every other value.[15]

16

THE WOMEN

1. 1907 Florence NIGHTINGALE
2. 1965 Dorothy HODGKIN
3. 1969 Dame Veronica WEDGWOOD
4. 1983 Mother TERESA (Honorary)
5. 1989 Dame Cicely SAUNDERS
6. 1990 Baroness THATCHER
7. 1991 Dame Joan SUTHERLAND
8. 1992 Dame Ninette DE VALOIS

Naturally, no woman has received the Order of Merit purely on account of her gender. The eight female recipients earned it in various capacities and it is in the chapters detailing particular fields of activity that I have described the achievements that brought them the honour.

In this chapter, I want to concentrate on why so few women have received the Order of Merit: eight is a fraction under 5 per cent of the total of 179 awards. If we exclude the 30 military Members – and no woman in the last century could realistically have been among them – the percentage rises fractionally to just over 5 per cent.

The Order was certainly not designed with women in mind, as a high-level exchange in February 1903 shows all too clearly. Anticipating an approach from the new Prime Minister, A. J. Balfour, suggesting **Florence Nightingale** for membership, the King's rivate Secretary quickly checked with the expert:

> Do you suppose that the Order of Merit can be given to *Women* as well as to men?[1]

51 Florence Nightingale, a bronze cast from a bust by Sir John Steell.

The instant response was that

> in framing the Statutes of the Order of Merit, I do not think it was contemplated to extend it to women, and the expression 'persons' was only intended for *men*, as in Statutes all members are referred to in a masculine sense . . . and the Order of Merit is now greatly prized for its rarity, and the more it is extended, the less it will be appreciated. Such is the way of the world.[2]

This brief correspondence concluded:

> The King however states very positively that women are *not* eligible for admittance to the Order, and so there is an end to the matter.[3]

It is difficult for us now to fathom the reasoning, if any, behind this sort of language, except to say that it is that of three men – the King and two close courtier-friends – who were in their sixties a hundred years ago.

The masculinity referred to in the above correspondence extended to the insignia, which was to be worn around the neck, hardly appropriate for formal female dress. Not until the 1935 Statute to expand membership in the ways described in Chapter 5, was the opportunity taken to acknowledge formally that there might be female Members. It was ordained that the Badge should be 'attached, in the case of women, to a similar riband tied in a bow on the left shoulder'.

It was Campbell-Bannerman who succeeded in wearing down the King regarding Florence Nightingale's receiving the OM. He mooted Florence Nightingale as one of

> two names which suggest themselves [the other was the equally aged botanist, Hooker]...when one looks back to the revolution which her services and example effected so far back as in the Crimean War, one wonders that nothing has been done to recognise her...I am sure it would be *most* popular.[4]

In line with his opposition to female suffrage or participation in the governance of the country, the King 'hung fire' over the proposal, 'being reluctant to give it [the OM] to women'.[5] But he finally agreed in November 1907. By a twist of fate, he now sits on his horse in Waterloo Place, eyes slightly cast down, facing but not looking at the standing statue opposite of 'Florence Nightingale, OM', her face averted.

Queen Victoria had given Nightingale a diamond brooch, designed by the Prince Consort, with 'Crimea' and 'Blessed are the merciful' engraved on it. Later, she was one of the first recipients of the Royal Red Cross when it was instituted in 1883 to reward the nursing services. Short of a peerage, on the lines of the rich philanthropist, Baroness Burdett-Coutts, there was no other suitable honour a woman could have received in the late nineteenth century.

Campbell-Bannerman was right about the popularity of the award. After welcoming the extension of 'that most coveted and most exceptional Order' to public service and to women, *The Times* declared:

> Of the paramount claims of Miss Nightingale to any honours that the Sovereign can bestow there is little need to speak...her name is one of the very few that is universally known, universally honoured.[6]

The Register of the Order of Merit in the Central Chancery of the Orders of Knighthood records her as 'Organiser of the nursing system during the Crimean War, 1854–1855' and it is not surprising that the King was asked whether she should be given the military insignia (with crossed swords). He replied that she should be a Civil and not Military Member.[7] It is therefore the male civilian Badge that now rests in the National Army Museum.

Florence Nightingale had been virtually confined to her bed in South Street, Mayfair, for many years and the King therefore commanded Sir Douglas Dawson (Comptroller of the Lord Chamberlain's Department) to present the insignia to her on his behalf. The famous scene has been described in every biography of her. Lytton Strachey called it

> a final revivification of the ancient myth... Propped up by pillows, she dimly recognised that some compliment was being paid her. 'Too kind – too kind,' she murmured; and she was not ironical.[8]

Strachey must have wondered what awaited her, since 'her conception of God was certainly not orthodox. She felt towards Him as she might have felt towards a glorified sanitary engineer.'[9]

Nightingale died on 13 August 1910. Following her death, there was consideration of avoiding a second 'embarrassment' by giving women their own Order of Merit. In 1911, a small committee, chaired by Sir Douglas Dawson and including the ubiquitous Lord Esher and H. Farnham Burke (Somerset Herald at the College of Arms), were asked to consider the creation of:

> A ladies Order of Merit to be conferred on ladies who have distinguished themselves by Services to the State in the cause of humanity, in Art, in Literature, etc. The Order to be of two Classes.[10]

Their views were sought on the name and precedence of the order and whether there should be titles to distinguish the two classes.

In their interim report, on 3 April 1911,[11] the committee deferred the question of name but recommended that it should be given precedence after the Order of the Crown of India, have a yellow riband with insignia of silver-gilt and enamel for the First Class and silver for the Second Class. The members would be styled simply Members of the First or Second Class. But, only a month later, Burke was told that the idea 'had been dropped. It is possible that later on the whole thing may be reconsidered.'[12]

The issue never was reconsidered and there remained the so-called problem of the 'eligibility' of women for *the* Order of Merit. In that long period between the appointment of the first woman in 1907 and the second in 1965, some other women had been suggested. In 1922, approaches were made to the Palace from various quarters on behalf of the 74-year-old Ellen

Terry, who was

> very poor, very deaf and nearly blind and can still make an audi-
> ence shout with enthusiasm... She will stand alone in at least two
> generations.[13]

The Palace response to another approach which had emphasised her
contribution to the war effort, was that

> it would not be possible to consider Ellen Terry for the Order of Merit. It
> would be altogether a new departure and, moreover, it is very question-
> able whether her case would come within the conditions of the Statutes
> of the Order.[14]

There was some effort to find women for the Order. On one of the
occasions when Morshead was producing a list of possibles for Hardinge,
he lamented: 'I have sought in vain for a woman. I tried to find a Scotsman
but...'[15]

An OM which was thought, at least by the recipient, to have been shared
with a woman was that conferred on Sidney Webb (Lord Passfield) in June
1944. The indomitable Beatrice, his partner in a lifelong working relationship of social history and reform as well as in marriage, had died in April
1943. Her biographer was quite clear on the point (if not so clear about the
Order):

> After her death, the Churchill Government conferred the Order of Merit
> upon her husband. This order is at present confined to the 'superior' sex;
> but Lord Passfield was assured that it was given in recognition of the
> social and political work of the partnership.[16]

For his part, Sidney went out of his way to make the point. His replies to
congratulatory letters included the phrase: 'My one impression is one of
vexation at my wife not being included in the Presentation.'[17]

Another woman who came near to the OM, in her lifetime, was Vita
Sackville-West, the poet and gardener. Her husband, Harold Nicolson, was
told over lunch at the Beefsteak Club in December 1944 by the King's Private
Secretary (Sir Alan Lascelles) that her name had been 'mentioned' for the
OM. Nicolson was excited:

> I do not think he would have said this to me had it not been 'mentioned'
> seriously. If she gets it, she will be overjoyed: the first woman since
> Florence Nightingale. But I shall say nothing to her, since if it does not
> go to her, she will be disappointed, and so far the idea has never entered
> her dear head.[18]

There is a footnote to say that nothing was heard of the proposal but that Vita was made a CH in January 1948.

Vita also much later, in 1960, gave a 'thumbs down' to her husband's reference to a possible OM for Edith Sitwell:

> I am not a mean-minded or envious person...Edith has built up her personality in many fortuitous ways – her strange appearance, her lovely hands, her Dante-esque headdress, and all the Sitwellian legend. But I cannot feel that she is a great poet...Not worthy of the OM.

She lamented:

> I cannot think of *anybody* worthy of the OM. What an awful reflection on English literature today![19]

I think this is a convenient point at which to compare the OM with the CH as regards the admission of women. Of the 307 CHs appointed since its institution in 1917, 29 have been women: just under 10 per cent. As I observed at the beginning of this chapter, the percentage of female OMs is around 5 per cent – not such a dramatic difference.

To return now to the seven women appointed OMs after that long gap from 1907 to 1965, all of them in the reign of the only female Sovereign of the Order. Between them, as we have seen from previous chapters, they have spanned the range of civilian achievement: a scientist (Hodgkin), a scholar (Wedgwood), a 'man' of affairs (Margaret Thatcher), two musicians (de Valois and Joan Sutherland) and two humanitarians (Mother Teresa and Cicely Saunders).

Whereas Nightingale had been 87 when appointed an OM, the others (bar one) have been appointed at much younger ages. De Valois was 94 but the average age of the other six was 62, well below that of the men: 69. Even when de Valois is included, the average age rises only to 67. Hodgkin, at 54, was among the dozen youngest OMs ever appointed.

The basic question remains: why so few women OMs? It is tempting to argue, as some women have to me, that it reflects the prejudice of a basically male establishment throughout the twentieth century. I suggest, however, that appointments to the Order have normally tried to reflect the society in which it found itself.

The century saw one woman Prime Minister out of 20 – and she did get the OM! Of 65 British scientists who gained Nobel Prizes, only one was a woman – and she also got the OM! There have been no female Presidents of the Royal Society, to which the first women were elected only in 1945. At the end of 2000, only 43 of the 1,198 Fellows of the Royal Society were women; in 2000, of the 42 new FRSs, two were women.[20]

It is possible to look back at the pioneers of women's participation in many aspects of national life. Florence Nightingale received the OM very much on that basis. Many other women, however, were pioneers by virtue of fighting the male establishment to an extent that was hardly likely to bring official honours in their lifetime.

To be the first women in a particular activity would not have been judged in its day by a male establishment sufficient to justify the new and exceptionally high OM, even in the woman's old age. Only in a couple of cases was it judged sufficient for a CH and they were both politicians: Nancy Astor, the first woman to sit in the House of Commons, and Margaret Bondfield, the first woman to chair the TUC and to be a Cabinet Minister and Privy Counsellor. The first woman doctor, Elizabeth Blackwell, died in 1910 and the pioneer doctor and first woman mayor, Elizabeth Garrett Anderson, died in 1917, only six months after the institution of the CH. Neither of them had the iconic status of Florence Nightingale.

A final word on women and the OM: on 4 August 2000, there was one vacancy in the Order of Merit. Queen Elizabeth The Queen Mother had many orders, not least the Garter and the Thistle, but the conferment of the OM on her hundredth birthday would have recognised her 'exceptionally meritorious' contribution to British national life during the twentieth century – as Duchess, Queen Consort (during a great conflict) and Queen Mother, choosing to support a husband and daughter in roles which they did not choose. Not only would the appointment have been vastly popular, which is not the object of such appointments, but, more importantly, the resulting coverage of the Order itself might have woken the public up to its true importance.

17

THE HONORARY MEMBERS

1. 1906 Field Marshal Prince YAMAGATA (Military)
2. 1906 Field Marshal Prince OYAMA (Military)
3. 1906 Admiral of the Fleet Marquis TOGO (Military)
4. 1918 Marshal of France Ferdinand FOCH (Military)
5. 1919 Marshal of France Joseph JOFFRE (Military)
6. 1945 General of the Army Dwight EISENHOWER (Military)
7. 1947 John G. WINANT (Civil)
8. 1955 Albert SCHWEITZER (Civil)
9. 1963 Sarvepalli RADHAKRISHNAN (Civil)
10. 1983 Mother TERESA (Civil)
11. 1995 Nelson MANDELA (Civil)

The honorary membership of the Order of Merit has never remotely developed like that of its model, the Pour le mérite. The 30 foreign members, equal in number to the Germans, are an integral part of that institution. The Statutes of the Order of Merit have never fixed the number of foreign Members but instead have always allowed for an unlimited number. In theory, they could have equalled their ordinary (mostly British) counterparts. In fact, there have been only 11 honorary members out of the total of 179.

The first six honorary members were all military: the Japanese, two field marshals and one admiral, in 1906; the two French marshals in 1918/19 and the American General of the Army in 1945. The next five were all civilian: the American wartime ambassador in 1947; the French philosopher and medical missionary in 1955; the Indian religious philosopher and statesman in 1963; the Albanian/Indian living saint in 1983; and the South African living saint in 1995.

The Japanese

The Japanese appointments may appear strange a century later and they need to be put into context more than any of the other honorary awards. Foch, Joffre and Eisenhower, with their direct connection with British war efforts, need no explanation. Yamagata, Oyama and Togo, without such direct connection, do.

The first years of the century had seen a determined effort to improve Anglo–Japanese relations. The co-operation during the Boxer Rising of 1900 had been followed by the formal alliance of 1902. Japan was emerging as a major power on the world scene and this was confirmed by her decisive defeat of Russia in the war of 1904–05. Britain's important interests in the East, not least in her Indian Empire and Asian colonies, impelled her to build on that alliance. The conferment of the Order of the Garter on the Emperor Mutsuhito in 1906 presented a ceremonial occasion to underline this co-operation.

The special Mission to present the Garter was led by the King's nephew, Prince Arthur of Connaught, and it included one of the original OMs, Admiral of the Fleet Sir Edward Seymour, who had led the international naval brigade (including a large Japanese component) sent to relieve the foreign legations in Peking during the Boxer Rising. As was common at the time, many British decorations were conferred on Japanese dignitaries, including ten Knights Grand Cross and five Knights Commanders. There were GCBs for the powerful Ministers of State for the Navy and the Army. Given that the whole level of awards had been placed so high, what could be given to the three very powerful men who had led Japan to victory in the war: Yamagata, Oyama, and Togo? The answer was the new prestigious Order of Merit, which the King/Founder and others regarded as superior to the routine orders.

The King's original intention had been to confer the OM on only Admiral Togo, the best known of the three in Britain because of his dramatic naval victory, and 'Marshal Commanding the Forces in Manchuria' – this was Oyama but his name was not even specified in the letter from the Private Secretary to the Assistant Private Secretary. A few days later the latter has added the name of Yamagata.[1] Obviously, the Palace found the proposed Japanese awards difficult to deal with in detail.

Prince Arthur duly conferred the three OMs in Japan on 21 February 1906. When it came to gazetting the awards later in the year, the King/Founder showed the esteem in which he held his new order: 'I do not wish the word Honorary to be used for 'Order of Merit', only the other orders. Of course,

the *Garter* is also *not* Honorary.' In other words, the foreign members of
those two orders were fully part of the fellowship.

Yamagata was the most powerful of the three, a soldier who was actively
engaged in politics (as a Special Adviser to the Emperor). He was regarded as
chiefly responsible for making the military class the most powerful faction in
the government. He had studied the military systems of France and Germany
and was, at various times, Chief of the General Staff and Minister for War,
for Home Affairs, for Justice and Prime Minister (from 1889–91 and 1898–
1900). In 1904, he was again Chief of the General Staff and after the war
he was made a prince. He remained a very powerful influence in Japanese
politics almost until his death in 1922.

Oyama, like Yamagata, had had European experience, as an observer
with the Prussian forces in the war with France in 1870. He rose to high
command both as Minister for War and as a commander in the field. He
was already a field marshal and a marquis by 1904. He commanded the
armies that defeated Russia and was raised to the rank of prince.

Togo had been trained in Britain from 1870–78 on *HMS Worcester* and
at the Royal Naval College, Greenwich, before being commissioned into
the Imperial Navy. Throughout the 1904–05 war, he had commanded
the Japanese fleet and, by blockading the Russian parts of Port Arthur and
Vladivostok, had secured the communications of the Japanese armies in
Korea and Manchuria. His largely British-built fleet crushed the exhausted
Russian Baltic fleet at the Battle of Tsushima on 27–28 May 1905.

Togo was made a count in 1907 and a marquis shortly before his death in
1934. He had been made a GCVO when Prince Arthur of Connaught visited
Japan again in 1912 for the funeral of Emperor Matsuhito.

Togo was taciturn and modest. A British diplomat in Japan in 1911
described his as 'the most silent man I ever met (he was alleged by the
Japanese never to say more than five words a day).'

The French

The French appointments after the First World War were much more appropriate. The two Marshals, **Joffre** and **Foch**, already GCBs, had commanded
the French armies alongside the British throughout the conflict and, in the
last stages, Foch had commanded British troops as well. He was famed in
Britain not only for his leadership in the final victory of 1918 but also for
his resolute message to Joffre in the first weeks of the war: 'My centre is
giving way, my right is in retreat; situation excellent. I shall attack.' After
the revival of the title 'Marshal of France', Joffre had been the first to receive
it; Foch received it later.

Within three weeks of the end of the war, King George V had honoured
Foch at a ceremony at the British Embassy in Paris on 29 November 1918.

The presentation took place at a reception following a dinner given by the Ambassador, Lord Derby. In French, the King said:

> I am happy to confer upon you the highest military distinction in my country as a sign of the esteem which my people have for you and for your leadership of the Allied Armies to victory.[2]

The event was special in two ways. It was witnessed by two future Sovereigns of the Order (the Prince of Wales, later King Edward VIII, and Prince Albert, later King George VI).

Père (or Papa) Joffre's turn came on a visit to Britain in the summer of 1919. After receiving an honorary degree at Oxford, he went to Buckingham Palace on 26 June to receive the OM from the King. He then lunched with the King and Queen and accompanied them to the Royal Tournament.

Foch, however, had one more British distinction to come, which placed him, as the commander at the end of a war, ahead of the commander at the beginning of it. On 19 July 1919, he was appointed a Field Marshal in the British Army; Joffre never was.

There might well have been a third French OM: Georges Clemenceau, Prime Minister from 1917–20. George V had wanted to make him a GCB but the answer to the British Ambassador's soundings 'had been in the negative [because] he had made a resolution never at anytime to accept any honour'. So when Lloyd George, in Paris in January 1920 for the ratification of the Treaty of Versailles, had wanted to obtain the King's permission to offer the OM to him, the Ambassador had advised him to sound Clemenceau first. The Frenchman 'told him that he would respectfully ask to decline. The actual offer therefore of the Order of Merit was never made.'[3]

The Americans

The last honorary military OM parallels that of Foch and the precedent was very much in George VI's mind when, a month after the end of the war against Germany, he decided to give the Order to General of Army **Dwight D. Eisenhower**, Supreme Commander, Allied Expeditionary Forces. A week later, Eisenhower was fêted in London. On the morning of 12 June 1945, he received at Guildhall the Honorary Freedom of the City of London and a sword of honour.

After telling the crowds from the balcony of the Mansion House that, 'I am now a Londoner myself. I have got just as much right to be down in that crowd yelling as you have,'[4] Eisenhower went to Buckingham Palace for tea with the King and Queen and Princess Elizabeth. Beforehand, the King took him aside and presented him with, as he later recalled, 'one of the most prized decorations any man can receive in Britain, the Order of Merit. As I recall, only 12 men in uniformed services and 12 civilians can hold the

52 General Dwight D. Eisenhower by George A. Campbell.

Order at any one time'[5] – almost correct. The King also handed Eisenhower a sealed letter, to be opened later. It was in manuscript and in very warm terms:

> the greatest possible pleasure to confer on you the Order of Merit ... complete confidence in your leadership of my forces under your command ... you established a tradition of trust and friendship between your people and mine ... sincerely glad to have this opportunity of showing my personal gratitude to you ... you will always be a very welcome guest, and friend in this country.[6]

The award was well received. *The Times* described the OM as 'existing to honour the highest form of public service'.

The OM was not Eisenhower's first British decoration but it was the one of which he was most proud. He had been made a GCB in 1943. When Eisenhower visited Canada in 1953, he wore the OM to the state dinner, telling his host, the Governor-General, that: 'he wanted to wear it rather than any other British decoration because it had been given him personally by the King.'[7] He had always regarded it as 'one of the most appreciated of all awards given to me by a Foreign Government.'[8]

Eisenhower is not a man of whom the reader needs to be told much. 'Ike' was of humble mid-Western farming stock, of Swiss-German origin. As a profile of him in 1951 recalled, he

> was a mere lieutenant-colonel at the outbreak of the last war, who finished it as the conqueror in Europe at the head of the mightiest army the world has seen and is now the Supreme Commander of the North Atlantic forces ... He has been accused of being pro-British: be that as it may, there is no doubt that we British are pro-Eisenhower.[9]

On Eisenhower's death in 1969, 25 years after his military peak and almost a decade after he had left the presidency, the British press were full of praise, more for his military than his civilian leadership: 'He supremely rose to the task of leading the British ... peerless qualities as chairman at headquarters';[10] 'It is as a supremely successful Supreme Commander that he will, above all, be remembered on this side of the Atlantic';[11] '... his greatest military achievement: the effective leadership of the most heterogeneous military force in history.'[12]

The first civilian honorary OM mirrored that of Dwight Eisenhower. As he had been the most prominent American military figure in Britain during the war, **John Gilbert Winant** ('Gil') had been the most prominent American civilian figure, as Ambassador to the Court of St James's from 1941–46.

Winant's official profile in Britain was always very high. When he arrived in February 1941, the arrangements were those for a head of state: he was met at the airport by the King's brother, the Duke of Kent, who accompanied him on an official train to Windsor, where King George VI was at the station to greet him and take him through crowded streets to the Castle. He summed it all up:

> It was the first time in the history of Great Britain that a King had gone to meet an Ambassador. He was returning the courtesy which President Roosevelt had shown Lord Halifax, and I did not even have a battleship![13] (Halifax had arrived in the Potomac on *King George V*.)

Of course, Winant had all the traditional access of an American Ambassador – intensified by the wartime conditions. He was everywhere: at the Palace, in Downing Street and frequently at Chequers. He knew everyone in the government but his circle went wider and included men of the intellectual left, like R. H. Tawney, H. G. Wells and Harold Laski. Roosevelt, who had after all appointed Winant in succession to the unsympathetic

Joseph Kennedy, thought he was 'really a most understanding person'.[14]
Mary Soames, Churchill's youngest daughter singled him out thus:

> the time of war brought to Winston and Clementine – and indeed to
> all our family – one very special friend: Gil Winant, the American
> Ambassador... Brilliant choice... Made friends with people in every
> walk of life. He was particularly beloved in the East End of London,
> where he was often to be seen in the thick of the air-raids. A man of
> quiet, intensely concentrated charm, Gil very quickly became a dear
> friend of us all, entering into our joys and sorrows, jokes and rows (in
> these last, always as a peace-maker).[15]

A successor as American Ambassador in 1991 was unimpressed:

> I have been reading [his] bland memoirs... Found fault with nobody:
> Roosevelt was saintly, so was Churchill. I would not endorse a Kitty
> Kelley approach to World War Two, but he is simply not credible.[16]

Perhaps the final word on the character of this honorary OM might appropriately come from another OM writing recently about a third OM – Roy
Jenkins on Churchill:

> He was staunchly pro-British, a man of quiet, unpretentious but not
> unnoticeable charm... Well before this [the foundering of Winant's mar-
> riage], Winant had fallen ethereally in love with Sarah Churchill, then
> in her late twenties, which helped to attract him to the Churchill family,
> to the British cause in general and to Chequers in particular. He was
> a helpful ambassador, but his look of calm asceticism concealed inner
> seething. He committed suicide in 1947.[17]

The esteem in which Winant was held in Britain at the end of the war is
shown by the comment on his appointment to the Order of Merit, which
(being honorary) was announced alongside, but not as part of, the New Year
Honours of 1947. In a leader, *The Times* commented that the honour was
'both a memorial of Anglo-American comradeship in danger and as a mark
of gratitude to an Ambassador for whom personal friendship in England
was, and remains, of the warmest'. A few months later, on his death, *The
Times* called the award 'a fitting tribute to the man who had shared our
darkest days with us'.[18]

The award for Winant gestated for a long time. In May 1946, George VI
mentioned it to the Prime Minister, who thought it an 'excellent idea'; he also
consulted the Foreign Secretary, who said it 'would be most suitable'.[19] He
received the insignia at Buckingham Palace on 16 January before lunching
with the King and Queen.

The post-war 'saints'

After the two world wars, honorary membership of the Order of Merit entered a new phase, albeit very limited: four appointments in 55 years, all to venerated rather than merely famous figures.

In 1953, **Dr Albert Schweitzer** was awarded the Nobel Peace Prize as the Founder of the Lambaréné Hospital in Gabon. In February 1955, shortly after his eightieth birthday, he was made an honorary OM. He was seen as a man who could have achieved greatness as a philosopher, a theologian or a musician (in all of which fields he had a doctorate) but who had chosen to qualify as a medical doctor before going in 1913 as a missionary to what was then French Equatorial Africa. Schweitzer had designed and largely built himself a hospital in the jungle, where he ministered to the medical and spiritual needs of the indigenous people. In recent years, he has sometimes been criticised as too autocratic and paternalistic, even racist: the 'great white', who never trained black doctors.

At the time of the award there were no doubts about Schweitzer's place in history. In a leading article headed 'Pour le mérite', a compliment to his Franco-German origins in Alsace and to the German order (which he received a couple of weeks later), *The Times* wrote:

> the Queen did what she alone is qualified to do: she associated the whole of the peoples of the British Commonwealth with the world's judgement that this is one of the great men of the age. Dr Schweitzer might claim more than one of the distinctions that the order exists to register – in theology and medicine, in music and philosophy; but without doubt he is honoured especially for his lifelong dedication to the relief of suffering. Therein he has only one peer among the past companions of the order, Florence Nightingale; and each is unique in its records, she as the only woman, he as the first civilian who has not been a subject of the British Crown.[20]

The next award of an honorary OM was a combination of the political and personal. On 12 June 1963, **President Sarvepalli Radhakrishnan** of India arrived in London on a state visit, the first to be paid to Britain by a Commonwealth Head of State. Instead of receiving the GCB or the Royal Victorian Chain, the customary awards for a visiting President on such occasions, he was singled out for this special distinction. The 'philosopher-king' was appropriately honoured.

The honour was greeted by *The Times* with a leading article headed 'Statesman and Scholar', which said:

> The mere fact that a man of his intellectual eminence and scholarly detachment should rise to hold such a position says much for the system

as well as for the man. Few other countries in the class known nowadays as emergent or newly independent can point to a man of similar calibre in such high office.

As to his philosophy, *The Times* explained that, in his writings on comparative religion,

> his concern was to present to the West the richness of eastern thought, neither aggressively nor apologetically, but because he believed that only in a true spiritual dialogue could East and West come to terms.[21]

Radhakrishnan came from a poor Brahmin family, although he accepted the fact that his father was probably not his natural parent.[22] He progressed up the official academic ladder to become George V Professor of Philosophy at Calcutta University. His first work was a study of the philosophy of (Sir) Rabindranath Tagore, whose Nobel Prize for Literature in 1913 had sent a wave of pride through intellectual India. In 1931, the year in which he came Vice-Chancellor of Andhra University, he was knighted, without prior consultation because he was a member of the Indian Education Service. He was a friend of Pandit Nehru and a supporter of the nationalist movement; the cricketing Governor of Bengal, Sir Stanley (FS) Jackson, commented: 'All the police reports are against him, but I like him.'

In 1926, Radhakrishnan began his life's work of interpreting Indian philosophy for the Western world by frequent lecturing in Britain and the United States, becoming Spalding Professor of the Eastern Religions and Ethics at Oxford (and a Fellow of All Souls) in 1936, a chair he held until 1952. He was the first Indian elected to the British Academy in 1939.

In 1947, independent India called Radhakrishnan to public service, initially to chair a commission on the universities and in 1949 to be Ambassador to the Soviet Union. He surprised Stalin by patting him on the cheek when he took his final leave in 1952; with tears in his eyes, the dictator said: 'You are the first person to treat me as a human being and not as a monster.'[23]

After serving as Vice President of India from 1952–62, Radhakrishnan became the second President in 1962. His period of office was dramatic, both externally and internally. There were wars with China and Pakistan. Two Prime Ministers, the veteran Nehru and his successor, Lal Bahadur Shastri, died in office. Radhakrishnan established the stabilising constitutional precedent of swearing-in the senior member of the Cabinet as Prime Minister until the ruling Congress Party had elected their new leader. His term ended in conflict with Indira Gandhi, Nehru's daughter and Shastri's successor and once a good friend; she did not attend his funeral.

Like Schweitzer, Radhakrishnan was elected to the German Order Pour le mérite and he received the Indian honour most closely equating to that and the OM, the Bharat Ratna, which is given for 'exceptional work for

53 Mother Teresa of Calcutta.

the advancement of art, literature and science and in recognition of public service of the highest order'. He qualified on more than one ground.

Twenty years after Radhakrishnan, it was another Indian (albeit by adoption) who was made an honorary OM: **Mother Teresa of Calcutta**. It was also on the occasion of a state visit, this time *to* India by the Queen. Although the recipient was far below Heads of State in terms of status, she was far above most of them in the respect she enjoyed from the world at large.

Like Schweitzer, Mother Teresa had recently (in 1979) received the Nobel Peace Prize, for her work in founding in Calcutta in 1949 the Roman Catholic order of Missionaries of Charity, which had spread to over 100 countries. For their work in Australia, she had received the OBE and been made an honorary Companion of the Order of Australia (AC). She had also been the first recipient in 1973 of the Nobel-like Templeton Prize for Progress in Religion, which was later awarded to other OMs: Radhakrishnan in 1975 and Dame Cecily Saunders in 1981. Like Radhakrishnan, she had received the Bharat Ratna.

Although, strictly speaking, the award was not the concern of the British Government, as a matter of convenience the British High Commissioner was asked by the Queen's Private Secretary to sound out Mother Teresa herself. She accepted the offer and, in her blue and white sari habit, overlaid with an old cardigan, received the insignia from the Queen at Rashtrapati Bhavan, the President's House in New Delhi. She was reported as regarding the Order as 'a great gift and a recognition of the problems of the poor. It's a beautiful gesture.'[24] Also that:

> I think things like this make the presence of the poor very real. People become more aware of the poor and it creates a greater concern.[25]

Mother Teresa died, at the age of 87, on 5 September 1997. There were lengthy and fulsome obituaries:

> More than anyone else of her time, Mother Teresa came to be regarded by millions as the embodiment of human goodness. By her compassion, humility and, it also has to be said, shrewd eye for publicity she raised public concern for the destitute; by devoting herself with single-minded vigour to the relief of human suffering, she galvanised individuals, both believers and non-believers, and even governments into action. Not since Albert Schweitzer has any one person had such an inspirational effect.[26]

This was the woman whom the Queen decided personally to include within her special fellowship.

When I come to the only living Honorary Member of the Order of Merit, **Nelson Mandela**, there is little that I can say that does not sound presumptuous or patronising, superficial or superfluous, trite or trivial. He is a secular saint and no less powerful for that, ranking not far below Mahatma Gandhi – and Gandhi did not spend 27 consecutive years in prison. As his period of incarceration in South Africa grew longer, so Mandela's hold on the imagination of the world grew stronger. His release from prison in February 1990 was one of the great news stories of recent years but what convinced most people of his greatness was what he chose to do with his freedom.

The absence of bitterness, the search for reconciliation and the negotiations with the apartheid government of F. W. de Klerk (with whom he shared the Nobel Peace Prize in 1993) for a peaceful transfer of power to the majority of the people – all these magnified the regard in which Mandela was already held when, in May 1994, he was sworn in as the first President of post-apartheid, non-racial South Africa. The inter-racial bloodbath, so often feared after the gruesome events in Sharpeville in 1961 and in Soweto in 1976, never happened.

Prince Philip represented the Queen at Nelson Mandela's inauguration and less than a year later, in March 1995, he accompanied Her Majesty

54 Nelson Mandela.

on a state visit to the 'new' South Africa, symbolising the long and close British connection with the country. Inevitably, there was speculation over the honour to be bestowed on the new President. A suggestion that the special nature of the visit and of the man might be marked with the OM found favour with the Queen and the Foreign Secretary, Douglas Hurd.

Although, strictly speaking, the OM is no concern of the government, the conferment of decorations on a state visit certainly is. As I have shown in Chapter 5, even in substantive appointments, the views of the Prime Minister cannot be wholly disregarded. Still less so is this the case with honorary appointments, where the British Head of State is making a small act of foreign policy. The subtlety of its being a 'personal' decision would not hold up, overseas or even in Britain, if the appointment were a controversial one. The British press eventually focused on the true reason for the OM: that a knighthood 'may not be sufficiently distinguished to mark the Queen's esteem, which suggests that an even more exclusive decoration has been chosen . . . the Order of Merit', which was 'markedly rarer than a knighthood'.[27] The Queen gave the insignia to the President in a low-key ceremony on the back porch of his office in Cape Town.

For the Mandela award, *The Times* reverted to the sort of reverential leading article language that it had used for Schweitzer:

> The Queen chose to decorate him in a manner commensurate with his stature as one of the foremost statesmen of the age. In bestowing on him the Order of Merit – an honour held only by Mother Teresa, among living non-Britons – she paid to South Africa's democratic revolution a rich and proper tribute.[28]

The might have beens

Why have there been relatively so few honorary Members of the Order of Merit – only 11 out of 179 in the first 100 years? The British have never been as keen as other countries to decorate foreigners, or to accept foreign awards. In general, British honorary awards require a link with Britain or services to British interests and not only services to British humanity at large. Albert Schweitzer's OM in 1955 was the royal exception that proved the governmental rule. There would be little more imagination about bringing foreigners into the companionship of the Order.

Let us look at some of the 'might have beens'. Britain was affected by the work of Marie Curie, the French/Polish double Nobel Prize winner, and Albert Einstein, a towering giant in twentieth-century physics, but there was insufficient link with Britain. It was otherwise with the Danish physicist, Niels Bohr. He studied with J. J. Thomson and Rutherford and, as a lecturer at Manchester University, formulated his model of the hydrogen atom, for which he received the Nobel Prize in 1922. During the Second World War, he escaped from occupied Denmark to Britain and went on to the United States, where he played a major role in the development of the atomic bomb. Dale described him as 'one of the world's great men of science, in the lineage of Newton, Rutherford and Einstein.'[29]

Guglielmo Marconi, the Italian radio pioneer and Nobel Prize-winner, had close links with Britain. He had a commercial enterprise in London, where he did much of his pioneering work; in 1901, he succeeded in sending a radio signal from Cornwall to Newfoundland. The GCVO he received from George V in 1914 might more appropriately have been the OM.

The OM could equally well have gone to the Norwegian humanitarian, explorer and diplomat, Fridtjof Nansen. He was his country's first Minister in London from 1906–08, but it was for his work as the League of Nations High Commissioner for Refugees after the First World War that the Order would have been appropriate. The repatriation of prisoners of war, the exchange of national groups after border changes (peaceful 'ethnic cleansing') and distress relief earned him the Nobel Prize for Peace in 1922. He gave his name to the Nansen Passport for displaced persons and the International Nansen Office for Refugees.

Not surprisingly, several Americans had links with Britain that could well have brought them the OM if there had been a more imaginative attitude. Its award to Eleanor Roosevelt after the Second World War would have recognised not only her own emerging role as one of the world's most distinguished women but also (posthumously) FDR's support for Britain in the war.

After the Second World War, the American field commander (Eisenhower) and the three British chiefs of staff (Alanbrooke, Portal and Cunningham) received the OM. As I have observed earlier, no British field commander did. Nor did the chairman of the American chiefs of staff, General of the Army George C. Marshall, with whom British co-operation had been close if not always easy. The close relationship was continued when he was Secretary of State (creating the Marshall Plan, which benefited Britain as well as continental Europe) and Secretary of Defense (during the Korean War). When he represented the United States at the Coronation in 1953, he could appropriately have been given the OM – of either variety: military or civil.

An American who actually came near to an OM is the portrait painter, John Singer Sargent, who lived and worked in London from 1885 until his death 40 years later. An RA (and nearly President of the Academy), he declined a knighthood from Campbell-Bannerman, preferring to retain his American citizenship. Asquith's attempt to get him the OM met with stiff opposition from George V: '[He] does not care about Sargent as an artist and he does not like him as a man and he is an American, though that of course is no bar to his being in the Order.'[30] Asquith vigorously rebutted the King's three points but to no avail.

Finally, I mention two notable Scottish emigrés who became Americans but retained strong links with Britain. Andrew Carnegie made a fortune from his Pittsburgh steel mills before giving away $ 350 million, much of it to build public libraries in Britain. He believed that 'the man who dies rich, dies in disgrace' and he certainly used his money 'towards the advancement of the Arts, Learning, Literature and Science', as provided for in the Statutes of the Order.

Alexander Graham Bell went to Canada before moving on to the United States and taking citizenship there. While still in Canada, he became the first person to transmit speech by electronic means – 'Mr Watson, come here, I want you' – to summon his assistant from the next room. Queen Victoria was impressed with a demonstration by Bell of the new 'telegram'.

It is a pity that these two famous former British subjects were not included within the fellowship of the Order of Merit, of which they would have been worthy Members.

18

STATISTICS: DOES 'OM' EQUAL 'OLD MAN'?

> To understand God's thoughts we must study statistics,
> for these are the measure of his purpose.
> (Attributed to Florence Nightingale, OM)

Since the statistics had to be calculated on a particular date, the chosen date was 6 February 2002, the fiftieth anniversary of the Queen's accession and only just short of the one-hundredth anniversary of the Order itself.

Numbers in the Order

There have been 176 Members of the Order of Merit. Of these, Edward VII appointed 27 in eight years, George V 37 in nearly 26 years, Edward VIII none in a year, and George VI 32 in 15 years: 96 in the first 50 years. Elizabeth II has appointed 80 in the following 50 years.

Of the 30 Military Members, only two have been appointed in this reign. There have been no military appointments since 1965.

The highest number of appointments in one year was naturally on its foundation: 12 in 1902. Since then, only once have six been appointed – in 1905; and only thrice have there been 5 – in 1946, 1969 and 1983. There have been appointments in 71 years but none in 29 years and twice there have been no appointments for three years in a row: 1932–34 and 1978–80.

The Order was not full until 1953, when for the first time it had 24 Members (and one Honorary). It has been kept fuller in the present reign than before. It was relatively 'under-used' in its first 50 years. At the end of each last year of a decade, the number of living Ordinary Members was: 1910–17; 1920–18; 1930–15; 1940–17; 1950–17; 1960–24; 1970–22; 1980–20; 1990–23; 2000–23.

Given the population of the United Kingdom over the years 1902–2002, the chance of being appointed to the Order was about 1 in 2 million.

The longest tenure of the Order so far has been Prince Philip, who by August 2006 had had it for over 38 years. Adrian had it for the next longest, 35 years and 55 days (1942–77). G. M. Trevelyan had it for 32 years and Masefield for 31. The shortest tenures have been those of Hume (22 days), Waverley (27 days), Pound (six weeks), Henry James (two months) and Hughes (two and a half months).

The average length of tenure of the 145 dead Ordinary Members was 11.83 years. On at least four occasions, the Order was conferred in clear anticipation of the recipient's early death: Henry James (1916), Waverley (1957), Hughes (1998) and Hume (1999).

Ages

Bernard Shaw said that OM equals 'Old Man' and Meredith supposedly said likewise. B. K. Nehru, a distinguished Indian High Commissioner to Britain, when presented with a high honour on his ninetieth birthday, said: 'They only give it to people who are so old that they are probably on the way out.' I fear that the statistics in this section will show they all had a point.

The average age of appointment to the Order has been 69.00: two in their forties; 27 in their fifties; 67 in their sixties; 57 in their seventies; 17 in their eighties; and six in their nineties. Of those six oldest, five were civilians, Hooker and Forster at 90 (on their birthdays); Gielgud at 92; de Valois at 94 and Denning at 98. The only military nonagenarian was Keppel at 93, in the original list. Of the six youngest, three were civilians: Prince Phillip (47), Britten (51) and Adrian (52), and three were military: Beatty (48) and Kitchener and Portal (52).

The average age of death of the 155 deceased Members was 81.31.

The average age of the 21 living Members is 78.9: one in his nineties; nine in their eighties; nine in their seventies; and two in their sixties.

Birthplaces

Where were the OMs born? Of course, the majority were born in the United Kingdom: 104 of those of the 165 Ordinary Members whose birthplaces I have traced.

Thirty-four Members were born overseas: 18 in what was then the Empire (seven in Australia, three each in New Zealand and India; two each in Canada and South Africa and one in Ceylon); and 16 foreign countries (nine in continental Europe, four in the USA, two in Latin America and one in Egypt).

The first Ordinary Member who was born *and* living permanently overseas was Smuts, in 1947, closely followed by Mackenzie King. A few others followed in the 1950s (Penfield and Burnet), the 1960s (Dixon), the 1970s (Beaglehole and Pearson), the 1980s (Nolan, although he moved to Britain) and the 1990s (Joan Sutherland).

Titles

For an Order that is often vaunted as an honour for those who do not want a title, it has contained a remarkably high number of titled Members. Leaving aside the 11 Honorary Members, only 40 (or 24 per cent) of the remaining 165 Ordinary Members were or are without a title of any kind. Most were already titled on becoming OMs but a few accepted a title afterwards.

All 24 Military Members were titled since we have yet to see a British five-star officer without one.

Between them, the 165 Ordinary Members have acquired a large number of other honours. Leaving aside the peerages, baronetcies and privy counsellorships, the knighthoods and other awards (many held by the same person) amount to 210.

Social origins

Class is notoriously difficult to classify, especially as social mobility increases. One man's working class is another's lower middle class; one's upper class is another's upper middle class. Successful men also have a tendency sometimes to improve on or even hide their origins. The analysis in this section is therefore not at all watertight but it does give an accurate general description of where in society the OMs have come from.

If the known occupations of their fathers are a guide, some 14 Members seemed to have come from the working or (at best) lower middle class, mostly in the earlier years of the Order. They include, with their fathers' occupations shown in brackets: Watts (poor piano and music teacher); Meredith (unsuccessful tailor); Holman Hunt (warehouseman); Crookes (tailor); Hardy (small builder/master mason); Elgar (organist, music seller and piano tuner); Geikie (musician); Lloyd George (shoemaker uncle and widowed mother); Barrie (handloom weaver); Samuel Alexander (saddler); Passfield (hairdresser mother); Henry Moore (coalminer); Nolan (tram driver); and Hughes (tobacconist and carpenter).

If we now go to the other end of the social spectrum we find two royals (Prince Philip and Lord Mountbatten) and one son of a Prime Minister (MacDonald). From there we find groups whose fathers were: based on the land (12 aristocrats, eight landowners, three farmers); in the armed forces (14); in the staple middle-class professions (19 lawyers, 12 clergymen, nine doctors); in business (28); in education (ten academics, six teachers); and a miscellany (five artists or architects, three MPs, three engineers, two civil servants) – an overwhelmingly middle-class picture.

Nationality

Most OMs were born and bred in the United Kingdom and I have already written of those who lived overseas and had nationalities of Commonwealth countries other than the UK. There were also those who came from overseas and in the days of shared British nationality were able to settle in the UK with no problem. Such were Samuel Alexander, Murray and Florey from Australia, Rutherford and Syme from New Zealand and Zuckerman and Aaron Klug from South Africa.

There were also a few Members who, by naturalisation, became eligible for appointment as Ordinary Members: Alma-Tadema (Netherlands), Henry James, Eliot, Penfield and Menuhin (USA), Prince Philip (Greece) and Berlin (Russia). Others came from families which had been naturalised in an earlier generation: Medawar and Michael Atiyah.

Education

The majority of OMs went to public schools: 85 out of the 148 whose schooling can readily be traced. Of these, ten went to Eton, five to Harrow, four each to Charterhouse and Cheltenham, three each to Winchester, Westminster and Merchant Taylor's and one or two to 17 other major public schools. Another 30 went to what could probably be described as minor public schools.

Twenty-four Members went to grammar schools and, particularly in the early days of the Order, another 22 had been educated at what were variously described as 'private schools', 'tutors', 'privately' or simply 'home'. Seventeen Members went to schools overseas.

The statistics on universities are rather more reliable than those on schools. Many went to two universities, most frequently (in earlier days) from Scotland or overseas to Oxford or Cambridge. I have traced 143 attendances at university:

- Cambridge – 47. Twenty-seven at Trinity College, five at St John's College and three or less at eight other colleges.
- Oxford – 40. Eight at Balliol College and three or less at 18 other colleges; three of them were Rhodes Scholars.
- Others in British Isles – 32. Eleven in London (five at University College); seven elsewhere in England and Wales; 11 in Scotland (five each at Edinburgh and Glasgow); three in Ireland (all at Trinity College, Dublin).
- Overseas – 24. Canada two; Australia four; New Zealand three; South Africa four; USA four; Germany and Austria six; France one.

The outstanding figure is obviously that of the 27 OMs attending Trinity College, Cambridge; far more than at any other single university institution.

It is in line with the College's boast that it has won more Nobel Prizes than France. There has always been a Trinity man among the 24 Members since the inclusion of Rayleigh in the original 12 and when Jeans was appointed in 1939, eight of the 24 came from Trinity.

For some OMs there was also professional education, beyond or instead of university. Twenty-seven had military training: 17 for the Navy, nine for the Army and one for the Air Force. Fourteen trained in the arts: 11 at art schools and three at the Royal College of Music. Twelve had legal training, for the Bar (five were at Lincoln's Inn) or as solicitors. Eight had medical training and two went to engineering schools.

Religion and sexuality

In a Britain where one's religion was often assumed to be 'Church of England', it is not always possible to be certain how many OMs were not Anglicans. Some were Catholics, including Elgar, Scott, Graham Sutherland, Cheshire, Greene and (obviously) Hume. A few were Jews, including Samuel Alexander, Herbert Samuel, Zuckerman, Berlin, Menuhin and Gombrich. In the days when people made a point of declaring themselves to be atheists or agnostics, those included Morley, Hardy, Vaughan Williams, Murray, Russell, Gooch, Moore and Medawar.

In that same Britain, for many years for good legal reasons, men were assumed to be heterosexual. Now, it is known that some OMs were not, including Britten, Forster, Ashton, Tippett and Gielgud. Over others, there has been progressive questioning and speculation about their sexuality: Kitchener, Henry James, Barrie and Mackenzie King.

19

THE LINKS

When it was suggested that the Order of Merit might forge closer links with its German model, the Order Pour le mérite, the Secretary of the British Order 'doubted if most of its members know each other by sight'. Historically, he was wrong. Although there was no formal meeting of the Order until 1977, the links between many of them as individuals had always been strong. This was because they were related or moved in the same political, social, scientific or artistic circles.

Family links

The closest relationship in the history of the Order was that of the historians, G. O. and G. M. Trevelyan, who were Members for nearly 50 of its 100 year existence: the father from 1911–28 and the son from 1930–62. There were two men whose sons-in-law also received the OM: Dale (and Todd) and Hopkins (and Priestley). Although there have been no sibling OMs, in one case it again approached it when Haldane's brother and sister both received the CH.

The only uncle and nephew OMs were Mountbatten and Prince Philip. Kelvin was the great-uncle of Malcolm MacDonald. There were a number of cousins, by marriage: Dorothy and Alan Hodgkin; Andrew Huxley and Veronica Wedgwood; and Andrew Huxley and G. M. Trevelyan.

It is rather surprising that, out of such a relatively small number, so many OMs are related; it is less surprising, however, when one realises how many came out of the Cambridge intellectual marriage market. Of course, in some cases, the relationship produced the same surname for OMs: the Trevelyans, the Hodgkins and the Mountbattens.

Friendships and other linkages

Apart from the links and often friendships that resulted from OMs being in the same field of activity, there were also friendships that owed nothing to that. For instance, at Merton College, Oxford, at the same time were two American undergraduates: Eliot and Penfield. The latter's closest friend at Princeton had been Winant and, in the Second World War, Penfield's daughter came to London to act as Winant's confidential secretary. Also on his staff was the young Roy Jenkins, doing a 'gentle research job' before joining the Army.

Lady Ottoline Morrell's famous bohemian and intellectual circle at Garsington included John, Russell, Eliot and de la Mare. Albany, the smart set of rooms off Piccadilly, has been home to at least five OMs: Berlin, Clark, Priestley, Greene and Margaret Thatcher.

In the days of grander and more frequent social gatherings in London, OMs would have seen a good deal of each other. For instance, at the annual dinner of the Royal Academy in 1960, there were 11 OMs (half the Order) and three future OMs. By 1986 and 1992, the number of OMs had dropped to two and four. Nevertheless, at the Lord Mayor of London's Millennium lunch, attended by the Queen, there were eight OMs (a third of the Order) among 300 guests at what was naturally hyped as the 'lunch of the century'.

A remarkable friendship between OMs was that of Ernst Gombrich and Max Perutz. They had been at the same school in Vienna but, with a five-year age difference, they did not know each other. Unable to live in their homeland after the Anschluss in 1938, these 'asylum seekers' pursued remarkable but separate careers in Britain, Gombrich as an art historian and philosopher and Perutz as a molecular biologist. They were honoured by Germany with the Order Pour le mérite before being appointed to the Order of Merit on the same day in 1988. They met for the first time as they waited to receive the insignia from the Queen and became good friends. Many of their fellow refugees from Hitler's demonic persecution were honoured in Britain but only these two received the highest intellectual accolade.

The scientists

In Chapter 9, we have already seen examples of scientist OMs working closely together. Many were taught by or worked for or with other OMs. For example, Sherrington taught Adrian – and later shared with him the 1932 Nobel Prize for Physiology or Medicine. Sherrington also taught Penfield, but died in 1952 before seeing his former pupil appointed as the next OM, in 1953. Twice more, the Nobel Prize for Physiology or Medicine was shared by OMs: by Burnet and Medawar in 1960 and by Andrew Huxley and Alan Hodgkin in 1963.

The Nobel Prizes have provided an important linkage with scientist OMs, although the two awards certainly do not go neatly hand-in-hand. Many more Britons (and other Commonwealth citizens) have won scientific Nobel Prizes than have received the OM; contrariwise, there have been OM scientists who never won a Nobel.

In fact 33 OMs have won the Nobel Prize. Twenty-six of them were scientists and, counting Frederick Sanger's two prizes, they were divided between Physics (six), Chemistry (ten) and Physiology or Medicine (11). Four OMs won the Literature Prize and three the Peace Prize.

In the field of Nobel Prizes for Literature, the Prize and the OM have followed each other more closely. Of the six British winners before 1980, four (Galsworthy, Eliot, Russell and Churchill) were OMs and the other two (Kipling and Shaw) could have been. Since 1980, the position has been less clear.

The three OMs who won the Nobel Peace Prize were not from Britain: Pearson (Canada) and two Honorary Members, Schweitzer and Mother Teresa.

The artists

Artistic OMs in the same field obviously knew each other but sometimes they co-operated across their disciplines. OM painters painted other OMs. Watts painted Lecky, Meredith and Roberts. Among his models (for the heroine in *Una and the Red Cross Knight*) was the mother of H. A. L. Fisher. Alma-Tadema painted Balfour. John painted Hardy, Lloyd George and Murray. Sutherland painted Churchill!

Spence assisted Lutyens with the drawings for New Delhi. At Chelsea College of Art in the late 1930s, Henry Moore was in charge of sculpture and Graham Sutherland of design. In 1941, a joint exhibition was held in Leeds by the youthful Henry Moore, OM, CH, Sutherland, OM and Clark, OM, CH.

Before the Second World War, Bloomsbury was thought of as the intellectual heart of London. During and after the war, Fitzrovia (north of Soho across Oxford Street but extending south into Soho itself) was the rather louche successor, frequented by Sutherland, Greene, John and Freud. Menuhin and Britten visited Belsen together, a gruesome experience which played its part years later in Britten's *War Requiem*.

Most recently, Norman Foster and Anthony Caro collaborated in creating a new Millennium pedestrian bridge across the Thames between St Paul's Cathedral and the Tate Modern Gallery, which had been designed by Scott and was the flagship of British atomic energy when Hinton headed it.

The writers

OMs have frequently written about each other. H. A. L. Fisher wrote a two-volume biography of Bryce. G. M. Trevelyan wrote a memoir of his father, G. O., and a study of Meredith.

In his *Great Contemporaries*, Churchill included profiles of Ypres, Morley, Foch, Haig, Balfour, Jacky Fisher and Baden-Powell. Berlin wrote a short memoir of an OM at a crucial moment in history: *Mr Churchill in 1940*. More recently, Jenkins wrote a much more substantial one-volume biography of Churchill, having written much earlier about Attlee and Balfour. Priestley, in *Particular Pleasures*, included sketches of Elgar, Walton, Olivier and Gielgud.

Writer OMs have always been quick to come together in intellectual protest. When authors campaigned in 1907 for the removal of the Lord Chamberlain's censorship powers over plays (which went 60 years later), five of them were future OMs: Hardy, Henry James, Barrie, Galsworthy and Murray.

In 1955, six existing OMs joined in the classic form of Establishment protest – a letter to *The Times* criticising a proposal that books should lose their favourable postal rates: Masefield, Dale, de la Mare, Eliot, G. M. Trevelyan and Vaughan Williams. A couple of years later, in 1958, a group of writers directed their fire at The Soviet Writers' Union about the treatment of Boris Pasternak and six existing or future OMs were among the signatories: Eliot, Forster, Greene, Clark, Priestley and Russell. On a few decades and a letter to *The Times* in 1986 still recruits OMs, expressing concern at the future of the much-loved round reading room of the British Museum: Berlin, Franks, Syme and Wedgwood.

On rare occasions, OMs indulged in more vigorous protest. Russell and Priestley were at the inaugural meeting of the Campaign for Nuclear Disarmament in 1958 and, three years later, John joined in an anti-nuclear demonstration in Trafalgar Square organised by Russell; it was the end of him, for he caught a chill and died.

Writer OMs were, however, quick to come to the aid of the country in the initial heady months of the First World War. Of the 25 authors who attended the first meeting of the War Propaganda Bureau in September 1914, five were OMs, present or future: Hardy, Barrie, Bridges, Galsworthy and Masefield.

'Scholar' OMs will have met frequently in the confines of the British Academy of which most were or are members. As the 'national academy for the humanities and social sciences', it is their natural gathering ground, much as the Royal Society is for scientific OMs. Indeed, the two great institutions are now side by side in Carlton House Terrace in London, separated only by the Duke of York's Column.

When the Royal Society of Literature instituted in 1961 the distinction of 'Companion of Literature' (C.Lit), the first five recipients included four

OMs: Churchill, Forster, Masefield and G. M. Trevelyan. Later, Clark and Greene were to receive the honour. A later President of the Society was Jenkins.

The famed Foyles Literary Luncheons had had (up to 1995) 27 OMs as guests of honour.

OMs have often worked across the artistic boundaries. There are the composers who based their works on those by fellow Members: Britten on Henry James' *Owen Wingrave* and *The Turn of the Screw* and on the poems of Eliot and de la Mare. Similarly, Britten composed the music for Priestley's *They Came To A City* and Walton did likewise for Olivier's films *Henry V*, *Richard III*, *Hamlet* and (to a small extent) *Battle of Britain*. Forster was the librettist for Britten's *Billy Budd*.

One interesting collaboration between OMs, amusingly described by Kenneth Rose in his biography of George V, was the miniature Dolls' House at Windsor Castle: Lutyens was the architect. Among the books, no bigger than large postage stamps, were poems by Hardy, a monograph on humanism by Haldane and a ghost story (*The Haunted Doll's House*) by M. R. James.

The rebuilding of Coventry Cathedral brought together Spence, the architect, Graham Sutherland, who designed the main tapestry, and Britten, who wrote his *War Requiem* for the rededication.

The men of affairs

The men who moved in the realms of politics and administration knew each other in varying degrees. British cabinets, especially in the first half of the century, often contained more than one OM, present or future. Even earlier, Rosebery's (1894–95) had three: Morley, Bryce and G. O. Trevelyan. Campbell-Bannerman's cabinet (1905–08) had four: Haldane, Lloyd George, Morley and Bryce. Asquith's (1908–16) had six: Lloyd George, Churchill, Haldane, Kitchener, Morley and Samuel.

In the second half of the century, OMs in cabinets were much rarer birds. In that period, only Churchill had it while actually serving, in his second premiership (1951–55). Altogether, 20 OMs served in cabinets: Kitchener, Morley, Bryce, G. O. Trevelyan, Haldane, Balfour, Lloyd George, H. A. L. Fisher, Chatfield, Passfield, Churchill, Halifax, Attlee, Waverley, Samuel, Alexander of Tunis, Malcolm MacDonald, Stockton, Margaret Thatcher and Jenkins. To these might be added Smuts, who sat in the Imperial War Cabinet in the First World War.

At a historical working breakfast in 1908 to discuss national insurance, there were Lloyd George, Churchill, Haldane and Passfield (Sidney Webb, with Beatrice). Three years later, the list of 254 men to whom it was proposed to offer peerages in order to ensure the passage of the Parliament Act in 1911 included seven present or future OMs: Hardy, G. O. Trevelyan, Barrie, Baden-Powell, Murray, Russell and Gooch.

At a cabinet meeting in the wartime government, Churchill pocketed a note from Malcolm MacDonald, whereupon Halifax sent a note to MacDonald:

> Be careful what you write to Winston. He'll publish it in his volumes about the war when it is over![1]

The Second World War brought together many of the OMs. In pictures from that time, there can be seen Churchill, Eisenhower, Mackenzie King and Smuts visiting the troops before D-Day. When it was all over, side by side at the saluting base for the Victory Parade in 1946, were Attlee, Churchill, Mackenzie King and Smuts; among the cars passing them was one in which the three Chiefs of Staff had squeezed: Portal, Alanbrooke and Cunningham. In the Imperial War Museum today sit the busts alongside each other of Churchill, Attlee, Waverley and Portal.

From 1957–60, the American and British governments were led by OMs, present and future. Eisenhower's second presidency coincided with the first half of Macmillan's premiership.

Sometimes, a crisis will bring OMs into the same frame, as when three appeared side by side in the *Illustrated London News* of 23 January 1965 during a crucial week of meetings about the future of the TSR-2 aircraft: Jenkins (Minister of Aviation), Portal (Chairman of the British Aircraft Corporation) and Edwards (Managing Director of BAC).

Margaret Thatcher's chemistry tutor at Oxford was Dorothy Hodgkin and, later, she was first given ministerial office by Harold Macmillan. More recently, she gave the inaugural James Bryce lecture at the Institute of United States Studies in London.

The universities

As we saw in the last chapter, Cambridge is a clear winner in the OM stakes. Within Cambridge, Trinity College has dominated in this field, as in others. To start with, the Founder, Edward VII was there. George VI was there, as was his grandson, Charles, an OM who is due to be the next Sovereign of the Order, as Charles III.

The Masters of Trinity have been OMs almost as often as the Presidents of the Royal Society (sometimes the same man anyway). Since 1918, six of the eight Masters have been chosen, by the Crown, from the ranks of the Order: Thomson, G. M. Trevelyan, Adrian, Alan Hodgkin, Andrew Huxley and Michael Atiyah. Even a Vice Master, Jackson (from 1914–21) was already an OM. The Order has become so associated with the Mastership that, on one occasion, those attending a memorial service included 'the Master of Trinity College OM and Lady Hodgkin'.

Cambridge, the university, had early OMs as Chancellor: Rayleigh from 1908–19, when he was succeeded (and in Edinburgh also) by his brother-in-law, Balfour (until 1930). After the brief chancellorship of Smuts (1948–50), there was a gap, before the elections again of OMs: Adrian (1967–76) and Prince Philip (since 1977).

The Cambridge dominance in the OM occasionally frightened the Palace. When Frazer and Rutherford were to be appointed in the 1925 New Year Honours, it was recorded:

> Lord Stamfordham . . . thought it would be better to put no description of these people in the *Gazette* – they are both Cambridge men [in fact both Fellows of Trinity] and this might be noticed.[2]

Many years later, this Cambridge neurosis was still there. When Whitehead was being considered for the Order, the Private Secretary at Number 10 cautioned:

> On the other hand, he is a Fellow of Trinity College, Cambridge, and it has not failed to be noticed that, of the 18 Members of the Order of Merit, 7 are Fellows of that College.[3]

A few months later, it was Holdsworth being considered and the Master of Trinity, G. M. Trevelyan, put his tongue firmly in his cheek before writing to the Palace:

> It would also not be a disadvantage from the public point of view if the number of Oxford OMs approached more nearly to those of Trinity College, Cambridge, though I should be personally sorry if they ever quite caught up.[4]

The Cambridge dominance in the Order persisted to the extent that when the 17 Nobel Laureates from that university signed the appeal for £250 million in 1996, eight of them were OMs.

The elite intellectual society at Cambridge, the Apostles, has included a number of future OMs in its ranks: G. O. Trevelyan, Jebb, Jackson, Whitehead, Russell, G. E. Moore, G. M. Trevelyan, Forster (and Keynes). Youthful camaraderie persisted until they were OMs; when told by the Palace in 1951 that Moore was to receive the Order, Trevelyan nostalgically recalled:

> I am very proud of the fact that I was twice on a Reading Party of five undergraduates, of whom three – Vaughan Williams, Moore and myself – have all got this award.[5]

Oxford cannot hold a candle to Cambridge where the Order of Merit is concerned. Nevertheless, at its pinnacle, Oxford shows up well. Since 1932, three Chancellors of the University have received the OM while in office, although, it needs to be said, for distinction beyond Oxford: Halifax (Chancellor from 1932–59) in 1946; Macmillan (1960–86) in 1976; and Jenkins (1987–2003) in 1993. The election of Macmillan in 1960 was awash with OMs. He was supported by Hinshelwood and Syme and secured 1,976 votes against 1,697 cast for Franks, who was supported by Dorothy Hodgkin and Clark.

Trinity College, Oxford, shared its Cambridge namesake's pride in the OM by commissioning a group portrait of honorary fellows who were Nobel laureates or holders of the OM, 'to remind undergraduates and graduate students that distinguished scholars (both scientists and arts men) have passed through the college, and to inspire emulation'; Clark and Syme are in the picture.

The oldest Scottish university, St Andrews, has also had OMs as Chancellor (Haig and Haldane) and as Lord Rector, elected by the students. Those elected include Balfour, Haig and Barrie, as well as Smuts, who defeated Halifax, Masefield and Baden-Powell. Kipling succeeded Barrie.

The university of Kent has named its four colleges after Eliot, Rutherford, Keynes – and Darwin. There will be many other universities with OMs in their past or present, including a number of Chancellors: James Black of Dundee, Denis Rooke of Loughborough, Michael Atiyah of Leicester (after George Porter and Alan Hodgkin), Owen Chadwick of East Anglia (after Franks). The country's 'intellectual academy' provides a ready source of recruitment for such distinguished honorific posts.

Miscellany

The original *Dictionary of National Biography* has been a trifle erratic in its treatment of the Order of Merit, all of whose British Members have featured in it. In some entries, the honour is mentioned; in others it is not. (A knighthood is never omitted.) In the 1941–50 and 1961–70 editions (but not 1951–60), OMs were singled out for special mention in the Prefatory Notes. In reply to a letter from me, the editor said: 'I agree that the OM is the most significant award of all' and his successor assured me that they did try to include it in their articles.

The Royal Society of Arts was founded in 1754 to encourage the arts, manufactures and commerce and its prestigious Albert Medal was instituted in 1864. It has been awarded to 26 OMs, 17 of whom were scientists. The President of the RSA today is Prince Philip.

20

THOSE WHO TURNED IT DOWN

When I told a recently-appointed OM about those who had declined it, he expressed surprise. He said that it had never crossed his mind to do so and nor, I think, the minds of most of the other recipients.

There are only three clearly recorded examples of refusal, all by men of letters: Rudyard Kipling (twice), A. E. Housman and Bernard Shaw. One occasion linked, uniquely, the three men I have mentioned. At the funeral of Thomas Hardy, OM, in 1928, the pallbearers included five literary figures: J. M. Barrie, already an OM, Galsworthy, soon to receive it, and the three who refused it: Kipling, Housman and Shaw.

Rudyard Kipling

Kipling turned down official honours time and time again and yet was the unofficial laureate of the British Empire at its apogee, when honours proliferated and seemed to be an important part of its cementing. (He had declined the official poet laureateship in 1895.) He did accept the Nobel Prize for Literature in 1907 for: 'the power of observation, originality of imagination, virility of ideas and remarkable talent for narration which characterize the creations of this world-famous author.' On hearing a rumour that he was to receive one of the first British Empire knighthoods, he told Bonar Law (the Conservative leader, who was Chancellor of the Exchequer in the coalition) that 'it must not be'.[1] When, by an administrative muddle, he was told that he was to be a CH, he got very testy with Bonar Law:

> How would *you* like to be waked up on a Sunday morning by a letter
> from the Acting Secretary of the Church Aid Society informing you that

your name was among the list of Bishops that had been recommended to the King?[2]

Kipling's name had been suggested for the OM for some time. In 1909, the persistent Esher told Knollys that Kipling had

> done more for the Empire than any living writer...mass of work of unequal value – some *very* bad...a few things of the highest national importance...has earned the OM for having – with his pen – accomplished as much for the Empire as Cromer or Kitchener [both OMs].[3]

The first formal offer of the OM reached Kipling at the end of 1921, when Stamfordham informed him that it would give the King

> much pleasure to confer upon you the Order of Merit in recognition of the eminent services you have rendered to the Science of Literature and of the almost unique estimation with which your works are regarded throughout the British Empire.[4]

His speedy letter of refusal struck Stamfordham as a 'very nice and respectful letter' because he described the King's approval of his work as 'the great honour of my life' while praying 'that HM may be graciously pleased to hold me excused'.[5]

Only a couple of years later, Stamfordham was telling Kipling that it would give the King, who had heard indirectly [in fact, from Baldwin] that he might have changed his mind, 'much pleasure to confer upon you the Order of Merit...delighted to do now what he so much wished to do at that time.'[6] Kipling again declined, saying that:

> I am convinced that whatever I may be able to do towards these ends, in the troublous times ahead, will be most serviceably carried through without acknowledgement in the public eye.[7]

Despite his double refusal of the special and personal royal honour, Kipling remained on close terms with George V. In May 1922, he wrote the King's speech at a war cemetery near Boulogne, which was described as 'among the finest pieces of prose among innumerable examples which he delivered'.[8] In 1932, Kipling wrote George V's first Christmas broadcast with a 'text of timeless simplicity...[which] bore the hallmark of the master'.[9] It is not surprising that the press called him 'the King's trumpeter'.

A. E. Housman

A. E. Housman, the classical scholar and poet (*A Shropshire Lad* appeared in 1896) was offered the OM once, in 1929, and turned it down in a rather oblique letter. He wrote to George V's Private Secretary, Lord Stamfordham:

> With all gratitude for His Majesty's most kind and flattering wish to confer upon me the Order of Merit I humbly beg permission to decline this high honour. I hope to escape the reproach of thanklessness or churlish behaviour by borrowing the words in which an equally loyal subject, Admiral Cornwallis, declined a similar mark of the Royal favour: 'I am, unhappily, of a turn of mind that would make my receiving that honour the most unpleasant thing imaginable.'[10]

Housman's claims on this occasion had been pressed by the Prime Minister, Stanley Baldwin, whose Private Secretary had written to the Palace: 'Housman...greatest living Latinist...*Shropshire Lad*...will be read forever – not...so sure of any other living poet...'[11] In late 1924, Stamfordham received unanimously favourable, if qualified, comment. From Sir Frederic Kenyon, the Director of the British Museum on Houseman and Murray who:

> have in them something of genius...he is much more of a recluse and might very likely refuse anything that was offered him: he is quite first-rate in scholarship in the narrower sense and a very sharp-tongued critic of others, especially Germans. His poetry is perfectly finished of its kind; you have probably seen his *Epitaph on a Mercenary Army* (the original BEF), which is the best thing of its kind in the language. He is not personally popular, because of his reserve and his sharp tongue: but his poetry is widely admired by all lovers of literature, and his scholarship is undeniable.[12]

Housman's name recedes until late 1928. Then, in response to an enquiry from Stamfordham, Owen Morshead, Librarian at Windsor Castle, opines that he is

> the greatest classic since Porson, and one of the finest poets we have ever had. His output...is small. He is 'caviare to the general' but so were Bradley and Grierson [appointed OMs in 1924 and 1928]; so are many nominees to this fine Order.[13]

and Geoffrey Dawson describes him as 'the first living pure scholar'.[14]

In a biography of Housman written by a friend shortly after his death in 1936, he is recounted as being really angry at being questioned about his refusal of the OM. In an appendix to the biography, Housman is reported as remarking, half-wistfully, 'You know, it is really a great distinction to have refused the OM.'[15]

George Bernard Shaw

Bernard Shaw, as one might expect, had fun with the honours system. Coming originally from John Bull's Other Island, British honours presented this professional Irishman with a problem anyway. As an absentee from his native land, he was understandably reluctant to accept the Presidency of the Irish Academy of Letters when it was founded in 1932. Although he was not even at the inaugural meeting, he held the office until relieved by W. B. Yeats in 1935 and, again, for another year after Yeats' death in 1939.

Shaw's Nobel Prize for Literature came in 1925, after his epic play *Saint Joan*: 'for his work which is marked by both idealism and humanity, its stimulating satire often being infused with a singular poetic beauty.'

In the 1920s, Shaw was already frequently in the 'OM frame', although usually put aside as 'too difficult'. In 1921, when pressing the case for J. M. Barrie, Lloyd George told Stamfordham that, although he would put Shaw ahead of Barrie as a writer, 'he could not expect the King to reward the author of the works which bore his name'.[16] At the same time, Stamfordham was told that Shaw was 'a genius in his way ... but ... of course impossible of honour'.[17]

A biographer wrote in Shaw's lifetime:

> Many friends pointed out that the Order of Merit was not open to his objections [to titles]. 'I have already conferred it on myself,' he replied. 'Besides, it has come to mean simply Old Man; and I have only one toe in the grave as yet.'[18]

Late in Shaw's life, the absence of official honours for him again appeared to embarrass a Labour Government that was now, for the first time, in power as well as office. In 1946, as his ninetieth birthday approached, he wrote to a friend:

> I have asked the Government, not for a title or a CH or OM, but for an Act which the Parliament of Eire has already passed for me.[19]

On 15 October 1946, Shaw was visited by Viscount Samuel, the Liberal leader in the House of Lords (and future OM), who sounded him on the possible award of the Order of Merit, although no actual offer was made. Samuel's immediately recorded recollection was that Shaw's response was:

> There are thousands of people doing excellent public service ... in complete obscurity, and will never get recognised and could not be. So why should others be singled out? ... Besides, if I were to accept, I might at any time do something monstrous that would bring discredit on the Order. I might even be hanged.[20]

Shaw promptly set about putting his views on the OM firmly on the record. To 'The Information Minister', who no longer existed, he wrote on 25 October:

> I have been sounded by a Privy Councillor (not a member of the Government) as to whether I would accept the Order of Merit if it were conferred on me. I must not treat this as public or official; but as it has been made a matter of reproach to the authorities that at ninety years of age I still remain undistinguished by any place in the Honours List the present Government may desire to make it known that there has been no omission or prejudice on its part, and that I was offered a knighthood by the Labour Prime Minister on my seventieth birthday 20 years ago, and that the superior distinction of the Order of Merit is now at my disposal. My formal reply runs as follows.

> 'Deeply grateful as I am for the award of the highest distinction within the gift of the Commonwealth, yet the nature of my calling is such that the Order of Merit in it cannot be determined within the span of a single human life. Either I shall be remembered as long as Aristophanes and rank with Shakespeare and Molière, or I shall be a forgotten clown before the end of the century. I dare not anticipate the verdict of history. I must remain simply Bernard Shaw.'[21]

Shaw died, still without the OM, in 1950.

Others

Because the confidential records of the Order of Merit for the present reign are still closed, it is difficult to be precise or definite about anyone who actually declined the OM in the last 50 years or who was not offered it because a refusal was virtually certain. It is likely that Francis Bacon would have been offered it, unless the inevitable refusal was not actually courted. His 'eligibility' was not in question. In a leading article in 1996, four years after his death, *The Times* commented:

> the obituaries were unanimous. Here was a painter of towering individuality, one of the greatest that this country has ever produced...the foremost British painter of the century...a modern British genius...[22]

Bacon's track record on honours was, however, as clear as his genius. One of his biographers wrote:

> Bacon was invited to become a Companion of Honour in 1977, although he had previously declined a knighthood...Bacon firmly stuck to his

principles of detachment from established society and refused this second accolade from his country. 'I always decline these honours,' he said. 'I never want them. I have no opinions on the honours system. It might be fine for other people but I want to stress I don't want anything for myself.'[23]

I have heard that, possibly in response to a tentative approach about the OM, he replied: 'I came into this world with no advantages and that's how I want to go out.'[24]

21

THE UNAPPOINTED – WHO WOULD NOT HAVE DISGRACED IT

In many of the previous chapters, I have already referred to those who, in various fields, were *not* appointed to the Order of Merit. In some cases, their omission seems – at least now – rather odd; in others, their appointment would have occasioned no great surprise, either at the time or in retrospect. In particular, I have already written of the omissions among the Military and Honorary Members and also among women.

In this chapter, I shall refer, inevitably briefly, to many of those who could have been appointed to the Order without bringing disgrace upon it. I think that most of them would have been up to its high standard. Many readers will not agree and many of them will know, at first- or second-hand, a lot more about the people in question than I do. I throw out these names, which by no means constitute a definitive list, to stimulate some thought about what the Order might have been and not just what it has actually been.

The reasons for the omissions will vary: they were not thought to be good enough, either against the competition in their field or against some notional absolute standard; they did not have good enough lobbyists on their behalf; there were no vacancies at the time or, despite what I said in Chapter 5, a balance needed to be kept between various fields of activity; or they died too young, especially by the standards of the decoration for Old Men.

A basic starting point is that many of the Companions of Honour appointed in the scientific or artistic fields (as distinct from the political) were potential OMs. I shall mention them as I pass from field to field, although I am deliberately excluding living CHs, since they are, theoretically, 'candidate OMs' at the moment.

Before I pass to the fields that formed the bases of my earlier chapters, I want to refer to cinema, radio and television. These were the new media of the twentieth century, with enormous effects on society, however much they have in turn been shunned by some of the intelligentsia. Yet no one specifically from these media has been honoured with the OM.

Reith, difficult man though he was, is still acknowledged as Auntie's Father; he received a peerage, a GCVO and eventually the Thistle but not the OM. Nor has any film director: Alfred Hitchcock, made a KBE only four months before his death at 80; David Lean, belatedly knighted at the age of 75, although his cause would probably not have been helped by his five marriages. James Logie Baird, who died at 58, would surely have been a strong candidate for the Order. He was the main British pioneer of television.

Charlie Chaplin, another belated KBE (two years before his death at 88) would have graced and, even in old age, amused the Order. Two members of it thought so: J. B. Priestley described him as 'the most famous clown the world has ever known'[1] and Mountbatten, in urging the Queen to knight him (four years before he was) described Chaplin as 'the greatest figure in cinema history. [He] would be thrilled to be recognised as an Englishman.'[2]

The Commonwealth

Before turning to the various fields, I want to say something about the Commonwealth, that is, the other countries of it besides the United Kingdom. Some citizens of what used to be called the 'Old Dominions' made their careers in Britain and received the OM: Rutherford, Florey and Zuckerman were notable examples. Rarely, however, have citizens actually living in those countries been made Ordinary (as distinct from Honorary) Members: Mackenzie King, Penfield and Pearson in Canada; Burnet, Dixon and Joan Sutherland in Australia (Nolan spent a lot of time and eventually settled in Britain); Beaglehole in New Zealand; and Smuts in South Africa.

The political figures in those countries, especially some of their early long-serving Prime Ministers (Laurier in Canada, Hughes and Bruce in Australia, Ward in New Zealand and Botha in South Africa), would not have qualified for the Order since they lacked literary 'cover'.

In Canada, however, there were: Sir William Osler, often called the 'father of modern medicine' (who ended his career, with a baronetcy, in the Regius Chair of Medicine at Oxford); Wilfred Grenfell 'of Labrador', who was knighted in the then independent Newfoundland for his medical missionary work; Frederick Banting, also knighted for his work in discovering insulin (for which his young co-discoverer, with whom he shared the money from his Nobel Prize, C. H. Best, eventually received a CH); and Vincent Massey, the first Canadian Governor-General of Canada and a learned patron of the arts.

In Australia, there were: Douglas Mawson, the geologist knighted at 32 for his work as leader of the 1911–14 Australasian Antarctic Expedition; Robert Garran, the legal 'father' of the Australian Constitution, who lived to be 90 and was not unrewarded (with a GCMG); Robert Menzies, Prime Minister for a total of 19 years, who delighted, since he was 'British to his boot straps', in receiving the Thistle; Zelman Cowen, the Governor-General who healed the wounds left by the controversial dismissal of the Prime Minister by his predecessor and who was debarred by his religion from enjoying the Garter bestowed on other holders of his vice-regal office; and Donald Bradman, who not only dominated cricket in a way no other player has matched but by the time of his death, aged 92, was widely regarded as the greatest living Australian – one obituary called him 'the king and president this country never had; and the Pope too: he was infallible'. Nelson Mandela called Bradman 'one of the divinities'.

In New Zealand, Bernard Freyberg, British-born but New Zealand-educated, a soldier wounded nine times and winning the VC and DSO (with three bars), who commanded the New Zealand Forces in the Second World War and was Governor-General after it; and Edmund Hillary, knighted at 33 for climbing Everest and much later made a Knight of the Garter (when the OM might have been more appropriate).

Undivided India was not a Dominion but it was a vast Empire with a strong literary and scientific community. There were: Sir C. V. Raman, who won the Nobel Prize for Physics in 1930 for his work on the diffusion of light (the 'Raman effect') and founded the Indian Academy of Sciences; Sir Muhammad Iqbal, Muslim thinker and poet, who might have been too controversial as President of the Muslim League when it adopted Pakistan as its objective; even Pandit Nehru, an architect of the modern Commonwealth, if he had lived into retirement or if he had been an executive president on the occasion of a state visit.

Lastly, there was Sir Rabindranath Tagore, poet and winner of the Nobel Prize for Literature – although possibly, after the Amritsar massacre in 1919 made him want to renounce his knighthood, he would not have accepted the higher non-titular honour. When he was suggested for the OM in 1938, although it was thought the approach would be regarded as a recognition of, and compliment to, Indian literature, the Viceroy (Lord Linlithgow) thought:

> the effect in India would not be good, as Tagore was now very old and his intellect was failing. He is somewhat troublesome in political matters, though he is no longer taken very seriously.[3]

The Order of Merit was constituted as an award open to the whole Empire and, later, Commonwealth. It has never been used in this way widely enough. I do not think this was because of a lack of suitable recipients. I think there was not enough imagination used in this particular aspect of the selection process.

The scientists

I look now at the scientists who might have been OMs. In 1967, the Post Office issued a set of stamps celebrating four 'aspects of British discovery which have changed the course of modern living': television, penicillin, radar and the jet engine. None of the four discoverers had (or had had) the OM: John Logie Baird (to whom I have already referred); Alexander Fleming (who nearly did get the OM); Robert Watson-Watt (who was knighted and received the largest sum awarded by the Royal Commission on Awards to Inventors after the Second World War); and Frank Whittle (also knighted and – 40 years after his work on the jet engine – honoured with the OM).

Earlier in the century, there were, at least, three scientists of distinction who lived well after the foundation of the OM but did not receive it. Sir William Ramsay, discoverer of argon and the first British winner of the Nobel Prize for Chemistry, in 1904; Sir Norman Lockyer, discoverer of helium, which Ramsay later isolated in the laboratory; and Sir Ronald Ross, the bacteriologist who proved that malaria is transmitted to human beings by mosquito bites and received an early Nobel Prize for Physiology and Medicine in 1902. Ramsay was considered in 1912 but fell foul because:

> his reputation, though great, has been largely made by the Press . . . below Raleigh, who has discovered the same things but has not talked about them . . . not of the same fine quality as Thomson.[4]

There have been several CH physicists. C. T. R. Wilson invented the cloud chamber named after him, which was the first instrument to detect the tracks of atomic particles. He shared the Nobel Prize in 1927 and, a modest man, received the CH in 1937. In a list of possible scientific OMs in 1944, it was said that:

> [his] work at the beginning of the century led to very important knowledge of electrons and [his] methods have been much used ever since.[5]

Sir Lawrence Bragg had shared the Nobel Prize in 1915 at the age of 25 (the youngest-ever winner) with his father, Sir William, for their work on 'the analysis of crystal structure by means of X-rays' – father received the OM in 1931, son the CH in 1967. They are the nearest rivals to the Trevelyan OMs. Sir James Chadwick discovered the neutron in 1932, receiving the Nobel Prize in 1935 and the CH in 1970, at the age of 79. Viscount Cherwell, as Professor Frederick Lindemann, held the Chair of Experimental Philosophy at Oxford and was Churchill's scientific adviser in the Second World War and during his peacetime government, for which he received a CH that was as much political as scientific.

R. V. Jones was the young boffin in the Second World War, who (in Churchill's words) 'broke the bloody beam' that guided German bombers to their British targets. A CB at 35, his CH, for overall contribution to science, came at 83, three years before he died.

Sir Nevill Mott had already been knighted before sharing the Nobel Prize in 1977 for his work on semiconductors, showing how a cheap and reliable material can be used to improve the performance of electrical currents. He was made a CH in 1995 at the age of 90, a year before he died.

Away from the physicists, the physiologist, A. V. Hill, shared the Nobel Prize in 1922, at the age of 36, for 'his discovery relating to the production of heat in the muscle'. For work in the war, he received the CH in 1946; he married Maynard Keynes' sister and both their sons and a son-in-law were FRSs.

Two noted nutritionists were CHs. Lord Boyd-Orr had won the DSO and MC as a doctor in the First World War and in the Second World War his views were at the base of national food policy. His work as the first Director-General of the United Nations Food and Agriculture Organisation was rewarded with a peerage and the Nobel Peace Prize in 1949. His CH followed belatedly in 1968, looking very much like a 'missed OM'. The other nutritionist was Elsie Widdowson, never a Dame but a CH at the age of 86, having been only 70 when elected FRS. Her work had made it possible for the first time to relate nutrient intakes to disease risks.

The biochemist, Rodney Porter, was killed in a road accident only three months after receiving the CH in 1985. (*The Times* obituary did not even catch up with the honour.) He had won the Nobel Prize for Medicine in 1972 and was set to pursue Medical Research Council work in his retirement.

Joseph Needham, both FRS and FBA, was an old-fashioned polymath: scientist, historian and Sinologist – and Master of Gonville and Caius College, Cambridge. His first wife was one of the first female FRSs and they were the first husband and wife in the Society, which she said would gratify his historical sense. The *Daily Telegraph* described Needham as 'one of the great British scholars, an Erasmus for our times'. When, having declined lesser honours, he accepted a CH at the age of 91, he said wryly: 'I suppose this means I am a failed OM.'[6]

In addition to the CH scientists, there were others whose possible claims on the OM were never met. Sir Edward Appleton, who discovered the level of the ionosphere that reflected radio waves, which is named after him and for which he received the Nobel Prize for Physics in 1947. He was knighted, finally with a GBE, for his work as the wartime Director of the Department of Scientific and Industrial Research.

Other administrator-scientists failed to make the OM-grade: Sir Frank Smith

> whose most important work has been in administration [including as Secretary of the Royal Society and Director of the National Physical

Laboratory] rather than in research ... I do not regard these as sufficient qualification for the OM.[7]

Also, Sir Henry Tizard who

has done extremely valuable work in aviation research; he is first class. In his case, there is a possible difficulty in that he has a strong enemy or at least opponent in Lord Cherwell, the scientific adviser to the Prime Minister.[8]

This last comment reflects the intense scientific rivalry in the Second World War. The ordinary honours system did both Smith and Tizard proud: a GCB for each and also a GBE for Smith.

Tizard was also given a 'thumbs down' by Sir John Anderson (Lord President of the Council, with special responsibility for scientific matters) in a conversation with the King's Private Secretary in 1944:

Anderson said to me emphatically that in his opinion neither Sir H. Tizard nor Sir R. Watson-Watt would ever attain the necessary standard for the OM.[9]

Perhaps Watson-Watt did not endear himself to the conservative Anderson by his socialist leanings and elaborate speech and writing: 'He never said in one word what could be said in a thousand,' said a colleague.[10]

Besides the Braggs, there were two other examples of very distinguished father and son scientists, with the sons, however, not following their fathers into the Order of Merit. On one occasion, the *Fourth* Lord Rayleigh was considered but in the view of the Secretary of the Royal Society:

[his] claims ... are not nearly so strong as those of either Eddington or Jeans. His contributions to scientific knowledge have not been either so brilliant or so numerous and very special recognition would I believe cause some surprise in the scientific world ... I have endeavoured to ensure that the great work of the father should not tend to belittle that of the son.[11]

J. J. Thomson's only son, George, also a physicist, shared the Nobel Prize in 1937, while his father was still alive, and was knighted for his work during the Second World War.

The hovercraft is a famous British invention of the twentieth century, even if its potential has not been fully realised. Its inventor, Christopher Cockerell, was knighted in 1969 but received no more, although he lived for another 30 years. It was not, however, for want of the suggestion being made.

Barnes Wallis was an engineer whose honours did not match his claims on the public imagination. His work on the airship R100, the Wellington bomber and the Ruhr dams bouncing bomb brought him a CBE and, eventually, a knighthood. There were those who lobbied for an OM for the man who, according to Tizard, had made 'the finest individual technical achievement of the war'.[12]

Two others might be mentioned as examples of how men of great distinction can remain, for whatever reason, outside the honours system. G. H. Hardy, the 'most renowned of the pure mathematicians' (in 1944),[13] held chairs at both Oxford and Cambridge between the two world wars and had great influence on many in his field (including the Indian mathematical genius Ramanujan). He died, aged 70, on the day he was to have received the Royal Society's highest honour, the Copley Medal.

Frederick Soddy, the chemist who won the Nobel Prize in 1921 for his work in radiochemistry, was a man of great foresight but a complicated and controversial character, who became increasingly concerned with the use to which atomic energy was being put.

The artists

If we turn to painting and sculpture, there are again a number of CHs who might have been in the running for the Order of Merit. There were painters: David Jones, who was also an engraver (a pupil of Gill) and writer – but lived only a few months after receiving the CH in 1974; Victor Pasmore, who began as a member of the Euston Road group and, with Kenneth Clark as his patron, painted landscapes and interiors before moving to abstractive art, painted mostly in the brilliant light of Malta, where he lived for his last 30 years; Carel Weight, whose urban scenes led to his being variously described as the 'John Betjeman' or 'Alfred Hitchcock' of British painting and who was made a CH only two years before his death at 88; and John Piper, whose paintings of churches and castles excited a great following and who was also admired for his stained glass – for him the CH, unlike a knighthood, 'doesn't distort the nomenclature'.

There was also the potter, Bernard Leach, who brought Japan into British drawing rooms and was made a CH in 1973, the year in which he made his last pot. There were the architect CHs: Hugh Casson (son of a CH, Sybil Thorndike), who made his name early with the Festival of Britain and went on to become President of the Royal Academy and something of a national treasure and whose delicate drawings delighted the nation; Denys Lasdun, best known for the National Theatre but probably most admired for the Royal College of Physicians building in Regent's Park and the University of East Anglia.

Two knighted artists are often talked of in the same terms as the OM artists. Stanley Spencer, whose honour beat death (at 68) by a few months and whose Resurrection paintings at Cookham and mural decorations in Burghclere Chapel in Hampshire continue to fascinate, as does his idiosyncratic lifestyle.

Jacob Epstein, the 'enfant terrible', who scandalised London with his well-endowed statues for the British Medical Association Building in the Strand (now the Zimbabwe Embassy), later came to be an establishment craftsman with, for instance, statues or drawings of a number of OMs: Samuel Alexander, Jacky Fisher, Portal, Menuhin, Waverley and Smuts. He is said to have remarked that he preferred a title before his name rather than initials after it. (His KBE gave him both.) In early consideration for the OM, he was: 'looked upon by the younger critics as the greatest of living sculptors – he also is impossible [to honour in this way].'[14] At the same time, Aston Webb is described as

> the parent of more public buildings than ever before entrusted to a single man – he is President of the Royal Academy, an energetic and sagacious reformer, a popular figure persona grata to the Sovereign, but as it happens not a great artist.[15]

A third knight, Thomas Brock (made a KCB rather than a KCVO for sculpting the Queen Victoria Memorial in front of Buckingham Palace), was considered for an OM, since the Memorial and other statues were 'really notable works; but of course he is now looked upon as *vieux jeu* and his days of active production have passed.'[16] In the *DNB* he is adjudged to be 'an artist of no great originality or inspiration'.[17]

There are other artists who were never knighted or made CHs but who would probably be accounted 'possible' OMs. Walter Sickert, a contemporary of Wilson Steer, OM (whom he now often beats in the sale room) and founder of the Camden Town Group; his works varied from London music hall to royalty: George V in a bowler hat and Edward VIII arriving for the opening of his only Parliament. Of course, he would not have endeared himself to Geoffrey Dawson, the editor of *The Times* whose views were frequently sought on OM appointments, by his

> frequent letters which offended Dawson's tidy mind by being almost illegibly written over large sheets of lined paper in thick black ink, apparently with a match-stick and usually with an impenetrable smudge over an operative word, a calligraphy which suited his savage *non sequiturs* on subjects far removed from painting.[18]

His unwelcoming behaviour was legendary and hardly designed to make friends. 'Goodbye! Come again when you can't stop quite so long' was one supposed farewell.

The ever-popular L. S. Lowry, the 'Matchstick Man', declined a knight-hood and a CH and, in his case, there is no reason to suppose the OM would have attracted him any more.

Oscar Kokoschka, the Austrian Expressionist, who had an affair with Alma Mahler, came to Britain as a refugee, taking British citizenship. At the age of 73, four years after Germany had given him the Pour le mérite, he was rewarded with a CBE, meagre recognition which caused *The Times* to comment that he was 'fated to be the prophet unhonoured, not exactly in his own country but in the country of his adoption'.[19] In a centenary exhibition catalogue at the Tate in 1986, he was described as 'one of the twentieth century's greatest figurative artists'.

The musicians and performers

The musical world has boasted a number of CHs: composers and con-ductors. Frederick Delius has already been referred to as more or less 'missing' the OM but his stock has grown since his own day. Sir Arthur Bliss was Master of the Queen's Music for the first 20 years of her reign and he combined a prolific composition with an important role in musical administration.

Knighted conductors are an integral part of the British musical scene and, every few years, one is elevated to a CH. Sometimes that honour, which is scarcely noted by the music-going public, comes rather late. Henry Wood had created the great festival of the Proms and to celebrate its fiftieth anniver-sary in 1944, the CH was bestowed – in the nick of time: two months before he died. His name had been 'mentioned' for the OM shortly before. The King's Private Secretary, however, was against it:

> [his] claims to an OM have often been discussed. As a grateful Promenader of nearly 40 years standing, my personal inclinations have sometimes been towards giving it to him. He has done a very great deal for music in this country; he is a widely popular figure; he is a 'Grand Old Man' – and all that. On the other hand, the 'eminent service' laid down in Statutes of the Order of Merit has always been held to be cre-ative, and not merely interpretative, service. I do not think conductors, as a class, ought to be eligible, any more than anthologists, as distinct from poets; or founders of art-galleries, as distinct from painters and sculptors.
>
> Moreover, qua conductor, Henry Wood is not eminent; he is only a very competent second-class conductor. Can his life-work of inducing the British public to go to listen to good music fairly be called creative? I have never been able to make up my mind about that...

P.S. I do not for a moment subscribe to the plea that a high honour should be awarded because it will give delight to the recipient's fan-public. Popularity is not enough.[20]

The CH was obviously Wood's *pis aller*.

Thomas Beecham's knighthood at 37 was quickly overtaken in the public imagination by his inherited baronetcy and the wealth flowing from all those pills; his wit was relished almost as much as his conducting. He waited another 40 years for his CH. Before that, in 1935, a terse note in the Royal Archives records: 'name has often been up...The King, I am sure, will not give him the OM.'[21]

Adrian Boult ascended the honours ladder, with a knighthood at 48 but no CH until he was 80; he died at 94. John Barbirolli was another whose CH came almost too late, after 25 years as conductor of the Halle Orchestra but only a year before his death at 70.

We cannot tell how Kathleen Ferrier's career would have developed. Was she, as some say, the finest British singer of classical music in the twentieth century or was she, as others maintain, not even the finest contralto? As a late-starter, with only a short international career, she reached only a CBE, on her deathbed at the age of 41, so any OM was a long way off.

The theatre has had many actor/knights and actress/dames but relatively few have gone on to a CH: Sybil Thorndike, Alec Guinness and John Gielgud (before going on even further to an OM). CHs have gone to those connected with the theatre, like Lilian Baylis, creator of the Old Vic, Annie Horniman, pioneer of the modern theatre repertory movement, and Gordon Craig, the designer, who was the son of Ellen Terry, father of Isadora Duncan's first child and cousin of John Gielgud.

The writers

Writers, of all descriptions, are difficult to classify, especially as their work frequently ranges over more than one field. The classification becomes even more difficult when considering which of them might have received the OM.

Early in the century, Augustine Birrell failed to secure the Order in 1911, when he was Chief Secretary for Ireland, despite the efforts of the Prime Minister, Asquith. George V was not impressed by the argument that 'personality ought to be considered and Birrell has much of it'; Asquith dropped the matter.[22] In advising the Palace, Balfour had been hesitant but nevertheless clear:

I have a great personal regard for him. His writings, like his conversation and his speeches, have an individuality, a special flavour, about them which I find very attractive. But I cannot think that he either is, or would claim to be, in the first rank of Literature. He has done nothing so far as I know but criticism; and his criticisms, though delightfully written, are not comparable either in range, or learning, or even in subtlety, to those of other living writers; and I am rather afraid that people will say that had Birrell not distinguished himself in the field of Politics, nobody would have thought of giving him the Order of Merit for his labours in the field of Literature.[23]

In May 1924, Joseph Conrad refused Ramsay MacDonald's offer of a knighthood:

> ... rather surprising that the staunch patriot refused the offer that King George V was willing to confer upon him ... Influenced perhaps by Kipling's and Galsworthy's refusals of knighthoods, a few years earlier, Conrad wanted to remain independent. He may not have wished to accept the honour from a Socialist government and aimed for bigger game, the Order of Merit and the Nobel Prize.[24]

Conrad died three months later and therefore received neither.

Arnold Bennett, the creator of the *Five Towns*, who similarly declined a knighthood, was a possible OM in his day. Esher thought he had: 'a touch of genius that is lacking in the excellent work of Galsworthy and Wells. All are uneven.'[25]

H. G. Wells, also contemptuous of a knighthood, might have reconciled his socialist and republican views with an OM – he is persistently said to have 'wanted' it – but in the early 1920s there was little inclination to give it to him. Stamfordham reported to George V that the Prime Minister, in recommending J. M. Barrie, 'would rule out Henry Wells, though admittedly an eminent writer.'[26] At the same time, the King's Press Secretary described Wells as: 'clever but he is not a genius and is tainted both as a person and a writer.'[27]

A couple of years later, Wells is admired but not favoured. Stamfordham told the Archbishop of Canterbury that: 'I expect you will agree with me that it would not do for the King to give them [Wells and Shaw] the decoration.'[28] From Paris, the Marquess of Crewe expressed: 'great admiration for Wells, who has made his own way unaided; but he has been mixed up in some serious scandals, and sober people would be shocked at his selection, no doubt.'[29]

Wells had many roles, not least as a prophet of the future, although he occasionally slipped. After saying in 1927 that the wireless had 'a very trivial future indeed', he went on to become a notable broadcaster. He achieved what has been denied to most OMs (and, indeed, the Order itself): a set of

British stamps, issued in 1995 to commemorate the centenary of the publication of *The Time Machine* and the fiftieth anniversary (almost) of his death.

Hilaire Belloc 'begged to refuse the honour' of the CH offered in 1943[30] with the result that when A. P. Herbert suggested him for the OM in 1952:

> A court personage said he had 'incontinently refused' the CH... Walter de la Mare was 'as much if not more deserving' of the OM.[31]

De la Mare received the OM the next year.

Two of the renowned writers of the mid-twentieth century were too young to be serious candidates for the OM, but who knows what would have happened if George Orwell and Dylan Thomas had lived to be older than 47 and 39 – and if Orwell had moved back towards the Establishment and Thomas had sobered up.

Evelyn Waugh died unhonoured at the age of 62. According to his son, Auberon:

> Once, the Prime Minister of the time – an infinitely depressing publisher some years his senior – wrote offering him the CBE... [H]e wrote back proudly that he would wait until he had earned his spurs.[32]

Apart from a knighthood, would he – as an increasingly 'grand old man' of English letters – have been offered a CH or OM?

C. P. Snow, who enjoyed honours and was ever-rumoured to have wanted the OM, died with a knighthood and a peerage – conferred more for his work in public administration than for his 'Lewis Eliot' sequence of novels: *Strangers and Brothers*. His main opponent in the famous debate over the 'Two Cultures' – scientific and artistic – was the Cambridge critic, F. R. Leavis, who was made a CH.

Later, in their mature years, the poets, Robert Graves and W. H. Auden surely came into the field of consideration for the OM. They successively held the chair of poetry at Oxford. Graves lived to be 90 and the *Oxford Companion to English Literature* simply records laconically that he 'received many honours and refused many'. Graves set out his forthright views on literary honours in 1954:

> The legitimacy of accepting official honours for poetry may seem a moot point but, in my opinion, as in Ben Jonson's, they should be politely declined... [Cabinet officials] have no more right to decide who is a true poet than the poet has to intervene in Cabinet meetings... [Just as DCM was devised to enhance VC and MM to enhance DCM] so the CH was first devised to enhance the dignity of the OM and inferior awards now enhance the dignity of the CH. [Bestowal of an award for poetry] – as opposed to scientific, military, or political services, which are more

easily assessable and in the public domain – is an act of criticism which no politician or permanent civil servant has any right to make.

Granted, Thomas Hardy, one of the most moral of poets, accepted the Order of Merit. But he knew that the award was conferred on him for his novels, which the Cabinet's advisers had read, rather than for his poems, which they had not; and, on the whole, civil servants are as likely to know a good novel from a bad one as are professional reviewers or publishers' readers.[33]

Shortly after delivering this indictment of literary honours, Graves stuck to his principles by declining a CBE and the CLit.

Auden's case was complicated, or perhaps made easier, by the fact that he took American citizenship, after having spent the war years there. Nevertheless, he spent his last years at Christ Church, Oxford. His memorial, in Westminster Abbey, is near those of the OM poets, Masefield and Eliot.

There were a number of writers (novelists, poets and playwrights) who were made CHs, in some cases after having taken or refused a knighthood. Among those who took the knighthood first were Hall Caine, A. P. Herbert and Henry Newbolt. Others were Laurence Binyon, Osbert and Sacheverell Sitwell (for whom, as baronets, a knighthood was rather irrelevant), Philip Larkin (who died six month after the CH) and Somerset Maugham and Anthony Powell, who had both declined knighthoods. Powell was certainly not short of lobbyists for his promotion to OM. Some years after his CH, Newbolt was suggested by Kipling for an OM: 'all that a scholar of English and a poet ought to be. He would represent the official side of Literature admirably...'[34]

Long before Maugham accepted the CH in 1954, John Masefield, Poet Laureate and an OM, had suggested him for the Order:

[He is a] successful playwright and the best writer of short stories now alive in the world... He has not yet done his best work...'[35]

Years later, Desmond MacCarthy, the critic, reviewed Maugham's work:

his best short stories would not be inferior to Maupassant's... and *Cakes and Ale* and *Of Human Bondage* must be reckoned I think among the best twentieth century novels... Nevertheless, both as a dramatist and a novelist, the bulk of his life's work has been of an inferior merit...[36]

For ten years or more from the mid-1930s to the mid-1940s, Max Beerbohm (as writer and cartoonist) excited the attention of those considering appointments to the OM. In 1936, a verdict was:

> Apart from his caricatures, he is, to my mind, the best writer of English alive today. The general public don't know much about him... several people in the present list of OMs I've never heard of myself.[37]

Beerbohm accepted a knighthood in 1939 and, during the war, returned to Britain from his retreat on the Italian Riviera. It was in 1943 that he came nearest to the OM. Morshead penned one of his longest notes to the Private Secretary:

> Suggestion... has great attraction... quality of his prose has perhaps never been excelled... dainty filigree... elegance... no less the epicure in his drawings... They are marked down for permanence... Max Beerbohm's OM would illumine the Honours List and furnish a nine days' topic... [O]n the debit side... [he] is finished... with this well-merited accolade [the knighthood] he took his curtain... [the OM now] would be an... admission of under-valuation... no small part of his talent has been devoted to guying the Royal Family, and particularly King Edward VII – the Founder of this very Order...
>
> I think it best to leave well alone... certain impish dandyism which is at variance with the dignity of the Order... One does not lightly risk playing battledore and shuttlecock with the OM... unreasonable that, having helped himself to his cake with such evident relish in past days, Sir Max Beerbohm should now be invited by the King to eat it.[38]

Sir Eric Maclagan (Director of the British Museum) was against Beehbohm's appointment:

> it might well make people ridicule the whole affair [of the OM], which would be deplorable. It is not, I think, the right place for the exquisite.[39]

Lascelles was convinced and concluded:

> Max OM would warm the heart but it would be just a little too august and weighty for his genius.[40]

The knighthood matched Beerbohm's whimsicality; the OM would have looked as though the Establishment took him seriously.

Only four years later, there was a last gasp for Beerbohm, now safely back in Italy. Morshead had forgotten, 'how we stand now... I'd include him in his mellow old age – even tho' he's been knighted.'[41] There was strong support from the critic, Desmond MacCarthy:

> among the best of English essayists and the most delicate of English
> humourists...His short stories in *Seven Men* are unique in English
> literature...few genuine men of letters...who would not agree with
> me in putting him at the head of your list.[42]

High praise, but to no avail. Beerbohm died, without the OM, in 1956.

After Max Beerbohm, Noel Coward. Louis Mountbatten intervened on
his behalf:

> Time and again he interceded to procure...the Order of Merit or a
> knighthood. 'He is determined that I should have an honour of some
> sort,' Coward wrote in his diary. 'He's a dear friend, I must say. He
> seems to mind about me being decorated much more than I do.'[43]

Coward received the knighthood but never the OM.

Incessant publicity, with biographical books and a film since her death,
may have made some wonder why Iris Murdoch was no more than a Dame.

Two writers perhaps deserved the OM for the immortal first lines in their
main novels: L. P. Hartley – 'The past is a foreign country: they do things
differently there' (*The Go-between*) and Rose Macaulay – ' "Take my camel,
dear," said my aunt Dot, as she climbed down from this animal on her return
from High Mass' (*The Towers of Trebizond*). Their actual rewards were
much less: CBE for Hartley and DBE for Macaulay.

Henry Williamson, the author of *Tarka the Otter* and pre-war supporter
of the Fascists, claimed that:

> Hardy, Galsworthy and Masefield – the old Order of Merit fellows [told
> him] You deserve the OM as much as we do.[44]

Perhaps that is what led him to wait

> with vain incredulity, on his eightieth birthday [in 1975], for the Order
> of Merit for which he never questioned his qualifications...it is a pretty
> irony that Oswald Mosley's initials rather than the nation's highest
> honour, should cling to Williamson's shade.[45]

An attempt was made earlier to get the OM for the Anglo-Irish novelist,
George Moore, who lived in what he called 'that long lack-lustre street',

Ebury, SW1. The move was

> scuppered by his 'old friend' Gosse [the literary critic], who showed
> Ramsay MacDonald, then Prime Minister, lubricious extracts from
> Moore novels.[46]

Before I leave the writers, I ought to recount the only example I found in
the OM archives of blatant and unsupported self-seeking. In 1904, Lewis
Morris wrote to the King's Private Secretary to put his claim to some recog-
nition beyond his existing knighthood since he had 'long been the most
popular of living writers of verse'. He was told his request had been noted.
In 1905, undeterred, he wrote again, enclosing his *Ode Recited on Laying the
Foundation Stone of the Sanatorium for West Wales by HRH The Princess
Christian* and reminding Knollys that, because of his work as unofficial Poet
Laureate, he 'might be thought to have earned a place in it' [the OM]. He
was told that: 'The King has not given any commands on the subject.' In
1906, still striving, he wrote to 'say that the possession of the OM . . . would
be very acceptable, as I believe [it would be] to the people of Wales'. This
time, the response was much firmer: the King 'regrets that he is not prepared
to have the pleasure of conferring upon you the Order of Merit'. Morris died
in 1907 and the Palace and the Order were at peace.[47]

The journalists

Journalists – a special breed of writers – have a long tradition, now perhaps
more often honoured in the breach than in the observance, of avoiding official honours, especially titles, for fear of compromising their impartiality
and freedom to criticise officialdom.

George Buckle, who had edited *The Times* for 25 years and spent the
next 20 completing the monumental biography of Disraeli and editing six
volumes of Queen Victoria's letters, twice declined a baronetcy – but might
have accepted an OM from the King.

C. P. Scott, who edited the *Manchester Guardian* for over half a century,
also declined a baronetcy and a knighthood but was mooted for the OM
from different quarters. Thomas Jones recorded:

> I find Scott refused several offer of Honours but I've always regretted
> that SB [Baldwin] did not suggest the OM as I urged him to do. To
> keep a great newspaper on the level of the *MG* day in day out for half
> a century ought to rank with e.g. writing a History of England. But SB
> likes Trevelyan and doesn't like Liberals with Principles.[48]

Max Beerbohm also urged it indirectly on Ramsay MacDonald in 1929.[49]
The OM would probably have sat historically quite well on a man whom *The*

Times recently described as: 'a pillar on whose stern commitment journalism aspires to rest.'[50]

A number of other leading journalists were happy to take the CH, in many cases preferring it to the increasingly routine journalistic knighthoods. They included:

- Helena Swanwick, who wrote on international and women's issues for over 30 years.
- E. V. Lucas, assistant editor of *Punch*, who was also an essayist, biographer and travel writer (the *Wanderer* books).
- J. A. Spender, editor of the Liberal *Westminster Gazette* for 25 years and thereafter author of a number of political books and biographies.
- H. A. Gwynne, editor of *The Morning Post* for 26 years until its merger with the *Daily Telegraph* in 1937.
- J. L. Garvin, editor of *The Observer* for 34 years (aiming 'to give the public what they don't want') with which he managed to combine editing the 1929 edition of the *Encyclopaedia Britannica*.
- Arthur Mann, editor of the *Yorkshire Post* for 20 years, who helped to precipitate the Abdication crisis by publishing a strong leader on the Bishop of Bradford's admonition of Edward VIII (and who, earlier, as editor of the *Evening Standard* had started Londoner's Diary).
- J. W. Robertson Scott, founder and for 20 years editor of *The Countryman*.
- James Bone, London editor of the *Manchester Guardian* for over 30 years and brother of Muirhead Bone, the artist ('We were born with pencils in our mouths').
- David Astor, the 'gentleman' editor of *The Observer* for over 25 years after the Second World War, whose mother (Nancy) had also been a CH.

The philosophers

There was no philosopher among the original Members of the Order of Merit and, as we saw in Chapter 4, *The Times* immediately suggested the name of Herbert Spencer to fill the void. He was 82, his output vast and his influence (at the time) immense. He advocated a minimal state, with the duty of simply policing at home and protecting against foreign aggression; a citizen could refuse to pay taxes, providing he surrendered the right to be protected by the state. He believed in the 'survival of the fittest' and Darwin described him as 'twenty times more intelligent than I am'.

There is a letter in the Royal Archives from a private individual suggesting that Spencer declined Edward VII's offer of the OM. There is, however, no official document to support this contention. The *DNB* states simply that from the time he refused the rectorship of St Andrews University in 1871, he could not be induced to accept any honour. He died only 18 months after the founding of the OM.

In 1928, Esher raised the idea of the OM for Randall Davidson (who had been Archbishop of Canterbury since 1903) for his ' "service to Christian philosophy" and to literature in his "sermons, speeches and writings" '. He queried why Balfour and Haldane had the Order; he supposed it was for, respectively, work on philosophic doubt and on Kantian discourse. And John Morley had got his OM for 'pagan philosophy'.[51] Later, in an OM 'round-up', Stamfordham consulted Balfour, without revealing what Esher had said about him.[52] The reply was that:

> Nobody would think of criticising Cantuar were he selected; but I should hardly have thought that he was, or that he claimed to be, an eminent theologian. He is a great Archbishop; but is he a great divine?[53]

No more was heard of the idea and Davidson died in 1930.

Twenty years later, a philosopher who would certainly not have disgraced the OM, if he could have been bothered to accept it, was Ludwig Wittgenstein. He and Sigmund Freud are considered by many to be outstanding among the thousands of refugees from Nazism. He is a giant of twentieth-century philosophy – and a very complex personality. It is tempting to linger longer on him than on many of the actual OMs.

Wittgenstein was a Catholic, but from an old-established and wealthy Jewish family in Austria. He turned from engineering to mathematics and came to Cambridge to study (supposedly) under Russell and Moore; his genius was suspected when he always looked puzzled in Moore's lectures; he was elected into the select group of the 'Apostles'. He fought for Austria in the First World War, gave away most of his inherited fortune and published in 1922, at the age of 33, his major work, *Tractatus Logico-Philosophicus*. Wittgenstein broke away to become an elementary school teacher, a monastery gardener (and nearly a monk) and an architect before returning to Cambridge, where he submitted his *Tractatus* as a doctoral thesis. He was examined by Russell and Moore and the latter's report is said to have been:

> It is my personal opinion that Mr Wittgenstein's thesis is a work of genius; but, be that as it may, it is certainly well up to the standard required for the Cambridge degree of Doctor of Philosophy.[54]

Wittgenstein clapped the examiners on the shoulder and exclaimed: 'Don't worry, I know you'll never understand it.'

Wittgenstein taught intermittently at Cambridge before becoming a British citizen in 1938 and succeeding Moore in the chair of philosophy in 1939. During the war, he worked as a hospital orderly (once pushing a young Brian Redhead into the operating theatre) and returned to his chair only briefly afterwards. One (disputed) account of an incident at a meeting in Cambridge at that time has become known as 'Wittgenstein's Poker', giving rise to a book of that name. Excited by what Karl Popper (who is mentioned below) was saying, Wittgenstein used a poker to emphasise his points. Russell told him to put it down and when Popper was asked to give an example of a moral principle, he replied: 'Not to threaten visiting speakers with pokers.' Wittgenstein walked out.

Wittgenstein was not an easy man. Moore wrote:

> he was much cleverer at philosophy than I was and not only cleverer, but also more profound, and with a much better insight.[55]

He avoided most Cambridge academics, except for some like G. H. Hardy, the mathematician (mentioned earlier). Russell complained that Wittgenstein would come to his rooms at midnight and pace up and down for hours threatening to commit suicide: 'So in spite of feeling sleepy, I did not like to turn him out.'[56] Not surprisingly, someone said: 'knowing Wittgenstein was the most exciting experience of my life, and I couldn't have stood it for one more day.'[57]

Wittgenstein's work has left us with wonderful soundbites: because the limits of language are the limits of thought; 'whereof one cannot speak, thereon one must remain silent'; and 'Death is not an event in life. We do not live to experience death.' Even his last words: 'Tell them I've had a wonderful life.' In 1952, the year after Wittgenstein's death, Lutyens' daughter, Elisabeth, wrote a motet with the fetching title, *Excerpta tractatus logico-philosophici*.

In the six years before Wittgenstein's death at 62, three much older philosophers received the OM: Whitehead (84), Russell (83) and Moore (78). There is no mention of Wittgenstein in the papers about their awards. Nevertheless, it is difficult to believe he would not have been offered the Order if he had lived to their ages. The conversation at any investiture defeats the imagination.

Other possible philosopher candidates were J. L. Austin, who had a chair at Oxford at 41 and examined meticulously ordinary linguistic usage to resolve philosophical questions – but died at 49; Gilbert Ryle, who edited *Mind* for many years and from his chair at Oxford for over 20 years helped to make that university a centre of English-speaking philosophy; and Elizabeth Anscombe, particularly if one is looking for those elusive female OMs, who was described by *The Times* on her death in 2001 as 'a giant of twentieth century philosophy'. She was one of Wittgenstein's literary executors and held a chair at Cambridge for many years, managing to combine producing influential books with having seven children.

Two knighted philosophers who did not make it to the OM (although they were certainly considered) were Alfred ('Freddie') Ayer and Karl Popper. Ayer's first youthful book, *Language, Truth and Logic*, aroused great hostility for its iconoclasm. Although he accepted a knighthood in 1970 on the grounds that honours were there and should be accepted because they reflected well on the academic world, he later regretted it and thought it was rather ridiculous. Popper, a Viennese refugee like Wittgenstein, was both FBA and FRS and went on from his knighthood to a CH, in 1982 – 12 years before his death. *The Open Society and Its Enemies*, published in 1945, was an influential polemic against Marxism and other totalitarian societies.

The classical scholars

A number of classical scholars received the CH but did not move on to the OM. Indeed, there has not been one in the Order since the death of Gilbert Murray in 1957.

An early CH was T. E. Page, who edited the renowned Loeb's *Classical Library* for the last 25 years of his life. After the Second World War there were a succession of CHs for scholars over a broad field. Arthur Waley (originally Schloss) was an orientalist, who taught himself Chinese and Japanese and brought translations of the poetry of those languages to a wide British public – without ever visiting either country. John Beazley, an archaeologist, devoted his life to Greek art and especially to Attic vase painting. Mortimer Wheeler, a more colourful archaeologist in both Britain and India, was an artillery brigadier in the Second World War and a populariser of his subject, not least in the TV game, 'Animal, Vegetable and Mineral'.

C. H. Dodd, a biblical scholar, directed the production of the *New English Bible* (and thereby earned – with C. H. Best, of insulin fame – the distinction of being a CH 'fore and aft'). Maurice Bowra went beyond his original Greek into later literature and was a living legend in mid-century Oxford; like some others, he was credited with having responded with his own surname, 'Heil Bowra', to Hitler's greeting him with 'Heil Hitler'. Bowra said the story 'brought me nothing but credit, but it was not true'.[58]

Literary critics also feature among the ranks of the CH. John Dover Wilson was an early appointment for his work on Shakespeare. Lord David Cecil was a distinguished literary biographer. I. A. Richards helped to develop the idea of Basic English and initiated the so-called 'New Criticism' movement; he left a chair at Cambridge for one at Harvard and was honoured on his retirement from there. F. R. Leavis was almost as much a sociologist as a literary critic, crusading against industrialisation and 'mass culture' and stressing the importance of impressing critical standards on the young.

There were other scholars whose names figure in the OM archives but who were never appointed to the Order. One such was Arthur Evans, the wealthy archaeologist of the Cretan civilisation at Knossos. He was much honoured: a knighthood, FRS (with its Copley Medal) and FBA:

> a great collector, but a bit of a dealer. A year ago, he undoubtedly would have deserved to be seriously considered: but the unfortunate affair last

spring, which brought him into the police-court, puts him out of court, at any rate for the present. Personally, I accept his assurances that he did nothing discreditable: but you could do nothing now without provoking unpleasant comment.[59]

That was in 1924. Evans lived to be 90 but died in 1941, still without the OM.

Frederic Kenyon, frequently consulted about candidates for the Order, was also considered for it himself. In 1933, however, when his name was put to Ramsay MacDonald in that connection, the Prime Minister 'says he has no remarks to make; which I take to mean that he does not feel any desire to press Kenyon's claims strongly.'[60] In 1941, Morshead pressed Kenyon's claims as:

> an extremely fine scholar ... [with M. R. James] knew more than any-one else about the textual sources of the Bible ... His inclusion would strengthen the Order.

Hardinge simply responded: 'Surely he is too old.'[61] He was 78, an age perfectly compatible with other appointments, before and after. Still, Kenyon was not unhonoured: KCB, GBE and, as icing, Gentleman Usher of the Purple Rod, a ceremonial office within the Order of the British Empire.

Aurel Stein was, in his day, a renowned archaeologist, who worked largely in Central Asia. Hungarian-born, his main achievement was three explorations, between 1901–16, of the ancient trade routes from China to the West, the careful records of which provided massive material for later scholars. In 1941, the India Office put his name for an OM to 10 Downing Street, who promptly passed it to the Palace. The King's Private Secretary doubted:

> whether [Stein] would ever have come up to the standard ... rather ridiculous to confer honours on people at the age of 80, when their powers must obviously have very substantially declined.[62]

A second approach in 1942, with the support of John Anderson and Malcolm Hailey, who rated Stein 'very highly indeed', did not move the Palace:

> I think His Majesty would take the line that if he had really been deserving of this distinction, his name would have been favourably considered a good many years ago.[63]

Stein remained with his KCIE, conferred in 1912, and died in 1943, a week after reaching Afghanistan, a lifelong ambition.

The historians

Britain was not short of good historians in the twentieth century and, as we have seen in Chapter 13, a number made their way into the Order of Merit. Many fell below it, however, and were honoured with knighthoods or CHs. In the period covered by the records I have seen, a number of knighted historians were considered for the OM, including those prominent in the economic and medieval fields.

The names of John Clapham, Frank Stenton and Maurice Powicke were looked at together in 1944, in correspondence between the Palace, G. M. Trevelyan and Richard Livingstone (the educationalist who was then Vice-Chancellor of Oxford University).[64] Trevelyan considered that Clapham's considerable works in economic history had an 'intellectual and literary quality' which probably placed him above Stenton but he had only recently been knighted and, by way of special pleading, Stenton came from the small University of Reading, without the resources of Oxford or Cambridge. He thought both were deserving of the OM.

Stenton's claims rested on his study of place names and his recently published *Anglo-Saxon England* but, in the application of ideas to history, Livingstone considered Powicke stood first. The verdicts in the *DNB* (1961–70) were that 'Powicke did more than most other British scholars in his generation to rescue medieval studies in this country from the insularity in which ... they had become embedded'; while 'Stenton's work was so securely-grounded in the evidence and his arguments were so meticulous, that it provided the starting point for all later discussion.' The special pleading is of some general interest to the Order of Merit, in which the vast majority of scholarly appointments go to the two oldest universities. Livingstone acknowledged the problem:

> the newer universities deserve any recognition they can get, for excellent work is done in them. On the other hand, the best men tend to get drawn to Oxford and Cambridge: the exceptions like Alexander at Manchester [an OM] are rare.

In the end, none of the three historians became OMs. Clapham died only two years later. Powicke and Stenton were both knighted within a couple of years and lived on for another twenty.

More recently, there was Richard Southern, who was described on his death in 2001 as

> the outstanding medieval historian of the postwar generation, shifting British medieval studies away from its preoccupation with the origins of constitutional government and inspiring a new concern with the whole Western cultural tradition.[65]

Southern was knighted and ought surely to have been considered for the OM. Perhaps he was; Tony Blair was an undergraduate at St John's College Oxford during his term as President.

In the specialised field of legal history, which Holdsworth eventually came to 'represent' in the Order, there was a man earlier who could have come to grace it. F. W. Maitland, however, died in 1906 at the age of 56 and so therefore would never have come seriously 'into view'.

Among other historians of the century, those knighted included names among which many readers will have their favourites, whom they may well think deserved also the higher honour of the OM: Lewis Namier, Keith Feiling, John Neale, Geoffrey Elton, Herbert Butterfield and so on. There were those, some previously knighted but some not, who were made CHs. Only two of these went on to the OM and have been considered in Chapter 13: G. P. Gooch and Kenneth Clark.

Among the others, Arthur Bryant was considered by some lucky to have gone beyond his knighthood but there is no denying the popular reach of most of his work. John Summerson's work was as curator of Sir John Soane's Museum for over 30 years and as an historian of architecture generally. Steven Runciman received both his knighthood and CH after the publication of his great three-volume, *History of the Crusades*, and as the higher honour came when he was 81, it is difficult to believe it was not deliberately instead of an OM. Son of a cabinet minister, he delighted in telling political and royal anecdotes; he claimed to have known every Prime Minister of the last century except Campbell-Bannerman, who died when he was three and Bonar Law, 'whom nobody knew'; he also described the face lift of Queen Elisabeth of the Belgians as having given her such an ecstatic smile that it had to be 'let down' before her husband's funeral.[66]

Of two unknighted CHs, Arnold Toynbee certainly declined a knighthood: a KCMG offered in 1945 for his work in the Foreign Office in both wars. He said it would complicate his relations with foreigners, especially Americans; a biographer, recalling American love of titles, wondered if it was not because the particular honour was only the same as that given to senior members of the Foreign Service. His fame rests largely on his 12-volume, *A Study of History*, sweeping across civilizations, and his CH came in 1956, when it had neared completion. Toynbee is among that small group who are thought to have considered themselves more deserving of the OM.

The other unknighted historian CH, A. L. Rowse, affected to despise honours.[67] Nevertheless, he is alleged to have told Veronica Wedgwood (in 1968) – 'You stole my OM' – and he was ready to accept the CH conferred on him in 1997, six months after a severe stroke and nine months before his death at the age of 93. It was an honour, as *The Times* put it, 'as belated as such recognition can well be' and was presented to him by the Lord Lieutenant of Cornwall; later he was visited by its Duke (the Prince of Wales). Son of a Cornish quarryman, Fellow of All Souls but never a professor, he identified (to his own and many other people's satisfaction) the 'Dark Lady' of Shakespeare's sonnets. *The Times* obituary (with a leading article tribute to 'The People's Don who proved Parnassus could be visited by all') ended:

> a cat that walked by itself. It will be a bad day for England and a worse one for historical scholarship when there are no more like him.[68]

I shall end this look at historians who might well have been OMs with one who certainly would have enhanced its standing but who was most unlikely to have accepted it: R. H. Tawney, a giant of economic history before and after the Second World War. Tawney spurned the Establishment (before it acquired that name) because it represented an inequitable society of which he deeply disapproved. He abhorred the hollow 'freedom to dine at the Ritz'. In return, the Establishment respected him. On his eightieth birthday in 1960, *The Times* did Tawney the unusual honour of a first leader, under the title 'Puritan Militant':

> No man alive has put more people into his spiritual and intellec-tual debt ... His writings have been seminal ... His personality no less than his pen has won him a unique position ... He is more of a saint than a socialist ... [his] brand of philosophical puritanism ... is a fiery repudiation of the meanness of 'I'm all right, Jack.'[69]

Tawney's Christian socialism was all-pervasive. He would not take his Oxford MA because it was paid for, he refused a commission in the First World War (in which he was wounded) and he would have no truck with honours. When Ramsay MacDonald offered him a peerage, he replied with, 'What harm have I ever done to the Labour Party?' and later, in a scathing article, wrote: 'Cruel boys tie tin cans to the tails of dogs; but even a mad dog does not tie a can to its own tail.'[70] There is no sign of a man described as 'the crowning figure of ethical socialism in the twentieth century' in any of the OM papers I have seen, even those during the Labour government of 1945–51. His *DNB* entry states that the offer of a *peerage* to Tawney was renewed by Attlee. Perhaps even the OM would have seemed to Tawney like a can tied to his own tail.

The men of affairs

For the purposes of this section, I am assuming that the relatively few people I mention could have been appointed to the Order of Merit, regardless of the strict ineligibility until 1935 of civil servants and until 1987 of politi-cal figures, unless they had philosophical or historical 'cover'. The blatant exceptions have already been noted in the chapters describing each category of OM.

In describing the relationship between the Sovereign and the Prime Minister in Chapter 5, I have shown how reluctant the latter was, in the early years of the Order, to believe that this juicy piece of patronage was theoretically beyond his control. That feeling extended to other prominent politicians, which is probably why, in January 1911, Churchill included in a letter to Asquith about honours to sweeten the Conservative Opposition the bald proposal of 'Order of Merit for Joe [Chamberlain]', the retired and paralysed former Colonial Secretary.[71]

In 1912, Edward Grey, the Foreign Secretary (who famously saw the lamps going out all over Europe in 1914, not to be lit again in our lifetime) became the first non-peer to receive the Garter since Castlereagh a century earlier. How much more appropriate would have been the OM, which he almost came to deserve for his enchanting book, *The Charm of Birds*.

Colonial administrators like Alfred Milner in South Africa (who was later Colonial Secretary) and Frederick Lugard in Hong Kong and, more particularly, Nigeria did not go unhonoured, with peerages and other high decorations. But, as outstanding figures in the Empire at its height, they would have given balance to the Order of Merit. Similarly, no Viceroy of India, as such, received the Order, although 15 years or so after giving up the office, Halifax and Mountbatten were so honoured. Of course, it can be argued rightly that Viceroys were heavily honoured already, with steps in the peerage and/or the Garter – and there was always the danger of automaticity.

An outstanding home civil servant wanted the OM but, wisely, Lloyd George did not try to get it for him in 1919. Maurice Hankey created (in 1916) the Cabinet Secretariat that has served British public life so well; as well as Secretary of the Cabinet, he was also Secretary of the Committee of Imperial Defence and Clerk of the Privy Council for 20 years. He was Secretary of the British Empire delegation to the Versailles Peace Conference in 1919, after which he received the GCB (and not the OM). Hankey also received a grant of £25,000, part of which he used (according to his *DNB* entry) to give a small box of cigars to his private secretary. Although an OM in 1919, when he was 42, would have been grossly premature, it would have been a fitting honour later for a creative public servant, either on his retirement in 1938 or even later; he lived until 1963.

A public servant, who moved from the career civil service to become an economist and social reformer, was William Beveridge, brother-in-law of R. H. Tawney. Lured to become Director of the London School of Economics by its founders, Sidney and Beatrice Webb, he was later Master of University College, Oxford. It was from that base that he launched in December 1942 the report on 'Social Insurance and Allied Services', which, despite initial lack of official enthusiasm, came to be adopted as the blueprint for the welfare state legislation of 1944–48. Whatever current views of it may be, its influence in the middle years of the century meant its author would not have been an unworthy OM.

The instinct to cross the thin political line was shown again by Churchill as Prime Minister, when he sought to secure an OM for Viscount Cecil of Chelwood. Robert Cecil was the third son of the Marquess of Salisbury, who had acquiesced so easily in the Order of Merit being 'the King's'. He was instrumental in the founding of the League of Nations and worked untiringly for it in and out of government office, winning the Nobel Peace Prize in 1937. From Washington in 1943, at the same time as pressing for the Order for Admiral Pound, Churchill telegraphed: 'I think [Cecil's] inclusion would add to the distinction of the List.'[72] The reply from the Palace was a polite rebuff:

> leaving aside the question of merit, His Majesty does not quite see how the type of services rendered by him could be reconciled with the Statutes of the Order.[73]

Cecil eventually received the CH at the age of 92: in 1956, the year after Churchill left office.

Another political figure missing from the list of OMs is Ernest Bevin. Leaving school at 11 to become a farm boy, he rose through the trade union movement, becoming famous as the 'Dockers' KC', before forming the largest union, the Transport and General Workers. In that capacity, Bevin declined a peerage offered to him in 1930 by Ramsay MacDonald. The toughness of character he had displayed as a trade union leader, he displayed when Churchill summoned him to the vital post of Minister of Labour in the wartime coalition, at the end of which he declined even a CH.

The same toughness came through as Foreign Secretary in the post-war Labour government, in which Bevin was a pivotal figure. He supported Attlee against all machinations, famously remarking when it was said that Herbert Morrison was his own worst enemy: 'Not while I'm alive, he ain't.'

As a young man, I learned that the Foreign Office owed to Bevin the practice of placing the 'Problem' at the head of a submission, followed immediately by 'Recommendation' and only then the 'Argument'. Not fond of reading long documents, he is supposed to have said: 'Tell me what the problem is and what you want me to do about it.' He defended the Foreign Office against many in the Labour Party who were suspicious of upper-crust diplomats and, anyway, thought it was time for some 'jobs for the boys'. Not surprisingly he earned the gratitude of the diplomats but also their respect for the way in which he defended British interests, most notably in the formation of NATO. He once summed up his foreign policy as being 'able to take a ticket at Victoria Station and go anywhere I damn well please.' Bevin would have loved Eurostar.

On Bevin's seventieth birthday, every member of the Foreign Office, from the Permanent Under-Secretary to the messengers, subscribed 6d for a present. He died only a month later and the question therefore never arose of an OM, on his retirement from politics or later, for a 'Grand Old Man' of foreign policy. His name now in the list of Members would be no disgrace.

Of the Prime Ministers of the earlier years of the century, who might reasonably be considered worthy of consideration for an OM for their length of time in office and overall contribution to British political life, two were looked after by the customary combination of an earldom and the Garter: Asquith and Baldwin.

A third, Ramsay MacDonald, a controversial but significant leader, refused a peerage and the Thistle, because both involved a title and the first might also have hindered the political career of his son, Malcolm. According to his daughter, he was offered a marquessate (!) but told her he was born 'Mr' – in Lossiemouth – and intended to die as such; he knew it was a pity that he could not become the 'Marquess of Lossie' (the title of a Scottish novel) and that she and her sisters would not be 'Ladies'.[74] It is strange, however, that George V, who considered Ramsay MacDonald a friend, did not offer him the non-titular OM; it shows, perhaps, how strong was that monarch's aversion to politicians in the Order. (Thirty years later Malcolm, with a filial aversion to titles, became an OM.)

Since it became easier, later in the century, and in other reigns, to adjust Prime Ministers, at least, in to the Order, few would quarrel objectively with the appointments of Churchill, Attlee and Thatcher, or Macmillan. Two others sought it, however. According to one of his private secretaries, Anthony Eden, who had refused the Garter (in Churchill's wake) in 1945 but was to receive it (again in Churchill's wake) in 1954, hankered after an OM (in 1952):

> [He] wants the Order of Merit and cannot have it because, as the Palace rightly point out, it is not meant for politicians.[75]

A brilliant premiership might have brought it, as well as the ritual earldom which Eden later took.

Harold Wilson was another Prime Minister whose mind turned to the OM. On his unexpected retirement in 1976, he toyed with the Garter, the OM or the Lords. According to his official biographer:

> One of those responsible at the palace claims that he originally asked for the GCVO, which had the attraction of being solely in the monarch's gift but which was felt to be entirely inappropriate. He was hurriedly offered the Garter, in case he next requested the Order of Merit, another distinction which did not seem entirely suitable.[76]

I ought to refer finally to the man without whom almost no book is complete: the maverick, T. E. Lawrence, whom Churchill described as not being in complete harmony with the normal. He was not the first or last man who loved backing into the limelight and there is a completely unauthenticated story that he did refuse the OM:

> The King sent for him to give him a knighthood [in fact, a CB] and was astonished when he begged to be let off. So the King offered him an OM. Lawrence turned that down also.[77]

It seems an unlikely story but where the truth lies is that, if he had been offered the OM (Military or Civil?), Lawrence probably would have turned it down. He is certainly one of the most celebrated British names of the twentieth century that is missing from the OM list. He did not lack OM friends, however: Hardy, Churchill and Forster.

I have deliberately referred in this chapter to many CHs because that order is so commonly bracketed with the OM. For many, indeed most, of them, however, there was little serious possibility of becoming OMs. In harsh terms, the CH was their ceiling, high though that was. They knew it and others knew it. This was particularly so in the early years of the CH, when there is little evidence in the Royal Archives of their being considered for the higher award. More recently, the CH has become a more recognised route to the top in the artistic and scientific fields.

As I said at the beginning of this chapter, the list of 'might have beens' is long and readers will add or subtract. I think that many of those, especially in the last 50 years (for which I have not seen the confidential papers), must have been considered for the Order of Merit. The wealth of talent reviewed in this chapter shows what a difficult task has always faced those who advise the Sovereign on appointments to the Order.

22

HOW ARE THEY REMEMBERED – IF THEY ARE?

The question is: 'Did I know anything or much about this member of the OM before I picked up this book?' Relatively few OMs are real household names, by which I mean that they can be mentioned in reasonably intelligent company without having to be explained or defined. I suggest that that select group would include 20 or so of the 150-odd dead recipients: Churchill, Rutherford, Baden-Powell, Haig, Kitchener, Lloyd George, Nightingale, Mountbatten, Elgar, Hardy, Henry James, Greene, Olivier, Mother Teresa, Lister, Attlee, Henry Moore, Cheshire.

Naturally, those Members nearer our own time are more likely to be recognised and remembered. It is history that is the great winnower of reputations. Since, in each successive generation, we are 'history', I know that readers will easily be able to add to or subtract from my list.

Within their own fields, OMs will naturally be well known. No music-lover would be ignorant of Elgar, Vaughan Williams, Britten, Walton, Tippett, Menuhin, de Valois or Ashton. No theatre-goer would need to be told about Olivier or Gielgud. No one interested in literature would require briefing on Hardy, Galsworthy, Eliot, Greene or Hughes. No student of history would fail to recognise G. M. Trevelyan or C. V. Wedgwood, but the names of Lecky and G. O. Trevelyan might nowadays not be so instantly acknowledged.

In the scientific field, where successive generations so clearly build on the work of their predecessors ('standing on the shoulders of giants'), those working in specific areas would be aware of the OM physicists, chemists, biologists and the like.

In advertisements for the BBC 2 series on 'Great Britons', four twentieth-century figures were featured: two OMs (Nightingale and Churchill), one whose public fame was of OM proportions (Fleming) and one CH who may yet live to be an OM (Stephen Hawking).

The best-known names will be found, on the whole, among the men of affairs, the military and those in the arts: musicians, performers, artists, novelists and poets. The least well-known names will generally be among the scientists and the scholars.

Those forgotten, except by people in very limited fields, would include Members such as Lecky, Jebb, Bradley, Grierson, Mackail, Hooker, Eddington and Taylor. Among the military, names that stir few memories now would include Keppel, Seymour, White, Wilson, Madden, Chetwode, Chatfield and Newall. A few years ago, I was asked to talk to a distinguished naval dining club on the 'forgotten' admiral OMs, about whom my audience knew virtually nothing. If they did not, why would non-sailors?

None of this listing of the 'forgotten' is meant to be impertinent by suggesting that these undoubtedly distinguished men, both civil and military, did not contribute greatly in their particular spheres. What I am suggesting, with the benefit of enormous hindsight, is that some do not match up to the *exceptionally* high standards set for the Order of Merit.

Statues and plaques

The classic, indeed classical, way of commemorating famous people was to erect a statue, often in their birthplace or near somewhere significant in their lives. Many of the early OMs are remembered in this way but the habit has become markedly less popular.

The erection of statues persisted with the most famous political and military figures and the area around Whitehall is full of them. Churchill and Smuts are in Parliament Square, Haig rides his much-criticised horse down Whitehall itself, as though it were taking him to Lutyens' Cenotaph past the statues of Alanbrooke – and Montgomery. Busts of Jellicoe, Beatty and Cunningham (unveiled by Prince Philip) look out, dwarf-like, on to a Trafalgar Square dominated by Nelson. Trenchard and Portal stare over the Thames from outside the Ministry of Defence. They cannot quite see Nelson Mandela, because he is round the side of the Royal Festival Hall.

I have already noted that the only four statues overlooking Horse Guards Parade are of OMs: Roberts and Wolseley on horseback guarding the archway, Kitchener dismounted guarding the garden door of 10 Downing Street and Mountbatten (the only one wearing his OM badge) on Foreign Office Green. As the Brigade of Guards perform on that parade ground, they will have come from Wellington Barracks, where Alexander of Tunis gazes at the renovated building.

Florence Nightingale stands in Waterloo Place – with her lamp – facing Edward VII, who reluctantly admitted her to the Order.

To find statues in Central London of the OM occupants of 10 Downing Street, such as Lloyd George, Balfour, Attlee or Macmillan, one has to venture into the Members' Lobby of the House of Commons. Margaret Thatcher will join them there one day but, meanwhile, the Guildhall of the City of London is likely to provide her statue with a temporary home.

Portland Place in London, close to Broadcasting House, provides a pointed contrast between statues to the 'remembered' and the 'forgotten'. There is a small bust of Lister and a large equestrian statue of Field Marshal Sir George White, VC, GCB, OM, GCSI, GCMG, GCIE, GCVO. Despite Balfour's doubts about White's receiving the OM, both were big men in the first decade of the last century. In 2006, however, Lister lives but White does not.

Outside Central London, there are statues of OMs in localities where they were born or with which they were closely associated. Attlee stands outside Limehouse Library, in the area he represented for three decades in the Commons. Baden-Powell appropriately guards the Scout headquarters named after him, in Kensington. Lloyd George is in the square of Caernarvon, for which he was the MP for 55 years, and a bust of him is outside the memorial museum at Llanystumdwy, near his burial place by the river from which he took his title. Hardy sits benignly in Dorchester – the 'Casterbridge' of his novels. And so on.

Graves and memorials

Our great churches house many OM graves and/or memorials. Westminster Abbey, the Valhalla of the Nation, is a Royal Peculiar (outside the jurisdiction of the Bishop of London) and, indeed, has a peculiarly close relationship with the Sovereign. So it is appropriate that 26 of the monarch's personal appointees to the Order of Merit should be buried or commemorated there. Churchill has his large marble slab near that of the Unknown Warrior.

Others are elsewhere in the floor or on the walls and they range from Attlee to Lloyd George, from Hardy to Masefield, from Britten to Olivier, from Lister to Rutherford, from Trenchard to Mountbatten. Parsons has a stained glass window. One slab reads 'Edward Elgar OM', his baronetcy and knighthood having got lost somewhere.

St Paul's Cathedral, the other Valhalla, has graves and memorials of OM soldiers (Roberts and Wolseley), sailors (Jellicoe and Beatty) and painters (Alma-Tadema and Holman Hunt).

Buildings

To many OMs there are memorials in bricks and mortar. Churchill has his college at Cambridge, founded towards the end of his life, with an OM (Cockcroft) as its first Master, appointed by the Crown. He has other solid, and powerful, memorials bearing his name: a British nuclear submarine and an American missile destroyer.

Lister has hospitals, and wards and blocks within hospitals, named after him. There is a Blackett Laboratory at Imperial College in London and a Sanger Laboratory in Cambridge. Sometimes the building is more modest, for instance a Bradley Room in Merton College, Oxford. Mountbatten gives his name to one of the principal rooms of the Royal Over-Seas League, in St James's, of which he was the Grand President for many years. There are London theatres called after the two actor OMs: Olivier and Gielgud.

The Queen Elizabeth II Conference Centre, opposite Westminster Abbey, has its rooms named after 'British figures who have made a significant contribution to modern society'. Of the eight modern figures, seven are OMs: Churchill, Whittle, Rutherford, Henry Moore, Mountbatten, Britten and Nightingale.

Foundations and trusts, sometimes operating from buildings bearing an OM's name, have been created to honour their work and the causes to which they were committed. Thus, the Attlee Foundation (of which I was a trustee for some years) is housed alongside Toynbee Hall in the East End of London, where the young 'Clem' had worked and developed a powerful social conscience.

Academic Memorials

With the strong academic streak running through the Order of Merit, particularly in the fields of 'Science' and 'Learning', it is not surprising that many positions in, or associated with, universities have been named after OMs: chairs, fellowships, lectureships, scholarships and prizes.

Oxford has the Foch Professor of French, twinned with the Haig Professor of English Literature in Paris. There is the Field Marshal Alexander Professor of Cardiovascular Medicine, as well as the Royal Society's Henry Dale research chair. A lectureship in American Foreign Policy, named after Winant, was endowed by his son.

At Cambridge, in addition to his college, there is the Churchill Professor of Mathematics for Operational Research. There is also a Smuts Professor of the History of the British Commonwealth and an Arthur Balfour Professor of Genetics. (I referred earlier to the King Edward VII Professor of English Literature.) In London, at Queen Mary and Westfield College, there is the Attlee Professor of Contemporary History.

The Royal Society has endowed a number of awards named after scientific OMs. The funds of the Rutherford Memorial are used for scholarships, a memorial lecture and the collection and copying of his correspondence; the lecture is given in a Commonwealth university outside Britain and at least one in three has to be delivered in his native New Zealand. The UK-Canada Rutherford Lecture, delivered alternately in the two countries, recalls his time at McGill before moving to Manchester and Cambridge. The Parsons

Memorial finances an annual lecture and medal. The Dorothy Hodgkin Fellowships support scientists (mostly women) in the early stages of their research careers. Florey Fellowships provide for young Australian biomedical students to follow his path to a British university. There is a lecture named after Florey, as there are ones in memory of Blackett and Medawar.

Medals bear OMs' names, such as the Kelvin, awarded by the Institution of Civil Engineers and the Eddington, from the Royal Astronomical Society. The T. S. Eliot Prize for Poetry, worth £10,000, was won by Ted Hughes shortly before his death. The Kitchener Scholarships, financed from the National Memorial Fund established after his death, are for the children of servicemen and women.

Banknotes and stamps

Two everyday items that bring some OMs to the attention of the public at large are banknotes and postage stamps. It is obviously rarer to appear on much-used notes than on the once-used stamps, although many more people collect stamps than banknotes. Since famous figures began to be placed on British banknotes, those chosen have included Shakespeare, Wren, Faraday, Dickens and Darwin (all eminently 'OM' in pre-OM days), as well as Nightingale and Elgar.

Famous people on stamps are a staple part of the philatelic industry. Churchill has appeared not only on British stamps (twice), as one would expect, but also on those of virtually every country in the world. Of the other OMs, Baden-Powell, as the founder of an international movement, has appeared on the stamps of many countries, including Britain.

Relatively few OMs have featured on British stamps, possibly because of our rather austere attitude on postal issues generally. The sailors, Fisher (wearing his OM Badge) and Cunningham were in the Maritime Heritage series in 1982 and the airmen, Trenchard and Portal, were in a series to commemorate the fiftieth anniversary of the formation of RAF Commands. Vaughan Williams had a stamp on his centenary and Elgar featured in a music series. A Tippett score was the background to a stamp on the British Council and a Nicholson still-life featured in a Europa issue.

Nightingale was on a British stamp on the one hundred and fiftieth anniversary of her birth and she has featured on other countries' issues as well. Hardy also had a single British stamp on his one hundred and fiftieth anniversary. Two stamps were issued for the centenary of Lister's discovery of antiseptic surgery. Not surprisingly, Dorothy Hodgkin was included in a series on Twentieth Century Women of Achievement in 1996.

Prince Philip has naturally appeared on stamps in Britain and other Commonwealth countries and, if he is featured in uniform, the OM makes a discreet appearance. Some OMs have been on other countries' stamps: Balfour on an Israeli issue on the fiftieth anniversary of 'his' declaration; Eliot, American by birth, a United States issue; Russell on an Indian issue, on his centenary, and Britten on an issue from the former German Democratic Republic.

OMs from other Commonwealth countries have fared well on stamps. Mackenzie King and Pearson have been in a Canadian Prime Ministers' issue and Penfield in a medical issue. Smuts has featured on South African stamps. On Rutherford's centenary, he was honoured by New Zealand, where he was born, by Canada, where he had worked, and by the Soviet Union (!) – but not by Britain where he had been a towering scientific figure. Parsons was on a stamp from Ireland, with which his family had close associations.

Honorary OMs have featured on stamps of their own countries. As a President, Eisenhower has been in more than one American issue. Foch and Joffre have been on French stamps, as has the Alsatian Schweitzer, whose 'other' country, Germany (both West and East) has also featured him. Togo was on a definitive, as distinct from a commemorative, Japanese stamp. Besides honouring Radhakrishnan and Mother Teresa, India issued a stamp for Mountbatten the year after his assassination, which is more than his own country has ever done.

Individual OMs have featured on the stamps of many countries. What of the Order of Merit itself? In 2002, there was not even a single stamp, let alone a series, to mark 100 years of Britain's premier society of honour. We shall see nothing to rival the elegant stamp issued by Germany in 1981, featuring the badge and ribbon of the Order Pour le mérite. The more glamorous, but less significant, British Orders of the Garter and the Thistle had special stamps to commemorate their six hundred and fiftieth and three hundredth anniversaries. In October 2001, the Post Office produced six stamps to celebrate the centenary of the Nobel Prizes and proudly announced that 94 of them had been won by UK citizens.

Yet, despite a very high-level approach, the Post Office was unable to fit a single OM stamp into its programme, even in the Golden Jubilee of the Sovereign of an Order, that is 'home-grown' and has gone to over 150 UK citizens. The issues for 2002 included coastlines, aircraft, London bridges, astronomy and mailboxes. The last laugh must be with Rudyard Kipling, who twice declined the OM but the centenary of whose *Just So* stories was celebrated in January 2002 with a set of *ten* stamps.

23

RARELY WITH THE JAM RATIONS

Honours have often got themselves a bad name because they seem to have been awarded profusely, indiscriminately and frequently to the undeserving. 'With the jam rations' was the slang term used by British servicemen, particularly in the First World War, to describe the shoals of gallantry awards that descended on the survivors: nearly 200,000 in the First World War but only a tenth of that number in the Second World War.

The proliferation of honours under Lloyd George, especially in the first years of the Order of the British Empire, did nothing to enhance the prestige of the system as a whole. Ever since, when a government wants to look bountiful or, to be fair, in times of national emergency needs to be more generous than usual, recourse has been made to the system of 'additional' appointments. These are over and above the theoretical numerical limits. Even the Order of the Companions of Honour, so often compared with the Order of Merit, has provision for 'Additional Members' and these have been appointed on the occasions of Coronations and Jubilees.

The Order of Merit has no such provision. Unless the Statutes are specifically changed, the limit, at any time and in any circumstances, is 24. Those appointed in Coronation and Jubilee Lists were Ordinary Members to fill existing vacancies, as were the only two royal Members. Since 1959, the Order has always been conferred on separate occasions from the New Year and Birthday Honours Lists.

The most usual way for an OM to be invested is by the Sovereign at Buckingham Palace, in early days frequently at a routine investiture of honours generally but more recently at a special private investiture. In 18 cases, it has been conferred by someone acting on behalf of the Sovereign, ranging from the Prince of Wales to a senior official to the postman. Those

18 conferments were all outside Buckingham Palace. So were 13 others, even though the Sovereign performed the ceremony. The venues varied: other royal residences or overseas, mostly in the Commonwealth but twice in France. As far as can be ascertained from the records, only three of these presentations were in public: to Foch, Smuts and Blackett.

A number of times, the OM has been announced or actually conferred (without formal warning) on an occasion special to the recipient and very definitely not with their jam rations. They ranged from Kitchener, on his victorious return from South Africa, to Attlee and Thatcher on their resignations as Prime Minister.

Many of the awards of the OM have been made to old or frail people, whose death was probably not far away. In five cases, however, the award was prompted by the actual expectation of death, which occurred within weeks, only three in the case of Basil Hume.

In one case, the award was approved but an unexpected heart attack intervened. J. M. Keynes, the great if not universally accepted economist, who was already a peer, was to have been appointed in the Birthday Honours List in June 1946 but he died on 21 April. He had learned of the honour with pleasure:

> He may have felt that it was what he 'desired perhaps more than anything else that remains to be got here'.[1]

Sadly, in his case, it was in the short run that he was dead.

24

THE INSIGNIA: WHERE HAVE ALL THE MEDALS GONE?

Originally, OM Badges were numbered. Twenty-eight Badges were supplied by Collingwood in 1902: 14 Military and 14 Civil. It is clear, however, that they were not issued in strict order, i.e. Military Number 1 or 15 to Roberts and Civil Number 1 or 15 to Rayleigh and so on, depending on whether the numbering started with the Military or Civil version.

Where I have been able to investigate the numbering, it follows no logic at all. Roberts' Badge is numbered 16, Wolseley's 17 and White's 28. Nightingale's is unnumbered. French's is numbered 14. Jellicoe's has no number, whereas Beatty's is numbered 30.

The original cypher on the reverse of the Badge was naturally Edward VII's and George V kept it that way. He decided to retain his father's cypher initially in 1910 and again in 1915:

> I pointed out to the King that the Order of Merit still has King Edward's Cypher, and His Majesty said that he did not wish this in any way altered. King Edward had founded the Order and it was only right, therefore, that his Cypher should remain there.[1]

Penfield was the first OM of the Queen's reign and received it on 7 July 1953. Her Majesty pointed out the new 'inscription': E II R:

> I said, 'Is it the first?' She hesitated and said 'One of the first.'[2]

The wearing of the OM on military uniform seems to have been a source of perennial discussion and was not firmly settled until it was almost too late to matter.

Edward VII was clear that the Order was not to be worn in miniature, with other decorations on the breast; he equated it, in that respect, with the three Great Orders – the Garter, Thistle and St Patrick. After hearing that some Members were having miniatures made, the Secretary of the Order sought and received the King's approval of a circular to the original 12 Members that he had

> received the King's command . . . [that OMs] will not at any time wear this Order in miniature, as is customary in the case of the lower grades of other Orders.[3]

What worried both the Admiralty and the War Office between 1915 and 1921 was whether the Badge itself, which was to be 'worn on all occasions' should be accompanied or, in the case of service dress, be supplanted by the ribbon on the breast. Precious few officers had the problem but those who did were concerned to get it right and both Service ministries received concerned letters from them. A pronouncement by George V in 1916, reversing an earlier decision, did not solve the problem:

> The King has decided that in future the Riband of the Order of Merit should be worn in Service and Undress and Uniform. Note. The Order of Merit ranks after the GCB and before the GCSI.[4]

By 1920, the situation was getting more complicated because of the variety of uniforms and because of Edward VII's views, which Sir Harry Legge recalled clearly:

> The Order of Merit should be worn on all occasions *private* as well as the public . . . [it] differs to (I think *all*) others in that it gives no precedence. King Edward made a special point of telling newly invested Members that they were 'to wear it always' and never missed an opportunity of instructing me to impress this on them.[5]

George V endorsed what Legge had said and the Lord Chamberlain's Office duly included in their new regulations for the wearing of orders and decorations a sentence:

> Nothing in the above shall affect in any way the practice of the Knights of the Orders of the Garter, Thistle and St Patrick, and Members of the Order of Merit with regard to wearing their insignia in accordance with previous custom.[6]

A proposal in 1921 that the OM should be worn 'on all occasions except with Service Dress', went back to the King, who approved:

> The Order of Merit is worn in Uniform on all occasions round the neck, except with Service Dress, and in Evening Dress on all occasions when Decorations are worn.[7]

Very senior officers continued to need reassurance about the correct wearing of the OM. After the Second World War, Portal sought and received detailed guidance from the Central Chancery. The essential point was that the Badge should be worn with all types of formal wear (including evening dress and morning dress) but only the ribbon (two inches wide in the case of the OM, rather than the customary one and a half inches) on the service dress.

By 1972, only two OMs were wearing it in uniform: Lord Mountbatten (Military) and Prince Philip (Civil). At the urging of the Secretary of the Central Chancery, they consulted together and

> agreed that the long-standing custom should be continued and that the ribbon would be worn [with Service or Undress Uniform].[8]

Today, by a strange quirk, the only OM seen frequently on a uniform is the Civil Badge of Prince Philip, which he now invariably wears instead of that of Grand Master of the Order of the British Empire, as he did from 1953 until the early 1970s. Since 2002, Prince Charles has also worn the Civil Badge in uniform.

While the military have fretted about the niceties of when and how the OM can be worn on uniform, the civilians have frequently adopted a nonchalant and haphazard approach, entirely suited to an intellectual élite.

There is a strange habit, throughout the honours system, of presenting neck decorations with a broad (one and a half inch) ribbon, which is never afterwards worn, instead of with a narrow 'miniature' (three-quarter inch) ribbon, on which the decoration is always worn thereafter in civilian or military dress. The result is that, unless the recipient has read the small print in the box of issue, the decoration, in this case the OM, frequently rests not, as it should, on a miniature ribbon just below the bow tie or the knot of an everyday tie but on its original long broad ribbon somewhere on the man's chest or stomach.

There are wonderful pictures of the great men, like Churchill and Attlee, with both the OM and CH dangling low down on their growing corpulence. In the uniform of Lord Warden of the Cinque Ports, Churchill wore those decorations on broad ribbons coming from somewhere under his epaulettes.

An occasional OM worries about how it should be worn properly. The urbane Clark sought reassurance before a state banquet:

> Mr Churchill, I remember, always wore all his decorations, which completely covered his ample bosom but it looked to me wrong. In my case, should I wear both the OM and the CH or only the OM?

After being told to restrict himself to the OM, he expressed sorrow about the CH,

> for which I have special affection (it came to me in happier times) and which has an aura of the seriousness that accompanied its installation – it was given, as you are sure to know, in order that Welsh ministers and non-conformists could be offered some honour that their consciences would not forbid them to accept.[9]

Much earlier in the century, the aged painter, Holman Hunt, was photographed in full court dress, buckle shoes, stockings and sword, with his OM hanging very low – in order that it could be seen below his luxuriant white beard.

The first Service and Luncheon for OMs in 1977, at which they were naturally to wear their Badges, produced an enquiry from Hinton that led to 14 of the Members being supplied with miniature width ribbon, so that they could be properly dressed for the occasion. Nevertheless, at a reception during a state visit a few years later, I saw one of those OMs wearing his Badge on a broad ribbon on his chest. The 'great and the good' (and he was pre-eminently that) are not so easily corralled.

Recently, after receiving his OM in South Africa, Nelson Mandela wore it on his stomach, dangling from the long wide ribbon he had been given with it. By the time he came to London on a return state visit in 1996, somebody had provided him with a miniature ribbon, on which his Badge hung, at a more elegant level, over one of the colourful shirts that are his trademark.

Where are the Badges of dead OMs now? Most of the Military ones have gone into museums or public collections. Thus, of the naval Badges, five are in the National Maritime Museum: Fisher, Jellicoe, Beatty, Pound and Cunningham and, when displayed, have had the OM at the top centre. For a time, the Museum also had the Civil Badge of John Masefield, the poet who wrote about the sea after ill-health had compelled him to give it up as a career.

Of the other six naval Badges, Mountbatten's is on display at his former home, Broadlands in Hampshire, and Wilson's is in a private collection. Of the remaining four, Madden's is still in the hands of his family, as may well be those of the other three: Keppel, Seymour and Chatfield.

Some of the army Badges have similarly found their way into the National Army Museum: Roberts and Wolseley, along with Nightingale's Civil Badge. The Museum did have White's but, when it was sent for sale by his family, it was bought by the museum of his old regiment, the Gordon Highlanders in Aberdeen. Haig's is in Edinburgh, at the Huntly House Museum.

The Imperial War Museum has the Badge of Ypres and, in its Cabinet War Rooms annexe in Whitehall, is the greatest prize of all: Churchill's, where it is part of the new museum in his memory. Alanbrooke's Badge is at the Royal Artillery Museum at Woolwich and two others (of Chetwode and Alexander) are possibly with the families. Kitchener's is presumed to be in the sea off the Orkneys. The three Air Force Badges are neatly and appropriately housed in the RAF Museum at Hendon: Newall, Portal and Trenchard.

The Japanese Embassy told me that Oyama's Badge was in an army museum, Yamagata's was with his family and the whereabouts of Togo's was unknown. *Both* of Eisenhower's Badges (original and duplicate) are in the USA. The Military Badge, uniquely bestowed for civilian services, on Baden-Powell, is with his family.

The location of Civil OM Badges is less easy to ascertain than the Military variety. They do not gravitate from the families to museums of the Services with which the recipients were identified. The interests of the many more civilian recipients range so widely that many institutions could be the eventual resting place of the Badge and any other decorations. The actual Badge will usually be of less interest to medal collectors, who tend to concentrate on military figures with tales of derring-do to accompany the ironware.

Trying to track down all the Civil Badges would be an impossibly time-consuming task but occasional enquiries produce results. The late Alan Clark told me:

> My father's papers are in *total* disorder. The archive room at Saltwood [in Kent] is, quite literally, knee-deep. So I can't at present help with the OM.[10]

That was over ten years after his father's death.

There are two OM Badges in the same display case in a house in Northumberland – Wallington Hall, the family house of the only father and son holders: G. O. and G. M. Trevelyan.

Those of two great scientists are lodged with their alma maters: Lister's in Edinburgh University Library and Rutherford's in the University of Canterbury in New Zealand. Eddington's was presented to his birthplace, Kendal, in Cumbria. Those of Lloyd George, MacDonald and Beaglehole were with their widows and the intention in the first case was that it should go into the museum near his burial place at Llanystumwdy, in North Wales.

The value in the saleroom of what is obviously the same sort of Badge depends mostly on the fame of the person it belonged to and partly to which Sovereign's cypher it bears (George VI's being the rarest).

The most unusual resting place for an OM Badge, of either variety, is probably that of Mother Teresa. Having little need to wear it on her nun's habit, she placed it around the neck of the Madonna in the chapel of the Missionaries of Charity in Calcutta. In the manuscript letter she sent to the Queen, she said:

> I thought it will give you joy to see the gift of the Queen of England on the neck of the Queen of Heaven and Earth. She looks so beautiful in our chapel each time, and that is often during the day I look at Her I pray for you.[11]

On the reverse of the photograph accompanying the letter, Mother Teresa had written: 'May She be a Mother to you and your people.'

55 Mother Teresa's OM insignia adorning a statue of the Virgin Mary in Calcutta.

On a few occasions, duplicate OM Badges have been supplied, either temporarily or permanently. In 1959, Burnet did not bring his own Badge on a visit from Australia because of the danger of losing it on a protracted journey and so was lent one by the Central Chancery for use at events during his stay here. Similarly, Cockcroft was reminded by the Central Chancery to let them have back the one they had lent him while his own was in America.

Other Badges were stolen: Jacky Fisher's in 1935, and his son received authority to purchase a new one from Collingwoods (the one that is now in the National Maritime Museum); Adrian's in 1955, when he had left a suitcase in an empty carriage at Liverpool Street Station for ten minutes; and Spence's in 1972, when he had to replace it at a cost of £188.43.

The most interesting 'duplicate' story arises from a premature gift to a son. Eisenhower gave his OM and GCB to his son but was reluctant to ask for them back when, in 1966, he wished to display them in the Eisenhower Museum at his birthplace in Abilene, Texas. His military aide therefore asked the British Embassy in Washington whether it would be possible to have duplicates of both awards. This posed the Palace with a tricky problem. A 'spare set' of the OM (or the GCB, come to that) was not normally provided:

> Nevertheless, the General is a personal friend of the Queen's (as he was of her father's). He is one of the surviving Great War leaders who commanded British and American troops in action. He is also a former Head of State. Therefore, provided that Her Majesty's Ambassador in Washington is prepared to say personally that this is a desirable thing to do, the Queen would be glad to sanction duplicates of the GCB and OM Insignia being sent to the General.[12]

Of course, the Ambassador gave the necessary assurance and the insignia were duly forwarded. The second OM now on display in Abilene naturally bears the cypher of Elizabeth II and not that of George VI, which was on Eisenhower's original Badge.

The returnability of the Badge was an issue from the very beginning. Within a month of the Order's foundation, the Treasury was enquiring of the Palace whether it was to be returned on death. The reply, from the Royal Yacht at Cowes, was unequivocal:

> The King says that the Order of Merit should *not* be returned on the demise of the owner
>
> 1. Because his Family would like to keep an order of that description
> 2. Because it gives no rank.
>
> Moreover the cost of it will be but trifling and VCs are not returned.[13]

As we have seen, however, the cost of the OM Badge – and its worth on the market – was rising inexorably. Collingwood's order book shows that they were charging, for the Civil Badge, £110 in 1959, £175 in 1969, £275 in 1973, £562 in 1976 and £1,826 in 1981. (By 2001, the cost had risen to £5,378.) In 1995, the market value of the Civil Badge was put at £2,000–3,000 and the increasingly rare Military Badge at £5,500–7,000. By comparison, the CH was being valued at £1,800.[14]

So, in the face of these increasing costs, it is not surprising that, in 1983, the Secretary of the Order raised the question whether the Badge should be returned, as the insignia of the Garter and the Thistle were. In 1991, the Queen approved an additional Statute (reproduced in Appendix B) requiring *future* Members, both Ordinary and Honorary, to arrange for the return of the Badge on their death and to give a written undertaking to that effect. The blow to the family has now been softened by a decision of the Queen in 2001 to receive the Badge back personally from a dead Member's heir, in the same way as she does for the heirs of Garter and Thistle Knights.

Like other orders, the Order of Merit provided, in its original Statute VIII, for the Sovereign to have the same Badge as Members 'save only those alterations which distinguish Our Royal Dignity'. This last proviso was removed when the Statutes were revised and consolidated in 1987 but the basic provision for the Sovereign to wear the Badge remains.

The Queen has shown an understandable reluctance to wear orders that came to her, at a young age, by virtue of assuming the sovereignty of them automatically on her accession. It is therefore hardly surprising that the Queen has never worn the insignia of the Order of Merit, despite suggestions from Lord Mountbatten that she should do so on the occasions of the quinquennial gathering of the Order on the grounds that she had earned it more than any of the Members. A compromise might have been for Her Majesty to wear a brooch, modelled on the OM Badge, in the style of those for regiments.

In declining to wear the Order of Merit, the Queen has followed in the tradition of her predecessors, none of whom ever wore it. She has, however, now been its Sovereign for over half its life and has appointed personally almost half its Members. Many people would think that, after more than 50 years of 'exceptionally meritorious service' to her peoples, she might unashamedly wear this particular Badge – 'For Merit'.

25

THE STANDING OF THE ORDER

The Sovereign's regard

The Order of Merit stands very high in the eyes of its Sovereign but much lower in those of the great majority of her subjects. They hardly know of its existence and, to many, OM is just another set of initials in that vast and perplexing field of honours abbreviations, such as OBE, CB, KCMG and LVO. Moreover, it brings no title, the mark to many observers of the highest echelons of those bewildering initials. There is no 'handle' to set it, with other 'high' decorations, apart from the mass of untitled gongs. More of that later.

The Sovereign's high regard is demonstrated in many ways. As shown in Chapter 5, she personally considers and decides on appointments to the Order, on the basis of advice carefully assembled by her Private Secretary. The prospective recipient is sounded by that Private Secretary and not by the Prime Minister's.

For many years, the appointments have been announced (from Buckingham Palace and not 10 Downing Street) separately from the routine honours lists and they are notified officially in separate issues of the *London Gazette*. The Sovereign confers the insignia at an individual investiture, rather than at one of the large ceremonies held by her or the Prince of Wales. Since it was decreed in 1991 that the insignia of future Members would have to be returned on death, the Sovereign has received it back personally from a close relative. For some years, OM has been in the very select band of honours included after an individual's name in the *Court Circular*, the only others being VC, GC, KG and KT.

In many respects, the Order of Merit is therefore like the Garter and Thistle and, to some extent, the Royal Victorian Order. It is unlike the other orders: Bath, St Michael and St George, British Empire and Companions of Honour (although CHs are usually invested individually). The Order of Merit is the only order which has a single officer, the Secretary and Registrar, formally outside the Central Chancery of the Orders of Knighthood; the history of that office and its holders is related in Appendix D.

The Sovereign has invariably been represented at the funeral or memorial service of a Member of the Order. Indeed, in two exceptional cases, the monarch has attended in person: Kitchener in 1916 and Churchill in 1965. The practice of the royal representative being normally another OM began more recently. Thus, by 1968, Cadogan, the diplomat, represented the Queen at the service for Spence, the architect. More recently, the representative has often been another OM from the same field, for example Ashton at the service for Walton; Henry Moore at the one for Clark; and Hinton at that for Penney. 'OM' is placed behind both names in the *Court Circular*, thus emphasising the special relevance of the representation. Additionally, Sir Edward Ford, during his long term as Secretary and Registrar, made a point of attending in order to represent the Order as such. There are still occasional exceptions to the practice: the Duchess of Kent represented the Queen at the funeral mass of Cardinal Basil Hume, who had received her as a convert into the Roman Catholic Church.

In two respects, the Sovereign accords the Order of Merit special treatment: she holds a lunch (sometimes preceded by a religious service) for Members every five years and she has formed a collection of drawings and photographs of Members. Each of these aspects of the Order deserves some description in detail.

The quinquennial 'reunions'

In 1977, the Queen made a decision that was to prove important in the development of the Order of Merit as a form of collegiate body. She accepted a suggestion from the new Secretary and Registrar, Sir Edward Ford, that the Members should be invited to celebrate the seventy-fifth anniversary of the institution of the Order – and her own silver jubilee. Not since the Athenaeum dinner in 1902 (described in Chapter 4) had the Members met together as such, although George V's physician, Lord Dawson, had once told the Private Secretary

> how much good would be done if men distinguished in science, art and literature were asked to Buckingham Palace.[1]

As late as the 1960s, the then Secretary and Registrar, Sir Norman Gwatkin, had dismissively said that the OMs would not come to a meeting of the Order even if asked. How wrong he was.

The responses of the Members to the royal invitation in 1977 were uniformly enthusiastic to what had been presented to them as a 'unique occasion'. The replies described the Queen's gesture as 'absolutely splendid' (Mountbatten), 'a lovely idea' (Zuckerman), 'extremely good' (MacDonald), 'another example of Her Majesty's generosity and sympathetic imagination' (Wedgwood) and a 'gracious act' (Macmillan). Edwards, as a relatively new Member, asked diffidently whether there was to be a presentation to the Queen. Burnet, the senior Member, was particularly sorry not to be able to make a second tiring and expensive journey from Australia in the same year.

On writing paper, headed 'Ben Nicholson OM', the painter excused himself on grounds of old age but praised the Queen's activities and indulged in a correspondence with Sir Edward Ford about the composition of the Order:

> my impression is that the selection of members has steadily improved!...I have the feeling that the 'OM' should (?) gradually become a *cultural* honour and that the Army, Navy, Air Force & politicians should be given a 'KG' – but this is all a world apart for me & I am obviously barking out of turn.[2]

After some hesitation, it was decided to hold a short service in the Chapel Royal of St James' Palace before the Queen's lunch at Buckingham Palace on 17 November 1977. A photograph was taken of the Queen, with Prince Philip and the other Members of the Order, immediately before the meal. The Members flanked the royal couple in their order of precedence within the Order, with the two senior present – Graham Sutherland and Henry Moore – taking pride of place. The only insignia worn was the badge of the Order. Thus, the pattern was set for the subsequent quinquennial gatherings.

The service included the music of Elgar, Vaughan Williams, Britten and Walton and a hymn written by Bridges. Prince Philip read the lesson: 'Let us now praise famous men' from *Ecclesiasticus*. At the lunch, Mountbatten made a short speech. He had failed to persuade more senior Members to make one, although they and others favoured the idea. Speaking as the only Member wearing the Military Badge, he expressed the thanks and appreciation of those present to the Queen and pointed out that Her Majesty had been 'Sovereign of the Order of Merit' longer than any living Member had held it. She had been none too keen on the idea of a speech but afterwards

> came up and said she had been very surprised to find that she was the Sovereign of the Order and was grateful to me for having pointed it out.[3]

The Times had no doubt of the significance of the occasion or of those present. The 'Home News' page was headed by an article by Philip Howard entitled 'The Queen invites her most meritorious'. Below the photograph of the Queen with the Members, he wrote (in between a brief account of the history of the Order):

> The Queen set a pretty precedent yesterday by inviting the 24 people whom she has selected personally as the most distinguished in her kingdom to celebrate the seventy-fifth anniversary of the Order of Merit with her.
>
> Although it confers no title, and has no robes, the Order of Merit is the most distinguished of all orders, since it has always been in the personal gift of the Sovereign.
>
> It was an intimate family occasion in the pretty Tudor chapel that has been the cradle of English church music. A row of the cleverest old faces in the United Kingdom sat opposite the Queen.
>
> They have even occasionally admitted statesmen, such as Churchill and Attlee, for distinction above and beyond the call of politics.
> . . .
> Some pessimists persuade themselves that we live in an age of decline and demerit. Yesterday's congregation of holders of the OM proved them wrong.[4]

In expressing their thanks for the occasion, some OMs added personal reflections. MacDonald was thrilled to see from the list of OMs that

> one of the original recipients was my great-great-uncle Lord Kelvin, whose Santa-Claus like figure I remember well from my childhood days.[5]

Edwards confessed that his chief reaction was

> the same that I had when first appointed – amazement that I should find myself amongst such company.[6]

Nicholson thought it was 'out of date' to have only three women members out of 24 and, moreover, 'the military, naval and air force (and political) achievements should be in a separate identified group'.[7] In any case, their achievements were already recognised by their military titles.

After the success of the 1977 gathering, the question was whether there should be more and, if so, how often. Todd once told me that he had suggested to Mountbatten, whom he obviously regarded as a key intermediary, that there should be 'more regular meetings of the Order'. (He had been a member of the German Order Pour le mérite for ten years and was familiar with its regular meetings.) Syme, as he told Berlin, was keen on annual gatherings

> for a jolly party, not necessarily with attendance by Royalty of any kind but simply in order to have a spread of some kind.

Berlin was doubtful, on both general and personal grounds:

> [W]e might be a rather geriatric body, hobbling on our sticks and saying to each other, as an old gentleman once did in Brooks's Club, to another one, in my presence, 'You still here? I thought you wouldn't get through the winter.'
>
> . . .
>
> If there were such a party I should come to it simply in order to see you [Edward Ford] and Freddy Ashton and Alan Hodgkin, but really for no other reason.[8]

Since there was not the compelling reason of its German model, the Order of Pour le mérite, to elect new members, the idea of annual reunions (even without the presence of the Sovereign) was not pursued. Left to themselves, Members might not be too keen; some lived abroad, some disliked 'going out' and some might not want the expense. After consultation, the Queen decided to invite the Members to meet every five years and that has been the pattern since.

On 1 April 1982, there was a lunch in the Waterloo Room at Windsor Castle, attended by 22 Members, many of whom (with their spouses) were conveyed from Buckingham Palace in a royal minibus. There was, however, no religious service. The senior Member, Macfarlane Burnet, was able to make the journey from Australia. The 88-year-old Macmillan was prompted, on glancing around him, to remark to another Member's wife: 'Proper old people's outing I call it, my dear.'[9]

By 1987, a new Honorary Member had joined the Order: Mother Teresa. The British Deputy High Commissioner in Calcutta was slightly puzzled at being asked to pass on her regrets at not being able to accept the invitation from the Palace but he guessed (correctly) that it was in connection with her OM. What she missed was a service, again in the Chapel Royal of St James' Palace, followed by a lunch at Buckingham Palace, on 23 June, the eighty-fifth anniversary of the Letters Patent establishing the Order.

Again, an article by Philip Howard featured prominently in *The Times*, under the heading 'Royal service honours a gathering of rare merit' but, overlooking the 1982 event, he began: 'The Queen met her intellectuals

56 The Queen with the Members of the Order of Merit, 23 June 1987.

yesterday, as she does every 10 years.' The article followed the lines of the earlier one, with such variations as:

> If you are keen on honours, the OM is the one to go for. The duties are light and privileges small...Other lesser but flashier honours make Whitehall seem a city of perpetual knights...
>
> Britain is notoriously wary of intellectuals, the arts, learning, literature and science. But, yesterday, at the highest level, in their own quiet way, they were not forgotten.[10]

A more detailed account, written by me, appeared in the *Journal of the Order and Medals Research Society*.[11] (The Secretary and Registrar of the Order sent a copy to every Member.) In addition to the music composed by OMs, there was the use made by Owen Chadwick in his address of the poetry of Eliot and Bridges. The lesson from the *Wisdom of Solomon*, read by Prince Philip, included a verse which neatly catalogued many of those aspects of human activity for excellence in which persons have been admitted to the Order of Merit, both the dead and, in the congregation, the living: 'a knowledge of the structure of the world and the operation of the elements' – the physicists and chemists; 'the beginning and end of epochs and their middle course' – the historians; 'the alternating solstices and changing seasons; the cycles of the years and the constellations' – the astronomers;

'the nature of living creatures and behaviour of wild beasts' – the zoologists, physiologists and biochemists; 'the violent force of winds and the thoughts of men' – the philosophers; and 'the varieties of plants and the virtues of roots' – the botanists.

Not fitting neatly into that reading but accommodated in the earlier 'Let us now praise famous men' were those from the arts ('such as found out musical tunes and recited verses in writing'); those exemplifying compassion and interest in the condition of their fellow men ('these were merciful men'); and those men of affairs ('such as did bear rule in their kingdoms, men renowned for their power, giving counsel by their understanding and declaring prophecies'). Missing altogether, from *Solomon's Wisdom*, from *Ecclesiasticus* and from the congregation in 1987, were the men of war. The last Member to wear the Military Badge, Mountbatten, had been killed by the IRA in 1979.

The next two gatherings were lunches only and received no detailed attention in the press. On 9 July 1992, there was a lunch at Buckingham Palace, attended by 20 Members and their spouses; the widowed Dorothy Hodgkin was accompanied by her son, her late husband having not attended previous lunches because he was a committed republican. On 8 April 1997, the lunch was held at Windsor Castle but was attended by only 17 Members and spouses; the remaining three (the Order was under strength at the time) could not be there.

On 31 October 2002, the centenary year of the Order was marked by a service in the Chapel Royal of St James' Palace, followed by a lunch in the state rooms of that palace. Only four people had attended the six events form 1977–2002: the Sovereign, two Members (Prince Philip and George Edwards) and the Secretary and Registrar. Despite the centenary, *The Times* mentioned the event only in the court circular, although it had marked the actual centenary in June by a not-wholly accurate article and it did later publish the 'group' photograph in its end-of-the year round-up.

As in 1987, I wrote an article for the *Journal of the Orders and Medals Research Society*.[12] It was likewise circulated to the Members of the Order by the Secretary and Registrar when he notified them of his retirement.

The service marked also the re-dedication of the chapel after the works that had been carried out there to commemorate the Golden Jubilee. Two particular features of it were the presence of an Honorary Member for the first time and of three very new Ordinary Members.

Nelson Mandela arrived early and I was asked to look after him. He is courteous to a fault and insisted on shaking hands with all the choristers as they finished their rehearsal. He talked to me with a respectful appraisal of the place in South African history of the only other OM from that country: Jan Smuts. He courteously introduced himself to the other OMs as they came in, as if they would not recognise arguably the greatest man in the world, especially clad in one of his eye-catching coloured shirts.

The three new British Members were the Prince of Wales, Lord May of Oxford, President of the Royal Society, and Lord Rothschild, the banker, philanthropist and patron of the arts. The Prince had been appointed on the day after the centenary of the Order in June 2002, and the two peers had been invested by the Queen with the insignia only minutes before they preceded her into the chapel for the centenary service.

As previously, the music at the service was by the five composer-OMs and the first lesson was that used in 1977: 'Let us now praise famous men'. It was read by the Sub-Dean of the Chapels Royal, Prebendary Willie Booth. Prince Philip, by now the senior Member, read the second lesson, from *Ephesians*, urging the putting on of 'the whole armour of God' in order to wrestle with 'principalities...powers...rulers of the darkness of the world...spiritual wickedness in high places.'

The Bishop of London, Dean of the Chapels Royal, conducted the service. In his address, Dr Richard Chartres said:

> The OM has established itself and confers an unparalleled mark of distinction. Part of its cachet is of course that it lies outside the normal honours system and is awarded by the sovereign personally, without political advice, as a recognition of a lifetime of achievement...especially during the half century of our present sovereign's reign the identity of the Order has developed...The opening to those with an distinguished record of public and humanitarian service has been one of the ways in which the OM has kept pace with changing circumstances.

The Bishop referred 'in the context of our present debates' to the honouring of two 'asylum seekers', Gombrich and Perutz. Both refugees from Nazi tyranny, they had never met until they waited together at Buckingham Palace to receive the OM from the Queen. Dr Chartres concluded:

> This Order established itself above fashion. Those who are enrolled here have known the struggle which is inseparable from a joyful creativity and the perseverance which leads to solid achievement. If such obvious truths are not articulated they will become invisible. Part of the vocation of monarchy is to identify and celebrate the values and truth which endure...it is good that there should be an order with some merit in it.

What was naturally evident at the centenary service was the age that usually accompanies membership of the Order. With an average age of 76, the Members comported themselves with a slow, and occasionally stooped, dignity. After the Service, the Queen gave the customary lunch for Members and their wives. For the first time, despite the significance of the centenary, the *Court Circular* did not list the Members of this special Order who had lunched with its Sovereign.

The evening before the Service and Lunch, there had been a less official gathering. The Athenaeum Club in Pall Mall gave a dinner in honour of the Members of the Order, 13 of whom attended. It replicated the dinner that the club had given on 25 July 1902 in honour of the original 12 Members, most of whom were also members of the club – as many later OMs have been. The 1902 dinner (described in Chapter 4) consisted of 11 courses and the wines included a pale East India sherry of 1866 and a Dow's port of 1875. Although, a century later, the dinner had been reduced to five courses, the wines included a 'Venerable 1902 Solera Pedro Ximinez, Pedro Domecq'.

The gatherings from 1977 to 2002 helped to form a collegiate notion for the Order. The idea had surfaced earlier, for instance, when Stamfordham consulted Bryce over the proposed appointment of Gilbert Murray in 1921 (which Lloyd George vetoed, as recounted in Chapter 5), saying that the King wanted to know

> whether this appointment would be acceptable to the small but distin-guished body that represent the Order.[13]

Bryce, with no apparent consultation, responded:

> I feel sure that the members of the Order of Merit & those certainly who belong to the classical and literary category would be very glad...[14]

The collegiate spirit struck OMs differently. Cheshire said that:

> The lunches are held every three [sic] years... We have no formal duties and don't all meet at any other time... Most of them are very intellectual and I'm not. We don't talk to each other all the time. It is not that sort of club.[15]

Another (more intellectual) OM told me that membership of the Order had brought him friends outside his own field.

The portraits and photographs

The story of the portraits and photographs of Members of the Order of Merit is, sadly, a mixed and broken one. It would be splendid if there were an unbroken record in the Royal Collection of contemporaneous drawings of the membership of this unique body. As it is, there are specially commis-sioned drawings, mostly by William Strang, of the Members from 1902–16.

There is then a break, with one or two exceptions, until the mid-1980s, when the then Secretary and Registrar began to assemble a collection of photographs, a task in which I was privileged to help.

Quite soon, however, the Queen decided that the concept of contemporaneous drawings should be reinstituted and so virtually every OM of the last 20 years has been drawn as well as photographed. It is unlikely that the practice will again be interrupted.

In 1906, Edward VII approved a suggestion from John Fortescue, the military historian, who had just been appointed Royal Librarian, that

> portraits of distinguished living men be drawn in pencil, chalk or crayon by a competent artist... a complete series of such portraits of the recipients of the Order of Merit, who may, I think, be taken as the most distinguished men in England.[16]

It was not all plain sailing, however, and, in just over a week towards the end of 1906, Fortescue wrote seven lengthy manuscript letters to Sir Arthur Davidson, the King's Assistant Private Secretary, about his pet project. There is a distinct strain of obsequiousness running through them that grates on the modern eye or ear, such as when he, 'the youngest and most insignificant of the King's servants', expresses his gratitude 'for the time which the King has condescended to give to the affairs of my little department.[17]

What worried Fortescue was that the King's selection of Emile Fuchs as the artist would be

> a great and lamentable blunder. He is regarded as an imposter; and our new coinage, for which he was responsible, is the laughing stock of Europe... the contempt – not jealousy – with which his name is received among artists. His work is thoroughly commonplace.
>
> . . .
>
> I doubt if Holman Hunt and Alma-Tadema, who both have the Order of Merit, would consent to sit to him, even for the King.[18]

Recognising that such arguments could hardly be deployed with the King, Fortescue urged Davidson to stress the importance of employing British artists to enhance the Royal Collection, as George III had done with Gainsborough and George IV with Lawrence:

> English artists have never forgiven Queen Victoria for her exclusive employment of foreigners, Winterhalter and Angeli, for royal portraits, when Englishmen like Millais and Watts were flourishing.
>
> . . .
>
> I do not think that the King in the slightest degree realises how much the neglect of British artists is resented and if Fuchs be now commissioned to do the proposed series for the Order of Merit, it will raise a real howl of

indignation ... He gives endless encouragement to British actors, none to British artists ... by employing [them] ... he would give them a lift which they would never forget.[19]

Arguing that regardless of his nationality, Fuchs was a 'self-advertising imposter', Fortescue ventured to suggest the names of Alphonse Legros, an elderly (British) artist of French birth who accepted few commissions, and William Strang, whose work was regarded as 'very fine indeed'. He concluded that:

it would be a misfortune if British artists had no share in depicting such a series of men as the recipients of the Order of Merit.[20]

Fortescue's persistent and vigorous advocacy paid off. The King agreed to consider the other artists, leaving the Royal Librarian:

a little astonished at my own temerity; but if I succeed in placing the portraits of the members of the Order of Merit in really good hands I shall have done the King a really good turn, both for himself and for his Library.[21]

Fortescue concluded his onslaught on Davidson by setting out how he foresaw expenditure on the new scheme:

£100 a year upon the drawing of new portraits ... the King has agreed that the drawing of a series of portraits of the recipients of the Order of Merit may be a permanent charge. The OMs are not numerous and with the expenditure of £100 a year we shall soon overtake them, for £100 means four or five portraits a year. Then it will only be a question of getting the portrait of each OM as he is appointed. Drawn by proper artists, these portraits will form a most valuable and interesting collection.

In 1907, the drawing began and, by 1914, 24 portraits had been completed, the majority of them in 1908. Strang, who had been elected ARA in 1906 (at the age of 47), drew 14 of them: Wolseley, Kitchener, Jacky Fisher, Meredith, Alma-Tadema, Cromer, Jackson, Wallace, Crookes, Hardy, Elgar, Wilson, Thomson and Geikie. (Strang particularly admired Hardy and drew or painted the writer on several occasions. He also drew, long before their appointment to the Order, other writers such as M. R. James and Masefield.) According to Jane Roberts, the Curator of the Print Room at Windsor, an earlier influence on Strang is discernible:

they are all on a pinkish background. It's very reminiscent of the greatest of royal portrait drawings, the Holbeins, which are also kept in the print room, and I believe Strang came here when he was first commissioned, probably to see the Holbeins.[22]

The other ten pre-1914 portraits were completed by four artists. Countess (later Lady) Feodora Gleichen, a sculptor and distant cousin of the King, drew Roberts, Hooker and Nightingale. Sir Charles Holroyd, the Director of the National Gallery, drew Rayleigh and G. O. Trevelyan. Elinor Hallé, daughter of the founder of the orchestra and a sculptor, enamellist and medallist, drew Seymour and Holman Hunt; later, she designed the collar of the Royal Victorian Order and the insignia of the Orders of the British Empire and the Companions of Honour. The last three of the 24 (Lister, Huggins and White) were drawn by Charles Ritchie.

Five OMs had died before the drawings were commissioned: Kelvin, Keppel, Watts, Jebb and Lecky; although the latter's widow presented a drawing by H. T. Wells, RA, to the Royal Collection.

Of the remaining five early portraits in the Collection, three are by T. P. Anderson (Ypres, Haldane and Haig). Another, of Henry James, is by John Singer Sargent; it was drawn in 1912 as a preliminary to the seventieth birthday portrait that is now in the National Portrait Gallery and was presented by the artist to the Collection two weeks after James' death.

The fifth is the only one to result from a royal commission. In August 1931, the Private Secretary wrote to Sir George Clausen, RA,[23] explaining that the King wished to include among the earlier OM portraits one of Jellicoe, who had received the honour shortly after the series had ended. There would be a fee of 25 guineas and the style would be at the artist's discretion. It was, however, not a royal command and Clausen should have no hesitation in declining if he preferred not to do it. He accepted and the portrait was done in 1932.

Two early OMs, both historians, are strangely absent from the collection. Morley outlived Strang but was never drawn, although he was active as a cabinet minister throughout the commissioning period. Bryce was Ambassador in Washington from 1907–13 but was available thereafter and also outlived Strang.

Apart from Jellicoe's there were no more commissioned OM portraits for nearly 75 years. So, leaving Morley and Bryce aside, portraits were not commissioned in respect of 85 OMs, although naturally many of them feature in the National Portrait Gallery

Why did the commissioning stop? The First World War must have turned the minds of many people, not least the King, elsewhere. Perhaps there was no money available. Fortescue, who might have been expected to pursue his brainchild if at all possible, remained Royal Librarian until 1926. Of the main artists, Strang (who, rather surprisingly, was never honoured with the Royal Victorian Order) lived until 1921, Gleichen until 1922 and Hallé until 1926.

In early 1942, there was an attempt to revive the OM portraits. The Central Institute of Art and Design, based at the National Gallery, raised with the Secretary of the Order, as 'a matter of national importance' the desirability of 'securing adequate portraits of all Members'.[24] It is not surprising that, ten days after the fall of Singapore and months before El Alamein and Stalingrad had begun to turn the tide of war, the Secretary 'doubted whether this is the right and opportune moment to carry out the scheme'.

The Institute, surprised to be told that any cost would have to fall to individual Members, agreed that the scheme would have to await the end of the war, unless a Member could be persuaded to give or bequeath about £3,000 to cover the cost of the drawings. The Secretary stressed that he had been 'strongly advised it would be best to postpone any question of approaching the Members ... till after the War.'

Nothing more happened on this front until the new-found collegiality of the Order in the quinquennial 'reunions' brought a revived interest in a permanent record of its Members. The early drawings were displayed at these gatherings and led to the new Secretary, Sir Edward Ford, beginning a photographic collection, which would bridge the gap in the portraits and become a complete set of images of the Members.

These photographs have been kept up to date and now comprise two sizeable leather-bound volumes in the Royal Collection, completed by the expert binder in the Royal Library, working under the direction of the then Librarian, Oliver Everett. The front covers are half Garter-blue and half crimson, with (appropriately) the *civil* badge of the Order in the centre above the words 'THE ORDER OF MERIT'. Inside are photographs of two OMs on each page, in the order of their appointment, with their names, decorations and dates of birth and death. Volume I takes the story to the end of the reign of George VI and the last photograph in it is that of Attlee. Volume II starts with Penfield, the first OM of Elizabeth II's reign.

Two slimmer accompanying volumes contain factual biographical details of the Members based on their entries in the *DNB* or *Who Was Who* or (for living Members) *Who's Who*. Again, the volumes divide into those appointed before and during the present reign.

The photographs were reasonably easy to trace, with the assistance of the National Portrait Gallery and similar institutions. The most difficult to find was that of the philosopher, Bradley. At his death in 1924, shortly after receiving the OM, the only picture of him that could be found was a passport photograph. From that, Merton College, Oxford (where he had lived in seclusion for many years), had a portrait painted and it is a photograph of that posthumous painting which rests in the album.

It was soon realised, however, that the photographs were only a substitute for the pre-1914 drawings. In 1988, therefore, the Queen revived the practice of having each new Member drawn shortly after his or her appointment. Additionally, there were to be portraits of existing Members and, of the new pencil drawings, nearly half are of such Members. They included ones of the Queen, as Sovereign of the Order, and of Prince Philip, as a Member. With only a couple of exceptions, each drawing is by a different artist and Royal patronage has therefore been more widely spread than in the original series. Only one is a self-portrait, a large etching by Lucian Freud.

Before the centenary of the Order in June 2002, portraits of another 44 Members had been added to the 30 drawn early in the century. Thus, nearly half of the Ordinary Members are included in this special collection.

The portraits have not always pleased the sitters. Menuhin disliked his so much that, not being able to destroy it, he sent another drawing to 'replace' it. (Would Churchill have liked his?) Another Member, Owen Chadwick, thought he resembled a green, tough, clerical Machiavelli; he thought it was great fun to be like that outside but he hoped he was not like it inside.

Unfortunately, no drawings, in either the first or second series, were commissioned of the 11 Honorary Members. Nelson Mandela has visited Britain often enough to have been drawn. An opportunity missed (so far).

Another failing of both series is that inevitably they depict Members in old age. It would be interesting, but probably expensive, to assemble a collection of portraits of Members in the prime of their lives, when they were engaged in the activity that later earned them the honour.

The centenary exhibition (2002)

Soon after the centenary celebrations at the end of October 2002, the Royal Collection mounted a small exhibition at Windsor Castle to commemorate the 100 years of the Order. Jane Roberts, the Curator of the Print Room (who is now also the Librarian) organised a display that included the three types of OM Badges: the Civil for men and for women and the Military.

There were portraits of 30 Members, ranging over the whole century. Because of the broken history of those portraits (described earlier), it had only a few of the early Members: Jacky Fisher and Henry James, Kitchener and Arthur Wilson, Hooker and Thomson, Elgar and Hardy, Nightingale and Lister. With these, there were displayed a musical score by Elgar, a Hardy manuscript and a copy of one of Nightingale's early reports inscribed to Queen Victoria.

Inevitably, there was a large gap in portraits from the Royal Library of Members from the middle years of the Order. The bulk therefore were from the specially commissioned drawings of recent years: Todd, Hume and Stoppard, Berlin and Denning, Wedgwood and Gombrich, Zuckerman and Crick, Huxley and Alan Hodgkin, Whittle and Edwards, Tippett and Sutherland, Menuhin and de Valois, Foster and Nolan and the only self-portrait (Freud).

A central display showed items from the Royal Collection relating to some of the Members missing elsewhere in the exhibition. There were manuscripts by Bridges and Masefield, as well as one by Ted Hughes of a 'celebratory pageant in six parts', written in 1986 for the sixtieth birthday of the Queen. An item on Queen Mary's Dolls' House in Windsor Castle recalled the eight OMs whose miniature books appear in it (as already recorded in Chapter 19).

Finally, there were special presentation copies of the memoirs of Churchill, Eisenhower and Thatcher. Churchill was George VI's 'devoted servant' and Eisenhower recalled 'my feelings of profound respect, admiration and devotion', while Margaret Thatcher conveyed 'my great admiration and deep personal thanks for the privilege of serving as your Prime Minister for eleven and a half years.'

Precedence – why not *above* the Bath?

In only one respect has the Sovereign not enhanced the image and standing of the Order of Merit. Its precedence has been retained immediately *below* that of the First Class of the Order of the Bath (GCB). It is an incomparably superior and more exclusive honour and this is clearly shown by the fact that *all* those who have held both distinctions received the OM *after* the GCB.

When Edward VII conferred the first honorary OMs on three Japanese military leaders in 1906, he conferred GCBs on their subordinates in the war against Russia. When, in 1918, George V conferred the OM on Marshal Foch (already a GCB), he described it as 'the highest military distinction in my country'.

More recently, on his fifty-fourth birthday in 2002, the Prince of Wales was promoted from Rear-Admiral to Vice-Admiral with corresponding advances in the Army and RAF. In three separate notifications in the same *London Gazette*, the Royal Navy and the Army put OM before GCB in their listings of his honours; only the RAF put OM in its technically correct position *after* GCB. The Prince himself, even in military uniform, prefers the civil OM badge to the technically higher one of Great Master of the Order of the Bath.

Another anomaly, given the small minority of military OMs over the years and their complete absence today, is that the Military Badge features on the seal of the Order. The military bias of the early twentieth century ought really to give way to the civilian reality of the twenty-first.

Public standing over the years

From its birth in 1902, the Order of Merit enjoyed an outstanding reputation in informed, or perhaps elite, circles. This is evident in many places in this book.

John Burns, the Socialist politician who served in the Liberal Cabinet until the First World War,

> had no patience with the trumpery of titles, the price for which is a premium paid by nonentities for a brief deferment of oblivion . . . He agreed there was one distinction worth having, the Order of Merit. Perhaps it was so entitled with a view to casting aspersions on all the others![25]

H. W. Massingham, the noted editor of *Nation*, told the King's Private Secretary in January 1922 that:

> The OM is a very great honour and the standard of admittance has been kept very high.[26]

The serious press was ready to devote space to vacancies in the Order. After the death of Bryce in January 1922, the *Manchester Guardian*, thinking that 'it may be of interest to note the views of some representative men with whom I discussed the subject', speculated with some prescience on future membership, suggesting the names of six who were to be admitted to it over the next few years.[27] At the same time, the *New Statesman* commented that because of the 'enormous depreciation in the prestige of all public honours . . . the public has been more interested in the bestowal of the letters "OM" . . . than in that of any other decoration or title.'[28] The journal looked askance, however, at the age of membership and the large number of vacancies (nine out of 24). It doubted whether the Order included the men of 'most important talent' or 'most remarkable achievement' but attributed this to the main qualification being a 'select, unchallenged reputation, which may have no staying power but over which there broods temporally the peace of finality'. It thought that perhaps too much was made of 'considerations which mankind ultimately brushes aside with impatience', such as public prominence, dignity and the resulting immunity from criticism, solid achievement and character.[29] Nevertheless:

> In John Gross's felicitous phrase, there was in Britain, during the first fifty years of this [the twentieth] century, an 'Order of Merit culture', largely liberal in tone, and [G. M.] Trevelyan, like his father, was at the very centre of it.[30]

By mid-century, an eminent American authority on British honours could describe the Order as:

> one of the most coveted distinctions in the whole hierarchy . . . Nothing but absolute supremacy and distinction in a particular field makes a man eligible to receive it.[31]

These words were echoed by Sir Ivan De La Bère, Secretary of the Central Chancery of the Orders of Knighthood, in his book *The Orders of Chivalry* (1961).

The reputation of the Order was such that the historian, Arthur Bryant (later to be a CH), described it in 1956 as one of the 'three British honours that transcend all others', along with the Garter and the Victoria Cross.[32] (Roberts is the only man to have held all three.) When, in 1957, Cockcroft received the Order, his fellow-scientist, Henry Tizard (who was a GCB), confessed that it was 'the one honour I should have coveted had I felt anywhere up to standard.'[33] John Betjeman was, typically, more extravagant: 'I'd like to be a Duke, but I'd sooner be an OM than anything.'[34] More loftily, G. M. Trevelyan, as 'doyen of the OMs', wrote:

> I have always watched the list with some anxiety lest some second-rate person in the vogue should lower the standard, but it does not happen, and I am particularly delighted that a high-flyer like you should raise the prestige of the Order.[35]

In the 1950s and 1960s, *The Times* frequently reported appointments to the Order with accompanying leading articles that extolled its standing. The appointment of Schweitzer in 1955:

> associated the whole of the peoples of the British Commonwealth with the world's judgment that this is one of the great men of the age.[36]

In 1960, when Hinshelwood and Sutherland became Members on the same day as new Garter Knights were appointed, the comment was that the Order was a

> less ancient company which, by the sustained distinction of its membership during its brief history, has come to enjoy equal renown ... no one has ever imputed a motive for an award less worthy than a sincere desire to recognize the merit for which it is named. In that the order is unique.[37]

'Its catholicity of recognition' was the theme of an article when Gooch and Henry Moore were admitted in 1963:

> Britain has no academy – no one society where the living are immortalized. The Order of Merit comes nearest to such a body.[38]

On the same occasion, however, *The Guardian* was more sceptical:

> [A] select company of men who deserve the highest honour but who
> cannot – or will not – be honoured in more pompous ways. It also looks
> like a gathering of venerable old men most of whose work is done.
> . . .
> [T]he timid system of advancing great artists and famous scholars from a
> middle-aged CH to a pensionable (or even later) OM, like civil servants
> 'getting their C', surely robs the honours of much of their effect.[39]

In an attack on the honours system in 1964, Anthony Wedgwood Benn
(fresh from renouncing his peerage) suggested that the Crown should be left
to dispense 'only the OM, CH and a simplified system of decorations for
gallantry.'[40] In 1966, the Queen agreed that the Palace should co-operate
with the BBC in the preparation of a short radio programme on the Order.
It was presented by Harold Abrahams, the respected administrator, broadcaster and athlete. He was allowed to see the early records of the Order but
not papers relating to 'contemplated awards'. The script was approved by
Sir Alan Lascelles, the retired Private Secretary to the Queen and the leading living authority on the significance and purpose of the Order. Not long
afterwards the serious Sunday newspapers displayed an interest in the Order,
producing articles on it in 1967. To *The Observer*, it was

> the badge of brainpower . . . which in the eyes of many carries the most
> prestige . . . some flavour of inverted snobbery in the simplicity of the
> OM . . . Many who scorn other honours are proud to be members.[41]

The root and branch critics of the honours system, however, have no time
even for the OM. The noted literary critic, Geoffrey Grigson, decried it along
with all other honours as telling

> lazy people of shaky self-confidence who can be admired. It tells English
> newspapermen (the least sophisticated, least educated journalists of
> Europe, least respectful of the intellect) who needn't be admired – when
> he dies especially.[42]

In the mid-1980s, two critics of the honours system had kind words for
the OM. Peter Hennessy, the contemporary historian, wrote that it

> really was what it said – meritorious . . . It is highly significant that the
> OM is the personal gift of the Sovereign and is limited to two dozen.[43]

John Grigg (another disclaiming peer) argued for a 'clean up of the great
British gong show' but reserved judgement on 'our most prestigious award

for talent and achievement' for which 'on the whole, selection has been good'.[44]

The Independent consistently argued for using the OM as the basis of a revised honours system. In demanding 'sweeping reform' in 1992, it argued for a single civilian award

> for outstanding distinction in literature, music, science, medicine, industry and so on [which] could be based on an expanded Order of Merit.[45]

A decade later, in a forthright article, The *Independent* wanted to do away 'with these baubles of our imperial past':

> Instead of all this nonsense, we should establish a single award, the Order of Merit. The OM would be given for exceptional service, with an emphasis on community and charity work, for exceptional contributions to the best that has been thought, said and done in the arts, science and sport and for exceptional bravery. The OM should then be awarded at a new democratic ceremony, performed at the House of Commons by the Speaker, dressed in clothes he would be happy to wear on public transport.[46]

The press would often accord the Order its true status by describing it as the 'highest accolade' or 'ultimate honour' or, as a crossword clue, 'chivalrous group ranked by their results'. A strange aberration was that by an art critic (who was later to write the report in *The Times* on the centenary exhibition of the Order):

> Henry Moore is said to have refused the two highest accolades the country can bestow on artists: a knighthood and election to the Royal Academy. Instead of being knighted, he accepted the Order of Merit, the 'artist's VC' ... [47]

'Instead of' reads rather oddly, as does 'artist's VC', somewhat as the Dickin Medal is described as the 'animal's VC'.

When *The Economist* speculated in 1991 on the composition of a revised Upper House, it thought that 'scientists who had been awarded the Order of Merit ... might deserve a place.'[48]

On the fortieth anniversary of the Queen's accession in 1992, a correspondent to *The Times* suggested a new order, 'through which recognition could be given to those who have made an outstanding contribution during her reign to the arts and sciences.'[49] The Order of Merit had been providing just such recognition for all those 40 years.

There has never been any doubt of the high regard in which its own Members hold the Order. This is evident from their comments throughout this book. It is an honour singled out by those who hold many. Just as Alanbrooke used only 'KG, OM' on the title page of his memoirs, so the same two abbreviations were used after Prince Philip's name on the marriage certificate of the Duke of York. To the Fifth Marquess of Salisbury, almost an hereditary KG himself, the Order of Merit was simply the 'premier society of honour'.[50]

Lack of general recognition

It is among the general public that there is almost complete ignorance of the true standing of the Order of Merit. Even among the 'informed' circles to whom I have referred, many groups are surprisingly not included. For instance, senior service officers to whom I have spoken had little or no knowledge of the Order to which a number of their most distinguished predecessors had belonged.

In reasonably sophisticated circles, I have found little knowledge of the Order and, in answer to queries on the subject of my book, my reply – 'The Order of Merit' – has usually had to be accompanied by an explanation of the significance of this honour.

Why is there such ignorance? One reason is its plain simple name. From the nineteenth century onwards, the noble orders of chivalry gradually gave way to, or shared the stage with, more democratic orders, membership of which was based (in theory, at least) on achievement and contribution to society rather than on birth. They became known as 'orders of merit'.

This poses a problem for the standing of an exclusive order that bears simply that generic name. It lacks the special glamour, in name as well as surrounding flummery, of the Garter or the Thistle, of the Aztec Eagle or the Million Elephants and the White Parasol. Many countries, particularly in Europe and Latin America, have an 'Order of Merit' to serve much wider purposes than our own. It was the name chosen by France and Norway when instituting second orders to supplement the overflowing Légion d'Honneur and St Olav.

Within the Commonwealth, where confusion with the British-based order is much more likely, there are Orders of Merit in Jamaica (Bob Marley, the reggae singer, had it), Antigua, Malta, South Africa and, most notably, in New Zealand. Perhaps unwisely, Order of New Zealand was chosen as the name of a select distinction, comparable with the CH. When therefore a name was later needed for a general omnibus order (to replace the discontinued Order of the British Empire), New Zealand was not able to follow the example of the Order of Canada and the Order of Australia by calling it the Order of New Zealand. Instead, it is the five-class New Zealand Order of

Merit. In Canada, recipients of the provincial Order of Manitoba put 'OM' after their names.

The main reason, however, why the pre-eminence of the Order of Merit is not popularly acknowledged is that it confers no title. Yet that is what is often cited as its raison d'être and great attraction, although three quarters of its Members have been titled.

The British are soppily – almost sloppily – in love with their knights. A knighthood is obvious and intrigues the unknighted. The 'Sir' attaches and is invariably used. The writer of a newspaper article or presenter of a radio or TV programme seems to feel obliged to refer to '*Sir* Charles' and this often prompts a reference to the knighthood as a sign of particular public recognition. The OM (or CH or even both) is ignored because it is cumbersome to deal with what the reader or listener or viewer may regard as just 'letters behind the name'. If, however, it is thought disrespectful not to use 'Sir', why is it not more disrespectful to omit the greatly more distinguished 'OM'?

It is not uncommon to describe a knighthood as the 'ultimate accolade', although it sometimes has to share that distinction with 'Desert Island Discs'. When a knighted OM like Aaron Klug appeared on this radio programme, there was mention of his knighthood, Nobel Prize and Presidency of the Royal Society but none of his Order of Merit.

Even when Richard Baker presented his erudite musical programmes, each composer, conductor or artist was respectfully accorded 'Sir' or 'Dame' but not an OM (or CH): *Sir* Edward Elgar – yes; Ralph Vaughan Williams, *OM* – no. All four main obituaries of Ninette de Valois were headed 'Dame', while only one used 'OM' as well. In one headline, she was 'dame of the dance' and we are all familiar with the overworked term 'knights of the theatre'.

A journalist with whom I once raised this ignoring of the OM responded that, 'for the creative artist titles are the only honours that tangibly enhance prestige and sales.' Perhaps that is why 'Sir' looms large on the front cover of the biography of a well-loved football manager. For a Canadian philanthropist (who already had a CBE as well as the Order of Canada), a knighthood meant that he had been 'accepted by Britain'.

In the days when everyone was accorded a prefix – 'Mr' or 'Dr' – it was natural to use 'Sir' where appropriate. Now, a 'Professor' or 'General' will normally be accorded that title. Even the most obscure major in an unfashionable corps can cling on to that rank, if only to be described as such in something like *Fawlty Towers*.

Now, when the casual telephone salesman is ready to use one's Christian name, it is hardly surprising that few journalists are prepared to settle for Mr Smith or Lady Jones. It has to be John Smith (rarely with the Mr) or Lady Mary Jones (always with the Lady). Of course, Sir Henry Brown has always had to be accorded title and first name, except by foreigners to whom he is often Sir Brown. To many it still seems impertinent or disrespectful to omit this particular mark of State esteem. Even 'knight', however, is not now good enough. Taking an unjustified leaf out of the peerage (who were traditionally part of the governance 'of the realm'), the media often pompously embellish the recipient as a 'knight of the realm'. Of course, most peers themselves are now usually called Lord John Smith and Baroness Mary Jones. Indeed, the situation probably needs formalising, at the expense of the purely courtesy titles which have hitherto been accorded to the younger children of dukes and marquesses (and, for arcane reasons, to the younger daughters of earls).

Knighthoods are even conferred posthumously on those who never had them. At a memorial service, there was a reading from the works of *Sir* Edmund Burke; the distinguished chemist who discovered isotopes (to whom I referred in Chapter 21) became *Sir* Frederick Soddy in *The Times'* 'Anniversaries' column; the same newspaper lauded the attractive Gibraltar football world cup stamps as depicting 'the great England captain and West Ham Player *Sir* Bobby Moore' (a title he would undoubtedly have secured had he survived until the Millennium honours list of 2000, which rewarded many overlooked 'icons'). Nearly a century after his execution, *Sir* Roger Casement is frequently accorded the title of which he was solemnly deprived before he was hanged. Another growing habit is to call 'Sir' those (usually CBEs) who are not knights, presumably in the belief that 'he's got some sort of honour – must be a knighthood'.

The ease with which 'Sir' or 'Dame' can be used before a name and the insistent desire of commentators to use these titles make the general recognition of the Order of Merit an uphill task but, as I shall now explain, it is one to which I have sometimes set my shoulder.

Efforts to secure greater recognition

Convinced – and irritated – that the Order of Merit is not properly recognised, I have, over many years, conducted a rather forlorn campaign to obtain better recognition. As I have shown in the previous section, many of those who write or talk about honours (either principally or incidentally) show little or no appreciation of the worth and standing of the Order.

It was naturally to *The Times* that I looked primarily for consistent recognition of the special place of the Order. For over 200 years it has been the leading newspaper of record in this country and has produced a 'Court' page: a 'tribal notice board' that has catalogued the births, marriages, deaths, appointments and activities of those who are now described as the 'Establishment'. The *Daily Telegraph* has followed a similar course.

The Times has made commendable efforts to identify OMs on its 'Court' page but, too often, it fails to do so. When, on one occasion, I drew attention to the numerous inconsistencies – with OMs recognised one day but not the next – I was assured by the editor's office that it was the policy to employ

'OM' on the Letters and Court pages 'and the omissions to which you draw attention were lapses, which are regretted'.[51] Sadly, however, the delivery has often fallen short of the promise. For many years, I noted the continuing omissions and inconsistencies but did not bother the editor again. I had no wish to seem a pedantic bore.

The arrival a few years ago of 'The Register' section of *The Times*, with its greatly expanded recording of events and people (especially obituaries), offered great hope of improved acknowledgement of the Order of Merit. The hope has not been wholly fulfilled. In the full and interesting listing of 'anniversaries', the births, deaths and achievements of OMs are regularly shown – always with any appropriate 'Lord' or 'Sir' but never with an 'OM'. It is the same with the daily list of current 'birthdays'. It never fails, however, to note a Nobel Prize. The centenary of the Order on 26 June 2002 was an ignored 'anniversary'.

In the news pages, the chances of finding an OM acknowledged are slender, although a title is always shown. Mother Teresa, especially as she nears sainthood, is frequently mentioned on those pages, always as 'Nobel Peace Prizewinner' but never as 'OM', yet this would demonstrate that Britain, and not simply the world at large, had honoured her in a unique way with its highest decoration.

The occasional serious journalist shows an interest in the Order, notably Anthony Howard, who consistently takes account of its history, significance and Members in what he writes; in comparing it and the Garter on one occasion, he described it 'the classier of the two'. Godfrey Smith is another columnist who shows a true appreciation of the worth of the OM. Naturally, Kenneth Rose, the historian, wrote frequently and knowledgeably about the Order in the 'Albany' column he founded in the *Sunday Telegraph*. Less well-informed journalists sometimes let their penchant for speculation get the better of them, as when the Peterborough column in the *Daily Telegraph* wrote that 'serious consideration' was being given to the Second World War ace, Group Captain 'Catseyes' Cunningham, as a successor to Ernst Gombrich. *The Times*' diary once hazarded that, 'to jazz up' the 'Order of Mortus', which had been 'devastated' by four deaths, Judi Dench was going to be appointed – to the bewilderment of Max Perutz who had 'no idea who she is' but to the delight of Cecily Saunders, who looked forward to meeting her fellow-dame at what the diarist called 'the regular OM knees-up at Buckingham Palace'.

The National Portrait Gallery, a great national institution that might be expected to acknowledge high national honours, usually fails to accord the letters 'OM' to those it portrays. For instance, in the *TLS* Literary Trail, staged to mark the centenary in 1902 of another great institution, knights and dames (with the strange exceptions of A. S. Byatt and Iris Murdoch) were accorded their titles but there was no sign of the OM behind the names of Hughes, Forster, Eliot, John and 'Sir Isaiah Berlin'.

Comprehensive and authoritative biographical reference works, such as those from Chambers or the Cambridge University Press, are scrupulous about recording knighthoods, peerages and Nobel Prizes. More often than not, however, OM is not mentioned. Of course, this leaves the untitled OM looking as though he or she had received no official recognition.

One such reference work that responded to my championship of the Order of Merit was the *Oxford Companion to English Literature*. The editor, Margaret Drabble, confessed to the recording of honours being somewhat random and was very ready to incorporate some 70 suggested emendations in the next printing.[52]

So, the effort to achieve proper recognition for the Order of Merit can go on but all in a random and haphazard sort of way.

The Order in fiction and in commerce

The Order of Merit has featured in fiction and a play with that title was produced on BBC radio in 1980. Written by Richard Austin, it is about a famous author to whose eightieth birthday party the Queen's letter offering him the OM is brought by her representative: 'a former diplomat – pompous, very smooth.' This is hardly the way an offer could or should be made and, indeed, before the author has the chance to accept or decline, he is toasted as 'Mr David Harvey, Order of Merit'. When he is asked why he did not refuse it, he responds:

> Because it would have been too bloody conventional and everyone would have expected it. At any rate, what harm does it do?[53]

Somerset Maugham, a CH but never an OM, drew a portrait in his *Cakes and Ale* (1930) of a Thomas Hardy lookalike author, called Edward Driffield, being presented with the OM by the Prime Minister, an event that has never taken place in real life. In *Vile Bodies* (1930), Evelyn Waugh described how a Prime Minister called 'Mr Outrage':

> sipped his champagne, fingered his ribbon of the Order of Merit, and resigned himself to the dust.[54]

By 1930, the only Prime Minister to have had the Order while in office was Lloyd George. Evelyn Waugh himself refused a CBE from a Prime Minister (and later OM) whom he regarded as a mere publisher and said he preferred to wait for his spurs (which never came).

Graham Greene, later to be an OM, refers in one of his early works, *It's A Battlefield* (1934), to a room that had contained (fictionally) three of his predecessors:

> Henry James had constructed his sentences like Chinese boxes which held at the centre a tiny colloquialism; Meredith had unloosed a torrent of epigrams; Hardy had wondered what it was all about.[55]

He also has a character, the writer Crabbe, who is described as having

> been very tiresome since they gave him the OM.
>
> . . .
>
> Although he was known to be difficult, he was still invited everywhere, partly because of his reputation and the Order of Merit . . . [56]

When Graham Greene died in 1991, his obituaries appeared by chance on the same day as a review of William Cooper's novel *Immortality at Any Price*, in which one of the main characters is an economist called Horsfall. The reviewer described Horsfall's 'rage at not getting the Nobel Prize, the OM or even the CH'. (At least Greene had both the latter.) He went on to refer to the 'hypothesis that Horsfall is some kind of version of C. P. (Sir Charles, Lord) Snow'.[57] Whether Snow ever expected the Nobel Prize, he is reputed to have coveted the OM.

Because of its prestige, there have been attempts to use 'Order of Merit' commercially. In 1943, a very reputable London printing firm was told by the Lord Chamberlain's Office that it would be 'extremely undesirable' to use the title of such 'a very highly prized distinction' in connection with any advertisement.[58] It was more difficult to deal with the use of the title and even of the insignia overseas. In 1966, in response to representations from the Secretary of the Order about the actions of a New York whisky firm, the Foreign Office pointed out the problems of preventing the use of such a generic title and even of pursuing, on slender legal grounds, the use of a representation of the insignia.[59]

'OM' is a term widely used beyond the confines of any order. It is a Sanskrit mantra, said to represent the first sound generated by the newly created universe and used by Geoffrey Moorhouse as the title of an Indian travel book. The initials are used for a French football team (Olympique Marseilles), a South African insurance company (Old Mutual) and a Swedish financial company (OM Group) that bid for the London Stock Exchange. In its literal sense, 'Order of Merit' stands clearly at the head of the examination results of professions like accountancy. 'OM1' was the registration number of a medium-sized and rather old saloon car seen on the A1 a few years ago. OMs are probably not the sort of people who acquire such a 'cherished' number.

26

THE FUTURE OF THE ORDER

The Order of Merit shot to fame overnight. It was immediately recognised as a superior honour from the head of state. The task has been to maintain that position. With a few possible exceptions, the quality of its membership has ensured the success of the original aspiration. The common denominator in respect of most appointments, particularly in the civil sphere, has been a powerful intellect, often with a touch of genius.

What of the future membership of the Order? Could the growing collegiate notion be extended to meetings every one or two years at which the existing members (under the chairmanship of a 'Chancellor' elected by themselves) made recommendations to the Sovereign? This would be a move towards the formal elections of the German Order Pour le mérite but without the advice of the Members becoming a formal mandatory election. Of course, there could be a problem over the weight that such recommendations should carry. Would tensions be created if they were rejected or deferred indefinitely by the Sovereign and her advisers? There would also have to be guidance of some kind to ensure (as in Germany) a fair balance between the various fields of endeavour.

Such participation by Members would help to increase the transparency that is now so often demanded in the public field and to remove the élitist image which still tends to surround the Order. The élitism, however, as has been demonstrated throughout this book, is one of merit. Its exclusivity seems to go against the modern notion of inclusivity, because its Members appear to stand out from the crowd: they are just plainly the best in their fields.

The Order has always been the most democratic of awards, provided the social system of the time has allowed the potential recipients to break through the layers of the old class system – and that was often easier than social commentators are ready to admit. In the first 50 years of the Order – in the old 'class-ridden' Britain – its Members included the sons of a piano tuner, a tailor, a weaver, a saddler, a hairdresser, a coal miner, a shoemaker, a sergeant major, a tram driver and a tobacconist.

In line with the increasing emphasis on rewarding voluntary 'humanitarian' work, more outstanding figures in that field are likely to be appointed to the Order – in the steps of Schweitzer, Cheshire, Mother Teresa and Cicely Saunders.

There are also bound to be more women and more from the ethnic minorities. As in other more substantial aspects of the national life, however, such appointments must avoid the impression of being 'token'. At lower levels of the honours system, unstated 'quotas' are probably necessary and acceptable but, at the level of the OM, they could quickly damage the true standing of the Order. True 'merit' acknowledged by all, should remain the sole criterion; as long as that is observed, the recipient will continue to be recognised as exceptional.

From ethnic communities in Britain, it is a short move to most countries of the overseas Commonwealth. As I commented in Chapter 21, opportunities were missed in not striving to find more suitable recipients of the Order from such countries. It is probably now too late. The ties between the 50-odd independent countries that now make up the Commonwealth are looser than previously. Less than a third of Commonwealth countries now owe allegiance to the monarch who personally confers the Order. In any case, the shared honours system – with the same orders and decorations being conferred on the basis of separate national channels of recommendation – has largely disappeared.

There needs to be special care to avoid any impression that an appointment stems mainly from too close a relationship with the royal family or the Establishment. The Garter and Thistle are there quite properly to reward such associations, as well as the much larger Royal Victorian Order. In respect of the Order of Merit, however, the monarch is very much a trustee for the nation when selecting recipients of its most highly regarded and exclusive honour.

There is sometimes a feeling that the Order should contain more people who have 'run things', as well as those who have worked mainly in some form of intellectual or artistic 'ivory tower'. In fact, the Order acquits itself quite well on this score. Apart from those who have 'run the country', there are other 'men of affairs' (described in Chapter 14) who were notable administrators, in Britain and overseas. The Presidents of the Royal Society (all OMs) have played an important role in the management of a great institution. Other OM-scientists have ventured into administration within their fields. The engineers were involved in running companies as well as research. Of course, in their day, the military OMs ran armies and navies.

Military appointments to the Order are dormant and, in fact, I think they are over. As I said in Chapter 8, nearly 40 years after the appointment of the last such Member – Mountbatten in 1965 – and over 20 years after his death, there is little prospect of any more unless there is another major world conflict. (There are now fewer VCs than OMs.)

The peacetime appointments between the two world wars did not greatly enhance the stature of the military side of the Order. Even leadership in the limited conflicts of the last 50 years has led – over and above the routine GCB – to the Garter and a peerage rather than the Order of Merit. In any case, the division between the military and civil aspects of national life, so apparent in 1902, is now deliberately less marked. The much-reduced armed services play their part in the emerging 'civil society'. There is therefore no reason why a senior officer honoured for 'exceptionally meritorious service' should not wear the same insignia as his civilian counterpart. As he rises through the ranks, he is appointed to the military division of the Orders of the British Empire and, later, of the Bath. There is, however, no distinctive military insignia within the Garter. Why should there any longer be within the equally prestigious Order of Merit?

The Central Chancery of the Orders of Knighthood now has – for historical record – only one military version of the OM Badge, with crossed swords between the arms of the cross. Two other such badges were dismantled. The end of the military OMs underlines my view that the Order should now be ranked above and not below the First Class of the Order of the Bath (GCB) and that the official seal of the Order should include the civil rather than the military badge.

Much is made of the advanced age of OMs on appointment. There are contrasting views. The Earl of Crawford and Balcarres, an early unofficial adviser on appointments, wrote that:

> the Order of Merit was established for terminal recognition rather than as an encouragement.[1]

Of course, 'safe' elderly nominations help to ensure the historical integrity of the Order. By the age of 80, a person's reputation is normally made, one way or the other. Nevertheless, elderly appointments mean that some worthy candidates miss the boat by dying young – at around 60! The experienced commentator, Anthony Howard, acknowledged that:

> the idea of this piece of Palace patronage is to reward a lifetime of achievement. But I am not sure the understrappers in charge of handing out these lollipops have not taken that 'lifetime' criterion too literally.[2]

Another writer compared the Order with the Nobel Prize, as

> an accolade for longevity ... while it is nice to salute old men, it is much
> better to give young men wings.[3]

The official approach has varied. Whereas during the 1980s there was
a reluctance to appoint anyone over 80, during the 1990s the age of 90
seemed to be an acceptable qualification. Is there an ideal age? Of course
not. Around the age of 65, however, a person's lifetime achievement ought
normally to be assessable.

Much more could be done to stimulate knowledge of, and interest in,
the Order. I hope that, in a small way, this book may help. Essentially,
however, it is in the hands of the Royal authorities to try to improve the
Order of Merit's standing at large.

Appointments are now announced on a random basis. Perhaps 26 June
(the anniversary of the institution of the Order) or 9 November (the birthday
of the founder, Edward VII) would be appropriate dates on which to make
appointments, much as they are made to the Garter on 23 April (St George's
Day) or to the Thistle on 30 November (St Andrew's Day).

When appointments are made, fuller information on the recipients could
be made available to the media. At present, the announcements in the
London Gazette give merely the names of new Members, almost on the
assumption that they are so distinguished that they will be well known to
the public. This is not always so, particularly in the case of the scientists.
In the original announcement from the Palace (of which the *Gazette* notice
is later confirmation), a short 'citation' could perhaps follow each name,
as was the custom in many of the earlier appointments. A fuller 'citation'
could be provided as background information, along with an account of the
history and importance of the Order itself.

The problem is whether the media would be interested, unless the new
Members were 'celebrities' for some reason or other. Possibly the serious
side of the media could be induced to report more fully on appointments to
the 'intellectual Garter'.

As to the investitures, photographs rarely appear of the actual presentation
of the insignia by the Queen. In recent years, only the dying Ted Hughes and
Basil Hume were judged newsworthy enough for this recognition. If such
photographs became the rule, rather than the exception, the special status
of the Order would be greatly enhanced.

Altogether, a certain reticence about promoting such an élite honour needs
to be overcome. If it is thrust at the public for the important and meritocratic
institution it is, they may eventually come to understand and appreciate it
properly.

As background to individual appointments, there could be a more consistent and permanent exposure of the Order. It has no permanent chapel,

with colourful banners and stall plates, which would be inappropriate to a society many of whose members would not want to have a coat of arms. Some might not be entirely happy with a religious chapel. Yet, the Chapel Royal of St James' Palace is the obvious home of the Order and could be marked out as such by a suitable plaque within it. It is where, in its new-found collegiate role, the Order has gathered.

Additionally, there could be a permanent, yet modest exhibition of the Order, in either St James' Palace or Windsor Castle, to both of which the public are increasingly admitted. It need contain only a brief history of the Order and its significance, male and female badges, the splendid book of photographs (perhaps open at the page of an OM whose birthday it was) and, of course, on a rotational basis, a couple of the early or modern drawings that now lie largely unseen in the Royal Collection. The exhibition could be supplemented with items about the Order: copies of extracts from the Royal Archives, from published memoirs or from the press. There could be copies of books, films and videos by or about Members.

In different circumstances, I might have enjoyed establishing and maintaining such an exhibition. As it is, an historically-minded Secretary and Registrar, who is not too busy with other activities, could well promote the Order in a singularly effective way. The story of the outstanding men and women who have made up the Order deserves to be told in a permanent form.

Beyond such a fixed museum or exhibition, more could be done to commemorate OMs around the country. Many already have memorials, ranging from institutions to statues to plaques. The blue plaques, so familiar in London, are not consistent in recording the OMs of those they honour. Such inconsistencies could be remedied and plaques could be placed where none exist at all in honour of OMs.

An elaborate system of specifically OM-related memorials was suggested in 1992 by Russell Malloch, a well-known authority on honours.[4] The problem about such a commendable idea is both expense and the administrative effort required. It is doubtful whether any likely Secretary and Registrar in the near future would have the time to stimulate and monitor such an enterprise.

Would some title or honorific overcome the problem of the Order being under-recognised? That is, if you can't beat them, join them. 'The Right Honourable' is associated with the Privy Council or, in one school of thought, with peers also; 'The Most Honourable' is the little-known prefix for a marquess; 'The Most Excellent' is linked with the full title of the Order of the British Empire; all such titles are longer-winded than the short and appealing 'Lord', 'Sir' or 'Dame'. In any case, *any* title could still deter precisely the recipients whom the Order most needs to honour – those for whom a title of any kind is fundamentally objectionable. Perhaps, a prospective Member could be given a choice whether or not to adopt a 'grand' title.

There is little doubt that the Order of Merit will survive any of the changes in the honours system that are increasingly mooted. As we have seen, in articles critical of the system, the OM is usually excepted from such criticism. Indeed, because of its appealing and simple title, it is frequently cited as the example for some sort of 'one honour' system. By all means, let it stand at the apex of such a system but to expand it to cover all the persons deserving of honour in society would be to destroy its unique rarity.

If a radical reform of the honours system led to the disappearance of titles and to those in the top two classes of the various orders remaining Mr or Mrs/Ms (as in most other countries), the Order of Merit would float naturally to the top of the honours bowl. With competition from lesser, but titular, honours removed, it would effortlessly be where it belongs.

The Order of Merit has entered its second century confident in having established itself as the premier British society of honour and the greatest distinction to which any subject of the Queen can aspire. All it needs is to be more widely acknowledged as such.

Appendix A
LETTERS PATENT OF 23 JUNE 1902 INSTITUTING THE ORDER OF MERIT

Edward VII, by the Grace of God, of the United Kingdom of Great Britain and Ireland, and of the British Dominions beyond the Seas, King, Defender of the Faith, to all to whom these Presents shall come, Greeting: Whereas We have resolved to institute an Order of Merit.

Know ye that We, for the purpose of carrying this Our Resolution into effect, have instituted, erected, constituted, and created, and by these presents for Us, Our heirs and successors, Do institute, erect, constitute, and create an Order of Merit, to be known by and have for ever hereafter the name, style, and designation of 'The Order of Merit'.

And We do ordain, direct, and appoint that the said Order shall consist of the Sovereign and of such Ordinary and Honorary Members as We, Our heirs and successors, shall from time to time appoint as by any Statute may be directed.

And We do further ordain, direct, and appoint that the said Members shall be of one class, to be styled and designated

Members of the 'Order of Merit'.

And We do ordain, direct, and appoint that We, Our heirs and successors, Kings and Queens Regnant of the United Kingdom aforesaid, shall be Sovereigns of the said Order.

And We do ordain, direct, and appoint that the said Order shall be governed by Statutes and Ordinances to be from time to time ordained, made, altered, and abrogated by Us, Our heirs and successors, Sovereigns of the said Order, at Our pleasure.

And We do further ordain, direct, and appoint that such persons only shall be competent to be Members of the said Order as shall possess the qualifications, to be defined in any Statute or Statutes to be hereafter made for the purpose, together with such Honorary Members as We, Our heirs and successors, may be pleased to appoint.

And whereas it is expedient for the dignity and service of the Order that there should be an officer attached thereto, We do, by these presents, for Us, Our heirs and successors, will and ordain that there shall be for ever hereafter belonging to the Order a Secretary and Registrar, whose duties shall be expressed and defined in and by the said Statutes.

And to the end that the Statutes of the Order may be legally established, We do hereby authorise and command that a Seal be immediately engraven, having thereon as follows, that is to say: upon a white field, a representation of the Badge to be worn by the Members of this Order, impaled with Our Royal Arms, with this circumscription, 'The Seal of the Order of Merit'. And Our Royal Will and Pleasure is that the said Seal shall hereafter be the Seal of the Order, and that the Statutes to be observed within the same, after having received Our Sign Manual and the counter-signature of one of Our Principal Secretaries of State, shall be established by and with the said Seal, which Statutes so given, and in future to be given, by Us, Our heirs and successors, to which the said Seal shall be affixed, shall be of the same validity, and read and taken as if the same and every article of them had been verbatim recited in these Our Letters Patent, and passed under the Great Seal of Our said United Kingdom of Great Britain and Ireland.

And lastly, We do hereby for Us, Our heirs and successors, grant that these Letters Patent or the enrolment or exemplification thereof shall be, in and by all things, good, firm, valid, sufficient, and effectual in the law, according to the true intent and meaning thereof, any omission, defect, or imperfection therein, or other matter, cause, or thing to the contrary thereof in anywise notwithstanding.

In witness whereof, We have caused these Our Letters to be made Patent. Witness Ourself at Westminster, the twenty third day of June, in the second year of Our Reign.

By Warrant under the King's Sign Manual
Muir Mackenzie

Appendix B

THE STATUTES

OF THE

ORDER OF MERIT

Instituted 23rd June, 1902.
Statute dated 25th July, 1907.
Statutes dated 16th December, 1935.
Statutes dated 7th November, 1969.
Statutes consolidated and revised 14th April, 1987.
Additional Statute dated 15th April, 1991.

ELIZABETH R.

ELIZABETH THE SECOND, by the Grace of God of the United Kingdom of Great Britain and Northern Ireland and of Her other Realms and Territories Queen, Head of the Commonwealth, Defender of the Faith, and Sovereign of the ORDER OF MERIT, to all to whom these Presents shall come:

Greeting!

WHEREAS Our Royal Great Grandfather, His Late Majesty King Edward the Seventh, by Letters Patent under the Great Seal of the United Kingdom, bearing date at Westminster the Twenty-third day of June, One thousand nine hundred and two, in the Second year of His Reign, did institute, erect, constitute, and create an Order, to be called and known for ever thereafter by the name, style and designation of THE ORDER OF MERIT whereof His said Majesty, His heirs and successors for ever should be Sovereigns, and did by the said Letters Patent ordain and declare that the said Order should be governed by Statutes and Ordinances to be established by the Sovereign and sealed by and with the Seal of the said Order:

Recites Letters Patent of 23rd June, 1902.

AND WHEREAS the Statutes of the said Order have from time to time been amended and re-enacted by Our Royal Predecessors and by Us:

WE deem it now expedient to assemble the said Statutes and to make such alterations as appear to Us necessary for the proper government of the Order:

NOW KNOW YE that, in pursuance and exercise of the power vested in Us by the said Letters Patent, We have abrogated and annulled and do hereby abrogate and repeal all and every the said Statutes and Ordinances so far as they are repugnant to or inconsistent with the following Statutes;

Repeals all former Statutes.

AND further Know all Ye to whom these Presents shall come that in substitution thereof We have made, ordained and established and by these Presents sealed with the Seal of the Order, do make, ordain and establish, the following

Statutes and Ordinances, which shall from henceforth be inviolably observed and kept within the same, namely:

Style and Designation of Order.

I.—It is ordained and enjoined that this Order shall be styled and designated in all acts, proceedings, and pleadings, "THE ORDER OF MERIT," as directed in the Letters Patent of the Second year of the Reign of Our Royal Predecessor King Edward the Seventh, and by no other designation.

Constitution of Order.

II.—It is ordained that the said Order shall consist of the SOVEREIGN and Members, Ordinary and Honorary.

Sovereigns of Order.

III.—It is ordained that We, Our heirs and successors, Kings or Queens Regnant of these Our Realms, are, and for ever shall be, Sovereigns of this Order, to whom doth and shall belong all power of annulling, interpreting, explaining, or augmenting these and every part of these Statutes.

Ordinary Members not to exceed 24 in number.

IV.—It is ordained that the Ordinary Members of the Order shall not exceed twenty-four in number.

Qualifications for admission to the Order.

V.—It is ordained that the persons to be admitted as Ordinary Members of this Order shall be such persons, subjects of Our Crown, as may have rendered exceptionally meritorious service in Our Crown Services, or towards the advancement of the Arts, Learning, Literature and Science, or such other exceptional service as We see fit to recognise.

Honorary Members.

VI.—It is ordained that the persons to be admitted as Honorary Members of the Order shall be such persons, who are not subjects of Our Crown, upon whom We may think fit to confer the honour of being received into the Order, and that the number of such Honorary Members may consist of as many such persons as We, Our heirs and successors shall think fit to appoint.

Manner of Appointment.

VII.—It is ordained that when We, Our heirs and successors, shall be pleased to nominate and appoint any person to be a Member of this Order, such appointment shall be made by Warrant under Our Royal Sign Manual, and sealed with the Seal of the Order.

Insignia of the Sovereign.

VIII.—It is ordained that the Insignia of the Sovereign of the said Order shall be of the material and fashion as are hereinafter appointed for the Members of the Order.

IX.—It is ordained that the Members of this Order shall wear the Badge of the Order, which shall consist of a Cross of red and blue enamel of eight points, having, within a laurel wreath upon a centre of blue enamel, the motto of the Order, that is to say: "For Merit", in letters of gold; on the reverse, within a laurel wreath, upon a centre of blue enamel, Our Royal Cypher in gold, the whole being surmounted by Our Imperial Crown enamelled in proper colours. Members who are men shall suspend the Badge from a parti-coloured riband of Garter blue and crimson, round the neck. Members who are women shall attach the Badge to a similar riband tied in a bow on the left shoulder. Members appointed for distinguished and meritorious services in Our Armed Forces shall wear a like Badge with the addition of two silver swords with gold hilts, placed saltirewise between the angles of the Cross.

Badge of the Order.

X.—It is ordained that upon the nomination of any person to be a Member of this Order, he, or she, shall be invested with the Insignia of his, or her, dignity in the Order by Us, Our heirs and successors, and that on the day of the investiture the person to be invested shall be introduced into the presence of the Sovereign by the Officer of the Order in attendance bearing the proper Insignia of the Order, when the Sovereign shall proceed to invest him, or her, with the Ensigns of the said Order with the Riband and Badge.

Investiture.

XI.—It is further ordained that it shall be competent for Us, Our heirs and successors, by a Warrant or Warrants under Our Sign Manual, and sealed with the Seal of this Order, to authorize some distinguished Officer in Our service, or other person to perform in Our name, and on Our behalf the ceremony of investing Members with the Insignia of their dignity, or to permit the ceremony of investiture to be dispensed with. And We reserve to Ourselves, Our heirs and successors, by Our or their Warrant or Warrants, as aforesaid, to permit and authorize the person or persons not invested by Us to wear the Insignia, and enjoy the privileges appertaining to their dignity.

Sovereign may delegate powers as to Investiture.

As to dispensing with Investiture.

XII.—It is ordained that for the greater honour and dignity of the Members of this Order, it shall be lawful for the Members of this Order to suspend a representation of their Riband and Badge from the bottom of the escutcheon containing their armorial bearings.

Members may suspend Badge from their Armorial Bearings.

Seal of the
Order.

XIII.—It is ordained that the Seal of this Order shall have engraved thereon as follows, that is to say: upon a white field, a representation of the Badge of the Order proper, impaled with Our Royal Arms, with the following circumscription, "The Seal of the Order of Merit", and that the Statutes of the said Order shall be sealed by and with the same.

Anniversary
of Order.

XIV.—It is ordained that the Twenty-sixth day of June every year shall be taken and deemed to be the anniversary of the institution of this Order.

Officer of the
Order.

XV.—It is ordained that the following Officer shall be appointed to this Order, that is to say, a Secretary and Registrar.

Secretary and
Registrar of
the Order.

XVI.—It is ordained that the Secretary and Registrar of the said Order shall be appointed from time to time by a Warrant under the Sign Manual of Us, Our heirs and successors, and shall hold the said Office during the pleasure of Us, Our heirs and successors.

His Insignia.

It is further ordained that he shall wear around his neck pendant to a chain of gold a like Badge to that appointed for Members of the Order, with the addition of two silver pens, saltirewise between the angles of the Cross.

His Duties.

To his custody shall be confided the Seal of the said Order, which he shall affix, or cause to be affixed, to all Statutes and other documents or instruments connected therewith. He shall, moreover, perform such duties as may be directed by the Sovereign or by these Statutes. He shall keep full lists of the Members of the Order. He shall carefully record all proceedings relative to the said Order that may take place, and he shall faithfully enter such proceedings in the Register of the Order, as well as all documents which may be transmitted to him for that purpose. We are further pleased to ordain that the Chancery of the said Order, wherein a record of all proceedings connected therewith shall be deposited and preserved, shall be in the Central Chancery of Our Orders of Knighthood.

Statutes to be
observed.

XVII.—We do hereby command and enjoin that these Statutes shall be of such and the same force, virtue and effect in every respect as if they had been duly made, and the said acts, deeds, matters and things had been duly done, on the Twenty-third day of June, One thousand nine hundred and two.

XVIII.—Lastly, We reserve to Ourselves, Our heirs and successors, full power of annulling, altering, abrogating, augmenting, interpreting, or dispensing with these Statutes and Regulations, or any part thereof, by a Notification under the Sign Manual of the Sovereign of the Order.

Power reserved to alter Statutes.

GIVEN under the Seal of the aforesaid Order of Merit, at Our Court at St. James's, this Fourteenth day of April, One thousand nine hundred and eighty-seven, in the Thirty-sixth year of Our Reign.

BY HER MAJESTY'S COMMAND,

EDWARD FORD

Secretary and Registrar.

ADDITIONAL STATUTE

ELIZABETH R.

ELIZABETH THE SECOND, by the Grace of God of the United Kingdom of Great Britain and Northern Ireland and of Her other Realms and Territories Queen, Head of the Commonwealth, Defender of the Faith, and Sovereign of the ORDER OF MERIT, to all to whom these Presents shall come:

Greeting!

WHEREAS by the Statutes of the ORDER OF MERIT dated the Fourteenth day of April, One thousand nine hundred and eighty-seven, power was reserved to the Sovereign of the Order of annulling, altering, abrogating, augmenting, interpreting or dispensing with the said Statutes, or any part thereof, by a notification under the Sign Manual of the Sovereign of the Order.

Recites Statutes of 14th April, 1987.

NOW THEREFORE, by virtue of the power and authority vested in Us as Sovereign of the said Order of Merit, We do hereby abrogate and annul Statute IX of the said Order, and in substitution therefor We do make, ordain and establish the following Statute:—

Cancelling of Statute IX.

IX.—It is ordained that the Members of this Order shall wear the Badge of the Order, which shall consist of a Cross of red and blue enamel of eight points, having, within a laurel wreath upon a centre of blue enamel, the motto of the Order, that is to say: "For Merit", in letters of gold; on the reverse, within a laurel wreath, upon a centre of blue enamel, Our Royal Cypher in gold, the whole being surmounted by Our Imperial Crown enamelled in proper colours. Members who are men shall suspend the Badge from a parti-coloured riband of Garter blue and crimson, round the neck. Members who are women shall attach the Badge to a similar riband tied in a bow on the left shoulder. Members appointed for distinguished and meritorious services in Our Armed Forces shall wear a like Badge with the addition of two silver swords with gold hilts, placed saltirewise between the angles of the Cross.

Badge of the Order.

Arrangements for Return of Badge of the Order.

It is further ordained that all Members, Ordinary and Honorary who, after the date of this Additional Statute, shall receive the Badges of this Order shall make arrangements for their return to the Central Chancery of Our Orders of Knighthood on their decease; and We are pleased to declare that every Member, Ordinary and Honorary, who receives the Badge of this Order shall upon receiving it, give a written undertaking and promise to fulfil the provisions of this Statute.

GIVEN under the Seal of the aforesaid Order of Merit at Our Court at Saint James's this Fifteenth day of April, One thousand nine hundred and ninety-one , in the Fortieth Year of Our Reign.

BY HER MAJESTY'S COMMAND,

EDWARD FORD

Secretary and Registrar.

Appendix C

MEMBERS OF THE ORDER OF MERIT: 1902–2002

Notes:

(1) *indicates a Military Member; ø indicates an Honorary Member.
(2) The styles, titles and decorations are those at death.
(3) Peerages and baronetcies are of first creation or for life, except where otherwise indicated.
(4) The term 'Lord' is used to describe the lowest level of peerage: 'Baron' formally.
(5) Membership of the Privy Council is indicated by PC after peers and by 'The Rt Hon' in other cases.
(6) The only non-state distinctions shown are FRS, FREng, FBA and RA.
(7) The designation is that at the time of, or immediately preceding, the award of the Order or it describes the profession of the recipient.

	Appointed	Recipient	Designation	Born	Died
	Reign of King Edward VII				
1	**1902** 26 June	*Field Marshal Frederick Sleigh, Earl ROBERTS OF KANDAHAR, VC, KG, PC, PC(I), KP, GCB, OM, GCSI, GCIE	Commander-in-Chief, British Army, 1901–04	30 Sep 1832	14 Nov 1914
2	26 June	*Field Marshal Garnet Joseph, Viscount WOLSELEY, PC, PC(I), KP, GCB, OM, GCMG	Commander-in-Chief, British Army, 1895–1900	4 June 1833	26 March 1913
3	26 June	*Field Marshal Herbert Horatio, Earl KITCHENER OF KHARTOUM, KG, PC, KP, GCB, OM, GCSI, GCMG, GCIE	Commander-in-Chief, South Africa, 1900–1902	24 June 1850	5 June 1916
4	26 June	John William (Third) Lord RAYLEIGH, PC, OM, FRS	Physicist; President, Royal Society, 1905–08	12 Nov 1842	30 June 1919
5	26 June	William, Lord KELVIN, PC, OM, GCVO, FRS	Physicist; President, Royal Society, 1890–95	26 June 1824	17 Dec 1907
6	26 June	Joseph, Lord LISTER, PC, OM, FRS	Surgeon; President, Royal Society, 1895–1900	25 April 1827	10 Feb 1912
7	26 June	*Admiral of the Fleet Hon Sir Henry KEPPEL, GCB, OM	Commander-in-Chief, Devonport, 1872–75	14 Jan 1809	17 Jan 1904
8	26 June	John, Viscount MORLEY OF BLACKBURN, PC, PC(I), OM FRS, FBA	Historian	24 Dec 1838	23 Sep 1923
9	26 June	The Rt Hon William Edward Hartpole LECKY, OM, FBA	Historian	26 March 1838	22 Oct 1903

	Appointed	Recipient	Designation	Born	Died
10	26 June	*Admiral of the Fleet the Rt Hon Sir Edward Hobart SEYMOUR, GCB, OM, GCVO	Commander-in-Chief, China Station, 1897–1901 (and Commander, International Naval Brigade during Boxer Rising, 1900)	30 April 1840	2 March 1929
11	26 June	Sir William HUGGINS, OM, KCB, FRS	Astronomer, President, Royal Society, 1900–05	7 Feb 1824	10 May 1910
12	26 June	George Frederic WATTS, OM, RA	Painter and sculptor	23 Feb 1817	1 July 1904
13	1905 30 June	*Field Marshal Sir George Stuart WHITE, VC, GCB, OM, GCSI, GCMG, GCIE, GCVO	Governor of Gibraltar, 1900–04 (and 'Defender of Ladysmith', 1899–1900)	6 July 1835	24 June 1912
14	30 June	*Admiral of the Fleet John Arbuthnot, Lord FISHER, GCB, OM, GCVO	First Sea Lord, 1904–10 and 1914–15	25 Jan 1841	10 July 1920
15	30 June	Sir Richard Claverhouse, JEBB, OM, FBA	Classical scholar; Regius Professor of Greek at Cambridge (1889–1905)	27 Aug 1841	9 Dec 1905
16	30 June	Sir Lawrence ALMA-TADEMA, OM, RA	Painter	8 Jan 1836	25 June 1912
17	30 June	George MEREDITH, OM	Novelist and poet	12 Feb 1828	18 May 1909
18	30 June	William HOLMAN HUNT, OM	Painter	2 April 1827	7 Sep 1910
19	1906 21 Feb	*øField Marshal Prince Aritomo YAMAGATA, OM	Chief of Japanese General Staff, 1904–05	15 May 1838	1 Feb 1922
20	21 Feb	* ø Field Marshal Prince Iwao OYAMA, OM	Commander-in-Chief, Japanese Field Armies, 1904–05	12 Nov 1842	10 Dec 1916

	Appointed		Recipient	Designation	Born	Died
21		21 Feb	*ø Admiral of the Fleet Marquis Heihachiro TOGO, OM, GCVO	Commander-in-Chief, Japanese Fleet, 1904–05	27 Jan 1848	30 May 1934
22		29 June	Evelyn, Earl of CROMER, PC, GCB, OM, GCMG, KCSI, CIE, FRS, FBA	Agent and Consul-General in Egypt, 1883–1907	26 Feb 1841	29 Jan 1917
23	1907	11 Feb	James, Viscount BRYCE, PC, PC(I), OM, GCVO, FRS, FBA	Jurist and historian; Chief Secretary for Ireland, 1905–07	10 May 1838	22 Jan 1922
24		30 June	Sir Joseph Dalton HOOKER, OM, GCSI, CB, FRS	Botanist; Director, Kew Gardens, 1865–85; President, Royal Society, 1873–78	30 June 1817	10 Dec 1911
25		29 Nov	Florence NIGHTINGALE, OM, RRC	Pioneer of modern nursing (and organiser of nursing system in Crimean War, 1854–55)	12 May 1820	13 Aug 1910
26	1908	26 June	Henry JACKSON, OM, FBA	Classical scholar; Regius Professor of Greek at Cambridge, 1906–21	12 March 1839	25 Sep 1921
27		9 Nov	Alfred Russel WALLACE, OM, FRS	Naturalist; President, Land Nationalisation Society	8 Jan 1823	7 Nov 1913

Reign of King George V

	Appointed		Recipient	Designation	Born	Died
28	1910	8 July	Sir William CROOKES, OM, FRS	Chemist; President, Royal Society, 1913–15	17 June 1832	4 April 1919
29	1911	8 July	Thomas HARDY, OM	Novelist and poet	2 June 1840	11 Jan 1928
30		19 June	The Rt Hon Sir George Otto TREVELYAN, (Second) Bt, PC(I), OM, FBA	Historian	20 July 1838	18 Aug 1928

	Appointed	Recipient	Designation	Born	Died
31	19 June	Sir Edward ELGAR, Bt, OM, GCVO	Composer	2 June 1857	23 Feb 1934
32	1912 8 March	*Admiral of the Fleet Sir Arthur Knyvet WILSON, (Third) Bt, VC, GCB, OM, GCVO	First Sea Lord, 1909–12	4 March 1842	25 May 1921
33	15 March	Sir Joseph John THOMSON, OM, FRS	Physicist; President, Royal Society, 1915–20	18 Dec 1856	30 Aug 1940
34	1914 1 Jan	Sir Archibald GEIKIE, OM, KCB, FRS	Geologist; President, Royal Society, 1908–13	28 Dec 1835	10 Nov 1924
35	3 Dec	*Field Marshal John Denton Pinkstone, Earl of YPRES, PC, KP, GCB, OM, GCVO, KCMG	Commander-in-Chief, British Expeditionary Force in France, 1914–15	28 Sep 1852	22 May 1925
36	1915 26 May	Richard Burdon, Viscount HALDANE, PC, KT, OM, FRS, FBA	Lord Chancellor, 1912–15 and 1924	30 Jul 1856	19 Aug 1928
37	1916 1 Jan	Henry JAMES, OM	Novelist	15 April 1843	28 Feb 1916
38	31 May	*Admiral of the Fleet John Rushworth, Earl JELLICOE, GCB, OM, GCVO	Commander-in-Chief, Grand Fleet, 1914–16	12 Oct 1861	20 Nov 1935
39	3 June	Arthur James, Earl of BALFOUR, KG, PC, PC(I), OM, FRS, FBA	Prime Minister, 1902–05; First Lord of the Admiralty, 1915–16	25 July 1848	19 March 1930
40	1918 29 Nov	*øField Marshal and Marshal of France Ferdinand FOCH, GCB, OM	Commander-in-Chief, Allied Armies in France since March 1918	2 Oct 1851	20 March 1929
41	1919 3 June	*Admiral of the Fleet David, Earl BEATTY, PC, GCB, OM, GCVO, DSO	Commander-in-Chief, Grand Fleet, 1916–19	17 Jan 1871	11 March 1936
42	3 June	*Field Marshal Douglas, Earl HAIG, KT, GCB, OM, GCVO, KCIE	Commander-in-Chief, British Army in France, 1915–19	19 June 1861	29 Jan 1928

	Appointed	Recipient	Designation	Born	Died
43	26 June	*øMarshal of France Joseph Jacques Césaire JOFFRE, GCB, OM	Commander-in-Chief, French Armies, 1915–17	4 Jan 1852	3 Jan 1931
44	5 Aug	David, Earl LLOYD GEORGE OF DWYFOR, PC, OM	Prime Minister, 1916–1922	17 Jan 1863	26 March 1945
1922					
45	2 Jan	Sir James Matthew BARRIE, Bt, OM	Novelist and dramatist	9 May 1860	19 June 1937
46 **1924**	3 June	Francis Herbert BRADLEY, OM, FBA	Philosopher	30 Jan 1846	18 Sep 1924
47	3 Jun	Sir Charles Scott SHERRINGTON, OM, GBE, FRS	Physiologist; President, Royal Society, 1920–25	27 Nov 1857	4 March 1952
48 **1925**	1 Jan	Sir James George FRAZER, OM, FRS, FBA	Anthropologist	1 Jan 1854	7 May 1941
49	1 Jan	Ernest, Lord RUTHERFORD OF NELSON, OM, FRS	Physicist; President, Royal Society, 1925–30	30 Aug 1871	19 Oct 1937
50 **1927**	3 June	The Hon Sir Charles Algernon PARSONS, OM, KCB, FRS	Engineer	13 June 1854	11 Feb 1931
51 **1928**	4 June	Sir George Abraham GRIERSON, OM, KCIE, FBA	Oriental scholar and philologist	7 Jan 1851	7 March 1941
52 **1929**	3 June	Robert BRIDGES, OM	Poet Laureate, 1913–30	23 Oct 1844	21 April 1930
53	3 June	John GALSWORTHY, OM	Novelists and dramatist	14 Aug 1867	31 Jan 1933
54 **1930**	3 June	Samuel ALEXANDER, OM, FBA	Philosopher	6 Jan 1859	13 Sep 1938
55	3 June	Montague Rhodes JAMES, OM, FBA	Medieval and classical scholar	1 Aug 1862	12 June 1936
56	3 June	George Macaulay TREVELYAN, OM, CBE, FRS, FBA	Historian	16 Feb 1876	20 July 1962
57 **1931**	1 Jan	*Admiral of the Fleet Sir Charles Edward MADDEN, Bt, GCB, OM, GCVO, KCMG	First Sea Lord, 1927–30	5 Sep 1862	5 June 1935

	Appointed		Recipient	Designation	Born	Died
58		1 Jan	Philip Wilson STEER, OM	Painter	28 Dec 1960	21 March 1942
59		3 June	Sir William Henry BRAGG, OM, KBE, FRS	Physicist; President, Royal Society, 1935–40	2 July 1862	12 March 1942
60	1935	1 Jan	John William MACKAIL, OM, FBA	Classical scholar; President, British Academy, 1932–36	26 Aug 1859	13 Dec 1945
61		3 June	John Edward MASEFIELD, OM	Poet Laureate, 1930–67	1 June 1878	12 May 1967
62		3 June	Ralph VAUGHAN WILLIAMS, OM	Composer	12 Oct 1872	26 Aug 1958
63		3 June	Sir Frederick Gowland HOPKINS, OM, FRS	Biochemist; President, Royal Society, 1930–35	20 June 1861	16 May 1947
64	1936	1 Jan	*Field Marshal Philip Walhouse, Lord CHETWODE, GCB, OM, GCSI, KCMG, DSO	Commander-in-Chief, India, 1930–35	21 Sep 1869	6 July 1950

Reign of King George VI

	Appointed		Recipient	Designation	Born	Died
65	1937	1 Feb	The Rt Hon Herbert Albert Laurens FISHER, OM, FRS, FBA	Historian	21 March 1865	18 April 1940
66		11 May	*Lieutenant-General Robert Stephenson Smyth, Lord BADEN-POWELL, OM, GCMG, GCVO, KCB	Founder of the Boy Scouts and Girl Guides	22 Feb 1857	8 Jan 1941
67	1938	9 June	Sir Arthur Stanley EDDINGTON, OM, FRS	Astronomer	28 Dec 1882	22 Nov 1944
68	1939	2 Jan	*Admiral of the Fleet Alfred Ernle Montacute, Lord CHATFIELD, PC, GCB, OM, KCMG, CVO	First Sea Lord, 1933–38	27 Sep 1873	15 Nov 1967
69		2 Jan	Sir James Hopwood JEANS, OM, FRS	Mathematician and astrophysicist	11 Sep 1877	16 Sep 1946

	Appointed		Recipient	Designation	Born	Died
70	1940	29 Oct	*Marshal of the Royal Air Force Cyril Louis Norton, Lord NEWALL, GCB, OM, GCMG, CBE, AM	Chief of the Air Staff, 1937–40	15 Feb 1886	30 Nov1963
71	1941	1 Jan	(George) Aimé MURRAY, OM, FBA	Classical scholar	2 Jan 1866	20 May 1957
72	1942	1 Jan	Sir Edwin Landseer LUTYENS, OM, KCIE, RA	Architect; President, Royal Academy, 1938–44	29 March 1869	1 Jan 1944
73		11 June	Augustus Edwin JOHN, OM, RA	Painter	4 Jan 1878	31 Oct 1961
74		11 June	Edgar Douglas, Lord ADRIAN, OM, FRS	Physiologist; President, Royal Society, 1950–55	30 Nov 1889	4 Aug 1977
75	1943	1 Jan	Sir William Searle HOLDSWORTH, OM, KC, FBA	Jurist	7 May 1871	2 Jan 1944
76		3 Sep	*Admiral of the Fleet Sir (Alfred) Dudley (Pickman Rogers) POUND, GCB, OM, GCVO	First Sea Lord, 1939–43	29 Aug 1877	21 Oct 1943
77	1944	8 June	Sidney James, Lord PASSFIELD, PC, OM	Social reformer and historian	13 July 1859	13 Oct 1947
78		8 June	Sir Henry Hallett DALE, OM, GBE, FRS	Pharmacologist; President, Royal Society, 1940–45	9 June 1875	23 July 1968
79		8 June	Sir Giles Gilbert SCOTT, OM, RA	Architect	9 Nov 1880	8 Feb 1960
80	1945	1 Jan	Alfred North WHITEHEAD, OM, FRS, FBA	Philosopher	15 Feb 1861	30 Dec 1947
81		12 June	*øGeneral of the Army Dwight David EISENHOWER, GCB, OM	Supreme Commander, Allied Expeditionary Force, 1944–45	14 Oct 1890	28 March 1969

	Appointed	Recipient	Designation	Born	Died
82	**1946** 1 Jan	The Rt Hon Sir Winston Leonard Spencer CHURCHILL, KG, OM, CH, FRS, FBA	Prime Minister, 1940–45 and 1951–55	30 Nov 1874	24 Jan 1965
83	1 Jan	*Marshal of the Royal Air Force Charles Frederick Algernon, Viscount PORTAL OF HUNGERFORD, KG, GCB, OM, DSO, MC	Chief of the Air Staff, 1940–45	21 May 1893	22 April 1971
84	13 June	*Field Marshal Alan Francis, Viscount ALANBROOKE, KG, GCB, OM, GCVO, DSO	Chief of the Imperial General Staff, 1941–46	23 July 1883	17 June 1963
85	13 June	*Admiral of the Fleet Andrew Browne, Viscount CUNNINGHAM OF HYNDHOPE, KT, GCB, OM, DSO	First Sea Lord, 1943–46	7 Jan 1883	12 June 1963
86	13 June	Edward Frederick Lindley, Earl of HALIFAX, KG, PC, OM, GCSI, GCMG, GCIE	Ambassador to the USA, 1941–46	16 April 1881	23 Dec 1959
87	**1947** 1 Jan	Field Marshal the Rt Hon Jan Christian SMUTS, OM, CH, FRS, KC	Prime Minister of South Africa, 1939–48 (and 1919–24)	24 May 1870	11 Sep 1950
88	1 Jan	ø The Hon John Gilbert WINANT, OM	United States Ambassador to the Court of St James's, 1941–46	23 Feb 1889	3 Nov 1947
89	17 Nov	The Rt Hon William Lyon MACKENZIE KING, PC(Can), OM, CMG	Prime Minister of Canada, 1935–48 (and 1921–26 and 1926–30)	17 Dec 1874	22 July 1950
90	**1948** 1 Jan	Thomas Stearns ELIOT, OM	Poet	26 Sep 1888	4 Jan 1965

	Appointed		Recipient	Designation	Born	Died
91	1949	9 Jan	Sir Robert ROBINSON, OM, FRS	Chemist; President, Royal Society, 1945–50	13 Sep 1886	8 Feb 1975
92		9 Jan	Bertrand Arthur William, (Third) Earl RUSSELL, OM, FRS, FBA	Philosopher	18 May 1872	2 Feb 1970
93	1951	1 Jan	The Rt Hon Sir Alexander George Montagu CADOGAN, OM, GCMG, KCB	Permanent Representative to the United Nations, 1946–50 (and Permanent Under Secretary, Foreign Office, 1938–46)	24 Nov 1884	9 July 1968
94		1 Jan	*Marshal of the Royal Air Force Hugh Montague, Viscount TRENCHARD, GCB, OM, GCVO, DSO	Chief of the Air Staff, 1918 and 1919–1929	3 Feb 1873	10 Feb 1956
95		7 June	George Edward Moore, OM, FBA	Philosopher	4 Nov 1873	24 Oct 1958
96		5 Nov	Clement Richard, Earl ATTLEE, KG, PC, OM, CH, FRS	Prime Minister, 1945–51 (and Deputy Prime Minister, 1942–45)	3 Jan 1883	8 Oct 1967

Reign of Queen Elizabeth II

	Appointed		Recipient	Designation	Born	Died
97	1953	1 Jan	Wilder Graves PENFIELD, CC, OM, CMG, FRS	Neurologist	26 Jan 1891	5 April 1976
98	1955	1 June	Walter John DE LA MARE, OM, CH	Poet	25 April 1873	22 June 1956
99		25 Feb	øAlbert SCHWEITZER, OM, FBA	French medical missionary, philosopher and musician	14 Jan 1875	4 Sep 1965
100	1956	31 May	(William) Malcolm, Lord HAILEY, PC, OM, GCSI, GCMG, GCIE	Administrator in India and colonial scholar	15 Feb 1872	1 June 1969
101	1957	1 Jan	Sir John Douglas COCKCROFT, OM, KCB, CBE, FRS	Physicist; Director, Atomic Energy Research Establishment, 1946–58	27 May 1897	18 Sep 1967

	Appointed	Recipient	Designation	Born	Died
102	8 Dec	John, Viscount WAVERLEY, PC, PC(I), GCB, OM, GCSI, GCIE, FRS	Civil servant and cabinet minister	8 July 1882	4 Jan 1958
103	**1958** 12 June	Sir (Frank) Macfarlane BURNET, OM, AK, KBE, FRS	Immunologist; Director, Institute for Medical Research, Melbourne, 1944–65	3 Sep 1899	31 Aug 1985
104	21 Nov	Herbert Louis, Viscount SAMUEL, PC, GCB, OM, GBE	Cabinet minister and philosopher (and Privy Counsellor for 50 years)	6 Nov 1870	5 Feb 1963
105	**1959** 1 Jan	*Field Marshal Harold Rupert Leofric George, Earl ALEXANDER OF TUNIS, KG, PC, PC(Can), GCB, OM, GCMG, CSI, DSO, MC	Second World War Commander (in Mediterranean)	10 Dec 1891	16 June 1969
106	**1960** 23 April	Sir Cyril Norman HINSHELWOOD, OM, FRS	Chemist; President, Royal Society, 1955–60	19 June 1897	9 Oct 1967
107	23 April	Graham Vivian SUTHERLAND, OM	Painter	24 Aug 1903	17 Feb 1980
108	**1962** 23 Nov	Sir Geoffrey de HAVILLAND, OM, CBE, AFC	Aviation pioneer and aircraft designer	27 July 1882	21 May 1965
109	23 Nov	Sir Basil Urwin SPENCE, OM, OBE, RA	Architect	13 Aug 1907	19 Nov 1976
110	**1963** 29 May	The Rt Hon Sir Owen DIXON, OM, GCMG, FBA	Jurist; Chief Justice of Australia, 1952–64	28 April 1886	8 July 1972
111	12 June	øDr (formerly Sir) Sarvepalli RADHAKRISHNAN, OM, FBA	Philosopher; President of India, 1962–67	5 Sep 1888	19 April 1975
112	16 Aug	George Peabody GOOCH, OM, CH, FBA	Historian	21 Oct 1873	31 Aug 1968

	Appointed		Recipient	Designation	Born	Died
113		16 Aug	Henry Spencer MOORE, OM, CH, FBA	Sculptor	30 July 1898	31 Aug 1986
114	1965	23 March	Edward Benjamin, Lord BRITTEN, OM, CH	Composer	22 Nov 1913	4 Dec 1976
115		23 March	Dorothy Mary Crowfoot HODGKIN, OM, FRS	Chemist	12 May 1910	29 July 1994
116		15 July	*Admiral of the Fleet Louis Francis Albert Victor Nicholas, Earl MOUNTBATTEN OF BURMA, KG, PC, GCB, OM, GCSI, GCIE, GCVO, DSO, FRS	Chief of the Defence Staff, 1959–65	25 June 1900	27 Aug 1979
117		15 July	Howard Walter, Lord FLOREY, OM, FRS	Pathologist; President, Royal Society, 1960–65	24 Sep 1898	21 Feb 1968
118	1967	20 Nov	Patrick Maynard Stuart, Lord BLACKETT, OM, CH, FRS	Physicist; President, Royal Society, 1965–70	18 Nov 1897	13 July 1974
119	1968	20 Nov	Sir William Turner WALTON, OM	Composer	29 March 1902	8 March 1983
120		23 April	Ben NICHOLSON, OM	Painter	10 April 1894	6 Feb 1982
121		23 Apr	Solly, Lord ZUCKERMAN, OM, KCB, FRS	Zoologist; Chief Scientific Adviser to the Government, 1964–71	30 May 1904	1 April 1993
122		10 June	His Royal Highness The Prince Philip, Duke of EDINBURGH, KG, PC, KT, OM, GBE, AC, QSO, FRS	Consort of the Sovereign	10 June 1921	-
123	1969	1 Jan	Edward Morgan FORSTER, OM. CH	Novelist	1 Jan 1879	7 June 1970
124		14 July	The Rt Hon Malcolm John MacDONALD, OM	Diplomat, 1941–69	17 Aug 1901	11 Jan 1981

	Appointed	Recipient	Designation	Born	Died
125	14 July	William George, Lord PENNEY, OM, KBE, FRS	Molecular physicist	24 June 1909	3 March 1991
126	14 July	Sir Geoffrey Ingram TAYLOR, OM, FRS	Mathematician, physicist and engineer	7 March 1886	29 June 1975
127	14 July	Dame Cicely Veronica WEDGWOOD, OM, DBE, FBA	Historian	20 July 1910	9 March 1997
128	1970 21 March	John Cawte BEAGLEHOLE, OM, CMG	Historian	13 June 1901	10 Oct 1971
129	1971 28 May	The Rt Hon Lester Bowles PEARSON, PC (Can), CC, OM, OBE	Prime Minister of Canada, 1963–68	23 April 1897	27 Dec 1972
130	28 May	Sir Isaiah BERLIN, OM, CBE, FBA	Philosopher	6 June 1909	5 Nov 1997
131	28 May	Sir George Robert EDWARDS, OM, CBE, FRS	Aeronautical engineer	9 July 1908	2 March 2003
132	1973 17 April	Sir Alan Lloyd HODGKIN, OM, KBE, FRS	Physiologist; President, Royal Society, 1970–75	5 Feb 1914	20 Dec 1998
133	17 April	Paul Adrian Maurice DIRAC, OM, FRS	Theoretical physicist and mathematician	8 Aug 1902	20 Oct 1984
134	1976 2 April	Maurice Harold, Earl of STOCKTON, PC, OM, FRS, FBA	Prime Minister, 1957–63	10 Feb 1894	29 Dec 1986
135	2 April	Christopher, Lord HINTON OF BANKSIDE, OM, KBE, FRS	Atomic power engineer	12 May 1901	22 June 1983
136	2 April	Kenneth Mackenzie, Lord CLARK, OM, CH, KCB, FBA	Art critic and historian	13 July 1903	21 May 1983
137	2 April	Sir Ronald SYME, OM, FBA	Ancient historian	11 March 1903	4 Sep 1989

	Appointed		Recipient	Designation	Born	Died
138	**1977**	24 Oct	Alexander Robertus, Lord TODD, OM, FRS	Chemist; President, Royal Society, 1975–80	2 Oct 1907	10 Jan 1997
139		24 Oct	Oliver Shewell, Lord FRANKS, PC, OM, GCMG, KCB, KCVO, CBE, FBA	Academic, administrator and diplomat	16 Feb 1905	15 Oct 1992
140		24 Oct	Sir Frederick William Mallandaine ASHTON, OM, CH, CBE	Founder-Choreographer, Royal Ballet (and Director, 1963–70)	17 Sep 1904	19 Aug 1988
141		24 Oct	John Boynton PRIESTLEY, OM	Dramatist and novelist	13 Sep 1894	14 Aug 1984
142	**1981**	6 Feb	Laurence Kerr, Lord OLIVIER, OM	Actor; First Director of National Theatre, 1962–73	22 May 1907	11 July 1989
143		6 Feb	Sir Peter Brian MEDAWAR, OM, CH, CBE, FRS, FBA	Zoologist and medical scientist	28 Feb 1915	2 Oct 1987
144		6 Feb	Group Captain Geoffrey Leonard, Lord CHESHIRE, VC, OM, DSO, DFC	Founder of Cheshire Foundation Homes for the disabled	7 Sep 1917	31 July 1992
145	**1983**	11 Nov	The Reverend William Owen CHADWICK, OM, KBE, FBA	Ecclesiastical historian	20 May 1916	–
146		11 Nov	Sir Andrew Fielding HUXLEY, OM, FRS	Physiologist; President, Royal Society, 1980–85	22 Nov 1917	–
147		11 Nov	Sir Sidney Robert NOLAN, OM, AC, CBE, RA	Painter	22 April 1917	27 Nov 1992
148		11 Nov	Sir Michael Kemp TIPPETT, OM. CH, CBE	Composer	2 Jan 1905	8 Jan 1998
149		18 Nov	ØMother TERESA (Agnes Gonxha Bojaxhiu), OM, AC, OBE	Missionary; Founder of Missionaries of Charity in Calcutta	27 Aug 1910	5 Sep 1997
150	**1986**	11 Feb	Henry Graham GREENE, OM, CH	Novelist	2 Oct 1904	3 April 1991

	Appointed		Recipient	Designation	Born	Died
151		11 Feb	Frederick SANGER, OM, CH, CBE, FRS	Biochemist	13 Aug 1918	–
152		11 Feb	Air Commodore Sir Frank WHITTLE, OM, KBE, CB, FRS	Engineer; inventor of the jet engine	1 June 1907	8 Aug 1996
153	1987	25 Feb	Yehudi, Lord MENUHIN, OM, KBE	Violinist and conductor	22 April 1916	12 March 1999
154	1988	15 Feb	Sir Ernst (Hans Josef) GOMBRICH, OM, CBE, FBA	Art historian and philosopher	30 March 1909	3 Nov 2001
155		15 Feb	Max Ferdinand PERUTZ, OM. CH, CBE, FRS	Molecular biologist	19 May 1914	6 Feb 2002
156	1989	30 Nov	Dame Cicely (Mary Strode) SAUNDERS, OM, DBE	Founder of the hospice movement	22 June 1918	14 July 2005
157		30 Nov	George, Lord PORTER OF LUDDENHAM, OM, FRS	Chemist; President, Royal Society, 1985–90	6 Dec 1920	31 Aug 2002
158	1990	7 Dec	Margaret Hilda, Baroness THATCHER, LG, PC, OM, FRS	Prime Minister, 1979–90	13 Oct 1925	–
159	1991	27 Nov	Dame Joan SUTHERLAND, OM, AC, DBE	Singer	7 Nov 1926	–
160		27 Nov	Francis Harry Compton CRICK, OM, FRS	Molecular biologist	8 June 1916	28 July 2004
161	1992	17 Nov	Dame Ninette de VALOIS, OM, CH, DBE	Founder of the Royal Ballet	6 June 1898	8 Mar 2001
162		17 Nov	Sir Michael Francis ATIYAH, OM, FRS	Mathematician; President, Royal Society, 1990–95	22 April 1929	–
163	1993	6 Dec	Lucian FREUD, OM, CH	Painter	8 Dec 1922	–
164		6 Dec	Roy Harris, Lord JENKINS OF HILLHEAD, PC, OM, FBA	Cabinet minister and historian	11 Nov 1920	5 Jan 2003

	Appointed		Recipient	Designation	Born	Died
165	1995	20 March	øNelson (Rolihlahla) MANDELA, OM, QC	President of South Africa, 1994–99	18 July 1918	–
166		23 Oct	Sir Aaron KLUG, OM, FRS	Molecular biologist; President, Royal Society, 1995–2000	11 Aug 1926	–
167	1996	9 Dec	Sir John GIELGUD, OM, CH	Actor	17 April 1904	21 May 2000
168	1997	25 Nov	Alfred Thompson, Lord DENNING, PC, OM	Jurist; Master of the Rolls, 1962–82	23 Jan 1899	5 March 1999
169		25 Nov	Norman Robert, Lord FOSTER OF THAMES BANK, OM, RA	Architect	1 June 1935	–
170		25 Nov	Sir Denis Eric ROOKE, OM, CBE, FREng, FRS	Engineer	2 April 1924	–
171	1998	10 Aug	Edward James (Ted) HUGHES, OM, OBE	Poet Laureate, 1984–98	17 Aug 1930	28 Oct 1998
172	1999	25 May	His Eminence Cardinal (George) Basil HUME, OM	Archbishop of Westminster, 1976–99	2 March 1923	17 June 1999
173	2000	9 May	Sir James Whyte BLACK, OM, FRS	Pharmacologist	14 June 1924	–
174		9 May	Sir Anthony Alfred CARO, OM, CBE	Sculptor	8 March 1924	–
175		9 May	Sir Roger PENROSE, OM, FRS	Mathematician	8 Aug 1931	–
176		9 May	Sir Tom STOPPARD, OM. CBE	Playwright	3 July 1937	–
177	2002	27 June	His Royal Highness The Prince Charles, Prince of WALES, KG, PC, KT, GCB, OM, AK, QSO	Heir to the Throne	14 Nov 1948	–
178		28 Oct	Robert McCredie, Lord MAY OF OXFORD, OM, AC	Zoologist; President, Royal Society, 2000–05	8 Jan 1936	–

	Appointed	Recipient	Designation	Born	Died
179	28 Oct	Nathaniel Charles Jacob, (Fourth) Lord ROTHSCHILD, OM, GBE, FBA	Banker, philanthropist and patron of the arts	29 April 1936	–

After the centenary year of the Order (2002), the following were appointed Members but have not been incorporated in the main body of the book. They are included here for purposes of record.

	Appointed	Recipient	Designation	Born	Died
180 **2005**	28 April	Sir David (Frederick) ATTENBOROUGH OM, CH, CVO, CBE, FRS	Broadcaster and naturalist	8 May 192	–
181	28 April	Betty, Baroness BOOTHROYD, PC, OM	Speaker of the House of Commons, 1992–2000	8 Oct 1929	–
182	28 April	Sir Michael (Eliot) HOWARD, OM, CH, CBE, MC, FBA	Historian	29 Nov 1922	–

Appendix D

THE SECRETARY AND REGISTRAR OF THE ORDER OF MERIT

The original Statute XVI read:

> It is ordained that the Comptroller of the Lord Chamberlain's Department of Our Household, for the time being, shall be the Secretary and Registrar of the said Order.

On 25 July 1907, that Statute was amended to read:

> It is ordained that the Secretary and Registrar of the said Order shall be appointed from time to time by a Warrant under the Sign Manual of Us or Our heirs and successors, and shall hold the said Office during the pleasure of Us, Our heirs and successors.

The first two Secretaries and Registrars held office under the provisions of the original Statute XVI – ex-officio, as Comptroller of the Lord Chamberlain's Department. The remaining six have been appointed by the Sovereign from Members, active or retired, of the Royal Household.

The Badge of the Secretary and Registrar is also provided for in Statute XVI. It is 'ordained that he shall wear around his neck pendant to a chain of gold a like Badge to that appointed for Members of the Order, with the addition of two silver pens, saltirewise between the angles of the Cross.' The chain and badge are retained for safe keeping in the Central Chancery, the Secretary and Registrar of the Order withdrawing them whenever he has occasion to wear them.

What does the Secretary and Registrar do? His duties are formally set out in Statute XVI as follows:

> To his custody shall be confided the Seal of the said Order, which he shall affix, or cause to be affixed, to all Statutes and other documents or instruments connected therewith. He shall, moreover, perform such duties as may be directed by the Sovereign or by these Statutes. He shall keep full lists of the Members of the Order. He shall carefully record all proceedings relative to the said Order that may take place, and he shall faithfully enter such proceedings in the Register of the Order, as well as all documents which may be transmitted to him for that purpose. We are further pleased to ordain that the Chancery of the said Order, wherein a record of all proceedings connected therewith shall be deposited and preserved, shall be in the Central Chancery of Our Orders of Knighthood.

Although they sound quite formidable, the Queen's Private Secretary described the office to a new incumbent thus:

> The duties are not onerous. When The Queen is about to make an appointment to the Order, it is my job to write and let you know. By this time, the recipient will have been sounded out by me and will have accepted, so all you have to do is to let him know formally. You also, in co-operation with the Central Chancery of the Orders of Knighthood, ensure that a list is published giving the names of the members.'[1]

The Secretary and Registrar countersigns the Warrant of Appointment of each OM, which is prepared by the Central Chancery. Since 1986, the Secretary and Registrar has also, as provided for in the Statutes, been in attendance on the Sovereign at the investiture of a Member of the Order. Previously, he had done so only occasionally. For many years, however, the Order was invariably conferred at one of the large regular investitures, where the attendance of the Secretary and Registrar was hardly appropriate. Even when the Order came to be conferred individually in the reign of King George VI, it occurred to no one (least of all the aged Sir Arthur Erskine, living in Perthshire) that the Officer of the Order should be there.

It was a different matter for Sir Edward Ford, so much more involved with the activities of the Order and living in London. As well as presenting each new OM to the Sovereign, he has also assiduously attended the memorial services for most of them, in addition to the Queen's formal representative.

It is during Sir Edward's tenure of office that the practice of quinquennial luncheons (with occasional religious services) has started. This, with his attendance at investitures, has given him closer personal contact with the OMs than any of his predecessors. As a former Assistant Private Secretary he has also taken a more active role in suggesting names that the Private Secretary might wish to consider submitting to the Queen for admission to the Order. He was instrumental in the collection at Windsor of photographs and drawings of Members being brought fully up-to-date.

Sir Edward was Secretary and Registrar for over 27 years, longer than any of his seven predecessors and he has taken a far closer interest in the Order. This was recognised by the Sovereign in promoting him to GCVO in the Birthday Honours List in 1998: the only Officer of the Order to be honoured specifically for his work in that role.

List of Secretaries and Registrars

1   *23 June 1902–11 June 1907*
   Major General Sir Arthur Edward Augustus ELLIS, GCVO, CSI

Born on 13 December 1837, he joined the 33rd Regiment in 1854 and served in the Crimean War. He became Equerry to the Prince of Wales in 1867, accompanied him on his visit to India in 1875, was promoted to Major General in 1885 and made a KCVO in 1897. From 1898–1901, he was Serjeant-at-Arms in the House of Lords. On the accession of King Edward VII, he became Comptroller of the Lord Chamberlain's Department and an Extra Equerry, posts that he held until his death in 1907. He had been made a GCVO in 1902.

In 1901, Ellis reorganised the antiquated Victorian court ceremonial – 'the masterly inactivity and fussiness of Windsor Castle' – replacing the tedious afternoon 'drawing rooms' with more lively evening 'courts'.

2   *18 June 1907–31 July 1907*
   Colonel Sir Douglas (Frederick Rawdon) DAWSON, KCVO, CMG

Born on 25 April 1854, he died on 20 January 1933. He was ex-officio Secretary and Registrar for only the few weeks between succeeding Sir Arthur Ellis as Secretary of the Lord Chamberlain's Department in June 1907 and the amendment of Statute XVI at the end of July. At that time, he happened also to be Secretary of the Order of the Garter, a post he held from 1904 until his death.

3   *1 August 1907–20 January 1924*
   Colonel the Honourable Sir Harry Charles LEGGE, GCVO

Born on 4 November 1852, he served in the Coldstream Guards from 1872–99. He became a Groom in Waiting to the Queen in 1889 and was Equerry in Waiting from 1893–1915, being made a KCVO in 1910. He was Paymaster of the King's Household from 1915–20, being promoted to GCVO in 1920. He was an Extra Equerry from 1915 until his death in 1924.

4   *4 July 1924–5 May 1939*
     Colonel the Honourable Sir Harry Julian STONOR, GCVO

Born on 17 November 1859, he was a Gentleman Usher from 1883–1936 and a Groom in Waiting from 1901–1936, being made a KCVO in 1933. He was an Extra Groom in Waiting from 1936 until his death in 1939.

5   *29 August 1939–24 July 1963*
     Colonel Sir Arthur (Edward) ERSKINE, GCVO, DSO

Born in 1881, he was a regular officer in the Royal Artillery and served in the First World War, being awarded the DSO in 1916. From 1919–24, he was Equerry in Ordinary and from 1924–41, he was Crown Equerry, being made CVO in 1926, KCVO in 1931 and GCVO in 1935. On retirement, he served as Secretary of the Ascot Authority from 1941–46. He was an Extra Equerry from 1941 until his death in 1963.

6   *16 August 1963–31 July 1971*
     Brigadier Sir Norman Wilmshurst GWATKIN, GCVO, KCMG, DSO

Born on 2 August 1899, he joined the Coldstream Guards in 1918 and was Adjutant of the Royal Military College, Sandhurst, from 1931–35. He became Assistant Comptroller of the Lord Chamberlain's Office in 1936, being made MVO in 1937. He served in the Second World War, commanded a brigade of the Guards Armoured Division and was awarded a DSO in 1944. He returned to the Lord Chamberlain's Office in 1946 and became Comptroller in 1960, being made CVO in 1946, KCVO in 1951, GCVO in 1963 and KCMG in 1964, when he retired. He was an Extra Equerry from 1950 until his death in 1971.

7   *24 September 1971–3 June 1975*
     Rear Admiral Sir Christopher Douglas BONHAM-CARTER, GCVO, CB

Born on 3 November 1907, he entered the Royal Navy in 1921 and served in the Second World War, being mentioned in despatches in 1943. Promoted captain in 1948, he commanded a frigate flotilla and a cruiser and served as Naval Attaché in Rome. From 1957–59, as a rear-admiral, he was Chief of Staff, Mediterranean, being made a CB in 1959. In retirement, he served as Treasurer to the Duke of Edinburgh from 1959–70, being made CVO in 1962, KCVO in 1968 and GCVO in 1970. He was an Extra Equerry to the Duke of Edinburgh until his death in 1975.

8   *1 August 1975–31 March 2003*
     Sir Edward William Spencer FORD, GCVO, KCB, ERD

Born on 24 July 1910, he acted as English tutor to King Farouk of Egypt before practising as a barrister from 1937–39. He served in the Grenadier

Guards in the Second World War, being twice mentioned in despatches. He was Assistant Private Secretary to King George VI and Queen Elizabeth II from 1946–67, being made MVO in 1949, CB in 1952, KCVO in 1957 and KCB in 1967. He was an Extra Equerry from 1955–2006. In retirement, he was Secretary to the Pilgrim Trust from 1967–75 and he played an active role in many charities. Shortly after the Queen's reference in a speech at Guildhall to 1992 having been her 'annus horribilis', the press revealed that the 'sympathetic correspondent' who had inspired the use of the phrase was Sir Edward Ford. On 31 March 2003, he was succeeded by Lord Fellowes. He died on 19 November 2006.

9   *31 March 2003–*
    Robert, Lord FELLOWES, PC, GCB, GCVO, QSO

Born on 11 December 1941, he was brought up on the royal estate at Sandringham, where his father was Land Agent. After serving in the Scots Guards, he worked in the City before becoming Assistant Private Secretary to the Queen on 6 February 1977. He was Private Secretary from 1990–99. He was made LVO in 1983, CB in 1987, KCVO in 1989, KCB in 1991, GCVO in 1996, GCB in 1998 and a life peer in 1999. He is now Chairman of Barclays Private Banking.

NOTES

RA – Royal Archives at Windsor Castle
CCOK – Central Chancery of the Orders of Knighthood

Chapter 1 Introduction

1 Gardiner, S., *Epstein* (London: Michael Joseph, 1992), p. 44.
2 Cannadine, David, *G. M. Trevelyan* (London: HarperCollins, 1992), p. 19.

Chapter 2 The Nineteenth Century Without an Order of Merit

1 Rose, Kenneth, *King George V* (London: Macmillan, 1983), p. 318.
2 J. Tyndall, *Faraday as a Discoverer* (London: RA Kessinger Publishing Co, 1868).
3 Behrman, S. N., *Conversations with Max* (London: Hamish Hamilton, 1960), Chapter 2.
4 RA PS GVI C 022/278C, note of 9 May 1944 from Sir Alan Lascelles to Owen Morshead.

Chapter 3 Moves Towards the Order of Merit

1 *The Barham Papers* (London: Naval Records Society, 1910), Vol. III, pp. 333 and 346.
2 Hansard (House of Commons), 22 March 1815, Vol. XXX, columns 332–333.
3 *Ibid.*, column 332.
4 Hansard (House of Commons), 18 April 1834, Vol. XXII, columns 954–955.
5 *Ibid.*, columns 959–960.
6 *Ibid.*, column 960.
7 Nicolas, N. Harris, Sir, *History of the Orders of Knighthood of the British Empire* (London, 1842), Vol. I, p. lxxxvii and Vol. III, pp. 266–267.
8 RA VIC/E 35/16, encl. to RA VIC/E 35/15, Sir Robert Peel to Prince Albert, 6 January 1847.
9 RA QV Journal, 27 August 1846.
10 Hansard (House of Lords), 21 February 1873, Vol. CCXIV, columns 773–782.
11 Hansard (House of Lords), 27 June 1873, Vol. CCXVI, columns 1466–1477.
12 Buckle, G. E., *The Life of Benjamin Disraeli* (London: John Murray, 1920), Vol. V, pp. 355–358.

13 *Queen Victoria's Letters*, Second Series, Vol. III (London: John Murray, 1928), pp. 668–669.
14 *Punch*, 13 February 1886, p. 78.
15 *Nature*, 16 June 1887, pp. 145–146.
16 RA VIC/L7/2, Sir James Linton to Princess Beatrice, 20 January 1887.
17 RA VIC/L7/3, Henry Manners to Sir Henry Ponsonby, 1 February 1887.
18 RA VIC/L7/4, *ibid.*
19 RA VIC/L7/6, Sir Henry Ponsonby to Sir James Linton, 4 February 1887.
20 RA VIC/L7/7, Sir James Linton to Sir Henry Ponsonby, 8 February 1887.
21 RA VIC/L7/8, Sir Owen Burne to Sir Henry Ponsonby, 11 February 1887.
22 RA VIC/A65/47, Lord Salisbury to the Queen, 3 March 1887.
23 Hatfield House Archives, The Queen to Lord Salisbury, 4 March 1887 (draft).
24 RA VIC/L7/11, Lord Salisbury to Sir Henry Ponsonby, 7 March 1887.
25 RA VIC/A66/5, Lord Salisbury to the Queen, 13 June 1887.
26 Hatfield House Archives, The Queen to Lord Salisbury, 25 July 1887.
27 RA VIC/L7/21, Lord Salisbury to the Queen, 5 January 1888.
28 RA VIC/QV Journal, 8 January 1888.
29 QVL, Third Series, Vol. II, pp. 85–86.
30 QVL, Third Series, Vol. III, p. 108.
31 *Ibid.*, p. 167.

Chapter 4 The Establishment of the Order of Merit

1 QVL, Third Series, Vol. III, pp. 192–193.
2 *Ibid.*, p. 37.
3 Hibbert, C., *Edward VII: A Portrait* (London: Allen Lane, 1977), pp. 197–198.
4 *Ibid.*, p 175
5 Maurois, A., *King Edward and His Times* (London: Cassell, 1933), p. 237.
6 *Compact Dictionary of National Biography*, p. 2616.
7 Lee, S., Sir, *King Edward VII: A Biography* (Basingstoke: Macmillan and Co, 1927), Vol. II, p. 743.
8 Letters to the author from Jane Langton (Royal Archives), 10 April 1985, and Robin Harcourt Williams (Hatfield House) 22 March 1985.
9 RA PS/GV/J 1729/25, letter of 15 March 1922.
10 RA PS/GV/J 1729/20, letter of 17 November 1921 from Earl of Rosebery to Lord Stamfordham.
11 CCOK, letter of 28 March 1902 from Sir Arthur Davidson to Sir Arthur Ellis.
12 RA VIC/R 22/82, submission of 17 April 1902 from Lord Salisbury to King Edward VII.
13 RA VIC/R 22/83, copy of letter from King Edward VII to Lord Salisbury (original is at Hatfield House).
14 Curzon Papers, India Office Library, letter of 29 April 1902 from St John Brodrick to Lord Curzon.
15 CCOK, letter of 24 May 1902 from Hon Schomberg McDonnell to Sir Arthur Ellis.
16 RA PS/GV/J 1729/25, letter of 15 March 1922 from A. J. Balfour to Lord Stamfordham.
17 CCOK, letter of 7 April 1902 from Hon Schomberg McDonell to Sir Arthur Ellis.
18 Letter of 6 Mar 1987 from Sir Colin Cole to the author.
19 Galloway, P., Stanley, D. and Martin, S., *Royal Service: The Royal Victorian Order, The Royal Victorian Medal, The Royal Victorian Chain*, Vol. I (London: Victorian Publishing, 1996), section on the Royal Victorian Chain by the author.

20 Letter of 14 May 1986 from Stephen C. Clark (Collingwood) to the author.

21 Letter of 18 September 1986 from G. P. Dyer (Royal Mint) to the author.

22 CCOK, letter of 13 April 1902 from Sir Arthur Ellis (Lord Chamberlain's Department) to Hon Schomberg McDonnell (PS to Prime Minister).

23 CCOK, letter of 25 July 1902 from Sir Arthur Ellis to Sir Francis Knollys.

24 CCOK, letter of 23 October 1902 from Lord Knollys to Sir Arthur Ellis and reply.

25 Squibb, G. D., *Precedence in England and Wales* (Oxford: Oxford University Press, 1981), pp. 41–42.

26 Kennedy, M., *Portrait of Elgar* (Oxford: Oxford University Press, 1968), p. 218.

27 Stuart, V., *The Beloved Little Admiral* (London: Robert Hale, 1967), p. 247.

Chapter 5 Development of the Order over the Years

1 RA VIC/R 26/34, letter of 5 June 1905 from A. J. Balfour to Lord Knollys.

2 Hatfield House Papers: letter of 20 June 1902 from Hon Schomberg McDonnell to Sir Francis Knollys.

3 RA PS/GV/J 1729/19, memorandum of 8 November 1921 by Lord Stamfordham.

4 RA PS/GV/J 1729/25, letter of 15 March 1922 from A.J. Balfour to Lord Stamfordham.

5 RA PS/GV/J 2331/49, note by Lord Stamfordham.

6 Nicolson, H., *King George V* (London: Constable & Co, 1952), p. 389.

7 RA PS/GV/J 2325/15, note of 16 April 1931 from C. P. Duff to Ramsay MacDonald.

8 Berriedale Keith, A., *The King and the Imperial Crown* (London: Longmans, Green & Co, 1936), pp. 341 and 345–346.

9 RA VIC/R29/58, letter of 28 October 1908 from Lord Knollys to King Edward VII.

10 Asquith Papers, Vol 1. Fol 76/77, letter of 1 November 1908 from Lord Knollys to Vaughan Nash.

11 Rose, K., *King George V* (Basingstoke: Macmillan, 1984), pp. 313–314.

12 RA PS/GV/J 629, telegram of 31 December 1913 from Lord Stamfordham to Sir Frederick Ponsonby.

13 RA PS/GV/J 1729/15, memorandum of 2 November 1921 by Lord Stamfordham.

14 RA PS/GV/J 1729/4, letter of 14 October 1921 from Lord Stamfordham to A. J. Balfour.

15 RA PS/GV/J 1729/5, letter of 15 October 1921 from A. J. Balfour to Lord Stamfordham.

16 RA PS/GV/J 1729/7, letter of 17 October 1921 from Lord Stamfordham to David Lloyd George.

17 RA PS/GV/J 1729/8, memorandum from Clive Wigram to Lord Stamfordham.

18 RA PS/GV/J 1729/10, manuscript note of 21 October 1921 by Lord Stamfordham.

19 RA PS/GV/J 1729/14, letter of 1 November 1921 from Lord Stamfordham to Viscount Knollys.

20 RA PS/GV/J 1729/17, memorandum of 5 November 1921 by Lord Stamfordham.

21 Wilson, D., *Gilbert Murray OM* (Oxford: Oxford University Press, 1987), p. 387.

22 RA PS/GV/J 1729/22, letter of 13 March 1922 from Lord Stamfordham to Sir Arthur Balfour.

23 RA PS/GV/J 1785A 28/29, memorandum of 26 December 1922 from Lord Stamfordham to Sir Francis Bryant and latter's marginal note.

24 RA PS/GV/J 1729/17, memorandum of 5 November 1921 by Lord Stamfordham.

25 Birkenhead, Lord, *Rudyard Kipling* (London: WH Allen, 1980), pp. 382–383.

26 RA PS/GV/J 2121/40, letter of 14 May 1927 from Lord Stamfordham to Stanley Baldwin.

27 RA PS/GV/J 2121/48, letter of 17 May 1927 from Sir Ronald Waterhouse to Lord Stamfordham.

28 RA PS/GV/J 2171/29, letter of 15 May 1928 from Lord Stamfordham to Sir Walter Lawrence.

29 RA PS/GV/J 2325/23, memorandum of 21 April 1931 from Owen Morshead to Sir Clive Wigram.

30 *Ibid.*

31 RA PS/GV/J 2325/27, comment of 24 April 1931 by Alexander Hardinge.

32 RA PS/GV/J 2325/54, memorandum of 12 May 1931.

33 RA PS/GVI/C 022/197-9, letter of 2 December 1940 from Sir Alexander Hardinge to Winston Churchill and reply of 3 December.

34 RA PS/GVI/C 022/44, telegram of 28 May 1943 from Sir Alexander Hardinge to Winston Churchill.

35 CCOK, note of 24 August 1942 from Miss H. M. Milsom to Major Harry Stockley.

36 Private note in private collection, quoted by permission of the Hon Lady Murray (daughter of Lord Hardinge of Penshurst).

37 *The Guardian*, 19 August 1963.

38 Hibbert, C., *Edward VII* (London: Allen Lane, 1977), p. 193.

39 CCOK, letter of 6 February 1908 from Hon Harry Legge to Sir Douglas Dawson and reply of 7 February.

40 CCOK, memorandum of 20 December 1910.

41 CCOK, undated memorandum from Lord Chamberlain's Office.

42 RA PS/GV/J 2504/1, letter of 27 November 1935 from Lord Wigram to Major Stockley (CCOK).

43 RA PS/GV/J 2504/5, letter of 10 December 1935 from Sir Warren Fisher to Lord Wigram.

44 RA PS/GV/J 2504/6, letter of 10 December 1935 from Robert Knox to Lord Wigram.

45 RA PS/GV/J 2504/8, letter of 11 December 1935 from Lord Wigram to Sir Warren Fisher.

46 CCOK, letter of 17 June 1969 from P. S. Milner-Barry to Sir Norman Gwatkin.

47 CCOK, letter of 21 June 1969 from Sir Michael Adeane to Sir Norman Gwatkin.

Chapter 6 The Original Members

1 *Rudyard Kipling's Verse* (London: Hodder & Stoughton, 1940), p. 204.

2 James, D., *Lord Roberts* (London: Hollis & Carter, 1954), p. 487.

3 Maurice, F., Sir and Arthur, G., Sir, *The Life of Lord Wolseley* (London: William Heinemann, 1924), p. 73.

4 *Ibid.*, pp. 136–137.

5 *Ibid.*, p. 334.

6 Magnus, P., *Kitchener: Portrait of an Imperialist* (London: John Murray, 1958), p. 289.

7 Lee, S., Sir, *King Edward VII* (Basingstoke: Macmillan and Co, 1925), Vol. I, pp. 174–175.

8 Stuart, V., *The Beloved Little Admiral* (London: Robert Hale 1967), p. 242.

9 *The Times*, 23 December 1968: letter from Sir George McRobert.

10 Russell, A., *Lord Kelvin: His Life and Work* (London: TC & EC Jack, 1912), p. 90.

11 Cameron, H.C., *Joseph Lister: The Friend of Man* (London: William Heinemann Medical Books Ltd, 1948), p. 157.

12 Fisher, R.B., *Joseph Lister* (London: Macdonald and Jane's, 1977), p. 315.

13 *The Times*, 12 February 1912.

14 *Compact DNB*, Vol. II, p. 2913.

15 *The Times*, 2 August 1995: letter from Lord Tugendhat.

16 Maurois, A., *King Edward and His Times* (London: Cassell, 1933), p. 184.

17 Rose, K., *King George V* (London: Papermac, 1984), p. 171.

18 RA PS/GV/J 2203/30, memorandum of 21 September 1928 from Viscount Esher to Lord Stamfordham.

19 RA PS/GV/J 248A/2, letter of 25 May 1911 from A. J. Balfour to Viscount Knollys.

20 McCartney, D., *W. E. H. Lecky: Historian and politician, 1838–1903* (Dublin: Lilliput, 1994).

21 Blunt, W., *England's Michelangelo* (London: Hamish Hamilton, 1975), p. 153.

22 *The Times*, 14 October 1997.

Chapter 8 The Military Men

1 Young, K., *Arthur James Balfour* (London: G. Bell & Sons, 1963), pp. 202–203.

2 Sir Anthony Caro in a Radio 4 programme on public sculpture, 30 April 1993.

3 Morris, J., *Fisher's Face* (London: Viking, 1995).

4 Marder, A. J. (Ed.), *Fear God and Dread Nought* (London: Cape, 1952), Vol. I, preface.

5 Fisher, Lord, *Memories* (London: Hodder and Stoughton, 1919), p. 3.

6 Magnus, P., *King Edward the Seventh* (London: John Murray, 1964), p. 440.

7 Rose, K., *King George V* (Basingstoke: Macmillan, 1984), p. 189.

8 Churchill, R. S., *Winston S. Churchill* (London: Heinemann, 1967), Vol II., pp. 538–539.

9 RA PS/GV/J 718/1, letter of 19 November 1914 from Maurice Bonham-Carter (10 Downing Street) to Lord Stamfordham.

10 Ponsonby, F., Sir, *Recollections of Three Reigns* (London: Eyre & Spottiswoode, 1951), p. 319.

11 Blake, R. (Ed.), *The Private Papers of Douglas Haig, 1914–1919* (London: Eyre & Spottiswoode, 1952), p. 344.

12 Holmes, R., *The Little Field Marshal: Sir John French* (London: Jonathan Cape, 1981), pp. 366–367.

13 Churchill, W., *The World Crisis* (London: Thornton Butterworth, 1927), Vol. III, p. 214.

14 Chalmers, W. S., *The Life and Letters of David Beatty* (London: Hodder and Stoughton, 1951), p. 319.

15 *Ibid.*, p. 427.

16 *Sunday Times*, 11 January 1981, review by Sir Michael Howard.

17 *The Times*, 13 April 1918.

18 *The Times* 31 January 1928.

19 Keegan, J., *The First World War* (London: Hutchinson, 1998), pp. 311 and 338.

20 Roskill, S., *Hankey: Man of Secrets, 1919–1931* (London: Collins, 1972), p. 508.

21 Jellicoe, Viscount, *The Grand Fleet, 1914–16* (London: Cassell and Company, 1919), p. 493.

22 RA VIC/Add A 15/9046, letter of 31 December 1935 from George V to Duke of Connaught.

23 *The Diplomatic Diaries of Oliver Harvey, 1937-40* (London: Collins, 1970), p. 254.

24 *Sunday Times*, 25 July 1976, review by Sir Michael Howard.

25 *The Times*, 4 December 1963, Marshal of the RAF Sir John Slessor.

26 Radio 4 programme on Churchill and 'Operation Catherine', 27 September 2001.

27 RA PS/GVI/C 022/42, telegram of 25 May 1943 from Prime Minister to Sir Alexander Hardinge.

28 RA PS/GVI/C 022/44, telegram of 28 May 1943 from Sir Alexander Hardinge to Prime Minister.

29 Viscount Cunningham of Hyndhope, *A Sailor's Odyssey* (London: Hutchinson, 1951), p. 584.

30 RA PS/GVI/C 022/374, minute of 19 April 1944 from Prime Minister to Sir Alan Lascelles.

31 RA PS/GVI/C 022/376, minute of 29 April 1945 from Prime Minister to Sir Alan Lascelles.

32 RA PS/GVI/C 022/381, letter of 26 October 1945 from T. L. Rowan (10 Downing Street) to Sir Alan Lascelles.

33 Hastings, M., *Bomber Command* (London: Michael Joseph, 1979).

34 *Sunday Times*, 19 March 1978, review by Sir Michael Howard.

35 *The Times*, 24 April 1971.

36 Bryant, A., *Triumph in the West* (London: Collins, 1959), p. 537.

37 Bryant, A., *The Turn of the Tide* (London, Collins, 1957), p. 32.

38 *Ibid.*, p. 32.

39 Sir David Fraser in *DNB 1961–1970*, pp. 147–148.

40 Viscount Cunningham of Hyndhope, *A Sailor's Odyssey* (London: Hutchinson, 1951), p. 623.

41 *The Times*, 11 February 1956.

42 Boyle, A., *Trenchard* (London: Collins, 1962), letter of 7 September 1940 from George VI to Viscount Trenchard, quoted on p. 723.

43 RA PS/GVI/C 022/173, letter of 19 April 1937 from Geoffrey Dawson to Sir Alexander Hardinge.

44 RA PS/GVI/C 022/12B, letter of 18 June 1941 from Sir Alexander Hardinge to Owen Morshead.

45 RA PS/GVI/C 022/542, letter of 3 October 1950 from MRAF Sir John Slessor to Sir Alan Lascelles.

46 RA PS/GVI/C 022/544, letter of 10 October 1950 from MRAF Viscount Trenchard to Sir Alan Lascelles.

47 *The Observer*, 6 July 1952.

48 Nicolson, N., *Alex* (London: Weidenfeld and Nicolson, 1973), pp. 239 and 281.

49 Macmillan, H., *The Blast of War* (Basingstoke: Macmillan, 1967), Vol. II, p. 304.

50 Lord Carrington on BBC2 chat show, June 1983.

51 Zeigler, P., *Mountbatten* (London: Collins, 1985), pp. 638–639

52 Bryant, A., *Triumph in the West* (London: Collins, 1959), pp. 58 and 321.

53 Warner, P., *Auchinleck: The Lonely Soldier* (London: Buchan & Enright, 1981), pp. 264–265.

54 Ziegler, p. 671.

55 *Ibid.*, p. 563.

Chapter 9 The Scientists

1 *Compact DNB*, p. 2927.

2 RA PS/GV/J 470/02, letter of 11 March 1912 from Viscount Haldane to Viscount Knollys.

3 *The Times*, 11 February 1993. Review by John Marenbon of Vol IV of *A History of the University of Cambridge*.

4 RA PS/GV/J 1757/17, letter of 2 June 1924 from Earl of Balfour to Lord Stamfordham.

5 RA PS/GV/J 1978/41, letter of 15 December 1924 from Lord Stamfordham to Randall Davidson.

6 RA PS/GV/J 1978/58, letter of 19 December 1924 from Lord Stamfordham to Sir Ernest Rutherford.

7 RA PS/GV/J 1978/59, letter of 20 December 1924 from Sir Ernest Rutherford to Lord Stamfordham.

8 Feather, N., *Lord Rutherford* (London: Priory Press, 1973), p. 173.

9 Snow, C. P., *Variety of Men* (Harmondsworth: Penguin, 1969), p. 15.

10 'The Listener', 21 December 1950. Text of Third Programme talk by Sir John Cockcroft.

11 Snow, p. 17.

12 *Ibid.*, p. 18.

13 *Ibid.*, p. 17.

14 O'Shea, P. P., *Ernest Rutherford: His Honours and Distinctions* (Notes & Records of the Royal Society, 1972), pp. 69–70.

15 Cockcroft talk.

16 *DNB*, 1941–1950, pp. 100–101.

17 RA PS/GV/J 2203/46, letter of 7 November 1928 from Lord Stamfordham to Earl of Balfour.

18 *The Times*, 19 September 1967.

19 *Sunday Times*, 20 June 1982, letter from Sir Harold Wilson.

20 CCOK, memorandum of 22 November 1967 from Sir Michael Adeane to Maj Gen Colquhoun.

21 *Sunday Telegraph*, 22 November 1992, Albany column.

22 Quoted in obituary in *The Independent*, 6 March 1991.

23 *Ibid.*

24 *Daily Telegraph*, 6 March 1991.

25 *The Times*, 30 June 1975.

26 Earl of Birkenhead, *The Prof in Two Worlds* (London: Collins, 1961), pp. 66–67.

27 *The Times*, 30 June 1975.

28 *Scientific American*, May 1963.

29 RA PS/GVI/C 022/025, letter of 9 April 1944 from Sir Alfred Egerton (Secretary of the Royal Society) to Sir Alan Lascelles.

30 RA PS/GVI/C 022/172, letter of 6 November 1936 from Lord Rutherford of Nelson to Stanley Baldwin.

31 RA PS/GVI/C 022/175, letter of 21 April 1938 from Sir Frank Smith to Sir Alexander Hardinge.

32 RA PS/GVI/C 022/181, letter of 2 December 1938 from Sir J. J. Thomson to Sir Alexander Hardinge.

33 *Compact DNB*, pp. 2586–2587.

34 *Ibid.*

35 *Ibid.*

36 RA PS/GV/J 461/2, letter of 16 June 1910 from Vaughan Nash to Lord Knollys.

37 CCOK, letter of 11 July 1910 from Sir William Crookes to Sir Douglas Dawson.

38 Fournier D'Albe, E.E., *The Life of Sir William Crookes* (London: T Fisher Unwin, 1923), p. 387.

39 RA PS/GVI/C 022/517, letter of 16 February 1949 from Sir Charles Darwin to Sir Alan Lascelles.

40 RA PS/GVI/C 022/537, letter of 28 June 1948 from Sir Alfred Egerton to Sir Alan Lascelles.

41 *The Guardian*, 23 April 1960.
42 *The Times*, 12 October 1967.
43 *Oxford Today*, Hilary Term, 1999.
44 *The Independent*, 1 August 1994, obituary by Max Perutz, OM.
45 *Ibid.*
46 *The Times*, 30 July 1994.
47 *The Guardian*, recounted in obituary, 15 January 1997.
48 *The Times*, 1 December 1977.
49 *The Guardian*, 15 January 1997.
50 *The Times*, 6 December 1985.
51 *The Times*, 1 December 1987.
52 *The Times*, 11 April 1988.
53 Church, R. (ed.), *The Spoken Word* (London: Collins, 1955), pp. 156–157.
54 *The Times*, 12 January 2000, interview with Anjana Ahuja.
55 *The Daily Telegraph*, 7 February 2002.
56 *The Times*, 16 December 1987.
57 *The* Times, 30 March 1977.
58 The *Times*, 7 February 2002.
59 *Ibid.*
60 *The Independent*, 7 February 2002.
61 *The Daily Telegraph*, 7 February 2002.
62 Crick, F., *What Mad Pursuit: A Personal View of Scientific Discovery* (London: Weidenfeld and Nicholson, 1988), p. 64.
63 *The Times*, 3 May 1994, quoted in an article by Lewis Wolpert.
64 *Compact DNB*, p. 2885.
65 *The Times*, 10 July 1997, review by Roger Bannister of *The Human Brain* by Susan Greenfield
66 RA PS GVI C 022/217, undated note.
67 *The Times*, 6 February 1978.
68 *Sunday Times*, 14 December 1980, interview with Danah Zohar.
69 *Biographical Memoirs of Fellows of the Royal Society*, Vol. 16 (1970), p. 159.
70 *Ibid.*, p 127
71 *TLS*, 13 January 1995, review of *Henry Wellcome* by Robert Rhodes James.
72 *Biographical Memoirs*, p. 153.
73 *The Times*, 24 and 25 July 1968.
74 *The Times*, 18 October 1988.
75 *Sunday Times*, 23 October 1988.
76 *The Times*, 12 June 1958.
77 Sexton, C., *The Seeds of Time* (Oxford, 1991), p. 77.
78 *Ibid.*, p. 143.
79 *Ibid.*
80 Sexton, Foreword
81 RA PS GVI C 022/381, letter of 26 October 1945 from T. L. Rowan to Sir Alan Lascelles.
82 Williams, T., *Howard Florey: Penicillin and After* (Oxford: Oxford University Press, 1984), pp. 204–205.
83 *History Today*, June 1984.
84 BBC, 'Horizon', 27 January 1986.
85 Lewis, J., *Something Hidden: A Biography of Wilder Penfield* (Toronto: Doubleday Canada, 1981), p. 218.
86 *Ibid.*, pp. 229–230.
87 CCOK, note by Sir Norman Gwatkin on letter of 3 March 1966 from Wilder Penfield.
88 Lewis, p. 284.
89 *The Times*, 17 April 1976.

90 RA VIC/R 28/55, letter of 10 June 1907 from Henry Campbell-Bannerman to Lord Knollys.
91 *TLS*, 1–7 July 1988, review by Mark Ridley of *The Correspondence of Charles Darwin: 1844–46*.
92 *Compact DNB*, p. 2702.
93 RA VIC/R 29/57, submission of 27 October 1908 from H. H. Asquith to King Edward VII.
94 RA VIC/R 29/59, undated note by King Edward VII.
95 RA VIC/R 29/62, letter of 29 October 1908 from H. H. Asquith to King Edward VII.
96 Asquith Papers 3 (Oxford: Bodleian Library), letter of 8 March 1912 from Lord Knollys to Maurice Bonham-Carter.
97 *Compact DNB*, p. 2946.
98 *Ibid.*
99 Radio 4, 25 February 2002.
100 RA PS/GV/J 629, letter of 31 December 1913 from Lord Stamfordham to Sir Archibald Geikie.
101 *Compact DNB*, p. 2649.
102 *The Independent*, 2 April 1993.
103 *The Times*, 2 February 1978.
104 Peyton, J., *Solly Zuckerman: A Scientist out of the Ordinary* (London: John Murray, 2001).
105 *The Independent*, 2 April 1993.
106 RA PS/GV/J 2121/29, letter of 11 May 1927 from Lord Rayleigh to Lord Stamfordham.
107 RA PS/GV/J 2121/35, letter of 13 May 1927 from J. J. Thomson to Lord Stamfordham.
108 RA PS/GV/J 2121/40 and 48, letter of 14 May 1927 from Lord Stamfordham to Stanley Baldwin and reply of 17 May from Sir Ronald Waterhouse.
109 RA PS/GV/J 2121/44 and 50, letter of 16 May 1927 from Lord Stamfordham to Sir Charles Parsons and reply of 17 May.
110 *DNB, 1961–1970*, p. 284.
111 *The Times*, 10 June 1960.
112 *Royal Society of Arts Journal*, September 1985, p. 720.
113 *The Times*, 10 July 1987.
114 *RSA Journal*, September 1985, pp. 719 and 722.
115 *The Times*, 16 November 1996.

Chapter 10 The Artists

1 Ash, R., *Alma-Tadema* (Princes Risborough: Shire Publications, 1973), pp. 35–36.
2 *Ibid.*, p. 42.
3 *Ibid.*, p. 37.
4 *Times Literary Supplement*, 28 February 1992.
5 *Compact Dictionary of National Biography*, p. 2710.
6 *The Times*, 22 May 1905.
7 *The Times*, 8 September 1910.
8 RA PS/GV/J 2262/30, memorandum of 20 May 1930 from Owen Morshead to Lord Stamfordham.
9 MacColl, D.S., *Life, Work and Setting of Philip Wilson Steer* (London: Faber and Faber, 1945), p. 149.
10 *The Times*, 28 January 1986, review by John Russell Taylor.
11 *The Times*, 14 May 1993, obituary of Maggie Hemingway.

12 *The Times*, 20 April 1972, review by Michael Holroyd of *Philip Wilson Steer 1860–1942* by Bruce Laughton.

13 Holroyd, M., *Augustus John, Vol. II* (London: Heinemann, 1975), p. 192.

14 *Ibid.*, p. 109.

15 John, A., *Chiaroscuro* (London: Jonathan Cape, 1952), p. 148.

16 RA PS/GVI/C 022/003, note of 3 October 1936 by Alan Lascelles.

17 RA PS/GVI/C 022/12B, letter of 18 June 1941 from Sir Alexander Hardinge to Owen Morshead.

18 RA PS/GVI/C 022/038, letter of 14 April 1942 from Sir Alexander Hardinge to Earl of Crawford and Balcarres.

19 Rose, K., *King George V* (London: Weidenfeld & Nicolson, 1983), p. 318.

20 Holroyd, pp. 101–104.

21 *Ibid.*, pp. 97–98.

22 Easton, M., *Augustus John* (London: National Portrait Gallery, 1975).

23 *Dictionary of National Biography, 1961–1970*, pp. 587–588.

24 The Guardian, 23 April 1960.

25 Berthoud, R., *Graham Sutherland* (London: Faber and Faber, 1982), pp. 240–241.

26 *Ibid.*

27 *Ibid.*

28 *The Times*, 3 August 1996, review by Richard Shone of National Portrait Gallery exhibition.

29 Berthoud, p. 299–300.

30 *Ibid.*

31 *The Times*, 13 January 1978.

32 Berthoud, p. 289.

33 *DNB 1971–1980*, pp. 826–827, note by John Hayes.

34 *The Times*, 3 August 1971.

35 *The Times*, 23 April 1968.

36 *DNB 1981–1985*, p. 296.

37 *Ibid.*, p. 297.

38 *The Times*, 23 October 1993, review by Waldemar Januszczak.

39 *The Melbourne Age*, 1 January 1963.

40 *The Daily Telegraph*, 30 November 1992.

41 *Sunday Times*, 4 October 1992.

42 *The Times*, 30 November 1992.

43 *Ibid.*

44 *The Economist*, 5 December 1992.

45 *Sunday Times*, 23 June 2002, review by Waldemar Januszczak.

46 *TLS*, 19 June 1987

47 *The Times*, 23 October 1982.

48 *The Times*, 17 June 1992.

49 *The Times*, 21 December 2001, article by Richard Cork.

50 Berthoud, R., *The Life of Henry Moore* (New York: EP Dutton, 1987), p. 302.

51 *The Times*, 16 August 1963.

52 RA PS/GVI/C 022/62A, note of 14 November 1944 from Sir Alan Lascelles to Sir Owen Morshead.

53 RA PS/GVI/C 022/63A, letter (manuscript) of 17 November 1944 from Sir Kenneth Clark to Sir Alan Lascelles.

54 Berthoud, p. 259.

55 *Ibid.*, p. 260.

56 *Ibid.*, p. 309.

57 *Ibid.*, p. 402.

58 *Daily Telegraph*, 1 September 1986.

59 *Die Welt*, 1 September 1986, article by Hanns Theodor Flemming.
60 *The Times*, 28 July 1998.
61 *The Times*, 23 February 1998, interview with Joanna Pitman.
62 Berthoud, p. 230.
63 *The Times*, 20 October 1989, review by John Russell Taylor.
64 *The Times*, 23 September 1989, note by David Lee.
65 Berthoud, p. 321.
66 *The Times*, 7 February 1998, interview with Dalya Alberge.
67 *The Times*, 3 March 1998, review by Richard Cork.
68 *Sunday Times*, 10 March 1991, interview with Hugh Pearman.
69 RA PS/GV/J 2203/30, letter of 21 September 1928 from Viscount Esher to Lord Stamfordham.
70 RA PS/GVI/C 022/207A, memorandum of 10 April 1937 from Owen Morshead to Sir Alexander Hardinge.
71 RA PS/GVI/C 022/207B, letter of 2 May 1937 from Owen Morshead to Sir Alexander Hardinge.
72 Hussey, C., *The Life of Sir Edwin Lutyens* (*Country Life*, 1950), p. 574.
73 Lutyens, M., Edwin Lutyens (London: Black Swan, 1991), p. 184.
74 *Ibid.*, p. 219.
75 *The Times*, 14 November 1981, article by Roderick Gradidge.
76 *Sunday Times*, 15 November 1981, article by Deyan Sudjic.
77 RA PS/GVI/C 022/288B, memorandum of 10 March 1944 from Owen Morshead to Sir Alan Lascelles.
78 RA PS/GVI/C 022/290A, memorandum of 10 March 1944 from Sir Alan Lascelles to 'OM'.
79 RA PS/GVI/C 022/304, submission of 9 May 1944 from Sir Alan Lascelles to King George VI.
80 *The Times Weekly Edition*, 14 June 1944.
81 *The Times*, 26 October 1978, article by Charles McKean.
82 *The Times*, 20 November 1976.
83 Spence, B., *Phoenix at Coventry* (London: Fontana, 1963), pp. 17–18.
84 *The Times*, 20 November 1976.
85 *Ibid.*
86 *The Times*, 18 June 2000, interview with Hugh Pearman.
87 *The Times*, 29 April 2002, article by Marcus Binney.
88 *The Times*, 4 December 2000, article by Richard Cork.
89 *The Times*, 13 November 1995, 9 June 1998 and 17 November 1998, articles by Marcus Binney.
90 *The Times*, 1 January 2000.

Chapter 11 The Musicians and Performers

1 RA PS/GV/J 248A/1–2, letters of 23 May 1911 from Viscount Morley of Blackburn and 25 May 1911 from A. J. Balfour to Lord Knollys.
2 RA PS/GV/J 248A/8, letter of 17 June 1911 from Sir Edward Elgar to Lord Knollys.
3 Kennedy, M., *Portrait of Elgar* (Oxford: Oxford University Press, 1968), p. 148.
4 *Ibid.*, p. 148.
5 *Times Educational Supplement*, 15 February 1957, article on centenary of Elgar's birth.
6 *The Times*, 7 August 1998, article by Daniel Johnson.
7 *The Times*, 24 February 1934.
8 *Compact DNB*, p. 2619.

9 *Times Educational Supplement*, 15 February 1957, article on centenary of Elgar's birth.
10 *Times Educational Supplement*, 17 October 1952.
11 *The Times*, 11 October 1952.
12 *The Times*, 27 August 1958, obituary quoting article by Ralph Vaughan Williams in *RCM Magazine* in 1912.
13 *Ibid.*
14 *The Spectator*, 18 July 1992.
15 Carpenter, H., *Benjamin Britten* (London: Faber and Faber, 1992), p. 448.
16 Headington, C., *Britten* (London: Eyre Methuen, 1981), pp, 106–107.
17 Carpenter, H., *Benjamin Britten* (London: Faber and Faber, 1992), p. 319.
18 Headington, C., *Britten* (London: Eyre Methuen, 1981), p. 108.
19 Hurd, M., *Britten* (London: Novello, 1966), p. 19.
20 Carpenter, H., *Benjamin Britten* (London: Faber and Faber, 1992), p. 579.
21 *Ibid.*
22 *Ibid.*, p. 580.
23 *Ibid.*
24 *The Guardian*, 6 December 1976.
25 Carpenter, H., *Benjamin Britten* (London: Faber and Faber, 1992), p. 585.
26 *The Times*, 29 March 1982.
27 Ottoway, H., *Walton* (London: Novello, 1972), p. 12.
28 *The Times*, 9 March 1983.
29 Tippett, M., *Those Twentieth Century Blues* (London: Hutchinson, 1991), pp. 114–115.
30 *Ibid.*, p. 220.
31 *The Times*, 10 January 1998.
32 *Ibid.*
33 *Daily Mail*, 21 September 1979.
34 *The Times*, 25 July 1970, article by Clive Barnes.
35 Royal Ballet Fiftieth Anniversary Season Programme, May 1981, article by John Percival.
36 *The Times*, 20 March 1978.
37 Medawar, J., *A Very Decided Preference* (Oxford University Press, 1990), p. 217.
38 *The Times*, 6 June 1983, profile by Brian Masters.
39 *The Times*, 9 March 2001.
40 *Radio Times*, 29 April 1986
41 *Daily Telegraph*, 13 March 1999, article by Norman Lebrecht.
42 Menuhin, Y., *Unfinished Journey* (London: Futura, 1978), preface by George Steiner.
43 *The Times*, 18 February 1959.
44 *The Times*, 1 January 1991.
45 *Daily Telegraph*, 21 February 1992.
46 *The Times*, 12 July 1989.
47 Medawar, J., *A Very Decided Preference* (Oxford: Oxford University Press, 1990), p. 216.
48 Personal information.
49 *The Spectator*, 28 May 1988.
50 *The Times*, 17 May 1982.
51 *The Guardian*, 12 July 1989.
52 *Royal Society of Arts Journal*, October 1989.
53 Morley, S., *John G* (London: Hodder & Stoughton, 2002), p. 452.
54 *Evening Standard*, 22 May 2000, article by John Mortimer.
55 *Sunday Times*, 14 February 1988.

Chapter 12 The Writers

1 *The Times*, 27 June 1902.

2 Cline, C. L., *The Letters of George Meredith*, Vol. III (Oxford: Oxford University Press, 1970), No. 2242, 21 June 1905 from Lord Knollys.

3 Meredith, W. M., *The Letters of George Meredith. Collected and Edited by his Son*, Vol. II (London: Constable, 1912), p. 574, 13 December 1905 to John Morley.

4 Information from Kenneth Rose to the author.

5 Sassoon, S., *Meredith* (London: Arrow Books, 1959), pp. 288–289.

6 *The Times*, 19 May 1909.

7 Trevelyan, G. M., *A Layman's Love of Letters*, Clark Lectures, 1953 (London: Longman, 1954), p. 110.

8 *The Spectator*, 7 March 1981, review by Michael Wharton of *God's Fifth Column* by William Gerhardie.

9 RA PS/GV/J 461/1, letter of 29 May 1909 from H. H. Asquith to Lord Knollys.

10 Hardy, F., *The Life of Thomas Hardy*, Vol. II (Basingstoke: Macmillan & Co, 1933), pp. 142–143.

11 Rose, K., *King George V* (London: Weidenfeld & Nicolson 1983), p. 313.

12 Hardy, F., *The Life of Thomas Hardy*, Vol. II (Basingstoke: Macmillan & Co, 1933), pp. 114–115.

13 *Oxford Companion to English Literature*, sixth edition (Oxford: Oxford University Press, 2000), p. 450.

14 *DNB 1922–1930*, p. 396.

15 Seymour-Smith, M., *Hardy* (London: Bloomsbury, 1994), p. 649.

16 Hepburn, J. (ed.), *Letters of Arnold Bennett*.

17 James, E., *Thomas Hardy 1840-1928* (London: British Library, 1990), p. 7, quoting Michael Millgate.

18 Cecil, Lord, D., *The English Poets* (London: William Collins, 1942), p. 42.

19 James, E., *Thomas Hardy 1840-1928* (London: British Library, 1990), p. 36.

20 Moore, H. T., *Henry James and His World* (London: Thames & Hudson, 1974), p. 111.

21 *The Times*, 21 August 1961, letter from Hamish Hamilton.

22 Rose, K., *King George V* (London: Weidenfeld & Nicolson 1983), p. 86–87.

23 RA PS/GV/J 845/1, letter of 11 December 1915 from A. J. Balfour to Lord Stamfordham.

24 Hassall, C., *Edward Marsh* (London: Longman, 1959), pp. 374–375, where the full text of the memorandum is given.

25 RA PS/GV/J 845/3, letter of 19 December 1915 from Asquith to Stamfordham.

26 RA PS/GV/J 845/7, lettter of 30 December 1915 from Lord Stamfordham to Henry James.

27 *The Times*, 1 January 1916.

28 RA PS/GV/J 845/16, n.d., letter from Viscount Bryce to Lord Stamfordham.

29 *The Times*, 29 February 1916.

30 *DNB 1912–1921*, p. 287.

31 *Ibid.*

32 *The Times*, 18 September 1997, obituary of Leon Edel.

33 *DNB 1912–1921*, p. 290.

34 *Ibid.*, p. 288.

35 Edel, L., *Henry James*, Vol. V (London: Rupert Hart-Davis, 1972), p. 565.

36 RA PS/GV/J 1752/57, undated memorandum from Sir Francis Bryant.

37 RA PS/GV/J 1752/105, memorandum of 22 December 1921 by Lord Stamfordham.

38 RA PS/GV/J 1752/107, letter of 23 December 1921 from John Murray to Lord Stamfordham.

39 RA PS/GVI/C 022/505, letter of 20 January 1948 from Sir Alan Lascelles to L. N. Helsby (10 Downing Street).
40 *The Nation & The Athenaeum*, 7 January 1922.
41 Dunbar, J., *JM Barrie* (London: Collins, 1970), p. 174.
42 *Ibid.*, p. 208.
43 Barrie, J. M., *The Greenwood Hat* (London: Peter Davies, 1937), pp. 168–169.
44 Asquith, C., *Portrait of Barrie* (London: James Barrie, 1954), p. 106.
45 Dunbar, pp. 199–200.
46 Birkin, A., *JM Barrie and The Lost Boys* (London: Constable, 1986), p. 295.
47 *The Observer*, 8 May 1960.
48 *Oxford Companion to English Literature*, sixth edition (Oxford: Oxford University Press, 2000), p. 70.
49 Marrot, H. V., *The Life and Letters of John Galsworthy* (London: William Heinemann, 1935), p. 435.
50 *Ibid.*, p. 436
51 *Ibid.*, p. 438
52 *Ibid.*, pp. 436–437.
53 RA PS/GV/J 2203/31, letter of 14 October 1928 from Rudyard Kipling to Lord Stamfordham.
54 RA PS/GV/J 2203/34, letter of 29 October 1928 from Robert Vansittart to Lord Stamfordham.
55 RA PS/GV/J 2213/66, memorandum (mid-May 1929) from Lord Stamfordham to King George V.
56 RA PS/GV/J 2213/67, letter of 19 May 1929 from Lord Stamfordham to John Galsworthy.
57 Marrot, p. 619.
58 *Ibid.*
59 Reynolds, M. E., *Memories of John Galsworthy* (London: Robert Hale, 1936), p. 128 (Reynolds was Galsworthy's sister).
60 *DNB 1931–1940*, p. 303.
61 *The Times*, 1 February 1933.
62 *Times Literary Supplement*, 4 September 1998, review by Robert Tanitch.
63 *DNB 1961–1970*, p. 383.
64 *Ibid.*, p. 382.
65 Gardner, P., *EM Forster* (London: Longman, 1977), p. 22.
66 *Ibid.*, p. 23.
67 *TLS*, 24 April 1998, review by Neil Powell of E. M. Forster's *The Prince's Tale*.
68 *The Spectator*, 31 October 1987, article by Mark Boxer.
69 *DNB 1961–1970*, p. 382.
70 Gardner, p. 29.
71 *Sunday Times*, 17 February 1980, interview with Sir Victor Pritchett.
72 Gardner p5
73 *Ibid.*, pp. 6 and 37.
74 *TLS*, 24 April 1998, review by Neil Powell of E. M. Forster's *The Prince's Tale*.
75 Forster, E. M., 'Art for art's sake', in *Two Cheers for Democracy* (London: Penguin, 1965), pp. 76–77.
76 Clark, K., *The Other Half* (London: John Murray, 1977), p. 198.
77 *Ibid.*, p. 197.
78 *The Observer*, 2 December 1951.
79 *DNB 1961–1970*, p. 383.
80 *The Listener*, 29 April 1985, review by John Drummond of Vol. II of Forster's *Letters*.
81 Priestley, J. B., *Margin Released* (London: Heinemann, 1962), p. 230.
82 *The Times*, 16 October 1976, extract from J. B. Priestley's *Instead of the Trees*.

83 Brome, V., *JB Priestley* (London: Hamish Hamilton, 1988), p. 454.

84 Collins, D., *Time and the Priestleys* (London: Alan Sutton, 1994), p. 224.

85 Radio interview on 25 October 1977.

86 *Yorkshire Post*, 16 August 1981.

87 Collins, p. 224.

88 Thatcher, M., *The Path to Power* (London: Harper Collins, 1995), p. 22.

89 *The Spectator*, 20 May 1989, article by Paul Johnson.

90 *Sunday Times*, 25 October 1998, review of *Priestley* by Judith Cook

91 *The Times*, 20 August 1996, letter from Sir Bob Scott.

92 *Sunday Times*, 14 December 1997, review by John Carey of *Priestley* by Judith Cook.

93 *The Times*, 16 January 1995, review by A. N. Wilson of Anthony Powell's *Journals 1982–1986*.

94 Church, R., *British Authors: A Twentieth Century Gallery* (London: Longmans Green, 1943), pp. 130–132.

95 *Sunday Times*, 23 October 1988, letter from Vincent Brome (biographer of Priestley).

96 *The Times*, April 1991, report by Simon Tait and John Phillips.

97 Greene, G., A Sort of Life (Harmondsworth: Penguin, 1972), p. 54.

98 *The Times*, 4 April 1991.

99 Philby, K., *My Silent War* (London: Panther, 1969), p. 7.

100 *New York Times*, 4 April 1991.

101 *Radio Times*, 18–25 April 1987, article by Nicholas Shakespeare.

102 *TLS*, 10–16 November 1989, review by Julian Symons of *Yours etc.*

103 *The Times*, 4 April 1991.

104 *The Times*, 27 November 1998, report by Ben Macintyre.

105 *The Times*, 11 July 2002.

106 *Sunday Times*, 31 January 1999.

107 *The Times*, 13 December 1997.

108 *The Times*, 2 July 2002, article by Benedict Nightingale.

109 RA PS/GV/J 2203/46, letter of 7 November 1928 from Lord Stamfordham to Earl of Balfour.

110 *DNB 1922–1930*, p. 115.

111 *Sunday Telegraph*, 9 August 1992, review by Caroline Moore of *Robert Bridges* by Catherine Phillips.

112 Church, R., *British Authors: A Twentieth Century Gallery* (London: Longmans Green, 1943), pp. 15 and 17.

113 *TLS*, 26 June 1953.

114 Review of *Robert Bridges* by Catherine Phillips, by Stephen Spender (*The Spectator*, 8 August 1992).

115 RA PS/GV/J 1978/40, letter of 14 December 1924 from Viscount Esher to Lord Stamfordham.

116 Nicolson, H., *King George the Fifth* (London: Constable, 1952) p. 511.

117 Church, p. 81.

118 *DNB 1961–1970*, p. 738.

119 Babington Smith, C., *John Masefield* (Oxford: Oxford University Press, 1978), p. 181.

120 *DNB 1961–1970*, p. 738.

121 Babington Smith, p. 199.

122 Lamont, C., *Remembering John Masefield* (London: Kaye & Ward, 1972), p. 16.

123 *The Times*, 1 June 1978, review by Robert Nye.

124 *Sunday Times*, 19 November 1978, review by John Carey of *John Masefield: The Sea Poems.*

125 RA PS/GV/J 1978/40, letter of 14 December 1924 from Viscount Esher to Lord Stamfordham.
126 RA PS/GVI/C 022/473, letter of 22 October 1940 from Sir Kenneth Clark to Sir Alexander Hardinge.
127 RA PS/GVI/C 022/476, letter of 10 July 1947 from Geoffrey Faber to Sir Alan Lascelles.
128 RA PS/GVI/C 022/483, letter of 1 October 1947 from John Masefield to Sir Alan Lascelles.
129 RA PS/GVI/C 022/485, letter of 2 October 1947 from Harold Nicolson to Sir Alan Lascelles.
130 RA PS/GVI/C 022/499, letter of 11 December 1947 from Sir Arthur Erskine to Sir Alan Lascelles.
131 RA PS/GVI/C 022/495A, letter of 2 December 1947 from L. N. Helsby (10 Downing Street) to Sir Alan Lascelles.
132 *Sunday Times*, 4 April 1999, article by John Carey.
133 *DNB 1961–1970*, p. 327.
134 *TLS*, 8 November 2002, review by Stefan Collini of *The Selected Works of Cyril Connolly*.
135 *DNB 1961–1970*, p. 328.
136 *Ibid.*, p. 327.
137 *Sunday Times*, 26 January 2003, column by Godfrey Smith.
138 Ackroyd, P., *TS Eliot* (London: Hamish Hamilton, 1984), pp. 303–304.
139 *The Times*, 5 January 1965.
140 *DNB 1961–1970*, p. 329.
141 *The Times*, 1 June 1953.
142 *The Times*, 23 June 1956.
143 Cecil, D., *The English Poets* (London: William Collins, 1942), pp. 46–47.
144 *DNB 1951–1960*, pp. 294–295.
145 Brain, R., *Tea with Walter de la Mare* (London: Faber and Faber, 1957).
146 *TLS*, 7 September 2001, review by Peter Parker of de la Mare's *Short Stories 1927–1956*.
147 *The Times*, 27 May 1993, review by Peter Ackroyd of *Imagination of the Heart* by Theresa Whistler.
148 *The Times*, 31 January 2003.
149 *The Times*, 20 December 1984.
150 *Sunday Times*, 5 and 12 August 2001.
151 *Chicago Tribune*, 2 November 1998, article by Julia Keller.
152 *TLS*, 24 March 2000.
153 *The Times*, 30 October 1998.
154 *Irish Times*, quoted on jacket of *Birthday Letters*.
155 *The Times*, 17 January 1998.

Chapter 13 The Scholars

1 RA PS/GV/J 1757/1 and 2, letters of 20 December 1921 and 29 January 1922 from Viscount Haldane to Lord Stamfordham.
2 RA PS/GV/J 1757/5, letter of 26 May 1924 from H. H. Asquith to Lord Stamfordham.
3 RA PS/GV/J 1757/6, letter of 28 May 1924 from Lord Stamfordham to F. H. Bradley.
4 *The Times*, 3 June 1924.
5 *The Times*, 24 September 1924.
6 Wollheim, R., *F. H. Bradley* (Harmondsworth: Penguin, 1969), p. 15.
7 *Ibid.*, p. 15.

8 Wollheim, R., *F. H. Bradley* (Harmondsworth: Penguin, 1969), p. 14.

9 *DNB 1931–1940*, p. 3.

10 *Ibid.*, p. 4.

11 RA PS/GVI/C 022/319, letter of 2 October 1942 from 12 philosophers to the Prime Minister.

12 RA PS/GVI/C 022/62A, memorandum of 14 November 1944 from Sir Alan Lascelles to Sir Owen Morshead.

13 Price, L., *Dialogues of Alfred North Whitehead* (New York: Mentor Books, 1956), pp. 35 and 249.

14 *Ibid.*, p. 249.

15 *Ibid.*, p. 232.

16 RA PS/GVI/C 022/516, letter of 14 February 1949 from J. R. H. Weaver to Sir Alan Lascelles, quoting Professor Henry Price.

17 RA PS/GVI/C 022/518, letter of 16 February 1949 from G. M. Trevelyan to Sir Alan Lascelles.

18 Russell, B., *The Autobiography of Bertrand Russell*, Vol. III (London: George Allen & Unwin, 1967), p. 26.

19 *The Autobiography of Bertrand Russell*, Vol. I (London: George Allen & Unwin, 1967), p. 39.

20 *The Times*, 7 January 1978, letter from Michael Burn.

21 *Sunday Times*, 10 February 1989, review by P. T. Martin of *The Great War of Words* by P. Buitenhuis.

22 Rowse, A. L., *Glimpses of the Great* (University Press of America, 1985), p. 1.

23 Crawshay-Williams, R., *Russell Remembered* (Oxford: Oxford University Press, 1970), p. 37.

24 *The Times*, 4 February 1970.

25 *The Times*, 19 July 1996, article by Sir Isaiah Berlin.

26 RA PS/GVI/C 022/559, letter of 16 February 1951 from Lord Brand to Major Edward Ford.

27 RA PS/GVI/C 022/561, letter of 20 February 1951 from G. M. Trevelyan to Sir Alan Lascelles.

28 RA PS/GVI/C 022/565, letter of 8 May 1951 from Isaiah Berlin to Sir Alan Lascelles.

29 *The Daily Telegraph*, 7 November 1997.

30 *The Times*, 31 October 1958, letter from Professor Richard Aaron.

31 *DNB 1951–1960*, pp. 745–746.

32 *Sunday Times*, 8 January 1984, review by P. N. Furbank of *The Collected Papers of Bertrand Russell*.

33 *DNB 1951–1960*, p. 747.

34 *Times Literary Supplement*, 29 January–4 February 1988, review by S. Blackburn of books on G. E. Moore.

35 *Observer*, 28 October 1979, review by B. Williams of *Moore* by P. Levy.

36 *TLS*, 29 May 1998.

37 *Sunday Times*, 31 March 1957.

38 Ignatieff, M., *Isaiah Berlin* (London: Chatto & Windus, 1998), p. 300.

39 *Ibid.*, p. 222.

40 *Ibid.*, p. 328.

41 Personal information.

42 *Oxford University Gazette*, 13 November 1997.

43 *The Daily Telegraph*, 7 November 1997.

44 Annan, N., *The Dons* (Chicago: University of Chicago Press, 1999), p. 222.

45 *Ibid.*, p. 155.

46 Personal information.

47 *Oxford Today*, Hilary 2002, article by Henry Hardy, p. 51.

48 *Isis*, 17 May 1985, p. 9.
49 *The Times*, 19 July 1996.
50 *The Times*, 7 November 1997.
51 *The Daily Telegraph*, 10 November 1997.
52 Price, L., *Dialogues of Alfred North Whitehead* (New York: Mentor Books, 1956), p. 183.
53 *DNB 1901–1911*, pp. 368–369.
54 Drabble, M. (ed.), *Oxford Companion to English Literature*, sixth edition (Oxford: Oxford University Press, 2000), p. 529.
55 *DNB 1912–1921*, p. 284.
56 Annan, N., *The Dons* (Chicago: University of Chicago Press, 1999), p. 240.
57 RA PS/GV/J 1765/5 and 6, letter of 25 September 1924 from Ramsay MacDonald to Lord Stamfordham enclosing letter of 24 September 1924 from Humphrey Ward to the Prime Minister.
58 RA PS/GV/J 1765/7, letter of 27 September 1924 from Lord Stamfordham to Ramsay MacDonald.
59 RA PS/GV/J 1978/13, letter of 19 November 1924 from Sir Frederic Kenyon to Lord Stamfordham.
60 RA PS/GV/J 1978/35, letter of 11 December 1924 from Lord Stamfordham to Earl of Balfour.
61 *DNB 1941–1950*, p. 275.
62 *Ibid.*, p. 273.
63 *Ibid.*, p. 275.
64 *The Spectator*, 7 July 1990, review by D. Cupitt of *The Making of The Golden Bough* by R. Fraser.
65 RA PS/GV/J 2171/81, memorandum of 24 May 1928.
66 RA PS/GV/J 2171/49, letter of 17 May 1928 from Earl of Balfour to Lord Stamfordham.
67 RA PS/GV/J 2171/41, letter of 16 May 1928 from Sir Walter Lawrence to Lord Stamfordham.
68 Collis, M., *The Journey Up* (London: Faber and Faber, 1970), pp. 24–25.
69 RA PS/GV/J 2203/41, letter of 2 November 1928 from Owen Morshead to Lord Stamfordham.
70 McBryde, G. (ed.) *Letters to a Friend From M. R. James* (London: Edward Arnold, 1956), p. 143.
71 Pfaff, R., *Montague Rhodes James* (Cambridge: Scholar Press, 1980), p. 387.
72 *Ibid.*
73 Cox, M., *M. R. James: An Informal Portrait* (Oxford: Oxford University Press, 1986), p. 177.
74 *Ibid.*, p. 101.
75 *Ibid.*, p. 140.
76 *The Times*, 21 July 1983.
77 RA PS/GV/J 1978/13, letter of 19 November 1924 from Sir Frederic Kenyon to Lord Stamfordham.
78 RA PS/GV/J 1978/35 and 39, letter of 11 December 1924 from Lord Stamfordham to Earl of Balfour and reply of 13 December.
79 *DNB 1941–1950*, p. 550.
80 Fisher, H. A. L., *An Unfinished Autobiography* (Oxford: Oxford University Press, 1940), p. 100.
81 *The Listener*, 12 March 1987, review by R. Blythe of *The Old Lie: The Great War and the Public School Ethos* by P. Parker.
82 *DNB 1941–1950*, p. 551.
83 RA PS/GV/J 1978/13, letter of 19 November 1924 from Sir Frederic Kenyon to Lord Stamfordham.

84 RA PS/GV/J 1978/14, letter of 21 November 1924 from Lord Stamfordham to Sir Frederic Kenyon.
85 RA PS/GVI/C 022/003, undated (1936) and unreferenced note in RA summarising history of OM candidates.
86 RA PS/GVI/C 022/173, letter of 19 April 1937 from Geoffrey Dawson to Sir Alexander Hardinge.
87 RA PS/GVI/C 022/194, letter of 22 November 1938 from John Masefield to Sir Alexander Hardinge.
88 RA PS/GVI/C 022/197-8, letter of 2 December 1940 from Sir Alexander Hardinge to Winston Churchill and reply of 3 December.
89 Wilson, D., *Gilbert Murray OM* (Oxford: Clarendon Press, 1987), p. 386.
90 *Ibid.*, p. 34.
91 *DNB 1951–1960*, p. 759.
92 Wilson, D., *Gilbert Murray OM* (Oxford: Clarendon Press, 1987), p. 54.
93 RA PS/GV/J 1729/1, letter of 1 October 1921 from A. J. Balfour to Lord Stamfordham.
94 Wilson, D., *Gilbert Murray OM* (Oxford: Clarendon Press, 1987), p. 193.
95 *Ibid.*, p. 230.
96 *Ibid.*
97 RA VIC/W 66/76a, letter of 2 June 1909 from Viscount Esher to Lord Knollys.
98 Buckle, G. E. (ed.), *Queen Victoria's Letters*, Third Series, Vol. I, 1891–1895 (London: John Murray, 1932), p. 178.
99 *Ibid.*, p. 381.
100 *DNB 1922–1930*, p. 131.
101 Hardinge of Penshurst, Lord, *Old Diplomacy* (London: John Murray, 1947) p. 132.
102 Wilson, B., *Friendly Relations: Britain's Ministers and Ambassadors to America (1791–1930)* (London: Lovat Dickson & Thompson, 1934), p. 295.
103 *Ibid.*, p. 305.
104 Ions, E., *James Bryce and American Democracy* (Basingstoke: Macmillan, 1968), p. 293.
105 Roskill , S., *Hankey: Man of Secrets*, Vol. II (London: Collins, 1972), pp. 256–257.
106 Ions, E., *James Bryce and American Democracy* (Basingstoke: Macmillan, 1968), p. 294.
107 RA VIC/W 66/76b, letter of 6 June 1909 from Viscount Morley of Blackburn to Lord Knollys.
108 RA PS/GV/J 248A/3, letter of 14 June 1911 from H. H. Asquith to Lord Knollys.
109 RA PS/GV/J 248A/9, letter of 19 June 1911 from Sir G. O. Trevelyan to Lord Knollys.
110 Cannadine, D., *G. M. Trevelyan* (London: Harper Collins, 1992) p. 27.
111 *DNB 1922–1930*, p. 833.
112 Magnus, P., *King Edward the Seventh* (London: John Murray, 1964), pp. 109 and 113.
113 Trevelyan, G. O., *Sir George Otto Trevelyan* (Harlow: Longmans, Green & Co, 1932), p. 138.
114 RA PS/GV/J 1978/13, letter of 19 November 1924 from Sir Frederic Kenyon to Lord Stamfordham.
115 RA PS/GV/J 2203/31, letter of 14 October 1928 from Rudyard Kipling to Lord Stamfordham.
116 RA PS/GV/J 2203/51, letter of 10 November 1928 from Earl of Balfour to Lord Stamfordham.
117 Cannadine, D., *G. M. Trevelyan: A Life in History* (London: Harper Collins, 1992), p. 18.

118 *Ibid.*, pp. 21–22.
119 *Ibid.*, p. xii.
120 *Ibid.*, p. 217.
121 Chadwick, O., *Freedom and the Historian* (Cambridge: Cambridge University Press, 1969).
122 Trevelyan, G. M., *An Autobiography* (Harlow: Longmans, Green & Co, 1949), p. 47.
123 Cannadine, D., *G. M. Trevelyan: A Life in History* (London: Harper Collins, 1992), pp. 38–39.
124 Cannadine, D., *G. M. Trevelyan: A Life in History* (London: Harper Collins, 1992), p. 124.
125 *Ibid.*, p. 125.
126 *The Times*, 14 February 1976, article by Lord Trevelyan.
127 *Ibid.*, pp. 227–228.
128 RA PS/GVI/C 022/005, letter of 26 October 1936 from Geoffrey Dawson to Major Alexander Hardinge.
129 RA PS/GVI/C 022/153, letter of 12 January 1937 from H. A. L. Fisher to Lord Wigram.
130 Ogg, D., *Herbert Fisher* (London: Edward Arnold, 1947), p. 133.
131 Fisher, H. A. L., *An Unfinished Autobiography* (Oxford: Oxford University Press, 1940), p. 109.
132 Church, R., *British Authors: A Twentieth Century Gallery* (Harlow: Longmans, Green & Co, 1943), pp. 98–99.
133 Private information.
134 RA PS/GVI/C 022/228, letter of 3 November 1936 from G. M. Trevelyan to Stanley Baldwin.
135 RA PS/GVI/C 022/229A, letter of 5 June 1941 from Owen Morshead to H. A. Hollond.
136 RA PS/GVI/C 022/229B, letter of 10 June 1941 from H. A. Hollond to Owen Morshead.
137 RA PS/GVI/C 022/230, letter of 12 June 1941 from Owen Morshead to Sir Alexander Hardinge.
138 RA PS/GVI/C 022/012B, letter of 18 June 1941 from Sir Alexander Hardinge to Owen Morshead.
139 Rowse, A. L., *A Cornishman Abroad* (London: Jonathan Cape, 1976), pp. 32–33.
140 *DNB 1941–1950*, p. 402.
141 *The Times*, 16 August 1963.
142 *The Guardian*, 16 August 1963.
143 Eyck, F., *Gooch: A Study in History and Politics* (Basingstoke: Macmillan, 1982), pp. 441–442.
144 *The Times*, 21 October 1963.
145 *The Times*, 2 September 1968.
146 *The Guardian*, 2 September 1968
147 Conversation with the author, 4 November 1974.
148 Ollard, R., *A Man of Contradictions: A Life of A. L. Rowse* (London: Penguin, 2000), pp. 246 and 315.
149 Letter of 9 October 1991 from A. L. Rowse to the author.
150 Letter of 29 October 1991 from A. L. Rowse to the author.
151 *The Independent*, 11 March 1997.
152 Church, R., *The Spoken Word* (London: Collins, 1955), pp. 308–309.
153 *Dominion* (Wellington), 24 March 1970.
154 *Landfall: A New Zealand Quarterly*, December 1971, p. 415.
155 Grayland, E., *More Famous New Zealanders* (Christchurch: Whitcombe & Tombs, 1972), p. 88.

156 Grayland, E., *More Famous New Zealanders* (Christchurch: Whitcombe & Tombs, 1972), p. 89.

157 Clark, K., *Another Part of the Wood* (London: John Murray, 1974), p. 211.

158 *Ibid.*, pp. 223–224.

159 *The Guardian*, 23 May 1983, tribute by Robert Waterhouse.

160 Clark, K., *Another Part of the Wood*, pp. 129 and 141.

161 *Ibid.*, pp. 175–176.

162 *Ibid.*, pp. 209–210.

163 *Ibid.*, p. 237.

164 *Ibid.*, p. 238.

165 Clark, K., *The Other Half* (London: John Murray, 1966), p. 10.

166 *Ibid.*, p. 21.

167 *Ibid.*, p. 76.

168 *Ibid.*, pp. 137–138.

169 *Ibid.*, p. 208.

170 *Ibid.*, p. 223.

171 Harris, N., *The Fly Away People (A Portrait Gallery of Outstanding Expatriate New Zealanders)* (London: Baynard-Hillier, 1971), p. 138.

172 *Te Marae* (London: New Zealand House, 1983), p. 3.

173 Hobson, H., *Indirect Journey* (London: Weidenfeld & Nicolson, 1978), p. 150.

174 Harris, N., *Fly Away People*, p. 143.

175 *The Times*, 4 April 1983, 'The Noblest Roman of Them All: 80th birthday profile', by Philip Howard.

176 *Oxford Magazine*, 13 November 1989, leading article.

177 *The Guardian*, 7 September 1989.

178 Edward Boyle, Lecture at the Royal Society of Arts, 4 December 1985.

179 *Orders and Medals Research Society Journal*, Spring 1977, article by the author on 'Honours for clergymen'.

180 *TLS*, 22 December 1995, review by Vivian Green.

181 BBC Radio 4, 5 April 1992.

182 *The Times*, 28 December 2001.

183 *TLS*, 3 July 1992, review by Antonia Phillips.

184 *The Independent*, 6 January 1990.

185 *The Times*, 6 November 2001.

186 *The Times*, 29 April 1984, profile by Clive Aslet.

187 *The Daily Telegraph*, 3 May 1993, interview with Sir Ernst Gombrich by Martin Gayford.

188 *The Independent*, 6 November 2001, obituary by Charles Hope.

Chapter 14 The Men of Affairs

1 RA PS/GV/J 926/2, letter of 1 June 1916 from A. J. Balfour to Lord Stamfordham.

2 RA PS/GV/J 926/3, letter of 2 June 1916 from Lord Stamfordham to A. J. Balfour.

3 RA PS/GV/J 1729/9, letter of 20 October 1921 from Sir Frederick Ponsonby to Sir Harry Legge.

4 RA PS/GV/J 1729/12, letter of 22 October 1921 from Sir Harry Legge to Sir Frederick Ponsonby.

5 RA PS/GV/J 1729/13, letter of 26 October 1921 from Sir Frederick Ponsonby to Sir Harry Legge.

6 RA PS/GV/J 2262/44 and 45, letter of 5 June 1930 from Lord Stamfordham to Geoffrey Dawson and reply of same day.

7 *Ibid.*

8 *CCOK*, letter of 26 May 1915 from Sir Harry Legge (Secretary of the Order of Merit) to Sir Douglas Dawson (Comptroller of the Lord Chamberlain's Department).

9 Haldane, R. B., *An Autobiography* (London: Hodder and Stoughton, 1929), p. 286.

10 RA PS/GV/J 1729/16, letter of 5 November 1921 from Earl of Rosebery to Lord Stamfordham.

11 *The Times*, 30 July 1956, centenary article by Lady Violet Bonham Carter.

12 *Ibid.*

13 Rose, K., *King George V* (London: Weidenfeld & Nicolson, 1983), p. 172.

14 Magnus, P., *King Edward the Seventh* (London: John Murray, 1964), p. 364.

15 Birkenhead, Earl of, *Contemporary Personalities* (London: Cassell, 1924), p. 78.

16 *Sunday Times*, 28 September 1980, review by Michael Howard of *Haldane: An Army Reformer* by E. M. Spiers.

17 *Ibid.*

18 *Ibid.*

19 Haldane, R. B., *An Autobiography* (London: Hodder and Stoughton, 1929), p. 285.

20 *Ibid.*

21 Nicolson, H., *King George the Fifth* (London: Constable, 1952), pp. 288–289.

22 Liddell Hart, B.H. *History of the First World War* (London: Cassell, 1970), p. 62.

23 Nicolson, H., *King George the Fifth* (London: Constable, 1952), p. 264.

24 Haldane, R. B., *An Autobiography* (London: Hodder and Stoughton, 1929), pp. 287–288.

25 *DNB* 1922–1930, p. 385.

26 RA PS/GV/J 2203/30, letter of 21 September 1928 from Viscount Esher to Lord Stamfordham.

27 *The Times*, 20 August 1928.

28 RA PS/GV/J 926/1, letter of 31 May 1916 from Lord Stamfordham to A. J. Balfour.

29 RA PS/GV/J 1729/25, letter of 15 March 1922 from Sir Arthur Balfour to Lord Stamfordham.

30 *DNB 1922–1930*, p. 43.

31 Birkenhead, Earl of, *Contemporary Personalities* (London: Cassell, 1924), p. 11.

32 Churchill, W. S., *Great Contemporaries* (Feltham: Odhams Press, 1947), p. 183.

33 *DNB 1922–1930*, p. 44.

34 Magnus, P., *King Edward the Seventh* (London: John Murray, 1964), p. 315.

35 *The Times*, 11 September 2001, article by Anthony Howard.

36 Rose, K., *King George V* (London: Weidenfeld & Nicolson, 1983), p. 269.

37 Churchill, W. S. *Great Contemporaries* (Feltham: Odhams Press, 1947), p. 224.

38 Dugdale, B., *Arthur James Balfour 1906–1930* (London: Hutchinson, 1939), pp. 256, 125 and 247.

39 Lloyd George, R., *Dame Margaret* (Melbourne: Allen & Unwin, 1947), p. 177.

40 BBC Radio 4, March 1986, interview with Lady Olwen Carey-Evans.

41 RA PS/GV/J 1487/1, letter of 5 August 1919 from Andrew Bonar Law to Lord Stamfordham.

42 RA PS/GV/J 1487/2, letter of 5 August 1919 from King George V to David Lloyd George.

43 Roskill, S., *Hankey: Man of Secrets*, Vol. II (London: Collins, 1972), p. 87.

44 Magnus, P., *King Edward the Seventh* (London: John Murray, 1964), pp. 430–431.

45 Churchill, W. S., *Victory* (Vol. 6 of Winston Churchill's War Speeches) (London: Cassell, 1946), pp. 89–90.

46 Churchill, W. S., *Victory* (Vol. 6 of Winston Churchill's War Speeches) (London: Cassell, 1946), p. 90.

47 *DNB 1941–1950*, p. 524.

48 *Ibid.*, p. 525.

49 Rose, K., *King George V* (London: Weidenfeld & Nicolson, 1983), pp. 200–201.

50 *Ibid.*, p. 247.

51 Jones, T., *A Diary with Letters 1931–1950* (Oxford: Oxford University Press, 1954), p. 169.

52 *The Times*, 7 December 1972, obituary of Frances, Countess Lloyd George.

53 *The Times*, 27 March 1945.

54 Churchill, W., *Victory* (Vol. 6 of Winston Churchill's War Speeches) (London: Cassell, 1946), p. 90.

55 RA PS/GVI/C 022/281, minute of 18 April 1944 from C. R. Attlee to W. S. Churchill.

56 RA PS/GVI/C 022/278C, note of 9 May 1944 from Sir Alan Lascelles to Owen Morshead.

57 *The Times Weekly Edition*, 14 June 1944.

58 MacKenzie, N., *The Letters of Sidney and Beatrice Webb*, Vol. III (Cambridge: Cambridge University Press/London School of Economics, 1978), p. 464.

59 Church, R., *The Spoken Word*, selection from *The Listener* (London: Collins, 1955), pp. 167–169.

60 *DNB 1941–1950*, p. 936.

61 *The Times*, 22 January 1958, article by Earl Attlee.

62 *Ibid.*

63 *DNB 1941–1950*, p. 939.

64 Seymour-Jones, C., *Beatrice Webb: Woman of Conflict* (London: Allison & Busby, 1992), reviews by Frances Partridge (*The Spectator*, 21 Mar 1992) and Anthony Howard (*Sunday Times*, 23 February 1992).

65 *Times Literary Supplement*, 17 March 2000, review by John Campbell of Professor Harrison's biography.

66 RA PS/GV/J 2203/29, memorandum of 18 September 1928 by Viscount Esher.

67 RA PS/GV/J 2203/30, letter of 21 September 1928 from Viscount Esher to Lord Stamfordham.

68 RA PS/GVI/C 022/194, letter of 22 November 1938 from John Masefield to Sir Alexander Hardinge.

69 RA PS/GVI/C 022/12b, letter of 18 June 1941 from Sir Alexander Hardinge to Owen Morshead.

70 RA PS/GVI/C 022/380, letter of 25 October 1945 from Sir Alan Lascelles to T. L. Rowan (10 Downing Street).

71 Gilbert, M., *Winston Churchill: Never Despair 1945–1965* (London: Minerva, 1990), p. 109.

72 RA PS/GVI/C 022/382, note of 8 November 1945 by Sir Alan Lascelles.

73 Gilbert, p. 178.

74 Wheeler Bennett, Sir J., *Action This Day: Working With Churchill* (London: Macmillan, 1968), p. 45.

75 Gilbert, pp. 823–824.

76 Rose, K., *King George V* (London: Weidenfeld & Nicolson, 1983), p. 264.

77 Gilbert, p. 1124.

78 Quoted by A. L. Rowse in *The English Spirit* (Basingstoke: Macmillan, 1944), p. 5.

79 *The Times*, 25 January 1965.

80 Churchill, W. S., *Thoughts and Adventures* (London: Odhams Press, 1947), p. 162.

81 *Evening Standard*, 13 January 1949.

82 *The Times*, 8 November 2002.
83 Cannadine, D., *In Churchill's Shadow* (Harmondsworth: Penguin, 2002), pp. 56–57.
84 Churchill, W. S., *Great Contemporaries* (London: Odhams Press, 1947), p. 259.
85 Information from Sir Edward Ford.
86 *Manchester Guardian Weekly*, 15 October 1953.
87 *The Times*, 17 October 2002, obituary of Grace Hamblin.
88 MacDonald, M., *Titans and Others* (London: Collins, 1972), p. 101.
89 Birkenhead, Earl of (ed.) 'Painting as a Pastime', in *The Hundred Best English Essays* (London: Cassell, 1929), p. 860.
90 *The Times*, 29 July 1964.
91 *The Times*, 25 January 1965.
92 Brain, R., *Tea with Walter de la Mare* (London: Faber and Faber, 1957), p. 62.
93 Jenkins, R., *Churchill* (Basingstoke: Macmillan, 2001), p. 591.
94 *The Times*, 7 January 1960, letter from Sir George Cunningham.
95 Birkenhead, Earl of, *Halifax* (London: Hamish Hamilton, 1965), pp. 310–311.
96 *Ibid.*, p. 312.
97 Roberts, A., *The Holy Fox* (London: Papermac, 1992), p. 70.
98 *Ibid.*, p. 308.
99 *Hansard* (House of Lords), 26 January 1960, columns 627–628.
100 Roberts, A., *The Holy Fox* (London: Papermac, 1992), p. 307.
101 RA PS/GVI/C 022/447, telegram of 2 January 1947 from Field Marshal J. C. Smuts to Sir Alan Lascelles.
102 *DNB 1941–1950*, p. 803.
103 *The Times*, 25 July 1950, letter from Sir Evelyn Wrench.
104 RA PS/GVI/C 022/455, letter of 10 October 1947 from Marquess of Salisbury to Sir Alan Lascelles.
105 RA PS/GVI/C 022/456, letter of 14 October 1947 from Sir Eric Machtig to Sir Alan Lascelles.
106 Pickersgill, J. W. and Forster, D. F., *The Mackenzie King Record*, Vol. 4 (Toronto: University of Toronto Press), pp. 90–92.
107 *Ibid.*, p. 100.
108 *Ibid.*, pp. 99–102.
109 Massey, V., *What's Past is Prologue* (Toronto: Macmillan, 1963), p. 504.
110 *DNB 1941–1950*, p. 459.
111 *Ibid.*, pp. 461–462.
112 *Ibid.*, p. 460.
113 Bradford S., *George VI* (London: Fontana, 1991), p. 372.
114 *The Times*, 24 July 1950.
115 *DNB 1941–1950*, p. 462.
116 Hutchison, B., *Mackenzie King: The Incredible Canadian* (London: Longmans Green, 1953), p. 450.
117 *The Times*, 22 November 1989, obituary of P. C. Stacey, author of *A Double Life, The Private World of Mackenzie King*.
118 RA PS/GVI/C 022/585, letter of 1 November 1951 from King George VI to C. R. Attlee.
119 BBC Radio 4, 11 August 1993, Tony Benn Tapes.
120 Wheeler-Bennett, J., *King George VI* (Basingstoke: Macmillan, 1958), p. 757.
121 *The Observer*, 26 September 1982, review of Kenneth Harris' *Attlee*.
122 *The Times*, 23 December 1976, letter from Sir William Hayter.
123 Attlee, C. R., *As It Happened* (London: William Heinemann, 1954), pp. 20–21.
124 Harris, K., *Attlee* (London: Weidenfeld & Nicolson, 1982), p. 569.
125 *Sunday Times*, 26 September 1982, review by John Vincent of Kenneth Harris' *Attlee*.

126 Williams, F., *A Prime Minister Remembers* (London: Heinemann, 1961), p. 4.
127 *The Times*, 26 May 1993, article by Robert Rhodes James.
128 *The Guardian*, 9 October 1967.
129 Dellar, G., *Attlee as I Knew Him* (London: Tower Hamlets Library Service, 1983), p. 11.
130 Thatcher, M., *The Path to Power* (London: Harper Collins, 1995), p. 69.
131 Dellar, p. 28.
132 *The Times*, 22 November 1958, leading article.
133 Samuel, Viscount, *Memoirs* (Cresset Press, 1945), p. 11.
134 *Sunday Times*, 5 March 1989.
135 BBC Radio 4, *Parliamentary Questions*, July 2002.
136 *DNB 1961–1970*, p. 922.
137 *Sunday Times*, 19 January 1992, review by Anthony Howard of Wasserstein's biography.
138 *Hansard* (Canadian House of Commons), 16 May 1973, p. 3832.
139 *The Times*, 28 May 1971.
140 Munro, J. A. and Inglis, A. I. (eds), *Mike: Memoirs of Lester Pearson, Vol. 3, 1957–1968* (London: Victor Gollancz, 1975), p. 302.
141 Munro, J. A. and Inglis, A. I. (eds), *The International Years*, Vol. 2 (1948–57) of *Memoirs of Lester B. Pearson* (London: Victor Gollancz, 1974), p. 103.
142 *DNB 1971–1980*, p. 663.
143 Munro, J. A. and Inglis, A. I. (eds), *Mike: Memoirs of Lester Pearson, Vol. 3, 1957–1968* (London: Victor Gollancz, 1975), p. 302.
144 *Ibid.*, p. 303.
145 *The Listener*, 8 January 1987, article by Peter Hennessy.
146 Horne, A., *Macmillan 1957–1968* (Basingstoke: Macmillan, 1989), p. 605.
147 *The Times*, 11 April 1964.
148 *The Times*, 15 January 1968.
149 *The Times*, 14 July 1973.
150 Horne, p. 572.
151 Edwards, R. D., *Harold Macmillan: A Life in Pictures* (Basingstoke: Macmillan, 1983), p. 167.
152 *Ibid.*, Introduction by Alistair Horne.
153 Horne, p. 572.
154 Private information.
155 *Daily Telegraph*, 2 April 1976.
156 Horne, p. 622.
157 *The Times*, 20 February 1984.
158 *The Times*, 26 April 1992, review by Anthony Howard of *The Macmillans* by R. Davenport-Hines.
159 Harris, K., *Attlee* (London: Weidenfeld & Nicolson, 1982), p. 557.
160 *The Listener*, 13 December 1984.
161 *DNB 1986–1990*, p. 279.
162 *Ibid.*, p. 280.
163 *The Times*, 20 March 2003.
164 *DNB 1986–1990*, p. 281.
165 Mallaby, G., *From My Level* (London: Hutchinson, 1965), p. 62.
166 *Sunday Times*, 9 October 1988, review by Enoch Powell.
167 *The Times*, 18 April 2003, article by Michael Binyon.
168 *The Times*, 18 April 2002, extract from *Queen and Country* by W. Shawcross.
169 *The Times*, 20 April 1989.
170 *Sunday Times*, 29 October 2000, extracts from J. Mortimer's *The Summer of a Doormouse*.
171 Jenkins, R., *A Life at the Centre* (London: Papermac, 1994), p. 57.

172 *Sunday Times*, 19 May 1996.
173 *The Times*, 23 July 1994, article by Roy Jenkins.
174 Hardinge, Lord, *Old Diplomacy* (London: John Murray, 1947), p. 125.
175 *DNB 1912–1921*, p. 25.
176 *The Times*, 16 September 1901.
177 Lee, Sir Sidney, *King Edward VII*, Vol. II (Basingstoke: Macmillan, 1927), pp. 534–535.
178 RA PS/GVI/C 022/405, letter of 9 April 1946 from Lord Keynes to Sir Alan Lascelles.
179 RA PS/GVI/C 022/408, note of 9 May 1946 from Sir Alan Lascelles to Captain Ritchie (Press Secretary to the King).
180 RA PS/GVI/C 022/545, letter of 10 October 1950 from Sir Alexander Cadogan to Sir Alan Lascelles.
181 Dilks, D. (ed.), *The Diaries of Sir Alexander Cadogan OM, 1938–1945* (London: Cassell, 1971), p. 631.
182 *Ibid.*, pp. 286–288.
183 *Ibid.*, p. 16.
184 *Balliol College Record*, July 1969, obituary notice by Lord Gore-Booth.
185 Dilks, p. 721.
186 *Ibid.*, p. 722.
187 *The Times*, 22 March 1950.
188 Dilks, p. 211.
189 RA PS/GVI/C 022/52, note of 5 November 1941 by Sir Alexander Hardinge.
190 *The Times*, 31 May 1956.
191 Cell, J.W., *Hailey: A study in British Imperialism 1872–1969* (Cambridge: Cambridge University Press, 1992).
192 *The Times*, 3 June 1969.
193 *Ibid.*
194 Cell, pp. xiii–xiv.
195 *DNB 1961–1970*, p. 473.
196 Wheeler-Bennett, J., *John Anderson, Viscount Waverley* (Basingstoke: Macmillan, 1962), pp. 403–406.
197 *The Times*, 9 December 1957.
198 Wheeler-Bennett, p. 16.
199 *Ibid.*, p. 39.
200 *Ibid.*, p. 301.
201 *Ibid.*, p. 354.
202 *Ibid.*, p. 375.
203 Clark, K., *The Other Half* (London: John Murray, 1977), p. 133.
204 *Sunday Times*, 5 January 1958.
205 *DNB 1951–1960*, p. 23.
206 *Sydney Morning Herald*, 30 May 1963.
207 *Melbourne Herald*, 30 May 1963.
208 *Melbourne Age*, 31 May 1963.
209 *Sydney Morning Herald*, 30 May 1963.
210 Menzies, R., Sir, *Measure of the Years* (Sydney: Cassell Australia, 1970), p. 244.
211 Letter of 31 May 1963 from Sir Owen Dixon to the author.
212 *The Times*, 10 July 1972
213 *The Times*, 10 June 1986
214 *The Times*, 16 April 2002
215 Allison, R. and Riddell S. (eds), *The Royal Encyclopaedia* (Basingstoke: Macmillan, 1991), p. 451.
216 *The Times*, 2 March 2002.
217 MacDonald, M., *People and Places* (London: Collins, 1969), p. 22.

218 MacDonald, M., *People and Places* (London: Collins, 1969), p. 128.
219 MacDonald, M., *Titans and Others* (London: Collins, 1972), p. 85.
220 *Ibid.*, pp. 176–179.
221 *DNB 1981–1985*, p. 256.
222 MacDonald, 1972, pp. 214–215.
223 Address at memorial service in Westminster Abbey, 3 March 1981.
224 *The Listener*, 7 February 1985, article by Peter Hennessy.
225 *The Times*, 6 July 1982.
226 *Sunday Telegraph*, quoting from *The Birth of NATO* by Sir N. Henderson.
227 Letter of 3 November 1977 from Lord Franks to the author.
228 *Daily Telegraph*, 16 October 1992.
229 *Ibid.*
230 Letter of 2 April 1957 from Sir Oliver Franks to the author.
231 *The Times*, 17 October 1992.
232 *The Times*, 6 March 1999.
233 Denning, Lord, *The Family Story* (London: Hamlyn, 1982).
234 Letter of 14 January 1983 from Lord Denning to the author.
235 *The Times*, 24 May 1982.
236 *The Times*, 26 January 1999.
237 *The Times*, 26 January 1999, article by Frances Gibb.
238 *The Independent*, 6 March 1999.

Chapter 15 The Humanitarians

1 *The Times*, 30 November 1907.
2 Letter of 12 May 1979 from (Patience) Lady Baden-Powell to the author.
3 RA PS/GV/J 2325/24, letter of 23 April 1931 from Owen Morshead to Sir Clive Wigram.
4 RA PS/GV/J 2203/44, letter of 4 November 1928 from Geoffrey Dawson to Lord Stamfordham.
5 RA PS/GVI/C 022/158, letter of 4 May 1937 from Lord Baden-Powell to Sir Alexander Hardinge.
6 *The Independent*, 1 August 1992.
7 *The Times*, 3 August 1992.
8 *The Times*, 26 December 1992.
9 Letter of 8 January 1990 from Dame Cicely Saunders to the author.
10 *The Times*, 18 June 1999.
11 *The Times*, 30 June 1999, letter from Lord St John of Fawsley.
12 *The Times*, 26 May 1999.
13 *The Times*, 18 June 1999.
14 *Daily Telegraph*, 4 June 1999.
15 *Daily Telegraph*, 18 June 1999.

Chapter 16 The Women

1 CCOK, letter of 19 February 1903 from Sir Francis Knollys to Sir Arthur Ellis (Secretary of the Order of Merit).
2 CCOK, letter of 20 February 1903 from Sir Arthur Ellis to Sir Francis Knollys.
3 CCOK, letter of 20 February 1903 from Sir Francis Knollys to Sir Arthur Ellis.
4 RA VIC/R 28/55, letter of 10 June 1907 from Sir Henry Campbell-Bannerman to Sir Francis Knollys.
5 Hibbert, C., *Edward VII* (London: Allen Lane, 1976), p. 283.
6 *The Times*, 30 November 1907.
7 CCOK, letter of 1 December 1907 from Sir Francis Knollys to Sir Douglas Dawson.

8 Strachey, L., *Eminent Victorians* (London: Chatto & Windus, 1974), p. 189.
9 *Ibid.*, p. 181.
10 CCOK, Undated Terms of Reference.
11 CCOK, report of meeting at Lord Chamberlain's Office, 3 April 1911.
12 Letter of 2 May 1911 from Sir Douglas Dawson to Mr H. Farnham Burke.
13 RA PS/GV/J 1766/7, letter of 20 February 1922 from Lilian Braithwaite to Sir Frederick Ponsonby (Keeper of the Privy Purse).
14 RA PS/GV/J 1766/2, letter of 17 February 1922 from Lord Stamfordham to Sir Arthur Stanley (Chairman, Joint Council, British Red Cross Society and Order of St John).
15 RA PS/GVI/C 022/11, letter of 3 June 1941 from Owen Morshead to Sir Alexander Hardinge.
16 Cole, M., *Beatrice Webb* (London: Longmans Green & Co, 1945), p. 187.
17 Mackenzie, N. (ed.), *The Letters of Sidney and Beatrice Webb, Vol. III,* (Cambridge: Cambridge University Press/London School of Economics, 1978), p. 464.
18 Nicolson, N. (ed.), *Diaries and Letters, 1939–45* of Harold Nicolson (London: Collins, 1967), p. 419.
19 Nicolson, N. (ed.), *Diaries and Letters, 1945–62* of Harold Nicolson (London: Collins, 1968), p. 382.
20 *Year Book of the Royal Society 2001.*

Chapter 17 The Honorary Members

1 CCOK, letter of 24 November 1905 from Lord Knollys to Sir Arthur Davidson and memorandum of 3 December 1905 by Davidson.
2 *The Times*, 2 December 1918.
3 RA PS/GV/J 1581/2, letter of 22 January 1920 from Lord Derby to Lord Cromer.
4 *The Times*, 13 June 1945.
5 Eisenhower, D. D., *At Ease: Stories I tell to Friends* (New York: Doubleday, 1967), pp. 279–280.
6 RA PS/GVI/C 022/369, letter of 12 June 1945 from King George VI to Dwight D. Eisenhower.
7 Massey, V., CH, *What's Past Is Prologue* (Toronto: Macmillan, 1963), p. 496.
8 Eisenhower, 1967.
9 *Sunday Times*, 28 October 1951.
10 *The Times*, 29 March 1969.
11 *The Guardian*, 29 March 1969.
12 *Daily Telegraph*, 29 March 1969.
13 Winant, J. G., *A Letter from Grosvenor Square* (London: Hodder & Stoughton, 1947), p. 19.
14 Churchill, W. S., *The Second World War, Vol. IV* (London: Cassell, 1951), p. 178.
15 Soames, C., *Clementine Churchill* (London: Cassell, 1979), p. 353.
16 Raymond Seitz in radio interview, 12 May 1991.
17 Jenkins, R., *Churchill* (Basingstoke: Macmillan, 2001), pp. 652–653.
18 *The Times*, 1 January 1947 and 5 November 1947.
19 RA PS/GVI/C 022/420, letter from Sir Orme Sargeant to Sir Alan Lascelles, 14 May 1946.
20 *The Times*, 20 October 1955.
21 *The Times*, 13 June 1963.
22 Gopal, S., *Radhakrishnan* (Delhi: Oxford University Press India, 1992), p. 10.

23 *Daily Telegraph*, 17 April 1975.
24 *Daily Telegraph*, 21 November 1983.
25 *The Guardian*, 25 November 1983.
26 *The Times*, 6 September 1997.
27 *The Times*, 18 and 20 March 1995.
28 *The Times*, 21 March 1995.
29 *The Times*, 26 November 1962.
30 RA PS/GV/J 248/A, letter of 13 June 1911 from Lord Knollys to Vaughan Nash (10 Downing Street).

Chapter 19 The Links

1 MacDonald, M., *Titans and Others* (London: Collins, 1972), p. 120.
2 RA PS/GV/J 1978/68, memorandum of 23 December 1924 from Lord Stamfordham to the Registrar and Secretary of the Order of Merit.
3 RA PS/GVI/C 022/309, letter of 14 August 1942 from J. M. Martin to Sir Alexander Hardinge.
4 RA PS/GVI/C 022/233, letter of 3 November 1942 from G. M. Trevelyan to Sir Alexander Hardinge.
5 RA PS/GVI/C 022/579, letter of 26 May 1951 from G. M. Trevelyan to Sir Alan Lascelles.

Chapter 20 Those Who Turned It Down

1 Carrington, C., *Rudyard Kipling* (London: Pelican Books, 1970), p. 526.
2 Lycett, A., *Rudyard Kipling* (London: Weidenfeld & Nicolson, 1999), p. 470, from letter of 2 July 1917 from Kipling to Bonar Law.
3 RA VIC/W 66/76a, letter of 2 June 1909 from Viscount Esher to Lord Knollys.
4 RA PS/GV/J 866/6, letter of 15 December 1921 from Lord Stamfordham to Rudyard Kipling.
5 RA PS/GV/J 866/7 and 8, letter of 17 December 1921 from Rudyard Kipling to Lord Stamfordham and latter's letter of 19 December 1921 to J. T. Davies (10 Downing Street).
6 RA PS/GV/J 866/21, letter of 18 January 1924 from Lord Stamfordham to Rudyard Kipling.
7 RA PS/GV/J 866/22, letter of 21 January 1924 from Rudyard Kipling to Lord Stamfordham.
8 Gore, J., *King George V: A Personal Memoir* (London: John Murray, 1941), p. 338.
9 Rose, K., *King George V* (Basingstoke: Macmillan, 1984), p. 394.
10 RA PS/GV/J 2203/115, letter of 23 February 1929 from A. E. Housman to Lord Stamfordham.
11 RA PS/GV/J 2203/34, letter of 29 October 1928 from Robert Vansittart to Lord Stamfordham.
12 RA PS/GV/J 1978/13, letter of 19 November 1924 from Sir Frederic Kenyon to Lord Stamfordham.
13 RA PS/GV/J 2203/41, letter of 2 November 1928 from Owen Morshead to Lord Stamfordham.
14 RA PS/GV/J 2203/44, letter of 4 November 1928 from Geoffrey Dawson to Lord Stamfordham.
15 Richards, G., *Housman 1897–1936* (Oxford: Oxford University Press, 1941), pp. 252–253 and 446.
16 RA PS/GV/J 1752/105, memorandum of 22 December 1921 by Lord Stamfordham.

17 RA PS/GV/J 1752/113, letter of 25 December 1921 from F. H. Mitchell (Press Secretary to the King) to Lord Stamfordham.
18 Pearson, H., *Bernard Shaw* (London: Collins, 1948), p. 403. (Originally published in 1942.)
19 Laurence, D. H. (ed.), *Bernard Shaw: Collected Letters, 1926–1950* (London: Viking, 1988), p. 769.
20 *Ibid.*, pp. 783–784.
21 *Ibid.*, p. 782.
22 *The Times*, 9 July 1996.
23 Sinclair, A., *Francis Bacon: His Life and Violent Times* (New York: Crown Publishers, 1993), p. 249.
24 Private information.

Chapter 21 The Unappointed –Who Would Not Have Disgraced It

1 Priestley, J. B., *Particular Pleasures* (London: Heinemann, 1975), p. 157.
2 Ziegler, P., *Mountbatten* (London: Collins, 1975), p. 671.
3 RA PS/GVI/C 022/107, memorandum of 28 August 1938 by Sir Alexander Hardinge.
4 RA PS/GVI/J 470/2, letter of 11 March 1912 from Viscount Haldane to Viscount Knollys.
5 RA PS/GVI/C 022/25, letter of 9 April 1944 from Sir Alfred Egerton (Secretary, Royal Society) to Sir Alan Lascelles.
6 *Independent Magazine*, 30 December 1995.
7 RA PS/GVI/C 022/180, letter of 2 December 1938 from Sir J. J. Thomson to Sir Alexander Hardinge.
8 RA PS/GVI/C 022/509, letter of 24 September 1941 from Sir William Bragg to Sir Alexander Hardinge.
9 RA PS/GVI/C 022/123B, note of 24 April 1944 by Sir Alan Lascelles.
10 *DNB 1971–1980*, p. 889. Entry by R. V. Jones, CH.
11 RA PS/GVI/C 022/69, letter of 24 April 1938 from Sir Frank Smith to Sir Alexander Hardinge.
12 *DNB 1971–1980*, p. 881. Entry by A. G. Pugsley.
13 RA PS/GVI/C 022/25, letter of 9 April 1944 from Sir Alfred Egerton (Secretary, Royal Society) to Sir Alan Lascelles.
14 RA PS/GV/J 1765/1, letter of 16 February 1922 from Earl of Crawford and Balcarres, Lord Stamfordham.
15 *Ibid.*
16 *Ibid.*
17 *Compact DNB*, p. 2533.
18 Greene, G., *A Sort of Life* (Harmondsworth: Penguin, 1974), p. 141.
19 *The Times*, February 1960.
20 RA PS/GVI/C 022/140, letter of 27 January 1944 from Sir Alan Lascelles to J. M. Martin (10 Downing Street).
21 RA PS/GVI/C 022/031, memorandum of 27 February 1935 from Sir Clive Wigram to the Keeper of the Privy Purse.
22 RA PS/GV/J 248 A, letters of 13 June 1911 from Lord Knollys to Vaughan Nash (10 Downing Street) and of 14 June from Nash to Knollys.
23 RA PS/GV/J 248A/2, letter of 25 May 1911 from A. J. Balfour to Lord Knollys.
24 Meyers, J., *Joseph Conrad* (London: John Murray, 1991), p. 355.
25 RA PS/GV/J 1978/40, letter of 14 December 1924 from Viscount Esher to Lord Stamfordham.
26 RA PS/GV/J 1752/105, memorandum of 22 December 1921 by Lord Stamfordham.

27 RA PS/GV/J 1752/113, letter of 25 December 1921 from F. H. Mitchell to Lord Stamfordham.
28 RA PS/GV/J 1978/41, letter of 15 December 1924 from Lord Stamfordham to Archbishop Randall Davidson.
29 RA PS/GV/J 1978/44, letter of 16 December 1924 from the Marquess of Crewe to Lord Stamfordham.
30 Morton, J. B., *Hilaire Belloc* (London: Hollis & Carter, 1955), p. 164.
31 Pound, R., *A. P. Herbert.*
32 *The Spectator*, 6 May 1966, article by Auberon Waugh.
33 Graves, R., *The Crowning Privilege: the Clark Lectures 1954–55* (London: Cassell, 1955), p. 20.
34 RA PS/GV/J 2203/31, letter of 14 October 1928 from Rudyard Kipling to Lord Stamfordham.
35 RA PS/GVI/C 022/194, letter of 22 November 1938 from John Masefield to Sir Alexander Hardinge.
36 RA PS/GVI/C 022/486–7, letter of 6 October 1947 from Desmond MacCarthy to Sir Alan Lascelles and enclosure.
37 RA PS/GVI/C 022/003 undated note.
38 RA PS/GVI/C 022/035A, memorandum of 24 October 1943 from Owen Morshead to Sir Alan Lascelles.
39 RA PS/GVI/C 022/034, note of October 1943 from Sir Eric Maclagan to Sir Alan Lascelles.
40 RA PS/GVI/C 022/067, letter of 26 October 1943 from Sir Alan Lascelles to R. M. Barrington-Ward (*The Times*).
41 RA PS/GVI/C 022/477B, memorandum of 4 August 1947 from Sir Owen Morshead to Sir Alan Lascelles.
42 RA PS/GVI/C 022/486–7, letter of 6 October 1947 from Desmond MacCarthy to Sir Alan Lascelles and enclosure.
43 Ziegler, P., *Mountbatten* (London: Collins, 1985), p. 671.
44 *Daily Telegraph*, 7 January 1989, article by Gordon Watkins.
45 *Sunday Times*, 20 June 1982, review by Frederic Raphael of *Henry: An Appreciation of Henry Williamson* by Daniel Farson.
46 *The Times*, 2 June 2000, review of *George Moore* by Adrian Frazier.
47 RA PP/EVII/B 6921, correspondence between Sir Lewis Morris and Lord Knollys, 1904–06.
48 Jones, T., *A Diary with Letters* (Oxford: Oxford University Press, 1954), p. 136.
49 *Daily Telegraph*, 28 August 1975, review by Anthony Powell.
50 *The Times*, 12 March 2002.
51 RA PS/GV/J 2203/30, letter of 21 September 1928 from Viscount Esher to Lord Stamfordham.
52 RA PS/GV/J 2203/46, letter of 7 November 1928 from Lord Stamfordham to Earl of Balfour.
53 RA PS/GV/J 2203/51, letter of 10 November 1928 from Earl of Balfour to Lord Stamfordham.
54 Ayer, A.J., *Wittgenstein* (London: Weidenfeld & Nicolson, 1985), p. 7.
55 *Ibid.*, p. 12.
56 *Ibid.*, p. 16.
57 *New Statesman*, 12 October 1990.
58 *DNB 1971–1980*, p. 76.
59 RA PS/GV/J 1978/13, letter of 19 November 1924 from Earl of Crawford and Balcarres to Lord Stamfordham.
60 RA PS/GVI/C 022/56, letter of 18 May 1933 from J. A. Barlow (10 Downing Street) to Sir Clive Wigram.

61 RA PS/GVI/C 022/11 and 12B, letter of 3 June 1941 from Owen Morshead to Sir Alexander Hardinge and reply of 18 June.

62 RA PS/GVI/C 022/088, letter of 12 December 1941 from Sir Alexander Hardinge to J. M. Martin (10 Downing Street).

63 RA PS/GVI/C 022/096, letter of 24 October 1942 from Sir Alexander Hardinge to Sir John Anderson.

64 RA PS/GVI/C 022/100 C,D,G,H, letters of March and May 1944 between Sir Alan Lascelles and G. M. Trevelyan and Sir Richard Livingstone.

65 *The Times*, 28 December 2001.

66 *The Times* and *The Independent*, 2 November 2000.

67 Personal correspondence with the author.

68 *The Times*, 6 October 1997.

69 *The Times*, 28 November 1960.

70 *Tribune*, 6 February 1953 (reproducing an article from the *Political Quarterly* in 1934).

71 Churchill, R. S, *Winston S. Churchill, Vol. II* (London: Heinemann, 1967), p. 349.

72 RA PS/GVI/C 022/42 and 44, telegram of 25 May 1943 from Winston Churchill to Sir Alexander Hardinge and reply of 28 May.

73 *Ibid*.

74 Author's conversation with Mrs Sheila Lochhead, 10 December 1985.

75 Shuckburgh, E., *Descent to Suez (Diaries 1951–1956)* (London: Weidenfeld & Nicolson, 1986), p. 70.

76 Ziegler, P., *Wilson* (London: Weidenfeld & Nicolson, 1993), p. 499.

77 *Daily Mail*, 27 November 1977, review by Peter Lewis of *Solitary in the Ranks* by H. Montgomery Hyde.

Chapter 23 Rarely with the Jam Rations

1 Harrod, R. F., *John Maynard Keynes* (London: Pelican Books, 1972), p. 114.

Chapter 24 The Insignia: Where Have All the Medals Gone?

1 CCOK, memorandum of 27 May 1915 from Sir Frederick Ponsonby (Keeper of the Privy Purse) to H. Trendell (Lord Chamberlain's Office).

2 Lewis, J. *Something Hidden: A Biography of Wilder Penfield* (Ontario: Doubleday Canada, 1981), p. 230.

3 CCOK, letter of 20 January 1903 from Sir Arthur Ellis to Sir Arthur Davidson.

4 CCOK, memorandum of 9 November 1916 from Sir Harry Legge.

5 CCOK, letter of 24 April 1920 from Sir Harry Legge to Sir Arthur Davidson.

6 CCOK, memorandum of 2 June 1920 from Douglas Dawson to Lord Stamfordham.

7 CCOK, memorandum of 13 May 1921; approved by the King on 23 May.

8 CCOK, letter of 10 March 1972 from Secretary of the Central Chancery to Secretary of the Order of Merit.

9 Letters of 16 and 18 June 1976 from Lord Clark to Sir Edward Ford.

10 Letter of 21 February 1994 from Alan Clark to the author.

11 Letter of 16 June 1984 from Mother Teresa to Her Majesty the Queen.

12 FO TPD 2/145/1, letter of 15 January 1967 from Sir Michael Adeane to Lees Mayall (Protocol Department, Foreign Office).

13 CCOK, letter of 22 July 1902 from Lord Knollys to Sir Arthur Ellis.

14 Gooding, N. (ed.), *The Medals Yearbook* (London: Naval & Military Press, 1995), pp. 7 and 10.

Chapter 25 The Standing of the Order

1 Prochoska, F., *The Republic of Britain* (Harmondsworth: Penguin, 2000), p. 166.
2 CCOK, letter of 4 October 1977 from Ben Nicholson to Sir Edward Ford.
3 CCOK, letter of 25 November 1977 from Earl Mountbatten of Burma to Sir Edward Ford.
4 *The Times*, 18 November 1977.
5 Responses to letter of 15 December 1977 from Sir Edward Ford to all OMs.
6 *Ibid*.
7 *Ibid*.
8 CCOK, letter of 21 June 1979 from Sir Isaiah Berlin to Sir Edward Ford.
9 Medawar, J., *A Very Decided Preference* (Oxford: Oxford University Press, 1990), p. 217.
10 *The Times*, 24 June 1987.
11 Martin, S., 'The Order of Merit: 85 Years Old', *Journal of the Orders and Medals Research Society* 27/3 (1988), pp. 182–187.
12 Martin, S., 'The Centenary of the Order of Merit: 1902–2002', *Journal of the Orders and Medals Research Society* 42/1 (2003), pp. 33–35.
13 RA PS/GV/J 1729/2, letter of 5 October 1921 from Lord Stamfordham to Viscount Bryce.
14 RA PS/GV/J 1729/3, letter of 13 October 1921 from Viscount Bryce to Lord Stamfordham.
15 *Daily Telegraph*, 21 December 1990.
16 RA VIC/X 32/268–274, letters of 28 November–7 December 1906 from Hon. John Fortescue to Sir Arthur Davidson.
17 *Ibid*.
18 *Ibid*.
19 *Ibid*.
20 *Ibid*.
21 *Ibid*.
22 *The Times*, 2 August 2002, quoted in article by Simon Tait.
23 RA PS/GV/J 2569/3, letter of 13 August 1931 from Private Secretary to Sir George Clausen.
24 CCOK, letters exchanged, from 24 February to 9 April 1942, between Charles Tennyson and Sir Arthur Erskine.
25 Kent, W., *John Burns, Labour's Lost Leader* (London: Williams & Norgate, 1950), p. 376.
26 RA PS/GV/J 866/11, letter of 12 January [1922] from H. W. Massingham to Lord Stamfordham.
27 RA PS/GV/J 1752/58.
28 RA PS/GV/J 1764/1, page from *The New Statesman*, 28 January 1922.
29 *Ibid*.
30 Cannadine, D., *G. M. Trevelyan* (London: Harper Collins, 1992), p. 22.
31 Risk, J. C., *British Orders and Decorations* (London: JB Hayward, 1973), p. 71. (Reprint of original 1946 edition.)
32 *Sunday Times*, 29 January 1956.
33 Hartcup, G. and Allibone, T. E., *Cockcroft and the Atom* (Bristol: Adam Hilger Ltd, 1984), p. 246.
34 *Ibid*., p. 215.
35 *Ibid*., p. 246.
36 *The Times*, 20 October 1955.
37 *The Times*, 23 April 1960.
38 *The Times*, 16 August 1963.
39 *The Guardian*, 16 August 1963.

40 *The Guardian*, 3 January 1964.
41 *The Observer*, 1 January 1967.
42 *New Statesman*, 20 January 1967.
43 *The Listener*, 13 June 1985.
44 *The Times*, 24 December 1986.
45 *The Independent*, 5 January 1992.
46 *The Independent*, 31 December 2001, article by Philip Collins.
47 *The Times*, 23 September 1988, review by Simon Tait.
48 *The Economist*, 6 July 1991.
49 *The Times*, 29 January 1992.
50 *Sunday Times*, 5 January 1958, tribute to Viscount Waverley OM.
51 Letter of 3 June 1981 from editorial office of *The Times* to the author.
52 Letters of 4 and 27 May 1987 from Miss Margaret Drabble to the author.
53 *The Order of Merit*, a play for radio by Richard Austin (BBC, Radio 4, 1 September 1980).
54 Waugh, E., *Vile Bodies* (Harmondsworth: Penguin, 1938), p. 131.
55 Greene, G., *It's a Battlefield* (London: Pan Books, 1953), p. 82.
56 *Ibid.*, p. 85.
57 *The Times*, 4 April 1991, review by Anthony Quinton.
58 CCOK, letter of 30 November 1943 from Sir Joseph Causton & Sons and LCO reply of 8 December.
59 CCOK, correspondence February–June 1966 between Sir Norman Gwatkin and A. L. Mayall (FCO).

Chapter 26 The Future of the Order

1 RA PS/GV/J 1765/1, letter of 16 February 1922 from Earl of Crawford and Calcarres to Lord Stamfordham.
2 *The Times*, 8 September 1999.
3 *The Times*, 14 October 1996, article by Nigel Hawkes.
4 *The Times*, 2 April 1992.

Appendix D

1 CCOK, letter of 17 September 1971 from Sir Michael Adeane to Rear-Admiral Sir Christopher Bonham-Carter.

BIBLIOGRAPHY

Ackroyd, P., *T. S. Eliot* (London: Hamish Hamilton, 1984).

Arthur, G., *Life of Lord Kitchener*, Vols I–III (London: Macmillan, 1920).

Arthur, G., *Lord Haig* (London: Heinemann, 1928).

Ash, R., *Alma-Tadema* (London: Shire Publications, 1973).

Ashby, E. and Anderson, M., *Portrait of Haldane* (London: Macmillan, 1974).

Asquith, C., *Portrait of Barrie* (London: James Barrie, 1954).

Attlee, C. R., *As It Happened* (London: Heinemann, 1954).

Augustiny, W., *The Road to Lambarené* (London: Frederick Muller, 1956).

Ayer, A. J., *Russell* (London: Fontana, 1972).

Barrie, J. M., *Courage: Rectorial Address at St Andrews University* (London: Hodder and Stoughton, 1922).

Barrie, J. M., *The Greenwood Hat, being a Memoir of James Anon* (London: Peter Davies, 1937).

Bateman, C., *G. F. Watts, RA* (London: George Bell, 1901).

Beauman, N., *E. M. Forster* (London: Hodder & Stoughton, 1993).

Berlin, I., *Mr Churchill in 1940* (London: John Murray, 1949).

Berthoud, R., *Graham Sutherland* (London: Faber & Faber, 1982).

Berthoud, R., *The Life of Henry Moore* (New York: EP Dutton, 1987).

Birkenhead, Earl of, *Halifax* (London: Hamish Hamilton, 1965).

Birkenhead, Lord, *Rudyard Kipling* (London: Weidenfeld & Nicolson, 1978).

Birkin, A., *J. M. Barrie and the Lost Boys* (London: Constable, 1979).

Blake, R. (ed.), *The Private Papers of Douglas Haig, 1914–1919* (London: Eyre & Spottiswoode 1952).

Blond, G., *Admiral Togo* (London: Jarrolds, 1961).

Blumenson, M., *Eisenhower* (London: Pan/Ballantine, 1973).

Blunt, W., *England's Michelangelo* (London: Hamish Hamilton, 1975).

Bowle, J., *Viscount Samuel* (London: Victor Gollancz, 1957).

Boyle, A., *Trenchard* (London: Collins, 1962).

Boyle, A., *No Passing Glory* (London: Collins, 1965).

Braddon, R., *Cheshire VC* (London: Evans Brothers, 1954).

Bragg, M., *Laurence Olivier* (London: Sceptre, 1989).

Bragg, W., *The Universe of Light* (London: G. Bell & Sons, 1945).

Brain, R., *Tea with Walter de la Mare* (London: Faber & Faber, 1957).

Braine, J., *J. B. Priestley* (London: Weidenfeld & Nicolson, 1978).

Brendon, P., *Eminent Edwardians* (London: Book Club Associates, 1979).

Brendon, P., *The Dark Valley – A Panorama of the 1930s* (London: Jonathan Cape, 2000).

Brome, V., *J. B. Priestley* (London: Hamish Hamilton, 1988).

Brooke-Hunt, V., *Lord Roberts* (London: James Nisbet, 1914).

Bryant, A., *The Turn of the Tide, 1939–1943* (London: Collins, 1957).

Bryant, A., *Triumph in the West, 1943–1946* (London: Collins, 1959).

Burke's Peerage, Baronetage and Knightage, various editions (London).

Burnet, M., *Genes, Dreams and Realities* (London: Penguin, 1973).

Cameron, H., *Joseph Lister* (London: Heinemann, 1948).

Campbell-Johnson, A., *Mission With Mountbatten* (London: Robert Hale, 1951).

Cannadine, D., *G. M. Trevelyan* (London: Harper Collins, 1992).

Carpenter, H., *Benjamin Britten* (London: Faber & Faber, 1992).

Carrington, C., *Rudyard Kipling* (London: Macmillan, 1955).

Cell, J.W., *Hailey* (Cambridge: Cambridge University Press, 1992).

Chalmers, Rear Admiral W. S., *The Life and Letters of David, Earl Beatty* (London: Hodder and Stoughton, 1951).

Charteris, J. G., *Haig* (London: Duckworth, 1933).

Cheshire, L., *The Face of Victory* (London: Hutchinson, 1961).

Cheshire, L., *The Hidden World* (London: Collins, 1981).

Churchill, R. S. and Gilbert, M., *Winston S. Churchill*, Vols I–VI and companion volumes of documents (London: Heinemann, 1966–1988).

Churchill, W. S., *Great Contemporaries* (London: Odhams Press, 1947).

Clark, K., *Another Part of the Wood* (London: John Murray, 1974).

Clark, K., *The Other Half* (London: John Murray, 1977).

Cokayne, G. E. (ed.), *The Complete Peerage of England, Scotland, Ireland, Great Britain & the United Kingdom, Extant & Extinct or Dormant*, second edition (London: ABC Publications, 1998).

Collins, D., *Time and the Priestleys* (London: Alan Sutton, 1994).

Colmer, J., *E. M. Forster – the personal voice* (London: Routledge & Kegan Paul, 1975).

Cooper, D., *Haig* (London: Faber & Faber, 1935).

Cox, M., *M. R. James* (Oxford: Oxford University Press, 1986).

Crawshay-Williams, R., *Russell Remembered* (Oxford: Oxford University Press, 1970).

Crook, M. J., *The Evolution of the Victoria Cross* (London: Midas, 1975).

Crystal, D. (ed.), *Cambridge Biographical Encyclopaedia* (Cambridge: Cambridge University Press, 1994).

Cunningham of Hyndhope, Viscount, *A Sailor's Odyssey* (London: Hutchinson, 1951).

Danchev, A., *Oliver Franks* (Oxford: Oxford University Press, 1993).

Danchev, A. and Todman, D. (eds), *War Diaries, 1939–1945 of Field Marshal Lord Alanbrooke* (London: Weidenfeld & Nicolson, 2001).

Day, J., *Vaughan Williams* (London: JM Dent, 1961).

Debrett's Peerage and Baronetage, various editions (London: Debrett's Limited).

De la Bère, I., *The Queen's Orders of Chivalry* (London: William Kimber, 1961).

Dellar, G. (ed.), *Attlee As I Knew Him* (Tower Hamlets Library Service, 1983).

Denning, Lord, *The Family Story* (London: Butterworth, 1981).

Desmond, A., *Huxley* (London: Penguin, 1998).

Dictionary of National Biography, various editions (Oxford: Oxford University Press).

Dilks, D. (ed), *The Diaries of Sir Alexander Cadogan, 1938–1945* (London: Cassell, 1971).

du Boulay, S., *Cicely Saunders* (London: Hodder and Stoughton, 1984).

Drabble, M. (ed.), *Oxford Companion to English Literature*, sixth edition, (Oxford: Oxford University Press, 2000).

Dugdale, B., Arthur James Balfour, Vols I–II (London: Hutchinson & Co, 1939).

Dukes, C., *Lord Lister* (London: Leonard Parsons, 1924).

Dunbar, J., *J. M. Barrie* (London: Collins, 1970).

Dupré, C., *John Galsworthy* (London: Collins, 1976).

Easton, M. and John, R., *Augustus John* (London: NPG, 1975).

Eddington, A., *The Nature of the Physical World* (London: JM Dent, 1935).

Eddington, A., *The Expanding Universe* (London: Pelican, 1940).

Edwards, R., *Harold Macmillan* (London: Macmillan, 1983).

Egremont, M., *Balfour* (London: Collins, 1980).

Eisenhower, D. D., *Crusade in Europe* (London: Heinemann, 1948).

Everett, O., *A Royal Miscellanny* (London: The Royal Collection, 1990).

Feather, N., *Lord Rutherford* (London: Priory Press, 1940).

Ferns, H. S. and Ostry, B., *The Age of Mackenzie King: The Rise of the Leader* (London: Heinemann, 1955).

Feschotte, J., *Albert Schweitzer* (London: Comet, 1956).

Fisher, Lord, *Memories* (London: Hodder and Stoughton, 1919).

Fisher, H. A. L., *An Unfinished Autobiography* (Oxford: Oxford University Press, 1940).

Foch, Marshal, *Memoirs* (London: Heinemann, 1931).

Frazer, J., *The Golden Bough* (London: Wordsworth Reference, 1993).

French, G., *The Life of Sir John French* (London: Cassell, 1931).

Galsworthy, J., *Glimpses & Reflections* (London: Heinemann, 1937).

Gardner, P., *E. M. Forster* (London: Longman, 1977).

Gooch, G. P., *Under Six Reigns* (London: Longmans, Green, 1958).

Gopal, S., *Radhakrishnan* (Delhi: Oxford University Press, 1989).

Gore, J., *King George V: A Personal Memoir* (London: John Murray, 1941).

Gransden, K. W., *E. M. Forster* (London: Oliver and Boyd, 1962).

Graves, R., *A. E. Housman* (London: Routledge & Kegan Paul, 1979).

Gray, J., *Isaiah Berlin* (London: Harper Collins, 1995).

Greene, G., *A Sort of Life* (London: Penguin, 1974).

Gross, J. (ed.), *Rudyard Kipling* (London: Weidenfeld & Nicolson, 1972).

Gwynedd, Viscount, *Dame Margaret* (London: George Allen and Unwin, 1947).

Haldane, R. B., *An Autobiography* (London: Hodder and Stoughton, 1929).

Halifax, Earl of, *Fullness of Days* (London: Collins, 1957).

Hansard (Lords and Commons), various editions (London: Stationery Office).

Hardinge of Penshurst, Lord, *Old Diplomacy* (London: John Murray, 1947).

Hardinge, H., *Loyal to Three Kings* (London: William Kimber, 1967).

Hardy, F., *The Life of Thomas Hardy*, Vols I–II (London: Macmillan, 1928–30).

Harper, G. M., *John Morley and Other Essays* (Oxford: Oxford University Press, 1920).

Harris, K., *Attlee* (London: Weidenfeld & Nicolson, 1982).

Harrod, R. F., *John Maynard Keynes* (London: Macmillan, 1951).

Hartcup, G. and Allibone, T.E., *Cockcroft and the Atom* (Bristol: Adam Hilger, 1984).

Harwood, R. (ed.), *The Ages of Gielgud* (London: Hodder and Stoughton, 1984).

Hayes, J., *The Art of Graham Sutherland* (Oxford: Phaidon, 1980).

Headington, C., *Britten* (London: Eyre Methuen, 1981).

Henderson, N., *Water Under the Bridges* (London: Hodder & Stoughton, 1945).

Hennessy, P., *The Statecraft of Clement Attlee* (Lecture at Queen Mary & Westfield College, 1995).

Hennessy, P. and Arends, A., *Mr Attlee's Engine Room* (London: Strathclyde Papers, 1983).

Hibbert, C., *Edward VII* (London: Allen Lane, 1976).

Hirst, F. W., Early Life and Letters of John Morley, Vols I–II (London: Macmillan, 1927).

Holloway, D., *John Galsworthy* (London: Morgan-Grampian, 1968).

Holman Hunt, D., *My Grandmothers and I* (London: Hamish Hamilton, 1960).

Holman Hunt, D., *My Grandfather, His Wives and Loves* (London: Hamish Hamilton, 1969).

Holmes, R., *The Little Field Marshal – Sir John French* (London: Jonathan Cape, 1981).

Holroyd, M., *Augustus John*, Vols I–II (London: Heinemann, 1974–75).

Horne, A., *Macmillan*, Vols I–II (Basingstoke: Macmillan, 1988–89).

Hough, R., *Mountbatten* (London: Weidenfeld & Nicolson, 1980).

Hurd, M., *Benjamin Britten* (London: Novello, 1978).

Hurd, M., *Tippett* (London: Novello, 1978).

Hutchison, B., *Mackenzie King* (London: Longmans, Green, 1953).

Ignatieff, M., *Isaiah Berlin* (London: Chatto & Windus, 1998).

Ions, E., *James Bryce and American Democracy, 1870–1922* (London: Macmillan, 1968).

Jackson, W. G. F., *Alexander of Tunis* (London: BT Batsford, 1971).

James, D., *Lord Roberts* (London: Hollis & Carter, 1954).

James, M. R., *Letters to a Friend* (London: Edward Arnold, 1956).

James, E., *Thomas Hardy* (London: British Library, 1990).

James, M. R., *Ghost Stories* (London: Tiger Books International 1991).

Jeans, J., *The Stars in Their Courses* (Harmondsworth: Penguin, 1939).

Jefferson, D. W., *Henry James* (London: Oliver and Boyd, 1960).

Jellicoe, Viscount, *The Grand Fleet, 1914–16* (London: Cassell, 1919).

Jenkins, R., *Mr Attlee* (London: William Heinemann, 1948).

Jenkins, R., *Asquith* (London: Collins, 1964).

Jenkins, R., *Baldwin* (London: Collins, 1987).

Jenkins, R., *A Life at the Centre* (Basingstoke: Macmillan, 1991).

Jenkins, R., *Churchill* (Basingstoke: Macmillan, 2001).

John, A., *Chiaroscuro* (London: Jonathan Cape, 1952).

John, A., *Finishing Touches* (London: Jonathan Cape, 1964).

Jones, T., Lloyd George (Oxford: Oxford University Press, 1951).

Jones, T., *A Diary With Letters, 1931–1950* (Oxford: Oxford University Press, 1954).

Keegan, J., *The First World War* (London: Hutchinson, 1998).

Kiernan, R. H., *General Smuts* (London: George G. Harrap, 1943).

King, F., *E. M. Forster and his World* (London: Thames and Hudson, 1978).

Kline, G. L., *Alfred North Whitehead – Essays on His Philosophy* (Englewood Cliffs, New Jersey: Prentice Hall, 1963).

Lamont, C., *Remembering John Masefield* (London: Kaye & Ward, 1972).

Laurence, D. H. (ed.), *Bernard Shaw – Collected Letters 1926–1950* (Viking, 1988).

Lee, S., *King Edward VII*, Vols I–II (London: Macmillan, 1925 and 1927).

Lees-Milne, J., *The Enigmatic Edwardian: The Life of Reginald, 2nd Viscount Esher* (London: Sidgwick & Jackson, 1986).

Leggett, H. W., *Bertrand Russell, OM* (London: Lincolns-Prager, 1949).

Levy, P., *Moore: G. E. Moore and the Cambridge Apostles* (London: Weidenfeld & Nicolson, 1979).

Lewis, J., *Something Hidden: A Biography of Wilder Penfield* (Toronto: Doubleday, 1981).

Liddell Hart, B. H., *Foch, Man of Orleans*, Vols I–II (Penguin, 1937).

Liddell Hart, B. H., *History of the First World War and History of the Second World War* (London: Cassell & Co, 1970).

Lloyd George, D., *The Truth About the Peace Treaties* (London: Victor Gollancz, 1938).

Lloyd George, D., *War Memoirs*, Vols I–II (London: Odhams Press, 1938).

Loftus Hare, W., *Watts, 1817–1904* (London: TC & EC Jack).

London Gazette, various issues.

Lutyens, M., *Edwin Lutyens* (London: John Murray, 1980).

Lycett, A., *Rudyard Kipling* (London: Weidenfeld & Nicolson, 1999).

McCann, K., *America's Man of Destiny: Eisenhower* (London: Heinemann, 1952).

MacCarthy, D., *Shaw* (London: MacGibbon & Kee, 1951).

MacDonald, M., *People and Places* (London: Collins, 1969).

MacDonald, M., *Titans and Others* (London: Collins, 1972).

Macmillan, H., *George Frederick Watts, RA* (London: JM Dent, 1903).

Macmillan, H., *Memoirs, 1914–1963*, Vols I–VI (London: Macmillan, 1966–73).

Macmillan, H., *War Diaries, 1943–1945* (Basingstoke: Macmillan, 1984).

Macmillan, H., *The Past Masters* (Basingstoke: Macmillan, 1975).

Magnus, P., *Kitchener* (London: John Murray, 1958).

Magnus, P., *King Edward the Seventh* (London: John Murray, 1964).

Malcolm, I., *Lord Balfour* (London: Macmillan, 1930).

Mandela, N., *Long Walk to Freedom* (London: Abacus, 1995).

Marchant, J., *History Through The Times* (London: Cassell, 1937).

Marder, A. J. (ed.), *Fear God and Dread Nought*, Vol. II, 1904–1914 (London: Jonathan Cape, 1956).

Marlow, A. N. (ed.), *Radhakrishnan: An Anthology* (London: George Allen and Unwin, 1952).

Masefield, J., *Grace Before Ploughing* (London: Heinemann, 1966).

Maurice, F., *Haldane*, Vols I–II (London: Faber & Faber, 1937–39).

Maurice, F. and Arthur, G., *The Life of Lord Wolseley* (London: Heinemann, 1924).

Maurois, A., *King Edward VII and His Times* (London: Cassell, 1933).

Medawar, J., *A Very Decided Preference* (Oxford University Press, 1990).

Medawar, P., *Memoir of a Thinking Radish* (Oxford: Oxford University Press, 1986).

Menuhin, Y., *Unfinished Journey* (London: Futura, 1978).

Morley, J., *On Compromise* (London: Macmillan, 1908).

Morley, J., *Recollections*, Vols I–II (London: Macmillan, 1918).

Morley, J., *Nineteenth-century Essays*; Selected and with an Introduction by Peter Stansky (Chicago: University of Chicago Press, 1970).

Morley, S., *John Gieldgud* (London: Hodder and Stoughton, 2001).

Mottram, R. H., *John Galsworthy* (London: Longmans, 1953).

Mountbatten, Earl, *Time Only To Look Forward* (London: Nicholas Kaye, 1949).

Mountbatten, Earl, *Eighty years in Pictures* (London: Book Club Associates, 1979).

Murray, G., *An Unfinished Autobiography* (London: George Allen and Unwin, 1960).

Murray, P. and Murray, L., *Dictionary of Art and Artists*, seventh edition (Harmondsworth: Penguin, 1997).

Nicholls, C. S. (ed.), *Hutchinson Encyclopaedia of Biography*, (Oxford: Helicon, 1996).

Nicolas, Sir N. H., *History of the Orders of Knighthood of the British Empire* (London: Chamberlayne, 1842).

Nicolson, H., *King George V* (London: Constable & Co, 1952).

Nicolson, H., *Diaries and Letters, 1930–45 and 1945–62* (edited by Nigel Nicolson) (London: Collins, 1967–68).

Nicolson, N., *Alex: The Life of Field Marshal Earl Alexander of Tunis* (London: Weidenfeld & Nicolson, 1973).

Nobel Foundation (ed.), *Nobel: The Man and His Prizes* (Amsterdam: Elsevier, 1962).

Ogg, D., *Herbert Fisher* (London: Edward Arnold, 1947).

Ollard, R., *A Man of Contradictions: A Life of A. L. Rowse* (Harmondsworth: Penguin, 1999).

O'Shea, P. P., *An Unknown Few* (Wellington, New Zealand: Government Printer, 1981).

Østergaard-Christensen, L., *At Work With Albert Schweitzer* (London: George Allen and Unwin, 1962).

Ottoway, H., *Walton* (London: Novello, 1977).

Page, N., *Thomas Hardy* (London: Routledge & Kegan Paul, 1977).

Patch, B., *Thirty Years With G. B. S.* (London: Victor Gollancz, 1951).

Patterson, S., *Royal Insignia* (London: Royal Collection, 1996).

Pearson, H., *Bernard Shaw* (London: Collins, 1942).

Pearson, L., Memoirs, Vols I–III (London: Victor Gollancz, 1973–75).

Perry, M. (ed.), *Chambers Biographical Dictionary*, sixth edition (London: Chambers, 1997).

Ponsonby, F., *Recollections of Three Reigns* (London: Eyre & Spottiswoode, 1951).

Porter, R. and Ogilvie, M. (eds), *Dictionary of Scientific Biography*, Vols I–II (Oxford: Helicon, 2000).

Prebble, J., *The King's Jaunt* (London: Collins, 1988).

Priestley, J. B., *Rain Upon Godshill* (London: Heinemann, 1939).

Priestley, J. B., *Midnight on the Desert* (London: Heinemann, 1940).

Priestley, J. B., *Theatre Outlook* (London: Nicholson & Watson, 1947).

Priestley, J. B., *Margin Released* (London: Heinemann, 1962).

Priestley, J. B., *Particular Pleasures* (London: Heinemann, 1975).

Queen Victoria's Letters (London: John Murray, various dates).

Raverat, G., *Period Piece* (London: Faber & Faber, 1952).

Ray, J., *Lloyd George and Churchill* (London: Heinemann, 1970).

Reynolds, E. E., *Baden-Powell* (Oxford University Press, 1942).

Reynolds, M. E., *Memories of John Galsworthy, by his sister* (London: Robert Hale, 1936).

Richards, G., *Housman, 1897–1936* (Oxford: Oxford University Press, 1941).

Risk, J. C., *The History of the Order of the Bath* (London: Spink & Son, 1972).

Roberts, A., *The Holy Fox: A Life of Lord Halifax* (London: Weidenfeld & Nicolson, 1991).

Roberts, Lord, *Forty-One Years in India*, Vols I–II (London: Richard Bentley, 1897).

Rose, K., *King George V* (London: Weidenfeld & Nicolson, 1983).

Rose, K., *Kings, Queens and Courtiers* (London: Weidenfeld & Nicolson, 1985).

Rosenthal, M., *The Character Factory: Baden-Powell and the Origins of the Boy Scout Movement* (London: Collins, 1986).

Royal Society, *Biographical Memoirs of Fellows of the Royal Society* (London: Royal Society).

Russell, A. E., *Lord Kelvin* (London: TC & EC Jack, 1912).

Russell, B., *Portraits from Memory* (London: George Allen and Unwin, 1956).

Russell, B., *Autobiography*, Vols I–III (London: George Allen and Unwin, 1967–69).

Ryan, A., *Bertrand Russell* (Oxford: Oxford University Press, 1993).

Samuel, Viscount, *Memoirs* (London: Cresset Press, 1945).

Samuel, Viscount, *Creative Man* (London: Cresset Press, 1949).

Samuel, Viscount, *Belief and Action* (London: Pan, 1953).

Samuel, Viscount, *Book of Quotations* (London: James Barrie, 1954).

Sampson, G., *Concise Cambridge History of English Literature* (Cambridge: Cambridge University Press, 1941).

Sassoon, S., *Meredith* (London: Constable, 1948).

Schweitzer, A., *On the Edge of the Primeval Forest* (London: A& C Black, 1955).

Scott-Kilvert, I., *A. E. Housman* (London: Longman, 1955).

Sewell, J. P. C., *Personal Letters of King Edward VII* (London: Hutchinson, 1931).

Seymer, L., *Florence Nightingale* (London: Faber & Faber, 1950).

Seymour-Smith, M., *Hardy* (London: Bloomsbury, 1994).

Sexton, C., *The Seeds of Time: Life of Sir Macfarlane Burnet* (Oxford: Oxford University Press, 1991).

Shaw, W., *The Knights of England*, Vols I–II (London: Heraldry Today, 1971).

Sherrington, C., *Man on his Nature* (Harmondsworth: Penguin, 1955).

Sinclair, A., *Francis Bacon* (New York: Crown Publishers, 1993).

Skidelsky, R., *John Maynard Keynes*, Vols I–III (Basingstoke: Macmillan, 1983–2001).

Smith, C. B., *John Masefield* (Oxford: Oxford University Press, 1978).

Smuts, J. C., *Jan Christian Smuts* (London: Cassell, 1952).

Soames, M., *Clementine Churchill* (London: Cassell, 1979).

Solomon, A. K., *Why Smash Atoms?* (London: Penguin, 1945).

Spence, B., *Phoenix at Coventry* (London: Fontana, 1963).

Stevenson, F., *Lloyd George: A Diary* (edited by A. J. P. Taylor) (London: Hutchinson, 1971).

Stuart, V., *The Beloved Little Admiral: Sir Henry Keppel* (London: Robert Hale, 1967).

Swinglehurst, E., *The Art of the Pre-Raphaelites* (London: Parragon, 1994).

Symons, A., *Behind the Blue Plaques of London, 1867–1994* (London: Polo Publishing, 1994).

Tate, A. (ed.), *T. S. Eliot: The Man and His Work* (Harmondsworth: Penguin Books, 1971).

Taylor, A. J. P. (ed.), *My Darling Pussy: The letters of Lloyd George and Frances Stevenson* (London: Weidenfeld & Nicolson, 1975).

Thomson, M., *David Lloyd George* (London: Hutchinson, 1947).

Tippett, M., *Those Twentieth Century Blues* (London: Hutchinson, 1991).

Trevelyan, G. M., *Sir George Otto Trevelyan* (London: Longmans, Green, 1932).

Trevelyan, G. M., *An Autobiography* (London: Longmans, Green, 1949).

Trevelyan, G. M., *A Layman's Love Letters* (London: Longmans, Green, 1954).

Trilling, L., *E. M. Forster* (London: Hogarth Press, 1944).

Vickers, H., *Royal Orders* (London: Boxtree, 1994).

Walden, B., *Walden on Attlee* (London: BBC, 1995).

Watts, G. F., The Hall of Fame (London: NPG, 1975).

Webb, S. and Webb, B., *Indian Diary* (edited by Niraja Jayal) (Oxford: Oxford University Press, 1990).

Weintraub, S., *The Importance of Being Edward: King in Waiting, 1841–1901* (London: John Murray, 2000).

Whealer, H., *The Story of Lord Roberts* (London: Harrap, 1915).

Wheeler-Bennett, J. W., *King George VI* (Basingstoke: Macmilllan, 1958).

Wheeler-Bennett, J. W., *John Anderson, Viscount Waverley* (Basingstoke: Macmillan, 1962).

Whitehead, A. N., *Dialogues* (New York: Mentor, 1956).

Whitaker's Almanack, various editions (London: Whitaker).

Whitaker's Peerage, Baronetage, Knightage & Companionage, various editions (London: Whitaker).

Who's Who, various editions (London: Routledge).

Who Was Who, various editions (London: Routledge).

Wilhelm, P., *The Nobel Prize* (London: Teleknowledge, 1983).

Williams, B., *Botha, Smuts and South Africa* (London: English Universities Press, 1946).

Williams, D., *George Meredith* (London: Hamish Hamilton, 1977).

Williams, F., *A Prime Minister Remembers: Memoirs of Earl Attlee* (Heinemann, 1961).

Williams, T. I., *Howard Florey: Penicillin and After* (Oxford: Oxford University Press, 1984).

Willis, I. C., *Florence Nightingale* (London: George Allen and Unwin, 1931).

Wilson, D., *Gilbert Murray, OM* (Oxford: Oxford University Press, 1987).

Wilson, J., *CB: a life of Sir Henry Campbell-Bannerman* (London: Constable, 1973).

Winant, J. G., *A Letter from Grosvenor Square* (London: Hodder & Stoughton, 1947).

Wollheim, R., *F. H. Bradley* (London: Peregrine, 1969).

Woodham-Smith, C., *Florence Nightingale* (London: Constable, 1950).

Ziegler, P., *Mountbatten* (London: Collins, 1985).

Ziegler, P., (ed.), *The Diaries of Lord Louis Mountbatten* (London: Collins, 1987–88).

Ziegler, P., *King Edward VIII* (London: Collins, 1990).

Ziegler, P., *Wilson* (London: Weidenfeld & Nicolson, 1993).

INDEX